PHILIP'S

STREET ATLAS
Wiltshire
and Swindon

First published 2002 by

Philip's, a division of
Octopus Publishing Group Ltd
2–4 Heron Quays, London E14 4JP

First colour edition 2002
First impression 2002

ISBN 0-540-08217-1 (hardback)
ISBN 0-540-08111-6 (spiral)

© Philip's 2002

 Ordnance Survey®

This product includes mapping data licensed from Ordnance Survey® with the permission of the Controller of Her Majesty's Stationery Office. © Crown copyright 2002. All rights reserved. Licence number 100011710.

Printed and bound in Spain
by Cayfosa-Quebecor

Contents

III   **Key to map symbols**

IV   **Key to map pages**

VI   **Route planning**

VIII   **Administrative and Postcode boundaries**

1   **Street maps** at 3½ inches to 1 mile

163   **Street maps** at 1¾ inches to 1 mile

213   **Street maps** at 3½ inches to 1 mile

218   **Town maps of** Andover and Frome

219   **Town map of** Bath at 7 inches to 1 mile

220   **Index** of towns and villages

223   **Index** of streets, hospitals, industrial estates, railway stations, schools, shopping centres, universities and places of interest

Digital Data

The exceptionally high-quality mapping found in this atlas is available as digital data in TIFF format, which is easily convertible to other bit mapped (raster) image formats.

The index is also available in digital form as a standard database table. It contains all the details found in the printed index together with the National Grid reference for the map square in which each entry is named.

For further information and to discuss your requirements, please contact Philip's on 020 7531 8439 or george.philip@philips-maps.co.uk

Key to map symbols

III

Motorway with junction number (22a)	
Primary route – dual/single carriageway	
A road – dual/single carriageway	
B road – dual/single carriageway	
Minor road – dual/single carriageway	
Other minor road – dual/single carriageway	
Road under construction	
Pedestrianised area	
DY7 **Postcode boundaries**	
County and unitary authority boundaries	
Railway	
Railway under construction	
Tramway, miniature railway	
Rural track, private road or narrow road in urban area	
Gate or obstruction to traffic (restrictions may not apply at all times or to all vehicles)	
Path, bridleway, byway open to all traffic, road used as a public path	

The representation in this atlas of a road, track or path is no evidence of the existence of a right of way

214
168
72
217

Adjoining page indicators
(The colour of the arrow indicates the scale of the adjoining page - see scales below)

The map area within the blue band is shown at a larger scale on the page, indicated by the blue block and arrow

Acad	**Academy**	Mkt	**Market**
Allot Gdns	**Allotments**	Meml	**Memorial**
Cemy	**Cemetery**	Mon	**Monument**
C Ctr	**Civic Centre**	Mus	**Museum**
CH	**Club House**	Obsy	**Observatory**
Coll	**College**	Pal	**Royal Palace**
Crem	**Crematorium**	PH	**Public House**
Ent	**Enterprise**	Recn Gd	**Recreation Ground**
Ex H	**Exhibition Hall**	Resr	**Reservoir**
Ind Est	**Industrial Estate**	Ret Pk	**Retail Park**
IRB Sta	**Inshore Rescue**	Sch	**School**
	Boat Station	Sh Ctr	**Shopping Centre**
Inst	**Institute**	TH	**Town Hall/House**
Ct	**Law Court**	Trad Est	**Trading Estate**
L Ctr	**Leisure Centre**	Univ	**University**
LC	**Level Crossing**	Wks	**Works**
Liby	**Library**	YH	**Youth Hostel**

Railway station Walsall	
Private railway station	
Bus, coach station	
Ambulance station	
Coastguard station	
Fire station	
Police station	
Accident and Emergency entrance to hospital	
H **Hospital**	
Place of worship	
i **Information Centre** (open all year)	
P **Parking**	
P&R **Park and Ride**	
PO **Post Office**	
Camping site	
Caravan site	
Golf course	
Picnic site	
Important buildings, schools, colleges, universities and hospitals Prim Sch	
River Medway **Water name**	
River, stream	
Lock, weir	
Water	
Tidal water	
Woods	
Houses	
Church **Non-Roman antiquity**	
ROMAN FORT **Roman antiquity**	

■ The small numbers around the edges of the maps identify the 1 kilometre National Grid lines ■ The dark grey border on the inside edge of some pages indicates that the mapping does not continue onto the adjacent page

The scale of the maps on the pages numbered in blue is 5.52 cm to 1 km • 3½ inches to 1 mile • 1: 18103

0	¼	½	¾	1 mile
0	250m	500m	750m	1 kilometre

The scale of the maps on pages numbered in green is 2.76 cm to 1 km • 1¾ inches to 1 mile • 1: 36206

0	¼	½	¾	1 mile
0	250m 500m 750m			1kilometre

The scale of the maps on the pages numbered in red is 11.04 cm to 1 km • 7 inches to 1 mile • 1: 9051.4

0	220 yards	440 yards	660 yards	½ mile
0	125m	250m	375m	½ kilometre

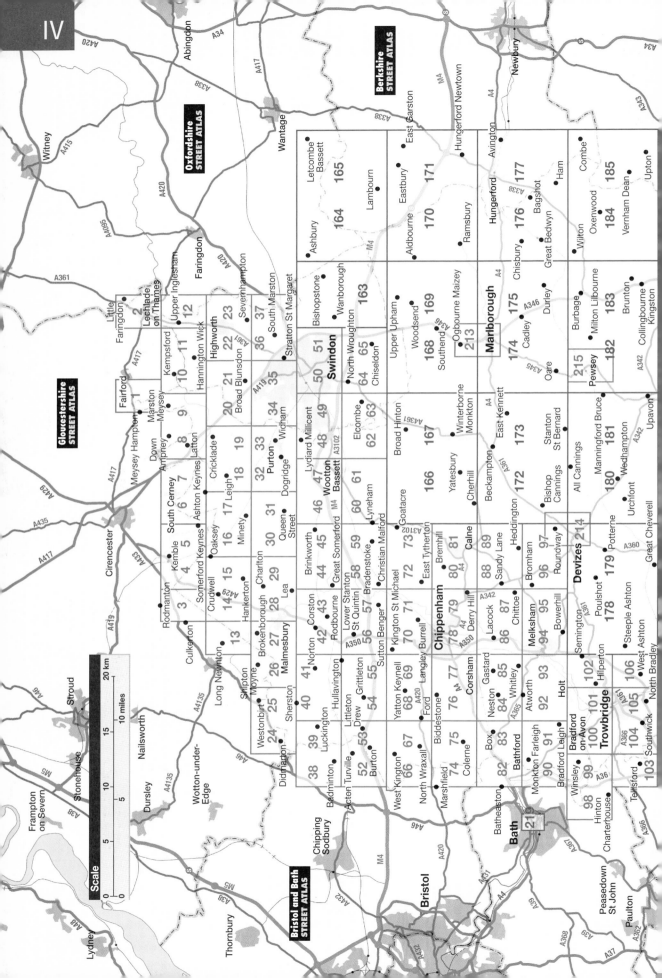

IV

Oxfordshire STREET ATLAS

Berkshire STREET ATLAS

Gloucestershire STREET ATLAS

Bristol and Bath STREET ATLAS

Scale

20 km
15
10
5
0

10 miles
5
0

North Hampshire STREET ATLAS

South Hampshire STREET ATLAS

Dorset STREET ATLAS

Key to map pages

Map pages at 1¾ inches to 1 mile

212

Map pages at 3½ inches to 1 mile

162

Map pages at 7 inches to 1 mile

219

Whitchurch Whitchurch Winchester Twyford Bishopstoke Eastleigh Netley Fawley Hythe Holbury Blackfield Southampton Dibden Purlieu Totton Romsey Bramshaw Lyndhurst Brockenhurst

Wildhern 193 Penton Mewsey 218 Andover Ludgershall 192 Kimpton Everleigh 191 216 North Tidworth Newton Toney Bulford Camp 199 135 Lopcombe Corner Middle Winterslow 149 West Dean 162 Platford 212 Nomansland

Coombe 190 Ablington 198 Durrington 217 Amesbury Boscombe 132 Idmiston 134 148 Pitton 147 Farley 154 155 West Grimstead 161 Whiteparish 160 Newton Lover 211 Woodgreen Godshill

West Chisenbury 189 Larkhill 197 Lake Stapleford—Upper Woodford 130 131 South Newton 145 146 Salisbury 152 153 Whaddon 158 159 Charlton-All-Saints 210 Breamore Fordingbridge

West Lavington 188 Tilshead Orcheston 196 Winterbourne Stoke Berwick St James 128 129 142 143 Wilton 144 Harnham 150 151 Homington 156 157 Downton Martin 209 Pentridge Damerham Ringwood

West Lavington 187 Chitterne 195 Codford St Mary Hanging Langford 201 Baverstock Barford St Martin Compton Chamberlayne 204 205 Mount Sorrel Ebbesbourne Wake 207 208 Woodyates Sixpenny Handley Farnham Verwood Ferndown

Edington Bratton 186 Heytesbury 194 Tytherington 200 Hindon Chilmark Tisbury 203 Semley 202 Berwick St John 206 Ashmore Cann Common Wimborne Minster

Westbury 109 113 Upton Scudamore Warminster 116 117 Sutton Veny Longbridge Deverill 120 121 Brixton Deverill Kingston Deverill 126 127 Pertwood West Knoyle 140 141 East Knoyle Sedgehill Motcombe Shaftesbury

Lower Rudge 107 111 Chapmanslade 114 115 Corsley Heath Horningsham 118 119 125 Kilmington 124 Mere 139 138 Zeals Stourton 137 Bourton Gillingham Wincanton Stalbridge Sturminster Newton

Frome 218 North Brewham 122 123 Maiden Bradley 136 Charlton Musgrove Milborne Port Sherborne

Shepton Mallet Evercreech South Brewham Bruton Castle Cary

Route planning

Scale

20 km

15

10 miles

10

5

5

0

0

Administrative and Postcode boundaries

Gloucestershire

SO|SP

Oxfordshire

Kemble
South Cerney
Down Ampney
Lechlade on Thames
GL 7
GL 8
Crickdale
Highworth
SN 6
Shipton Moyne
SN16
Minety
SN26
Malmesbury
Purton
SN25
Stratton St Margaret
Sherston
SN 5
SN 2
Swindon
SN 1
SN 3
OX12
Great Somerford
Swindon
SN 6
SN 7
South Gloucestershire
GL 9
Wootton Bassett
Lyneham
Nettleton
North Wiltshire
SN15
SN 4
Chiseldon
Lambourn
SN14
Broad Hinton
Aldbourne
Chippenham
Compton Bassett
Berkshire
Colerne
Corsham
SN11
Ramsbury
SN13
Calne
Marlborough
RG17
BA 1
Beckhampton
Hungerford
Bath
Bathford
BA15
SN12
Melksham
Kennet
SN 8
BA 2
Holt
Wootton Rivers
Bath & North East Somerset
BA 2
Bradford on Avon
BA14
Devizes
Burbage
Trowbridge
Pewsey
SN10
SN 9
Urchfont
Collingbourne Ducis
Vernham Dean
BA13
Upavon
Westbury
Market Lavington
Somerset
West Wiltshire
Wiltshire
Frome
BA11
Netheravon
North Tidworth
Ludgershall
SP11
Warminster
BA12
SP10
Durrington
SP 9
Andover
Chitterne
Shrewton
Heytesbury
Maiden Bradley
Amesbury
SP 4
Hampshire
BA10
Salisbury
BA 9
Hindon
SP 3
Wilton
SP 8
Mere
SP 1
Tisbury
Fovant
SP 2
Salisbury
SP 5
SP 7
Coombe Bissett
Alderbury
Shaftesbury
Whiteparish
Ludwell
Downton
S051
Ashmore
Sixpenny Handley
SP 6
Dorset
DT11
BH21
Fordingbridge
S043

ST|SU

Scale
0   5   10   15   20   25   30km
0   5   10   15   20 miles

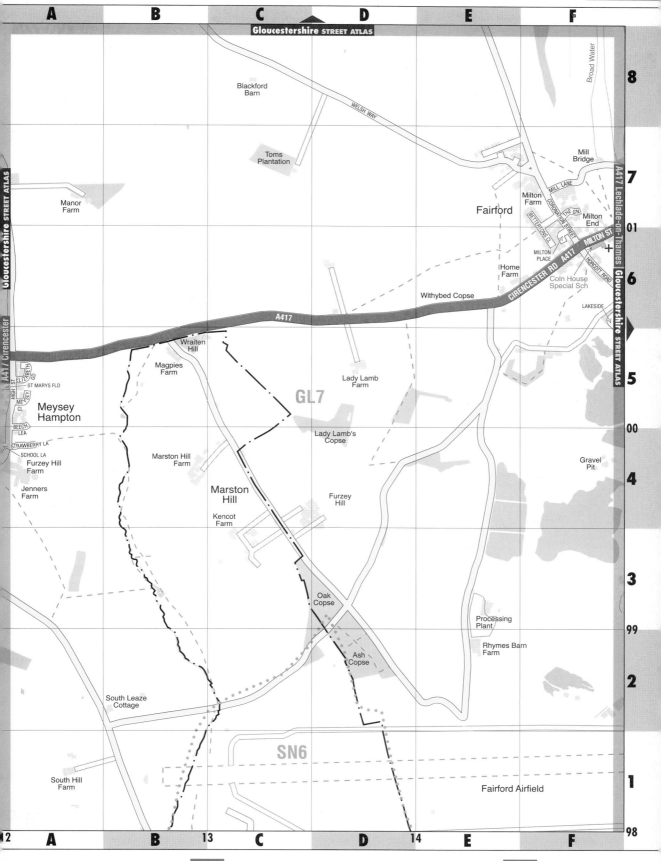

Broad Water

8

Blackford
Barn

WELSH WAY

Toms
Plantation

Mill
Bridge

7

MILL LANE

Milton
Farm

CORONATION STREET

THE GN

Milton
End

A417 Lechlade-on-Thames

Manor
Farm

Fairford

BETTERTONS CL

Milton
End

Gloucestershire STREET ATLAS

01

MILTON
PLACE

MILTON ST

Milton
End

A417 / Cirencester

CIRENCESTER RD

A417

Home
Farm

Coln House
Special Sch

HORCOTT ROAD

6

Withybed Copse

A417

LAKESIDE

Wraiten
Hill

A417

Magpies
Farm

Lady Lamb
Farm

GL7

5

A417 / Cirencester

HIGH ST

ELI

ST MARYS FLD

ME
CL

Meysey
Hampton

BEECH
LEA

STRAWBERRY LA

SCHOOL LA

Furzey Hill
Farm

Lady Lamb's
Copse

00

Jenners
Farm

Marston Hill
Farm

Gravel
Pit

4

Marston
Hill

Kencot
Farm

Furzey
Hill

3

Oak
Copse

Processing
Plant

99

Rhymes Barn
Farm

Ash
Copse

2

South Leaze
Cottage

SN6

South Hill
Farm

Fairford Airfield

1

98

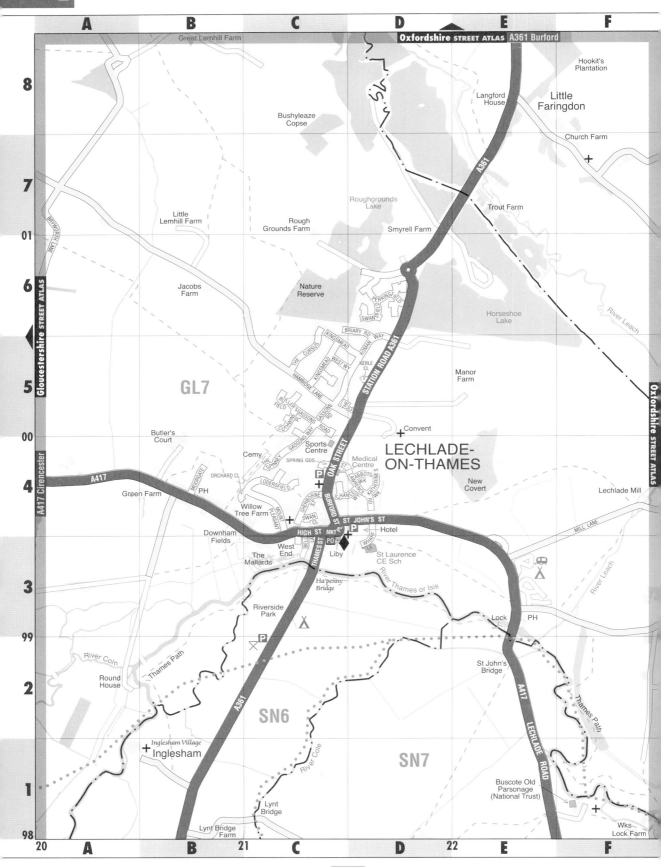

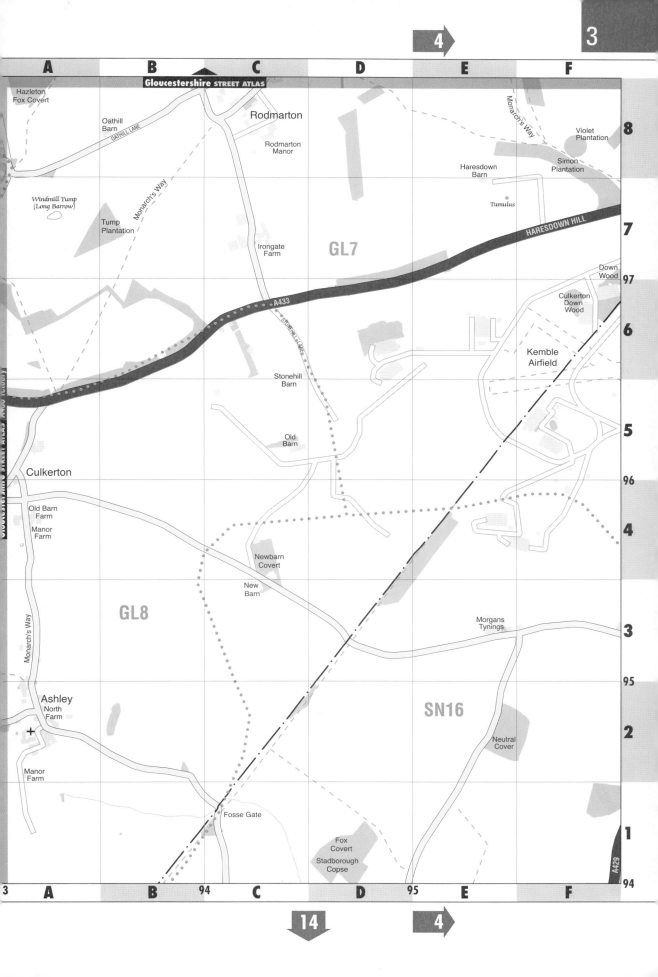

Gloucestershire STREET ATLAS

| A | B | C | D | E | F |

Hazleton
Fox Covert

Oathill
Barn
OATHILL LANE

Rodmarton

Rodmarton
Manor

Monarch's Way

Violet
Plantation

8

Haresdown
Barn

Simon
Plantation

Windmill Tump
(Long Barrow)

Monarch's Way

Tumulus

Tump
Plantation

Irongate
Farm

GL7

HARESDOWN HILL

7

Down
Wood

97

A433

STONEHILL LANE

Culkerton
Down
Wood

6

Stonehill
Barn

Kemble
Airfield

5

Old
Barn

96

Culkerton

4

Old Barn
Farm

Manor
Farm

Newbarn
Covert

New
Barn

GL8

Morgans
Tynings

3

Monarch's Way

95

Ashley
North
Farm

SN16

Neutral
Cover

2

Manor
Farm

Fosse Gate

1

Fox
Covert

Stadborough
Copse

A429

94

| A | B | 94 | C | D | 95 | E | F |

A   B   C   D   E   F

A433 Cirencester (A429)

Gloucestershire STREET ATLAS

8

Fan Grove

Burnt
Covert

Field
Barn

Clayfurlong
Farm

A433

Jackaments
Bottom

Kemble

Jackaments
Bottom Farm

Limekiln
Hill

Sixteen
Acre Covert

PH

WINDMILL

Kemble

PO

GLEBE
LA

STATION ROAD

Kemble
CP Sch

7

Kemble

SCHOOL RD

WEST HAY GR

WEST LANE

STATION ROAD

LINES RD

CHURCH RD

97

Jackaments
Barn

A429

Home
Farm

THE OAKS

TAMESIS DR

OLD

CARAGE LA

+

Prospect
Farm

Highstubs
Plantation

6

Kemble
Airfield

Kemble
Wood

GL7

Beanfield
Plantation

Pat-Yat

5

Kemble
Airfield

Rendall's
Barn

96

Odd
Farm

Bob's
Copse

Kemble Wick

4

A429

Lower
Odd
Farm

Factory

3

Woodlands

Dean
Plantation

95

Lime
Plantation

2

Devil's Copse

Laynes
Farm

Norwood Castle
(site of)

Chelworth
Lawns

Dean
Farm

Quelfurlong
Farm

THE GROVE

Chelworth

1

Chelworth
House

Chelworth
Manor Farm

Laynes
Farm

SN16

94

96   A   B   97   C   D   98   E   F

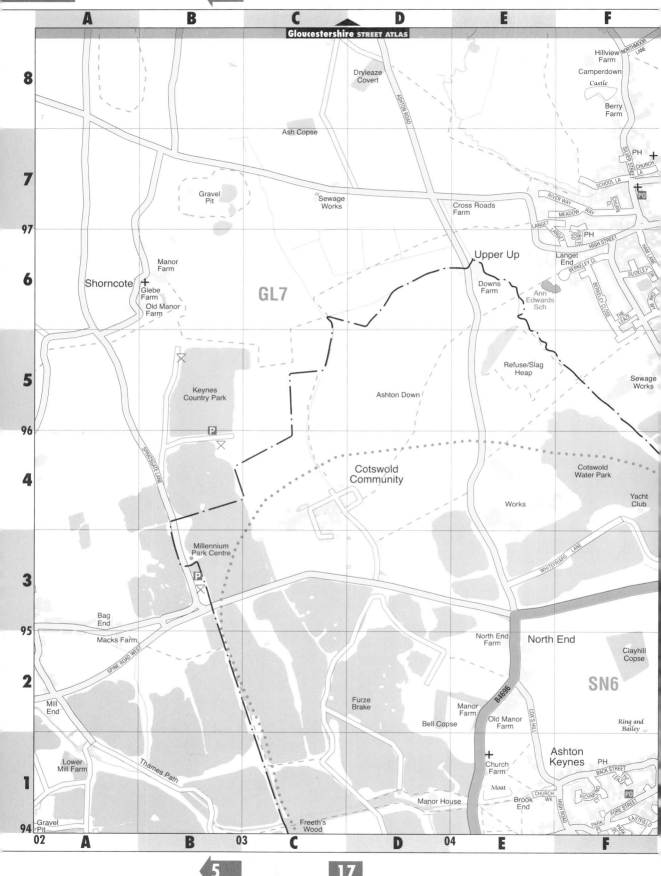

Gloucestershire STREET ATLAS

Hillview
Farm

NORTHMOOR LANE

Camperdown
Castle

Berry
Farm

PH

SILVER STREET

CHURCH LA

SCHOOL LA

PO

RIVER WAY

MEADOW WAY

CHURN CL

LANGET

LANGET (GD)

JUBILEE

PH

HIGH STREET

HART LANE

Dryleaze
Covert

ASHTON ROAD

Ash Copse

Gravel
Pit

Sewage
Works

Cross Roads
Farm

Upper Up

Langet
End

BERKELEY CL

Langet End

SUDELEY

BERKELEY CLOSE

THE LEAZE

WK

Shorncote

Manor
Farm

Glebe
Farm

Old Manor
Farm

GL7

Downs
Farm

Ann
Edwards
Sch

BERKELEY CL

Keynes
Country Park

P

Ashton Down

Refuse/Slag
Heap

Sewage
Works

SPRATSGATE LANE

Cotswold
Community

Cotswold
Water Park

Yacht
Club

WHITEFRIARS LANE

Works

Millennium
Park Centre

P

Bag
End

Macks Farm

North End
Farm

North End

Clayhill
Copse

SN6

SPINE ROAD WEST

Mill
End

Furze
Brake

Manor
Farm

Bell Copse

Old Manor
Farm

B4696

COX'S HILL

Ring and
Bailey

Lower
Mill Farm

Thames Path

Church
Farm

Moat

Ashton
Keynes

PH

BACK STREET

THE

PO

Manor House

CHURCH WK

Brook
End

HIGH ROAD

RICHMOND CL

FORE STREET

PARK PL

EASTFIELD

PARK

Gravel
Pit

Freeth's
Wood

02   A   B   03   C   D   04   E   F

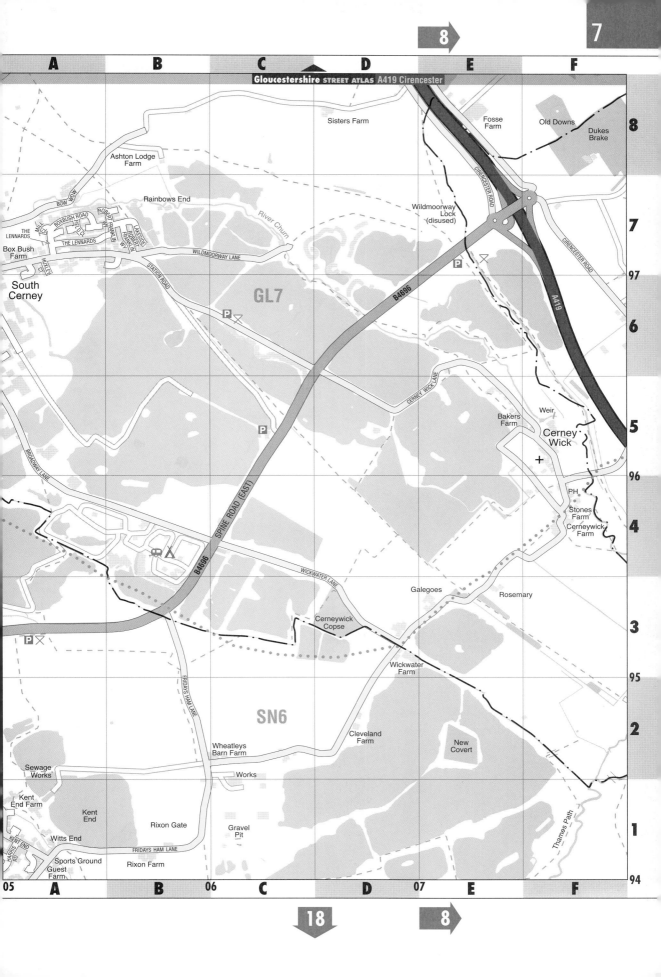

| A | B | C | D | E | F |

Gloucestershire STREET ATLAS A419 Cirencester

Sisters Farm

Fosse Farm

Old Downs

Dukes Brake

8

Ashton Lodge Farm

Rainbows End

Wildmoorway Lock (disused)

CIRENCESTER ROAD

7

BOW WOW

Boxbush Road

THE LENNARDS

Box Bush Farm

THE LENNARDS

MILL

ROBERT FRANKLIN WY

LAKESIDE

ROBERT FRANKLIN

River Churn

Wildmoorway Lane

STATION ROAD

B4696

CIRENCESTER ROAD

A419

97

South Cerney

GL7

6

HUXLEY CT

P

P

B4696

CERNEY WICK LANE

Bakers Farm

Weir

Cerney Wick

5

BROADWAY LANE

P

SPINE ROAD (EAST)

+

96

B4696

Wickwater Lane

PH

Stones Farm

Cerneywick Farm

4

P

Galegoes

Rosemary

3

FRIDAYS HAM LANE

Cerneywick Copse

Wickwater Farm

95

SN6

Cleveland Farm

New Covert

2

Sewage Works

Wheatleys Barn Farm

Works

Kent End Farm

Kent End

Rixon Gate

Gravel Pit

1

KENT END

HARRIS RD

Witts End

FRIDAYS HAM LANE

Sports Ground Guest Farm

Rixon Farm

94

| A | B | 06 | C | D | 07 | E | F |

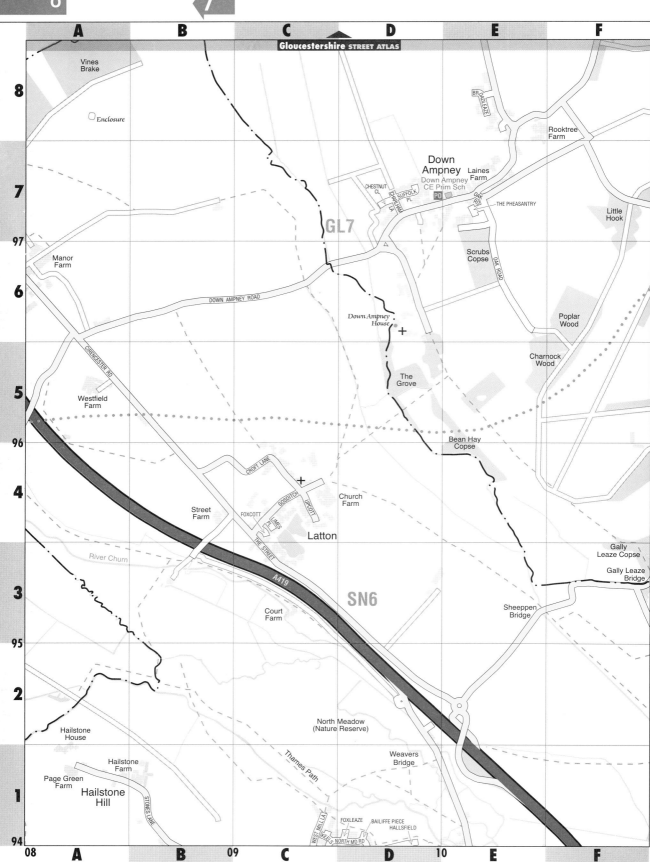

8

Vines
Brake

Enclosure

Down
Ampney

Down Ampney
CE Prim Sch

BR OAKLEAZE

Rooktree
Farm

7

CHESTNUT
CL

SUFFOLK
PL

CHARLHAM
LA

PO

Laines
Farm

OAK
RD

THE PHEASANTRY

Little
Hook

97

GL7

Manor
Farm

Scrubs
Copse

OAK ROAD

6

DOWN AMPNEY ROAD

Down Ampney
House

+

Poplar
Wood

Charnock
Wood

The
Grove

5

CIRENCESTER RD

Westfield
Farm

Bean Hay
Copse

96

Croft Lane

+

Church
Farm

4

Street
Farm

FOXCOTT

GOSDITCH

UPCOTT

LIMES

PL

THE STREET

Latton

Gally
Leaze Copse

Gally Leaze
Bridge

River Churn

A419

3

SN6

Sheeppen
Bridge

Court
Farm

95

2

North Meadow
(Nature Reserve)

Hailstone
House

Weavers
Bridge

Hailstone
Farm

Thames Path

1

Page Green
Farm

Hailstone
Hill

STONES LANE

WEST MILL LA

FOXLEAZE

KEELS

NORTH MD RD

BAILIFFE PIECE
HALLSFIELD

94

A **B** **C** **D** **E** **F**

8

Dunfield

GL7

Cox's
Farm

7

Middle
Farm

Willow
End

TOP ROAD

THE KNOLL

WELFORD RD

97

PH

HIGH STREET

BROADWAY

CHAPEL CL

CHAPEL CL

1 JOHN OF GAUNT RD
2 SWYNFORD CL
3 WAKEFIELD CL
4 NORTHEN CL
5 LANCASTER RD

OAKLEY FLATS

Paradise
Farm

PH

FORD

TUCKWELL RD

HAM LANE

Kempsford

6

THE WHARFINGS

WHARF LA

PO

Stubbs Farm

ST MARY'S CL

Manor
Farm

Blackburr
Farm

5

Sewage
Works

River Thames or Isis

96

Manor
Farm

Thames Path

PH

BLACKFORD LANE

Blackford
Farm

THE STREET

LONG ROW

CHURCH VIEW

Castle
Eaton

4

SCHOOL LANE

PO

Castle
Eaton Farm

SN6

Thames Path

3

95

The Well
Cottage

Frogpit

2

Droveway

Lushill Farm

Lus Hill

1

94

14 **A** **B** 15 **C** **D** 16 **E** **F**

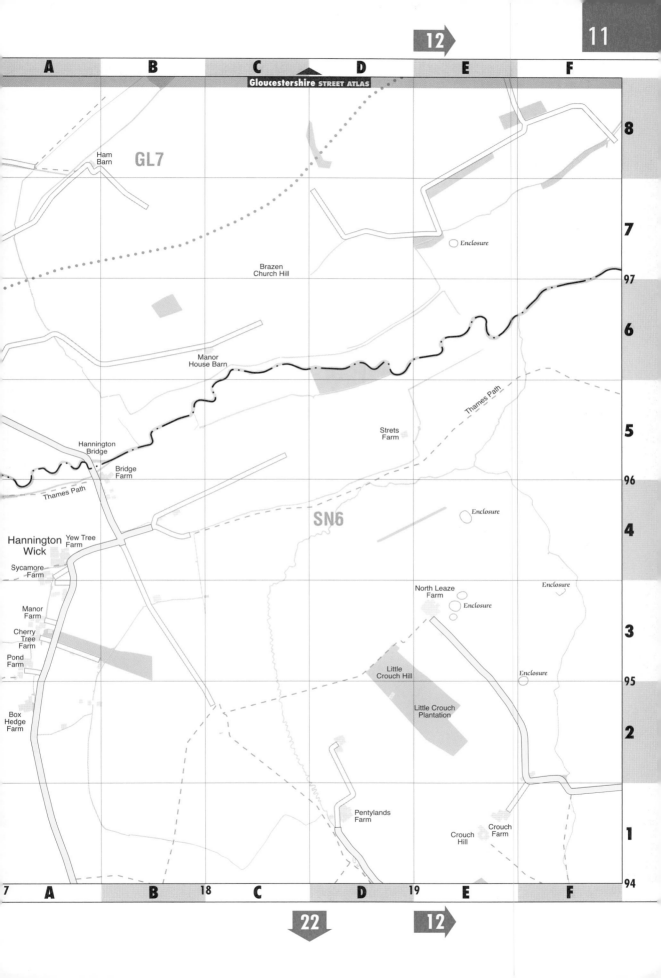

12

Gloucestershire STREET ATLAS

GL7

Ham
Barn

Brazen
Church Hill

Enclosure

8

7

97

6

Manor
House Barn

Thames Path

Strets
Farm

Hannington
Bridge

Bridge
Farm

Thames Path

5

96

SN6

Enclosure

4

Hannington
Wick

Yew Tree
Farm

Sycamore
Farm

North Leaze
Farm

Enclosure

Enclosure

Manor
Farm

Enclosure

Cherry
Tree
Farm

Pond
Farm

3

Little
Crouch Hill

Enclosure

95

Box
Hedge
Farm

Little Crouch
Plantation

2

Pentylands
Farm

Crouch
Hill

Crouch
Farm

1

94

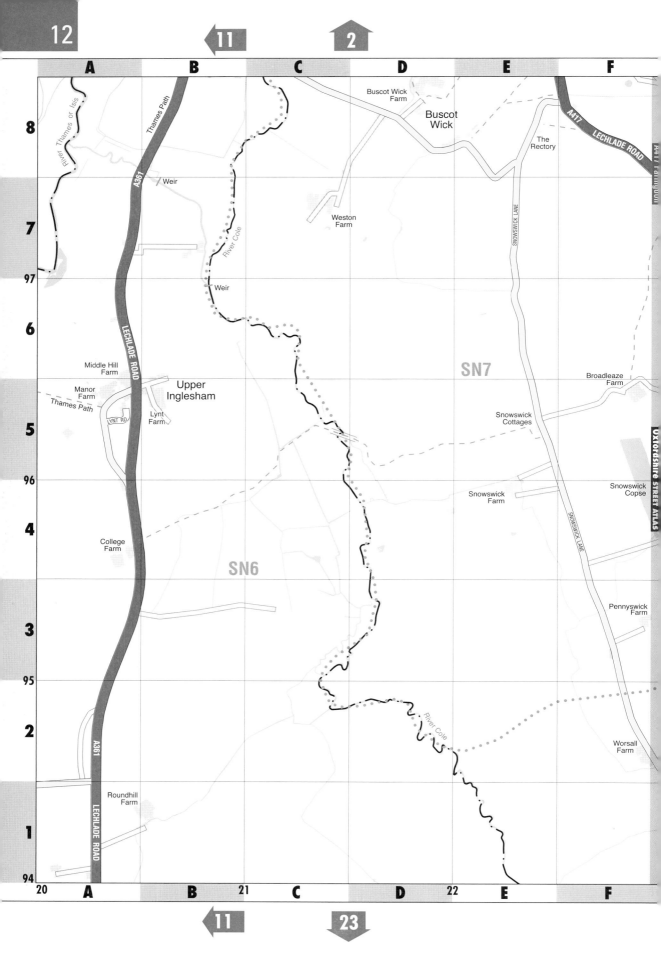

River Thames or Isis

Thames Path

A361

Weir

Buscot Wick Farm

Buscot Wick

The Rectory

A417 LECHLADE ROAD

A411 Faringdon

River Cole

Weston Farm

Weir

SNOWSWICK LANE

SN7

Broadleaze Farm

LECHLADE ROAD

Middle Hill Farm

Upper Inglesham

Manor Farm

Thames Path

LYNT RD

Lynt Farm

Snowswick Cottages

Snowswick Copse

Oxfordshire Street Atlas

College Farm

SN6

Snowswick Farm

SNOWSWICK LANE

Pennyswick Farm

River Cole

Worsall Farm

A361

Roundhill Farm

River Cole

LECHLADE ROAD

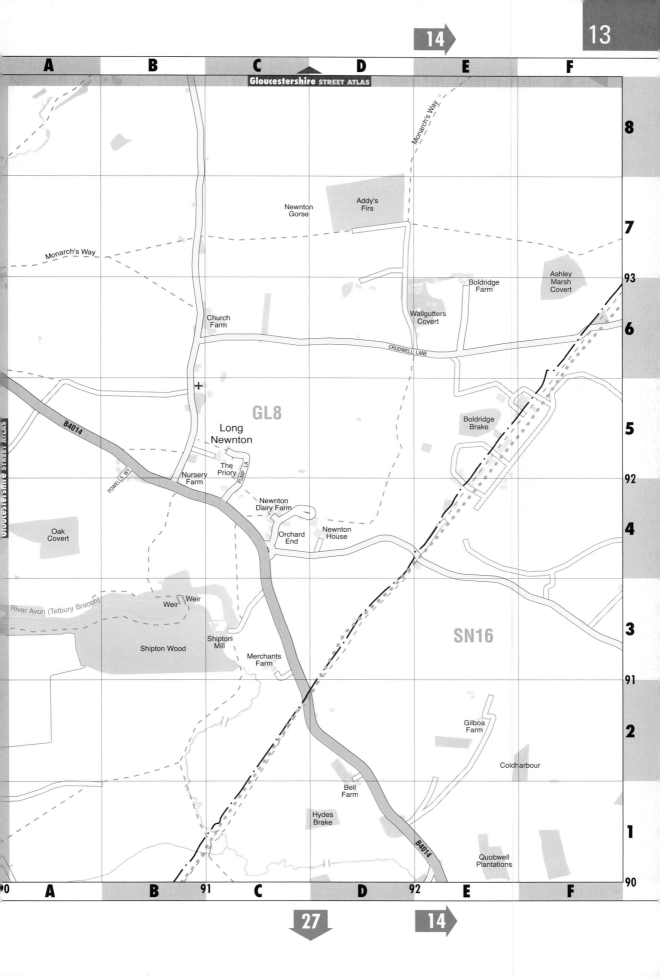

A   B   C   D   E   F

Gloucestershire STREET ATLAS

Monarch's Way

8

Newnton Gorse

Addy's Firs

7

Monarch's Way

93

Boldridge Farm

Ashley Marsh Covert

Church Farm

Wallgutters Covert

CRUDWELL LANE

6

GL8

Boldridge Brake

5

Long Newnton

Nursery Farm

The Priory

PUMP LA

POWELL'S WY

92

B4014

Newnton Dairy Farm

Oak Covert

Orchard End

Newnton House

4

River Avon (Tetbury Branch)

Weir Weir

SN16

3

Shipton Wood

Shipton Mill

Merchants Farm

91

Gilboa Farm

2

Coldharbour

Bell Farm

Hydes Brake

1

B4014

Quobwell Plantations

90

A   B   C   D   E   F

90   91   92

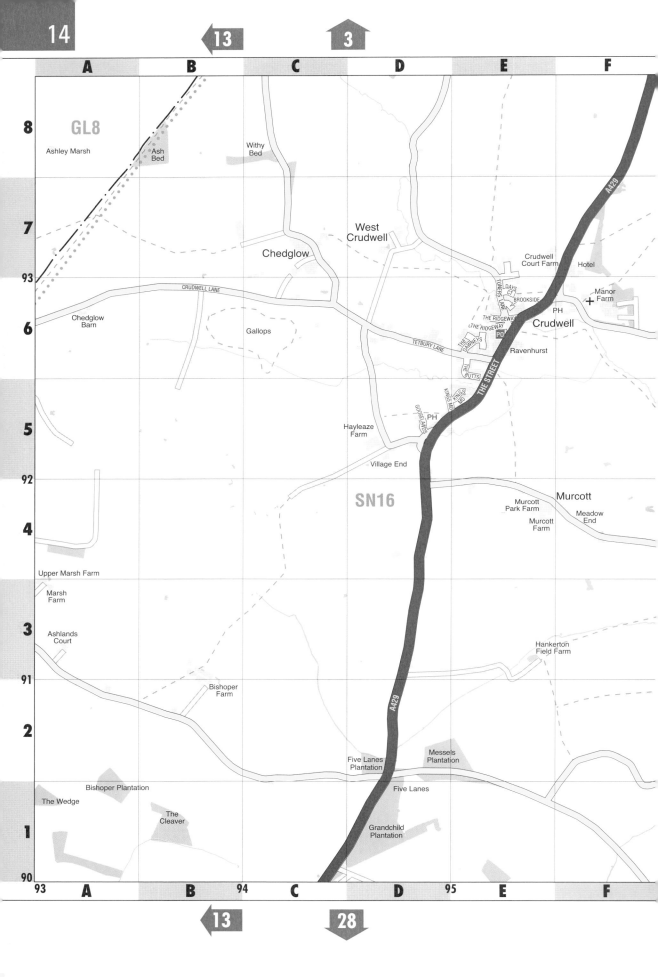

GL8

Ashley Marsh

Ash Bed

Withy Bed

West Crudwell

Chedglow

CRUDWELL LANE

Chedglow Barn

Gallops

Crudwell Court Farm

Hotel

DAYS CT

TURNERS LANE

BROOKSIDE

THE RIDGEWAY

'THE RIGDEWAY'

PH

Crudwell

MANOR Farm

TETBURY LANE

THE DAWNEYS

PO

Ravenhurst

THE BUTTS

THE STREET

KINGS MD

KINGS MD

Hayleaze Farm

GOOSELANDS

PH

Village End

SN16

Murcott Park Farm

Murcott

Murcott Farm

Meadow End

Upper Marsh Farm

Marsh Farm

Ashlands Court

Hankerton Field Farm

Bishoper Farm

A429

Five Lanes Plantation

Messels Plantation

Bishoper Plantation

The Wedge

The Cleaver

Five Lanes

Grandchild Plantation

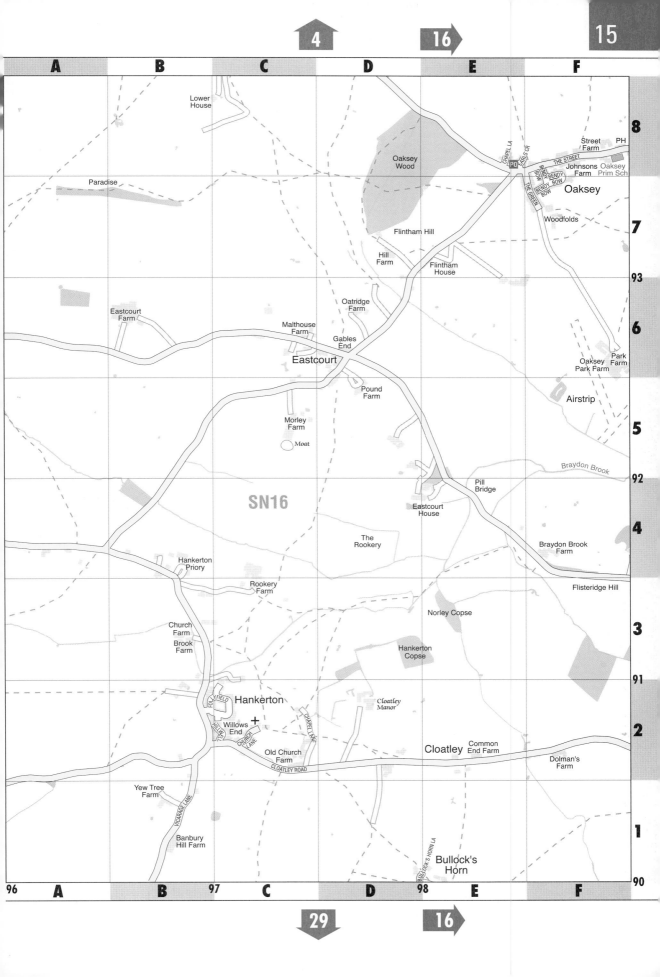

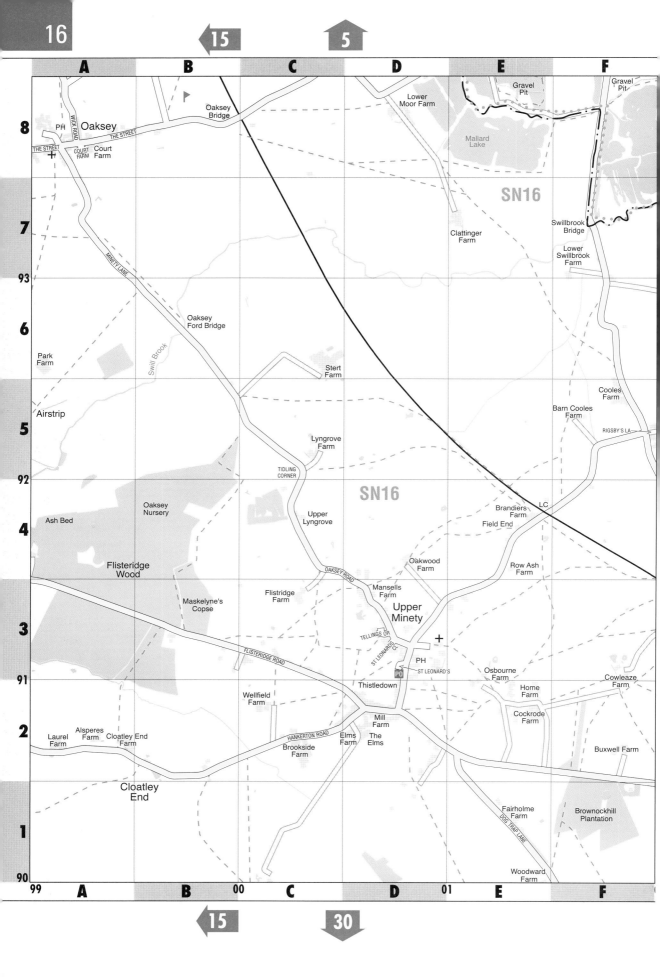

A   B   C   D   E   F

8   Oaksey
PH
THE STREET
THE STREET   COURT   Court
FARM   Farm
WICK ROAD
Oaksey
Bridge
Lower
Moor Farm

Gravel
Pit
Gravel
Pit

SN16

7   MINETY LANE   Clattinger
Farm
Swillbrook
Bridge
Lower
Swillbrook
Farm

93

6   Oaksey
Ford Bridge
Swill Brook
Park
Farm
Stert
Farm
Cooles
Farm

5   Airstrip
Lyngrove
Farm
Barn Cooles
Farm
RIGSBY'S LA

92   TIDLING
CORNER
SN16

4   Ash Bed
Oaksey
Nursery
Upper
Lyngrove
Brandiers
Farm
Field End
LC

Flisteridge
Wood
Oakwood
Farm
Row Ash
Farm

3   Maskelyne's
Copse
Flistridge
Farm
OAKSEY ROAD
Mansells
Farm
Upper
Minety

FLISTERIDGE ROAD
TELLINGS DR
ST LEONARD'S CL
PH
PO   ST LEONARD'S
Osbourne
Farm
Cowleaze
Farm

91   Thistledown
Home
Farm

Wellfield
Farm
Mill
Farm
Cockrode
Farm

2   Laurel
Farm
Alsperes
Farm
Cloatley End
Farm
HANKERTON ROAD
Brookside
Farm
Elms
Farm
The
Elms
Buxwell Farm

Cloatley
End
Fairholme
Farm
DOG TRAP LANE
Brownockhill
Plantation

1

90   Woodward
Farm

99   A   00   B   C   D   01   E   F

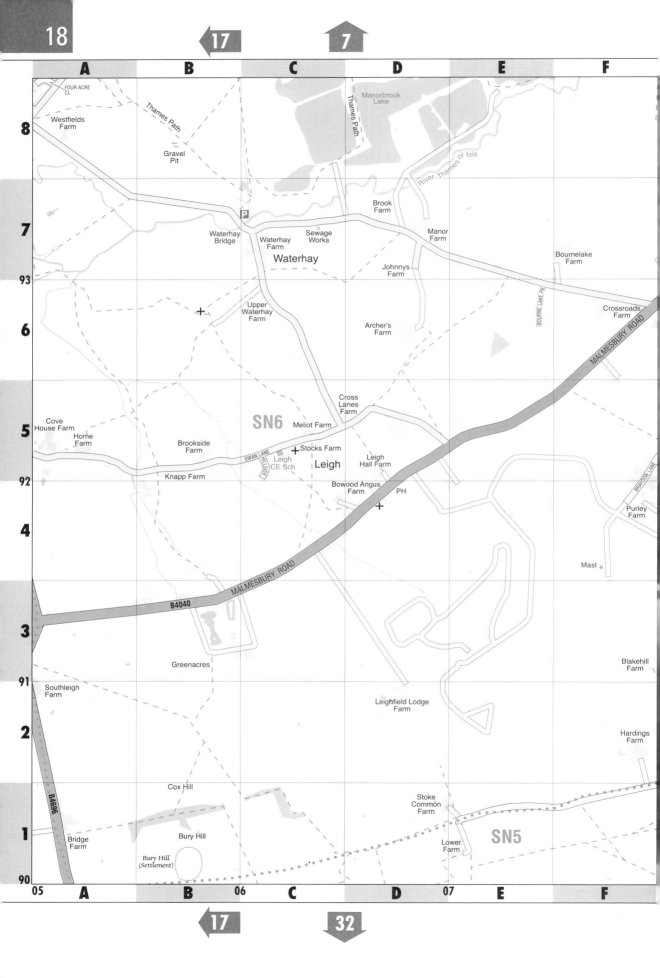

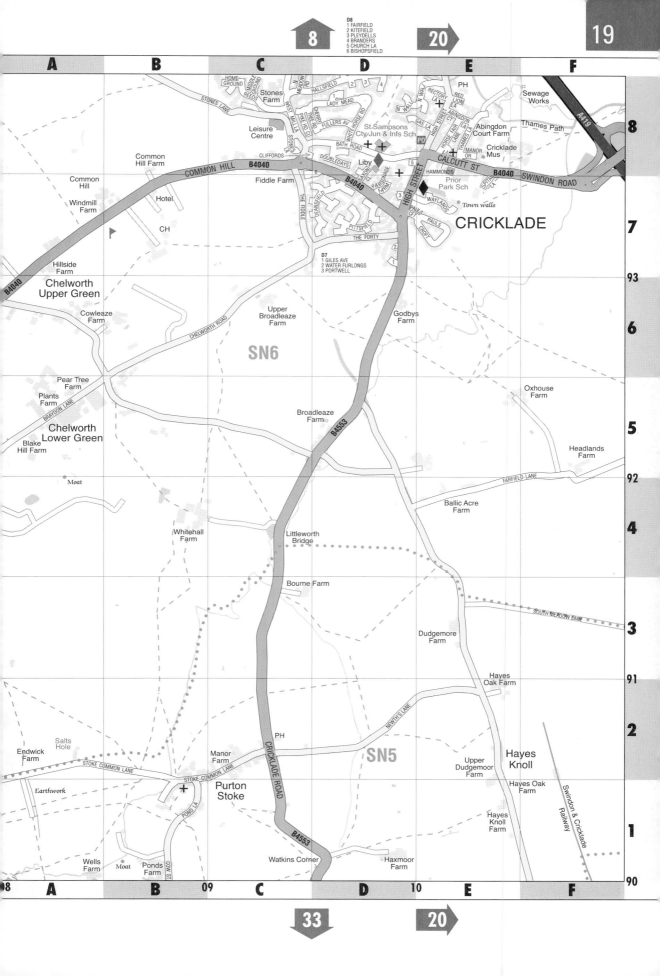

8

20

19

D8
1 FAIRFIELD
2 KITEFIELD
3 PLEYDELLS
4 BRANDERS
5 CHURCH LA
6 BISHOPSFIELD

A   B   C   D   E   F

Sewage
Works

A419

Home
Ground

Hallsfield

PH

RECTORY

RED
LION
LA

Abingdon

Thames Path

8

Stones
Reeds

Stones
Farm

Lady Mead

N MEADOW RD

WEST MILL LA

PIKE HO CL

CHERRY TREE CL

WHITE HORSE RD

FULLERS AV

ABINGDON

N WALL

N WALL

HIGH STREET

HORSE FAIR LA

GAS LA

THAMES LA

Abingdon
Court Farm

Leisure
Centre

St.Sampsons
Cty.Jun & Infs Sch

PO

Cricklade
Mus

MANOR
OR

Common
Hill Farm

CLIFFORDS

Liby

CALCUTT ST

SPITAL LA

B4040

SWINDON ROAD

8

Common
Hill

Windmill
Farm

COMMON HILL

B4040

Fiddle Farm

DOUBLEDAYS

BATH ROAD

STONES

Parsonage
Farm

B4040

HAMMONDS

Prior
Park Sch

HIGH STREET

7

Hotel

THE FIDDLE

MANSFIELD

PITTSFIELD

WAYLANDS

PAULS

PAULS CFT

CROFT

Town walls

CRICKLADE

CH

THE FORTY

D7
1 GILES AVE
2 WATER FURLONGS
3 PORTWELL

Hillside
Farm

B4040

93

Chelworth
Upper Green

Cowleaze
Farm

Upper
Broadleaze
Farm

CHELWORTH ROAD

Godbys
Farm

6

SN6

Pear Tree
Farm

Oxhouse
Farm

Plants
Farm

BRAYDON LANE

Broadleaze
Farm

B4553

5

Chelworth
Lower Green

Headlands
Farm

Blake
Hill Farm

FARFIELD LANE

92

Moat

Ballic Acre
Farm

4

Whitehall
Farm

Littleworth
Bridge

Bourne Farm

SOUTH MEADOW LANE

3

Dudgemore
Farm

Hayes
Oak Farm

91

Salts
Hole

NEWTH'S LANE

2

Endwick
Farm

STOKE COMMON LANE

Manor
Farm

PH

CRICKLADE ROAD

SN5

Upper
Dudgemoor
Farm

Hayes
Knoll

Earthwork

STOKE COMMON LANE

Purton
Stoke

POND LA

Hayes Oak
Farm

Swindon & Cricklade Railway

Wells
Farm

Moat

Ponds
Farm

COW ST

B4553

Watkins Corner

Haxmoor
Farm

Hayes
Knoll
Farm

1

08   A   B   09   C   D   10   E   F   90

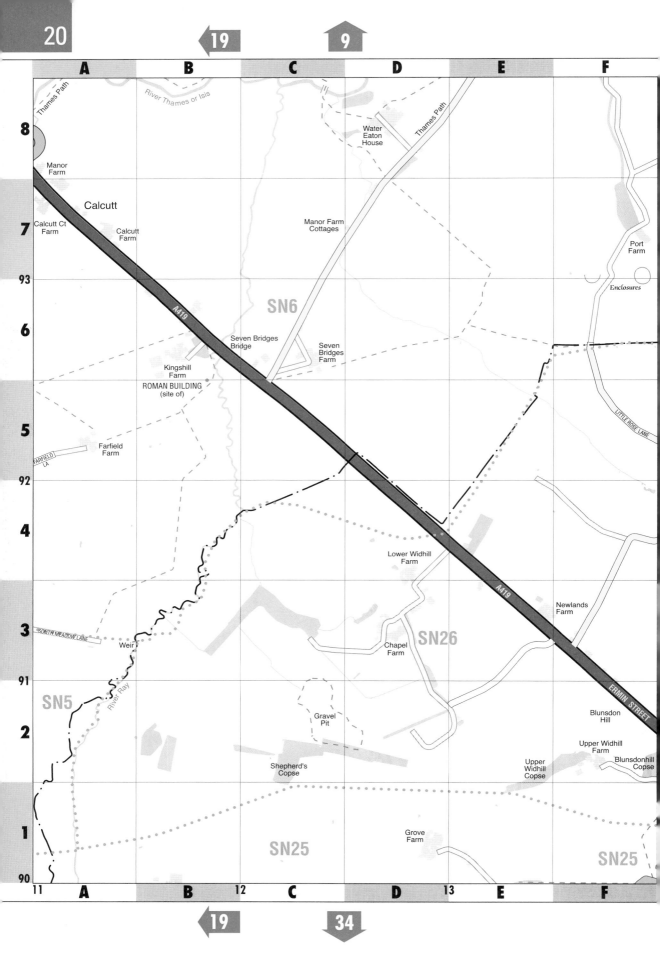

A B C D E F

Thames Path

River Thames or Isis

Water Eaton House

Thames Path

8

Manor Farm

Calcutt

Manor Farm Cottages

Port Farm

7

Calcutt Ct Farm

Calcutt Farm

A419

Enclosures

93

SN6

6

Seven Bridges Bridge

Seven Bridges Farm

LITTLE ROSE LANE

Kingshill Farm

ROMAN BUILDING (site of)

5

FARFIELD LA

Farfield Farm

92

4

Lower Widhill Farm

A419

Newlands Farm

3

SOUTH MEADOW LANE

Weir

SN26

Chapel Farm

Blunsdon Hill

91

River Ray

SN5

Gravel Pit

Upper Widhill Farm

Blunsdonhill Copse

2

Upper Widhill Copse

Shepherd's Copse

ERMIN STREET

1

Grove Farm

SN25

SN25

90

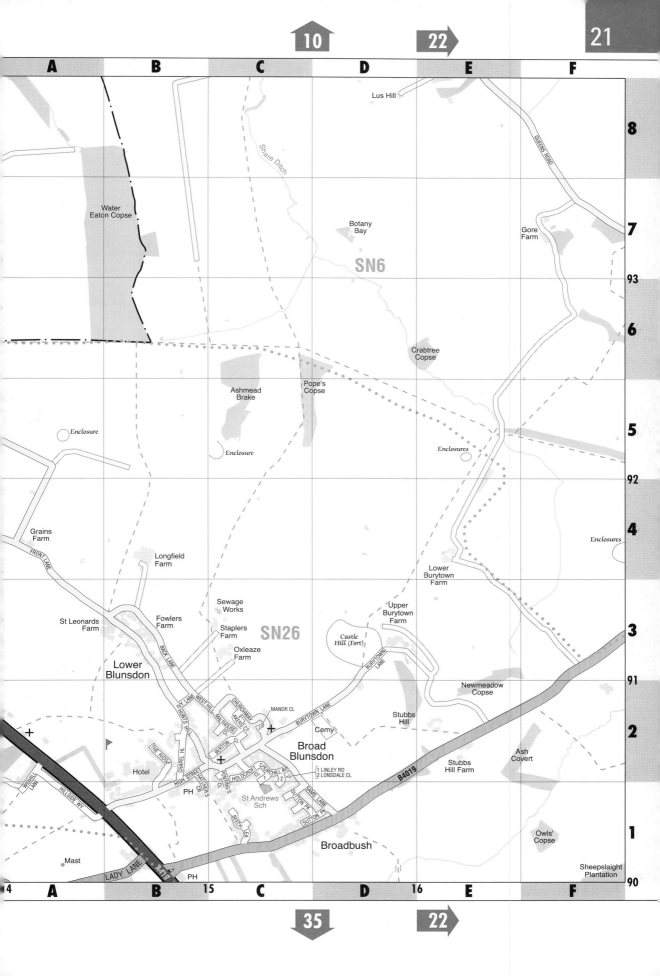

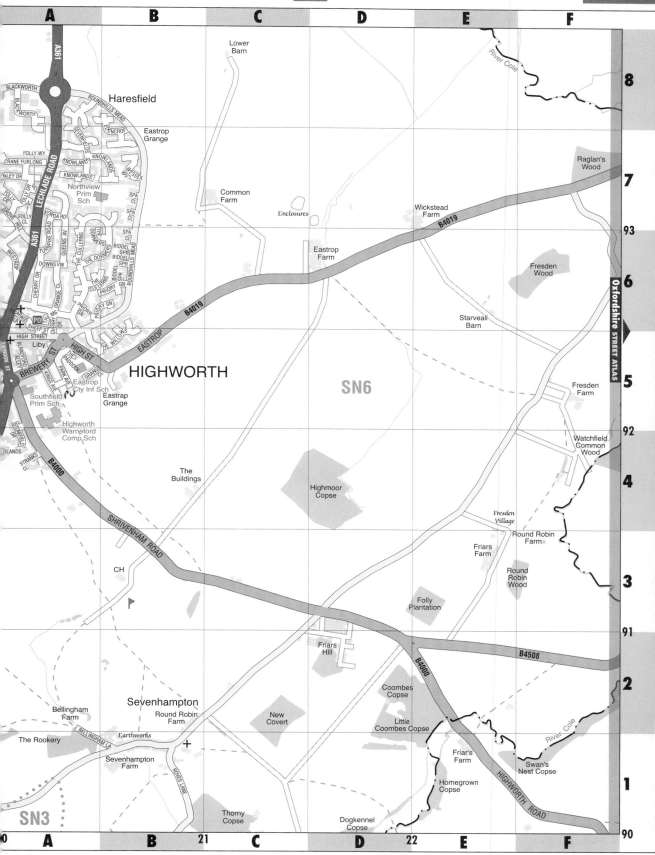

A   B   C   D   E   F

8

Lower
Barn

River Cole

Haresfield

BLACKWORTH

Eastrop
Grange

Raglan's
Wood

7

Common
Farm

Enclosures

Wickstead
Farm

B4019

93

Eastrop
Farm

Fresden
Wood

B4019

6

Starveall
Barn

HIGHWORTH

Fresden
Farm

SN6

5

Eastrop
Cty Inf Sch

Eastrap
Grange

92

Highworth
Warneford
Comp Sch

Watchfield
Common
Wood

The
Buildings

Highmoor
Copse

4

B4000

SHRIVENHAM ROAD

Fresden
Village

Round Robin
Farm

CH

Friars
Farm

Round
Robin
Wood

3

Folly
Plantation

91

Friars
Hill

B4000

B4508

2

Coombes
Copse

Sevenhampton

Bellingham
Farm

Round Robin
Farm

New
Covert

Little
Coombes Copse

River Cole

BELLINGHAM LA

Earthworks

The Rookery

Friar's
Farm

Swan's
Nest Copse

Sevenhampton
Farm

RIVES LANE

Homegrown
Copse

HIGHWORTH ROAD

1

SN3

Thorny
Copse

Dogkennel
Copse

90

A   B   21   C   D   22   E   F

Dovecote

Park Wood Farm

Apsimore Wood

Park Wood

Tumuli

Waste Barn

Didmarton Grove

GL8

89

Barn Farm

Avenue Farm

Glebe Barn Farm

Knockdown

Knockdown Farm

Oldbury on the Hill

Woodway Cottages

A433

PH

Warren Farm

Manor Farm

Earthworks

GL9

Bury Hill

Woodhayes House

Lower Oldbury Farm

88

Creephole

Joyce's Pool

BERTHA'S FIELD

PH

ST ARILD'S RD

CHAPEL WK

Whitehouse Farm

THE STREET

Sewage Works

A433 Bath (A46)

A433

Didmarton

Seven Mile Plantation

Worcester Lodge

Ashen Bottom

River Avon (Sherston Branch)

87

Crow Down Springs

Bullpark Wood

SN14

Northend Farm

Church Leaze Farm

Sopworth Brake

Sopworth

CHURCH LA

Street Farm

MANOR COTTS

Chilbury Hill

Manor Farm

86

81 · A · 82 · B · C · 82 · D · 83 · E · F

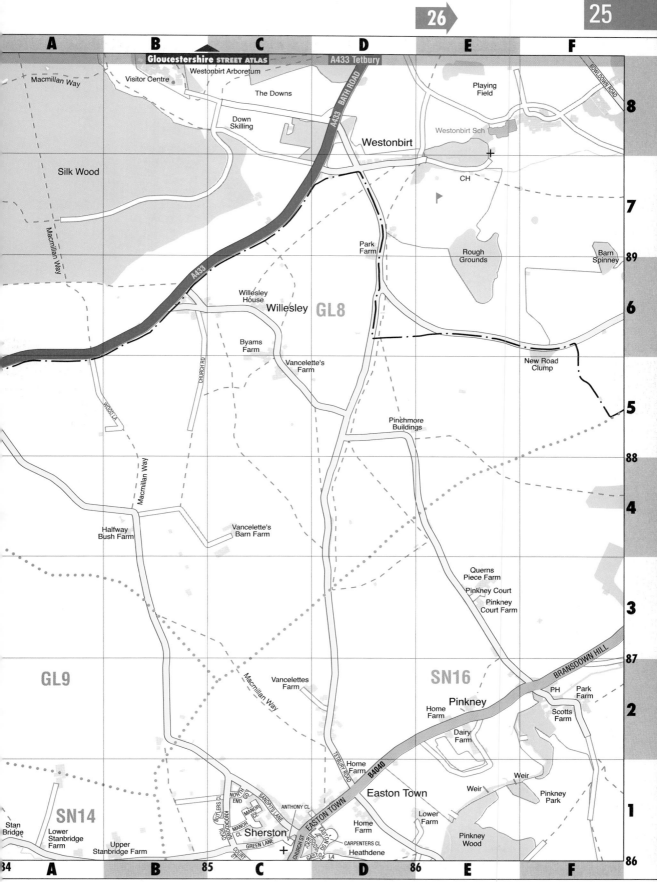

Gloucestershire STREET ATLAS

A433 Tetbury

A **B** **C** **D** **E** **F**

Macmillan Way

Visitor Centre

Westonbirt Arboretum

The Downs

Playing
Field

BOWLDOWN ROAD

8

Down
Skilling

Westonbirt Sch

Westonbirt

CH

Silk Wood

7

A433 BATH ROAD

Park
Farm

Rough
Grounds

Barn
Spinney

89

Macmillan Way

Willesley
House

Willesley

GL8

6

A433

New Road
Clump

Byams
Farm

CHURCH RD

Vancelette's
Farm

5

WOOD LA

Pinchmore
Buildings

88

Macmillan Way

4

Halfway
Bush Farm

Vancelette's
Barn Farm

Querns
Piece Farm

Pinkney Court

Pinkney
Court Farm

3

BRANSDOWN HILL

87

GL9

Macmillan Way

Vancelettes
Farm

SN16

Pinkney

PH

Park
Farm

Home
Farm

Scotts
Farm

2

Dairy
Farm

TETBURY ROAD

B4040

Home
Farm

Weir

Weir

Pinkney
Park

Easton Town

Lower
Farm

SN14

EASTON TOWN

Pinkney
Wood

1

Stan
Bridge

Lower
Stanbridge
Farm

NORTH
END

SANDPITS LANE

ANTHONY CL

Home
Farm

PITLERS CL

MANOR
CL

Sherston

CHURCH ST

CARPENTERS CL

Heathdene

Upper
Stanbridge Farm

GREEN LANE

GASTON
RD SOUTH

LA

86

A **B** **C** **D** **E** **F**

84   85   86

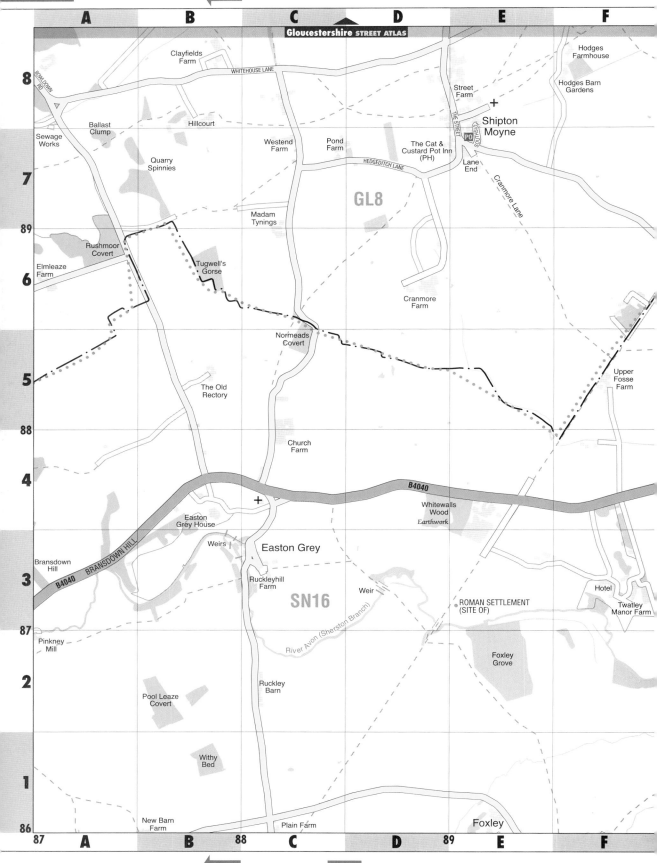

Gloucestershire STREET ATLAS

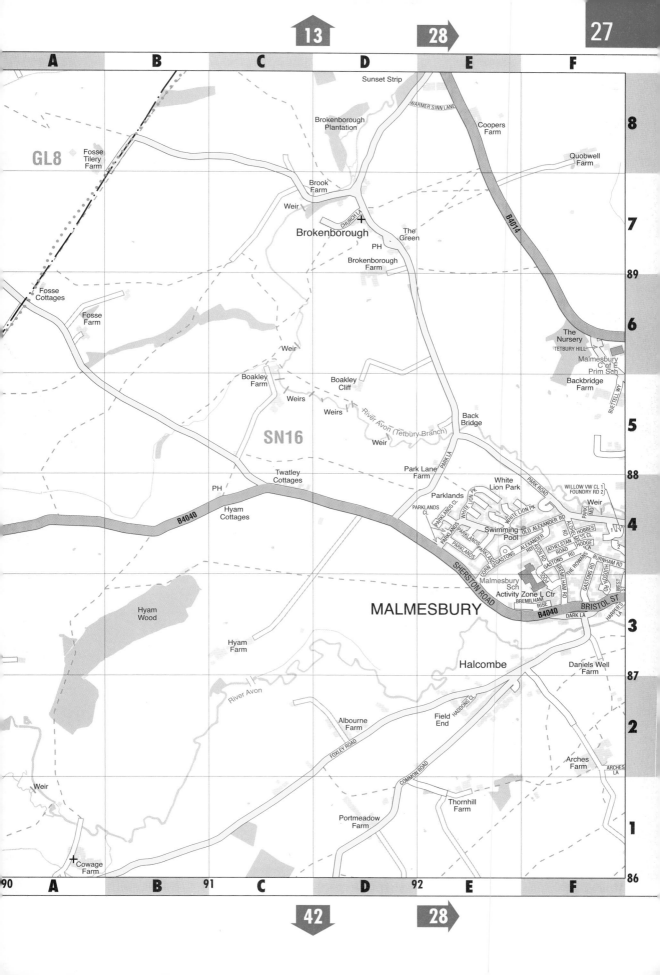

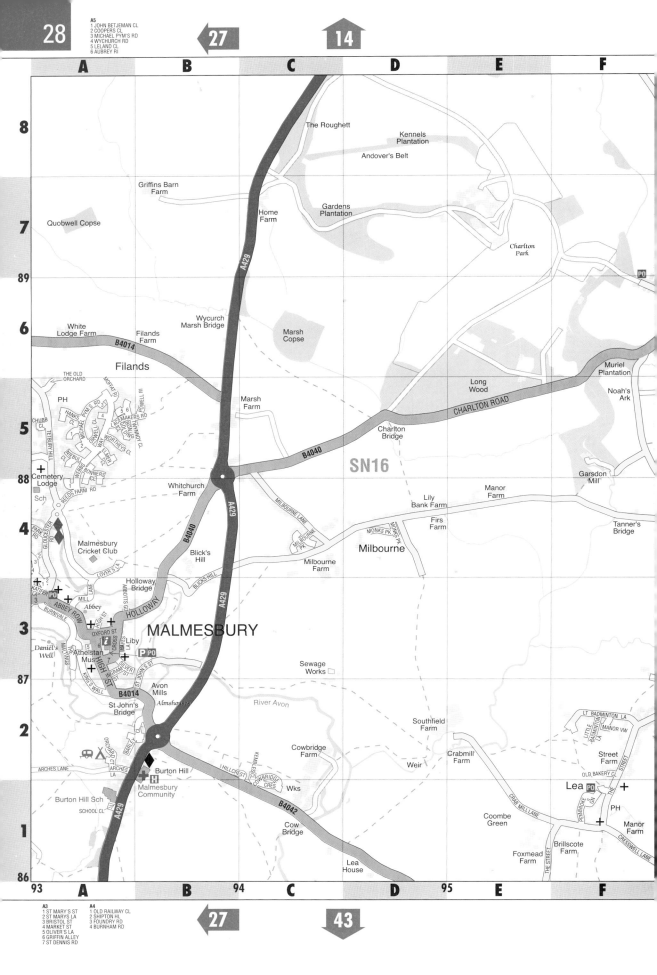

28

A5
1 JOHN BETJEMAN CL
2 COOPERS CL
3 MICHAEL PYM'S RD
4 WYCHURCH RD
5 LELAND CL
6 AUBREY RI

27

14

A B C D E F

8

The Roughett

Kennels
Plantation

Andover's Belt

7

Griffins Barn
Farm

Gardens
Plantation

Home
Farm

Quobwell Copse

Charlton
Park

89

White
Lodge Farm

Filands
Farm

Wycurch
Marsh Bridge

6

B4014

Marsh
Copse

Muriel
Plantation

Filands

THE OLD
ORCHARD

Marsh
Farm

Long
Wood

CHARLTON ROAD

Noah's
Ark

PH

MOFFAT RI
POWELL RI

5

HANKS
CL

LACEMAKERS RD
GOLDING

TWINNOY CL

Charlton
Bridge

Lily
Bank Farm

Manor
Farm

Garsdon
Mill

CHUBB
CL

MICHAEL PYM'S RD
POWELL CL
WAY WORTHEYS CL
ELMER
WEBBS

B4040

SN16

Firs
Farm

TETBURY HILL

INEBULL

BONNERS
CT

88

Cemetery
Lodge

REEDS FARM RD
BONNERS CL

Whitchurch
Farm

MILBOURNE LANE

Tanner's
Bridge

Sch

MILBOURNE
PK

MONKS PK

4

GLOUCESTER RD

PARK
RD

Malmesbury
Cricket Club

B4040

Blick's
Hill

MILBOURNE
PK

MONKS PK

Milbourne

Daniel's
Well

LOVER'S LA

Holloway
Bridge

BLICKS HILL

Milbourne
Farm

A429

MILL LANE

ABBOTTS GD

HOLLOWAY

MATTINGS

Abbey

BURNIVALE

ABBEY ROW

PO

OXFORD ST

3

MALMESBURY

CROSS

Liby

Sewage
Works

Athelstan
Mus

HIGH ST

HAYES LA

P PO

Daniel's
Well

KING'S WALL

INGRAM ST

SILVER ST
ST JOHN'S ST

87

B4014

Avon
Mills

Almshouses

River Avon

Southfield
Farm

St John's
Bridge

ORCHARD RD

BARTE CL

LT. BADMINTON LA

2

ARCHES
LA

Cowbridge
Farm

MANOR VW

LITTLE
BADMINTON
LA

ARCHES LANE

HILLCREST

KEMBLES CL

COWBRIDGE
CRES

Weir

Crabmill
Farm

Street
Farm

Burton Hill

OLD BAKERY CL

THE STREET

Wks

Malmesbury
Community

Lea

PO

A429

SCHOOL CL

B4042

CRAB MILL LANE

PENBROKE
GDNS

PH

Burton Hill Sch

Manor
Farm

Cow
Bridge

Coombe
Green

1

Foxmead
Farm

Brillscote
Farm

THE STREET

CRESSWELL LANE

86

Lea
House

93 A 94 B C 95 D E F

A3
1 ST MARY'S ST
2 ST MARYS LA
3 BRISTOL ST
4 MARKET ST
5 OLIVER'S LA
6 GRIFFIN ALLEY
7 ST DENNIS RD

A4
1 OLD RAILWAY CL
2 SHIPTON HL
3 FOUNDRY RD
4 BURNHAM RD

27

43

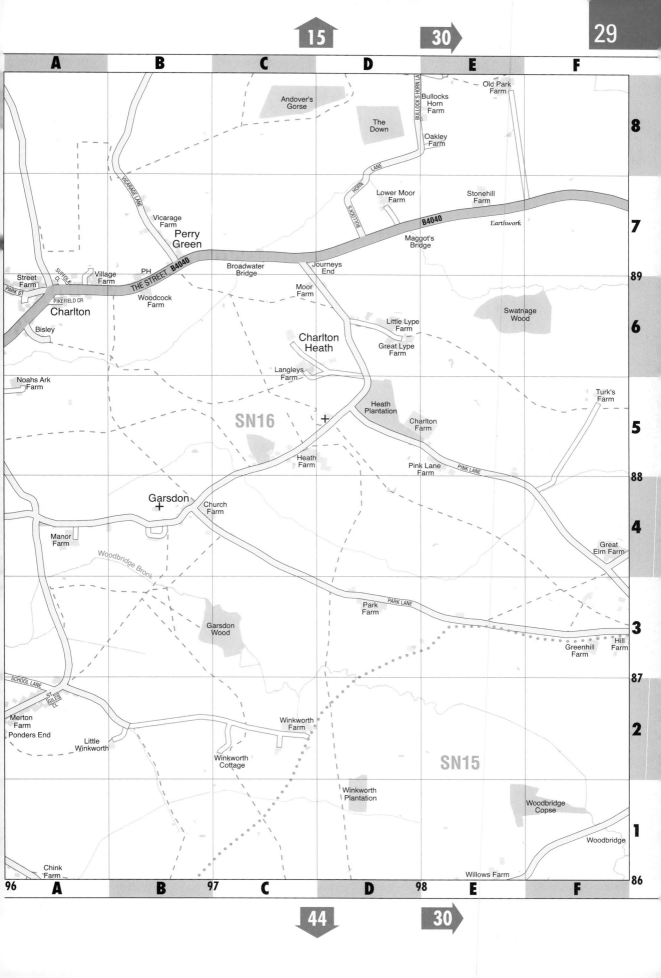

A B C D E F

8

7

B4040

89

SN16

6

Park Copse

Square Plantation

Woodward Farm

Perlieu Plantation

Kemble's Farm

DOG TRAP LANE

Stone Hill

Stonehill Wood

Cockroost Farm

Purlieus Farm

B4040

Summer House Farm

Bick Farm Cottages

Water Twr

Cocked Hat Wood

Bicks Farm

Pond Hill Farm

Long Wood

Pond Farm

Braydon Wood

Nineteen Acre Wood

5

Great Withy Wood

88

Braydon Pond

Pond Lodge

Worthy Hill Farm

4

Braydon Wood

PARK LANE

New House Farm

Braydon Wood

3

PARK LANE

87

Woodhill Farm

Somerford Farm

Milbourne Common Wood

2

Fernhill Farm

Wood Hill

Sundays Hill

Tanglin Farm

SN15

Horsells Farm

1

Rouselands Farm

Dollaker's Green

Sundey Hill Farm

86

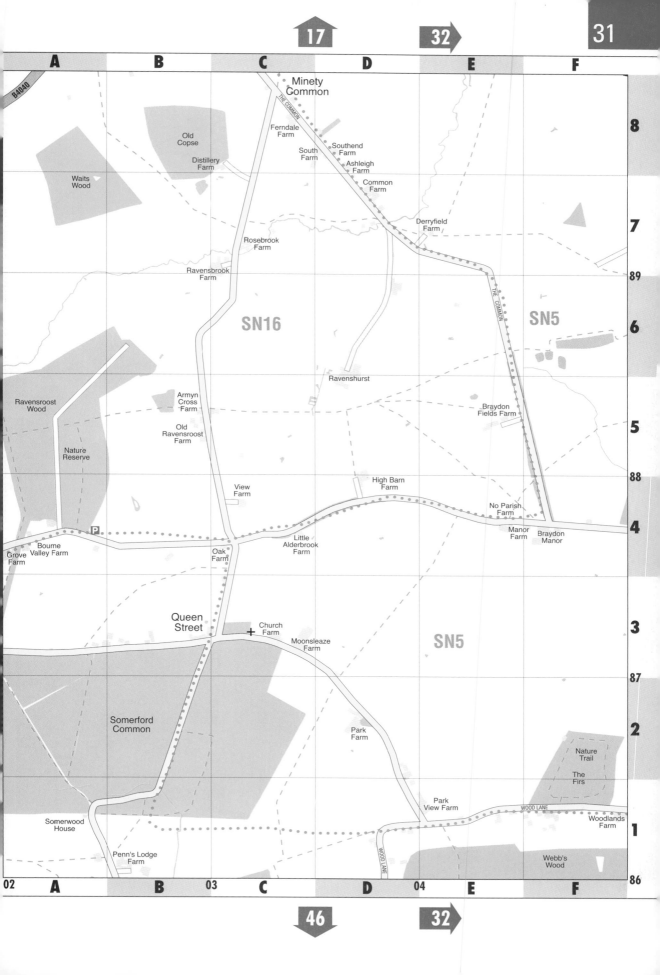

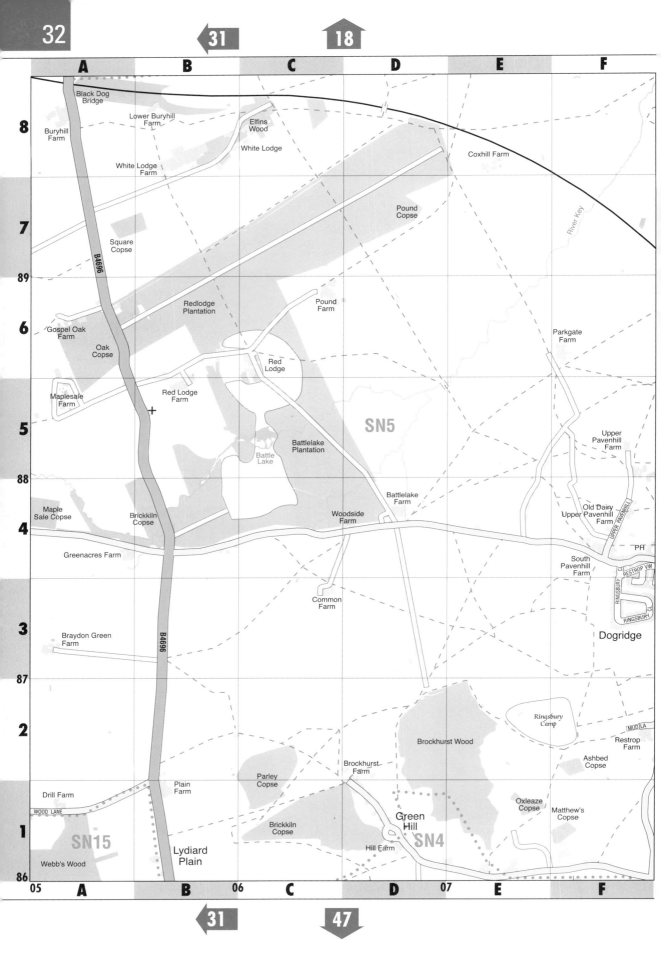

A B C D E F

8

7

89

6

5

88

4

3

87

2

1

86

Black Dog Bridge

Buryhill Farm

Lower Buryhill Farm

Elfins Wood

White Lodge

White Lodge Farm

Coxhill Farm

Pound Copse

River Key

B4696

Square Copse

Redlodge Plantation

Pound Farm

Parkgate Farm

Gospel Oak Farm

Oak Copse

Red Lodge

Maplesale Farm

Red Lodge Farm

Battle Lake

Battlelake Plantation

SN5

Upper Pavenhill Farm

Maple Sale Copse

Brickkiln Copse

Battlelake Farm

Woodside Farm

Old Dairy Upper Pavenhill Farm

UPPER PAVENHILL

PH

Greenacres Farm

Common Farm

South Pavenhill Farm

RINGSBURY CL

RESTROP VW

Braydon Green Farm

B4696

Dogridge

RINGSBURY CL

Ringsbury Camp

MUD LA

Restrop Farm

Brockhurst Wood

Ashbed Copse

Drill Farm

WOOD LANE

Plain Farm

Parley Copse

Brockhurst Farm

Oxleaze Copse

Matthew's Copse

SN15

Brickkiln Copse

Green Hill

SN4

Webb's Wood

Lydiard Plain

Hill Farm

05 A B 06 C D 07 E F

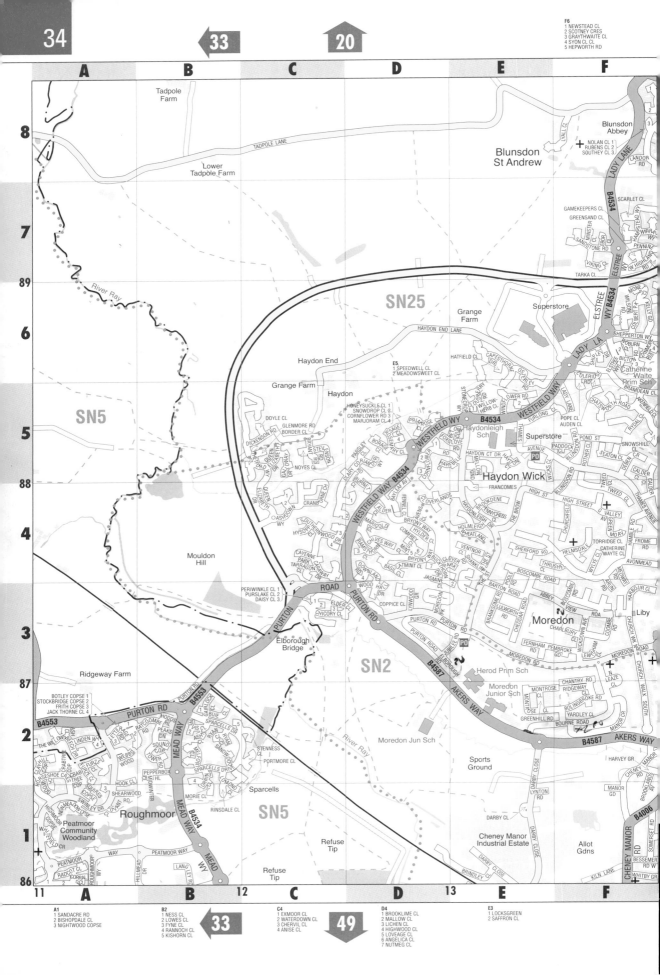

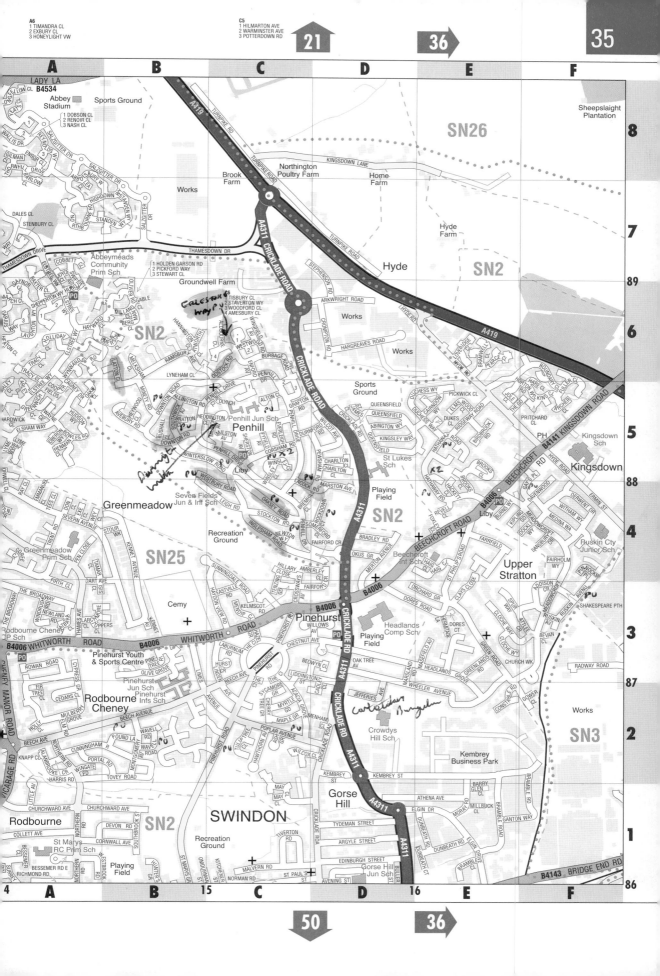

A   B   C   D   E   F

8

Sheepslaight Plantation

SN26

SN6

The Cottage Park Farm
Park Farm

Great Wood

South Field Copse

HIGHWORTH ROAD

Beech Farm

HIGHWORTH RD

Sports Ground

Hunt's Copse

South Marston Park

Broadmoor Rd

7

Kingsdown Crem

SN2

A361

Woodside Road

Stirling Road

Broadmoor Road

Woodside Rd

Broadmoor Copse

Marston Copse

89

B4141

South Marston Park Industrial Estate

Stirling Road

Lancaster Pl

Lancaster Ms

Burton Grove Farm

6

Kingsdown Road

SN25

HIGHWORTH RD

Stirling Road

Viscount Way

Kingsdown Farm

5

SN2

1 BROCKLEY RI
2 HORNSEY GD
3 CHOBHAM CL
4 WALWAYNE FLD

HIGHWORTH RD

A361

Motor Works

Quarry Farm

QUARRYBROOK CLOSE

BYRON COURT

CHAPEL LA

South Marston

88

Hadleigh Ri
Retingham Way
Bedding Cl
Ross Gd

Kingsdown

Wynndale Cl

Greenfields
PO
PH

CHURCH FARM LN

Sevor Farm

NIGHTINGALE LANE

4

Briery Cl

Ermin Street

HIGHWORTH ROAD

St Margarets

H

Belmont Cl

Delamere Drive

B4006

Sewage Works

Yew Tree Farm

St Julians Farm

YEW TREE GD

Downderry

Hotel

MANOR PK

Playing Field

South Marston Arms & Leisure Club

Pigeon House Farm

SN3

SWINDON

Stratton St Margaret

Parsonage Road

Hobley Dr

Ermin St

Grange Inf Sch

Gifford Road

Godwin Road

A419

Sewage Works

Works

Manor Farm

3

Works

Radway Road

B4006

Swindon Road

Pigeon House Lane

Carman Cl

Cemy

Oxleaze Farm

South Marston Farm

87

Works

Bridgeman Cl

Lower Stratton

Grange Junior Sch

Ermin Street

Kenwin Cl

Blake Cres

Watefmead

Park St

Hatherhal Cl

Priory Farm

Marston Farm

2

Tilley's La

Chamberlain Rd

Casson Rd

Bunce

Marshfield

Bourton Av

Overton Cl

Yiewsley Cres

Griffiths Close

Hotel

A420

Home Farm

St Margarets Retail Park

SN4

1

Cameron Cl

B4143

B4006

SWINDON RD

Winchester Cl

Burgess Cl

PO

Sandgate

OXFORD ROAD

Castle Vw

Whelstone

Cullerne Road

Hill View Road

WANBOROUGH ROAD

MERLIN WY A420

86

A4312

Slade Dr

Colebrook Road

Nythe Road

Hill View Road

Trajan Road

17   A   B   18   C   D   19   E   F

A2
1 STRATTON OR
2 CALLAGHAN CL
3 GOULDING CL
4 SHAPLANDS
5 THE PADDOCKS

B2
1 ST MARGARET'S GN
2 FRANKTON GD

B3
1 BROWNING CL
2 WARNER CL
3 COTTARS CL
4 BARON CL
5 BOWMAN CL
6 CRISPIN CL
7 CHURCH WAY
8 FRANK WARMAN CT

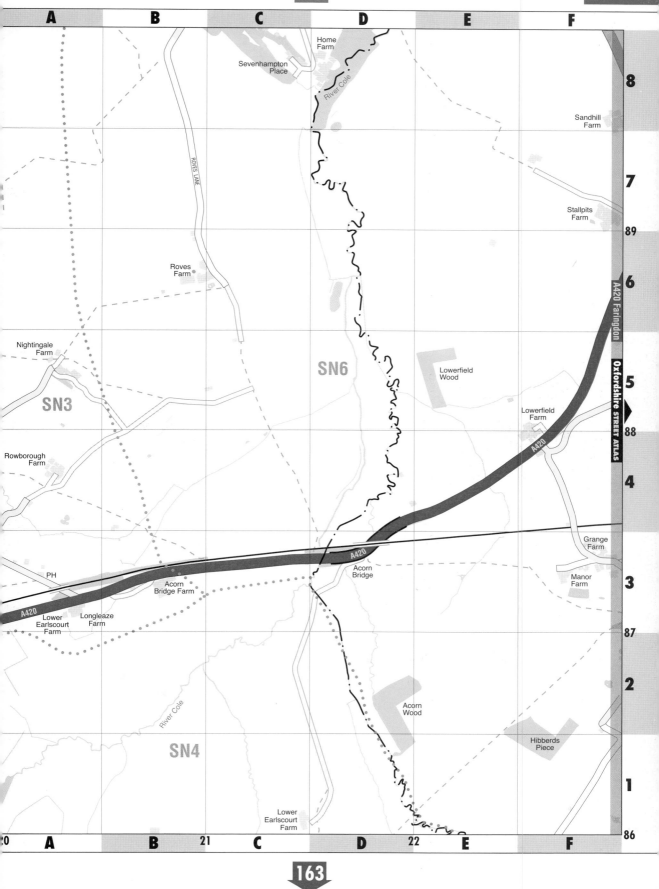

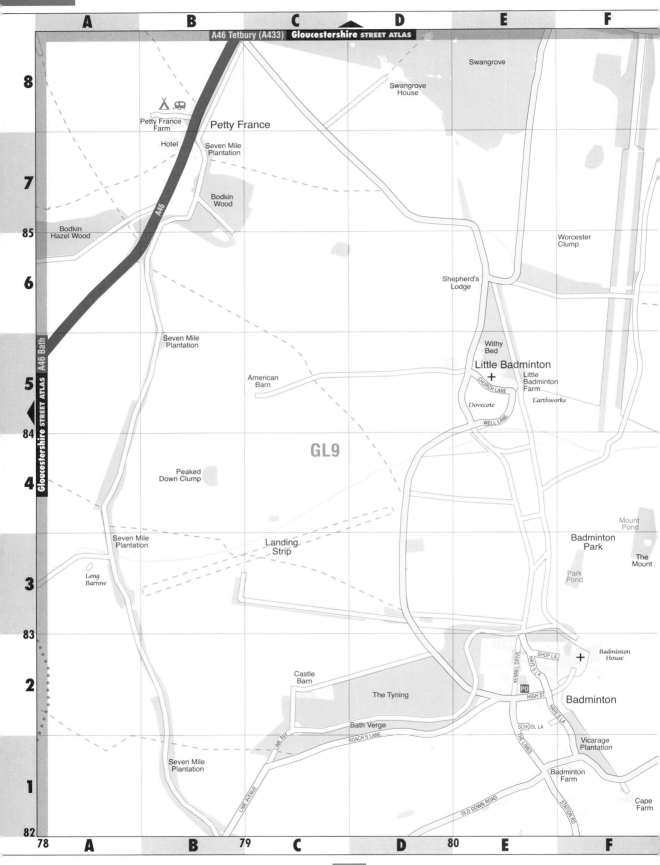

Swangrove

Swangrove
House

Petty France
Farm

Petty France

Hotel

Seven Mile
Plantation

Bodkin
Wood

Worcester
Clump

Bodkin
Hazel Wood

A46

Shepherd's
Lodge

Seven Mile
Plantation

Withy
Bed

Little Badminton

American
Barn

CHURCH LANE

Little
Badminton
Farm

Dovecote

Earthworks

WELL LANE

GL9

Peaked
Down Clump

A46 Bath

Gloucestershire STREET ATLAS

Seven Mile
Plantation

Landing
Strip

Mount
Pond

Badminton
Park

The
Mount

Long
Barrow

Park
Pond

Badminton
House

SHOP LA

KENNEL DRIVE

HAYE'S LA

Castle
Barn

The Tyning

PO

HIGH ST

Badminton

HAYE'S LA

Bath Verge

LIME AVE

ROACH'S LANE

SCHOOL LA

Vicarage
Plantation

THE LIMES

Seven Mile
Plantation

LIME AVENUE

Badminton
Farm

STATION RD

OLD DOWN ROAD

Cape
Farm

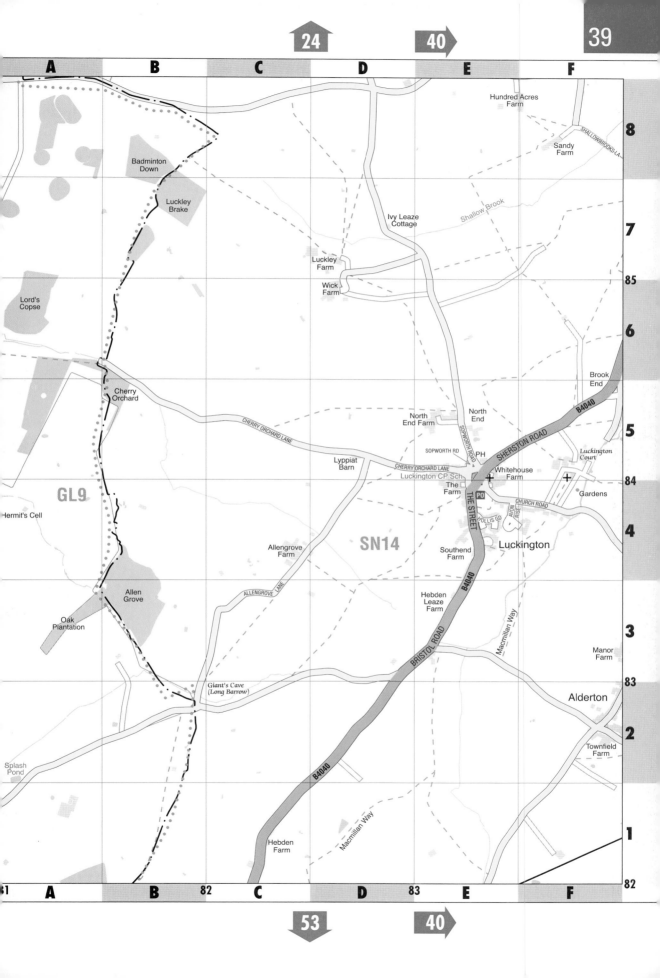

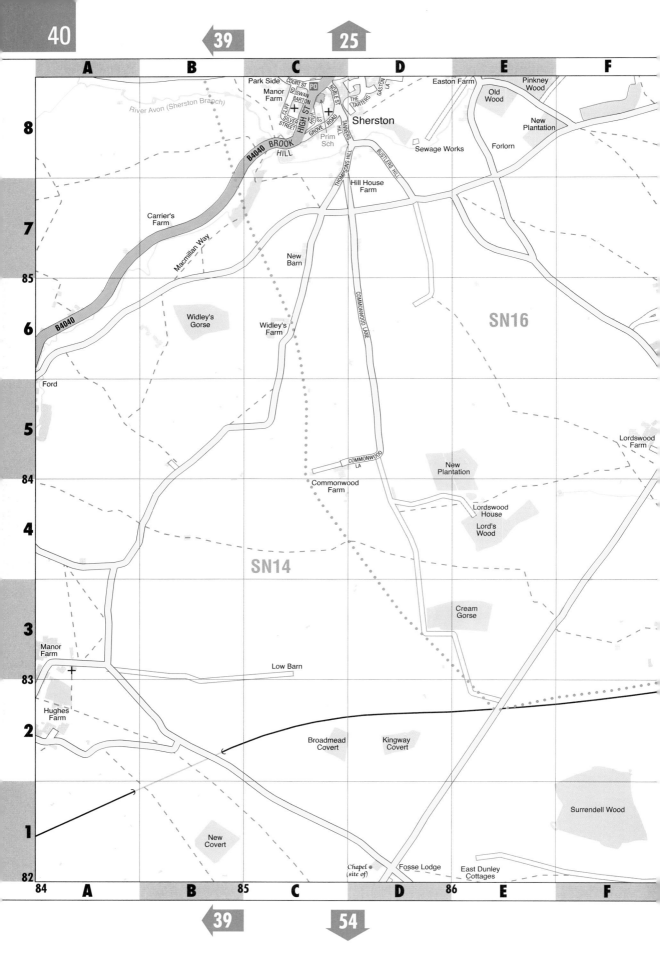

A B C D E F

River Avon (Sherston Branch)

Park Side
Manor
Farm
Easton Farm
Pinkney
Wood
Old
Wood
New
Plantation

COURT ST
SWAN
GASTON LA
THE
TARTERS
NOBLE ST
HIGH ST
CLIFF
SILVER
STREET
GROVE
ROAD
PO
Sherston

8

Prim
Sch
Sewage Works
Forlorn

B4040 BROOK
HILL

BUSTERS HILL
THOMPSONS HILL

Carrier's
Farm
Hill House
Farm

7

Macmillan Way
New
Barn

85
SN16

6
B4040
Widley's
Gorse
Widley's
Farm
COMMONWOOD LANE

Ford

5
Lordswood
Farm

84
COMMONWOOD
LA
New
Plantation

Commonwood
Farm
Lordswood
House

4
Lord's
Wood

SN14

Cream
Gorse

3
Manor
Farm

83
Low Barn

Hughes
Farm

2
Broadmead
Covert
Kingway
Covert

Surrendell Wood

1
New
Covert

Chapel
(site of)
Fosse Lodge
East Dunley
Cottages

82
84 A B 85 C D 86 E F

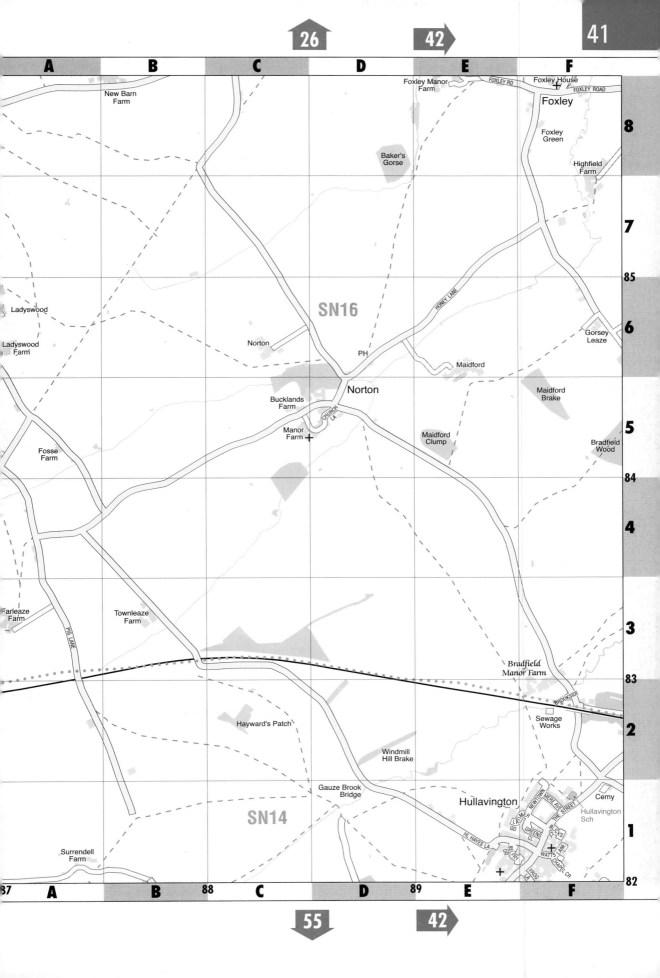

A B C D E F

8
7
85
6
5
84
4
3
83
2
1
82

New Barn Farm

Foxley Manor Farm

FOXLEY RD

Foxley House

FOXLEY ROAD

Foxley

Foxley Green

Baker's Gorse

Highfield Farm

SN16

HONEY LANE

Ladyswood

Ladyswood Farm

Norton

PH

Maidford

Gorsey Leaze

Norton

Bucklands Farm

CHURCH LA

Maidford Clump

Maidford Brake

Bradfield Wood

Manor Farm

Fosse Farm

Farleaze Farm

PIG LANE

Townleaze Farm

Hayward's Patch

Bradfield Manor Farm

BROOKSIDE

Sewage Works

Windmill Hill Brake

Gauze Brook Bridge

SN14

Hullavington

NEWTOWN

MERE AVE

THE STREET

Cemy

Hullavington Sch

LIME GD

GREENS CL

BUCKS CL

HL HAYES LA

BELFRY DRI

WATTS

CHAPEL CR

FROG LA

Surrendell Farm

87 A B 88 C D 89 E F

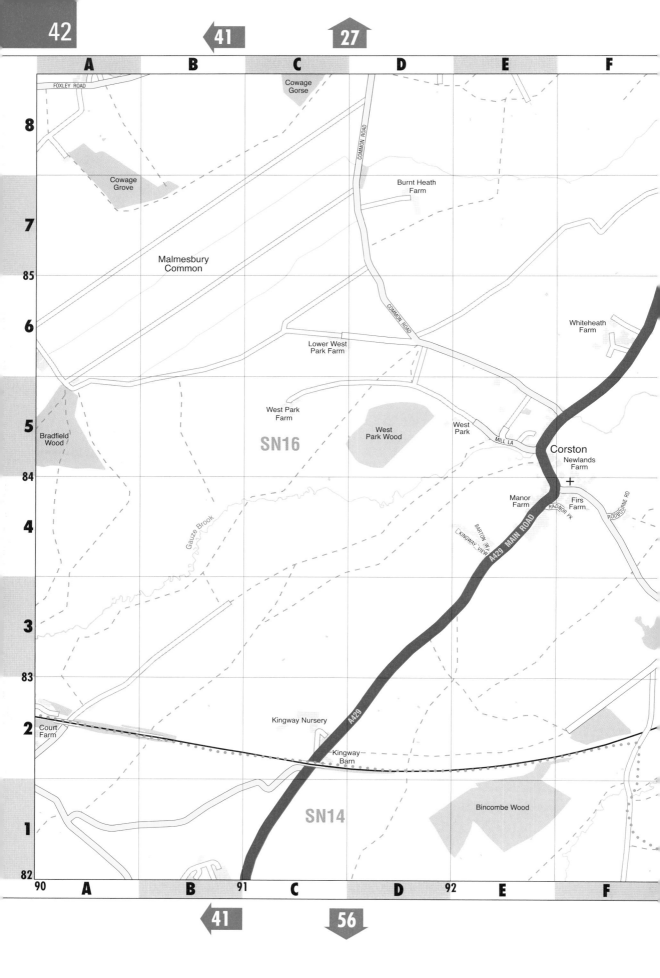

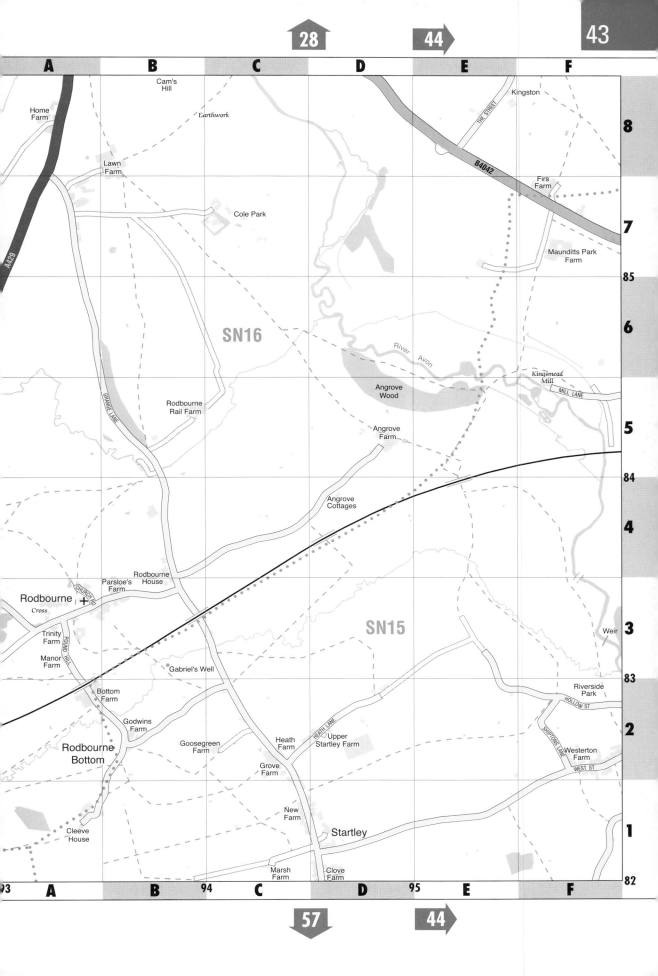

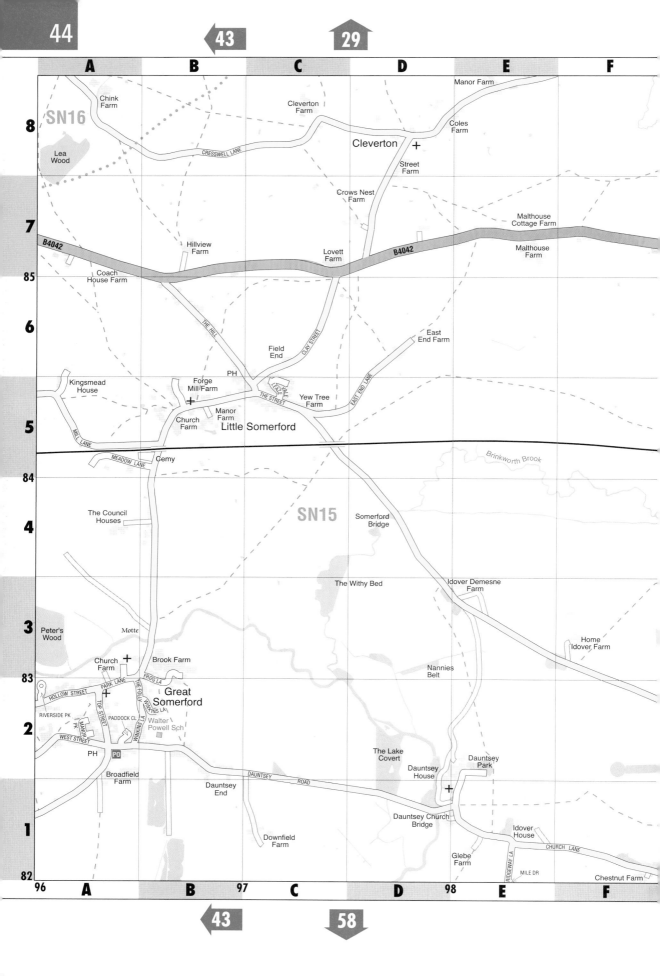

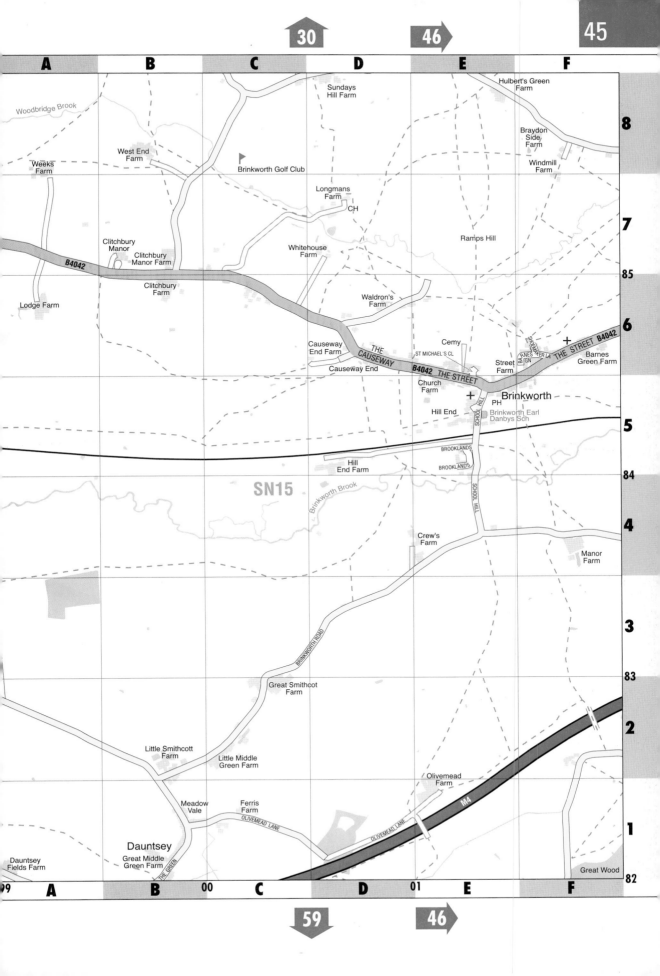

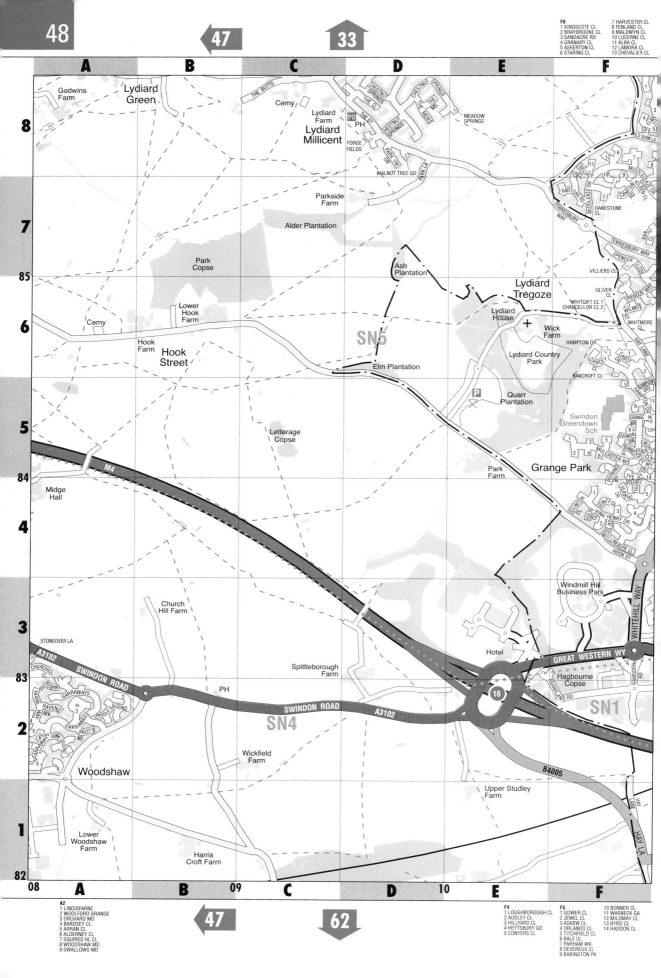

F8
1 KINGSCOTE CL
2 BRAYBROOKE CL
3 SANDACRE RD
4 GRANARY CL
5 ASKERTON CL
6 STARING CL
7 HARVESTER CL
8 FENLAND CL
9 MALDWYN CL
10 LUCERNE CL
11 ALBA CL
12 LAMORA CL
13 CHEVALIER CL

Godwins Farm

Lydiard Green

THE BUTTS

Cemy

Lydiard Farm

Lydiard Millicent

CHESTNUT SPRINGS

THE ST

THE CL

CHESTNUT SPRINGS

THE MS

THE MEWS

CHESTNUT SPRINGS

MEADOW SPRINGS

MEADOW SPRINGS

PO

PH

FORGE FIELDS

PARK DR

PARK VW

PARK LA

WALNUT TREE GD

THE OLD SHAW LA

TALLIS

MIDDLELEZE DR

CATTLIN GREEN CL

GARTONS RD

MIDDLELEZE DR

DANESTONE

TEWKESBURY WAY

EAST LT

Parkside Farm

Alder Plantation

TEWKESBURY WAY

SPENCER CLOSE

VILLIERS CL

Park Copse

Ash Plantation

Lydiard Tregoze

VILLIERS CL

OLIVER CL

WHITGIFT CL 1
CHANCELLOR CL 2

TREGOZE WAY

WILMOT CL

WHITMORE CL

Cemy

Lower Hook Farm

Lydiard House

Wick Farm

HAMPTON DR

HAY LANE

Cemy

Hook Farm

Hook Street

SN5

Elm Plantation

Lydiard Country Park

BANCROFT CL

DARCY

CABOT

HAMPTON DR

Midge Hall

M4

Letterage Copse

P

Quarr Plantation

Swindon Greendown Sch

Park Farm

Grange Park

MULCASTER AVE

GRANGE PK

GRINDAL

SIMKINS SD

SERLEY

TYE

THURLOW

HANKS CL

CLINTON

KING HENRY DR

ROSS CL

LINEACRE WY

HOOK ST

Church Hill Farm

Windmill Hill Business Park

WHITEHILL WAY

STONEOVER LA

A3102

SWINDON ROAD

CHURCHILL

REDBRIDGE

GARRAWAYS

RAVENS WK

HARTE WY

GARRAWAYS

BAILEY'S

HOME GROUND

TOWER ROUND

FAIRE WY

2

3

Spittleborough Farm

PH

SWINDON ROAD

A3102

Hotel

16

Hagbourne Copse

FRANKLAND RD

RAMSDEN

GREAT WESTERN WY

SN1

SN4

Woodshaw

Wickfield Farm

B4005

Upper Studley Farm

HAY LA

Lower Woodshaw Farm

Harris Croft Farm

A2
1 LINDISFARNE
2 WOOLFORD GRANGE
3 ORCHARD MD
4 BARDSEY CL
5 ARRAN CL
6 ALDERNEY CL
7 SQUIRES HL CL
8 WOODSHAW MD
9 SWALLOWS MD

F4
1 LOUGHBOROUGH CL
2 AUDLEY CL
3 HILLYARD CL
4 HEYTSBURY GD
5 CONYERS CL

F5
1 GOWER CL
2 JEWEL CL
3 ASKEW CL
4 ORLANDO CL
5 TITCHFIELD CL
6 BALE CL
7 PARHAM WK
8 DEVEREUX CL
9 BABINGTON PK
10 BONNER CL
11 WARBECK GA
12 MILDMAY CL
13 BYRD CL
14 HADDON CL

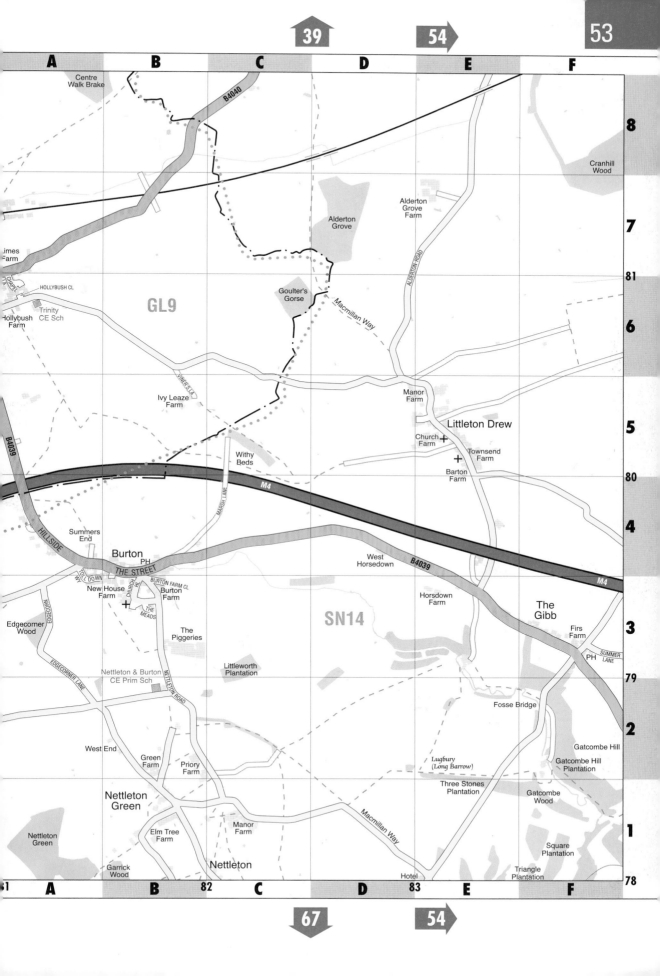

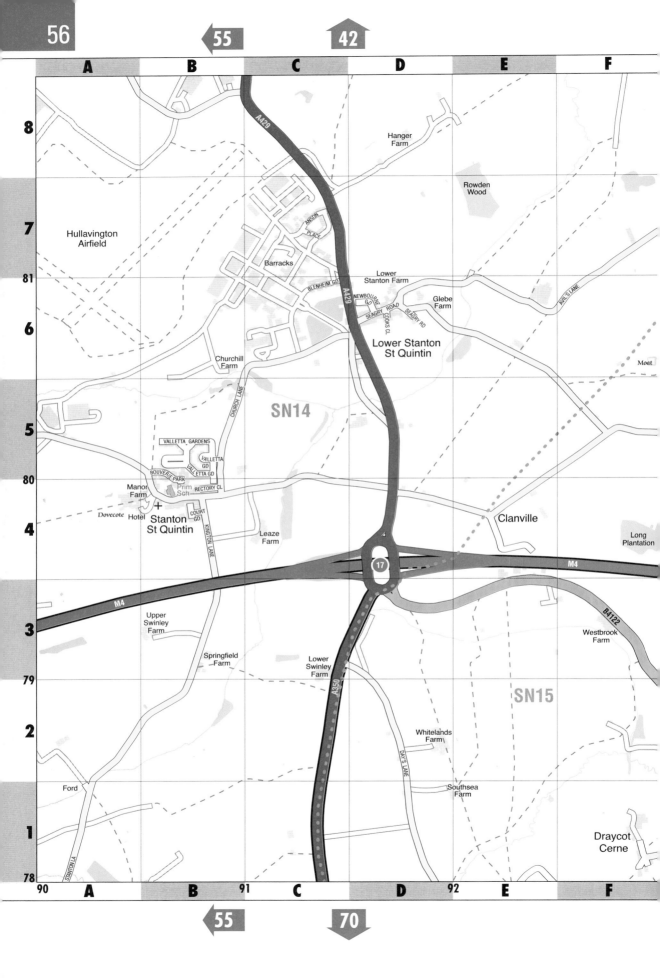

A B C D E F

Startley Farm

Seagry Heath

Honey Acre Farm

New Leaze Farm

8

Seagry Wood

Upper Farm

Albany Farm

7

AVIL'S LANE

Avil's Farm

Lower Seagry Farm

Lower Seagry

Trinity Farm

81

Seagry House

Five Thorn Farm

FIVE THORN LANE

CHURCH ACRE

Vicarage Cottages

HENN LANE

BROADLEAZE

Upper Seagry

Church Farm
Tithe Barn

6

Upper Seagry Sch

Moat

Manor Farm

Nables Farm

Woodman Croft Covert

Greenfields Farm

Ell Wood

Mill House

Weir

5

SCOTLAND HILL

North Draycot Park Farm

Hardinge

SN15

River Avon

80

M4

4

Long Plantation

The Cottage

Brookside

SEAGRY HILL

Summerlands Farm

Weirs

AVONWEIR LA

Malford Farm

3

MAIN ROAD

B4069

Christian Malford

79

River Avon

Draycott Park Farm

Draycot House

WILLOWBROOK END

Sutton Benger

MANOR FARM DR

PO

Church Farm

BARRETT LA

Church Piece

CHURCH PIECE

B4069

2

Weir

HIGH STREET

PH

Hotel
Sutton Benger CE Sch

SUTTON LA

SUTTON LA

B4122

Arms Farm

PH

CHESTNUT ROAD

QUEENS

SEAGRY RD

PARK LA

GREGORY CL

Sewage Works

CORONATION CL

LEE CR

COWLEY WAY

NEVILLE TR

WESTLAKE PL

SUTTON LANE

B4069

The Old Rectory

B4069

78

93 A B 94 C D 95 E F

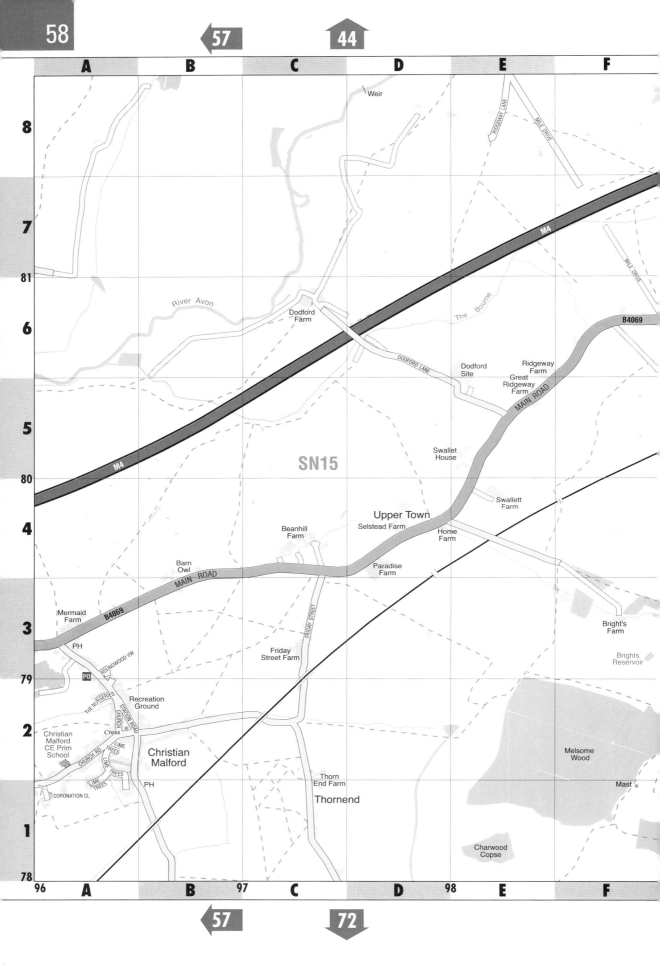

A B C D E F

8
7
81
6
5
80
4
3
79
2
1
78

Weir

RIDGEWAY LANE
MILE DRIVE

M4

River Avon

The Bourne

B4069

Dodford
Farm

DODFORD LANE

Dodford
Site

Dodford
Farm

Ridgeway
Farm

Great
Ridgeway
Farm

MAIN ROAD

MILE DRIVE

SN15

Swallet
House

Swallett
Farm

Upper Town

Beanhill
Farm

Selstead Farm

Home
Farm

Barn
Owl

MAIN ROAD

Paradise
Farm

Mermaid
Farm

B4069

PH

FRIDAY STREET

Bright's
Farm

Brights
Reservoir

PO

ROUNDWOOD VW

Friday
Street Farm

THE NURSERIES

STATION ROAD

Recreation
Ground

Christian
Malford
CE Prim
School

CHURCH RD

CHURCH

Cross

LIME
TREES

LIME
TREES

Christian
Malford

PH

LIME
TREES

CORONATION CL

Melsome
Wood

Mast

Thorn
End Farm

Thornend

Charwood
Copse

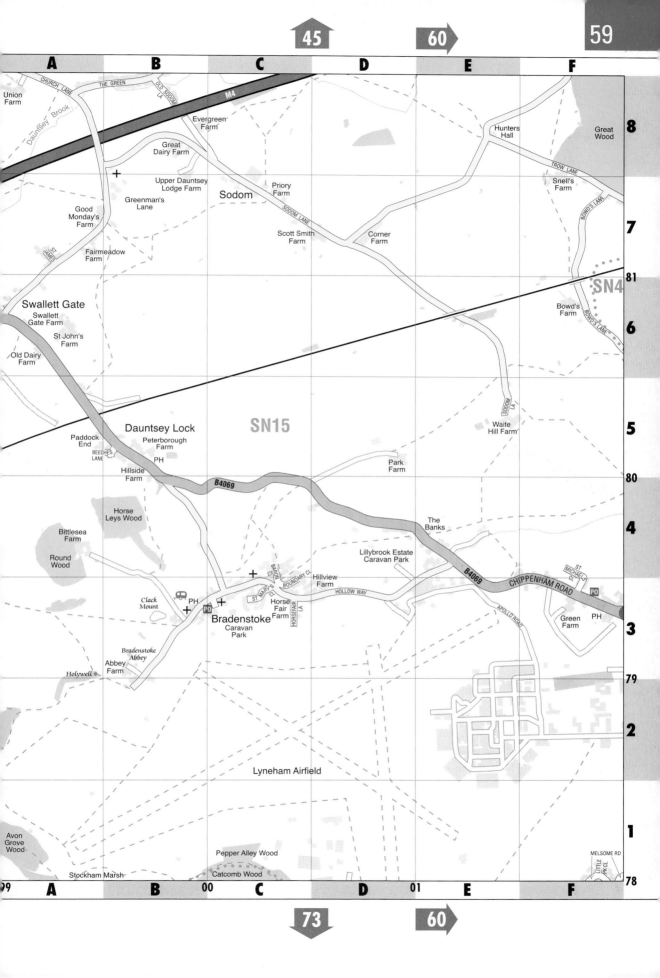

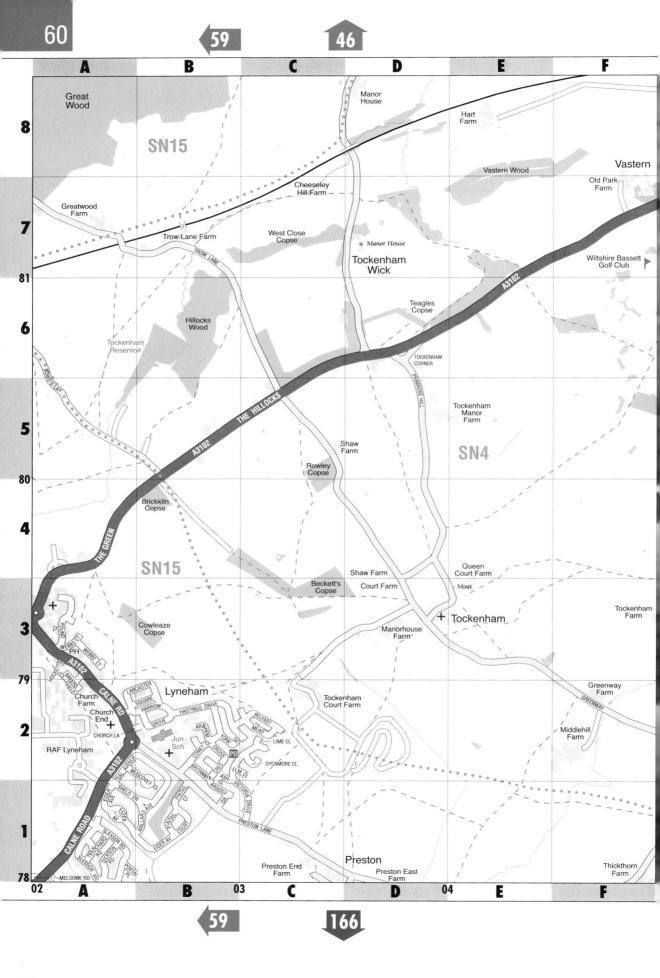

A B C D E F

Wootton Bassett

Skew Bridge

Knights Farm

SKEW BR CL
WESTBURY PARK
MORSTONE RD
ELM PK
NEW ROAD
PIPERS CL
STATION RD

HUNTS MILL ROAD

VASTERN WHARF
A3102

Huntsmill Farm

DUNNINGTON RD
GLENVILLE CL
TEMPLAR'S
FIRS

Brynard's Hill

Greenhill Common Farm

Brinkworth Brook

MARLBOROUGH ROAD

CH

Lanes Farm

Kendricks Farm

Meadow Farm

Meux Farm

Little Park Farm

Vale Farm

Wootton Fields Farm

Ashdown Farm
BROADTOWN LA

Lower Greenhill Farm

SN4

Barn Hill Farm

BREACH LANE

Upper Greenhill Farm

Lower Ham Farm

Hambrook Farm

Clyffe Pypard Wood

The Barton

Upper Ham Farm

Common Farm

Parsonage Farm

New House South Farm

Manor Farm

Thornhill

SN15

North Farm

WITHY BED

WOOD STREET

Wood Street Farm

8

7

81

6

5

80

4

3

79

2

1

78

5 A B 06 C D 07 E F

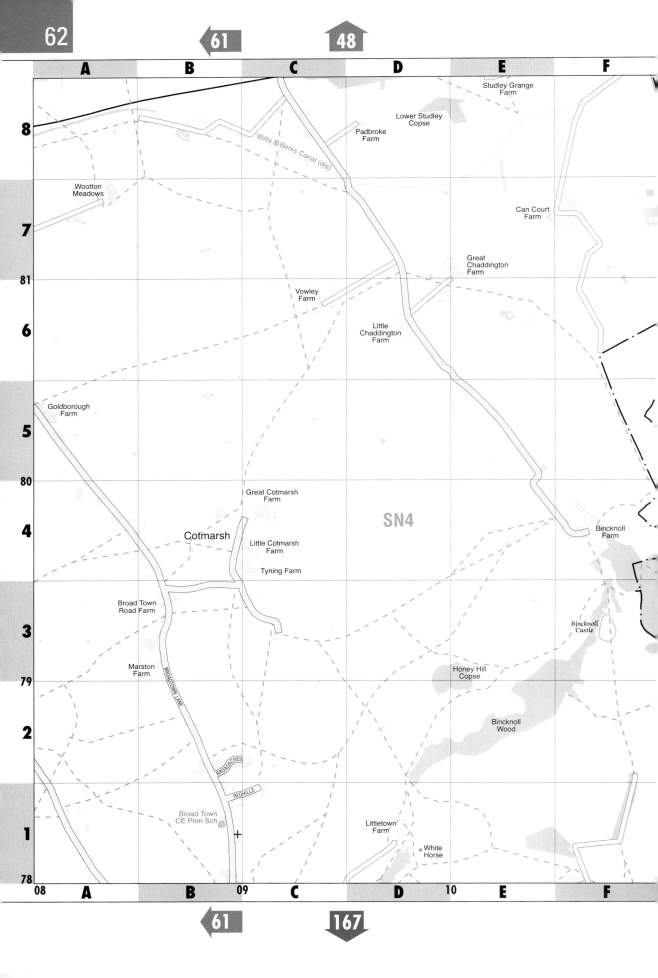

A B C D E F

8
7
81
6
5
80
4
3
79
2
1
78

14 A B 15 C D 16 E F

SN1
SN3
SN4
SN3

WOODLAND VIEW
Wroughton Covert
Croft Wood
BRETTINGHAM GATE
Bird Sanctuary
Nightingale Farm
CROFT RD
A4361
SWINDON RD
MOORE CL
Refuse Tip
BURDEROP CL
THE MOUNTINGS
North Wroughton
Sewage Works
Wroughton Cty Junior Sch
Sports Centre
Ridgeway Sch
LISTER ROAD
PETER CL
HACKPEN CL
MARINE CL
ST ANDREWS CL
BERKELEY ROAD
ARTIS CL
BAILEY'S WAY
Berkeley Farm
Burderop Wood
M4
MAUNSELL WY
FALKIRK RD
BONESS ROAD
HALIFAX CL
DUNBAR ROAD
BEAUFORT RD
BARCELONA RD
JOHN RD
KENNET RD
BLENHEIM CL
STIRLING RD
ANTHONY ROAD
LANCASTER RD
KEARS WAY
PLUMMER CL
PERRY'S LANE
MILL CLOSE
WEIRSIDE AV
COVENTRY CL
Works
Hotel
Wood Farm
BMI The Ridgeway
MOORMEAD RD
Ladder Hill
Lodge Farm
B4005 WHARF ROAD
CORONATION RD
Wroughton Cty Inf Sch
1 BARRETT WAY
2 SPENCERS ORCHARD
THREE TUNS ROUNDABOUT
H
DEVIZES RD
PH
MARLBOROUGH ROAD
Burderop Park
CHIL
A4361 HIGH STREET
PO
Wroughton
THE PITCHENS
WILLOW WK
MANOR CL
PRIMS HILL
ROBERTS CL
BAKERS RD
GREEN'S LANE
THE PITCHENS
WANSDT CL
WINSMORE CL
COOMBE CL
B4005 BRIMBLE HILL
SNAPPS CL
OVERTOWN HILL
DAIRY ROAD
Coombe Bottom
Moorleaze Farm
Overtown House
Overtown
Great Moorleaze Farm
Coombe Bottom
Overtown Farm
BERANBURH FIELD
Burderop Hackpen

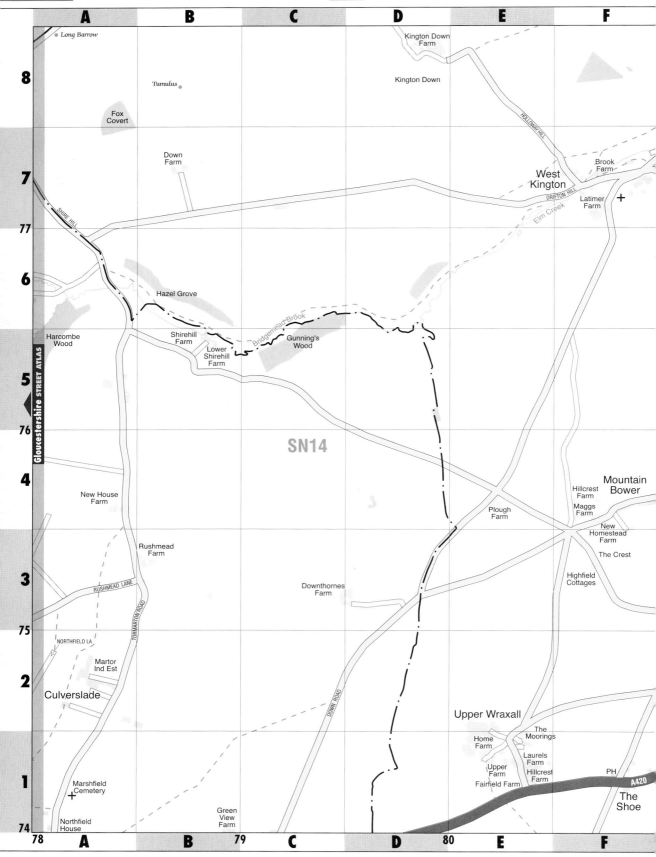

Long Barrow

Kington Down Farm

Tumulus

Kington Down

8

Fox Covert

HOLLOWAY HILL

Down Farm

Brook Farm

West Kington

7

SHIRE HILL

DRIFTON HILL

Latimer Farm

Elm Creek

77

6

Hazel Grove

Harcombe Wood

Shirehill Farm

Bridgemead Brook

Gunning's Wood

Gloucestershire STREET ATLAS

Lower Shirehill Farm

5

76

SN14

4

New House Farm

Mountain Bower

Hillcrest Farm

Maggs Farm

Plough Farm

New Homestead Farm

The Crest

Rushmead Farm

Downthornes Farm

Highfield Cottages

3

RUSHMEAD LANE

75

TORMARTON ROAD

NORTHFIELD LA

DOWN ROAD

Martor Ind Est

2

Culverslade

Upper Wraxall

Home Farm

The Moorings

Laurels Farm

Upper Farm

Hillcrest Farm

PH

A420

1

Marshfield Cemetery

Fairfield Farm

The Shoe

Green View Farm

Northfield House

74

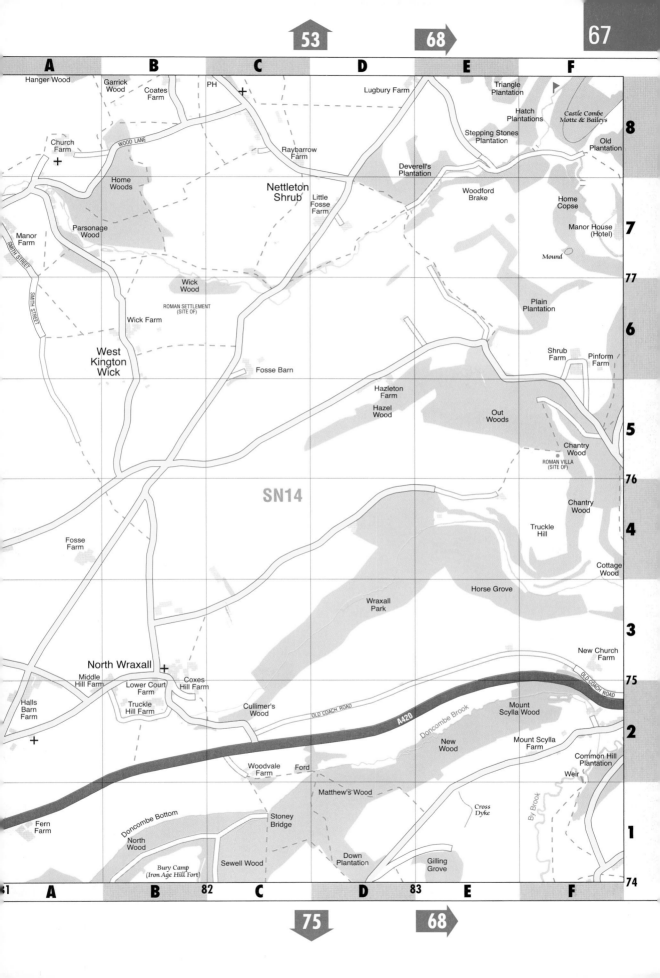

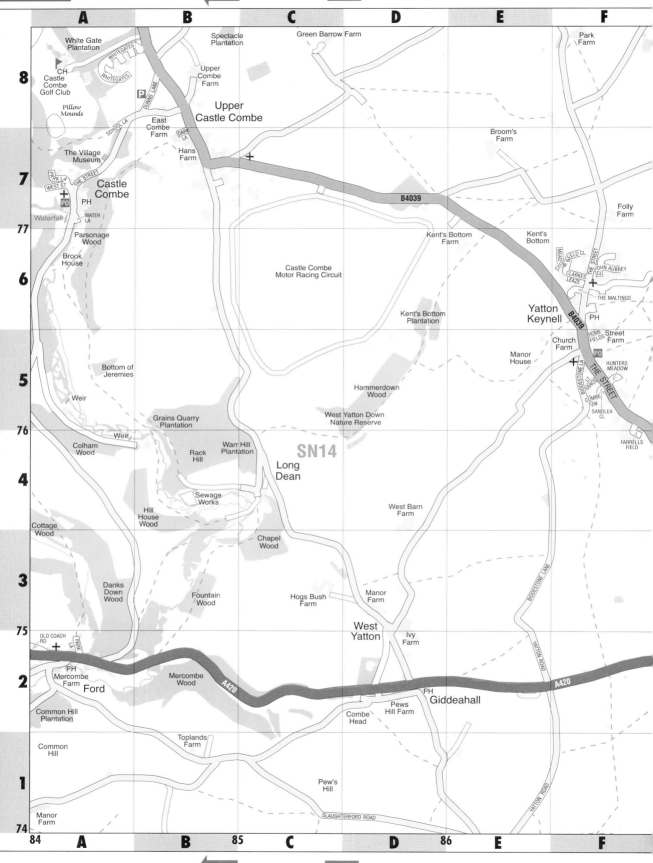

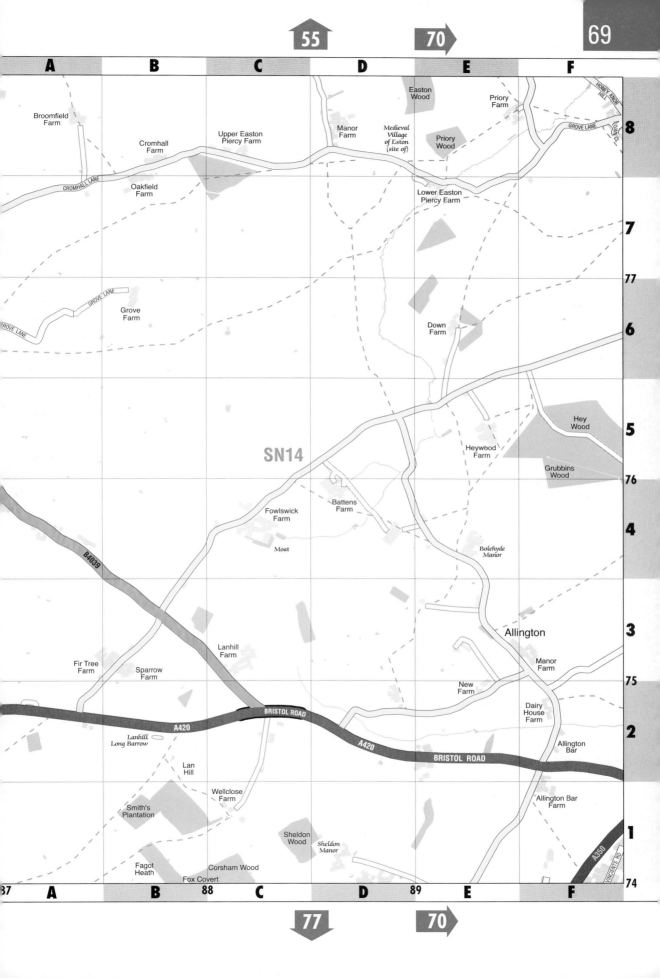

A B C D E F

8

7

77

6

5

76

4

3

75

2

1

74

Broomfield Farm

Cromhall Farm

CROMHALL LANE

Oakfield Farm

Upper Easton Piercy Farm

Manor Farm

Easton Wood

Medieval Village of Eston (site of)

Priory Wood

Priory Farm

HONEY KNOB HILL

TOWN CL

GROVE LANE

Lower Easton Piercy Farm

GROVE LANE

GROVE LANE

Grove Farm

Down Farm

SN14

Hey Wood

Heywood Farm

Grubbins Wood

Fowlswick Farm

Battens Farm

Moat

Bolehyde Manor

B4039

Fir Tree Farm

Sparrow Farm

Lanhill Farm

Allington

Manor Farm

New Farm

Dairy House Farm

Allington Bar

75

A420

BRISTOL ROAD

Lanhill Long Barrow

Lan Hill

A420

BRISTOL ROAD

Allington Bar Farm

A350

VINCENTS RD

Wellclose Farm

Smith's Plantation

Sheldon Wood

Sheldon Manor

Fagot Heath

Corsham Wood

Fox Covert

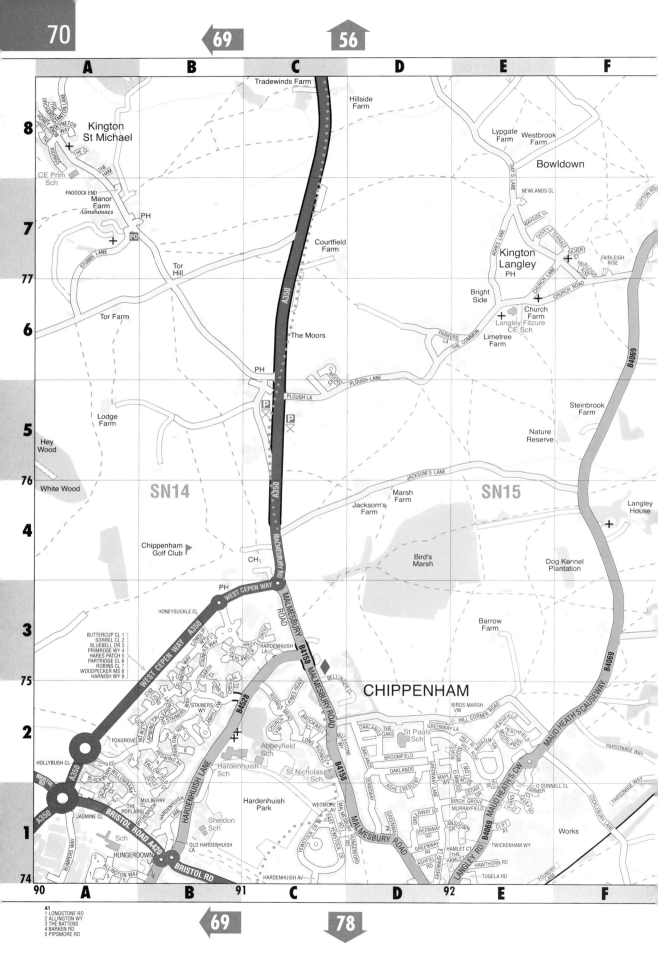

A **B** **C** **D** **E** **F**

8

Kington
St Michael

CE Prim
Sch

PADDOCK END
Manor
Farm
Almshouses

Orchard Close · Skyneton Lane
Honey Knob Hill · THE RIDINGS
THE CL
THE HAM

PH

PO

7

STUBBS LANE

Tor
Hill

Lypgate
Farm

Westbrook
Farm

Bowldown

NEWLANDS CL

DAY'S LANE

ASHES LANE

WAYSIDE CL

DOVEY'S TERRACE

SILVER
ST

FAIR LEIGH
RISE

FAIRLEIGH
RISE

SUTTON RD

Kington
Langley
PH

CHURCH LANE

CHURCH ROAD

77

Tor Farm

Courtfield
Farm

A350

Bright
Side

Langley
CE Sch

Church
Farm
Fitzure

6

The Moors

PARKERS
LA

THE COMMON

Limetree
Farm

B4069

Steinbrook
Farm

PH

PLOUGH LANE

MOORS
CL

PLOUGH LA

P

P

A350

Langley
House

5

Hey
Wood

Lodge
Farm

Nature
Reserve

76

White Wood

SN14

JACKSOM'S LANE

Marsh
Farm

Jacksom's
Farm

SN15

4

Chippenham
Golf Club

MALMESBURY RD

A350

CH

Bird's
Marsh

Dog Kennel
Plantation

B4069

3

PH

WEST CEPEN WAY

HONEYSUCKLE CL

A350

WEST CEPEN WAY

COWSLIP
WY

COWSLIP

CELANDINE WAY

STAINERS WAY

GARTH

SUTHERLAND DR

ARGYL DRIVE

HARDENHUISH
LA

B4158

BELLINGER CL

Barrow
Farm

MAUD HEATH'S CAUSEWAY

PARSONAGE WY

75

BUTTERCUP CL 1
SORREL CL 2
BLUEBELL DR 3
PRIMROSE WY 4
HARES PATCH 5
PARTRIDGE CL 6
ROBINS CL 7
WOODPECKER MS 8
HARNISH WY 9

STAINERS
WY

LAMBILL CW

CORB CL

CHEVRAL CL

B4528

RIDINGS MEAD

LADIES HEAD

CHURCH
VW

BROOMWELL

LONG
RIDINGS

MILESTONE
WY

CHIPPENHAM

MALMESBURY ROAD

BIRDS MARSH
VW

Birds Marsh
VW

Hill Corner Road

HEATHFIELD

HEATHFIELD

MEADLANDS

O DONNELL CL

FARMER

PARSONAGE WY

2

HOLLYBUSH CL

A350

FOXGROVE

BLACKBERRY CL

ASH CL

WILLOWBANK

REDWING AV

FALLOW
FIELD

FOX CL

BARN ROW RD

STAINERS
WY

GPSY
PDOCK

SKEPPE
EPPS RD

LAPWING CW

8

Abbeyfield
Sch

Hardenhuish
Sch

St Nicholas
Sch

OAKLANDS

THE
OAKS

St Pauls
Sch

Greenway la

OAKLANDS

BROOMFIELD

DENNSWAY

ASHE CRESCENT

GREENWAY LANE

HILL PL

HILL RISE

BARROW

NORTH

ELMWOOD

MAPLE
WY

CEDAR
GR

BIRCH GROVE

MURRAYFIELD

EVANS
CL

SAXBY
RD

MAUD HEATHS CW

COCKLEBURY LANE

Works

1

BRISTOL
RD

A350

JASMINE CL

BRISTOL ROAD A420

HARDENHUISH LANE

MULBERRY
CL

THE POPLARS

ACACIA
CL

Sheldon
Sch

Hardenhuish
Park

OLD HARDENHUISH
LANE

WEDMORE
AV

EAST TYNSTOCK CR

YENSTOCK CR

MALMESBURY RD

HUNGERFORD

MALMESBURY ROAD

GREENWAY
GD

GREENWAY
GD

LANSDOWN

GREENWAY
AV

ASHFIELD
RD

HAMLET CT

THE
HAMLET

HAWTHORN RD

TWICKENHAM WY

LANGLEY RD

B4069

CLIFT

FOUNDRY
LANE

74

Sch

HUNGERDOWN
LANE

ALLINGTON WAY

BRISTOL RD

HARDENHUISH AV

TUGELA RD

BUMPERS WY

90 **A** **B** **91** **C** **D** **92** **E** **F**

A1
1 LONGSTONE RD
2 ALLINGTON WY
3 THE BATTENS
4 BARKEN RD
5 PIPSMORE RD

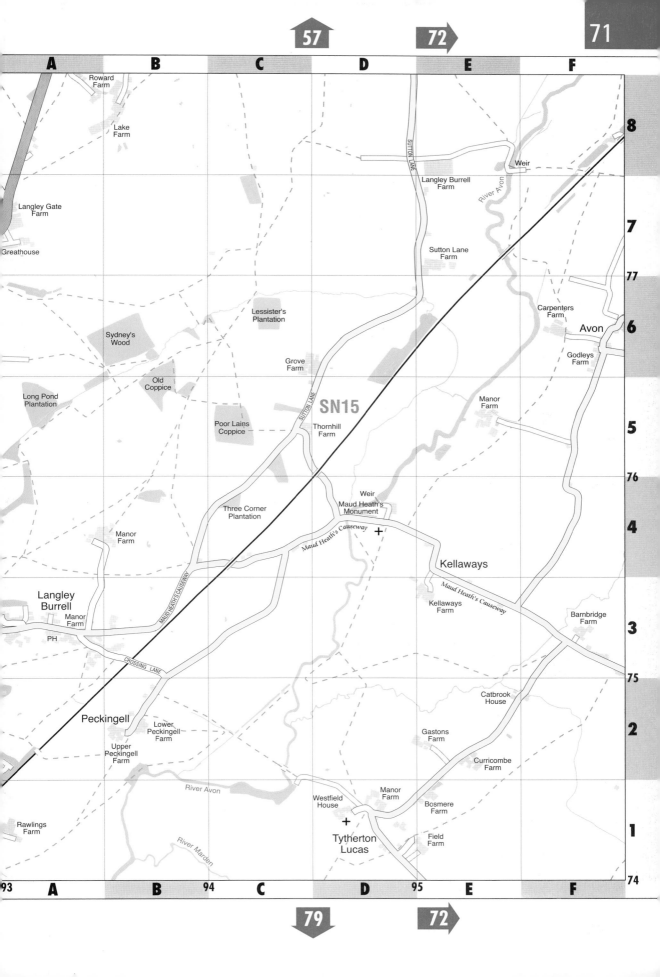

A **B** **C** **D** **E** **F**

8

Christian Farm

Godsell Farm

Barn. Farm

Brook Farm

Park Farm

Foxham Farm

Elm Farm

Heathercote

7

West End Farm

Foxham

Lock Farm

PO

SN15

West End

Gate Farm

PH

Summerleaze Farm

Cadenham Park Farm

77

Cadenham Manor

6

Teal Farm

HARE STREET

Old Canal

5

Hare Street Farm

76

4

Wagon House Farm

Charlcutt Farm

Tucks Farm

SN15

Charlcutt

Chestermans Farm

Charlcutt Hill

The Farm

3

Bremhill Grove Farm

Pinnigers Farm

SN11

Maud Heath's Causeway

East Tytherton

Bremhill Grove Bridge

75

Maud Heath Prim Sch

Maud Heath's Causeway

2

Bremhill Grove

Honeybed Wood

Wick Bridge

Field Farm

Hanger Park Farm

1

Wick Bridge Farm

Wick Farm

Bremhill Wick

Hill Top Farm

TURF HOUSE LANE

74

Avon Grove Wood

Godsell Cottages

Catcomb Wood

Lyneham Airfield

SN15

FREEGROVE RD

WHITCOMBE CL.

8

Mast

Catcomb Old Farm

New Zealand Farm

New Zealand

Lyneham Farm

A3102

Wood Farm

VICTORIA CL

QUAKERS WALK

7

Goatacre

GOATACRE LANE

ILES CT

Stockham Marsh Farm

77

Court Farm

COMBE LANE

Catcomb Farm

Haygrove Wood

6

Catcomb

Catcomb House Farm

SN11

Beacon Hill

Beacon Hill Farm

SNOW HILL

5

Spirthill Farm

Siderow Farm

76

Leekshedge Farm

4

Spirthill

SWINDON ROAD

CHURCH RD

PH

3

COMPTON RD

75

Turnham Wood

Jubilee Plantation

Cowage Brook

Nine Acre Wood

Hilmarton Manor

Manor Park Farm

2

A3102

Bremhill House

Cowick Farm

Lower Penn Farm

1

Cowage Wood

74

Marshfield

A420 Bristol

A420

Down Road

Star Farm

Star La

Bond's Wood

HAYFIELD
HAY STREET
HAYFIELD
CHIPPENHAM ROAD
FAIRFIELD CL
BARN
CHIPPENHAM RD
WITHYMEAD
WITHYMEAD RD
Garston Farm

East End

MKT PL
TORRARTON RD
MARKET END
WEST LA
CHURCH LA
PLACE

Marshfield CE Prim Sch

Pitt Farm

Newleaze Wood

Woodlands Farm

8

Ringswell

Sewage Works

Doncombe Hill

Pinewood Way

Pinewood Way

Northwoo Farm

7

Cloud Wood

Doncombe Scrubs

Pinewood Way

73

Henleyhill Barn

FR LINDEN DR
WALNUT DR
HOLLY DR
LARCH
CYPRESS WLK
LAUREL DRIVE
ASPEN CL

Henley Hill

Marshfield Wood

6

Henleyhill Plantation

Gloucestershire STREET ATLAS

Raizes Wood

SN14

5

Raizes Plantation

The Raizes

72

Ashwicke Grange

West Lodge

Barracks

4

Grange Plantation

Ashwick Hall International Sch of Choueifat

Centre Plantation

Colerne Airfield

Ashwicke Home Farm

East Lodge

Motcombe Farm

Clift Wood

ASHWICKE ROAD

Colerne Rugby Football Club

BATH ROAD

3

Cherry Wood

Diamond Wood

Ranch House Farm

71

Longley Wood

Motcombe Wood

OAKFORD LANE

Bandywell Wood

Lictum Spring

2

Dicknick Wood

Rocky Wood

The Rocks

Hunters Hall

Breach Wood

Orchard Wood

Ryder's Wood

BA1

Abbotscombe Wood

Fewells Wood

Moonshine Wood

Brokenboro Wood

Draught Wood

ROAD HILL

Westwood Farm

West Wood

SN13

1

Oakford Farm

Rodney Wood

Three Shire Stones

70

A **B** **C** **D** **E** **F**

8

Slaughterford
Backpath Wood
HAM LANE
Little Glebe
Cemy
SLAUGHTERFORD RD
YATTON ROAD
Field Farm
Biddestone
CHURCH ROAD
THE GREEN
Home Farm
Pool Farm PH
Biddestone Manor

Weir
By Brook
GERMAIN'S LANE
WEAVERN LANE
Honeybrook Farm
WEAVERN LA
White Cliff Wood

7

SN14
Field Farm
Mountjoy Farm
THE BUTTS
BUTTS CL
PRINCES
LIT CHURCH

73

Macmillan Way

6

Field Barn Farm
WEAVERN LANE
Jubilee Wood
The Grove

Husseyhill Wood
Mound
Home Farm
Hartham Farm
Leigh Wood

5

Erkwell Wood
Square Covert
Tyning Wood
HARTHAM LANE

72

WEAVERN LANE
Weavern Farm
Hartham Park

4

Tyning Wood
Tyning Wood
Tyning Wood
Prestley Wood
MIDDLEWICK LANE
Church Farm

Hungerford Wood
The Larches
Pickwick Lodge Farm
Long Plantation

3

Upper Pickwick
Broad Wood
SN13
Middlewick
MIDDLEWICK LANE

Rudloe Wood
Pickwick
DOVECOTE DR
Corsham Regis Sch
PRIORY STREET
YORK CL
MANOR RD
KINGS AVENUE
QUEENS AVENUE

71

2

RAF Rudloe Manor
ACADEMY DRIVE
WOODLANDS
BATH RD A4
CHARLES ST
WELLER RD
ARNOLDS MEA
PICKWICK ROAD
B3353

1

Lower Rudloe Farm
BOX HILL
A4
LEAFY LANE
ASHWOOD RD
PINE CL
PINE CLOSE
LONG CLOSE AV
LEYLANDS RD
TOGHILL CR
Rudloe
BATH ROAD
Half Way Firs
BRADFORD ROAD
B3109
Underground Quarry
SUMSIONS DR
PARK LANE
MASONS WY
PICTOR CL
PEL CIR
PEEL CIR
Corsham
WEST PARK ROAD
HATTON WAY
The Corsham Sch
Springfield Sports Centre
Sports Ground
VALLEY ROAD
PROVIDENCE
ERNESTON CR
PAUL ST
THE TYNINGS

Hotel

70

69

F5
1 TOWCESTER PL
2 TAUNTON CL
3 GOODWOOD WY
4 HAYDOCK CL
5 METHUEN PK
6 LINGFIELD CL

78

F6
1 FARLEIGH CL
2 HAZEL COPSE
3 DERRIADS LA
4 HEXHAM CL
5 DEVON CL
6 NEWTON ABBOT CL

7 CATTERICK CL
8 PHEASANT CL
9 NEWMARKET CL
10 KEMPTON PK CT

77

A B C D E F

8
7
73
6
5
72
4
3
71
2
1
70

Chapscroft Wood
Fox Covert
Corsham Wood
Sheldon Farm
Sheldon Corner
FROGWELL
Southernwood Farm
TOWNSEND PL
A350
WEST CEPEN WAY
VINCIENTS ROAD
BUMPERS WAY
CRUSE
FROGWELL
BUMPERS WAY
MOSS MEAD
PHILLIPS
CHAMBERLAIN RD
BRINKWORTH CL

Starveall Farm
CHIPPENHAM LANE
Priors Copse
Nature Trail
BRITTAIN CL
TURPIN WY
CLARENCE RD
LENTON CL
KENSING WY
AVENUE
HERON WY
CONISTON
TRURO WK

Chiverlins House
SN14
Middlehill Cottage
Holy Well
DRAKE CRES
OAK RD
PLUMPTON CL
WOLVERTON
BRIGHTON WY
AINTREE
SANDOWN DRIVE
SED GEFIELD
WYM
EPSOM DR
CHIPPENHAM

Beckhill Wood
Stowell Farm
WEST CEPEN WY
TYN DR
EXETER
HAM
WARWICK CL
BERKELEY WY
AYR CL
TOWCESTER CL
NEWBURY DR
SANDOWN DRIVE

Jubilee Wood
BATH RD
5

Briary Wood
Chequers Hill Plantation
Chequers Farm
Mynte Farm
A4
Superstore
72

BATH ROAD
The Folly
A350
4

Mynte Wood
EASTON LANE

PH
SN13
Cross Keys
3

Corsham Park
Pheasant Covert
Easton Farm
71

COULSTON ROAD
CROSS KEYS ROAD
BENCES
Corsham Court
The Heywood Preparatory Sch
Bath Academy Of Art
Westrop Plantation
Easton
Easton Court Farm
Easton
2

THE LAGGAR
IVY FIELD
BENCES LA
HIGH STREET
NEWLANDS ROAD
TH
CHURCH ST
Corsham Lake
Park Farm
Westrop
Thingley Court Farm
1

POST OFFICE
PICKWICK SOUTH
Liby
St Patricks RC Sch
Corsham Town Football Club
LACOCK ROAD
Thingley Farm
SN15

SOUTH ST
GROVE RD
STATION RD
PILL
B3353
POUND
Corsham Sports & Cricket Club
Corsham CP Sch
LADBROOK LANE
Thingley
70

87 A 88 B C 89 D E F

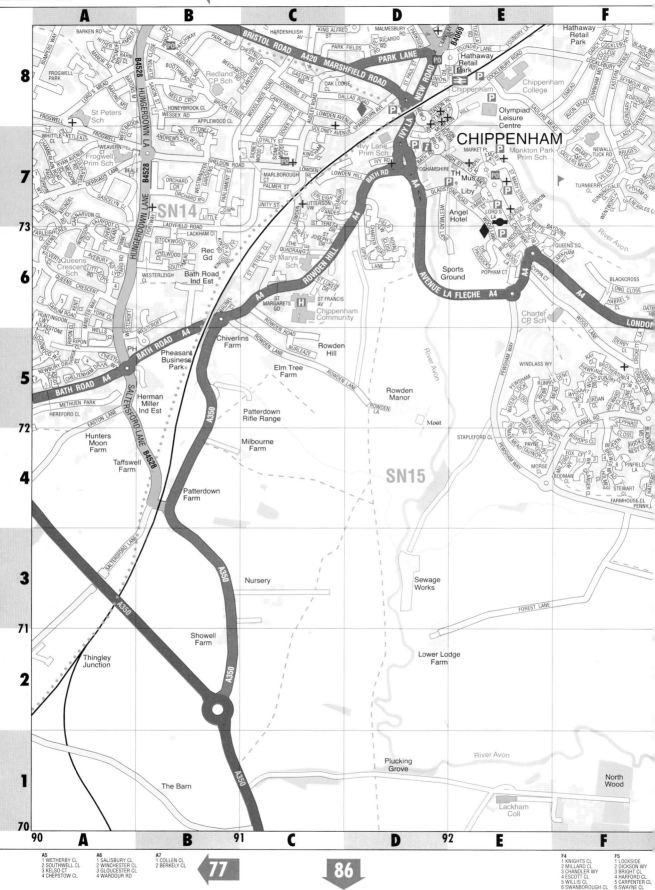

Map Labels

CHIPPENHAM

SN14

SN15

Hathaway Retail Park

Chippenham College

Olympiad Leisure Centre

Monkton Park Prim Sch

Angel Hotel

Sports Ground

Charter CP Sch

River Avon

LONDON

Pheasant Business Park

Herman Miller Ind Est

Hunters Moon Farm

Taffswell Farm

Patterdown Farm

Patterdown Rifle Range

Milbourne Farm

Nursery

Showell Farm

Thingley Junction

The Barn

Sewage Works

Forest Lane

Lower Lodge Farm

Plucking Grove

North Wood

Lackham Coll

Rowden Manor

Moat

Rowden Hill

Elm Tree Farm

Chiverlins Farm

Rowden Community / Chippenham Community

St Margarets GD

St Marys Sch

The Quadrang

Frogwell Park

St Peters Sch

Frogwell Prim Sch

Queens Crescent Sch

Sarum Road

Redland CP Sch

Ivy Lane Prim Sch

Bath Road Ind Est

Street index

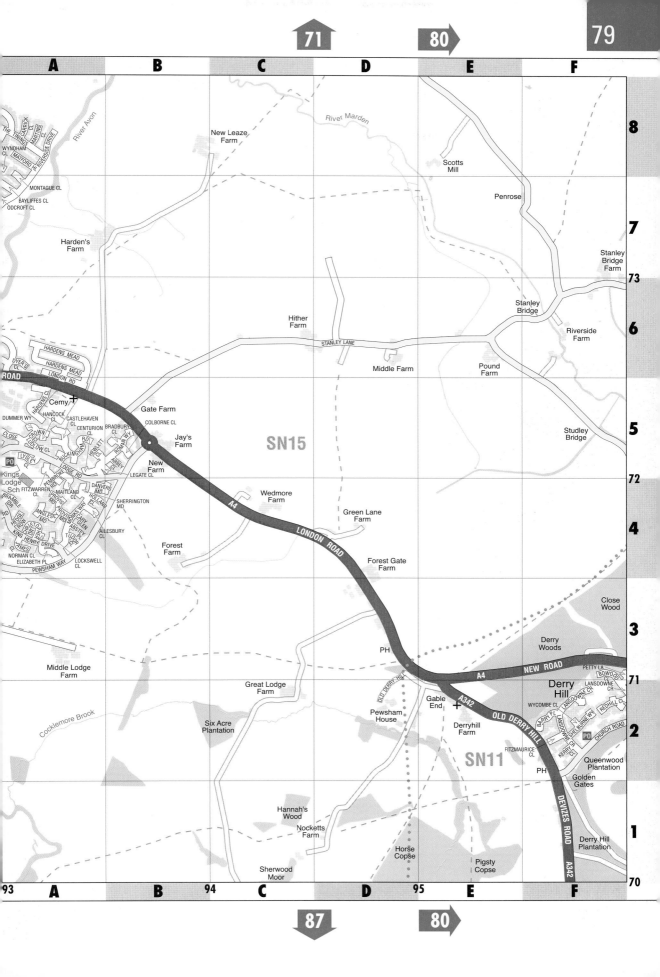

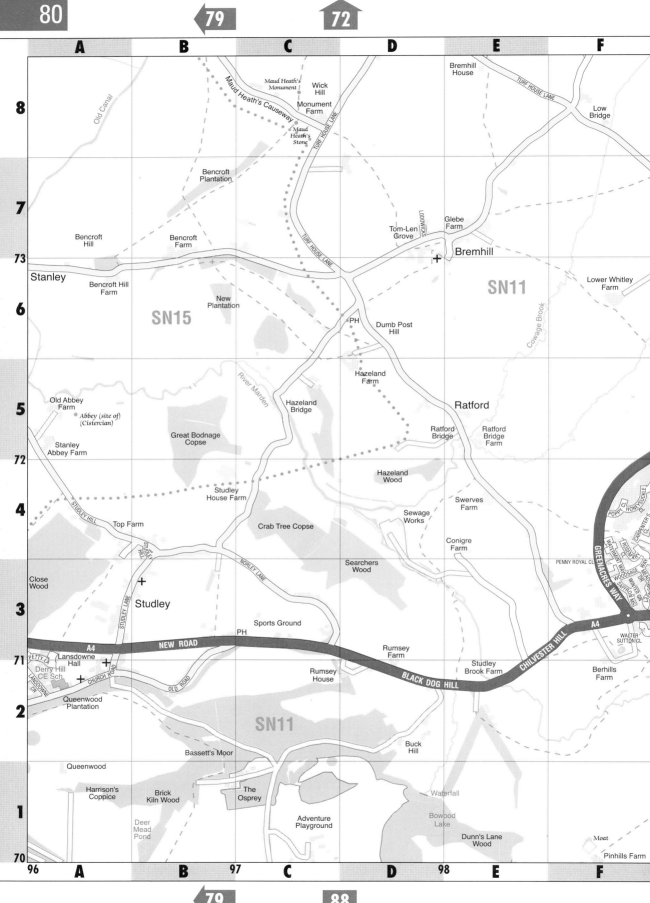

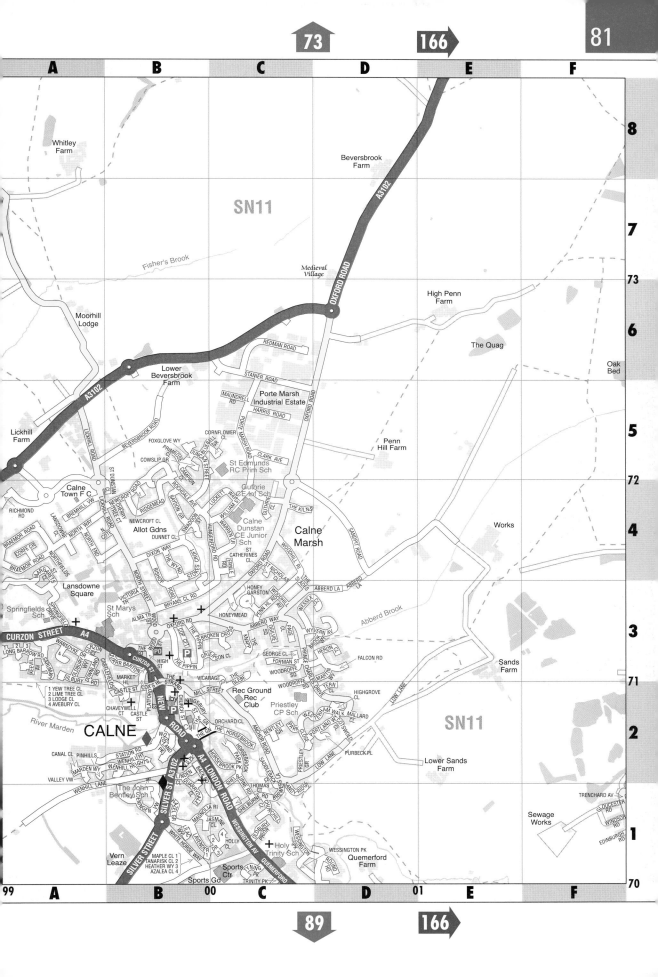

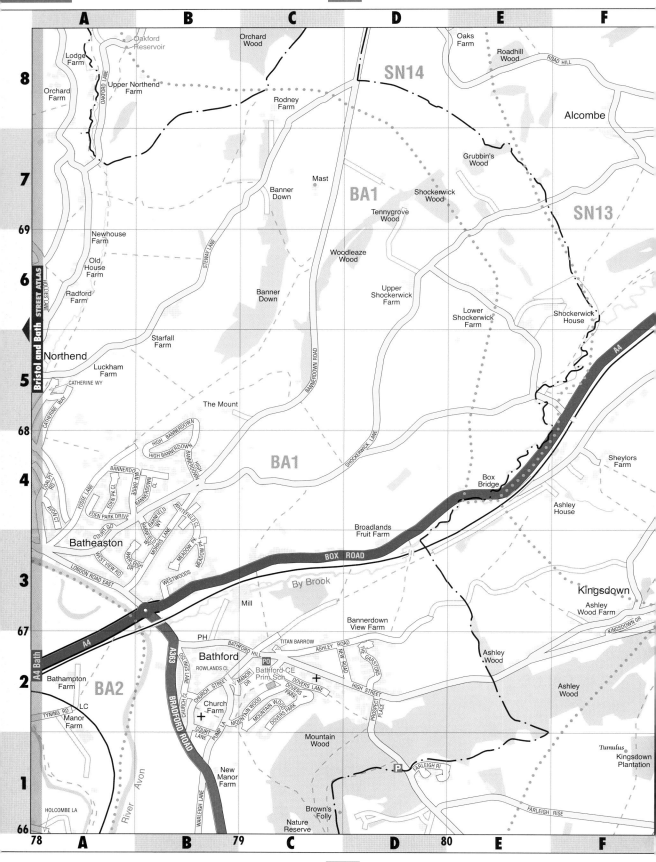

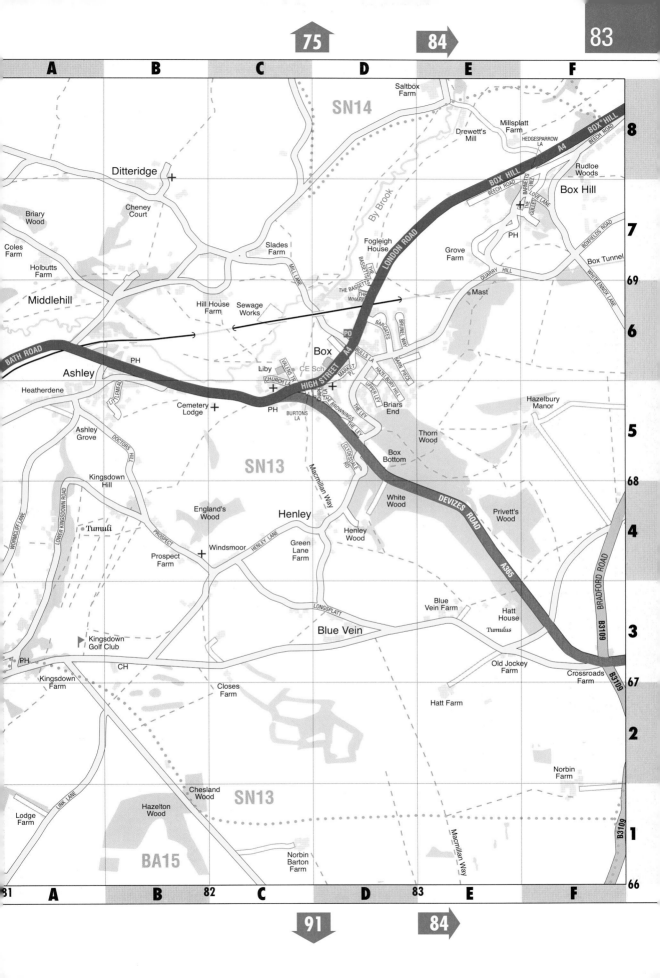

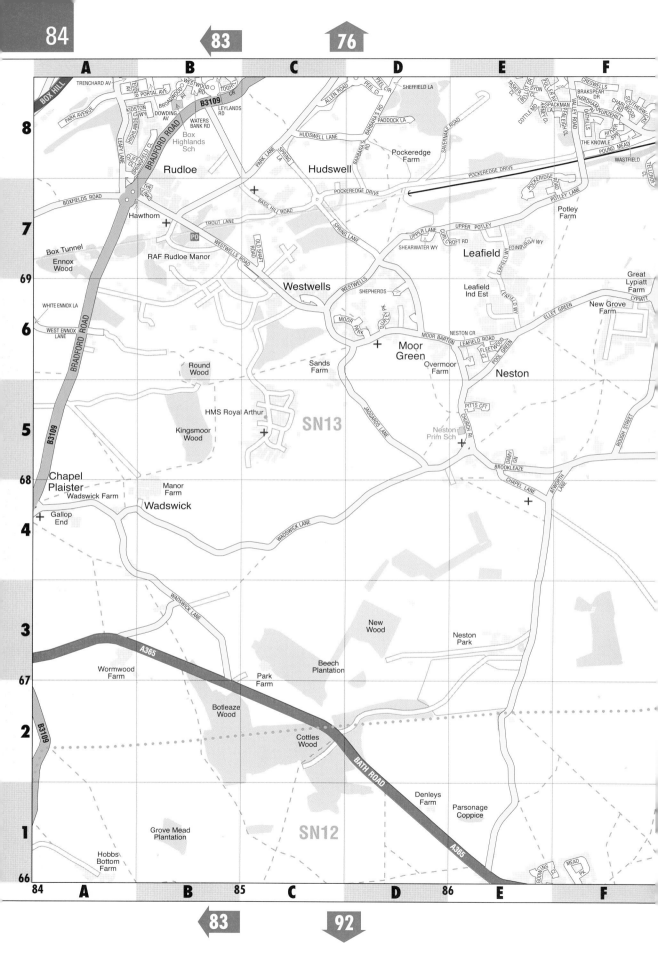

77
86

CORSHAM

8

7

69

6

5

68

4

67

3

2

1

66

SN13

SN15

SN12

Gastard

Chapel Knapp

Monk's Park

The Linleys

The Ridge

Whitley

A   B   C   D   E   F

Williams GR

SOUTH HASTINGS RD

STATION ROAD

STOKES ROAD

NURSERY GD

POUND PILL

B3353

PROSPECT

Cemy

Ladbrook Farm

LADBROOK LANE

Sewage Works

LACOCK RD

CORSHAM ROAD

Courtlands

Thingley Bridge Farm

Byde Mill Farm

New Farm

Cleevedale Rd

PO

Elm Hayes

Lypiatt Rd

Dicketts Road

LUDMEAD

BROADMEAD

WOODBOROUGH RD

BROADMEAD

BROOK DRIVE

BROOK DRIVE

BROOK DRIVE

Meadowcroft Farm

LADBROOK LANE

Sewage Works

Pandown Farm

Catherine Court Farm

Coppershell Farm

Willgarrup Farm

Sandpitts Farm

Lypiatt Road

Little Lypiatt Farm

Linleys Farm

SILVER STREET

B3353

Lanes End Farm

Moonrakers Farm

MONK'S LANE

THE CL

VELLEY HILL

LANES END

Court Farm

Attwood Farm

Ridge Farm

Ridgeside Farm

MONKS PK GD

GREEN ROAD

Boyds Farm

VELLEY HILL

Chapel Knapp Farm

WICK LANE

Pond Close Farm

GREEN ROAD

B3353

GOODES HILL

Catridge Farm

Daniel's Wood

Mast

Brittle Wood

GOODES HILL

Westlands Farm

WESTLANDS LANE

Beardwell Farm

West Hill

LITTLEWORTH LANE

PH

PO

Top Lane

WHITES CL

CORSHAM ROAD

B3353

Purlpit Bridge

WEST HILL

PEARTREE CL

PLANE TREE CL

SPRINGFIELD GD

FIRST LANE

ORANGE CL

GRANGE RD

SLACKFIELD RD

MIDDLE LANE

EDEN GR

EDEN GR

Applecroft Farm

PURLPIT

MOUNT PLEASANT

Slade's Farm

Whitley Farm

ASH CL

KENNEL AV

A   B   88   C   D   89   E   F

93
86

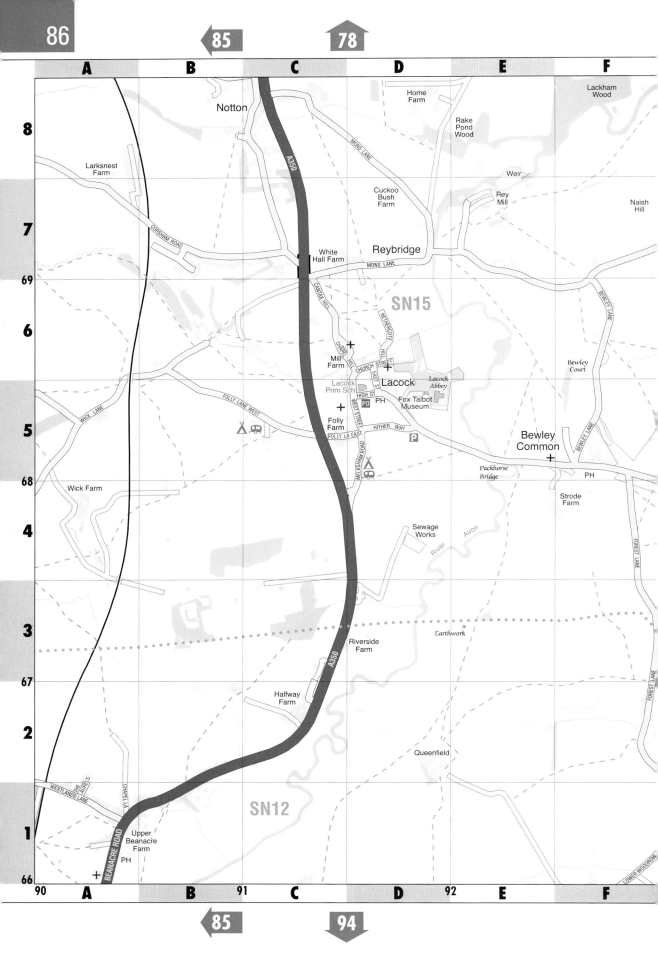

A **B** **C** **D** **E** **F**

8

7

69

6

5

68

4

3

67

2

1

66

90 91 92

Larksnest
Farm

CORSHAM ROAD

Notton

Home
Farm

Rake
Pond
Wood

Lackham
Wood

Weir

Rey
Mill

Naish
Hill

Cuckoo
Bush
Farm

A350

White
Hall Farm

Reybridge

MONS LANE

MONS LANE

SN15

CANTAX HILL

NETHERCOTE

Bewley
Court

Mill
Farm

CHAPEL HILL

CHURCH STREET

EAST ST

HIGH ST

Lacock
Prim Sch

Lacock

Lacock
Abbey

Bewley
Common

PO

PH

Fox Talbot
Museum

WICK LANE

FOLLY LANE WEST

WEST STREET

Folly
Farm

HITHER WAY

FOLLY LA EAST

Wick Farm

P

BEWLEY LANE

PH

Packhorse
Bridge

Strode
Farm

MELKSHAM ROAD

Sewage
Works

River Avon

Earthwork

FOREST LANE

Riverside
Farm

A350

Halfway
Farm

Queenfield

SN12

WESTLANDS LANE

THE LAURELS

CHAPEL CL

BEANACRE ROAD

Upper
Beanacre
Farm

PH

LOWER WOODROW

79
88

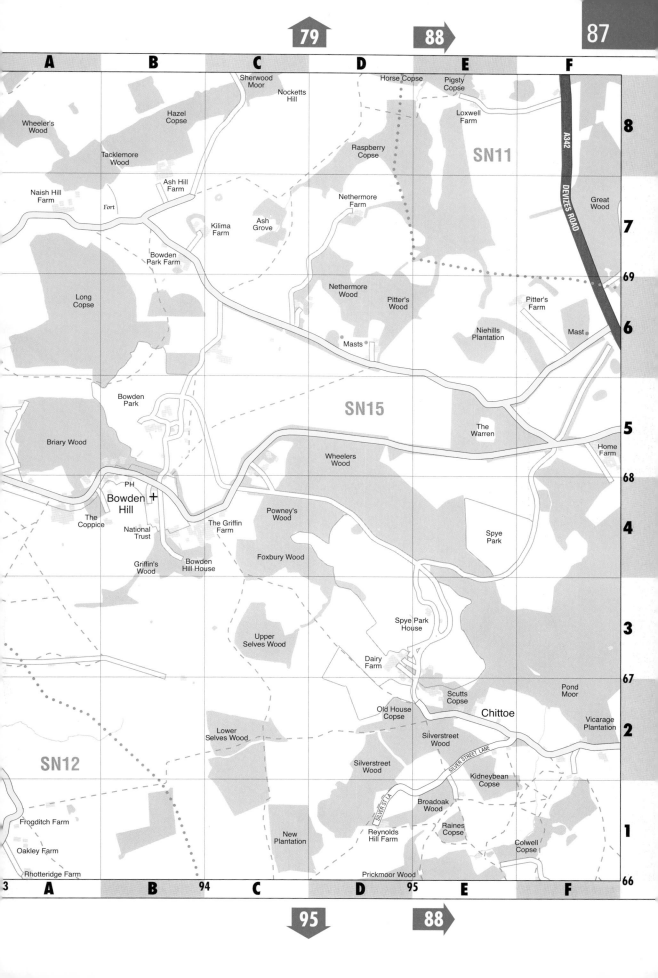

95
88

87
80

A
B
C
D
E
F
8
7
69
6
5
68
4
3
67
2
1
66
96
97
98
Bowood Park
Bowood House
Bowood Gardens
Pinhills Farm
Home Farm
CH
Bowood Golf & Country Club
Bowood Lake
Monk's Hill Wood
Wash Way Wood
Pilpot Wood
Clark's Hill
Hill-top Plantation
Pilpot Wood
Coombe Grove
Great Wood
Cuff's Corner
Holland's Moor
SN11
Mile End Farm
A342
ROMAN VILLA (SITE OF)
PH
Nuthills Farm
Home Wood
Whetham Wood
Whetham
Leigh Wood
Pillow Mound
Sandy Lane
Whetham Farm
Stable Moor
New Moor Copse
Hopyard Copse
Weavers Bridge
Leech Pool
Wans House
St Edith's Leigh Wood
BACK LANE
A3102
DEVIZES ROAD
SN15
Deepet's Wood Copse
Broads Green Farm
Broad's Green
Hayfield Copse
Pond Moor
Bell Farm
Marsh End Farm
Wick Farm
Common Farm
Chittoe Heath Plantation
Chittoe Heath
CHITTOE HEATH
Heddington Wick
Manor Farm
Gable End
Gore Farm
Turnpike Farm
A3102
WESTBROOK ROAD
A342
Wyatts Lake Farm

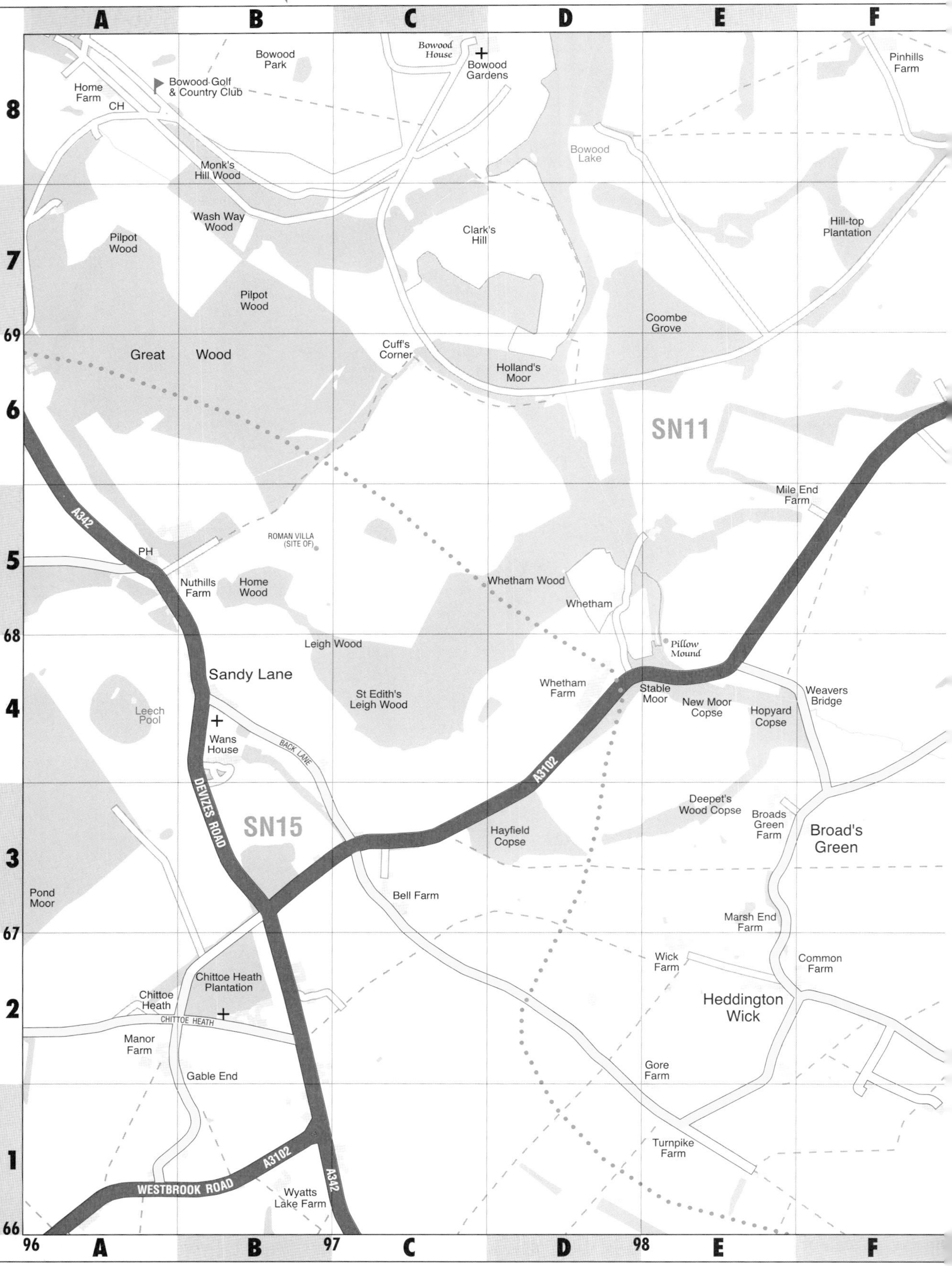

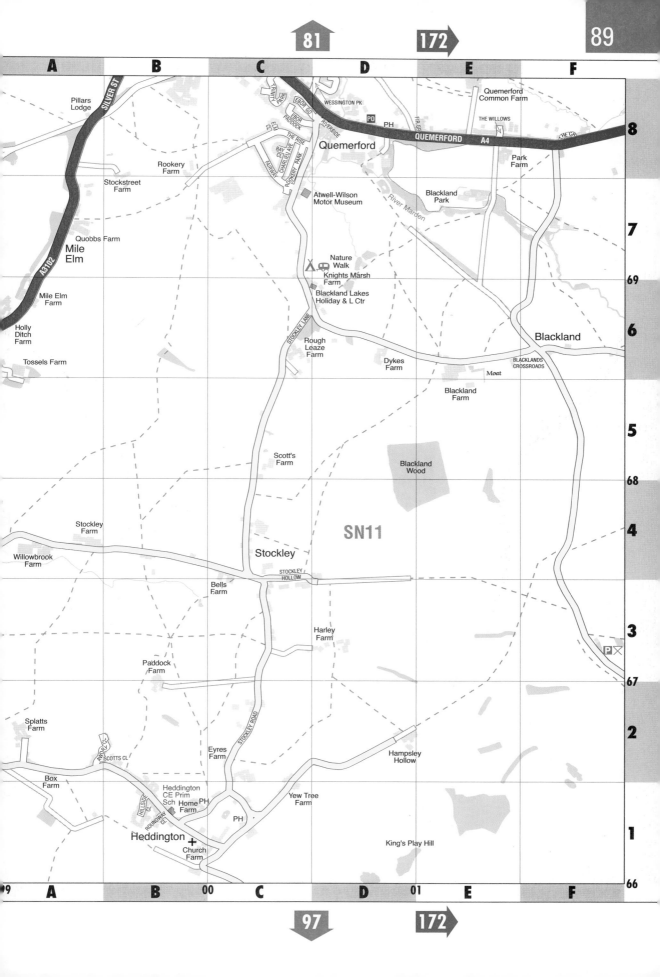

A B C D E F

8

7

69

6

5

68

4

3

67

2

1

66

Pillars
Lodge

SILVER ST

Stockstreet
Farm

Rookery
Farm

Quobbs Farm

Mile
Elm

A3102

Mile Elm
Farm

Holly
Ditch
Farm

Tossels Farm

TRINITY PK
EBOR GD
ELM CL
PADDOCK
THE RISE
BAY CL
FAIRWAY
CHARLES LANE
ROOKERY PARK

RIVERSIDE

WESSINGTON PK

PO

PH

Quemerford

QUEMERFORD   A4

FIR GD

Quemerford
Common Farm

THE WILLOWS

Park
Farm

THE CL

Atwell-Wilson
Motor Museum

River Marden

Blackland
Park

Nature
Walk

Knights Marsh
Farm

Blackland Lakes
Holiday & L Ctr

STOCKLEY LANE

Rough
Leaze
Farm

Dykes
Farm

Blackland

BLACKLANDS
CROSSROADS

Moat

Blackland
Farm

Scott's
Farm

Blackland
Wood

SN11

Stockley Farm

Willowbrook
Farm

Stockley

STOCKLEY
HOLLOW

Bells
Farm

Harley
Farm

P ✕

Paddock
Farm

Splatts
Farm

IVY DR CL
SCOTTS CL
STOCKLEY ROAD

Eyres
Farm

Hampsley
Hollow

Box
Farm

Heddington
CE Prim
Sch

HILLSIDE CL
ROUNDWAY CL

Home
Farm

PH

PH

Yew Tree
Farm

Heddington

Church
Farm

King's Play Hill

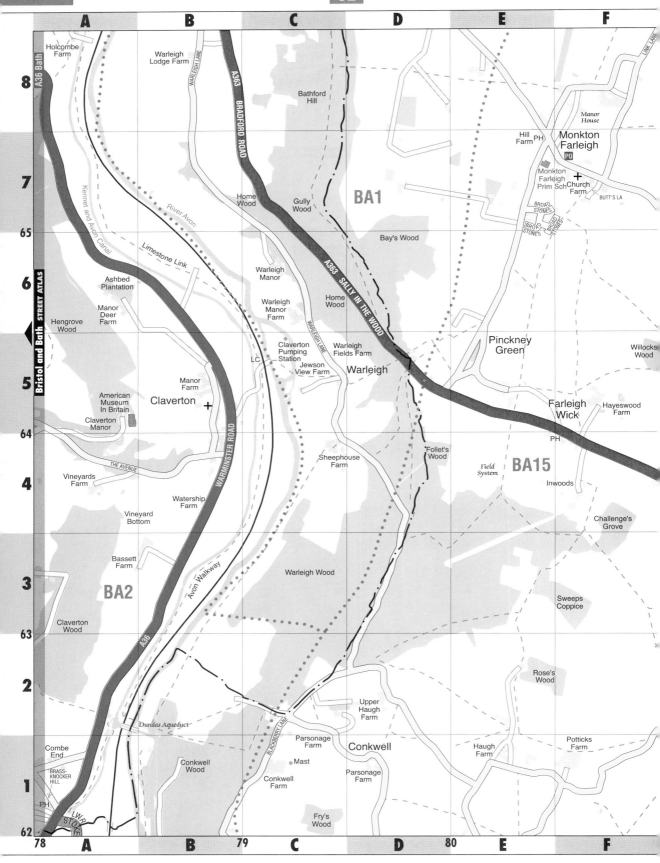

Bristol and Bath STREET ATLAS

A36 Bath

Holcombe Farm

Warleigh Lodge Farm

WARLEIGH LANE

A363 BRADFORD ROAD

Bathford Hill

Kennet and Avon Canal

River Avon

Home Wood

Gully Wood

BA1

Manor House

Hill Farm PH

Monkton Farleigh

Monkton Farleigh Prim Sch

Church Farm

BUTT'S LA

BROAD STONES

BROAD STONES

Limestone Link

Bay's Wood

Ashbed Plantation

Warleigh Manor

Home Wood

A363 SALLY IN THE WOOD

Hengrove Wood

Manor Deer Farm

Warleigh Manor Farm

WARLEIGH LANE

Claverton Pumping Station

LC

Warleigh Fields Farm

Warleigh

Pinckney Green

Willocks Wood

Jewson View Farm

Manor Farm

Claverton

American Museum In Britain

Claverton Manor

WARMINSTER ROAD

Farleigh Wick

Hayeswood Farm

PH

THE AVENUE

Vineyards Farm

Sheephouse Farm

Follet's Wood

Field System

BA15

Inwoods

Watership Farm

Vineyard Bottom

Challenge's Grove

Bassett Farm

Avon Walkway

Warleigh Wood

BA2

Claverton Wood

A36

Sweeps Coppice

Rose's Wood

Upper Haugh Farm

Dundas Aqueduct

Potticks Farm

BLACKBERRY LANE

Parsonage Farm

Conkwell

Haugh Farm

Combe End

BRASS-KNOCKER HILL

Conkwell Wood

Mast

Parsonage Farm

PH

LWR STOKE

Conkwell Farm

Fry's Wood

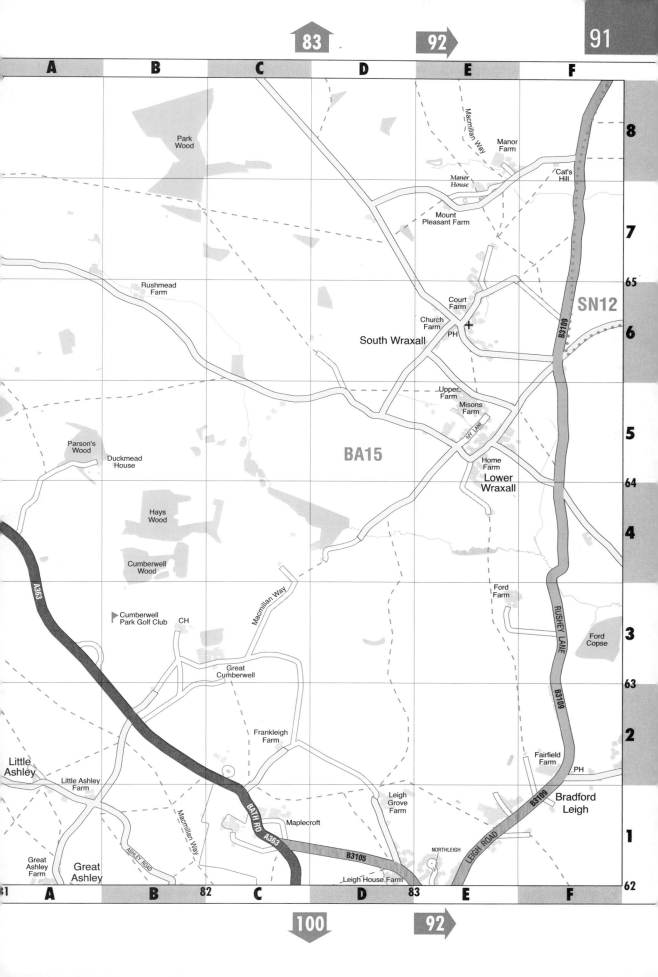

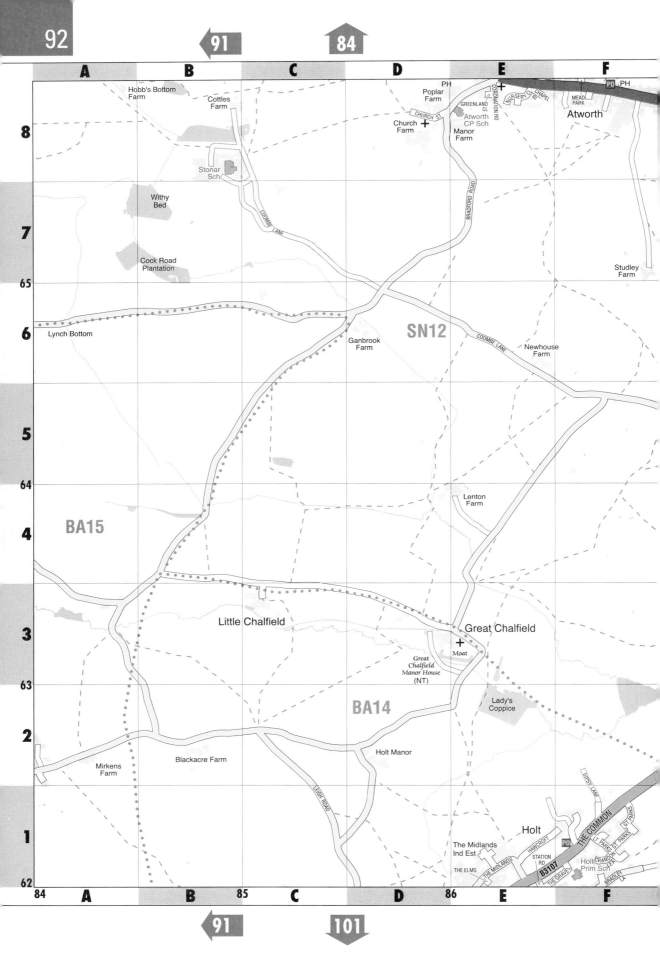

A B C D E F

8

7

65

6

5

64

4

3

63

2

1

62

Hobb's Bottom Farm

Cottles Farm

Poplar Farm

PH

Church St

Church Farm

Greenland CL

Atworth CP Sch

Manor Farm

Coronation Rd

Nursery Ch

Chapel

PO PH

MEAD PARK

Atworth

Stonar Sch

Withy Bed

Coombe Lane

Bradford Road

Cock Road Plantation

Studley Farm

Lynch Bottom

Ganbrook Farm

SN12

Coombe Lane

Newhouse Farm

BA15

Lenton Farm

Little Chalfield

Great Chalfield

Moat

Great Chalfield Manor House (NT)

BA14

Lady's Coppice

Mirkens Farm

Blackacre Farm

Leigh Road

Holt Manor

Gipsy Lane

The Common

Holt

The Midlands Ind Est

Hawcroft

Station Rd

PO

Lt Parks

Gt Parks

Holt Prim Sch

Cranson

Bradley La

THE ELMS

THE MIDLANDS

B3107

THE GRAVEL

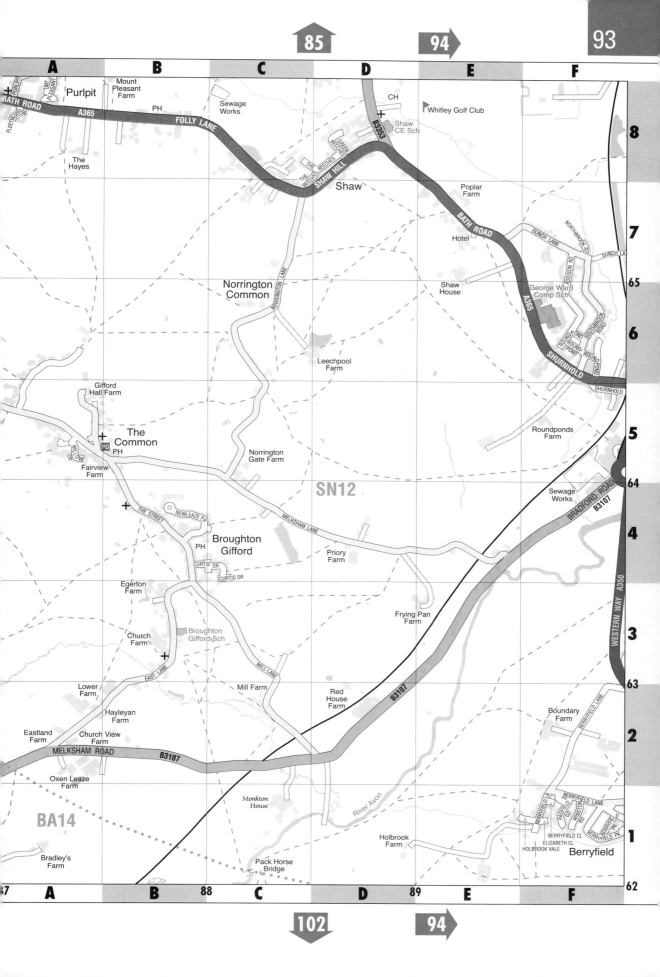

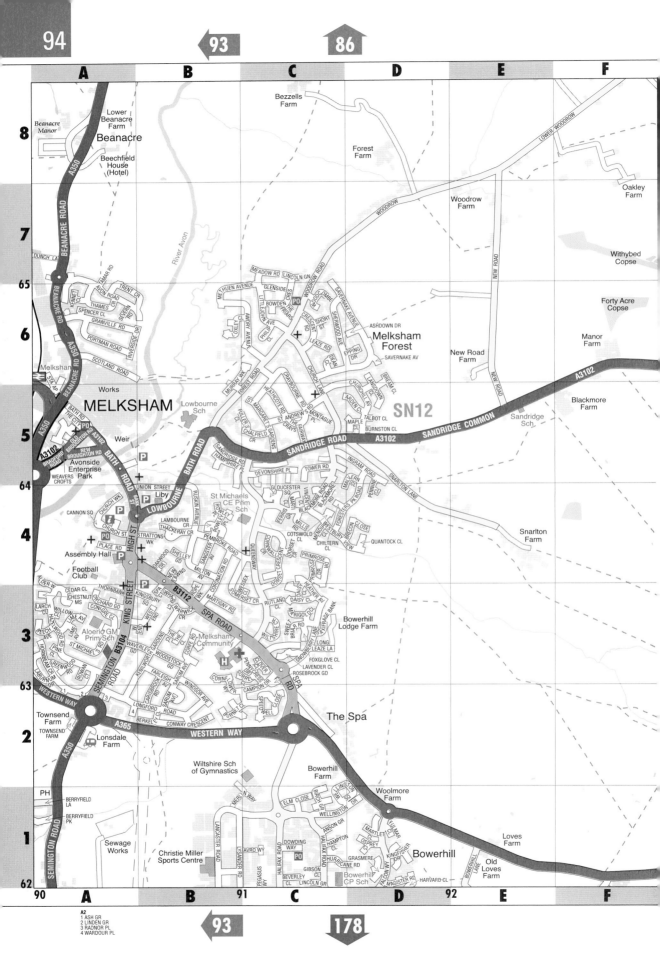

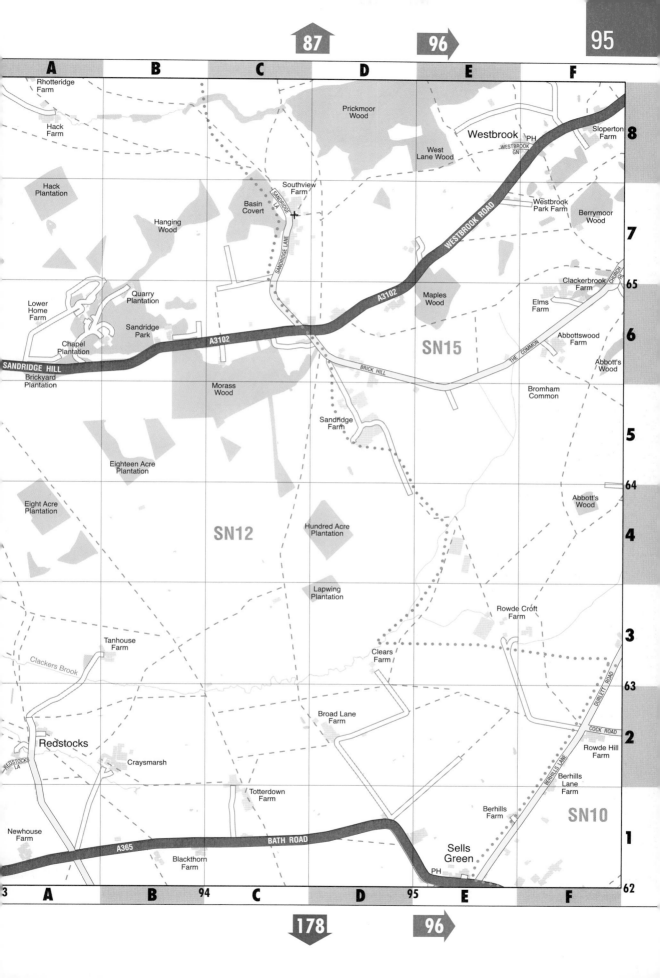

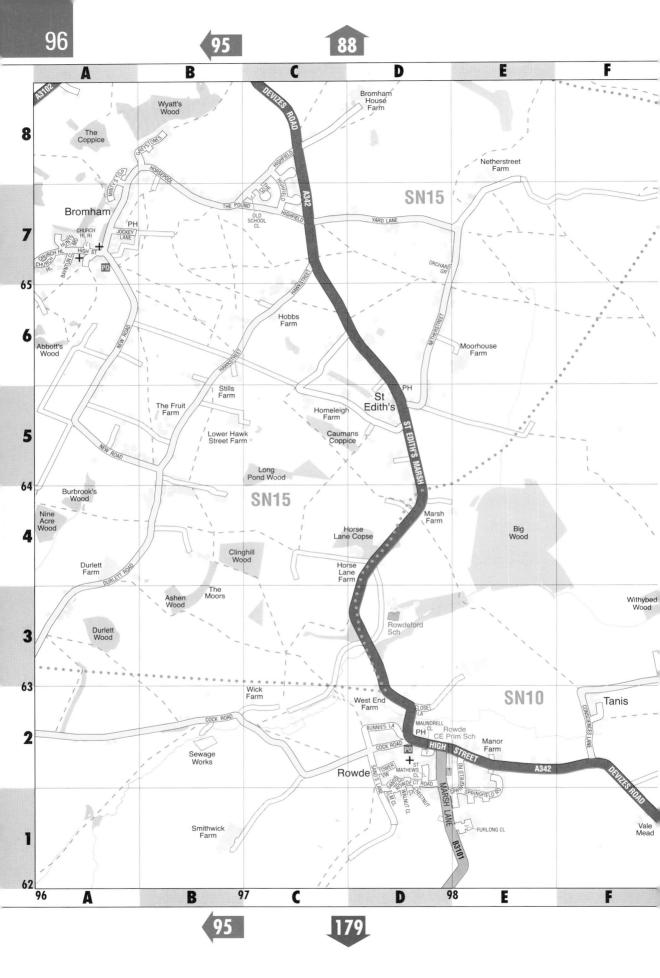

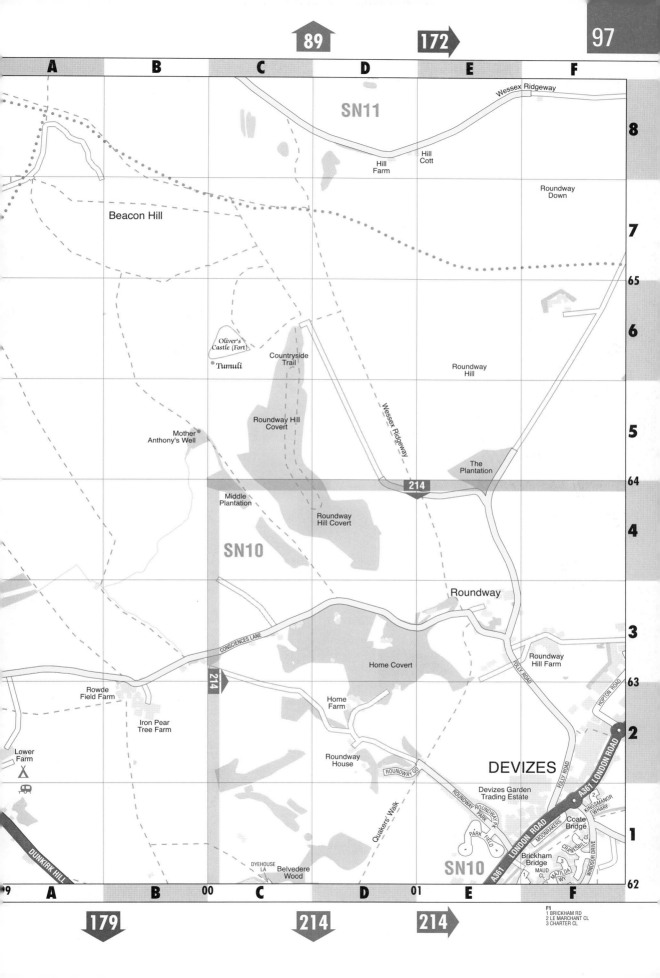

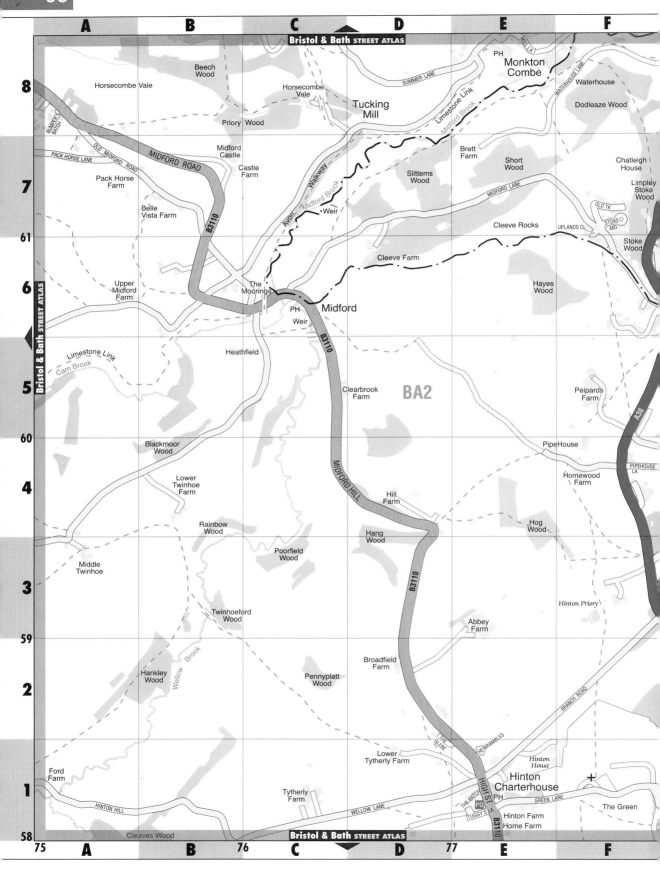

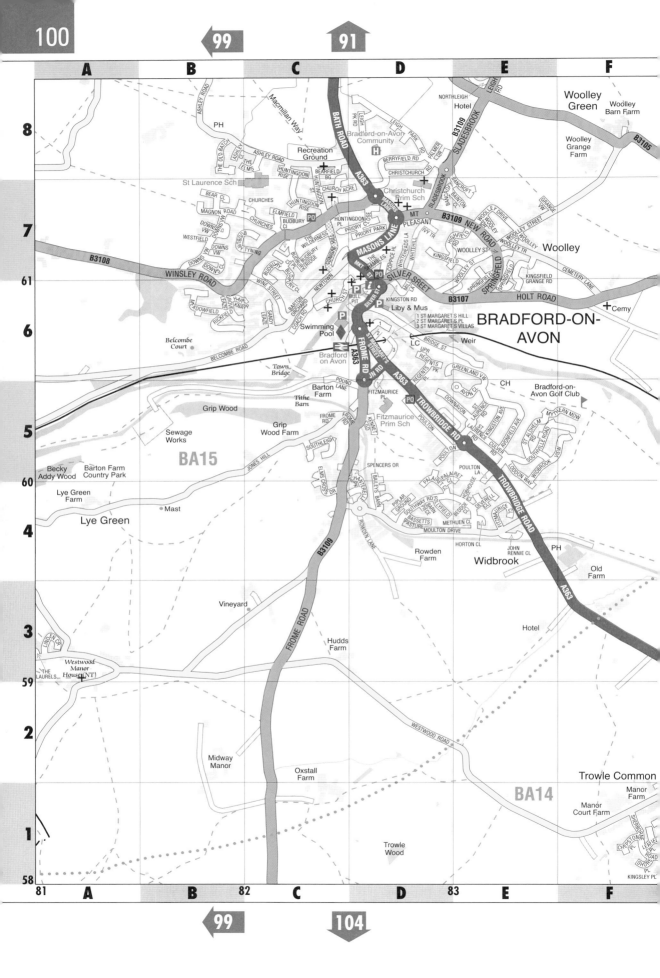

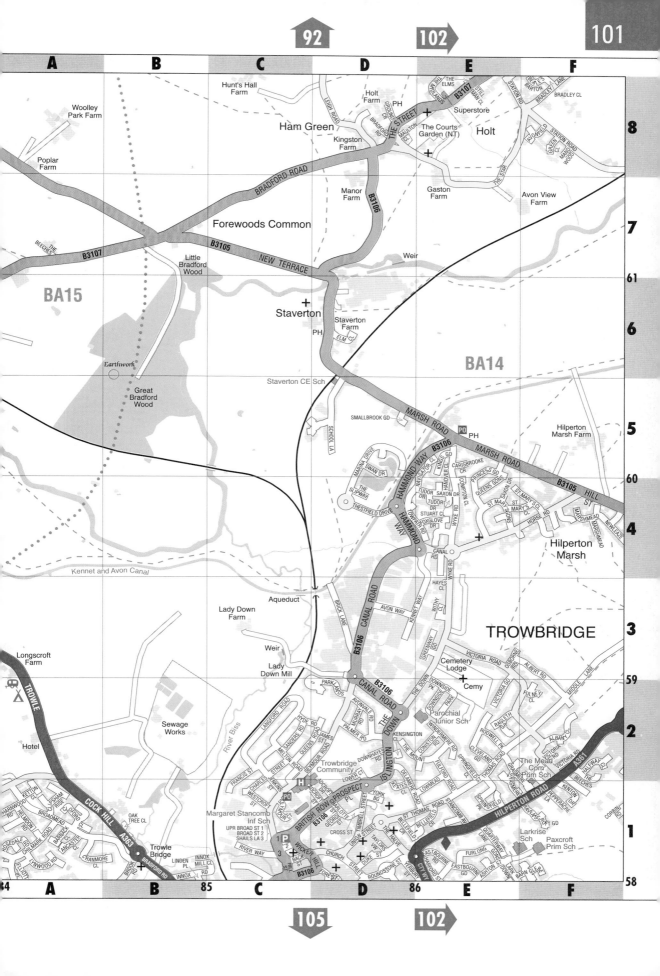

Woolley
Park Farm

Poplar
Farm

THE BEECHES
B3107

BA15

Hunt's Hall
Farm

Holt
Farm

Ham Green

Kingston
Farm

LEIGH ROAD

BRADFORD RD

THE STREET

MAULTON

B3106

THE MIDLANDS

THE ELMS

PH

STATION RD

MANS CL

BRADLEY RD

BELLE'S
LANE

B3107

BRADLEY CL

Superstore

The Courts
Garden (NT)

Holt

GREEN
CL

STATION ROAD

MANS
WOOD

8

Manor
Farm

B3106

Gaston
Farm

Avon View
Farm

THE STAR

BRADFORD ROAD

Forewoods Common

B3107

Little
Bradford
Wood

B3105

NEW TERRACE

Weir

7

61

Earthwork

Staverton

Great
Bradford
Wood

PH

Staverton
Farm

ELM CL

6

BA14

Staverton CE Sch

SMALLBROOK GD

MARSH ROAD

PO

PH

Hilperton
Marsh Farm

5

SCHOOL LA

MARTINA DRIVE

SWAN DR

THE
SLIPWAY

THESTFIELD DRIVE

HAMMOND WAY

KINGS CL

HANOVER CL

CARISBROOKE
CR

COMPTON CL

TUDOR
DR

SAXON DR

STUART CL

TUDOR
DR

FOXGLOVE
DR

WYKE RD

PRINCESS GD

QUEENS GDNS

ST MARYS GDNS

ST
MARY'S CL

ST MARY'S CL

HORSE RD

MARSHMEAD

MARSHMEAD

NEWLEAZE

B3105

HILL

ST

60

HAMMOND
WAY

TONGDAY RD

CANAL
RD

CANAL RD

HAYES
CL

WYKE RD

Hilperton
Marsh

4

Kennet and Avon Canal

Aqueduct

Lady Down
Farm

BRICK LANE

B3106

CANAL ROAD

AVON WAY

KENNET WAY

WITHY
CL

TROWBRIDGE

3

Longscroft
Farm

TROWLE

Hotel

Weir

Lady
Down Mill

River Biss

Sewage
Works

PARK KNAPS

B3106

CANAL ROAD

THE DOWN

ISLINGTON

Cemetery
Lodge

VICTORIA ROAD

DOWNSIDE

DOWNSIDE
PK

DOWNSIDE
PARK

Cemy

Parochial
Junior Sch

KENSINGTON

THE MOUNT

WINDERMERE RD

CONISTON RD

GREENWAY

ALBERT RD

VICTORIA RD

OSBORNE

RAGLETH
RD

RODWELL PK

CLEVELAND RD

THOMAS ST

SPRINGFIELD RD

GRASMERE

FULNEY
CL

MIDDLE LANE

The Mead
Com
Prim Sch

ALBANY

VICTORIA RD

A361

59

2

KETTON

IPSHAM
RISK

HARNWOOD
RD

CHILMARK RD

TREMOON
RD

BARWICK

BROADMEAD

ROSEDALE
CL

LANCASTER

ELLIOTT

LYNWOOD

COCK HILL

A363

OAK
TREE CL

CRANMORE
CL

LINDEN
PL

INNOX
MILL CL

BRADFORD RD

INNOX
RD

Trowle
Bridge

Margaret Stancomb
Inf Sch

UPR BROAD ST 1
BROAD ST 2
SHAILS LA 3

RIVER WAY

LANGFORD
ROAD

FRANCIS ST

CHARLES
ST

WESTCROFT
ST

HYDE RD

MURRAY RD

SANDERS
RD

QUEENS
RD

SEYMOUR RD

PALMER RD

HAMES

JEWKINS
ST

DOWNHAYES
RD

Trowbridge
Community

LOWER CT

PO

H

BACK
ST

WICKER HILL

B3106

BRITISH ROW

PROSPECT
PL

GEORGE ST

CROSS ST

YORK
BG

UNION STREET

CHURCH
ST

FORE ST

TIMBRELL
ST

BELLEFIELD
CR

ST THOMAS

DUKE ST

ROUNDSTONE ST

CITY WY

CASTLE ST

VICTORIA RD

THE
BEECHES

PEPPERACRE
LA

HILPERTON ROAD

HAYCROFT
RD

EASTBOURNE
RD

GREENWAY

LARKRISE
GD

COURTENAY
RD

ASHTON
CL

CORBIN
RD

KENTON
DR

Larkrise
Sch

Paxcroft
Prim Sch

BARN GLEBE

FURLONG

HALFWAY

1

B3106

58

105

102

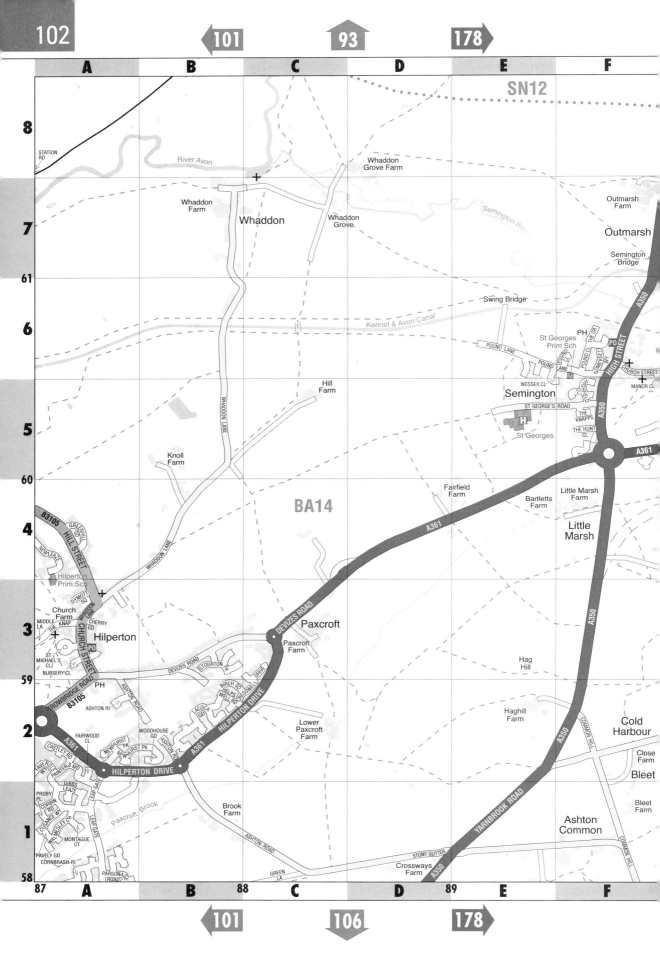

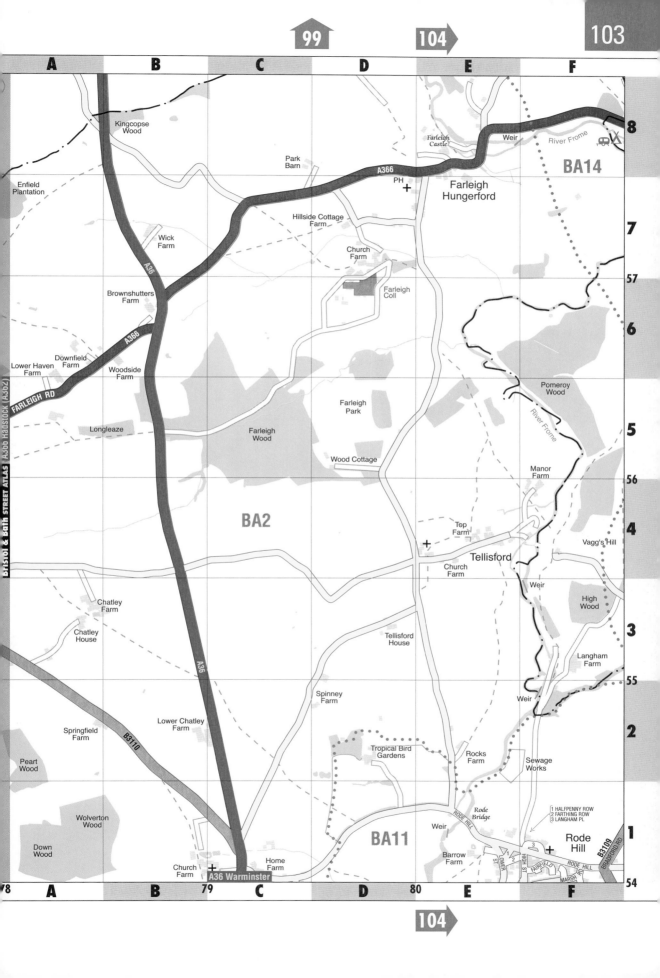

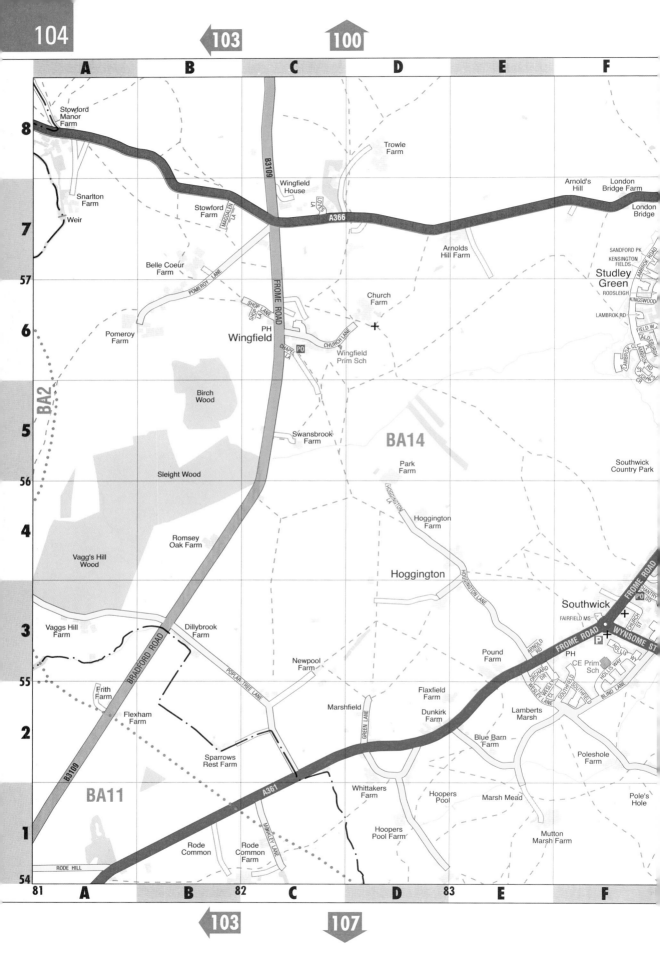

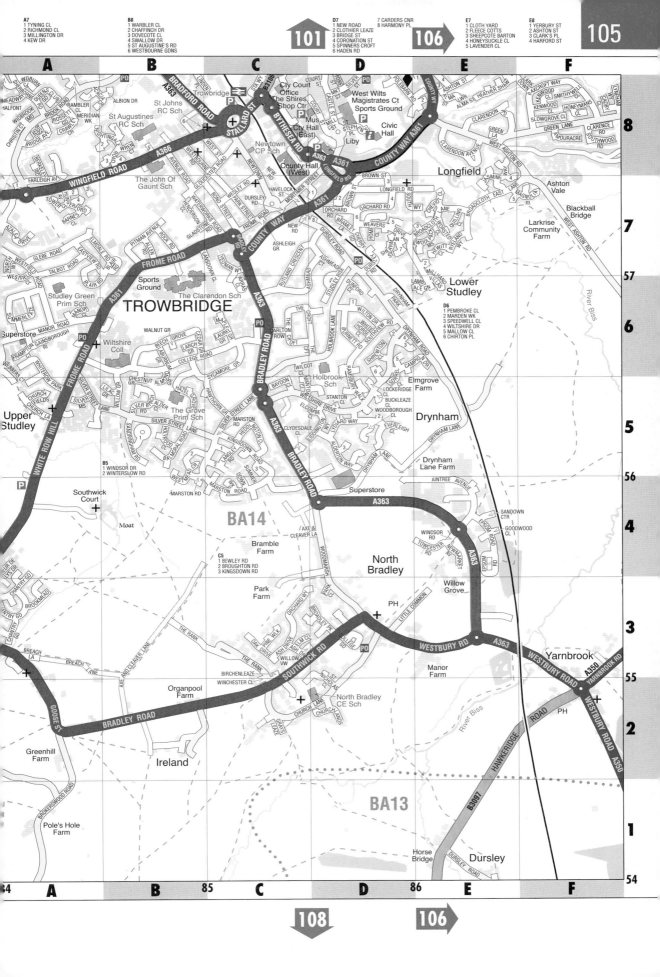

A7
1 TYNING CL
2 RICHMOND CL
3 MILLINGTON DR
4 KEW DR

B8
1 WARBLER CL
2 CHAFFINCH DR
3 DOVECOTE CL
4 SWALLOW DR
5 ST AUGUSTINE'S RD
6 WESTBOURNE GDNS

D7
1 NEW ROAD
2 CLOTHIER LEAZE
3 BRIDGE ST
4 CORONATION ST
5 SPINNERS CROFT
6 HADEN RD

7 CARDERS CNR
8 HARMONY PL

E7
1 CLOTH YARD
2 FLEECE COTTS
3 SHEEPCOTE BARTON
4 HONEYSUCKLE CL
5 LAVENDER CL

E8
1 YERBURY ST
2 ASHTON ST
3 CLARK'S PL
4 HARFORD ST

101   106   105

BA14

BA13

TROWBRIDGE

A **B** **C** **D** **E** **F**

8

Rode Common Farm

BA14

Parsonage Farm

Farm Pool

7

The Devils Bed and Bolster

Mount Pleasant

53

Moberley Pond

Castley Farm

Norris Hill Farm

Overcourt Farm

High Wood

6

Seymours Court

Duck Pool Farm

Silver Street Farm

Woodland Park

Seymours Court Farm

CASLEY LANE

DUCK POOL LANE

RUDGE LANE

Lady Wood

Hazel Wood

Upper Castley Farm

Waterslade

RIDGE HILL

Church Farm

Wishing Well Farm

5

Rudge

Round Wood

BA11

Lower Rudge Hill Farm

FAIRWOOD ROAD

Brokerswood

52

SCOTLAND LANE

Lower Rudge

PH

4

Lower Rudge Farm

PH

Cowards Farm

Ford

Carter's Bridge

BA13

White Row Farm

Scotland Farm

Stourton Bushes

3

Edgell's Wood

Standerwick Court

RIDGE LANE

51

Salmond's Copse

Trees Farm

Tennis Corner Farm

Tennis Corner Wood

LC

A36

Palmers Farm

TENNIS CORNER DROVE

Fairwood Farm

2

Standerwick

RIDGE ROAD

PH

Round Wood

Hilleaze Farm

Barber's Wood

Cuzners Farm

B3099

MARSH ROAD

1

Frome Market

BERKLEY STREET

Foxes Drove Farm

Five Lords Farm

CLIVEY

B3099

Dilton Marsh

Poplar Farm

Clivey Farm

50

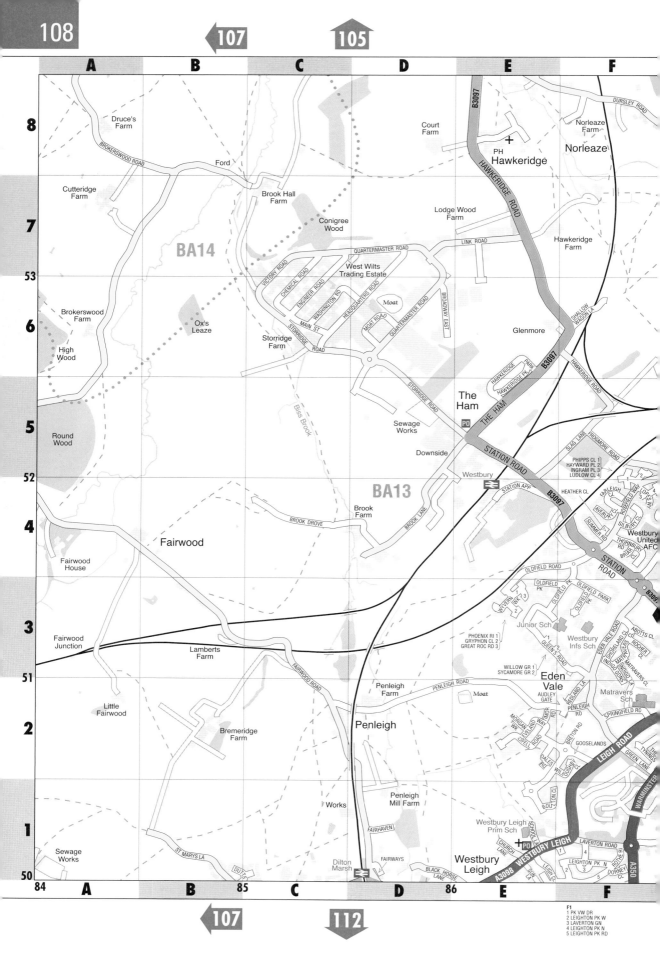

A **B** **C** **D** **E** **F**

8

Druce's Farm

Norleaze Farm

Court Farm

PH Hawkeridge

Norleaze

BROKERSWOOD ROAD

Ford

B3097

HAWKERIDGE ROAD

DURSLEY ROAD

Cutteridge Farm

Brook Hall Farm

Lodge Wood Farm

Hawkeridge Farm

7

Conigree Wood

LINK ROAD

BA14

QUARTERMASTER ROAD

53

VICTORY ROAD
CHEMICAL ROAD
ENGINEER ROAD

West Wilts Trading Estate

WASHINGTON RD
HEADQUARTERS ROAD

Moat

SHALLOW WAGON LA

B3097

HAWKERIDGE ROAD

6

Brokerswood Farm

Ox's Leaze

MAIN ST

Storridge Farm

STORRIDGE ROAD

QUARTERMASTER ROAD

BROADWAY EAST

MOAT ROAD

Glenmore

HAWKERIDGE PARK
B3097

High Wood

Biss Brook

STORRIDGE ROAD

The Ham

THE HAM

SLAG LANE
FROGMORE ROAD

5

Round Wood

Sewage Works

PO

STATION ROAD

PHIPPS CL 1
HAYWARD PL 2
INGRAM PL 3
LUDLOW CL 4

Downside

FARLEIGH
ROSEFIELD WAY
TOPS WY

52

Westbury

STATION APP

B3097

HEATHER CL

AVERY RD
SILBURY CL

STATION

BA13

Brook Farm

BROOK LANE

Westbury United AFC

SUMMER RD
THORNBURY
BRIDE

4

Fairwood

BROOK DROVE

ROAD

Fairwood House

OLDFIELD ROAD

OLDFIELD PK

OLDFIELD PARK
OLDFIELD PK

3

Fairwood Junction

Lamberts Farm

FAIRWOOD ROAD

WATVERN WK

Junior Sch

PHOENIX RI 1
GRYPHON CL 2
GREAT ROC RD 3

Westbury Infs Sch

QUEEN'S RD

AROTTS CL
ROCHER CL

51

Little Fairwood

Penleigh Farm

PENLEIGH ROAD

Moat

WILLOW GR 1
SYCAMORE GR 2

Eden Vale

AUDLEY GATE

REDLAND LA
PENLEIGH RD

Matravers Sch

SPRINGFIELD RD

2

Bremeridge Farm

Penleigh

MORGAN WK
WELLAND CL
GIFELL RD

BRETON RD

GOOSELANDS

LEIGH ROAD
THE TYNINGS
GREEN LANE

WARMINSTER

A350

1

Sewage Works

Works

Penleigh Mill Farm

FAIRHAVEN

Westbury Leigh Prim Sch

PO

WESTBURY LEIGH

LAVERTON ROAD

ST MARYS LA

DUTS

FAIRWAYS

BLACK HORSE LANE

CHURCH LANE
SCHOOL RD

Westbury Leigh

A3098 WESTBURY LEIGH

LEIGHTON PK N
SUN

LEIGHTON PK
DORNEY CL
ROCHE RI

50

Sewage Works

Dilton Marsh

84 **A** **B** 85 **C** **D** 86 **E** **F**

F1
1 PK VW DR
2 LEIGHTON PK W
3 LAVERTON GN
4 LEIGHTON PK N
5 LEIGHTON PK RD

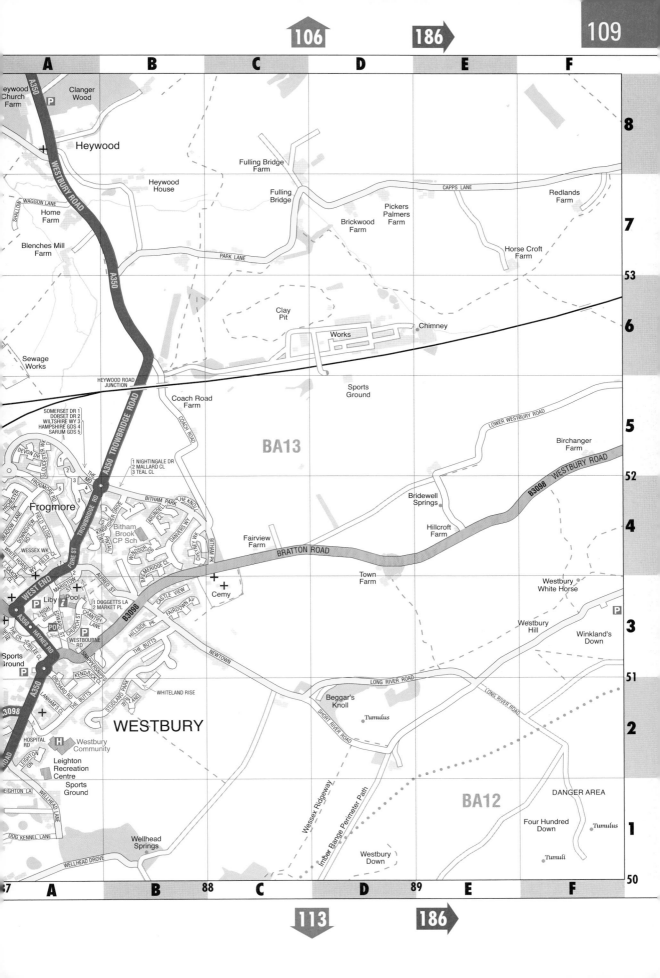

A B C D E F

8

Heywood Church Farm

P

Clanger Wood

Heywood

WESTBURY ROAD

A350

SHALLOW

WAGGON LANE

Home Farm

Heywood House

Fulling Bridge Farm

Fulling Bridge

CAPPS LANE

Redlands Farm

7

Blenches Mill Farm

PARK LANE

Brickwood Farm

Pickers Palmers Farm

Horse Croft Farm

53

Clay Pit

Chimney

6

Sewage Works

Works

A350 TROWBRIDGE ROAD

HEYWOOD ROAD JUNCTION

Coach Road Farm

Sports Ground

Lower Westbury Road

5

SOMERSET DR 1
DORSET DR 2
WILTSHIRE WY 3
HAMPSHIRE GDS 4
SARUM GDS 5

COACH ROAD

BA13

Birchanger Farm

DEVON DR

DORCHESTER WK

1 NIGHTINGALE DR
2 MALLARD CL
3 TEAL CL

THE MD

A350 TROWBRIDGE ROAD

B3098 WESTBURY ROAD

52

HIGHFIELD PK

MEADOW WAY

DOWNSVIEW

FIELD CLOSE

Frogmore

BITHAM PARK

KINGFISHER DRIVE

THE KNOLL

ARUNDEL CL

Bitham Brook CP Sch

DANVERS WY

Bridewell Springs

Hillcroft Farm

4

WHITE HORSE WY

SAXON WY

WESSEX WK

FIELD CL

WINDSOR CL

PINTAIL

CHENEY WY

BITHAM PK

Fairview Farm

BRATTON ROAD

Town Farm

Westbury White Horse

West End

FORE ST

MARISTON ST

ALFRED ST

BREMERIDGE CL

CASTLE VIEW

FAIRDOWN AV

Cemy

Westbury Hill

Westbury Hill

P

3

Liby

Pool

HIGH ST

CHANTRY LANE

1 DOGGETTS LA
2 MARKET PL

HILLSIDE PK

THE BUTTS

Winkland's Down

P

HAYNES RD

EDWARD ST

CHURCH ST

Westbourne Rd

BINCKNOLL

NEWTOWN

A350

B3098

51

B3098

ORCHARD RD

KENDRICK CL

THE BUTTS

STUDLAND PARK

WHITELAND RISE

LONG RIVER ROAD

LONG RIVER ROAD

2

LANHAM'S CL

Beggar's Knoll

SHORT RIVER ROAD

WESTBURY

Tumulus

BA12

DANGER AREA

HOSPITAL RD

H

Westbury Community

Leighton Recreation Centre

Wessex Ridgeway

Imber Range Perimeter Path

Four Hundred Down

Tumulus

LEIGHTON GN

WELLHEAD LANE

Sports Ground

DOG KENNEL LANE

Wellhead Springs

Tumuli

1

LEIGHTON LA

WELLHEAD DROVE

Westbury Down

50

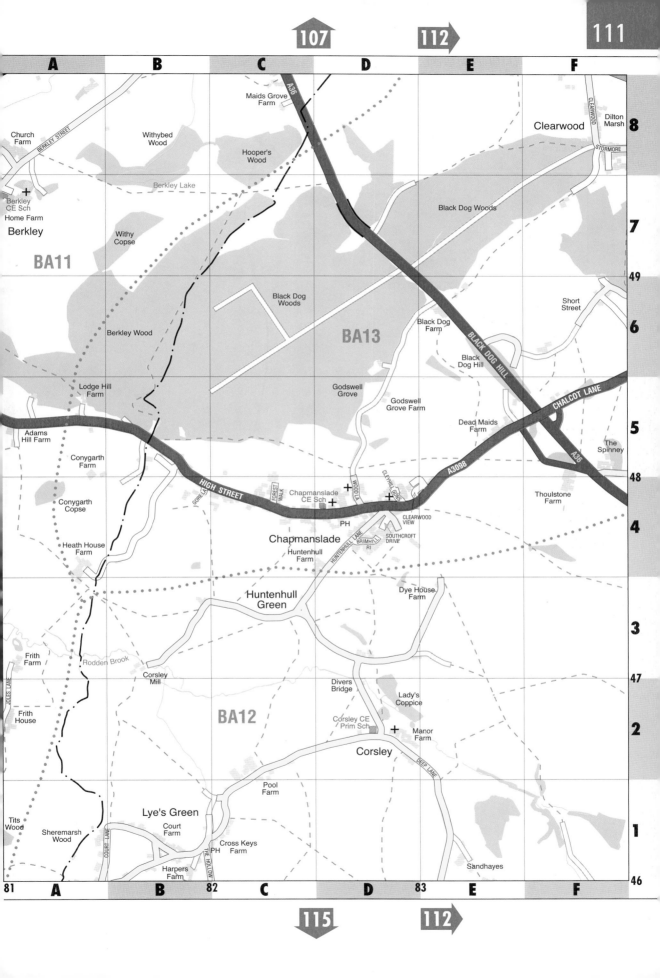

A B C D E F

8 Clearwood
Dilton Marsh
CLEARWOOD
STORMORE
Church Farm
BERKLEY STREET
Maids Grove Farm
Withybed Wood
Hooper's Wood
Black Dog Woods

7 Berkley Lake
Berkley CE Sch
Home Farm
Berkley
Withy Copse

BA11

49

6 Black Dog Woods
BA13
Black Dog Farm
Berkley Wood
Short Street
BLACK DOG HILL

5 Lodge Hill Farm
Godswell Grove
Godswell Grove Farm
Black Dog Hill
Dead Maids Farm
CHALCOT LANE
The Spinney
Adams Hill Farm
A36

48 Conygarth Farm
HIGH STREET
GORE LA
FOREST WALK
Chapmanslade CE Sch
WOOD LA
CLEYHILL GDNS
A3098
Thoulstone Farm

4 Conygarth Copse
PH
CLEARWOOD VIEW
SOUTHCROFT DRIVE
Chapmanslade
HUNTENHULL LANE
BRIMHILL RI
Heath House Farm
Huntenhull Farm

3 Huntenhull Green
Dye House Farm
Frith Farm
Rodden Brook
Corsley Mill

47 Divers Bridge
Lady's Coppice
Frith House
JOLES LANE
BA12
Corsley CE Prim Sch

2 Manor Farm
Corsley
DEEP LANE

Pool Farm

1 Lye's Green
Court Farm
Cross Keys Farm
Tits Wood
Sheremarsh Wood
COURT LANE
THE HOLLOW
PH
Harpers Farm
Sandhayes

46
81 A B 82 C D 83 E F

111
108

A **B** **C** **D** **E** **F**

CLIVEY
B3099
Dilton Marsh Farm
SHEPHERDS MD
RD PIT
STORMORE
GREENACRES
+ Stormore

Dilton Marsh
ATYEO CL
PARK RD
THE AV
WOODLAND VW
ALAN POWELL CR
MARSH LA
PO
ATYEO CL
+
Dilton Marsh CE Cont Prim Sch

HIGH STREET
ST MARYS ST
SILVER ST
LYES GR
PH
WHITECROFT
ORCHARD CL
C/CA CLOSE
FRIARS CL
PETTICOAT LANE

B3099
A3098
TOWER HILL
HONEY LANE
MILL LANE

WESTBURY LEIGH
A3098
+
Penknap
SAND HOLE LANE

8

Hisomley
THE HOLLOW

Titford Farm
Dilton Vale
OLD DILTON ROAD

SAND HOLE LANE

WELLHEAD DROVE
A350
WARMINSTER ROAD

Chalcot Wood

Chalcot Park

Chalcot Park Farm

Firn Farm

+
Dilton Farm
Old Dilton

7

49

Chalcot House
A3098
DILTON CT

Dilton Court

BA13

CHALCOT LANE

Biss Bottom

6

5

CH

Hedge Croft Wood

Upton Scudamore
Millards Farm
Biss Farm
PH
Tumulus
THE OR
BISS CL

48

Thoulstone Cottages

Temple Farm
+

4

Clear Wood

A36

BA12

Tumuli

A350

3

47

Norridge Farm

BATH ROAD

2

Motel

B3414
BATH ROAD
A36

1

Norridge Wood

Brick Hill

Refuse Tip
FURNAX LA

46

84 **A** **B** 85 **C** **D** 86 **E** **F**

110

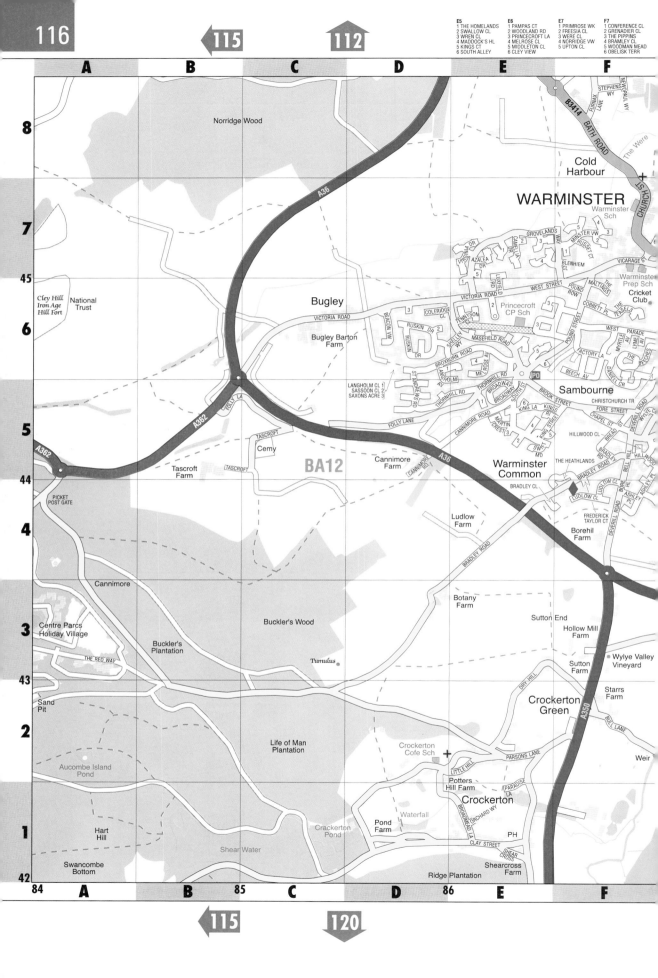

Norridge Wood

Cold Harbour

WARMINSTER

Warminster Sch

Cley Hill
Iron Age
Hill Fort

National
Trust

Bugley

Bugley Barton
Farm

Warminster
Prep Sch

Cricket
Club

VICTORIA ROAD

COLERIDGE CL

WEST STREET

Princecroft
CP Sch

THE
MALTINGS

Sambourne

CHRISTCHURCH TR

FORE STREET

LANGHOLM CL 1
SASSOON CL 2
SAXONS ACRE 3

FOLLY LANE

Cemy

TASCROFT

Tascroft
Farm

TASCROFT

BA12

Cannimore
Farm

Warminster
Common

THE HEATHLANDS

BRADLEY CL

Ludlow
Farm

FREDERICK
TAYLOR CT

Borehil
Farm

PICKET
POST GATE

Cannimore

Botany
Farm

Sutton End

Hollow Mill
Farm

Centre Parcs
Holiday Village

Buckler's
Plantation

Buckler's Wood

THE RED WAY

Tumulus

Sutton
Farm

Wylye Valley
Vineyard

Sand
Pit

Crockerton
Green

Starrs
Farm

Life of Man
Plantation

Crockerton
Cofe Sch

PARSONS LANE

Weir

Aucombe Island
Pond

Potters
Hill Farm

Crockerton

Hart
Hill

Crackerton
Pond

Pond
Farm

Waterfall

PH

Swancombe
Bottom

Shear Water

Ridge Plantation

Shearcross
Farm

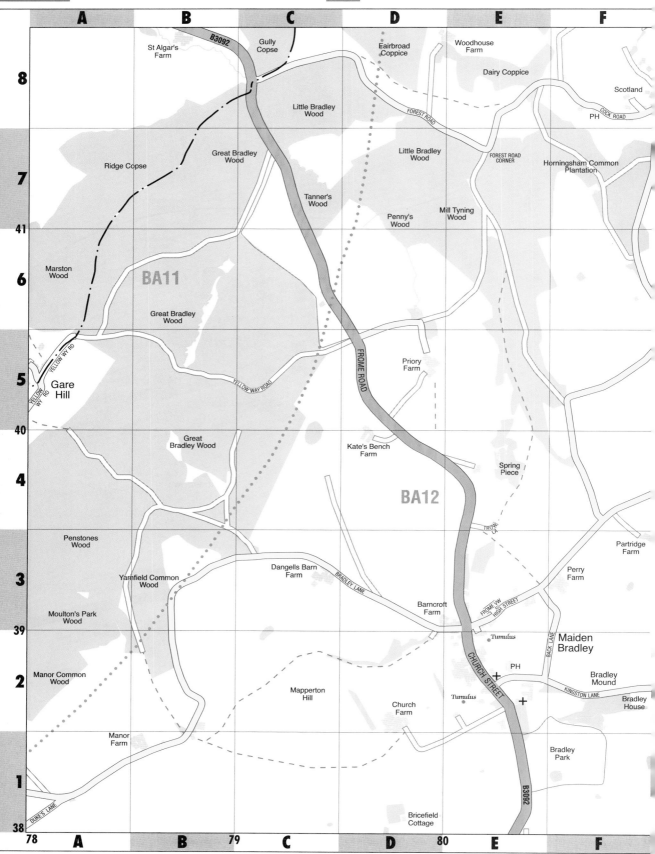

A B C D E F

Upper Pond
Weir
My Lady's
Bridge

Swancombe
Bottom

8

Newbury
ROWE'S HL
WHITE STREET
ROWE'S HL
Dertley
Plain

LODGE ROAD

Park
Farm

Round Hill
Plantation

West
Common

Mill
Farm

WATER LANE

Horningsham
CP Sch

Mill Pond

CHURCH STREET

GENTLE STREET

Hitcombe
Bottom

7

CHAPEL STREET

PO

Town Well

Horningsham

Parsonage
Farm

41

POTTLE STREET

6

POTTLE STREET

Round Hill
Farm

Everett's
Wood

Lower Barn
Farm

5

BA12

Charlock Hill
Thicket

40

Baycliffe
Farm

4

Bidcombe
Wood

Bidcombe
Hill

Woodcombe Bottom

3

Tumulus

Proutly Wood

Brimsdown
Hill

Tumulus

Woodcombe
Wood

39

Marcombe
Wood

Tumulus

Mound

Whitecliff
Down

2

Brimsdown
Hill

Sewage
Works

Little Marcombe
Wood

Holcombe
Hall

Bidcombe
Down

Bushcombe
Bottom

Brimble Hill
Wood

Newmead
Cottages

Earthwork

Hiscombe
Wood

Cross
Dyke

1

Newmead
Farm

Whitepits
Down

Tumuli

Tumuli

Earthworks

38

119
116

119
126

A **B** **C** **D** **E** **F**

Southleigh Wood

Henge   DEVERILL ROAD   The Beeches

Lynchets

South Leigh Farm

Pickle Farm

WALNUT CL
HIGH ST
D'MOCKS LA

8

Sand Pit

Long Ivor Farm

7

Sandhill Farm

Longbridge Hill

41

SAND ST

PH

BA12

6

Sturgess Farm

Cow Down

Settlement

Whiten Hill   Haycombe Hill Bungalow

Manor Farm

A350

Tumulus

Haycombe Hill Farm

Littlecombe Hill

5

40

Field Barn Farm

Tumulus

Sutton Bottom

4

Lord's Hill Farm

Parsonage Down

3

Westcombe

39

SP3

Little Down

A350

Tumuli

Parsonage Down Farm

2

Tumulus

Beech Clump

Burnbake

Tumuli

1

Tumulus

38

A B C D E F

8
7
37
6
5
36
4
35
3
2
1
34

Hick's Park Wood

Hents Hill Farm

CANNWOOD LANE

Canwood Farm.

Walters Farm

Forest Gate Farm

Lark Farm

Lipgate Farm

HAMMER STREET

Green Acres

SOCK'S LANE

Horseshoe Farm

Brewham House

Border Farm

Longfield Farm

JAMES'S HILL

Jerrards Farm

Treetops Farm

PH

North Brewham

Cooks Farm

TILE HILL

Brewham Lodge Farm

River Brue

Bridge Farm

Mill Farm

Earthwork

+

PH

Street Farm

CHARCROFT HILL

STREET LANE

BA10

36

South Brewham

Brook Farm

Haven Farm

STREET LANE

Charcroft Farm

Holland Farm

King's Wood

CHARCROFT HILL

Shave Farm

SHAVE LANE

Jack's Castle Plantation

Macmillan Way

Tumulus

Hookgate Farm

Hilcombe Farm

TOWER ROAD

P

Convent Bottom

Alfred's Tower

Crawley House Farm

KINGSETTLE HILL

Hilcombe Hanging

Cards Farm

Brewham Brake Farm

Leland Trail

Berridge

Tower Road Farm

Hardway House

Pillinge Farm

Park Farm

Brewham Wood

Beaumont's Wood

Hardway

PH

Aaron's Hill

Moss Cottage

Picketts Farm

Picket's Copse

PEN HILL

72 A B 73 C D 74 E F

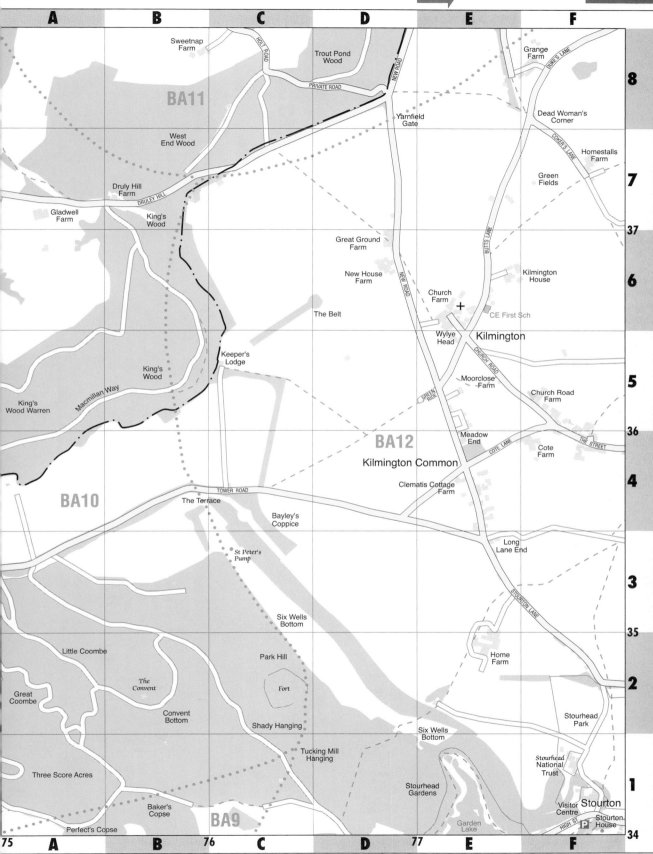

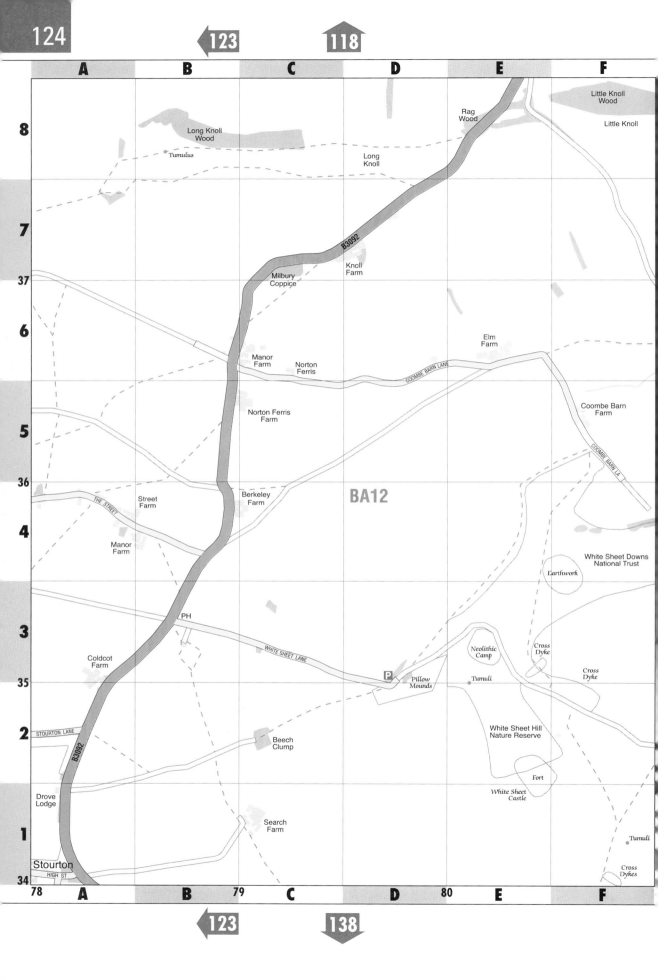

A B C D E F

8   Little Knoll
    Wood
    Long Knoll   Rag   Little Knoll
    Wood   Wood
    Tumulus
                      Long
                      Knoll
7   B3092
37   Knoll
    Milbury   Farm
    Coppice
6   Elm
                                 Farm
    Manor   Norton
    Farm   Ferris   COOMBE BARN LANE
                                          Coombe Barn
    Norton Ferris   Farm
5   Farm   COOMBE BARN LA
36
    THE STREET   Berkeley   BA12
    Street   Farm
    Farm
4   White Sheet Downs
    Manor   National Trust
    Farm   Earthwork
                                     Neolithic   Cross
3   PH   Camp   Dyke
    WHITE SHEET LANE   Cross
    Coldcot   Dyke
35 Farm   P
                         Pillow   Tumuli
                         Mounds
2   STOURTON LANE   White Sheet Hill
    B3092   Beech   Nature Reserve
                 Clump
                                     Fort
    Drove   White Sheet
    Lodge   Castle
1   Search
                   Farm   Tumuli
    Stourton
34 HIGH ST   Cross
                                                Dykes
78   A   B   79   C   D   80   E   F

A B C D E F

Bidcombe Down
Earthworks
Whitepits Down
8

Dairy Farm
Tumulus

River Wylye
7

37

Truncombe Wood
Peter's Penning
Tumulus
Bath Wilts & North Dorset Gliding Club
6
Court Hill
Court Hill Plantation

Rodmead Farm
Tumulus

The Park
Tumulus
Danes' Bottom
5

Rodmead Hill
36

BA12

Tumuli
Earthwork
Tumuli
Cleeve
Danes' Bottom
Tumulus
4
Rodmead Wood
Tumulus
Earthwork
Tumulus
South Down

Cross Dyke
Mere Down
3

The Drusses
Tumuli
35

Tumulus
B3095
Pond Bottom
Mast
2
Tumulus
Mere Down Farm

Cross Dyke
Tumulus
Mere Down
Earthworks
Tumuli
Tumulus
1
Danger Area
Tumulus

Great Bottom
Charnage Down
34

1 A B 82 C D 83 E F

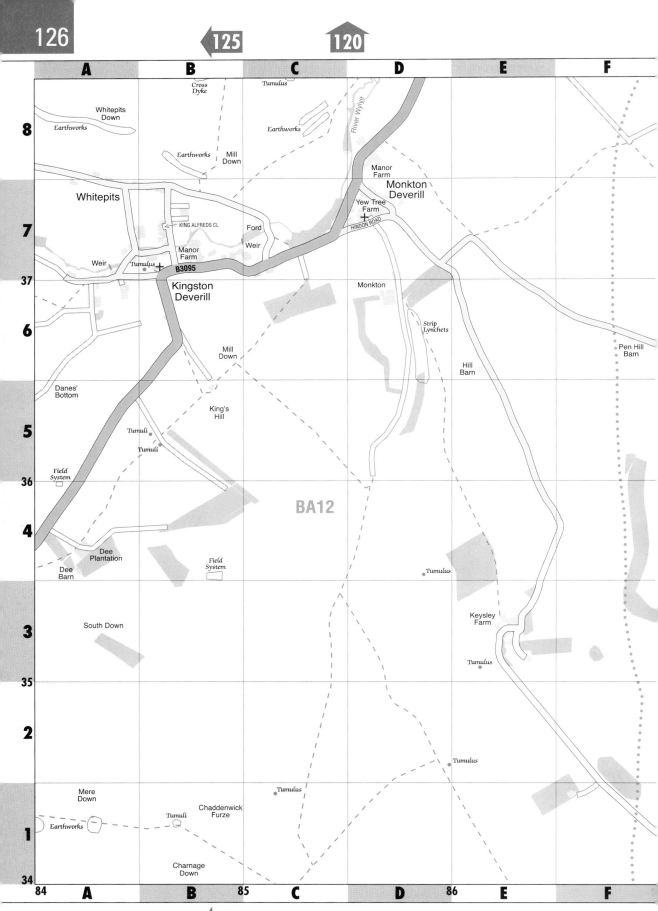

A B C D E F

8

Whitepits
Down
Earthworks

*Cross
Dyke*

Tumulus

Earthworks

River Wylye

Manor
Farm

Monkton
Deverill

Earthworks

Mill
Down

Whitepits

KING ALFREDS CL

Ford

Weir

Yew Tree
Farm

HINDON ROAD

7

Weir

Tumulus

Manor
Farm

Weir

B3095

Kingston
Deverill

37

Monkton

*Strip
Lynchets*

6

Mill
Down

Hill
Barn

Pen Hill
Barn

*Danes'
Bottom*

King's
Hill

5

Tumuli

Tumuli

*Field
System*

36

BA12

4

*Dee
Plantation*

Tumulus

*Dee
Barn*

*Field
System*

Keysley
Farm

3

South Down

Tumulus

35

Tumulus

2

Tumulus

Mere
Down

Tumulus

1

Earthworks

Tumuli

Chaddenwick
Furze

34

Charnage
Down

84 A B 85 C D 86 E F

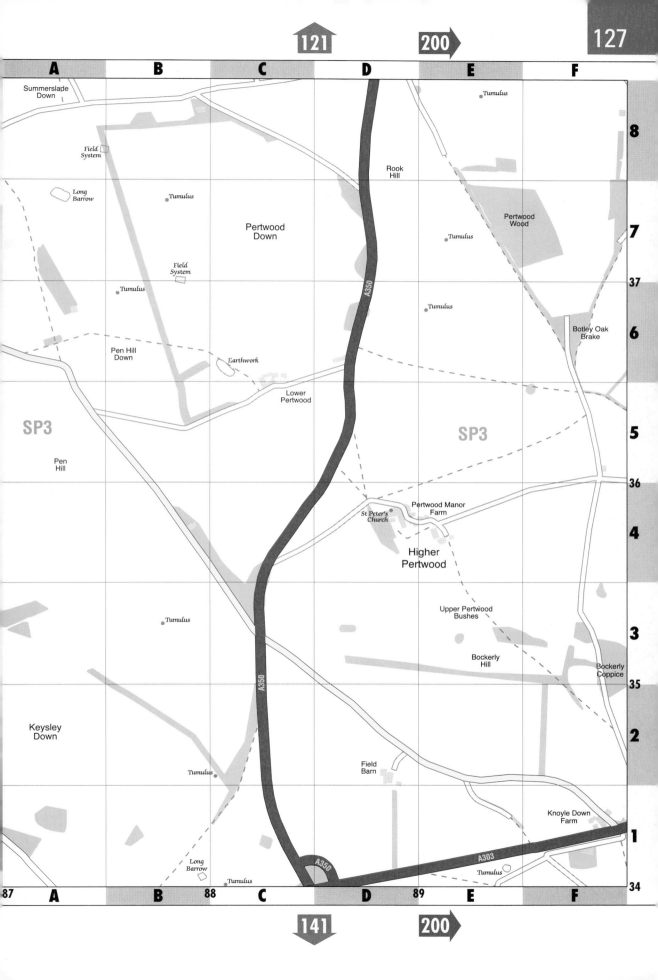

A B C D E F

8

Summerslade Down

Field System

Long Barrow

Tumulus

Pertwood Down

Field System

Tumulus

Rook Hill

Tumulus

Pertwood Wood

Tumulus

7

37

Botley Oak Brake

6

Pen Hill Down

Earthwork

Lower Pertwood

SP3

Pen Hill

SP3

5

36

Pertwood Manor Farm

St Peter's Church

Higher Pertwood

4

Tumulus

Upper Pertwood Bushes

Bockerly Hill

Bockerly Coppice

3

35

Keysley Down

Field Barn

2

Tumulus

Knoyle Down Farm

1

A350

Long Barrow

Tumulus

A350

A303

Tumulus

34

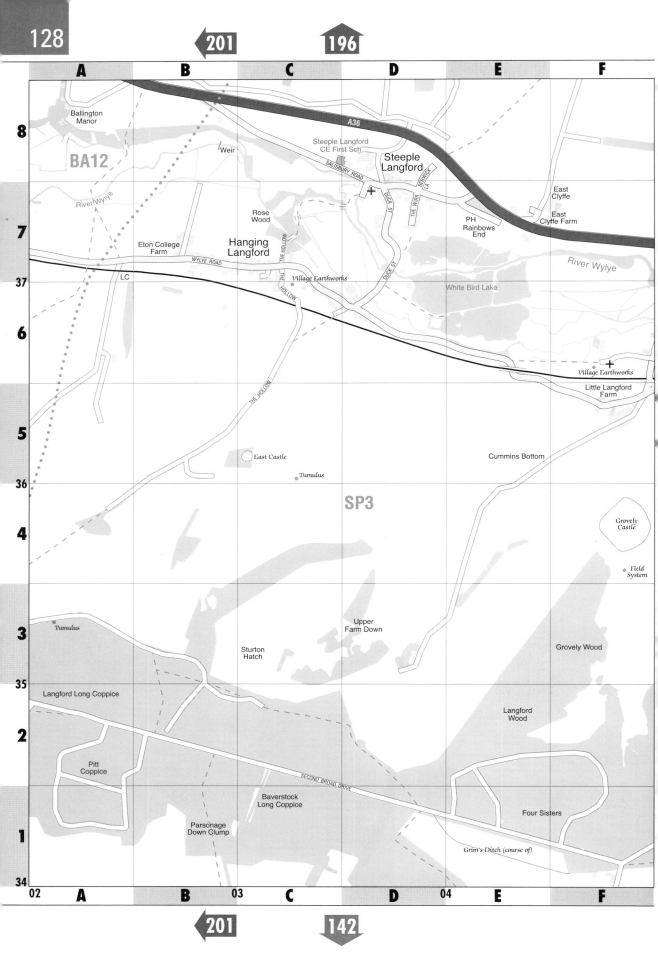

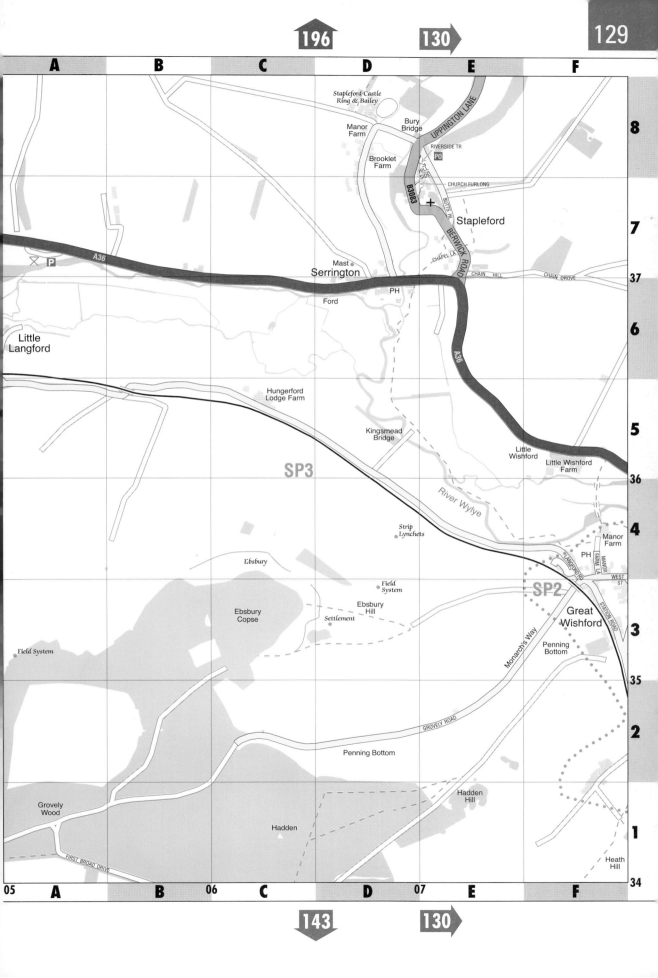

A **B** **C** **D** **E** **F**

8

Stapleford Castle
Ring & Bailey

Manor
Farm

Bury
Bridge

UPPINGTON LANE

RIVERSIDE TR

PO

Brooklet
Farm

HILL SIDE

CHURCH FURLONG

B3063

BUTS HL

Stapleford

7

CHAPEL LA

BERWICK ROAD

Mast

Serrington

CHAIN HILL

CHAIN DROVE

37

PH

Ford

A36

6

Little
Langford

A36

Hungerford
Lodge Farm

5

Kingsmead
Bridge

Little
Wishford

Little Wishford
Farm

SP3

River Wylye

36

Strip
Lynchets

Manor
Farm

4

Ebsbury

Field
System

LANGFORD RD

PH

MANOR FARM LA

WEST ST

SP2

Ebsbury
Copse

Ebsbury
Hill

Settlement

Great
Wishford

Penning
Bottom

3

Field System

Monarch's Way

35

Penning Bottom

GROVELY ROAD

2

Grovely
Road

Hadden
Hill

Grovely
Wood

Hadden

1

FIRST BROAD DRIVE

Heath
Hill

34

A   B   C   D   E   F

8

Eighteen Acre
Plantation

Stapleford Down

Camp
Plantation

7   SP3

Camp
Cottages

Tumulus

37

Monarch's Way

CHAIN DROVE

6   Stoford Hill
Buildings

A360

Tumulus

SP4

Monarch's Way

5

36   Stoford Bottom

MOUNT PLEASANT

Enclosure

RIVERSIDE CL

4   PH

Wishford
Prim Sch   Stoford
Bridge

Charity
Farm   Newton Barrow

WEST ST   Masts

Stoford

Wishford Farm   Village Earthworks

Town
End   SP2

SOUTH ST

35

3   Stoford
Farm

VALE VIEW RD

2   HIGHLAND VIEW
OAK CL
ASHLEIGH CLOSE
ST ANDREW'S RD
EDGE SIDE RD   South
Newton

A36

A360

PH

1

SP3   Manor
Farm

34   Mill Farm

08   A   B   09   C   D   10   E   F

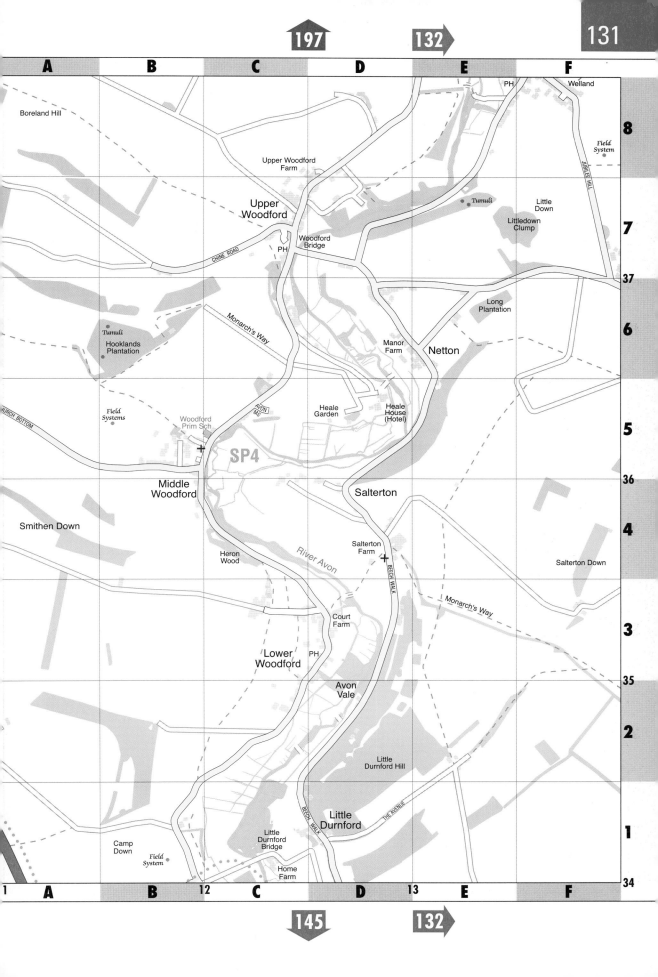

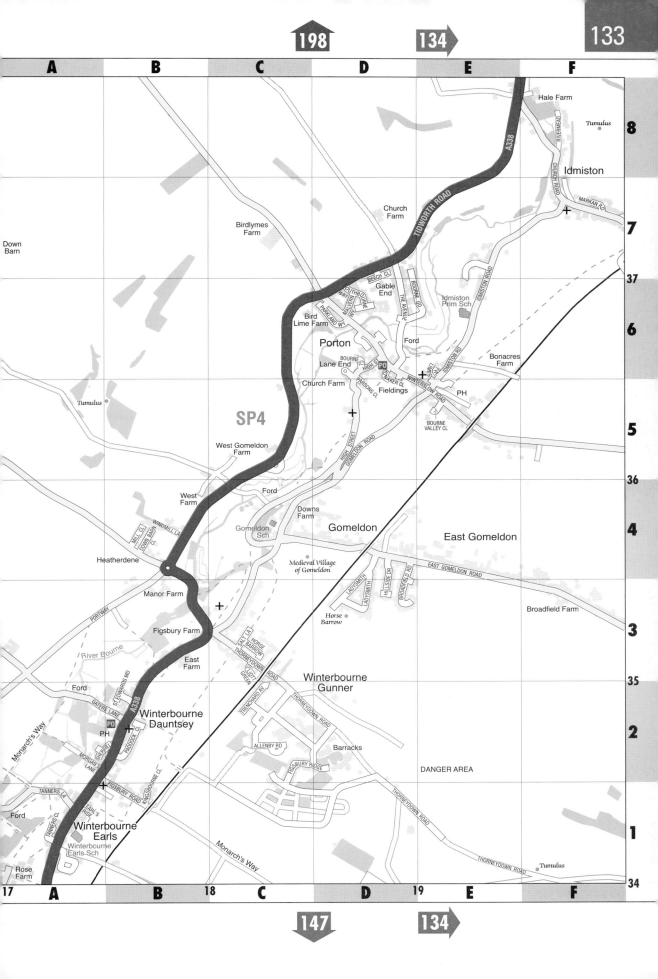

A B C D E F

8

Down
Barn

Hale Farm

Tumulus

Idmiston

MARKAN RD

7

37

Birdlymes
Farm

Church
Farm

A338 TIDWORTH ROAD

RIVERMEAD

CHURCH ROAD

IDMISTON ROAD

Idmiston
Prim Sch

BEECH CL

Gable
End

SOUTHBOURNE WAY

MALVEN WY

PARKLAND WY

THE AVENUE

BOURNE RD

6

Bird
Lime Farm

Porton

Ford

Bonacres
Farm

Tumulus

SP4

BOURNE
Lane End

Church Farm

BAKER CL

PARSONS CL

HIGH ST

PO

WINTERSLOW ROAD

ESWL7

PH

BOURNE
VALLEY CL

Fieldings

5

West Gomeldon
Farm

West
Farm

Ford

HIGH STREET

GOMELDON ROAD

36

Downs
Farm

Gomeldon

East Gomeldon

4

MILL CL

DOWN BARN CL

WINDMILL LA

Heatherdene

Gomeldon
Sch

Medieval Village
of Gomeldon

LADYSMITH

LADYSMITH

HILLSIDE DR

BROADFIELD RD

EAST GOMELDON ROAD

Broadfield Farm

Manor Farm

PORTWAY

Horse
Barrow

3

Figsbury Farm

River Bourne

East
Farm

ST EDWARDS RD

A338

LA LA

HORSE
BARROW

THORNEYDOWN

THORNEYDOWN ROAD

(FOOTPATH)
GREEN

Winterbourne
Gunner

35

Ford

GATERS LANE

Winterbourne
Dauntsey

PO

PH

MORGAN'S LANE

SHERFIELD

PADDOCK CL

KINGSBOURNE CL

FIGSBURY ROAD

TRENCHARD AV

ALLENBY RD

FIGSBURY RIDGE

Barracks

DANGER AREA

2

Monarch's Way

TANNERS LA

TANNERS CL

EARL'S RISE

Winterbourne
Earls

Winterbourne
Earls Sch

Ford

Rose
Farm

Monarch's Way

THORNEYDOWN ROAD

THORNEYDOWN ROAD

Tumulus

1

34

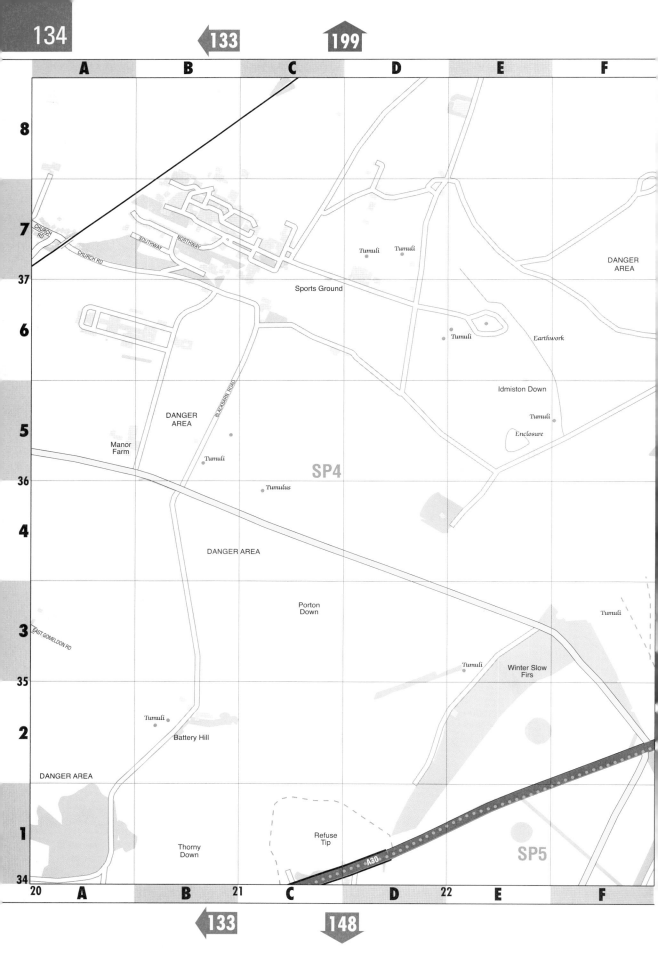
A   B   C   D   E   F

8

7

CHURCH RD

CHURCH RD

SOUTHWAY

NORTHWAY

37

Sports Ground

Tumuli   Tumuli

DANGER AREA

6

Tumuli

Earthwork

Idmiston Down

DANGER AREA

BLACKBARN ROAD

5

Tumuli

Enclosure

Manor Farm

Tumuli

SP4

36

Tumulus

4

DANGER AREA

3

EAST GOMELDON RD

Porton Down

Tumuli

Tumuli

35

Tumuli

Winter Slow Firs

2

Tumuli

Battery Hill

DANGER AREA

1

Refuse Tip

A30

SP5

Thorny Down

34

20   A   B   21   C   D   22   E   F

A B C D E F

8

7

37

6

North Hampshire STREET ATLAS A343 Andover

5

36

4

35

3

2

1

34

Earthwork

Isle of
Wight Hill

DANGER
AREA

Boscombe
Down East

Enclosure

Forty Acre
Plantation

Earthwork

SP4

Tumulus

Franklin's
Well

Earthwork

Earthwork

A343

Little Firs
Farm

Blake's
Firs

Easton
Down

Earthwork

Roche
Court Down

Earthwork

LOPCOMBE
CORNER

Lopcombe
Corner
Farm

A30

Firs Farm

Popple Down
Farm

Valley
Farm

A30 Stockbridge

Tumuli

Easton
Down
Farm

The Pheasant
Hotel

A30

SP5

Gutteridge
Farm

Popple
Light Copse

Ashley's
Copse

Howe
Copse

Roche Court

Ramshill
Copse

23 A B 24 C D 25 E F

BA10

Walk
Copse

Walk
Farm

Coach Road
Farm

Bedlam Green
Farm

Blackslough
Wood

PEN HILL

Leland Trail
Macmillan Way

New Park
Farm

Newpark
Pond

Newpark
Wood

Barrow Lane
Farm

Barrow Water
Farm

GREY'S
CORNER

Horseacres
Farm

Cherry Tree
Farm

Barrow Corner
Farm

Barrow

Coneygore Wood

BARROW WATER LANE

BARROW LANE

Homestead
Farm

Stavordale
Priory

Motte &
Bailey

Somerlea
Farm

Canons
Farm

BA9

Cockroad Wood

Sewage
Works

Common
Farm

Brickhouse
Farm

PH

Charlton
Musgrove

Higher Shalford
Farm

SHALFORD LANE

Thorney Copse
Farm

Monarch's Way

Pen
Forest

B3081

Knapp
Farm

Rectory
Farm

Southmarsh

PARSONAGE LANE

RECTORY LANE

Monarch's Way

Home
Farm

South Marsh
Farm

Hillside
Farm

Greenlands
Farm

Bridle
Farm

Lower Church
Farm

Bitwood
Farm

Belmont
Farm

Encie
Farm

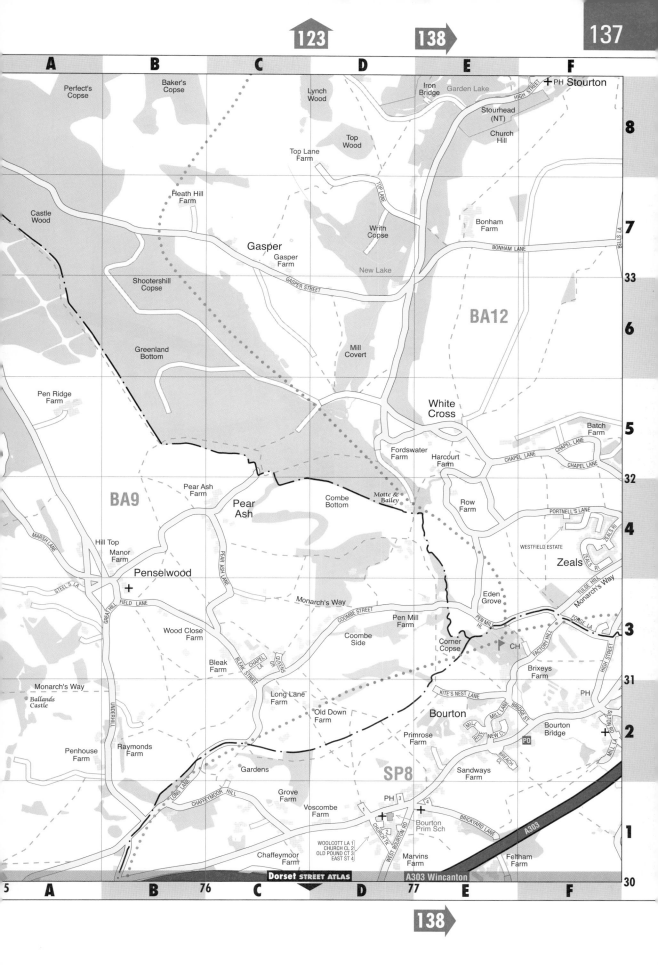

A B C D E F

8
7
33
6
5
32
4
3
31
2
1
30

+ PH Stourton

Perfect's Copse

Baker's Copse

Lynch Wood

Iron Bridge
Garden Lake

HIGH STREET

Stourhead (NT)

Church Hill

Top Wood

Top Lane Farm

Castle Wood

Heath Hill Farm

TOP LANE

Writh Copse

Bonham Farm

BELLS LA

BONHAM LANE

Gasper

Gasper Farm

GASPER STREET

New Lake

BA12

Shootershill Copse

Greenland Bottom

Mill Covert

White Cross

Pen Ridge Farm

Fordswater Farm

Harcourt Farm

Batch Farm

CHAPEL LANE

CHAPEL LANE

CHAPEL LANE

Pear Ash Farm

Combe Bottom

Motte & Bailey

Row Farm

PORTNELL'S LANE

BA9

Pear Ash

MARSH LANE

Hill Top

Manor Farm

ZEALS RI

Westfield Estate

Zeals

PEAR ASH LANE

STEEL'S LA

Penselwood

+

FIELD LANE

GREAT HILL

Monarch's Way

COOMBE STREET

Pen Mill Farm

Eden Grove

TULSE HILL

Monarch's Way

PEN MILL HL

FORGE LA

HIGH STREET

Wood Close Farm

Coombe Side

Corner Copse

CH

FACTORY HILL

Brixeys Farm

Monarch's Way

Ballands Castle

UNDERHILL

Bleak Farm

CHAPEL LA

QUEENS GR

BLEAK STREET

Long Lane Farm

KITE'S NEST LANE

Bourton

MILL LANE

BRIDGE ST

PH

Bourton Bridge

MILL LA

SUTTON RD

+

Penhouse Farm

Raymonds Farm

Old Down Farm

Primrose Farm

MILL
IRIS
NEW CL

PO

SP8

Sandways Farm

BREACH CL

Gardens

LONG LANE

CHAFFEYMOOR HILL

Grove Farm

Voscombe Farm

PH 3

BRICKYARD LANE

A303

+
Bourton Prim Sch

Feltham Farm

WOOLCOTT LA 1
CHURCH CL 2
OLD POUND CT 3
EAST ST 4

CHURCH TK

WEST BOURTON RD

Marvins Farm

Chaffeymoor Farm

A B C D E F

8

7

33

6

5

32

4

3

31

2

1

30

BELLS LANE

B3092

CRAB LANE

CRAB LANE

B3092

BA12

Long Cross

St Martin Farm

Zeals First Sch

PH

ZEALS GN DR

Zeals

CHAPEL LANE

BOTTNELL'S LA

LULSE HILL

NEW ROAD

BELLS LANE

A303

Zeals Fish Farm

Wolverton

Monarch's Way

NEW RD

Queen Oak

FANTLEY LANE

TAN LA

CHURCH ROAD

DUNN'S LANE

Fitz Farm

FANTLEY LANE

Bagmore Farm

SP8

Bagmore Wood

Silton Wood

Redmoor Farm

SLODBROOK LANE

Zeals Knoll

Nor Wood

Lower Zeals

Manor Farm

Zeals House

Castle Ground Farm

South Lodge

Mapperton Hill Farm

MAPPERTON HILL

Ridge Hill Farm

A303

Wood Farm

Cross Dykes

MANOR ROAD

MERE BY-PASS

A303

Mere Castle (site of)

Tumuli

Recn Go

Long Hill

Quarry Fields Industrial Estate

Quarry Cottages

CADDY LA

UNDERHILL

HOMEFIELD

LONG HL

HILLSIDE CL

PROSPECT PL

BRAMLEY

TITH

B3095 CASTLE STREET

TOWNSEND CL

Town End

Greenhouses

B3092

B3092

78 A B 79 C D 80 E F

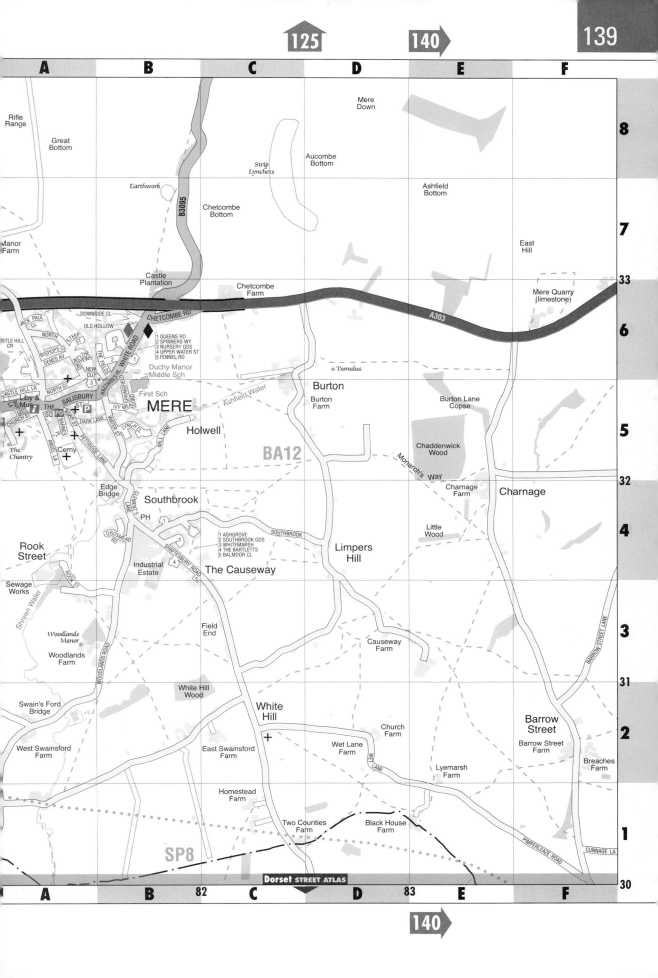

A   B   C   D   E   F

8

Rifle
Range

Great
Bottom

Mere
Down

Strip
Lynchets

Aucombe
Bottom

Ashfield
Bottom

Earthwork

Manor
Farm

Chetcombe
Bottom

East
Hill

7

Castle
Plantation

Chetcombe
Farm

Mere Quarry
(limestone)

33

B3095

A303

6

DOWNSIDE CL

JACK PAUL
CL

NORTH

STEEP ST

BISHOPS CL

THE REVIEWS

THE FIELDS

OLD HOLLOW

CHETCOMBE RD

1 QUEENS RD
2 SPINNERS WY
3 NURSERY GDS
4 UPPER WATER ST
5 FENNEL RD

CASTLE HILL CR

DENES AV

NORTH ST

NEW CUT

HAZZARD'S HL

HIGHFIELD

WHITE ROAD

Duchy Manor
Middle Sch

Tumulus

First Sch

Ashfield Water

Burton

Burton Lane
Copse

Liby &
Mus

SALISBURY

ST

P

THE SQ

PO

BOAR ST

IVY MEAD

WATER ST

MILL LANE

MERE

Burton
Farm

CASTLE HILL LA

CHURCH ST

PL

BARNES

Dark Lane

LYNCH CL

Holwell

Chaddenwick
Wood

5

The
Chantry

Cemy

ANGEL LA

PETRIDGE LANE

BA12

Monarch's Way

Charnage
Farm

Charnage

32

Edge
Bridge

CLEMENT'S LANE

Southbrook

PH

1

2

3

1 ASHGROVE
2 SOUTHBROOK GDS
3 WHITEMARSH
4 THE BARTLETTS
5 BALMOOR CL

SOUTHBROOK

Little
Wood

4

Rook
Street

LORDSMEAD RD

ROOK ST

Industrial
Estate

4

SHAFTESBURY ROAD

The Causeway

Limpers
Hill

Sewage
Works

Shreen Water

Woodlands
Manor

WOODLANDS ROAD

Field
End

Causeway
Farm

BARROW STREET LANE

3

Woodlands
Farm

31

Swain's Ford
Bridge

White Hill
Wood

White
Hill

Barrow
Street

2

West Swainsford
Farm

East Swainsford
Farm

Wet Lane
Farm

Church
Farm

WET LANE

Barrow Street
Farm

Lyemarsh
Farm

Breaches
Farm

Homestead
Farm

1

SP8

Two Counties
Farm

Black House
Farm

PIMPERLEAZE ROAD

CUNNAGE LA

30

A   82   B   C   D   83   E   F

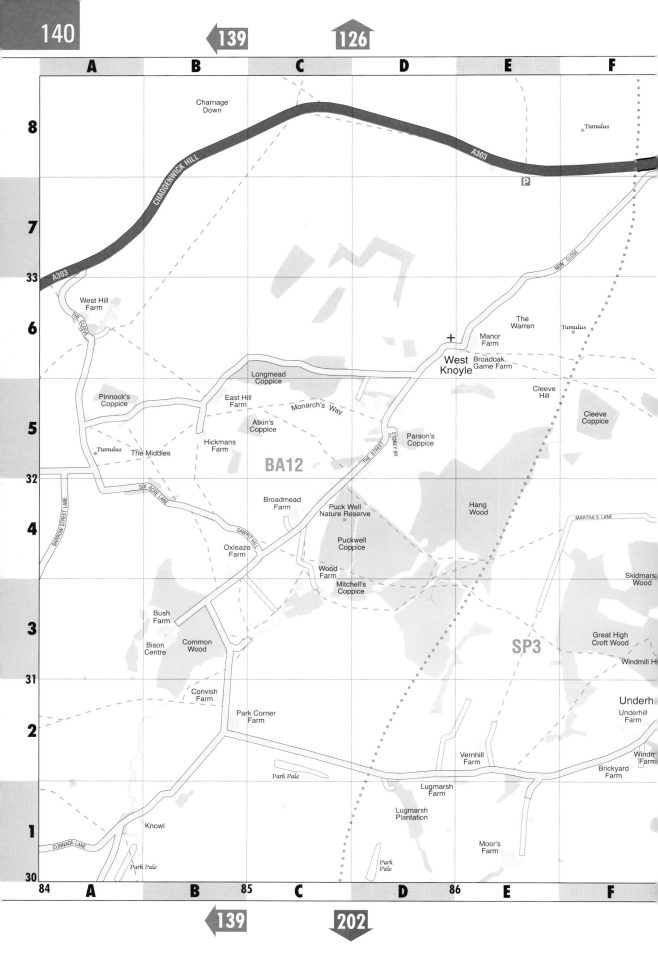

8
Charnage Down
Tumulus

A303
CHADDENWICK HILL
P

7

A303

33

West Hill Farm

THE CLEEVE

6
The Warren
Tumulus
+
Manor Farm
West Knoyle
Broadoak Game Farm
NEW CLOSE
Cleeve Hill

Longmead Coppice

Pinnock's Coppice
East Hill Farm
Monarch's Way
Cleeve Coppice

5
Atkin's Coppice

Hickmans Farm
Parson's Coppice

Tumulus
The Middles
BA12
THE STREET
STONEY BR

32
SIX ACRE LANE
Broadmead Farm
Puck Well Nature Reserve
Hang Wood
MARTHA'S LANE

BARROW STREET LANE

4
SAWPIT HILL
Puckwell Coppice
Skidmars Wood

Oxleaze Farm
Wood Farm
Mitchell's Coppice

3
Bush Farm
Great High Croft Wood

Bison Centre
Common Wood
SP3
Windmill H

31
Convish Farm
Underh

2
Park Corner Farm
Underhill Farm

Vernhill Farm
Windm Farm

Park Pale
Lugmarsh Farm
Brickyard Farm

1
Lugmarsh Plantation

Knowl
CUNNAGE LANE
Moor's Farm

Park Pale
Park Pale

30

A B C D E F

Keysley
Down

A303

Willoughby
Hedge

B3089

8

Two Mile
Down

Chapel Field
Barn

7

Kemps
Barn

B3089

Tumulus 33

Holden
Farm

6

Monarch's Way

Monarch's Way

A350

Peaked Field
Coppice

Upton Bottom
Farm

5

SP3

32

WISE LANE

Upton

SUTTON BOTTOM

Haddon
Hill

Haddon
Acre

4

Sheephouse
Farm

TOUCHORNE LANE

Milton

Terrace
Wood

PH

Clouds
Farm

Milton
Farm

Steeple
Close

The
Green

Barns
Hill

Warminster
Plantation

Coombe Bottom

Hindon
Plantation

Knoyle Corner

31

NEW ROAD

Mill

WISE LANE

Clouds
House

Park
Farm

Knoyle Ridge

2

East
Knoyle

SANDPIT RD

PO

HINDON ROAD

Summerleaze
Pond

Sandpit
Coppice

CHURCH RAILS

✦

Wessex Ridgeway

Holloway

HOLLOWAY LANE

✦

MILLBROOK LA

THE STREET

A350

1

Great Ground
Coppice

Park
Coppice

PH

MILLBROOK LANE

Sewage
Works

30

A   B   C   D   E   F

8

Monarch's Way

Firfields

Grovely
Lodge

7

Field
System

Monarch's Way

Grovely
Farm

33

Land Girl
Plantation

6

Field
System

BAVERSTOCK LANE

Crouch's
Down

SP3

5

32

Baverstock

Crowdell's
Copse

Manor Farm

4

Enclosure

+

Cemy

LC

SANDHILLS RD

B3089   HINDON ROAD

PH

HORSE-SHOE LANE

Weir

Weir

Hurdcott
House

3

LC

Weir

Horse Shoe
Bridge

Rookery
Plantation

Hurdcott
Home Farm

31

Weir

2

Horse Shoe Copse

Barford
Heath

1

Stone
(site of King's Elm)

30

Compton
Park

+

Pond Copse

02   A   B   03   C   D   04   E   F

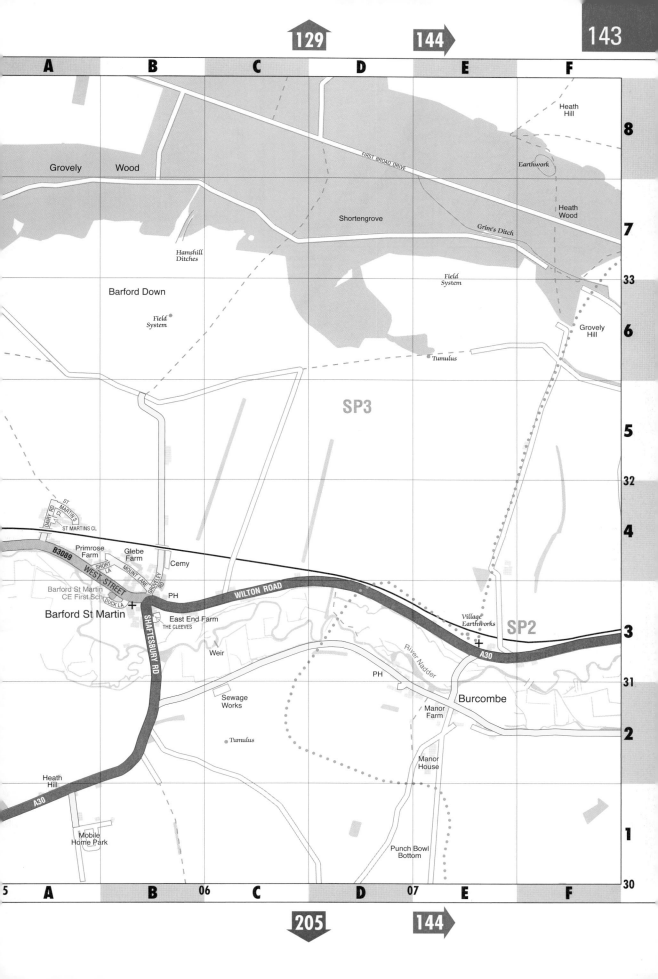

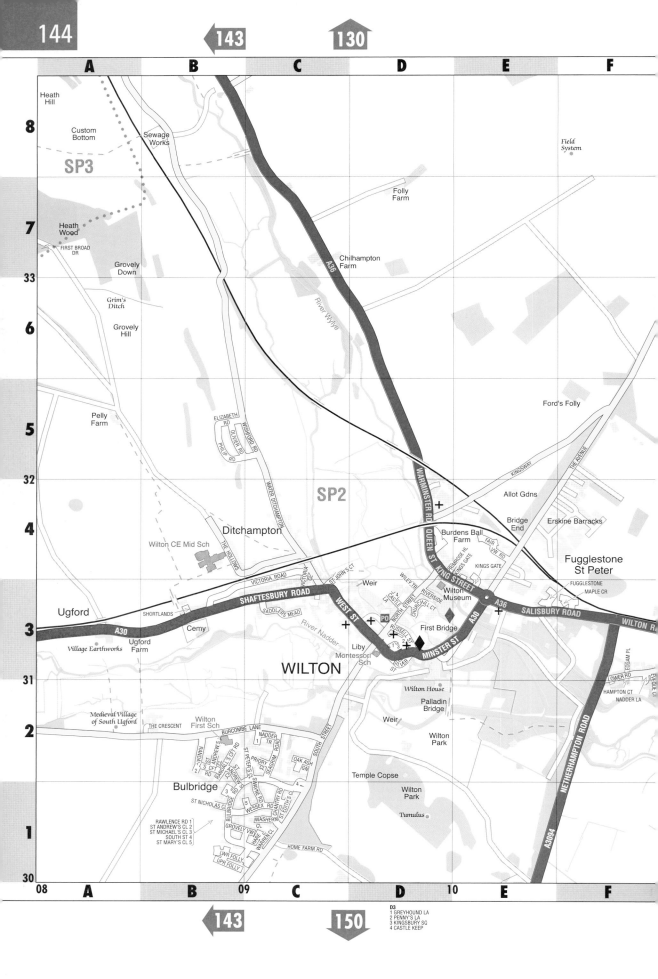

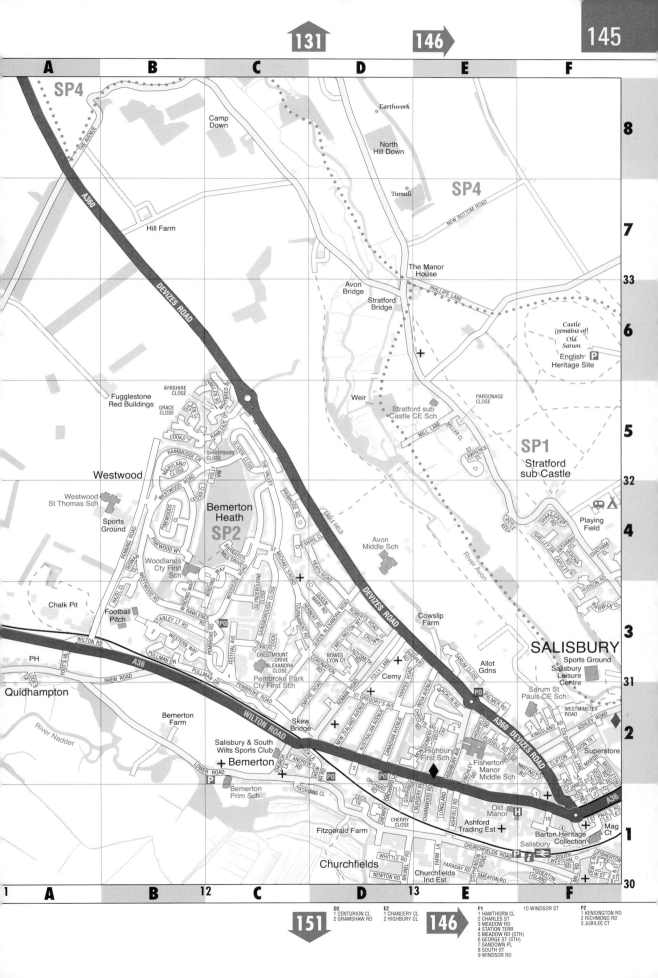

A   B   C   D   E   F

8

Salisbury City Football Club

NORTHSIDE

White Heathers
Hurdcott
River Side

Rockshill Plantation

Monarch's Way

Sewage Works

PH

Old Sarum Barracks

Old Sarum Flying Club

SOUTHSIDE

SPITFIRE ROAD

GREEN LANE CL

7

PORTWAY

Landing Strip

SP4

MANOR FARM RD

Ford

BROKEN CROSS

33

A338

6

Old Sarum Farm

PH

Castle Hill

GREEN LANE

A345

A30

LONDON RD A30

St Thomas's Bridge

5

St Osmund's Close

SP1

HARTLEY WAY   APPLESHAW WAY

PEARCE WAY

A30

32

Salisbury Rugby Club

BROADLANDS CL

WOODVILL   ST JUDES

A30

River Bourne

Cockey Down

4

FAIRFIELD RD

Bishopdown

THISTLEBARROW ROAD

Wyndham Park Sch

BURAH

St Josephs Secondary Sch

CHESTNUT

3

South Wilts Grammar Sch

Victoria Park

St Marks CE Junior Sch

Salisbury Crematorium Cemy

ASTON MEAD

REDFORD CLOSE

Laverstock & Ford Sports Club

St Edmunds Girls Sch

Wyvern Coll

St Andrews Sch

SP5

31

BUTTS ROAD

A345

CASTLE ROAD

La Retraite Sch

TOWER MEWS

GLENMORE ROAD

STOCKWOOD

WESTFIELD CLOSE

St Andrews

2

Scamell's Road

CHURCHILL WY NORTH

Chafyn Grove Sch

CHURCHILL WY WEST

SALISBURY

COW LA

Laverstock Down

Laverstock

1

SP2

Mus, Liby & Art Gall

Swimming Baths

Council Offices

Arts Ctr

ROSEMARY CL
WILLIAM CL

Laverstock Mill Bridge

NAPIER RD

PH

Burroughs Hill

Pillow Mounds

30

THE MALTINGS

BOAR ROW   WINCHESTER STREET

Godolphin Prep Sch

Douglas Hse

SP1

RIVERBOURNE RD

14   A   15   B   C   16   D   E   F

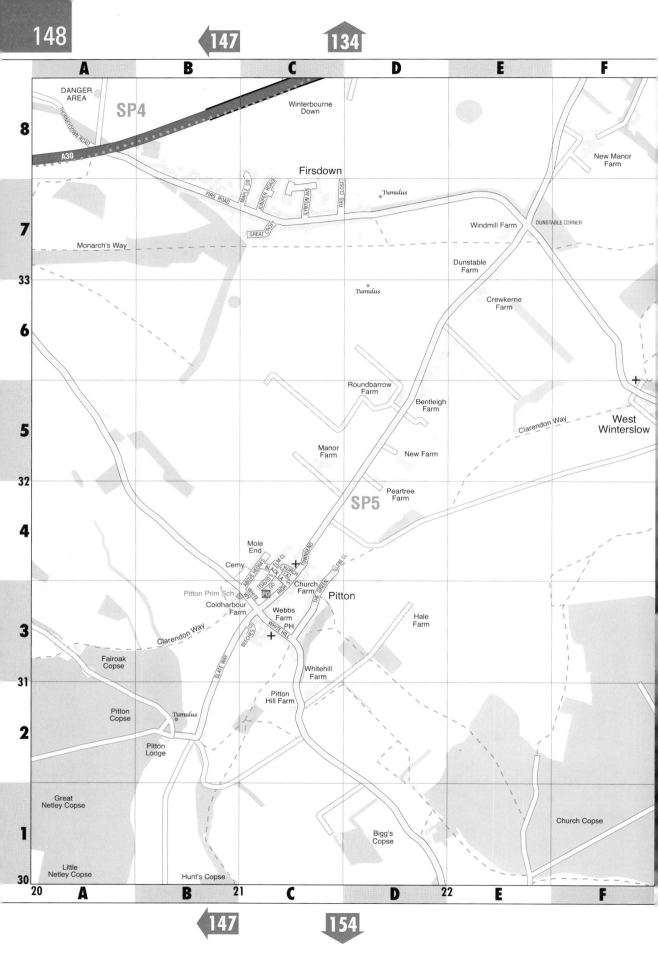

147
134

A B C D E F

DANGER
AREA

SP4

8

THORNEDOWN ROAD

A30

Winterbourne
Down

Firsdown

FIRS ROAD

MAPLE DR

JUNIPER ROAD

LYNTON AVE

FIRS CLOSE

GREAT CROFT

7

New Manor
Farm

Tumulus

Windmill Farm

DUNSTABLE CORNER

Monarch's Way

33

Dunstable
Farm

Crewkerne
Farm

Tumulus

6

Roundbarrow
Farm

Bentleigh
Farm

West
Winterslow

Clarendon Way

5

Manor
Farm

New Farm

32

Peartree
Farm

SP5

4

Mole
End

Cemy

ABOVE HEDGES

ELM CL

BLACK LA

CHURCH

TOWNSEND

GLEBE CL

Church
Farm

Pitton

Coldharbour
Farm

Pitton Prim Sch

PO

DAVID'S GD

WHITE WAY

HIGH

THE GREEN

Webbs
Farm
PH

Hale
Farm

3

BEECHES CT

WHITE HILL

Fairoak
Copse

Clarendon Way

SLATE WAY

Whitehill
Farm

31

Pitton
Copse

Tumulus

Pitton
Hill Farm

2

Pitton
Lodge

Great
Netley Copse

Bigg's
Copse

Church Copse

1

Little
Netley Copse

Hunt's Copse

30

20 A B 21 C D 22 E F

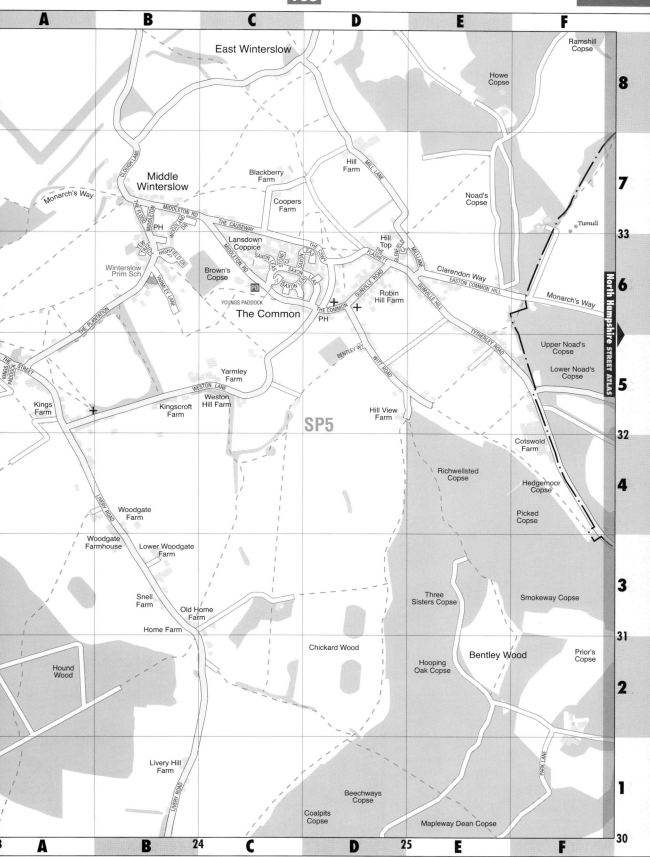

East Winterslow

Ramshill Copse

Howe Copse

Noad's Copse

Middle Winterslow

Blackberry Farm

Hill Farm

MILL LANE

Monarch's Way

Coopers Farm

MIDDLETON RD

THE CAUSEWAY

PH

THE FLOOD

MIDDLETON

WOODLAND DR

Lansdown Coppice

Hill Top

Tumuli

33

NEW TREE CL

HIGHFIELD CR

MIDDLETON RD

SAXON LEAS

STONE CL

SAXON LEAS

THE CSWY

Clarendon Way

Winterslow Prim Sch

Brown's Copse

SAXON LEAS

THE FLASHETT

GLENFIELD

MILL LANE

Easton Common Hill

North Hampshire STREET ATLAS

YARMLEY LANE

PO

YOUNGS PADDOCK

SAXON LEAS

Robin Hill Farm

GUNVILLE HILL

Monarch's Way

6

THE PLANTATION

The Common

THE COMMON

PH

GUNVILLE ROAD

Upper Noad's Copse

KINGS PADDOCK

Yarmley Farm

BENTLEY WY

TYTHERLEY ROAD

Lower Noad's Copse

THE DOCK STREET

WESTON LANE

Weston Hill Farm

WITT ROAD

SP5

Hill View Farm

5

Kings Farm

Kingscroft Farm

Cotswold Farm

32

Richwellsted Copse

Hedgemoor Copse

4

LIVERY ROAD

Woodgate Farm

Picked Copse

Woodgate Farmhouse

Lower Woodgate Farm

Three Sisters Copse

Smokeway Copse

3

Snell Farm

Old Home Farm

Bentley Wood

Prior's Copse

Home Farm

Chickard Wood

Hooping Oak Copse

31

Hound Wood

PARK LANE

2

Livery Hill Farm

LIVERY ROAD

Beechways Copse

1

Coalpits Copse

Mapleway Dean Copse

30

A   B   C   D   E   F

8

7

29

6

5

28

4

3

27

2

1

26

PH

A3094   NETHERHAMPTON ROAD

Home
Farm

HOME FARM ROAD

The Kennels

Warren Down

SP2

Hare Warren

Neale's Barrow

OLD SHAFTESBURY DROVE

Tumuli

Netherhampton
Down

Salisbury
Racecourse

Down
Barn

North
Down

PORTFIELD ROAD

SP5

DROVE LANE

Manor
Farm

Manor
Farm

Stratford
Tony

Manor
Farm

CHURCH LANE

MILL LANE

Throope Manor
House

Ragland's Hill

Coombe
Farm

STRATFORD TONY ROAD

DROVE
CL

A354

PH

Cranbourne
Farm

Coombe
Bridge

BLANDFORD RD

THORNE CL

PO

Coombe
Bissett

Coombe
Bissett Sch

08   A   B   09   C   D   10   E   F

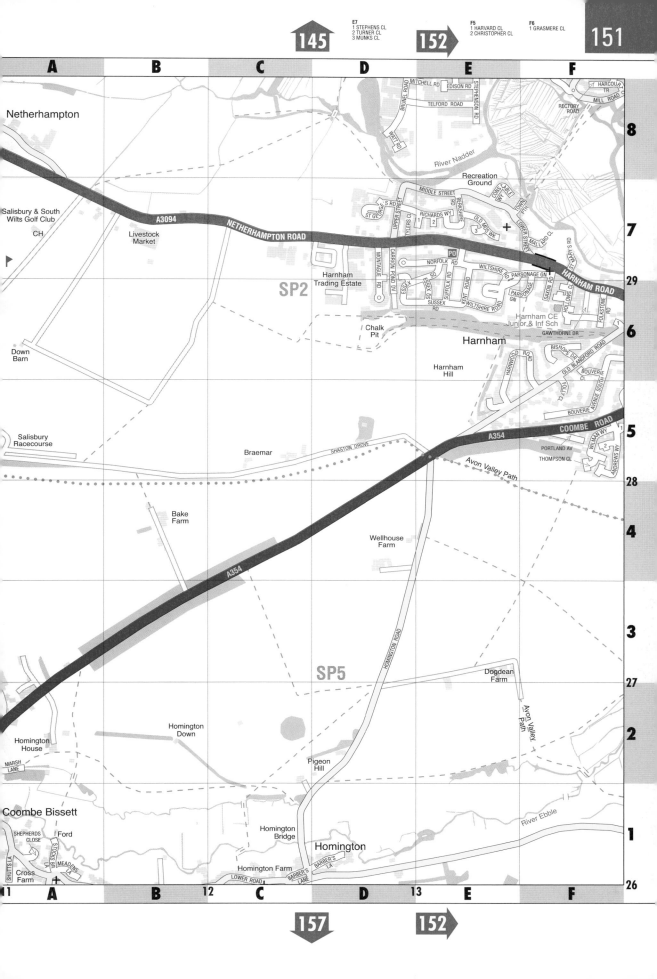

145　　152　　151

E7
1 STEPHENS CL
2 TURNER CL
3 MUNKS CL

F5
1 HARVARD CL
2 CHRISTOPHER CL

F6
1 GRASMERE CL

A　　B　　C　　D　　E　　F

MITCHELL RD
EDISON RD
STEPHENSON RD
BRUNEL ROAD
TELFORD ROAD
HARCOURT TR
MILL ROAD
RECTORY ROAD
WATT RD

Netherhampton

River Nadder

Recreation Ground

Middle Street
ST GEORGE'S RD
UPPER STREET
TYLERS CL
BERKSHIRE RD
RICHARDS WY
OLD MILL WK
CONSTABLE WY
TURNER
LOWER MALL
CARD CL

Salisbury & South Wilts Golf Club

CH

A3094

NETHERHAMPTON ROAD

PO

NORFOLK RD
ESSEX SQ
KENT RD
SUFFOLK RD
SUSSEX RD
WILTSHIRE RD
MONTAGUE RD
CARRION POND DV
PARSONAGE GN
WILTSHIRE ROAD
SAXON RD
HOLLOWS CL
PARSONAGE GN
HARNHAM ROAD
FOLKSTONE RD
ST MARY'S RD

SP2

Harnham Trading Estate

Livestock Market

29

Chalk Pit

Harnham CE Junior & Inf Sch

GAWTHORNE DR

Harnham

6

Down Barn

Harnham Hill

HARNHAM ROAD
BISHOPS DR
OLD BLANDFORD ROAD
BOUVERIE CL
BOUVERIE AVENUE SOUTH

Braemar

SHASTON DROVE

A354

COOMBE ROAD

PORTLAND AV
THOMPSON CL
WILMAN WY
ANDREWS WY

Salisbury Racecourse

5

Avon Valley Path

28

Bake Farm

4

Wellhouse Farm

A354

3

HOMINGTON ROAD

SP5

Dogdean Farm

27

Avon Valley Path

Homington Down

2

Homington House

MARSH LANE

Pigeon Hill

Coombe Bissett

River Ebble

1

SHEPHERDS CLOSE
Ford
STOCKS BR LA
MEADENS LA

Homington Bridge

Homington

Cross Farm

Homington Farm
BARBER'S LANE
BARBER'S LA

LOWER ROAD

SHUTTS LA

26

11　　A　　B　　12　　C　　D　　13　　E　　F

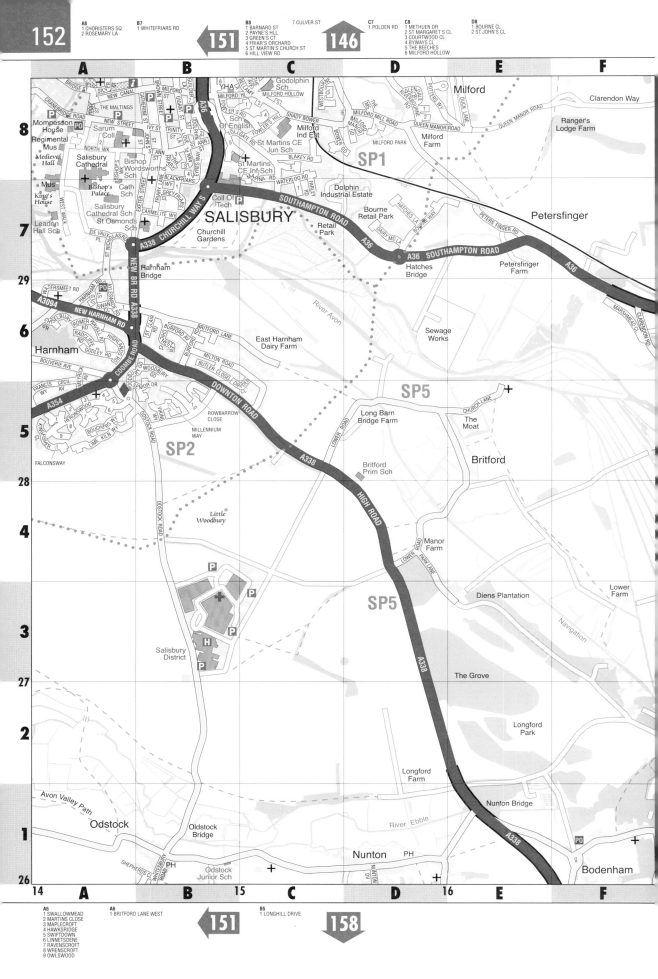

A B C D E F

8

Little Netley Copse
Crendle Bottom
Hunt's Copse
Grimsditch Copse
Farley
Farleys All Saints Prim Sch

7

Bests Farm
PH
PO
THE STREET
PENNY'S LA
OAK CL
CHURCH ROAD
PITTON ROAD
PARSONAGE HILL
BEN LANE

29

Knightwood Farm
LUCEWOOD LANE
Woodfields Farm
March Farm
Bracken Farm
Farley Copse

6

The Plantation
Nightwood Copse
Pitchers Farm
Adams Mere Farm
Brown's Copse
GRIMSTEAD ROAD

5

Upper Brickwood Farm
Old Brickwood Farm
Hazel Hill Wood
SP5
Hazel Hill Farm
Lyvers Farm
Meadow End

28

Pope's Bottom
CLARENDON ROAD
Drove End
Furzy Close Copse
Whitehouse Farm
Horse Close Copse
Dairy Farm
Whitehouse Farm
East Grimstead
Pucks Hill Farm

4

LONG DROVE
GREEN DROVE

Walden House
Walden Farm
BUTTER FURLONG ROAD
Manor Farm

3

West Common Plantation

27

Nursery Farm
GREENFIELDS

Crockford Copse
CROCKFORD ROAD
CHAPEL HILL
West Grimstead
Thicket Copse

2

Whaddon Common
Emmotts Farm
GRIMSTEAD ROAD
Hill Top
Hedge End
CHURCH ST
Redlynch Plantation

1

Oakridge Copse
Broadmead Farm
WINDWHISTLE LANE
Gallows Hayes Copse
GRIMSTEAD ROAD

26

20 A B 21 C D 22 E F

A B C D E F

8

Livery
Farm

The
Livery

Coalpits
Copse

Dean
Copse

Farley
Farm

PARK LANE

Park
Copse

Blackmoor Copse

Bentley
Wood

Bentley Wood
Nature Reserve

Redridge
Copse

Beechwood
Copse

7

LIVERY ROAD

LIVERY RD

29

Barnridge
Copse

Hatchers
Farm

Howe
Copse East

6

LONG DROVE

Keepers
Cott

Howe
Farm

Barnridge
Farm

Dean
View Farm

Beegarden
Copse

Howe Copse West

Hatchers
Copse

Heath Copse

5

Hawks
Grove

Dean
Copse

New Berryfield
Copse

28

SP5

Donkey
Copse

Pilgrims
Croft

Upper
Highwood Copse

Pegsbrook
Copse

DEAN ROAD

4

Lower
Highwood Copse

Churchway
Copse

Fine
Wood

Motte

PO

3

West
Dean

DEAN ROAD

Green Acre

HL MOODY'S

LC

Dean

27

MOODY'S HILL

Orchard
Farm

RECTORY H...

HILLSIDE C...

2

ASHMORE LANE

West Dean
Farm

Dean
Hill

1

26

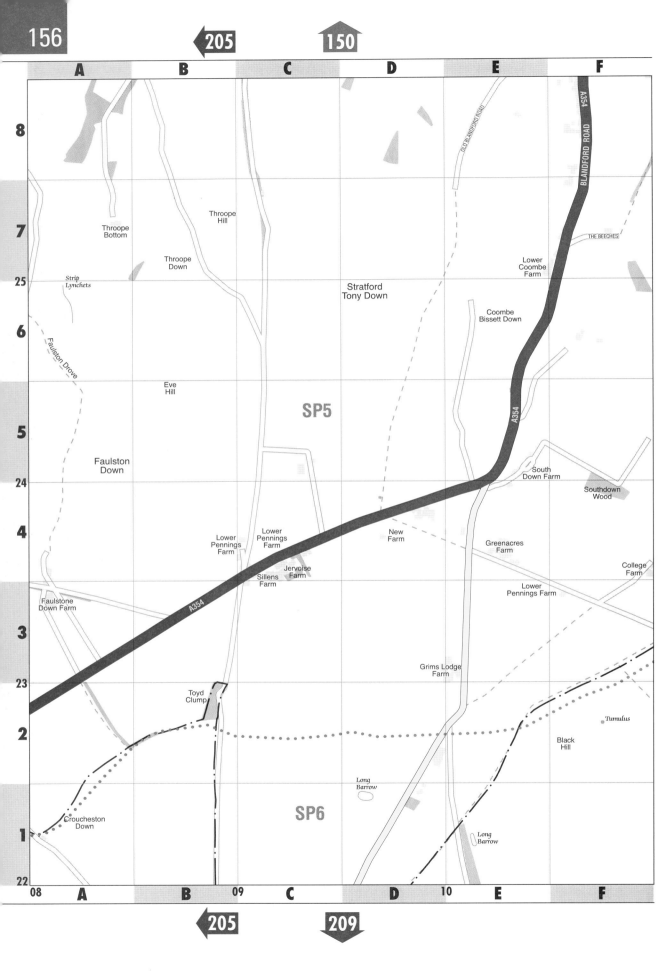

8

Throope
Bottom

Throope
Hill

Throope
Down

25

Strip
Lynchets

7

Stratford
Tony Down

Lower
Coombe
Farm

THE BEECHES

6

Faulston Drove

Coombe
Bissett Down

Eve
Hill

SP5

A354

BLANDFORD ROAD

A354

5

Faulston
Down

24

South
Down Farm

Southdown
Wood

4

Lower
Pennings
Farm

Lower
Pennings
Farm

New
Farm

Greenacres
Farm

College
Farm

Sillens
Farm

Jervoise
Farm

Lower
Pennings Farm

Faulstone
Down Farm

A354

3

Grims Lodge
Farm

23

Toyd
Clump

Tumulus

2

Black
Hill

Long
Barrow

SP6

1

Croucheston
Down

Long
Barrow

22

A   B   C   D   E   F

8

HOMINGTON ROAD

Homington

Flowers
Bottom

Crichton Plantation

7

Tumulus

25

Odstock
Down

Snakesfield
Plantation

6

Homington
Down

Pheasantry Copse

Down Barn

Little Yews Plantation

5

Little
Yews

24

Pennings
Farm

SP5

4

Catherines
Plantation

Yews
Farm

NUNTON DROVE

Grim's Ditch

3

Great Yews

23

Long
Barrow

Charlton
Furze

2

Round Clump

SP6

Long
Plantation

Galops

1

22

PENNINGS DROVE

New Hall

Nunton

A338

THE HIGHWAY

Bodenham Hill
Plantation

Matrimony
Farm

Fir Plantation

Earthworks

Charlton
Plantation

Odstock Copse

Nunton
Copse

Clearbury
Plantation

NUNTON DRIVE

NUNTON DRIVE

Charlton
Manor Farm

Clearbury
Ring

SP5

THE HIGHWAY

NUNTON
DROVE

Clearbury Down

North
Field Copse

Warren
Plantation

The Giant's Grave
(Long Barrow)

Giant's Grave
Plantation

The Giant's
Chair (Tumulus)

New Court
Down Barn

New Court
Down

Avon Valley Path

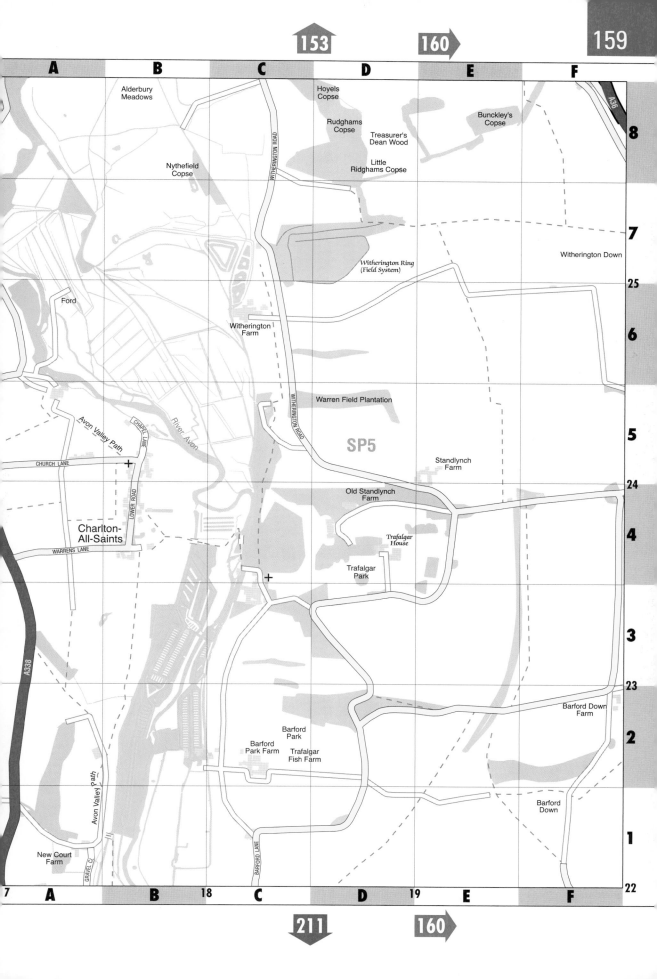

159
154

A   B   C   D   E   F

8

WINDWHISTLE LANE

7

Grimstead
Beeches
(N.T.)

25

A36

Pepperbox
Hill

6

P

The Pepperbox
(NT)

Witherington
Down

Brickworth
Down

Upper
Bushes

Nature
Reserve

5

Field
System

Mast

SP5

Quarry
Pit

Lower
Bush Farm

Brock
Farm

Brickworth
House

24

Leg
Plantation

Privett
Farm

Brickworth
Down Farm

A36

BRICKWORTH LA

Brickworth
Farm

Standlynch
Down

4

A27

Clover
Farm

Cheyney's
Wood

Clapgate
Copse

Battscroft
Copse

Little Clapgate
Copse

3

Long
Copse

Hundred Acre
Copse

Sandland
Copse

23

LANGFORD LANE

Langford
Lane Wood

Goose
Eye Copse

Church
Copse

2

Barford Down

LANGFORD LANE

Langford
Copse

Studlands
Copse

Round Copse
North

1

Hanghill
Copse

Whipshill
Copse

Popplehill
Copse

Moor
Farm

22

20   A   B   21   C   D   22   E   F

159
211

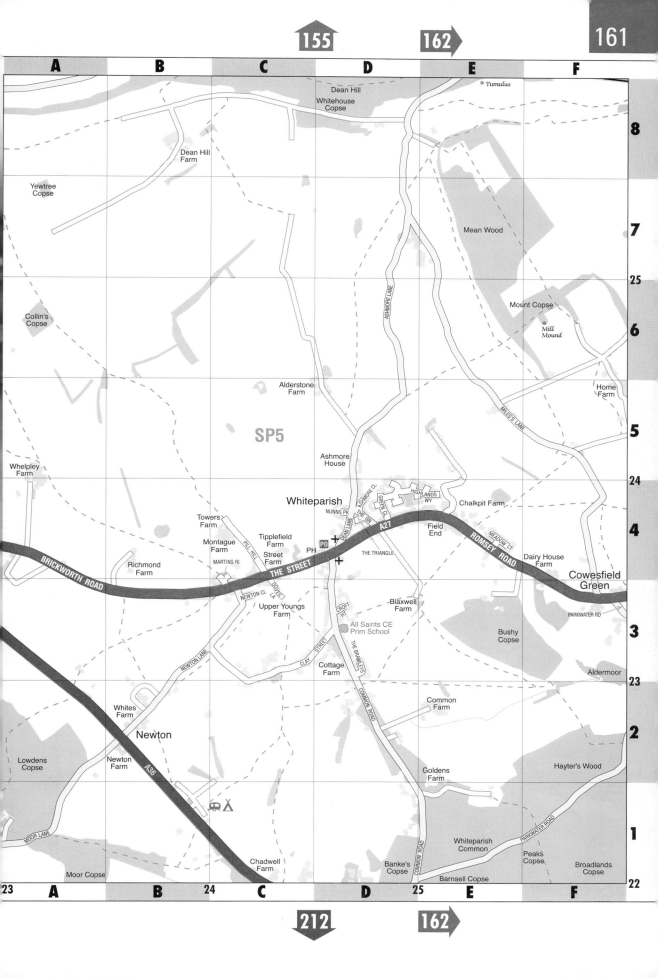

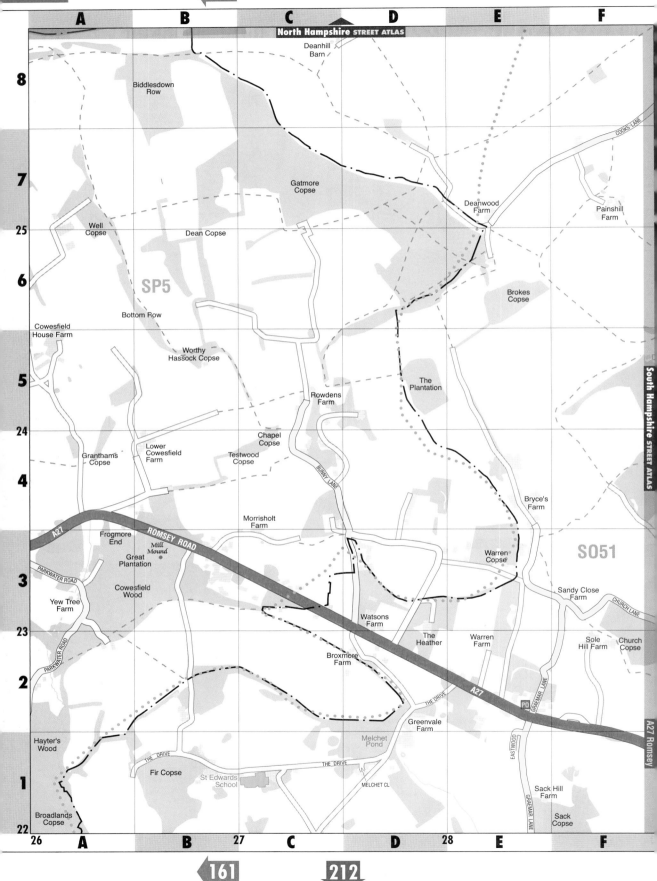

A   B   C   D   E   F

8

7

25

6

SP5

Biddlesdown Row

Deanhill Barn

Gatmore Copse

Well Copse

Dean Copse

Deanwood Farm

Painshill Farm

Brokes Copse

Bottom Row

Cowesfield House Farm

Worthy Hassock Copse

The Plantation

5

24

Rowdens Farm

Granthams Copse

Lower Cowesfield Farm

Chapel Copse

Testwood Copse

BUNNY LANE

Bryce's Farm

4

Morrisholt Farm

Warren Copse

SO51

A27

ROMSEY ROAD

Frogmore End

Mill Mound

Great Plantation

Sandy Close Farm

CHURCH LANE

3

PARKWATER ROAD

Yew Tree Farm

Cowesfield Wood

Watsons Farm

The Heather

Warren Farm

Sole Hill Farm

Church Copse

23

PARKWATER ROAD

Broxmore Farm

GRAEMAR LANE

2

THE DRIVE

A27

PO

EASTWOOD

Greenvale Farm

Melchet Pond

Hayter's Wood

THE DRIVE

Fir Copse

St Edwards School

THE DRIVE

MELCHET CL

Sack Hill Farm

GRAEMAR LANE

1

A27 Romsey

22

Broadlands Copse

Sack Copse

South Hampshire STREET ATLAS

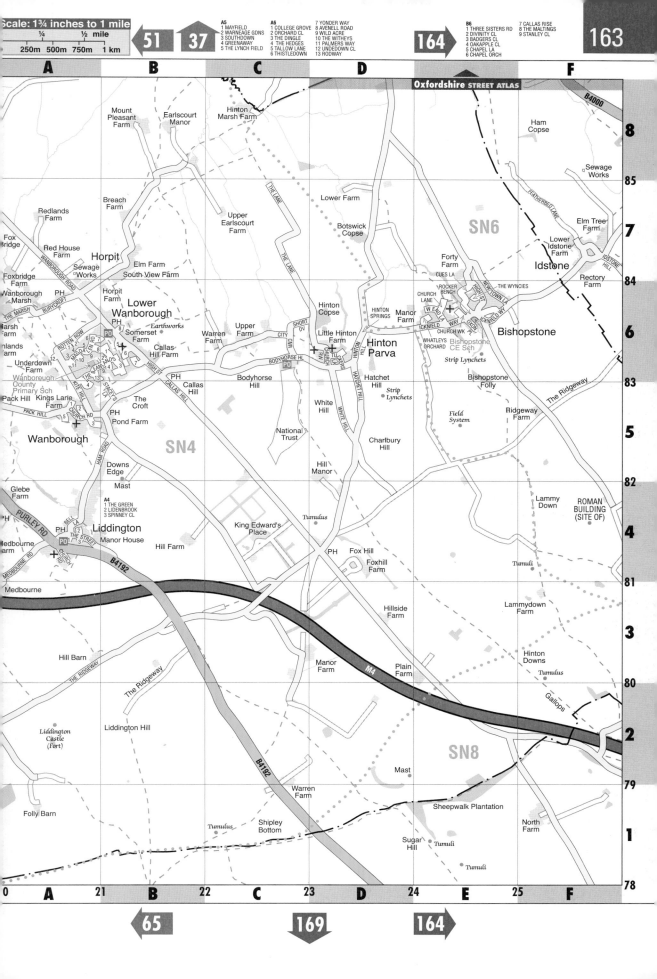

Scale: 1¾ inches to 1 mile

0   ¼   ½   mile
0 250m 500m 750m 1 km

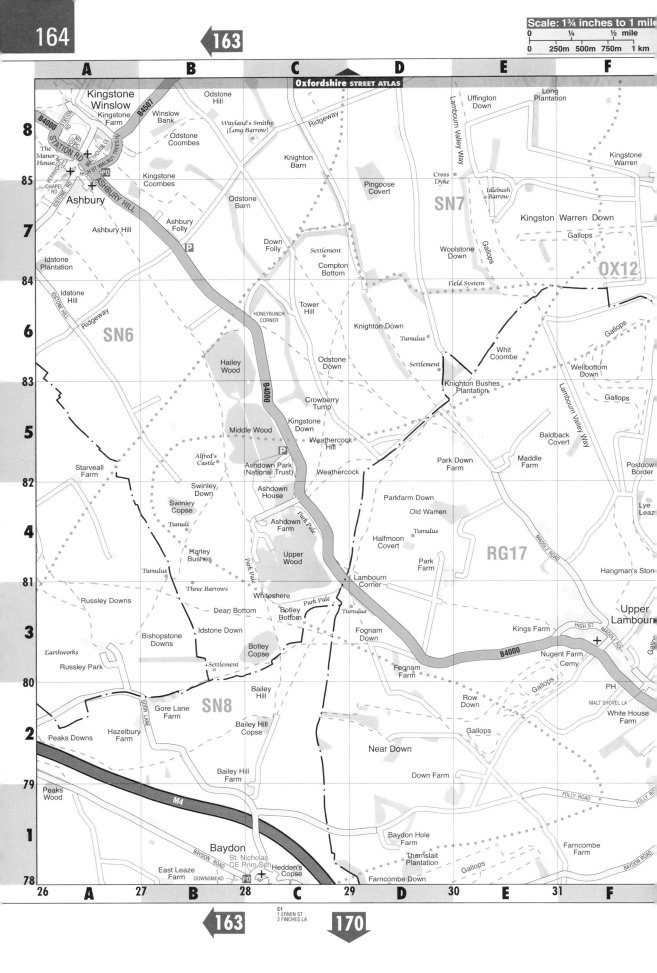

C1
1 ERMIN ST
2 FINCHES LA

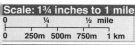
Scale: 1¾ inches to 1 mile

0   ¼   ½   mile
0   250m 500m 750m 1 km

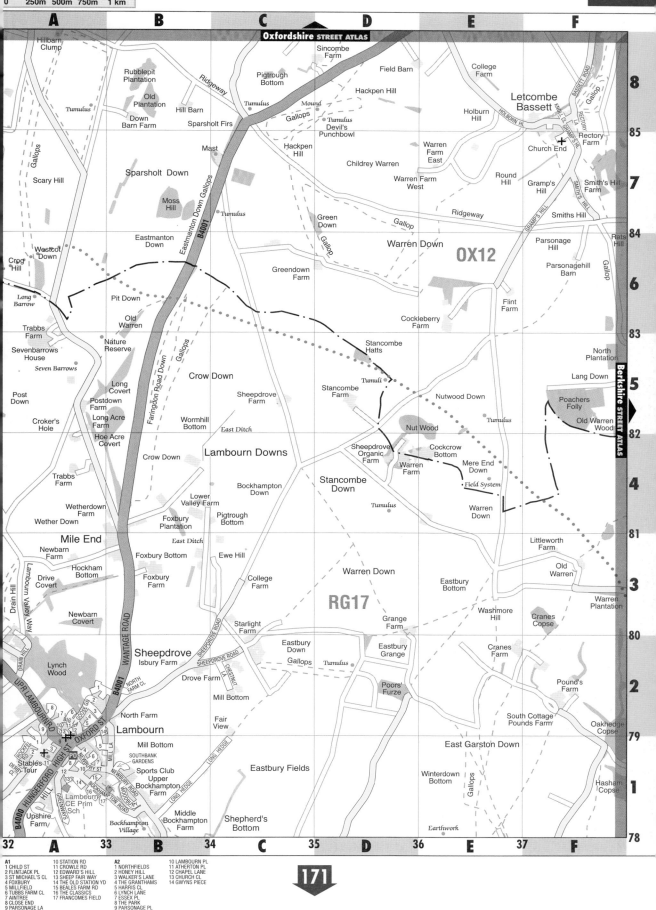

Berkshire STREET ATLAS

A1
1 CHILD ST
2 FLINTJACK PL
3 ST MICHAEL'S CL
4 FOXBURY
5 MILLFIELD
6 TUBBS FARM CL
7 AINTREE
8 CLOSE END
9 PARSONAGE LA

10 STATION RD
11 CROWLE RD
12 EDWARD'S HILL
13 SHEEP FAIR WAY
14 THE OLD STATION YD
15 BEALES FARM RD
16 THE CLASSICS
17 FRANCOMES FIELD

A2
1 NORTHFIELDS
2 HONEY HILL
3 WALKER'S LANE
4 THE GRANTHAMS
5 HARRIS CL
6 LYNCH LANE
7 ESSEX PL
8 THE PARK
9 PARSONAGE PL

10 LAMBOURN PL
11 ATHERTON PL
12 CHAPEL LANE
13 CHURCH CL
14 GWYNS PIECE

171

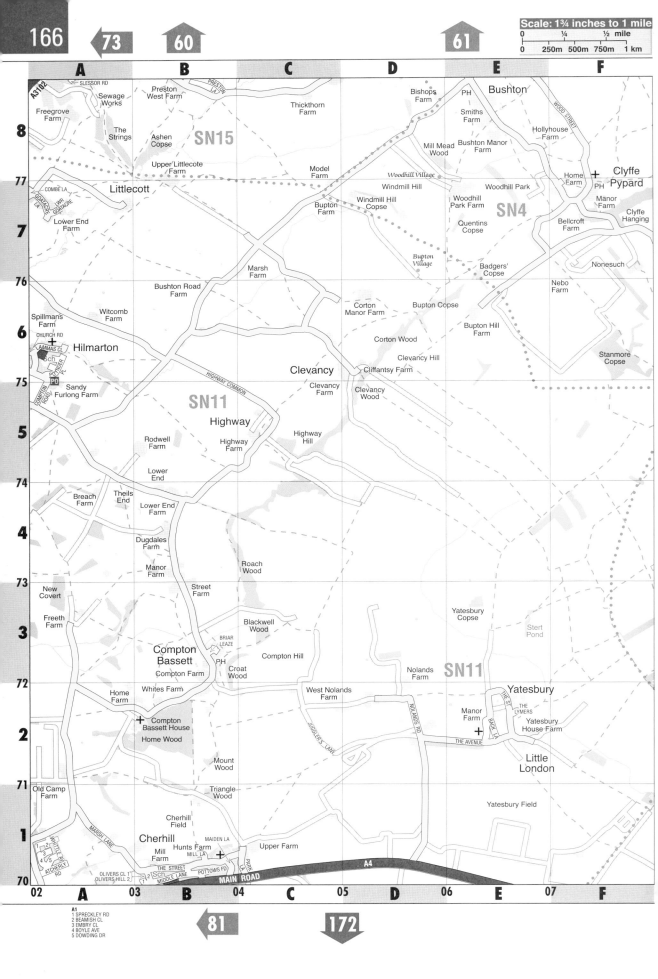

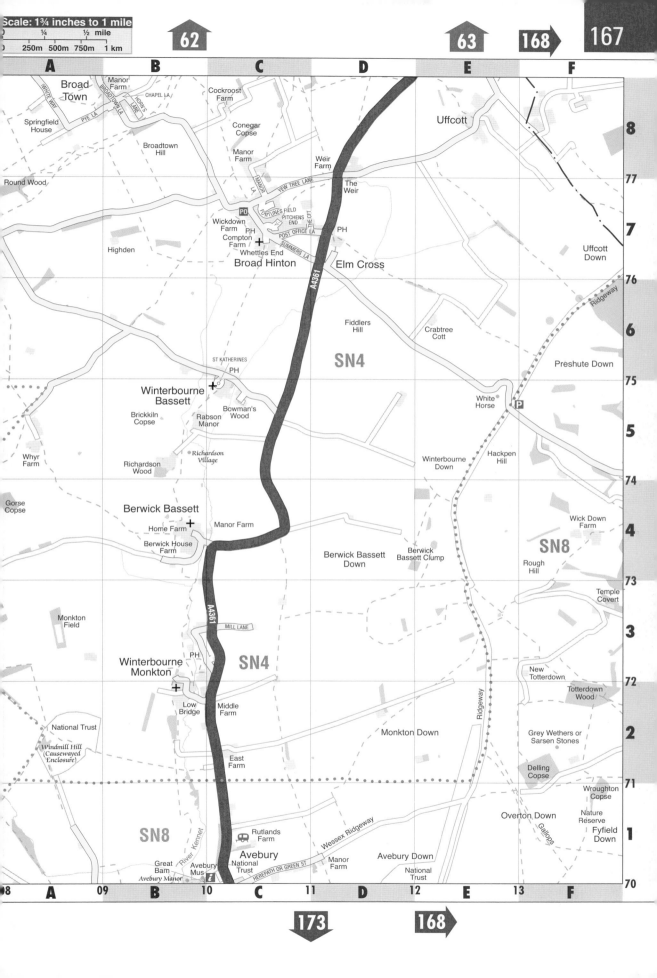

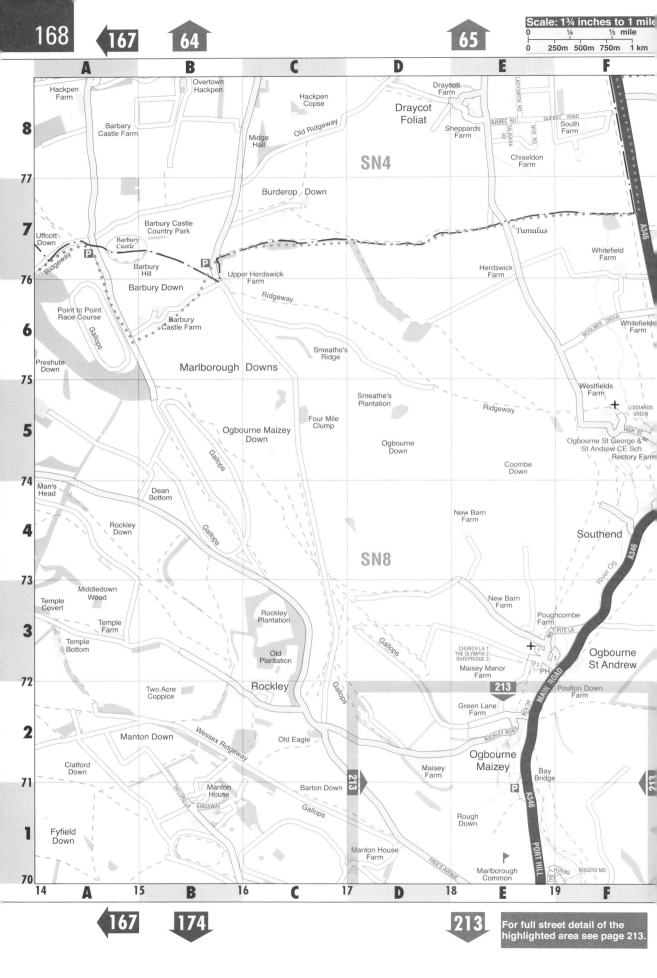

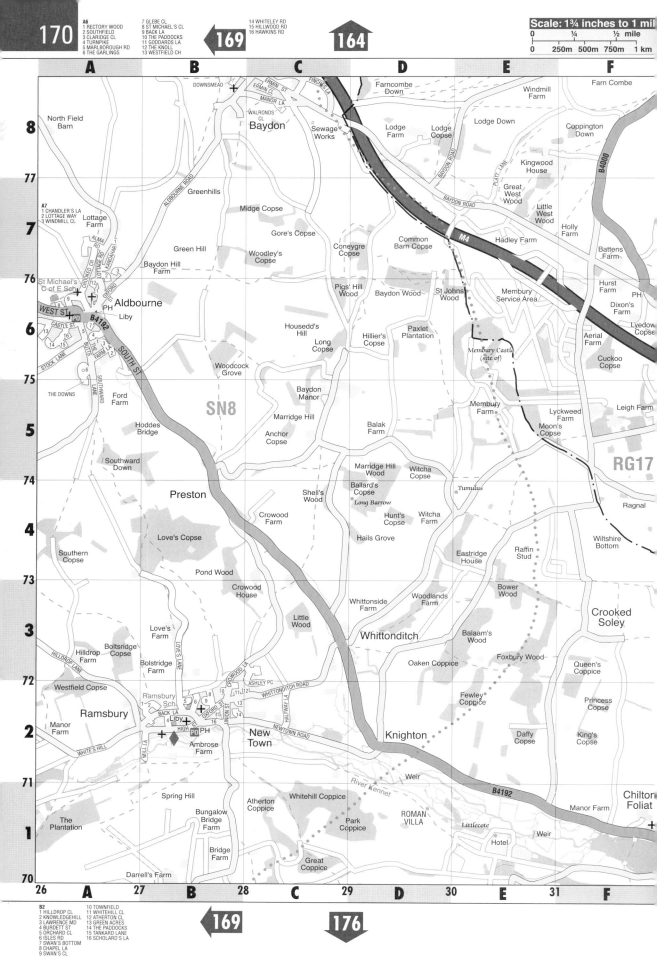

170

A6
1 RECTORY WOOD
2 SOUTHFIELD
3 CLARIDGE CL
4 TURNPIKE
5 MARLBOROUGH RD
6 THE GARLINGS

7 GLEBE CL
8 ST MICHAEL'S CL
9 BACK LA
10 THE PADDOCKS
11 GODDARDS LA
12 THE KNOLL
13 WESTFIELD CH

14 WHITELEY RD
15 HILLWOOD RD
16 HAWKINS RD

◀ 169

▲ 164

Scale: 1¾ inches to 1 mil
0   ¼   ½ mile
0   250m 500m 750m 1 km

Farn Combe

North Field Barn

DOWNSMEAD

ERMIN ST
ERMIN CL
MANOR LA
WALRONDS CL

Baydon

Farncombe Down

Windmill Farm

Coppington Down

FINCHES LA

Sewage Works

Lodge Farm

Lodge Copse

Lodge Down

Kingwood House

B4000

A7
1 CHANDLER'S LA
2 LOTTAGE WAY
3 WINDMILL CL

Greenhills

Midge Copse

Great West Wood

Little West Wood

Holly Farm

Lottage Farm

ALDBOURNE ROAD

Green Hill

Gore's Copse

Woodley's Copse

Coneygre Copse

Common Barn Copse

Baydon Wood

M4

BAYDON ROAD

Hadley Farm

PLATT LANE

Battens Farm

ALMA RD
LOTTAGE RD
CROOKED CR
KANDAHAR

Baydon Hill Farm

OXFORD ST

St Michael's C of E Sch

Aldbourne

PH
Liby

WEST ST
CASTLE ST
PO
B4192
STOCK LANE
BUTTS

SOUTH ST

Pigs' Hill Wood

Housedd's Hill

Hillier's Copse

Paxlet Plantation

St Johns Wood

Membury Service Area

Hurst Farm

PH

Dixon's Farm

Lyedown Copse

Aerial Farm

Long Copse

Membury Castle (site of)

Cuckoo Copse

Woodcock Grove

THE DOWNS

Ford Farm

SOUTHWARD LANE

SN8

Baydon Manor

Marridge Hill

Membury Farm

Leigh Farm

Lyckweed Farm

Moon's Copse

RG17

Hoddes Bridge

Anchor Copse

Balak Farm

Southward Down

Marridge Hill Wood

Witcha Copse

Tumulus

Preston

Shell's Wood

Ballard's Copse

Long Barrow

Hunt's Copse

Witcha Farm

Ragnal

Crowood Farm

Love's Copse

Hails Grove

Eastridge House

Raffin Stud

Wiltshire Bottom

Southern Copse

Pond Wood

Whittonside Farm

Woodlands Farm

Bower Wood

Crooked Soley

Love's Farm

Crowood House

Little Wood

Whittonditch

Balaam's Wood

Foxbury Wood

Queen's Coppice

Hilldrop Farm

Boltsridge Copse

HILLDROP LANE

LOVE'S LANE

Bolstridge Farm

CROWOOD LA

Oaken Coppice

Fewley Coppice

Princess Copse

Westfield Copse

Ramsbury Sch

ASHLEY PC

WHITTONDITCH ROAD

HALFWAY LA

Manor Farm

BACK LA
Liby
OXFORD ST
UNION ST

NEWTOWN ROAD

New Town

Knighton

Daffy Copse

King's Copse

Ramsbury

PH
PO

Ambrose Farm

MILL LA

WHITE'S HILL

Spring Hill

Atherton Coppice

Whitehill Coppice

River Kennet

Weir

B4192

Manor Farm

Chilton Foliat

The Plantation

Bungalow Bridge Farm

Park Coppice

ROMAN VILLA

Littlecote

Hotel

Weir

Bridge Farm

Darrell's Farm

Great Coppice

B2
1 HILLDROP CL
2 KNOWLEDGEHILL
3 LAWRENCE MD
4 BURDETT ST
5 ORCHARD CL
6 ISLES RD
7 SWAN'S BOTTOM
8 CHAPEL LA
9 SWAN'S CL

10 TOWNFIELD
11 WHITEHILL CL
12 ATHERTON CL
13 GREEN ACRES
14 THE PADDOCKS
15 TANKARD LANE
16 SCHOLARD'S LA

◀ 169

▼ 176

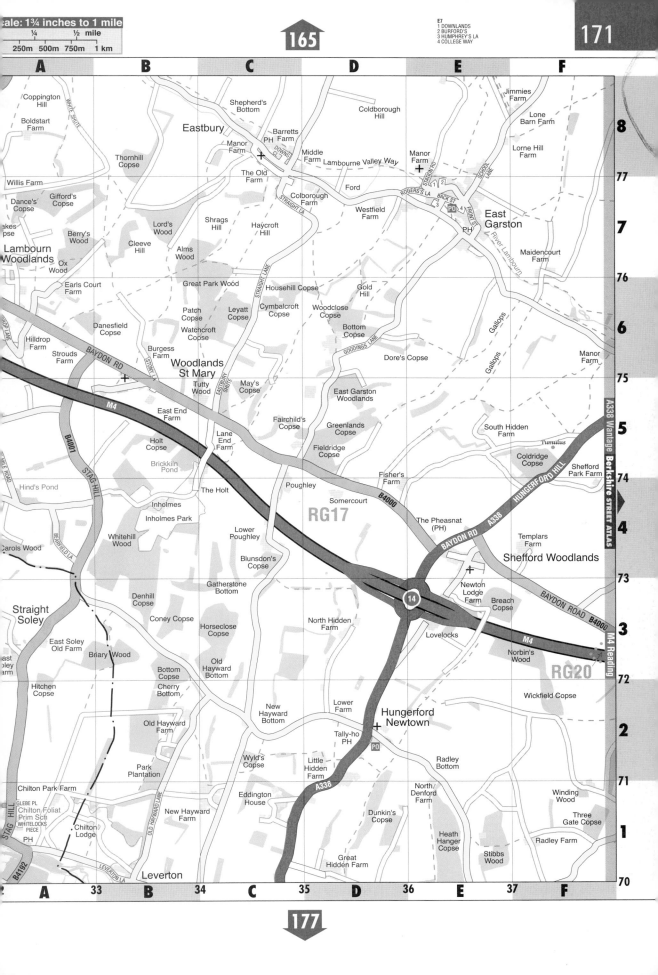

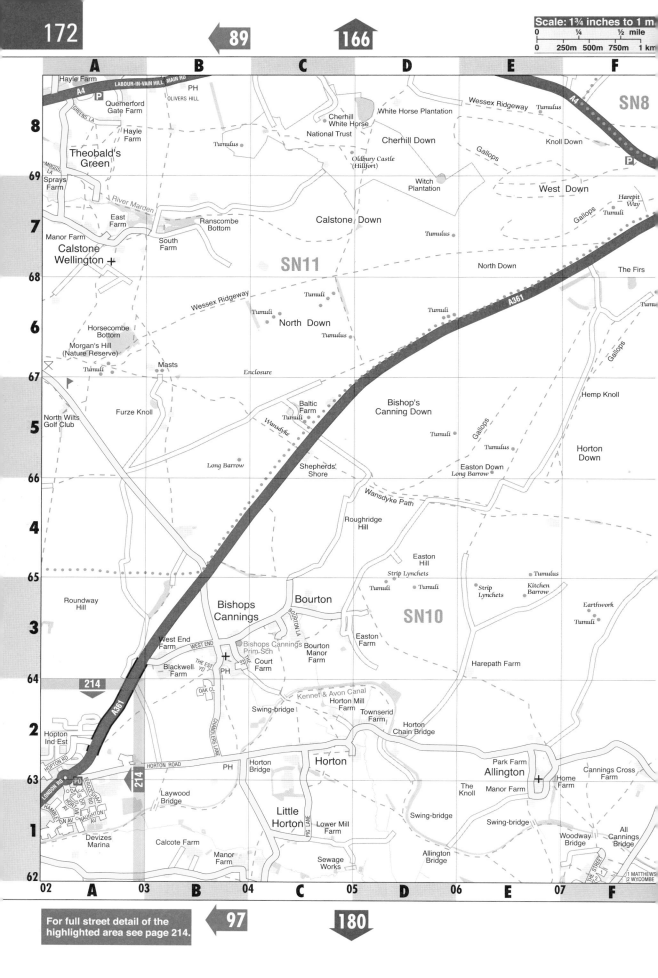

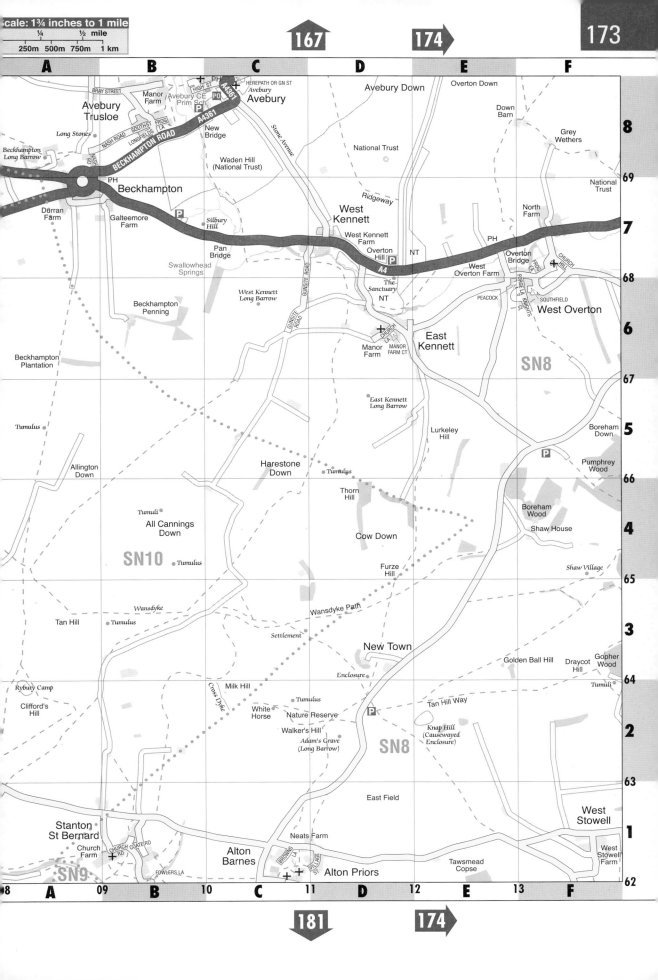

A B C D E F

8

Avebury Down
Overton Down

Bray Street
Manor Farm
Avebury CE Prim Sch
HIGH ST
HEREPATH OR GN ST
Avebury
Avebury

Down Barn

Grey Wethers

Avebury Trusloe
Long Stones

National Trust

69

Beckhampton Long Barrow
New Bridge
Waden Hill (National Trust)
Stone Avenue

National Trust

7

Durran Farm
PH
Beckhampton
Galteemore Farm
Silbury Hill
Ridgeway
West Kennett
West Kennett Farm
Overton Hill
NT
North Farm
PH
Overton Bridge
CHURCH HILL

68

Swallowhead Springs
Pan Bridge
GUNSITE ROAD
West Kennett Long Barrow
The Sanctuary NT
West Overton Farm
PEACOCK
FORGE LA
KNIGHTS CL
Southfield
West Overton

6

Beckhampton Penning
GUNSITE ROAD
Church La
Manor Farm
MANOR FARM CT
East Kennett

SN8

67

Beckhampton Plantation
East Kennett Long Barrow

5

Tumulus
Lurkeley Hill
Boreham Down

Allington Down
Harestone Down
Tumulus
Pumphrey Wood

66

Tumuli
Thorn Hill
Boreham Wood
Shaw House

4

All Cannings Down
Cow Down

SN10
Tumulus
Furze Hill
Shaw Village

65

Wansdyke
Tumulus
Wansdyke Path
Tan Hill

3

Tan Hill
Settlement
New Town
Golden Ball Hill
Draycot Hill
Gopher Wood

Enclosure
Tumuli

64

Rybury Camp
Cross Dyke
Milk Hill
Tan Hill Way

Clifford's Hill
White Horse
Tumulus
Nature Reserve
Knap Hill (Causewayed Enclosure)

2

Walker's Hill
Adam's Grave (Long Barrow)
SN8

63

East Field
West Stowell

1

Stanton St Bernard
Neats Farm
West Stowell Farm

Church Farm
CHURCH RD
COATE RD
Alton Barnes
BROWNS LA
ST VILLAGE
Tawsmead Copse

SN9
FOWLERS LA
Alton Priors

62

08   A   09   B   10   C   11   D   12   E   13   F

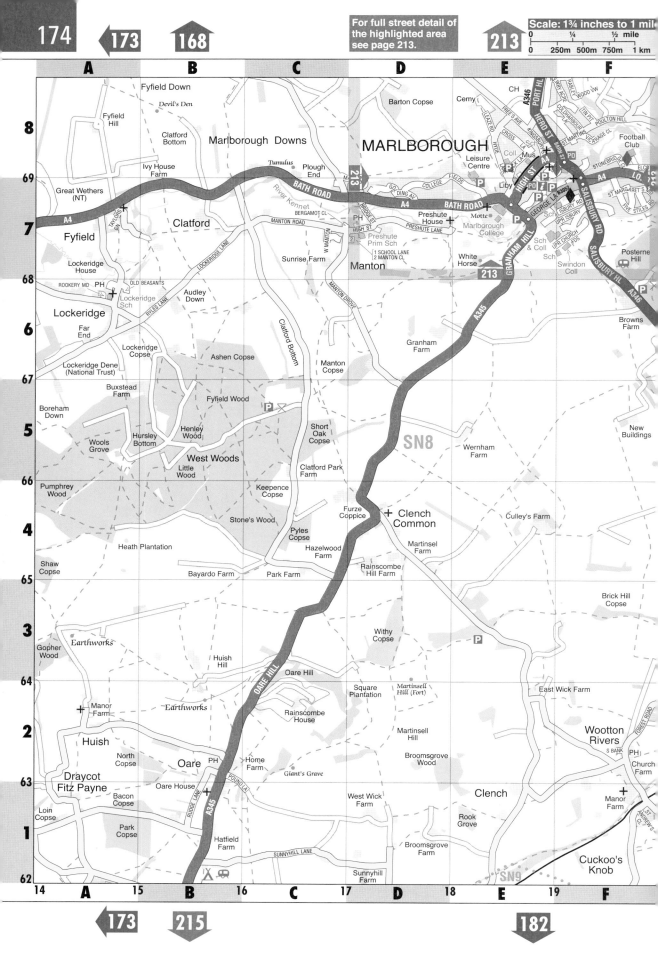

Scale: 1¾ inches to 1 mile
¼   ½ mile
250m 500m 750m 1 km

A   **B**   **C**   **D**   **E**   **F**

Mildenhall
Glebe Farm
HOME FARM CL
GREENWAY RD
THICKETTS ROAD
PH
Durnsford Farm
Grove Farm
KINGS DRIVE
STONE LA
River Kennet
Park Farm
8
WERG
Black Field
Stitchcombe Farm
Stitchcombe
Briary Wood
1 LAUREL DR
2 FOREST DALE RD
3 ELCOT ORCH
CHURCH
BERRYCROFT
CVNIETO ROMAN TOWN
Coombe Farm
Hens Wood
69
Sewage Works
Elcot Farm
Church Farm
St Johns Sch
COCK-A-TROOP LANE
CHOPPING KNIFE LANE
COCK-A-TROOP LA
Oxleaze Copse
7
HAZEL CL
Earthworks
Mast
Folly Copse
Forest Hill Farm
A4
East Croft Coppice
Knowle Hens Wood
Savernake
H
Forest Hill
Puthall Farm
Henset Village
68
Furze Coppice
LOOP RD
GRAND AVENUE
A4
Red Vein Bottom
Ashlade Firs
Little Frith
Voronzoff Wood
Knowle Farm
6
WHITE ROAD
LONG HARRY
High Trees
Braydon Hook
ASHLADE FIRS ROAD
Luton Lye Cotts
Horseleaze Wood
AMITY DRIVE
Timbridge Farm
Crabtree Cotts
Chapel
Cobham Frith
67
Gt Lodge Bottom
Eight Walks
GREAT LODGE DRIVE
SAWPIT DRIVE
GREAT LODGE DR
BUNKER RD
Savernake Lodge
Belmore Copse
5
Great Lodge Farm
GT LODGE DR
Savernake Forest
GRAND AVENUE
Birch Copse
Sainsbury Park Farm
Cadley
Tumuli
SN8
ASHLADE FIRS ROAD
LONDON RIDE
66
Kingstones Farm
Tumulus
King Oak
Nature Reserve
DRURY LANE
The Warren
Bedwyn Common
4
Queen Oak
THREE OAK HILL DRIVE
Warren Farm
St Katharines
Park Farm
Mast
CHARCOAL BURNERS RD
Column
St. Katharines Sch
65
Hat Gate Cottage
P
Leigh Hill
Column Ride
GRAND AVENUE
Tottenham Park
3
The Pit Plantation
THREE OAK HILL DRIVE
Terrace Hill
Durley
COLUMN RIDE
64
Crooks Copse
Long Copse
Leigh Hill Copse
Home Farm
Tottenham House
Haw Wood
Apshill Copse
Tumuli
Square Copse
Deer Park
2
Brimslade Farm
Kennet & Avon Canal
Burbage Wharf
Heathy Close
Ram Alley Copse
MARLBOROUGH RD
SAVERNAKE ROAD
Langfield Copse
63
Round Copse
Ram Alley
Hotel
The Long House
A346
Bowden Farm
STEEPE WY
PH
Stibb Green
Ladywell Copse
Wolfhall Bridge
1
HIGH ST
THE WITHIES
Freewarren Bridge
DARK LA
62

20   **A**   **21**   **B**   **22**   **C**   **23**   **D**   **24**   **E**   **25**   **F**

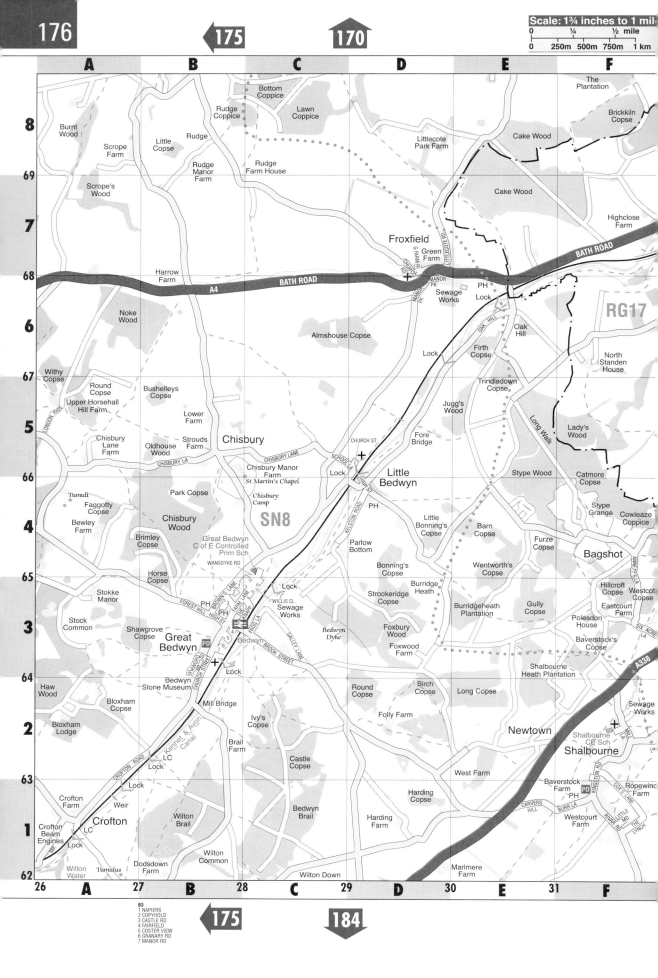

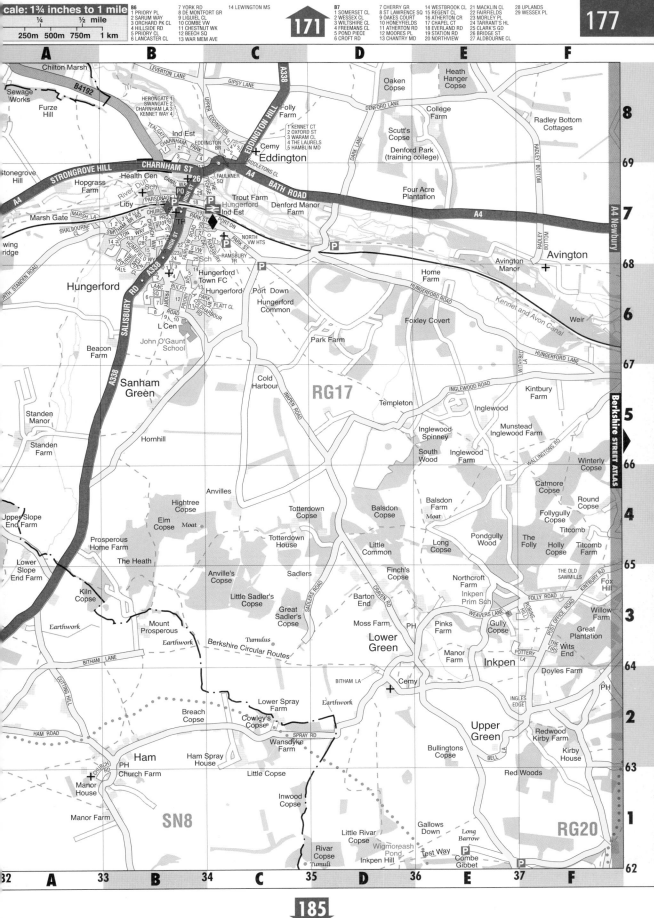

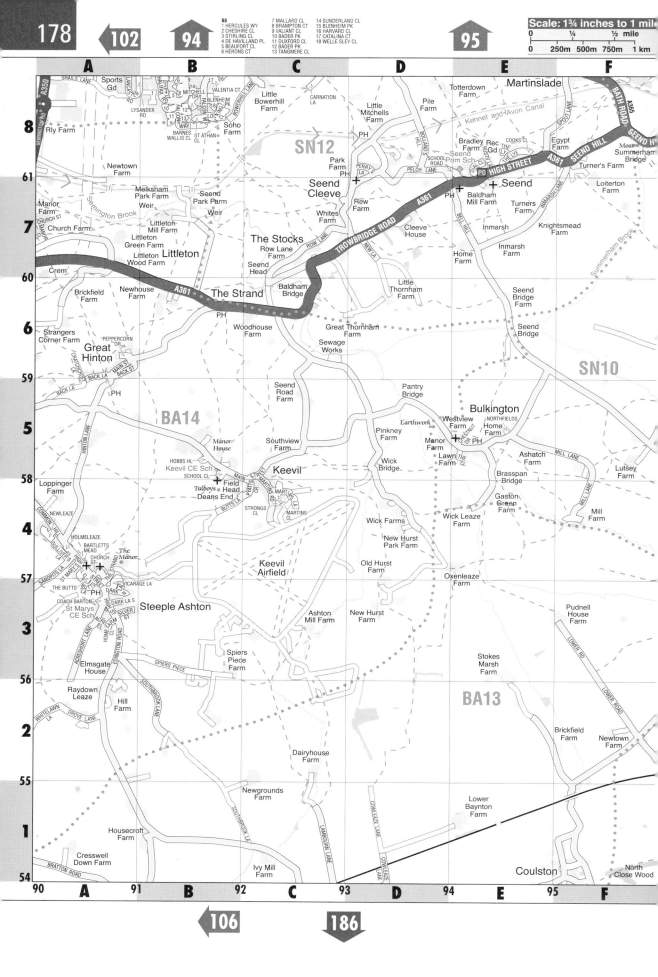

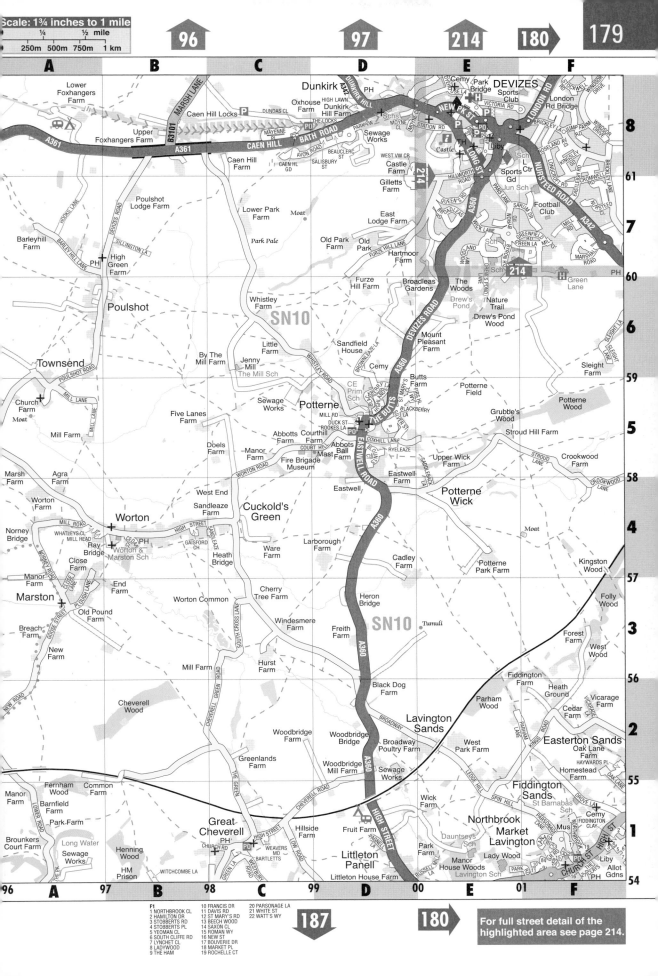

A B C D E F

8
61
7
60
6
59
5
58
4
57
3
56
2
55
1
54

Lower Foxhangers Farm
Caen Hill Locks
DUNDAS CL
Oxhouse Farm
HIGH LAWN
Dunkirk Hill Farm
Dunkirk
PH
DEVIZES
Park Bridge
Sports Club
London Rd Bridge
STOCKWELL
WINDSOR DRIVE
LONDON RD
Upper Foxhangers Farm
THE LOCKS
MAYENNE PL
AVON ROAD
CAEN HILL
BATH ROAD
PARK WAY
Sewage Works
Schs
MOYNE CL
STATION RD
VICTORIA RD
NEW PK ST
Castle
Liby
Cemy
PARK BRIDGE CL
USE LA
H
PO
i
ROSELAND AV
BRICKLEY CL
LONGCROFT
KINGSLEY RD
EASTLAND
CROMWELL RD
BRICKLEY LA
CLUMP FARM
WINDSOR DRIVE
A361
B3101
A342
A361
CAEN HILL
SALISBURY ST
CAEN HL GD
BEAUCLERC ST
CASTLE ST
Caen Hill Farm
Gilletts Farm
WEST VW CR
Castle Farm
QUEEN'S RD
BROAD LEAS
HILLWORTH ROAD
LONG ST
PANS LANE
SARUM DR
A360
A361
Sports Gd
L Ctr
Jun Sch
Football Club
Sch
GREENFIELD RD
GREEN LA
WICK LANE
BYRON RD
MILL RD
NURSTEED RD
NURSTEED ROAD
A342
Barleyhill Farm
BARLEY HILL LA
HOOKS LANE
SILLINGTON LA
DEVIZES ROAD
Poulshot Lodge Farm
Lower Park Farm
Moat
Park Pale
Old Park Farm
Old Park
East Lodge Farm
FURZE HILL LANE
Hartmoor Farm
Broadleas Gardens
The Woods
Drew's Pond
Nature Trail
Drew's Pond Wood
SLEIGHT LA
Sleight Farm
High Green Farm
PH
SN10
Whistley Farm
Little Farm
Jenny Mill
The Mill Sch
Sandfield House
BROWNLEAZE LA
Cemy
Mount Pleasant Farm
Butts Farm
Potterne Field
Grubbe's Wood
Potterne Wood
Townsend
POULSHOT ROAD
Poulshot
By The Mill Farm
WHISTLEY ROAD
CE Prim Sch
ST MARY'S CL
FIRST HL
BLACKBERRY LA
SILVER'S LA
Stroud Hill Farm
Crookwood Farm
Church Farm
MILL LANE
Moat
Mill Farm
Five Lanes Farm
Sewage Works
Potterne
MILL RD
DUCK ST
ROOKES LA
THE BUTTS
POT
Abbotts Courthill Farm
COURT HILL
Abbots Ball Farm
Mast
COXHILL LANE
RYELEAZE
Upper Wick Farm
SADDLEBACK LA
STROUD LANE
Crookwood Farm
CROOKWOOD LANE
Marsh Farm
Agra Farm
Doels Farm
Manor Farm
Fire Brigade Museum
WORTON ROAD
Eastwell
EASTWELL ROAD
Eastwell Farm
Potterne Wick
Moat
Norney Bridge
Worton Farm
MILL ROAD
WHATLEYS CL
MILL HEAD
Worton
Ray Bridge
CEO
PH
Worton & Marston Sch
HIGH STREET
GAISFORD CH
West End
Sandleaze Farm
SANDLEAZE LA
Heath Bridge
Cuckold's Green
Ware Farm
Larborough Farm
Cadley Farm
A360
Potterne Park Farm
Kingston Wood
Folly Wood
Close Farm
CLOSE LANE
PLOUGH LANE
End Farm
Worton Common
Cherry Tree Farm
Heron Bridge
SN10
Forest Farm
West Wood
Manor Farm
Marston
GOOSE STREET
NORNEY ROAD
Old Pound Farm
SOUTH CROSS LANE
Windesmere Farm
Freith Farm
Tumuli
Breach Farm
New Farm
NEW ROAD
Mill Farm
Hurst Farm
Black Dog Farm
Fiddington Farm
Heath Ground
Vicarage Farm
VICARAGE
Cedar Farm
Cheverell Wood
CHEVERELL GREEN ROAD
THE GREEN
Woodbridge Farm
Woodbridge Bridge
Broadway Poultry Farm
BROADWAY
Lavington Sands
Parham Wood
West Park Farm
PARHAM RD
KING'S ROAD
Easterton Sands
Oak Lane Farm
HAYWARDS PL
Homestead Farm
OAK LANE
Manor Farm
Fernham Wood
Common Farm
Greenlands Farm
Woodbridge Mill Farm
Sewage Works
A360
HIGH STREET
Wick Farm
LEDGE HILL
SPIN HILL
Fiddington Sands
St Barnabas Sch
DROVE LA
Barnfield Farm
Park Farm
CHEVERELL ROAD
Great Cheverell
PH
CHURCH RD
PO
HIGH STREET
LOW ROAD
Hillside Farm
Fruit Farm
Park Farm
PERSONAGE LANE
Dauntseys Sch
Northbrook Market Lavington
NADA
St Barnabas
Cemy
Fiddington Clay
Mus
Brounkers Court Farm
Long Water
Sewage Works
Henning Wood
HM Prison
WITCHCOMBE LA
Manor Road
GREEN LA
WEAVERS MD
BARTLETTS
WESTBURY ROAD
RUSSELL'S RD
Littleton Panell
Littleton House Farm
Manor House Woods
Lavington Sch
Lady Wood
Park
CHURCH ST
HIGH ST
Liby
PH
Allot Gdns
Manor Farm
LOWER ROAD
THE PK
Park Farm

96 97 98 99 00 01
A B C D E F

F1
1 NORTHBROOK CL
2 HAMILTON DR
3 STOBBERTS RD
4 STOBBERTS PL
5 YEOMAN CL
6 SOUTH CLIFFE RD
7 LYNCHET CL
8 LADYWOOD
9 THE HAM
10 FRANCIS DR
11 DAVIS RD
12 ST MARY'S RD
13 BEECH WOOD
14 SAXON CL
15 ROMAN WY
16 NEW ST
17 BOUVERIE DR
18 MARKET PL
19 ROCHELLE CT
20 PARSONAGE LA
21 WHITE ST
22 WATT'S WY

For full street detail of the highlighted area see page 214.

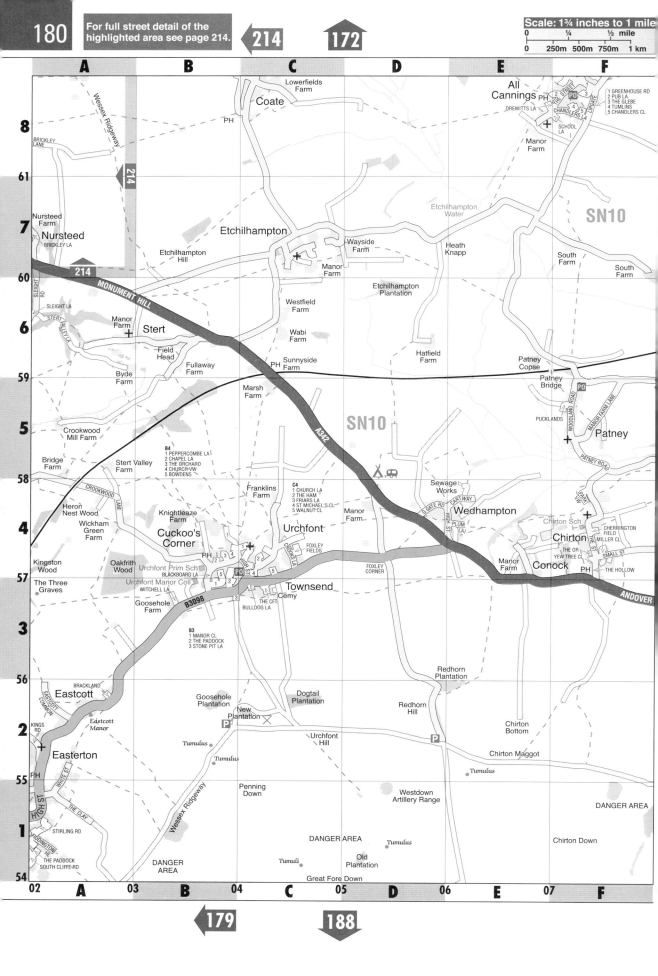

180

For full street detail of the highlighted area see page 214.

214

172

Scale: 1¾ inches to 1 mile
0   ¼   ½   mile
0   250m 500m 750m   1 km

A   B   C   D   E   F

8

61

7

60

6

59

5

58

4

57

3

56

2

55

1

54

Brickley Lane

Wessex Ridgeway

214

Nursteed Farm
Nursteed
BRICKLEY LA

Lowerfields Farm
Coate
PH

All Cannings PH
1 GREENHOUSE RD
2 PUB LA
3 THE GLEBE
4 TUMLINS
5 CHANDLERS CL
THE STREET
CHANDLERS LA
LIPGATE
DREWITTS LA
SCHOOL LA
Manor Farm

SN10

214

Etchilhampton
Etchilhampton Hill

MONUMENT HILL

SLEIGHT RD
SLEIGHT LA

STERT VALLEY LA

Manor Farm
Stert

Field Head

Byde Farm

Fullaway Farm

Crookwood Mill Farm

Bridge Farm

Stert Valley Farm

CROOKWOOD LANE

Heron Nest Wood

Wickham Green Farm

Kingston Wood

The Three Graves

Etchilhampton Water

Wayside Farm

Manor Farm

Westfield Farm

Wabi Farm

Sunnyside Farm
PH

Marsh Farm

Heath Knapp

Etchilhampton Plantation

Hatfield Farm

South Farm

South Farm

Patney Copse

Patney Bridge
PO

WOODLAND ROAD
MANOR FARM LANE

PUCKLANDS

Patney

PATNEY ROAD

SN10

A342

B4
1 PEPPERCOMBE LA
2 CHAPEL LA
3 THE ORCHARD
4 CHURCH VW
5 BOWDENS

Franklins Farm

C4
1 CHURCH LA
2 THE HAM
3 FRIARS LA
4 ST MICHAEL'S CL
5 WALNUT CL

Manor Farm

S GATE RD
CART WAY

Sewage Works

Wedhampton

HIGH ST
PLUM LA

Chirton Sch

Chirton

CHERRINGTON FIELD
MILLER CL

PARK VW

THE ST

Knightleaze Farm
BLACKBOARD LA

Cuckoo's Corner

Oakfrith Wood

Urchfont Prim Sch

Urchfont Manor Coll
WITCHELL LA

Goosehole Farm

B3098

Urchfont
PH
HIGH ST
CROSS LA

FOXLEY FIELDS

FOXLEY CORNER

PO

Townsend
Cemy
THE CFT
BULLDOG LA

B3
1 MANOR CL
2 THE PADDOCK
3 STONE PIT LA

Manor Farm

THE OR
YEW TREE CL

SMALL ST

Conock
PH
THE HOLLOW

ANDOVER

Eastcott
BRACKLAND

EASTCOTT COMMON

KINGS RD

Eastcott Manor

Easterton
PH

HIGH ST
HODINGTON HL
STIRLING RD
WHITE ST
THE CLAY

THE PADDOCK
SOUTH CLIFFE RD

Wessex Ridgeway

Goosehole Plantation

New Plantation
P

Dogtail Plantation

Urchfont Hill

Tumulus
Tumulus

Penning Down

Redhorn Plantation

Redhorn Hill
P

Westdown Artillery Range

Chirton Bottom

Chirton Maggot

Tumulus

DANGER AREA

Chirton Down

DANGER AREA

Tumulus

Old Plantation

Tumuli

DANGER AREA

Great Fore Down

02   A   03   B   04   C   05   D   06   E   07   F

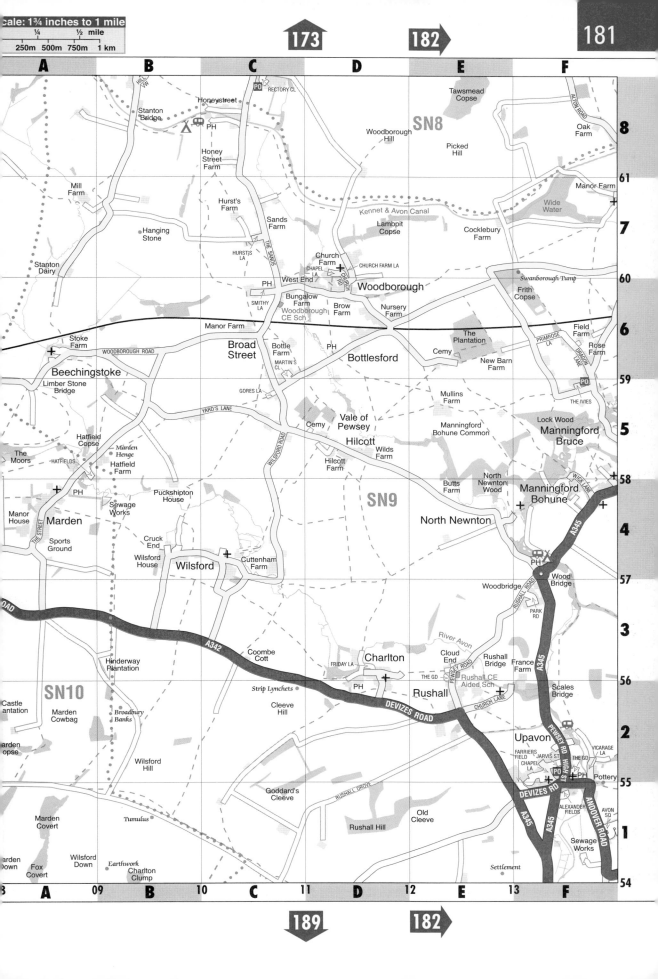

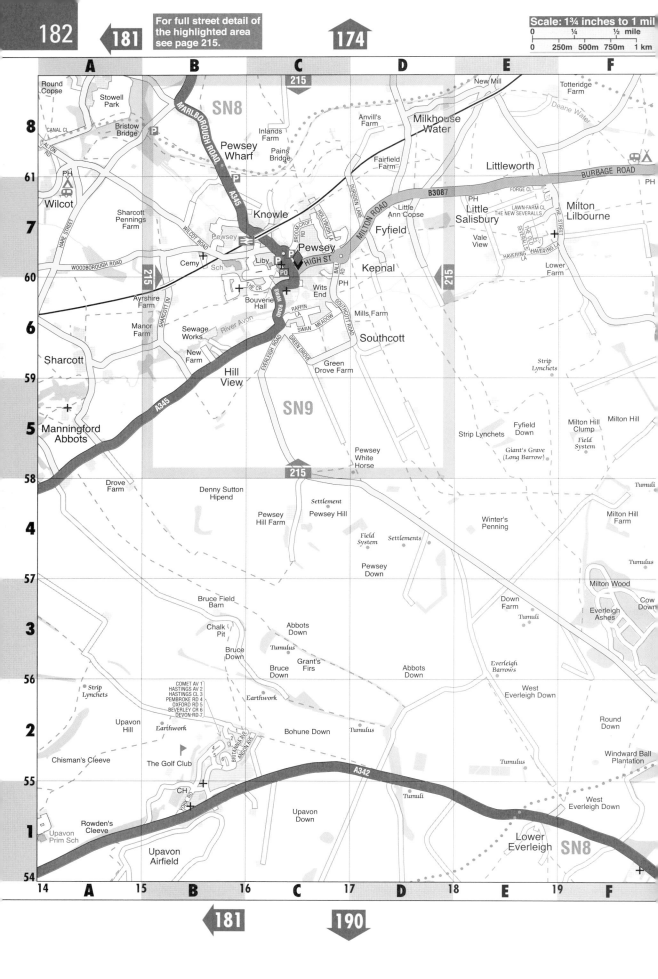

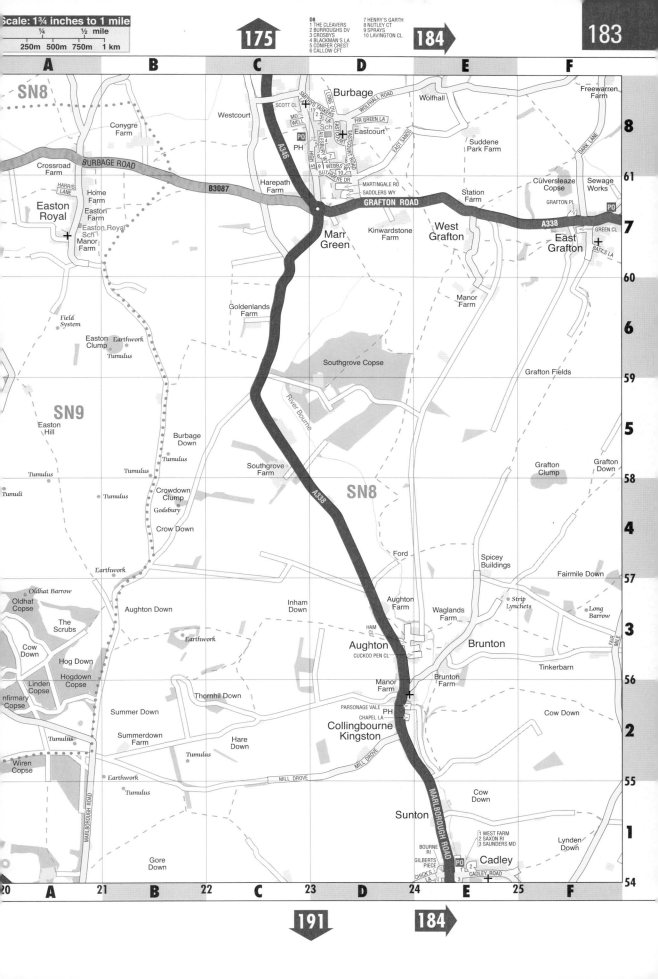

184

◄ 183

176 ▼

Scale: 1¾ inches to 1 mile

0   ¼   ½   mile
0   250m 500m 750m 1 km

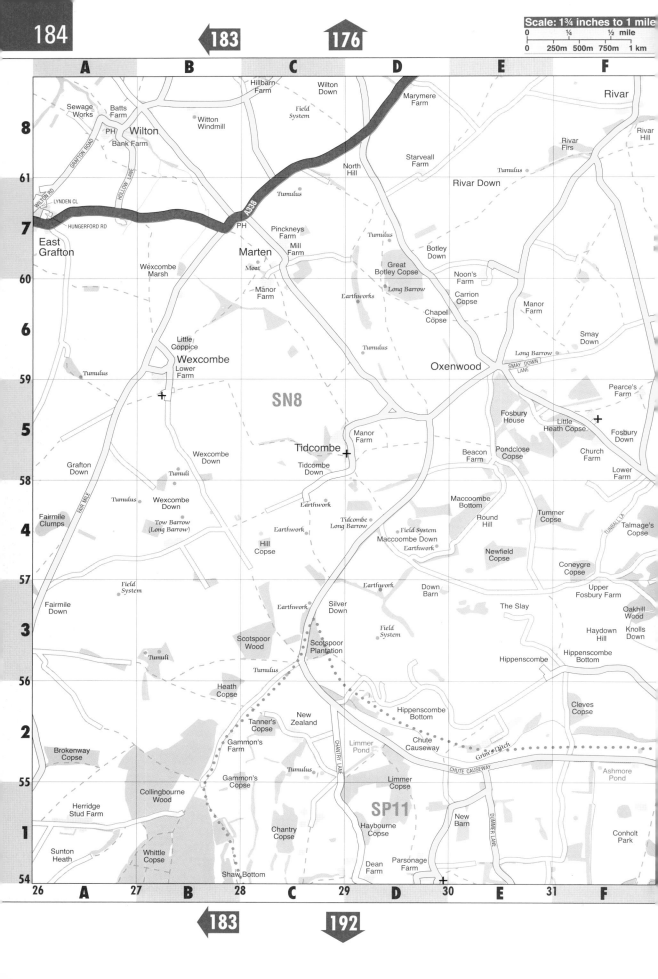

North Hampshire STREET ATLAS

SN8

RG17

SP11

Ashley Down
Inlands Copse
New Buildings
Henley
Tumulus
Fosbury
East Down
Oakhill Wood
Fosbury Hill Fort
Field System
Conholt Bottom
Conholt House
Garden Copse
Conholt Park
Hampshire Gate
Bevisbury Hill Fort

Ham Hill
Earthwork
Town Farm
WOODCOTE ROAD
Buttermere Pond
Grange Farm
Buttermere
HUNGERFORD ROAD
Bishop's Barn
Manor Farm
Ballyack House
Kent's Copse
Upper Horns Farm
Willis Farm
Upper Row Farm
Bulpitt's Copse
Skites Copse
Vernham Row
CHURCH LA
Box Farm
BOWERS LA
Bank Copse
THE DELL
Sargents Farm
BACK LA
BULPITTS HILL
PO
PH
Vernham Bank
Boats Copse
Thornycombe Wood
CONHOLT HILL
Kiblet Down
CONHOLT LANE
Lower Conholt Farm
Oakdown Copse
Forty Acre Wood
Well Bottom
Conholt Down
Cow Down

Three Cornered Covert
Pigtrough Copse
Belvedere Wood
Nut Covert
CHURCH LA
HEATH LANE
WHITE FARM LA
DOWNS LANE
Buttermere Bottom
Buttermere Wood
Grant's Copse
Rockmoor Down
Heath Plantation
Rockmoor Pond
ROCKMOOR LANE
Winterside Farm
Wissenden Farm
Halls Farm
Harts Bottom
Drove Farm
HAYDOWN LEAS
HATCHBURY LA
SHEPHERDS RI
SCHOOL·CL
Vernham Dean Sch
Vernham Dean
BOTISDONE CL
Ankers Farm
Mascombe Copse
Rushmore Down
Enclosure

Wright's Copse
Wright's Farm
Summer Hill
Sheepless Hill
Test Way
Wadsmere Down
Summerton's Down
Rockmoor Plantation
Combe Wood
Birch Copse
Hart Hill Down
Well Wood
Littledown
Vernham Street
Vernham Manor
Assam Wood
Upton Manor
Upton
PH
Little Bourne Farm
Rushmore Farm

Fort
Walbury Hill
Combe
Lower Farm
Manor Farm
Combe Bottom
Hogs Hole
Limber Copse
Highdown
Combe Bottom
Down Copse
Cleve Hill
Manor House
PO
Linkenholt
Netherton
Earthworks
Netherton House
Manor Farm
Test Way
Farm Copse
Wilster Copse
Parsonage Farm
Clinchorn Farm
Netherton Hanging Copse
Sawyers Wood
Grim's Ditch
Day's Copse
Test Way
Ambley Farm
Ambley Wood
DUNSTAN'S DROVE
Lower Down Copse

Moordown Farm
ASHLEY DROVE
Field System
Conholt Bottom

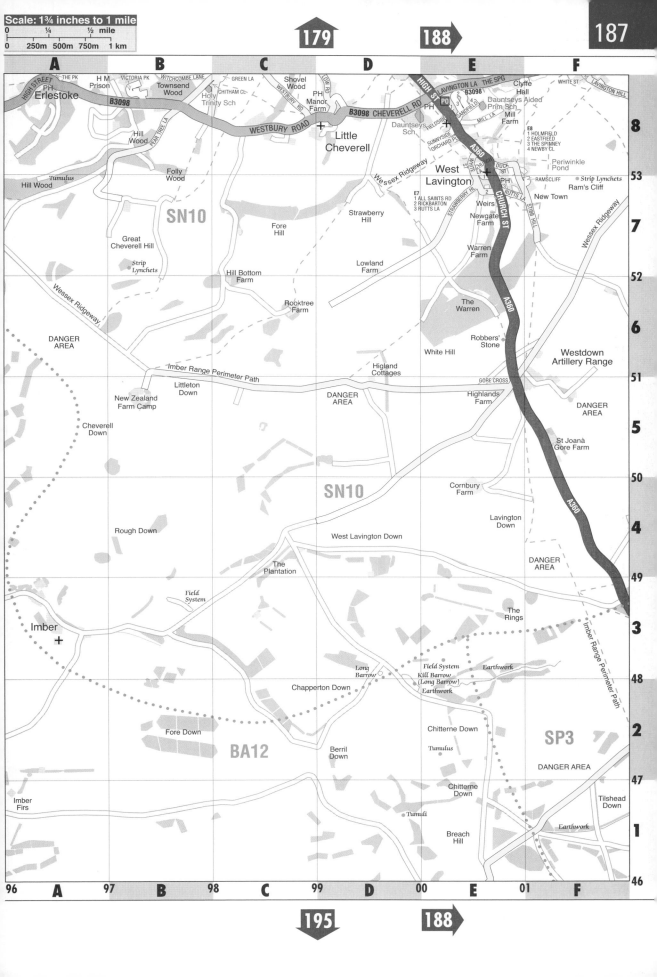

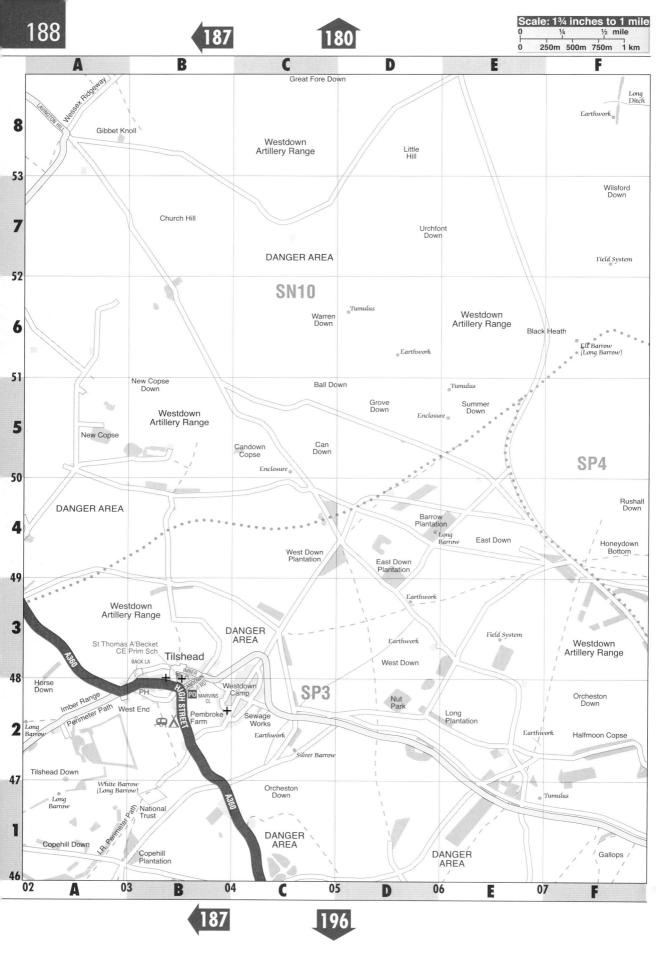

188

187

180

Scale: 1¾ inches to 1 mile

0   ¼   ½ mile
0   250m   500m   750m   1 km

A   B   C   D   E   F

8

Wessex Ridgeway

Lavington Hill

Great Fore Down

Long Ditch

Earthwork

Gibbet Knoll

Westdown
Artillery Range

Little
Hill

Wilsford
Down

53

7

Church Hill

Urchfont
Down

Field System

52

DANGER AREA

SN10

6

Warren
Down

Tumulus

Westdown
Artillery Range

Black Heath

Elf Barrow
(Long Barrow)

Earthwork

51

New Copse
Down

Ball Down

Tumulus

Grove
Down

Summer
Down

5

Westdown
Artillery Range

Enclosure

SP4

New Copse

Candown
Copse

Can
Down

50

Enclosure

Rushall
Down

4

DANGER AREA

Barrow
Plantation

Long
Barrow

East Down

Honeydown
Bottom

West Down
Plantation

East Down
Plantation

49

Earthwork

3

Westdown
Artillery Range

DANGER
AREA

Field System

Westdown
Artillery Range

St Thomas A'Becket
CE Prim Sch

Tilshead

Earthwork

BACK LA

West Down

48

Horse
Down

Imber Range

Perimeter Path

PH

West End

PO

MARVINS
CL

Westdown
Camp

SP3

Nut
Park

Orcheston
Down

IMBER

CANDOWN RD

HIGH STREET

A360

Pembroke
Farm

Sewage
Works

Long
Plantation

Earthwork

Halfmoon Copse

2

Long
Barrow

Earthwork

Silver Barrow

Tilshead Down

47

Long
Barrow

White Barrow
(Long Barrow)

National
Trust

Orcheston
Down

Tumulus

Copehill Down

I.R. Perimeter Path

Copehill
Plantation

A360

DANGER
AREA

DANGER
AREA

Gallops

1

46

02   A   **03**   B   **04**   C   **05**   D   **06**   E   **07**   F

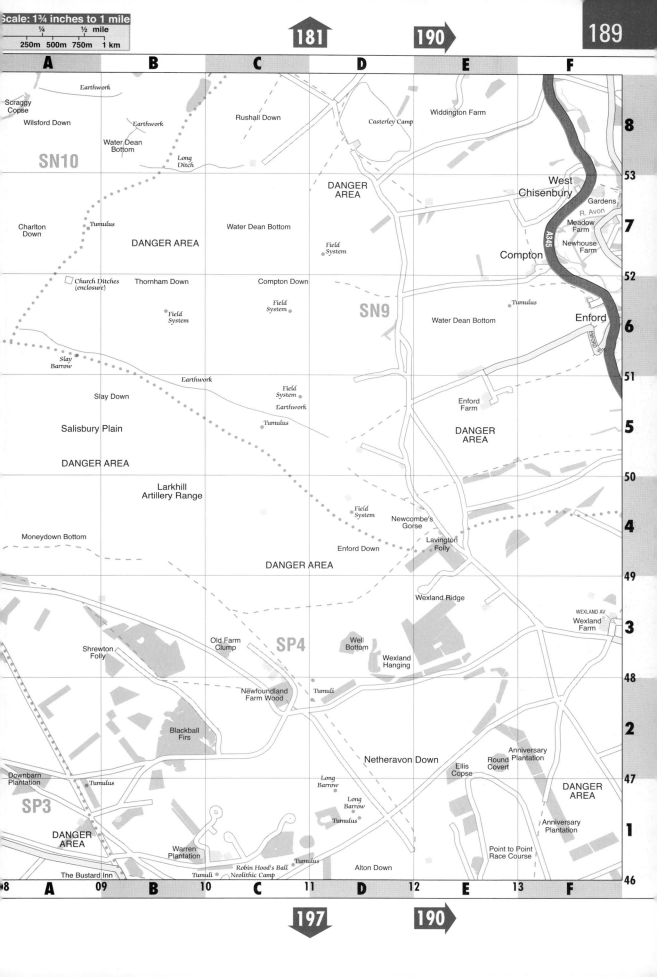

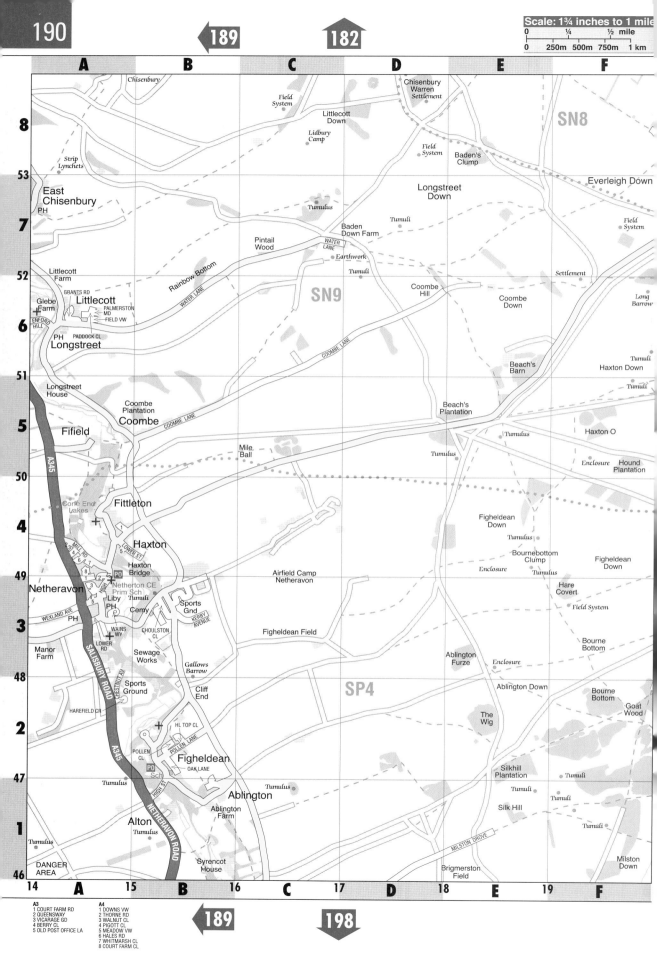

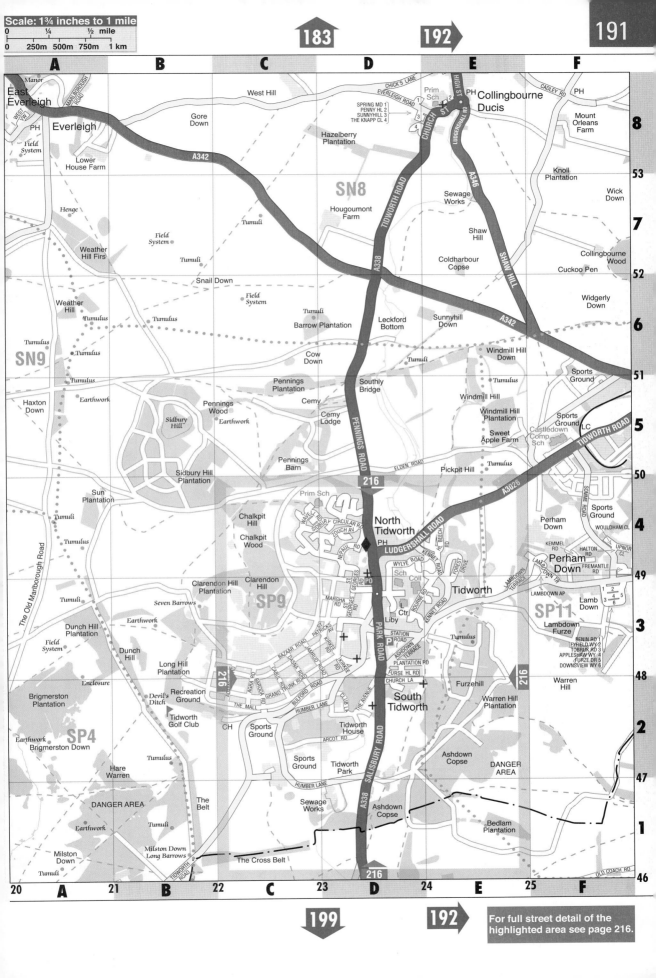

Scale: 1¾ inches to 1 mile

0   ¼   ½ mile
0 250m 500m 750m 1 km

A   B   C   D   E   F

Manor
East Everleigh
West Hill
CHICK'S LANE
EVERLEIGH ROAD
PH
Prim Sch
HIGH ST
PH
Collingbourne Ducis
CADLEY RD
PH

Everleigh
PH
WEST VW
MARLBOROUGH ROAD
Gore Down
CHURCH ST
LUDGERSHALL RD
Mount Orleans Farm

Field System
Lower House Farm
A342
Hazelberry Plantation
SPRING MD 1
PENNY HL 2
SUNNYHILL 3
THE KNAPP CL 4
A346
Knoll Plantation

Henge
SN8
Wick Down

Weather Hill Firs
Field System
Tumuli
Hougoumont Farm
TIDWORTH ROAD
Shaw Hill
Coldharbour Copse
Collingbourne Wood

Weather Hill
Tumulus
Tumulus
Field System
Snail Down
A338
Barrow Plantation
Leckford Bottom
Sunnyhill Down
SHAW HILL
Cuckoo Pen
A342

SN9
Tumulus
Tumulus
Tumuli
Cow Down
Southly Bridge
Windmill Hill Down
Widgerly Down

Haxton Down
Tumulus
Earthwork
Pennings Plantation
Cemy
Windmill Hill
Sports Ground

Sidbury Hill
Earthwork
Pennings Wood
Cemy Lodge
PENNINGS ROAD
ELDEN ROAD
Windmill Hill Plantation
Sports Ground
Castledown Comp Sch
LC
TIDWORTH ROAD

Sun Plantation
Sidbury Hill Plantation
Pennings Barn
216
Sweet Apple Farm
Pickpit Hill
Tumulus
A3026

The Old Marlborough Road
Chalkpit Hill
Prim Sch
WAVE RD
SIDBURY RD
CIRCULAR RD
North Tidworth
PH
LUDGERSHALL ROAD
BEECH RD
Perham Down
WOULDHAM CL

Tumulus
Chalkpit Wood
ZOUCH AV
NEPAUL RD
WYLYE ROAD
Sch
KENNET ROAD
FOREST DRIVE
KEMMEL RD
HALTON RD
UPNOR CL

Clarendon Hill Plantation
Clarendon Hill
ST GEORGES RD
PO
Coll
Tidworth
LAMBDOWN TR
Perham Down
FREMANTLE RD

Dunch Hill Plantation
Seven Barrows
SP9
MARGHA RD
BOURNE RD
L Ctr
Liby
KENNET ROAD
LAMBDOWN AP
Lamb Down
SP11

Tumulus
Earthwork
PATRICKS AV
STATION ROAD
Tumulus
Lambdown Furze
BENIN RD 1
FYFIELD WY 2
TOBRUK RD 3
APPLESHAW WY 4
FURZE DR 5
DOWNSVIEW WY 6

Field System
Dunch Hill
Long Hill Plantation
216
BAZAAR ROAD
DASMA RD
ASHDOWN TERRACE
PLANTATION RD
FURSE HL RD
CHURCH LA
Furzehill
216
Warren Hill

Brigmerston Plantation
Devil's Ditch
Recreation Ground
DR BARODA RD
GRAY RD
CABUL ROAD
GRAND TRUNK ROAD
BULFORD ROAD
HUMBER LANE
South Tidworth
Warren Hill Plantation

SP4
Tidworth Golf Club
THE MALL
CH
KIRKE RD
THE AVENUE
CLUB LA
Ashdown Copse
DANGER AREA

Earthwork
Brigmerston Down
Hare Warren
Tumulus
Sports Ground
ARCOT RD
Tidworth House
Tidworth Park
Bedlam Plantation

DANGER AREA
The Belt
Sports Ground
HUMBER LANE
A338
SALISBURY ROAD

Earthwork
Milston Down
Tumuli
Milston Down Long Barrows
TIDWORTH ROAD
Sewage Works
The Cross Belt
Ashdown Copse
OLD COACH RD

8
53
7
52
6
51
5
50
4
49
3
48
2
47
1
46

For full street detail of the highlighted area see page 216.

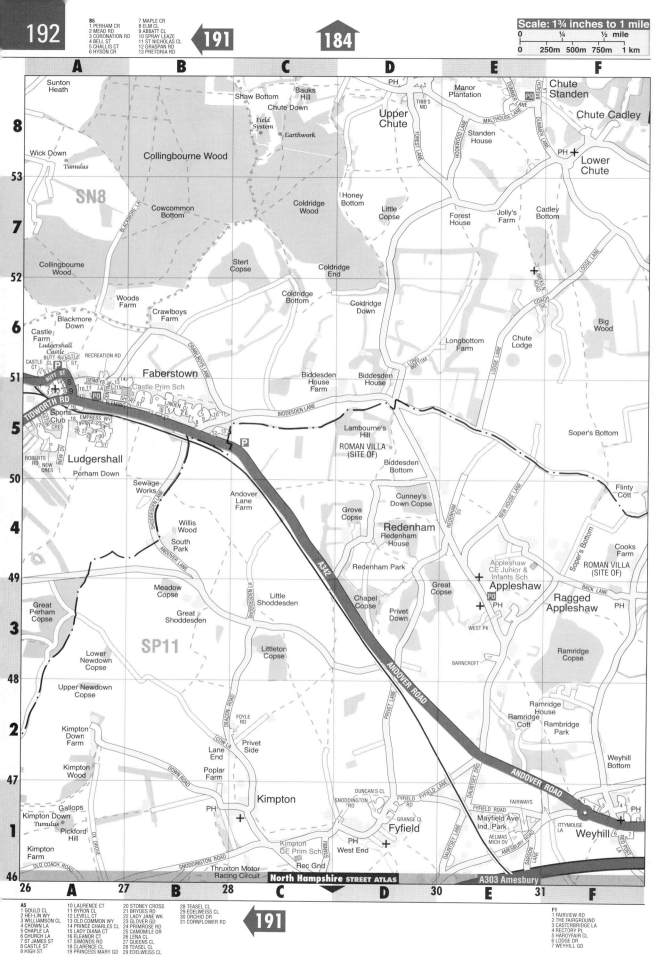

192

B5
1 PERHAM CR
2 MEAD RD
3 CORONATION RD
4 BELL ST
5 CHALLIS CT
6 HYSON CR
7 MAPLE CR
8 ELM CL
9 ABBATT CL
10 SPRAY LEAZE
11 ST NICHOLAS CL
12 GRASPAN RD
13 PRETORIA RD

191

184

Scale: 1¾ inches to 1 mile
0   ¼   ½ mile
0 250m 500m 750m 1 km

Sunton Heath
Shaw Bottom
Bauks Hill
Chute Down
Upper Chute
Manor Plantation
Chute Standen
Chute Cadley
PH
TIBB'S MD
DUMMER LANE
BREACH
PO
Wick Down
Tumulus
Collingbourne Wood
SN8
Field System
Earthwork
FOREST LANE
HOOKWOOD LANE
MALTHOUSE LANE
Standen House
DUMMER LANE
PH
Lower Chute
Cowcommon Bottom
Coldridge Wood
Honey Bottom
Little Copse
Forest House
Jolly's Farm
Cadley Bottom
BLACKMORE LA
Collingbourne Wood
Stert Copse
Coldridge End
LODGE LANE
MEKLIN ROAD
COACH HL
Big Wood
Woods Farm
Crawlboys Farm
Coldridge Bottom
Coldridge Down
Longbottom Farm
Chute Lodge
Blackmore Down
CRAWLBOYS LANE
LONG BOTTOM
LODGE LANE
Soper's Bottom
Castle Farm
Ludgershall Castle
RECREATION RD
Faberstown
Biddesden House Farm
Biddesden House
CASTLE BUTT
CASTLE
DEWEYS LA
CENTRAL LA
Castle Prim Sch
BIDDESDEN LANE
CASTLE CT
BUTT ST
PO
SHORT ST
LINDEN CL
FLEMING LA
TIDWORTH RD
Sports Club
EMPRESS WY
CRES
Lambourne's Hill
ROMAN VILLA (SITE OF)
Biddesden Bottom
Soper's Bottom
Flinty Cott
P
ROBERTS RD
NEW DV
Ludgershall
NEW CRES
Perham Down
Sewage Works
Andover Lane Farm
Grove Copse
Cunney's Down Copse
Redenham
Redenham House
REDENHAM DV
NEW HOUSE LANE
Soper's Bottom
Cooks Farm
ROMAN VILLA (SITE OF)
Great Perham Copse
SHODDESDEN LANE
Willis Wood
South Park
ANDOVER LANE
Meadow Copse
Great Shoddesden
SHODDESDEN LA
Little Shoddesden
A342
Redenham Park
Chapel Copse
Privet Down
Great Copse
REDENHAM DV
Appleshaw CE Junior & Infants Sch
Appleshaw
PO
PH
BACK LANE
Ragged Appleshaw
PH
Ramridge Copse
SP11
Littleton Copse
Privet Lane
WEST PK
BARNCROFT
Lower Newdown Copse
Great Shoddesden
Littleton Copse
Ramridge House
Ramridge Cott
Ramridge Park
Upper Newdown Copse
DEACON ROAD
FOYLE RD
PRIVET LANE
ANDOVER ROAD
Weyhill Bottom
Kimpton Down Farm
COW LA
Lane End
Privet Side
Poplar Farm
DAUNTSEY DRO
FYFIELD LANE
FYFIELD RD
Mayfield Ave Ind Park
FAIRWAYS
ITTYMOUSE LA
Kimpton Wood
DOWN ROAD
Kimpton
PH
DUNCAN'S CL
SNODDINGTON RD
GRANGE CL
Fyfield
FYFIELD ROAD
AELMAS MICH DV
AMESBURY ROAD
SARSON LANE
Weyhill
PH
RED POST LA
Gallops
Kimpton Down
Tumulus
Pickford Hill
OX DROVE
PH
Kimpton CE Prim Sch
STANBU
West End
PH
Rec Gnd
DAUNTSEY LANE
Kimpton Farm
OLD COACH ROAD
SNODDINGTON ROAD
Thruxton Motor Racing Circuit
North Hampshire STREET ATLAS
A303 Amesbury

A5
1 GOULD CL
2 HEI-LIN WY
3 WILLIAMSON CL
4 CROWN LA
5 CHAPLE LA
6 CHURCH LA
7 ST JAMES ST
8 CASTLE ST
9 HIGH ST
10 LAURENCE CT
11 BYRON CL
12 LEVELL CT
13 OLD COMMON WY
14 PRINCE CHARLES CL
15 LADY DIANA CT
16 ELEANOR CT
17 SIMONDS RD
18 CLARENCE CL
19 PRINCESS MARY GD
20 STONEY CROSS
21 BRYDES RD
22 LADY JANE WK
23 GLOVER GD
24 PRIMROSE RD
25 CAMOMILE DR
26 LENA CL
27 QUEENS RD
28 TEASEL CL
29 EDELWEISS CL
28 TEASEL CL
29 EDELWEISS CL
30 ORCHID DR
31 CORNFLOWER RD
F1
1 FAIRVIEW RD
2 THE FAIRGROUND
3 CASTERBRIDGE LA
4 RECTORY PL
5 HARDYFAIR CL
6 LODGE DR
7 WEYHILL GD

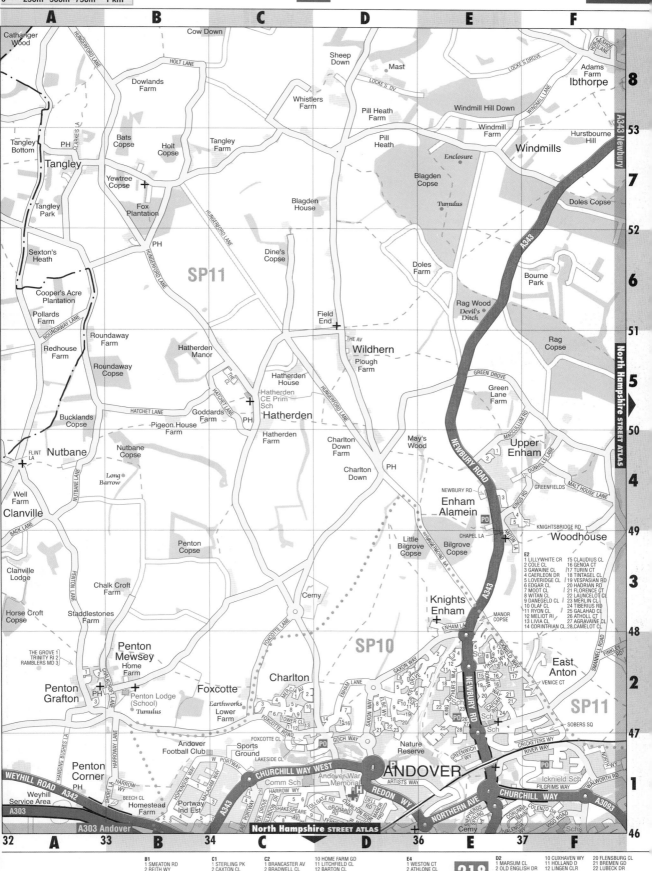

Cathanger Wood
Tangley Bottom
PH
Tangley
Tangley Park
Sexton's Heath
Cooper's Acre Plantation
Pollards Farm
Redhouse Farm
Bucklands Copse
Nutbane
FLINT LA
Well Farm
Clanville
Clanville Lodge
Horse Croft Copse

HUNGERFORD LANE
CLARKE'S LA
Dowlands Farm
HOLT LANE
Bats Copse
Holt Copse
Yewtree Copse
Fox Plantation
PH
PH
SP11
Roundaway Farm
Roundaway Copse
Staddlestones Farm
Long Barrow
Nutbane Copse
Nutbane Farm
ROUNDAWAY LANE
HATCHET LANE
Goddards Farm
Pigeon House Farm
Chalk Croft Farm
Penton Copse

Cow Down
HOLT LANE
Whistlers Farm
Tangley Farm
Blagden House
Dine's Copse
Field End
THE AV
Wildhern
Plough Farm
Hatherden Manor
Hatherden House
Hatherden CE Prim Sch
Hatherden
Hatherden Farm
Charlton Down Farm
Charlton Down
PH
May's Wood

Sheep Down
Mast
Pill Heath Farm
Pill Heath
Enclosure
Blagden Copse
Tumulus
Doles Farm
Little Bilgrove Copse
Bilgrove Copse
HUNGERFORD LA

LOCKE'S DROVE
LOCKE'S DV
Windmill Hill Down
Windmill Farm
Windmills
Green Drove
Green Lane Farm
NEWBURY ROAD
Upper Enham
Enham Alamein
NEWBURY RD
PO
Knights Enham
ENHAM LA
MANOR COPSE

Adams Farm
Ibthorpe
Hurstbourne Hill
Doles Copse
Bourne Park
Rag Wood
Devil's Ditch
Rag Copse
MACCULLUM CL
DUNHILLS LANE
KINGS RD
GREENFIELDS
MALT HOUSE LANE
Woodhouse
KNIGHTSBRIDGE RD
CHAPEL LA
A343

A343 Newbury
North Hampshire STREET ATLAS
8
53
7
52
6
51
5
50
4
49
3
48

E2
1 LILLYWHITE CR   15 CLAUDIUS CL
2 COLE CL   16 GENOA CT
3 GAWAINE CL   17 TURIN CT
4 CAERLEON DR   18 TINTAGEL CL
5 LOVERIDGE CL   19 VESPASIAN RD
6 EDGAR CL   20 HADRIAN RD
7 MOOT CL   21 FLORENCE CT
8 WITAN CL   22 LAUNCELOT CL
9 DANEGELD CL   23 MERLIN CL
10 OLAF CL   24 TIBERIUS RD
11 RYON CL   25 GALAHAD CL
12 MELIOT RI   26 ATHOLL CT
13 LIVIA CL   27 AGRAVAINE CL
14 CORINTHIAN CL   28 CAMELOT CL

THE GROVE 1
TRINITY RI 2
RAMBLERS MD 3
Penton Mewsey
Home Farm
PH
CHALKCROFT LANE
Penton Lodge (School)
Tumulus
Penton Grafton
Foxcotte
Lower Farm
Earthworks
Andover Football Club
Penton Corner
PH
Weyhill Service Area
A303
WEYHILL ROAD A342
Homestead Farm
PENTON LANE
BACK LANE
NUTBANE LANE
HANGING BUSHES LA
HARROWAY LANE
SHORT LA
HARROW WY
HOPKINSON WY
MACADAM WY
BEECH CL
Portway Ind Est
EAST PORTWAY
Sports Ground
LAKESIDE CL
FOXCOTTE CL
FOXCOTTE ROAD
FOXCOTTE LANE
Charlton
MERCIA AV
TOWER CL
SAXON WAY
ENHAM LANE
GOCH WAY
PO
Nature Reserve
PO
ARTISTS WAY
ANDOVER
Andover War Memorial
REDON WY
CHURCHILL WAY WEST
Comm Sch
HARROW WY
PORTWAY
GROVE RD
TOLLGATE RD
CHARLTON RD
SHAKESPEARE
ORCHARD
DELL RD
MANOR RD
NORTHERN AVE
SHEPHERDS SPRING
Cemy
VALENCIA
WALENGER
CORUNNA
NEWBURY RD
SAXON WAY
ELBE WY
KING ARTHUR'S WAY
ICKNIELD WAY
ROMAN WAY
VIKING WAY
MEL DRIVE
CAESAR
Sch
Sch
Sch
VENICE CT
East Anton
SP11
SMANNELL ROAD
FINKLEY RD
SOBERS SQ
CRICKETERS WY
RIVER WAY
Icknield Sch
PO
CHURCHILL WAY
A3093
GREENWICH
GREENWICH WY
PILGRIMS WY
COLENZO DR
VIGO ROAD
WALWORTH RD
NORTH WY
Schs
SP10

32   33   34   35   36   37
46
47
A   B   C   D   E   F

B1
1 SMEATON RD
2 REITH WY
3 JOULE RD
4 WHITTLE RD
5 ROYCE CL

C1
1 STERLING PK
2 CAXTON CL
3 MITCHELL CL
4 WATT CL
5 CHAUCER AV
6 MILTON AV
7 SOPWITH PK
8 BRACKENBURY
9 MAY TREE RD

C2
1 BRANCASTER AV
2 BRADWELL CL
3 RICHBOROUGH DR
4 ETHELBERT DR
5 HENGEST CL
6 RECULVER WY
7 BEDE DR
8 PORCHESTER CL
9 AUGUSTINE WY

10 HOME FARM GD
11 LITCHFIELD CL
12 BARTON CL
13 DACRE CL

E4
1 WESTON CT
2 ATHLONE CL
3 LANDALE CL
4 ALAMEIN RD
5 TOBRUK CL

D2
1 MARSUM CL
2 OLD ENGLISH DR
3 JUTLAND CR
4 RUNE DR
5 MONEYER RD
6 ANDEFERAS RD
7 ALDRIN CL
8 BORKUM CL
9 HATTEM PL

10 CUXHAVEN WY
11 HOLLAND D
12 LINGEN CLR
13 MINDEN CL
14 ST THOMAS CL
15 COLLINS CL
16 ARMSTRONG RI
17 ALTONIA GD
18 EMDEN RD
19 VERDEN WY

20 FLENSBURG CL
21 BREMEN GD
22 LUBECK CL
23 HAMBURG CL

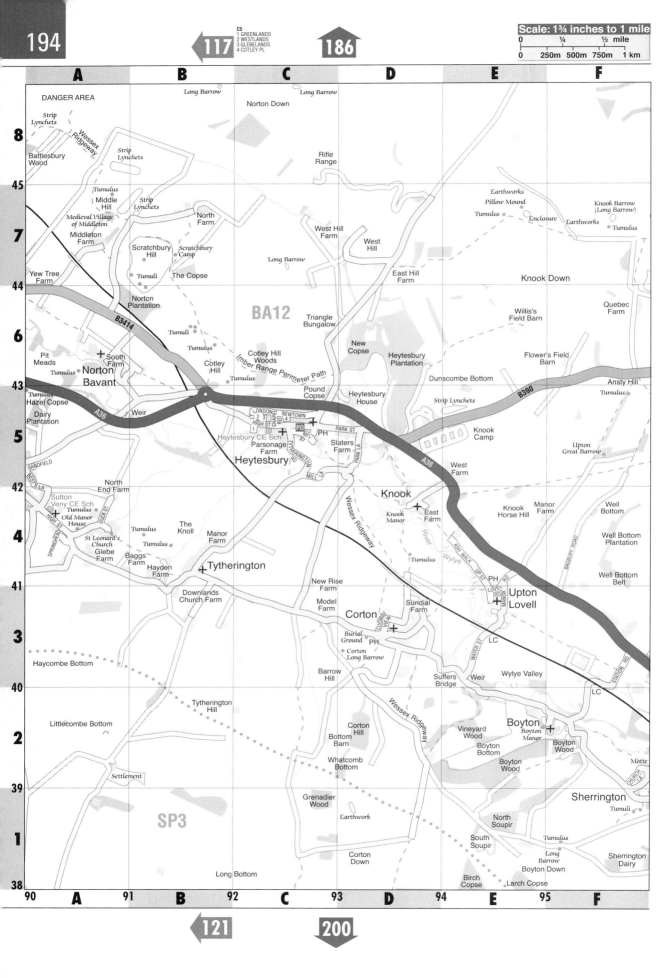

Scale: 1¾ inches to 1 mile

¼   ½ mile

250m   500m   750m   1 km

A   B   C   D   E   F

SP3

Tumulus

8

Breakheart
Bottom

DANGER AREA

Middle
Barn

45

Castle
Barrow

Earthworks
Breakheart
Hill

Imber Range Perimeter Path

7

Settlement

Chitterne
Farm

ABDON CL

ook Castle
Settlement

Manor
Farm

TOWNSEND

PITTS LA

44

Chitterne

Elm
Farm

Valley
Farm

Glebe
Farm

PH
ST MARY'S CL

BIDDEN

B390

Middle Barn

6

ANSTY HILL

Chittterne Brook

CODFORD ROAD

Clump
Farm

SHREWTON ROAD

B390

43

Field System

Codford Down

Tumuli

Wind Farm

Clay Pit Hill

5

Vraxworthy
Plantation

Auckland
Farm

East
Codford Down

42

Manor
Farm

BA12

4

East Codford
Down

41

Green Road

Chitterne Road

Punch Bowl
Bottom

Codford Circle or
Wilsbury Ring

Hare
Covert

Deptford
Down

3

Ashdown
Farm

Tethers
End

NEW RD

Codford St Peter

Stony
Hill

Codford St Mary
CE Sch

Little
Wood

RICKWORTH PL

East
Codford
Farm

Lamb
Down

Parry's
Field Barn

40

PH

HIGH ST

HIGH STREET

CHEAPSIDE

PO

OXYARD

CHURCH LA

Codford St Mary

SHERRINGTON LA

BURY MD 1
CHERRY OR 2
DOUGHTY'S LA 3

MALMPIT HI

Tumulus

Foxhole
Bottom

Codford Rising Sun
(Hill Figure)

Starveall

Gilbert's
Plantation

2

LC

Deptford
Field Barn

CHURCH
LA TON HI

Long
Barrow

River Wylye

A36

Tumulus

Manor
Farm

39

Dairy Cottage
New Farm

Stockton
House

White
Farm

Deptford

WESTCOMBE LA

Little
Down

Stockton

PH

Manor
Farm

The
Glebe

WATERMEADOW LA

Fisherton
de la Mere
Aqueduct (dis)

Village
Earthworks

A36

Tumulus

1

Shute
Plantation

Sherrington
Plantation

LC

Bapton

A303

A36

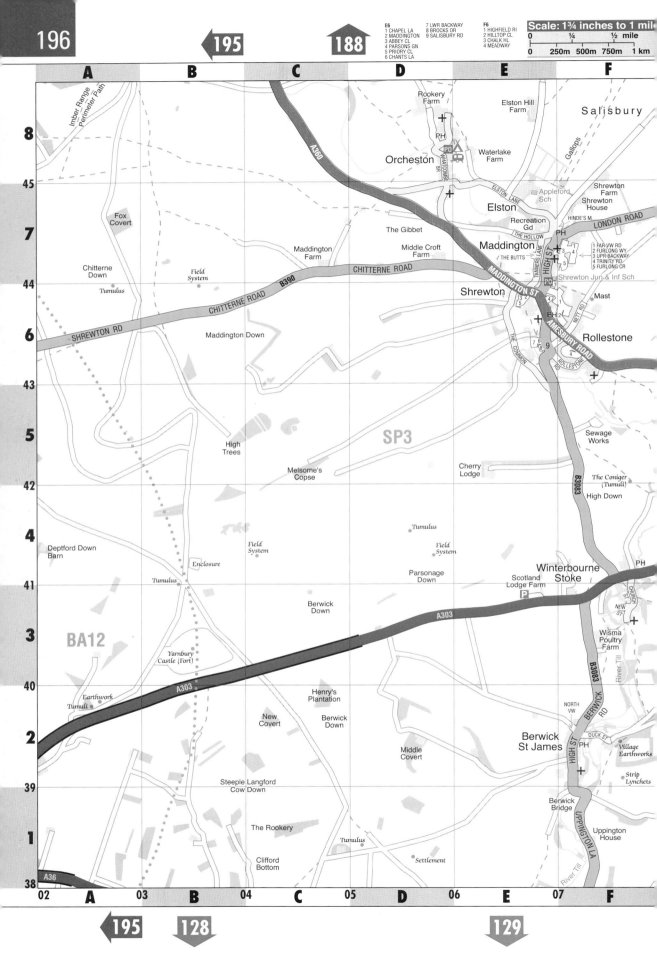

195
188

E6
1 CHAPEL LA
2 MADDINGTON
3 ABBEY CL
4 PARSONS GN
5 PRIORY CL
6 CHANTS LA
7 LWR BACKWAY
8 BROCKS OR
9 SALISBURY RD

F6
1 HIGHFIELD RI
2 HILLTOP CL
3 CHALK HL
4 MEADWAY

Scale: 1¾ inches to 1 mile
0   ¼   ½   mile
0 250m 500m 750m 1 km

Salisbury

Rookery Farm

Elston Hill Farm

PH

Orcheston

Waterlake Farm

Appleford Sch

Shrewton Farm

Elston

Shrewton House

HINDE'S M

The Gibbet

Recreation Gd

THE HOLLOW

Maddington Farm

Middle Croft Farm

PH

London Road

Maddington

THE BUTTS

MADDINGTON ST

HIGH ST

1 FAR-VW RD
2 FURLONG WY
3 UPR BACKWAY
4 TRINITY RD
5 FURLONG CR

TANNERS LANE

Shrewton Jun & Inf Sch

Chitterne Down

Field System

CHITTERNE ROAD

Shrewton

Mast

Tumulus

B390

CHITTERNE ROAD

PH

NETT RD

SHREWTON RD

Maddington Down

AMESBURY ROAD

Rollestone

THE COMMON

ROLLESTONE RD

SP3

Sewage Works

High Trees

Melsome's Copse

Cherry Lodge

The Coniger (Tumuli)

High Down

B3083

Deptford Down Barn

Field System

Enclosure

Field System

Tumulus

Winterbourne Stoke

PH

Tumulus

Parsonage Down

Scotland Lodge Farm

P

CHURCH ST

NEW ST

BA12

Berwick Down

Wisma Poultry Farm

B3083

River Till

Yarnbury Castle (Fort)

A303

Henry's Plantation

NORTH VW

BERWICK RD

Earthwork

Tumuli

New Covert

Berwick Down

Middle Covert

Berwick St James

PH

HIGH ST

DUCK ST

Village Earthworks

Strip Lynchets

Steeple Langford Cow Down

Berwick Bridge

UPPINGTON LA

Uppington House

The Rookery

Tumulus

Settlement

Clifford Bottom

River Till

A36

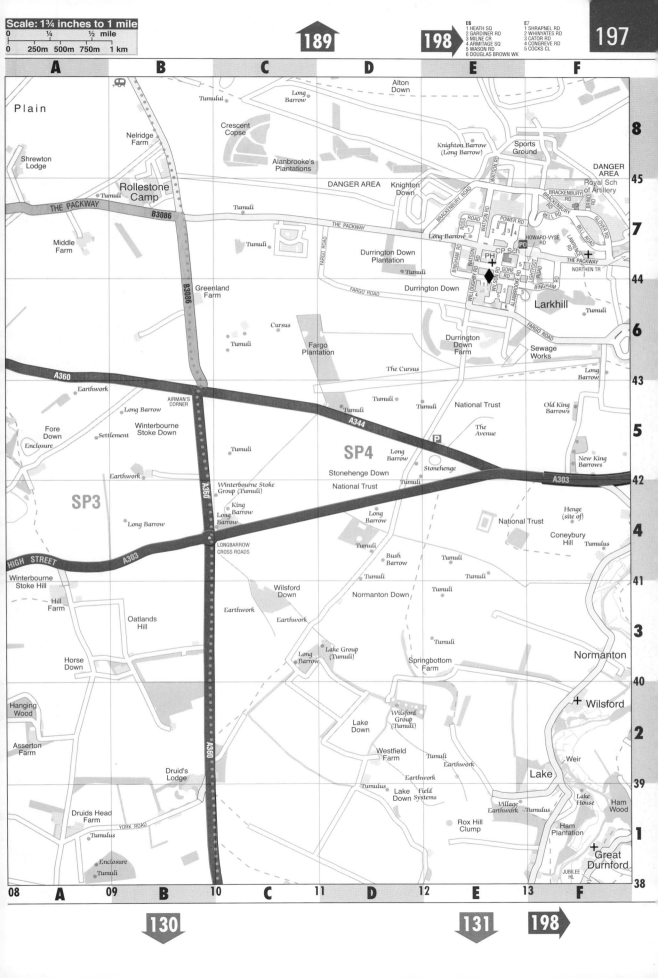

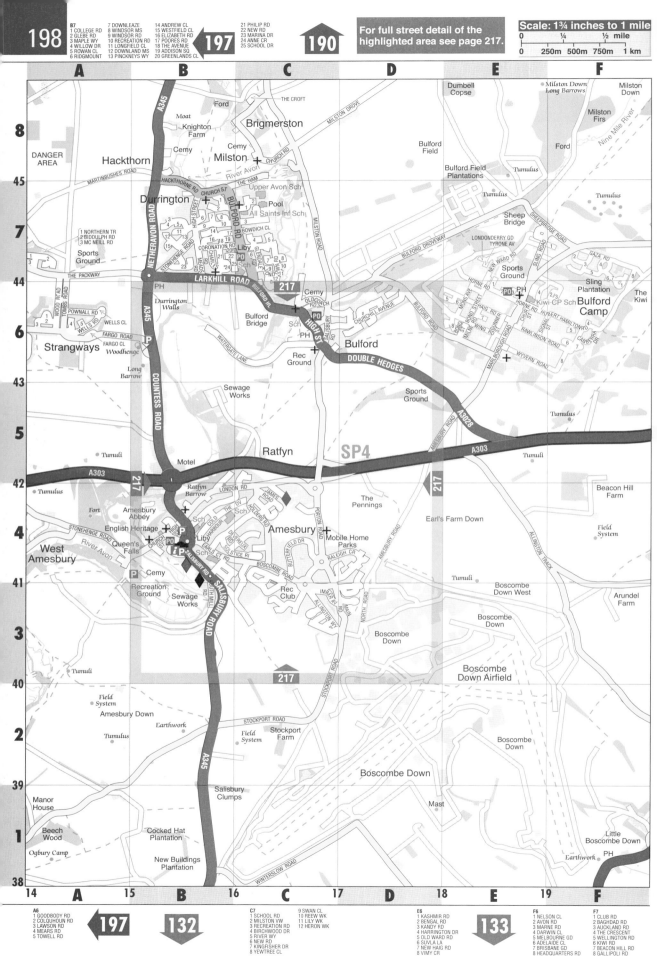

198

B7
1 COLLEGE RD
2 GLEBE RD
3 MAPLE WY
4 WILLOW DR
5 ROWAN CL
6 RIDGMOUNT

7 DOWNLEAZE
8 WINDSOR MS
9 WINDSOR RD
10 RECREATION RD
11 LONGFIELD CL
12 DOWNLAND MS
13 PINCKNEYS WY

14 ANDREW CL
15 WESTFIELD RD
16 ELIZABETH RD
17 POORES RD
18 THE AVENUE
19 ADDISON SQ
20 GREENLANDS CL

21 PHILIP RD
22 NEW RD
23 MARINA DR
24 ANNE CR
25 SCHOOL DR

197

190

For full street detail of the
highlighted area see page 217.

Scale: 1¾ inches to 1 mile
0   ¼   ½ mile
0   250m 500m 750m   1 km

197

132

133

A6
1 GOODBODY RD
2 COLQUHOUN RD
3 LAWSON RD
4 MEARS RD
5 TOWELL RD

C7
1 SCHOOL RD
2 MILSTON VW
3 RECREATION RD
4 BIRCHWOOD DR
5 RIVER WY
6 NEW RD
7 KINGFISHER DR
8 YEWTREE CL

9 SWAN CL
10 REEW WK
11 LILY WK
12 HERON WK

E6
1 KASHMIR RD
2 BENGAL RD
3 KANDY RD
4 HARRINGTON DR
5 OLD WARD RD
6 SUVLA LA
7 NEW HAIG RD
8 VIMY CR

F6
1 NELSON CL
2 AVON RD
3 MARNE RD
4 DARWIN CL
5 MELBOURNE GD
6 ADELAIDE CL
7 BRISBANE GD
8 HEADQUARTERS RD

F7
1 CLUB RD
2 BAGHDAD RD
3 AUCKLAND RD
4 THE CRESCENT
5 WELLINGTON RD
6 KIWI RD
7 BEACON HILL RD
8 GALLIPOLI RD

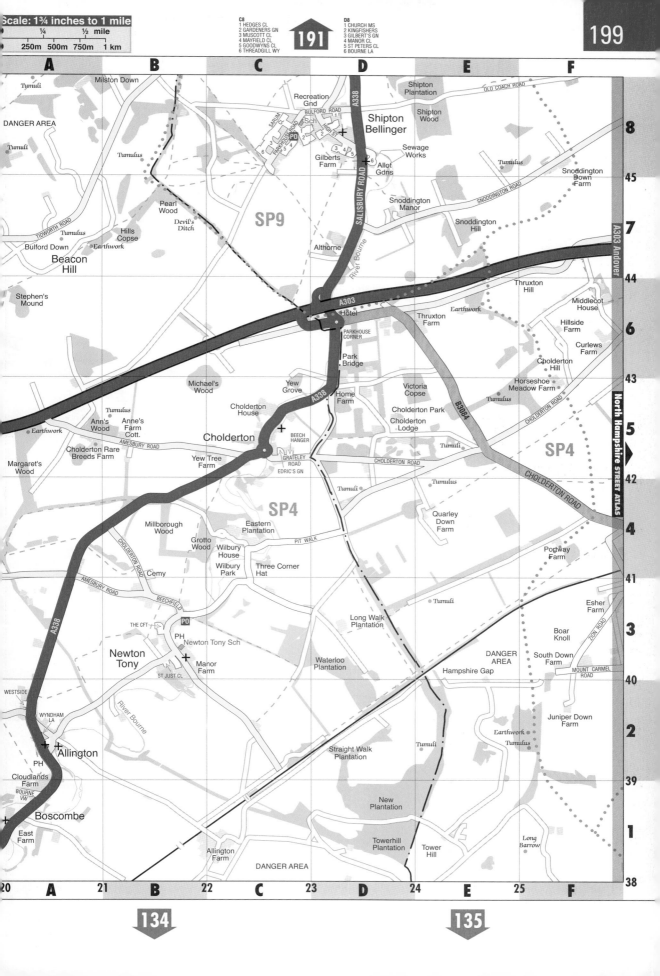

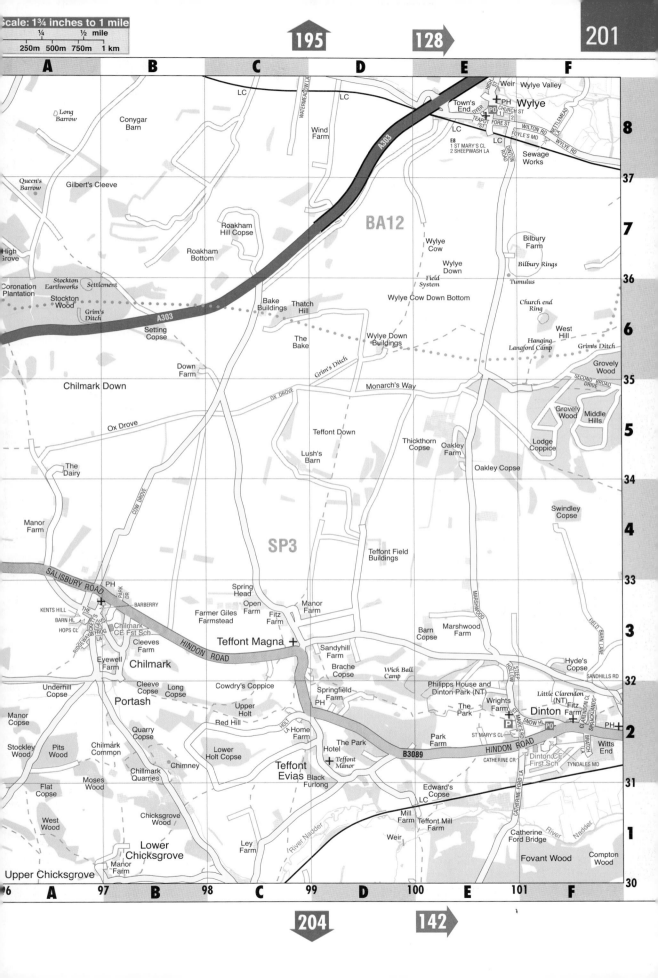

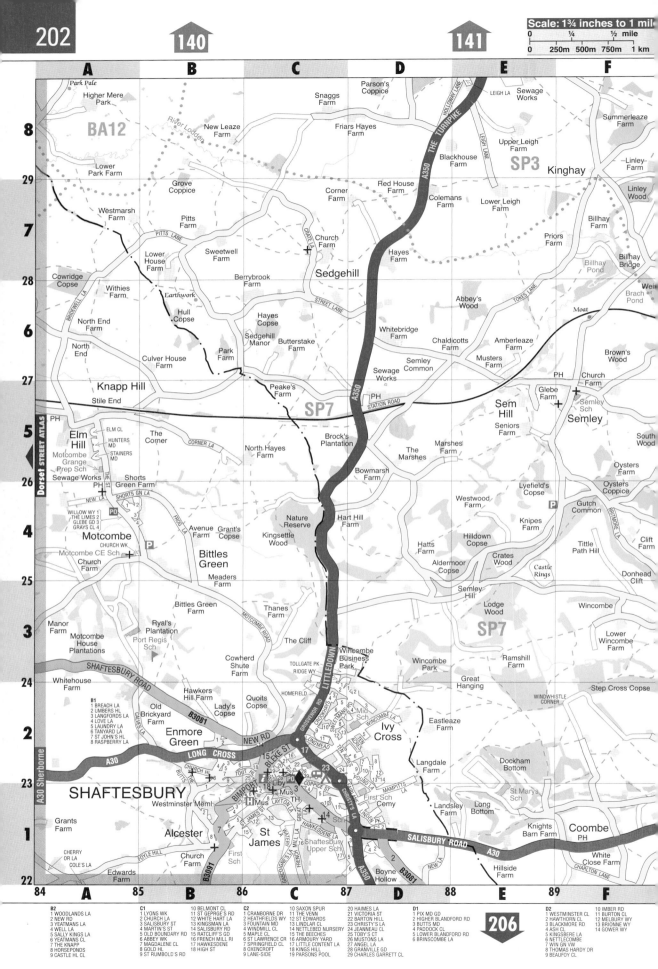

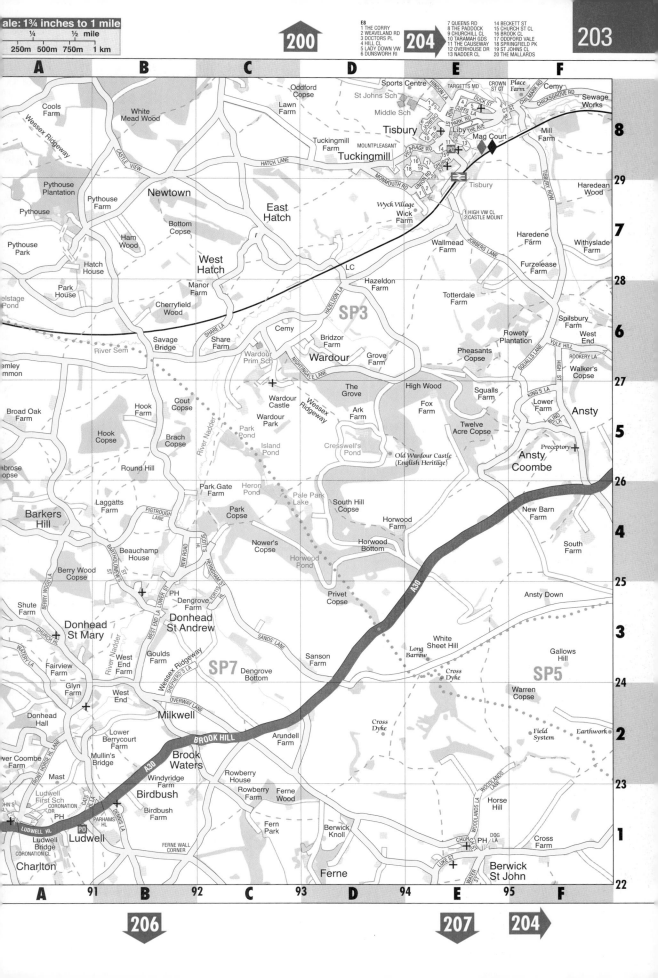

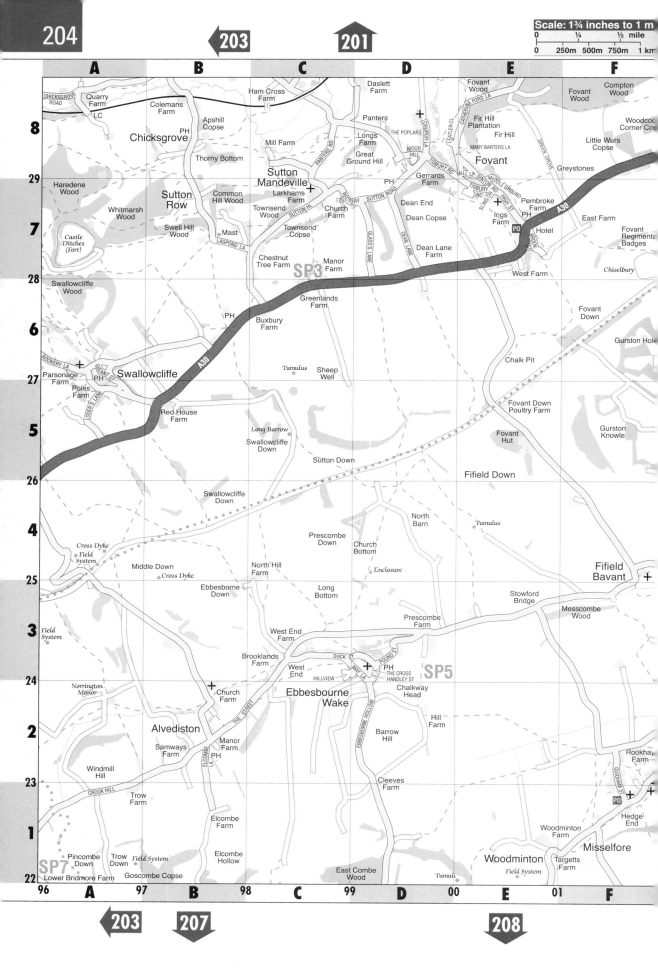

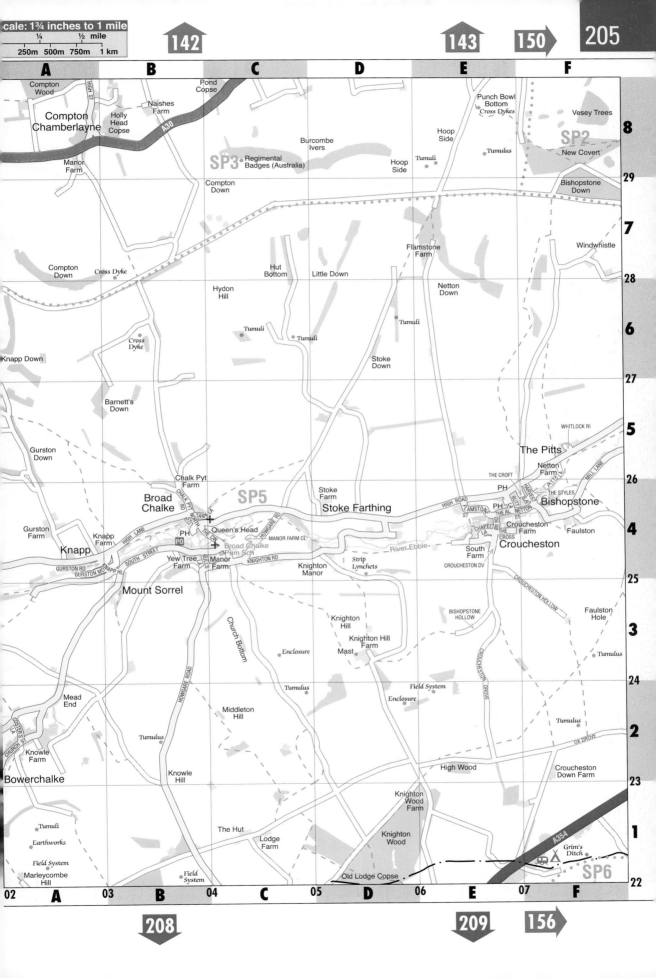

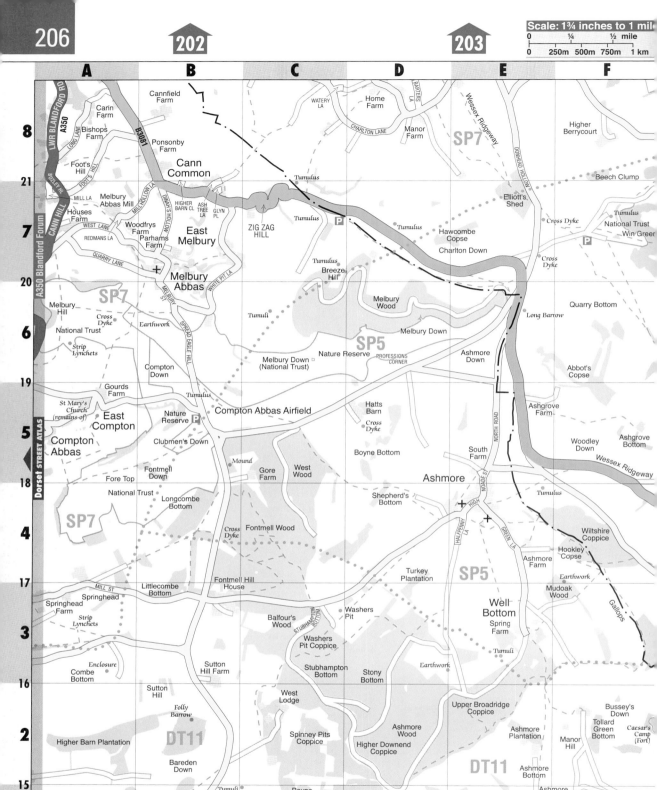

A   B   C   D   E   F

LWR BLANDFORD RD
A350
Long Lane
Cann
Bishops
Farm
Foot's
Hill
MILL LA

Cannfield
Farm

Ponsonby
Farm

Cann
Common

Watery LA

Home
Farm

CHARLTON LANE

Manor
Farm

BARTERS LA

Wessex Ridgeway

DONHEAD HOLLOW

SP7

Higher
Berrycourt

Beech Clump

8

21

Houses
Farm
Melbury
Abbas Mill
WEST LANE
Woodfrys
Farm
REDMANS LA
Parhams
Farm
QUARRY LANE

B3081
HIGHER
BARN CL
ASH
TREE
LA
GLYN
PL

East
Melbury

ZIG ZAG
HILL

Tumulus

Tumulus

Tumulus

P

Hawcombe
Copse

Charlton Down

Elliott's
Shed

Cross Dyke

Cross
Dyke

P

Tumulus
National Trust
Win Green

7

CANN HILL
A350 Blandford Forum
Melbury
Hill
National Trust
Cross
Dyke
Earthwork
Strip
Lynchets

MELBURY ST
SPREAD EAGLE HILL

Melbury
Abbas

WHITE PIT LA

SP7

Breeze
Hill

Tumuli

Melbury
Wood

Melbury Down

Melbury Down
(National Trust)

SP5

Nature Reserve
PROFESSIONS
CORNER

Ashmore
Down

Long Barrow

Quarry Bottom

Abbot's
Copse

20

6

19

Dorset STREET ATLAS

Compton
Down

Gourds
Farm

St Mary's
Church
(remains of)

East
Compton

Nature
Reserve
P

Tumulus

Compton Abbas Airfield

Hatts
Barn
Cross
Dyke

North Road

Ashgrove
Farm

Ashgrove
Bottom

Woodley
Down

5

18

Compton
Abbas

Fore Top
National Trust

SP7

Clubmen's Down

Fontmell
Down

Longcombe
Bottom

Mound

Gore
Farm

West
Wood

Boyne Bottom

Shepherd's
Bottom

Ashmore

South
Farm

HIGH ST

Tumulus

Wessex Ridgeway

Wiltshire
Coppice

Hookley
Copse

4

17

Springhead
Farm
Springhead
MILL ST
Strip
Lynchets

Littlecombe
Bottom

Cross
Dyke

Fontmell
Wood

Fontmell Hill
House

Turkey
Plantation

HALFPENNY LA
GREEN LA

SP5

Ashmore
Farm

Earthwork

Mudoak
Wood

Gallops

3

Enclosure
Combe
Bottom

Sutton
Hill Farm

Balfour's
Wood

Washers
Pit

STUBHAMPTON BOTTOM

Washers
Pit Coppice

Stubhampton
Bottom

Stony
Bottom

Earthwork

Tumuli

Well
Bottom

Spring
Farm

16

2

Higher Barn Plantation

DT11

Sutton
Hill

Folly
Barrow

Bareden
Down

West
Lodge

Spinney Pits
Coppice

Ashmore
Wood

Higher Downend
Coppice

Upper Broadridge
Coppice

Ashmore
Plantation

DT11

Ashmore
Bottom

Bussey's
Down
Tollard
Green
Bottom
Caesar's
Camp
(Fort)

Manor
Hill

Ashmore
Barn
Farm

15

Wales Wood

Bareden Wood

Iwerne Hill

TOWER HILL

BOYNES LANE

Tumuli

Common
Bushes

Payne
Coppice

Great Peakey
Coppice

Wessex Ridgeway

Hanging
Coppice

Earl's
Hill

Tumuli

Tumuli

ASHMORE BOTTOM

Bussey
Stool Farm

1

14

Brookman's
Valley

Hill
Farm

Stubhampton
Down

Dungrove
Hill

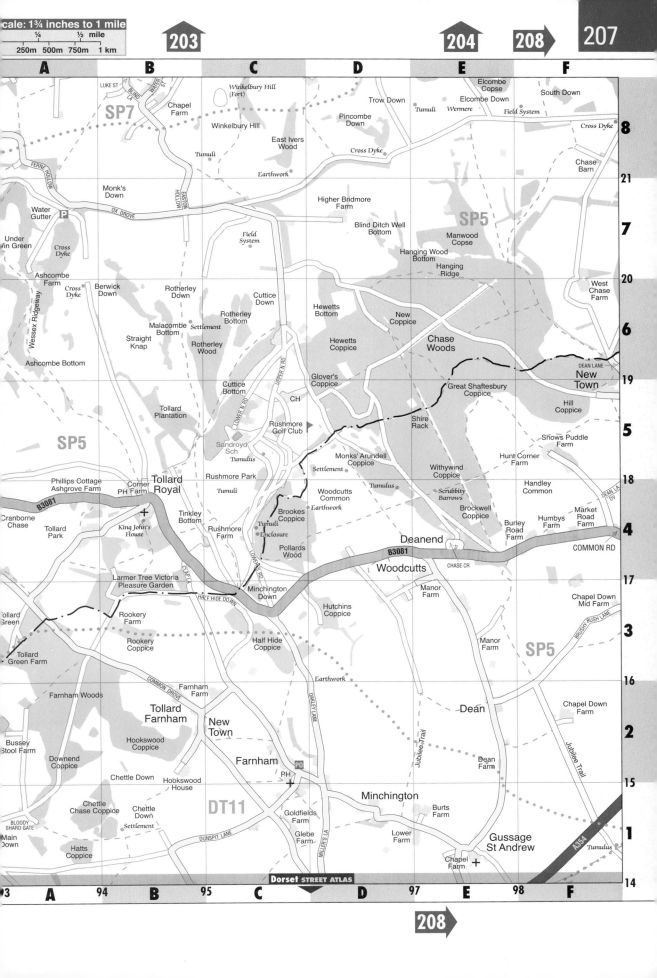

scale: 1¾ inches to 1 mile

¼ ½ mile
250m 500m 750m 1 km

203

204

208

207

A B C D E F

8

LUKE ST
WATER ST
BLIND LA
SP7
Chapel Farm
Winkelbury Hill (Fort)
Winkelbury Hill
East Ivers Wood
Tumuli
Earthwork
Pincombe Down
Trow Down
Tumuli
Wernere
Cross Dyke
Elcombe Copse
Elcombe Down
Field System
South Down
Cross Dyke
Chase Barn

21

FERNE HOLLOW
Monk's Down
OX DROVE
EASTON HOLLOW
Higher Bridmore Farm
Blind Ditch Well Bottom
Manwood Copse
SP5

7

Water Gutter
P
Under Win Green
Cross Dyke
Ashcombe Farm
Berwick Down
Cross Dyke
Field System
Rotherley Down
Cuttice Down
Hewetts Bottom
Hanging Wood Bottom
Hanging Ridge
New Coppice

20

Wessex Ridgeway
Ashcombe Bottom
Straight Knap
Malacombe Bottom
Settlement
Rotherley Bottom
Rotherley Wood
Hewetts Coppice
Glover's Coppice
Chase Woods
Great Shaftesbury Coppice
West Chase Farm
DEAN LANE
New Town

6

19

SP5
Tollard Plantation
Cuttice Bottom
LOWER N RD
UPPER N RD
CH
Rushmore Golf Club
Monks' Arundell Coppice
Shire Rack
Withywind Coppice
Snows Puddle Farm
Hunt Corner Farm
Hill Coppice

5

Phillips Cottage
Ashgrove Farm
Tollard Royal
Corner PH Farm
Sandroyd Sch
Tumulus
Rushmore Park
Tumuli
Settlement
Woodcutts Common
Tumulus
Scrubbity Barrows
Handley Common

18

B3081
Cranborne Chase
Tollard Park
King John's House
Tinkley Bottom
Rushmore Farm
LOWERS RD
Tumuli
Enclosure
Brookes Coppice
Earthwork
Brockwell Coppice
Burley Road Farm
Humbys Farm
Market Road Farm
DEAN LA DV
COMMON RD

4

Deanend
Pollards Wood
B3081
Woodcutts
CHASE CR

17

Larmer Tree Victoria Pleasure Garden
CLAPTA
Half Hide Down
Minchington Down
Hutchins Coppice
Manor Farm
Chapel Down Mid Farm
BRUSHY BUSH LANE

3

Tollard Green
Rookery Farm
Rookery Coppice
Half Hide Coppice
Manor Farm
SP5

16

Tollard Green Farm
COMMON DROVE
Farnham Woods
Farnham Farm
Earthwork
Jubilee Trail
Dean
Chapel Down Farm
Jubilee Trail

2

Bussey Stool Farm
Tollard Farnham
Hookswood Coppice
New Town
OAKLEY LANE
Dean Farm

15

Downend Coppice
Chettle Down
Hookswood House
Farnham
PO
PH
Minchington
Burts Farm
Gussage St Andrew
A354

1

BLOODY SHARD GATE
Chettle Chase Coppice
Chettle Down
Settlement
DT11
DUNSPIT LANE
Goldfields Farm
Glebe Farm
MILLER'S LA
Lower Farm
Chapel Farm
Tumulus

Main Down
Hatts Coppice

14

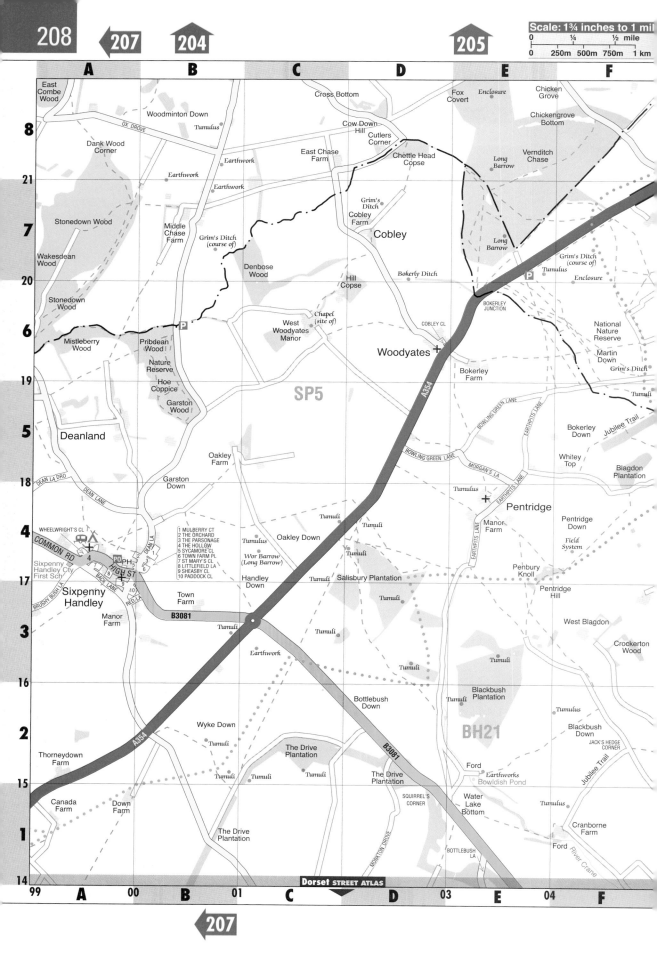

Scale: 1¾ inches to 1 mil
0 ¼ ½ mile
0 250m 500m 750m 1 km

East Combe Wood

Woodminton Down

Cross Bottom

Fox Covert

Enclosure

Chicken Grove

Chickengrove Bottom

OX DROVE

Tumulus

Cow Down Hill

Cutlers Corner

Dank Wood Corner

Earthwork

East Chase Farm

Chettle Head Copse

Long Barrow

Vernditch Chase

Earthwork

Earthwork

Grim's Ditch

Stonedown Wood

Middle Chase Farm

Grim's Ditch (course of)

Cobley Farm

Cobley

Long Barrow

Grim's Ditch (course of)

Wakesdean Wood

Denbose Wood

Hill Copse

Bokerly Ditch

Tumulus

Enclosure

Stonedown Wood

Chapel (site of)

West Woodyates Manor

COBLEY CL

National Nature Reserve

Mistleberry Wood

Pribdean Wood

Woodyates

BOKERLEY JUNCTION

Martin Down

Nature Reserve

Bokerley Farm

Grim's Ditch

Hoe Coppice

SP5

Bokerley Down

Jubilee Trail

Garston Wood

BOWLING GREEN LANE

Whitey Top

Blagdon Plantation

Deanland

Oakley Farm

EARTHPIT'S LANE

MORGAN'S LA

Tumulus

EARTHPIT'S LANE

Pentridge

DEAN LA DRO

Garston Down

Pentridge Down

DEAN LANE

Field System

WHEELWRIGHT'S CL

1 MULBERRY CT
2 THE ORCHARD
3 THE PARSONAGE
4 THE HOLLOW
5 SYCAMORE CL
6 TOWN FARM PL
7 ST MARY'S CL
8 LITTLEFIELD LA
9 SHEASBY CL
10 PADDOCK CL

Tumulus

Oakley Down

Tumuli

EARTHPIT'S LANE

Manor Farm

Pentridge Down

COMMON RD

Tumuli

Penbury Knoll

Sixpenny Handley Cty First Sch

PO PH

HIGH ST

BACK LANE

Wor Barrow (Long Barrow)

Handley Down

Tumuli

Salisbury Plantation

Pentridge Hill

Sixpenny Handley

Town Farm

BRUSKY BUSH LA

RED LA

B3081

Tumuli

Tumuli

Manor Farm

Tumuli

Earthwork

West Blagdon

Crockerton Wood

Tumuli

A354

Wyke Down

Tumuli

Bottlebush Down

Tumuli

Blackbush Plantation

BH21

Tumuli

Blackbush Down

Thorneydown Farm

Tumuli

The Drive Plantation

B3081

Tumuli

JACK'S HEDGE CORNER

Tumuli

Tumuli

The Drive Plantation

Ford

Earthworks

Jubilee Trail

Canada Farm

Down Farm

Water Lake Bottom

Bowldish Pond

Tumulus

Cranborne Farm

SQUIRREL'S CORNER

MONKTON DROVE

The Drive Plantation

BOTTLEBUSH LA

Ford

River Crane

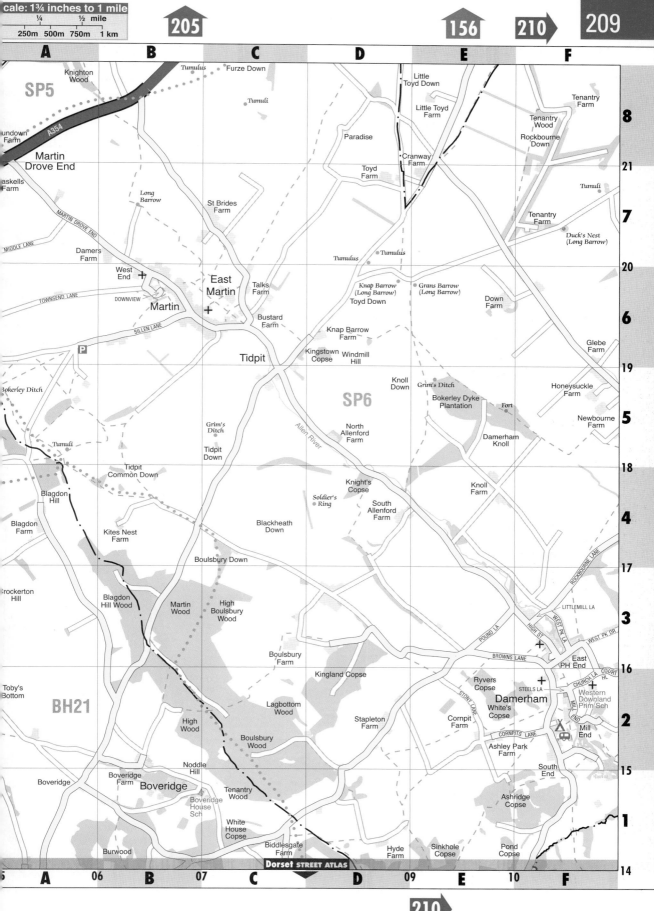

scale: 1¾ inches to 1 mile
¼   ½   mile
250m 500m 750m 1 km

A   B   C   D   E   F

SP5

Knighton Wood

Tumulus   Furze Down

Little Toyd Down

Little Toyd Farm

Tenantry Farm

Tenantry Wood

Rockbourne Down

Tumuli

oundown Farm

A354

Paradise

Cranway Farm

8

Martin Drove End

21

askells Farm

Toyd Farm

Tumuli

Tenantry Farm

7

MARTIN DROVE END

Long Barrow

St Brides Farm

MIDDLE LANE

Damers Farm

West End

DOWNVIEW

East Martin

Martin

TOWNSEND LANE

SILLEN LANE

Talks Farm

Tumulus   Tumulus

Knap Barrow (Long Barrow)

Grans Barrow (Long Barrow)

Duck's Nest (Long Barrow)

Down Farm

20

6

Bustard Farm

Toyd Down

Tidpit

Knap Barrow Farm

Kingstown Copse   Windmill Hill

Knoll Down

Grim's Ditch

Bokerley Dyke Plantation

Glebe Farm

Honeysuckle Farm

19

okerley Ditch

SP6

Fort

Newbourne Farm

5

Grim's Ditch

Tidpit Down

North Allenford Farm

Allen River

Damerham Knoll

Tumuli

Tidpit Common Down

Soldier's Ring

Knight's Copse

South Allenford Farm

Knoll Farm

18

Blagdon Hill

Blagdon Farm

Kites Nest Farm

Blackheath Down

4

Boulsbury Down

17

rockerton Hill

Blagdon Hill Wood

Martin Wood

High Boulsbury Wood

ROCKBOURNE LANE

LITTLEMILL LA

WEST PK LA

3

POUND LA

HIGH ST

WEST PK DR

Boulsbury Farm

Kingland Copse

BROWNS LANE

East PH End

16

Toby's Bottom

BH21

High Wood

Boulsbury Wood

Lagbottom Wood

Stapleton Farm

Ryvers Copse

STEELS LA

White's Copse

STONY LANE

Cornpit Farm

Western Downland Prim Sch

CHURCH LA

COURT HL

Damerham

CORNPITS LANE

MILL END

Mill End

2

Noddle Hill

South End

15

Boveridge

Boveridge Farm

Boveridge

Tenantry Wood

Boveridge House Sch

White House Copse

Ashley Park Farm

Ashridge Copse

1

Burwood

Biddlesgate Farm

Hyde Farm

Sinkhole Copse

Pond Copse

14

Dorset STREET ATLAS

A   06   B   07   C   D   09   E   10   F

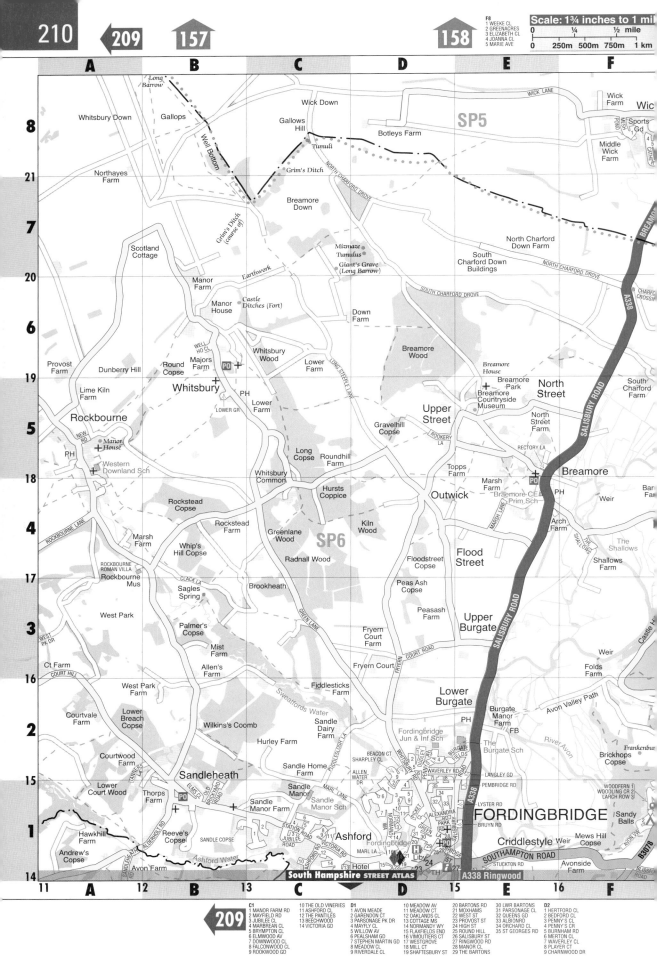

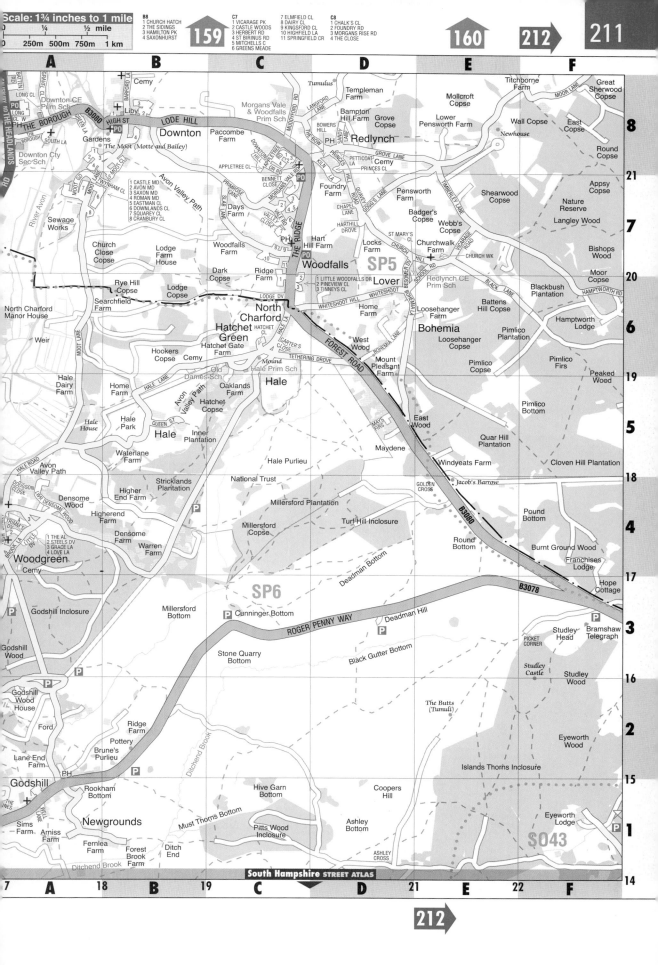

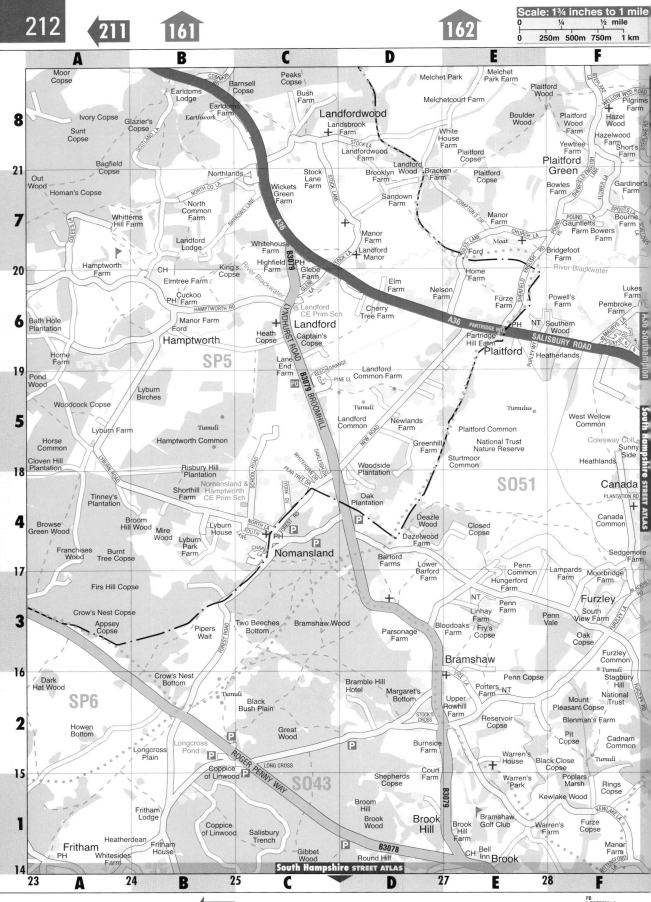

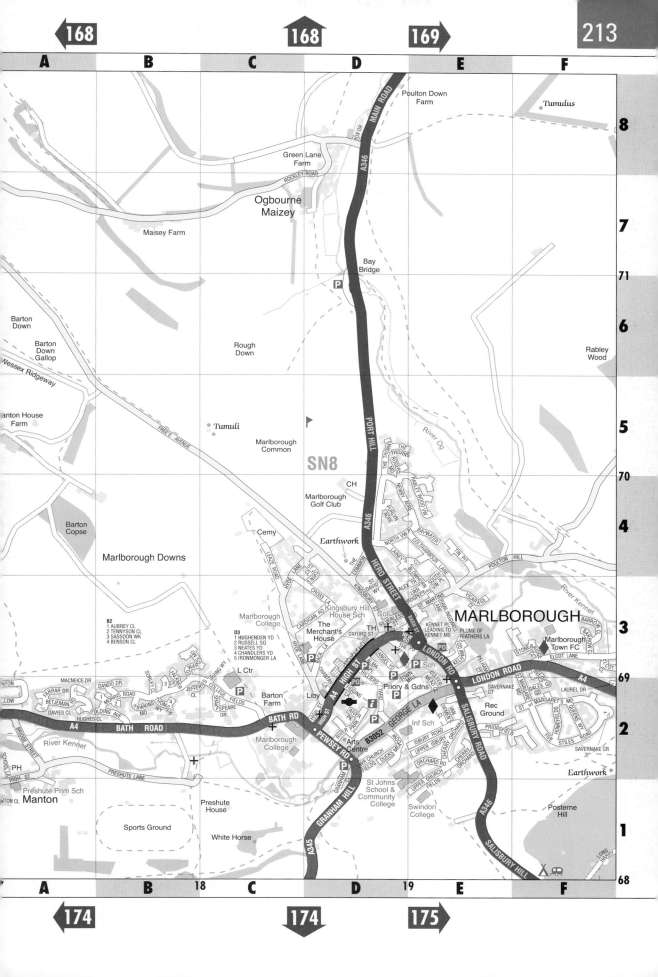

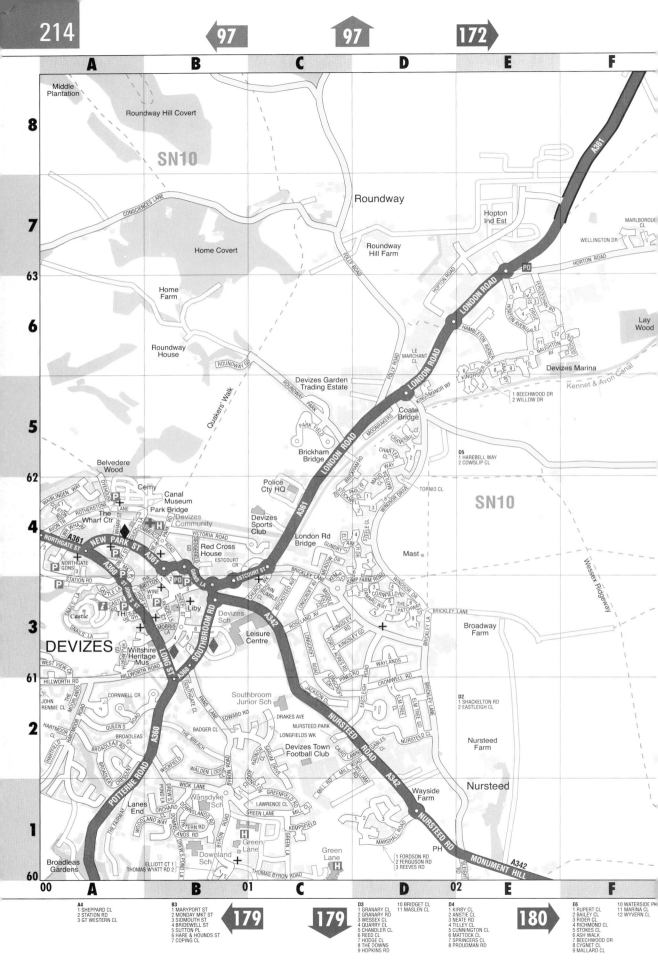

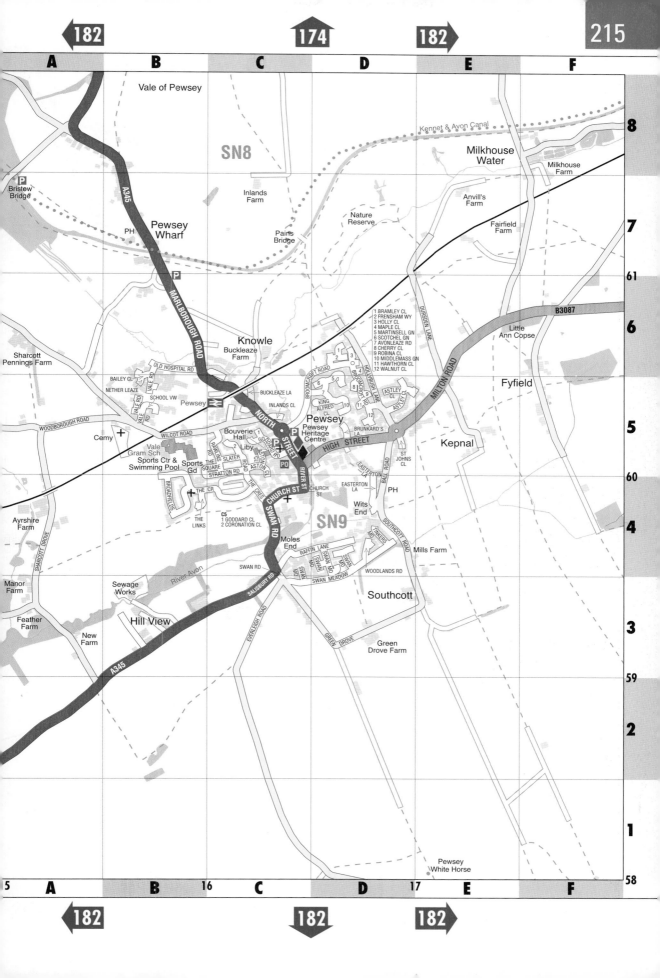

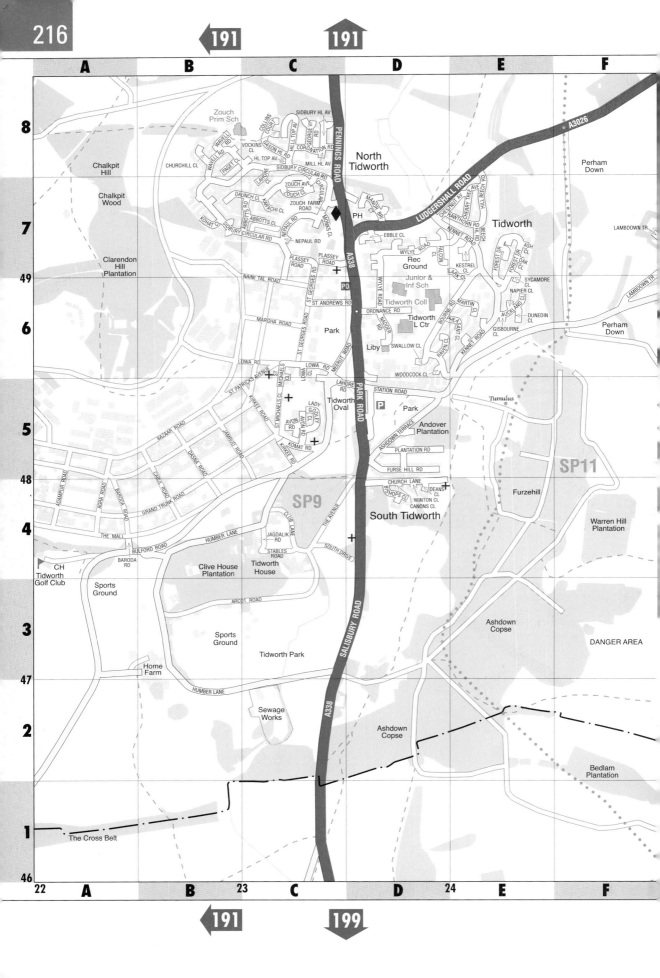

SP4

Amesbury

Bulford

Ratfyn

B3
1 SCHOOL LA
2 SMITHFIELD ST
3 CHAPLINS PL
4 NURSERY CL
5 JOHN GAY RD
6 HAYWAIN
7 LYNCHFIELD RD

C2
1 MILLGREEN RD
2 BEAULIEU RD
3 PAINS WY
4 FLIT CROFT
5 HARVARD WY
6 TUCKER CL
7 WITTENHAM VW
8 DIDDLEDOWN RD

C3
1 FINNIS RD
2 CHERRY TREE WY
3 GENEVILLE RI
4 LAWRENCE CL
5 RINGWOOD AV

D2
1 LIGHTNING RD
2 HAVARD WY
3 MCKIE RD
4 LEONARD CHESHIRE CL
5 BEYER RD
6 BAWDSEY RD

D3
1 BEAUCHAMP DR
2 CARLTON CL
3 WESTLAND CL
4 FOSTERS BUSHES
5 HURLEY CL
6 JAVELIN CL
7 MOYNE GD
8 LUMLEY WK
9 TEMPEST RD
10 CANTERBURY CL

E3
1 VIRGINIA CL
2 VERNON CL
3 CHESTERFIELD CL
4 PURVIS CL
5 CONISTON CL
6 NICOLSON CL
7 BURWOOD CL
8 HEYFORD CL
9 BARNES WALLIS CL
10 THURLOW CL

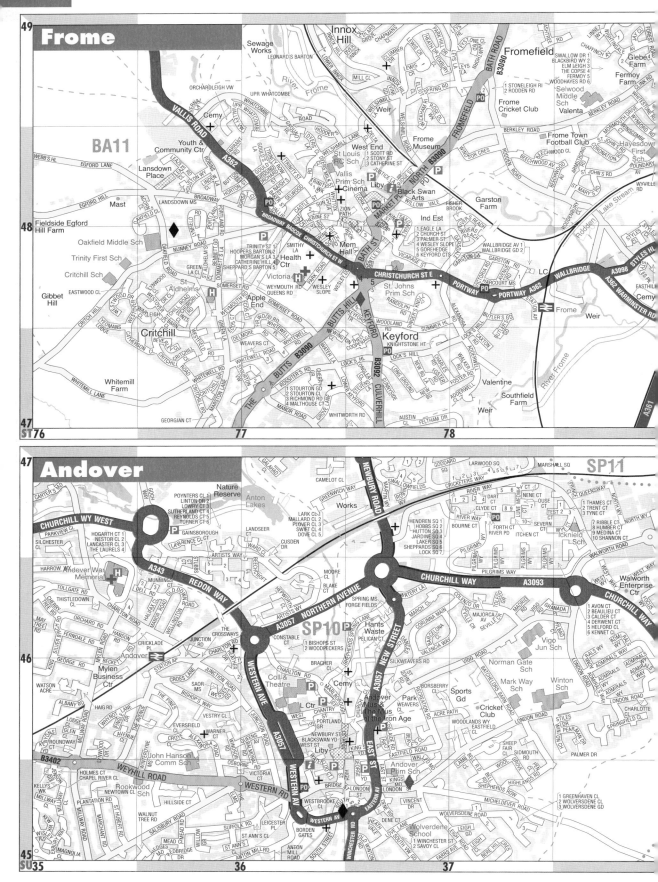

Frome

BA11

Andover

SP11

SP10

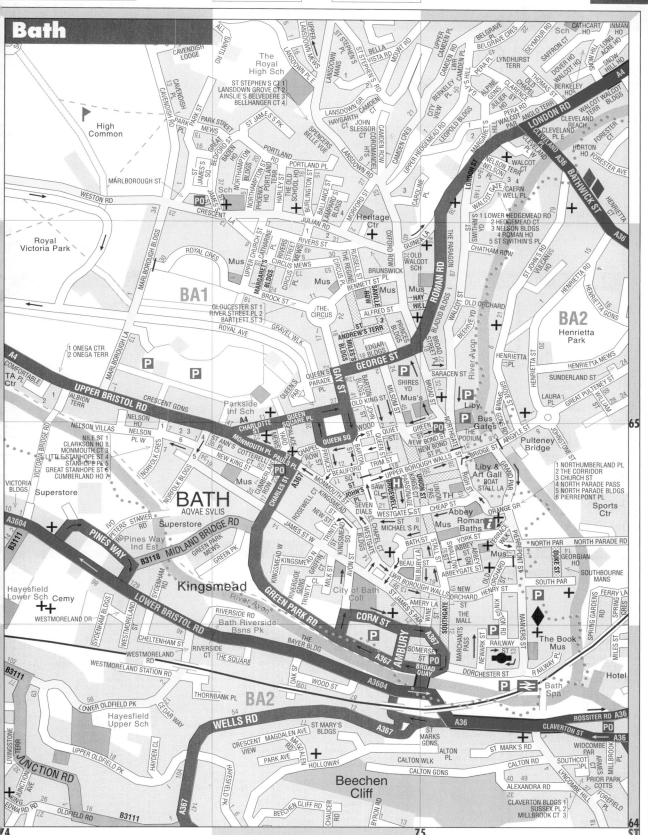

Index

Church Rd **6** Beckenham BR2.........**53** C6

Place name	**Location number**	**Locality, town or village**	**Postcode district**	**Page and grid square**
May be abbreviated on the map	Present when a number indicates the place's position in a crowded area of mapping	Shown when more than one place has the same name	District for the indexed place	Page number and grid reference for the standard mapping

Public and commercial buildings are highlighted in magenta   **Places of interest** are highlighted in blue with a star★

Abbreviations used in the index

Acad	**Academy**	Comm	**Common**	Gd	**Ground**	L	**Leisure**	Prom	**Promenade**
App	**Approach**	Cott	**Cottage**	Gdn	**Garden**	La	**Lane**	Rd	**Road**
Arc	**Arcade**	Cres	**Crescent**	Gn	**Green**	Liby	**Library**	Recn	**Recreation**
Ave	**Avenue**	Cswy	**Causeway**	Gr	**Grove**	Mdw	**Meadow**	Ret	**Retail**
Bglw	**Bungalow**	Ct	**Court**	H	**Hall**	Meml	**Memorial**	Sh	**Shopping**
Bldg	**Building**	Ctr	**Centre**	Ho	**House**	Mkt	**Market**	Sq	**Square**
Bsns, Bus	**Business**	Ctry	**Country**	Hospl	**Hospital**	Mus	**Museum**	St	**Street**
Bvd	**Boulevard**	Cty	**County**	HQ	**Headquarters**	Orch	**Orchard**	Sta	**Station**
Cath	**Cathedral**	Dr	**Drive**	Hts	**Heights**	Pal	**Palace**	Terr	**Terrace**
Cir	**Circus**	Dro	**Drove**	Ind	**Industrial**	Par	**Parade**	TH	**Town Hall**
Cl	**Close**	Ed	**Education**	Inst	**Institute**	Pas	**Passage**	Univ	**University**
Cnr	**Corner**	Emb	**Embankment**	Int	**International**	Pk	**Park**	Wk, Wlk	**Walk**
Coll	**College**	Est	**Estate**	Intc	**Interchange**	Pl	**Place**	Wr	**Water**
Com	**Community**	Ex	**Exhibition**	Junc	**Junction**	Prec	**Precinct**	Yd	**Yard**

Index of localities, towns and villages

A

Ablington 190 B1
Acton Turville 52 F6
Alcester 202 B1
Alcombe 82 F8
Aldbourne 170 A6
Alderbury 153 C3
Alderton 39 F2
All Cannings 180 E8
Allington 69 E3
Allington 172 E2
Allington 199 A2
Allington Bar 69 F2
Alton 190 B1
Alton Barnes 173 C1
Alton Priors 173 D1
Alvediston 204 B2
Amesbury 217 C4
Ansty 203 F5
Ansty Coombe 203 F5
Appleshaw 192 E3
Ashbury 164 A7
Ashford 210 C1
Ashley 3 A2
Ashley 83 A6
Ashmore 206 D5
Ashton Common 102 F1
Ashton Keynes 6 F1
Atworth 92 F8
Aughton 183 D3
Avebury 173 C8
Avebury Trusloe 173 B8

Avington 177 F7
Avon 71 F6
Avoncliff 99 F4
Axford 169 D1

B

Badbury 65 F5
Badbury Wick 65 D8
Badminton 38 F2
Bagshot 176 F4
Ballard's Ash 47 D5
Bapton 195 D1
Barford St Martin 143 A3
Barkers Hill 203 A4
Barrow 136 C5
Barrow Street 139 F2
Batheaston 82 A3
Bathford 82 B2
Baverstock 142 B4
Baydon 170 C8
Beanacre 94 A8
Beckhampton 173 B7
Beechingstoke 181 A6
Bemerton 145 C2
Bemerton Heath 145 C4
Berkley 111 A7
Berkley Down 110 C5
Berryfield 93 F1
Berwick Bassett 167 B4
Berwick St James 196 E2
Berwick St John 203 E1

Berwick St Leonard ...200 C4
Bewley Common 86 E5
Biddestone 76 F8
Birdbush 203 B1
Bishopdown 146 C4
Bishops Cannings 172 B3
Bishopstone 163 E6
Bishopstone 205 F4
Bishopstrow 117 E4
Bittles Green 202 B4
Blackland 89 F6
Bleet 102 F2
Blue Vein 83 D3
Blunsdon St Andrew ...34 E8
Bodenham 152 F1
Bohemia 211 E6
Boreham 117 C5
Boscombe 199 A1
Bottlesford 181 D6
Bourton 137 E2
Bourton 172 C3
Boveridge 209 B1
Bowden Hill 87 B4
Bowerchalke 205 A2
Bowerhill 94 D1
Bowldown 70 E8
Box 83 D6
Box Hill 83 F7
Boyton 194 E2
Bradenstoke 59 C3
Bradford Leigh 91 F1
Bradford-on-Avon 100 E6
Bramshaw 212 E3
Bratton 186 B7

Breamore 210 F5
Bremhill 80 E7
Brigmerston 198 C8
Brinkworth 45 E5
Britford 152 E5
Brixton Deverill 120 E2
Broad Blunsdon 21 C2
Broad Chalke 205 B4
Broad Hinton 167 C7
Broad Street 181 C6
Broad Town 167 A8
Broad's Green 88 F3
Broadbush 21 D1
Brokenborough 27 D7
Brokerswood 107 F5
Bromham 96 A7
Brook 212 E1
Brook Hill 212 D1
Brook Waters 203 B2
Broomfield 55 A1
Broughton Gifford 93 C4
Brunton 183 E3
Bugley 116 C6
Bulbridge 144 B1
Bulford 217 E8
Bulford Camp 198 F6
Bulkington 178 E5
Bullenhill 106 E8
Bullock's Horn 15 E1
Burbage 183 D8
Burcombe 143 E2
Burton 53 B4
Burton 139 D5
Buscot Wick 12 D8

Bushton 166 E8
Buttermere 185 B8

C

Cadley 175 A5
Calcutt 20 A7
Callow Hill 46 D6
Calne 81 B2
Calne Marsh 81 C4
Calstone Wellington ..172 A7
Canada 212 F4
Cann Common 206 B8
Castle Combe 68 A7
Castle Eaton 10 B4
Catcomb 73 D6
Cerney Wick 7 F5
Chalford 113 A8
Chapel Barton 115 D6
Chapel Knapp 85 D5
Chapel Plaister 84 A5
Chapmanslade 111 C4
Charlcutt 72 F4
Charlton 29 A6
Charlton 181 D3
Charlton 193 C2
Charlton 203 A1
Charlton Heath 29 D6
Charlton Musgrove ...136 B4
Charlton-All-Saints ..159 A4
Charnage 139 E4
Chedglow 14 C7

Chelworth 4 C1
Chelworth Lower Green 19 A5
Chelworth Upper Green 19 A6
Cherhill 166 B1
Chicklade 200 A5
Chicksgrove 204 B8
Chilmark 201 B3
Chilton Foliat 170 F1
Chippenham 78 E7
Chirton 180 F4
Chisbury 176 B5
Chiseldon 65 D3
Chitterne 195 C7
Chittoe 87 E2
Cholderton 199 C5
Christian Malford 58 B2
Churchfields 145 D1
Chute Cadley 192 F8
Chute Standen 192 F8
Clanville 56 E4
Clanville 193 A4
Clatford 174 B7
Claverton 90 B5
Clearwood 111 E8
Clench 174 E1
Clench Common 174 D4
Clevancy 166 C6
Cleverton 44 D8
Cloatley 15 E2
Cloatley End 16 B1
Clyffe Pypard 166 F8
Coate 51 C2
Coate 180 C8
Cobley 208 D7
Codford St Mary 195 B2
Codford St Peter 195 A3
Cold Harbour 102 F2
Cold Harbour 116 F8
Colerne 75 B3
Collingbourne Ducis 191 E8
Collingbourne Kingston 183 D2
Combe 185 F8
Common Platt 33 F2
Compton 189 F7
Compton Abbas 206 A5
Compton Bassett 166 B3
Compton Chamberlayne 205 A8
Conkwell 90 D1
Conock 180 E4
Coombe 190 B5
Coombe 202 F1
Coombe Bissett 150 F1
Coped Hall 47 F4
Corsham 85 A8
Corsley 111 D2
Corsley Heath 115 B8
Corston 42 E5
Corton 194 D3
Cotmarsh 62 B4
Cotswold Community 6 D4
Coulston 178 E1
Covingham 51 D7
Cowesfield Green 161 F4
Cricklade 19 E7
Criddlestyle 210 E1
Crockerton 116 E1
Crockerton Green 116 F2
Crofton 176 A1
Crooked Soley 170 F3
Cross Keys 77 A3
Croucheston 205 F4
Crudwell 14 E6
Cuckold's Green 179 C4
Cuckoo's Corner 180 B4
Cuckoo's Knob 174 F1
Culkerton 3 A5
Culverslade 66 A2

D
Damerham 209 F2
Dauntsey 45 B1
Dauntsey Lock 59 B5
Dean 207 E2
Deanend 207 E4
Deanland 208 A5
Deptford 195 E1
Derry Fields 17 F8
Derry Hill 79 F2
Dertfords 115 B7
Devizes 214 A3
Didmarton 24 C3
Dilton Marsh 112 B8
Dinton 201 F2
Ditchampton 144 C4
Ditteridge 83 B8
Dogridge 32 F3
Donhead St Andrew 203 B3
Donhead St Mary 203 A3
Dorcan 51 D5
Down Ampney 8 D7
Downton 211 B8
Draycot Cerne 56 F1

Draycot Fitz Payne 174 A2
Draycot Foliat 168 D8
Drynham 105 E5
Dunfield 10 A8
Dunge 106 E1
Dunkirk 179 D8
Durley 175 D3
Durnford 198 B7
Dursley 105 E1

E
East Anton 193 F2
East Chisenbury 190 A7
East Compton 206 A5
East Everleigh 191 A8
East Garston 171 E7
East Gomeldon 133 E4
East Grafton 183 F7
East Grimstead 154 F4
East Hatch 203 C7
East Kennett 173 E6
East Knoyle 141 C2
East Martin 209 C6
East Melbury 206 B7
East Town 106 E4
East Tytherton 72 B2
East Winterslow 149 C8
East Woodlands 114 B5
Eastbury 171 C8
Eastcott 180 A2
Eastcourt 15 D6
Easterton 180 A2
Easterton Sands 179 F2
Eastleaze 49 B6
Easton 77 D2
Easton Grey 26 C3
Easton Royal 183 A7
Easton Town 25 D1
Eastrip 75 D4
Ebbesbourne Wake 204 C3
Eddington 177 C8
Eden Vale 108 E3
Edington 186 C8
Elcombe 63 E5
Eldene 51 C5
Elliots Green 114 D8
Elm Cross 167 D7
Elm Hill 202 A5
Elston 196 E7
Enford 189 F6
Enham Alamein 193 E4
Enmore Green 202 B2
Erlestoke 187 A8
Etchilhampton 180 C7
Even Swindon 49 E6
Everleigh 191 A8
Ewen 5 C8

F
Faberstown 192 B6
Fairford 1 E7
Fairwood 108 B4
Farleigh Hungerford 103 E7
Farleigh Wick 90 F5
Farley 154 D8
Farnham 207 C2
Ferne 203 D1
Fiddington Sands 179 F1
Fifield 190 A5
Fifield Bavant 204 F4
Figheldean 190 B2
Filands 28 A6
Firsdown 148 C8
Fisherton de la Mere 195 D1
Fittleton 190 A4
Flaxlands 47 D6
Flood Street 210 E4
Fonthill Bishop 200 D3
Fonthill Gifford 200 B2
Ford 68 A2
Ford 146 D7
Fordingbridge 210 E1
Forest Hill 175 B7
Forewoods Common 101 C7
Fosbury 185 A5
Foscote 54 E3
Fovant 204 E8
Foxcotte 193 C2
Foxham 72 D7
Foxley 41 F8
Fresh Brook 49 A4
Freshford 99 B5
Fritham 212 A1
Frogmore 109 A4
Frome 110 A5
Fromefield 110 A6
Froxfield 176 D7
Fugglestone St Peter 144 F4
Furzley 212 F3
Fyfield 192 D1
Fyfield 215 E5

G
Gare Hill 118 A5
Garsdon 29 B4
Gasper 137 C7
Gastard 85 D6
Giddeahall 68 D2
Goatacre 73 F7
Godshill 211 A1
Gomeldon 133 D4
Gorse Hill 35 D1
Grange Park 48 F5
Great Ashley 91 A1
Great Bedwyn 176 B3
Great Chalfield 92 E3
Great Cheverell 179 C1
Great Durnford 197 F1
Great Hinton 178 A6
Great Somerford 44 B2
Great Wishford 129 F3
Greatfield 47 F8
Green Hill 32 D1
Greenmeadow 35 B4
Greenwich 200 C3
Grittenham 46 C2
Grittleton 54 C5
Gussage St Andrew 207 E1

H
Hackthorn 198 A8
Hailstone Hill 8 A1
Halcombe 27 E3
Hale 211 C5
Half Way Firs 76 C1
Halfway 113 A4
Ham 177 B2
Ham Green 101 C8
Hampshire Gate 185 A1
Hampton 22 D5
Hampton Hill 22 E5
Hamptworth 212 B6
Hanging Langford 128 C7
Hankerton 15 C2
Hannington 22 B7
Hannington Wick 11 A4
Hardway 122 A6
Haresfield 23 B8
Harnham 151 E6
Hatchet Green 211 C6
Hatherden 193 C5
Hawkeridge 108 E8
Haxton 190 B4
Haydon Wick 34 E3
Hayes Knoll 19 E2
Heddington 89 B1
Heddington Wick 88 E2
Henley 83 C4
Henley 185 A6
Heytesbury 194 C5
Heywood 109 A8
Higher Pertwood 127 E4
Highway 166 B5
Highworth 23 B5
Hilcott 181 D5
Hill Corner 110 E7
Hill Deverill 120 F5
Hill View 215 B3
Hilmarton 166 A6
Hilperton 102 A3
Hilperton Marsh 101 F4
Hindon 200 B3
Hinton Charterhouse 98 E1
Hinton Parva 163 D6
Hisomley 112 C7
Hodson 65 A5
Hoggington 104 D4
Holloway 141 A4
Holt 92 E1
Holwell 139 B5
Homington 151 D1
Hook 47 F6
Hook Street 48 B6
Horningsham 119 A7
Horpit 163 B7
Horton 172 C2
Hudswell 84 C8
Huish 174 A2
Hullavington 41 E1
Hungerford 177 A6
Hungerford Newtown 171 D2
Huntenhull Green 111 C3
Hurdcott 146 F8
Hyde 35 D7

I
Ibthorpe 193 F8
Idmiston 133 F8
Idstone 163 F7
Imber 187 A3
Inglesham 2 B1

Inkpen 177 E3
Ireland 105 B2
Ivy Cross 202 D2

K
Keevil 178 D5
Kellaways 71 E4
Kemble 4 E4
Kemble Wick 4 E4
Kempsford 10 E6
Kepnal 215 E5
Kilmington 123 E5
Kilmington Common 123 D4
Kimpton 192 C1
Kinghay 202 F8
Kingsdown 35 F5
Kingsdown 82 F3
Kingshill 50 B5
Kingston Deverill 126 B6
Kingstone Winslow 164 A8
Kington Langley 70 E7
Kington St Michael 70 A8
Knapp 205 A4
Knapp Hill 202 A5
Knighton 170 D2
Knights Enham 193 E3
Knook 194 D4
Knowle 215 C6

L
Lacock 86 D5
Lake 197 F2
Lambourn 165 B2
Lambourn Woodlands 171 A7
Landford 212 C6
Landfordwood 212 D8
Lane End 115 A8
Langley Burrell 71 A3
Larkhill 197 F6
Latton 8 C4
Laverstock 146 E2
Lavington Sands 179 E2
Lawn 50 F3
Lea 28 F1
Leafield 84 E7
Lechlade-on-Thames 2 D4
Leigh 18 C5
Leigh Delamere 55 C3
Letcombe Bassett 165 F8
Leverton 171 B1
Liddington 163 B4
Liden 51 D3
Limpers Hill 139 D4
Limpley Stoke 99 A6
Linkenholt 185 E5
Little Ashley 91 A2
Little Badminton 38 E5
Little Bedwyn 176 B5
Little Chalfield 92 C3
Little Cheverell 187 D8
Little Durnford 131 D1
Little Faringdon 2 F8
Little Horton 172 C1
Little Langford 129 A6
Little London 166 E2
Little Marsh 102 F1
Little Salisbury 182 E7
Little Somerford 44 B5
Littlecott 166 A7
Littlecott 190 A6
Littledown 185 D4
Littleton 178 B7
Littleton Drew 53 E5
Littleton Panell 179 D1
Littleworth 182 E8
Lockeridge 174 A6
Long Cross 138 B5
Long Dean 68 C4
Long Newnton 13 C5
Longbridge Deverill 120 F6
Longfield 105 B2
Longhedge 115 D5
Longstreet 190 A6
Lover 211 D6
Lower Blunsdon 21 B3
Lower Burgate 210 D2
Lower Chicksgrove 201 B1
Lower Chute 192 F8
Lower Everleigh 182 E1
Lower Green 177 D3
Lower Moor 17 A4
Lower Rudge 107 D4
Lower Seagry 57 F7
Lower Stanton St Quintin 56 D6
Lower Stratton 36 B2
Lower Studley 105 E6
Lower Wanborough 163 B6
Lower Woodford 131 C3
Lower Wraxall 91 E5

Lower Zeals 138 D5
Luckington 39 E4
Ludgershall 192 A5
Ludwell 203 A1
Lydiard Green 48 B8
Lydiard Millicent 33 D1
Lydiard Plain 32 B1
Lydiard Tregoze 48 E6
Lye Green 100 A4
Lye's Green 111 B1
Lyneham 60 B2

M
Maddington 196 E7
Maiden Bradley 118 F2
Malmesbury 28 B3
Manningford Abbots 182 A5
Manningford Bohune 181 F4
Manningford Bruce 181 F5
Manton 213 A1
Marden 181 A4
Market Lavington 179 E1
Marlborough 213 F3
Marr Green 183 D7
Marshfield 74 A8
Marston 179 A3
Marston Hill 1 C4
Marston Meysey 9 C7
Marten 184 C7
Martin 209 B6
Martin Drove End 209 A8
Martinslade 178 E8
Melbury Abbas 206 B7
Melksham 94 A5
Melksham Forest 94 D6
Mere 139 B5
Meysey Hampton 1 A5
Middle Winterslow 149 B7
Middle Woodford 131 B4
Middlehill 83 A6
Middlewick 76 D3
Midford 98 C6
Milbourne 28 D4
Mildenhall 175 A8
Mile Elm 89 A7
Mile End 165 A3
Milford 152 E8
Milkhouse Water 215 E8
Milston 198 B8
Milton 141 B3
Milton Lilbourne 182 F7
Minchington 207 D1
Minety 17 B2
Minety Common 31 C8
Misselfore 204 F1
Monk's Park 85 A6
Monkton Combe 98 E8
Monkton Deverill 126 D2
Monkton Farleigh 90 F7
Moor Green 84 D6
Moredon 34 E3
Motcombe 202 A4
Mount Sorrel 205 B3
Mountain Bower 66 F4
Murcott 14 F4

N
Neston 84 E6
Netheravon 190 A3
Netherhampton 151 A8
Netherton 185 F4
Nettleton 53 C1
Nettleton Green 53 B1
Nettleton Shrub 67 C7
Netton 131 E6
New Town 50 D6
New Town 170 C2
New Town 173 D3
New Town 207 C2
New Town 207 F6
Newbury 119 C8
Newgrounds 211 B1
Newton 161 B2
Newton Tony 199 B3
Newtown 176 E2
Newtown 203 B7
Nine Elms 49 A8
Nomansland 212 C4
Norleaze 108 F8
Normanton 197 F3
Norrington Common 93 C6
North Bradley 105 D4
North Brewham 122 A6
North Charford 211 C6
North End 6 E2
North Newnton 181 A4
North Street 210 E5
North Tidworth 216 D8
North Wraxall 67 B3
North Wroughton 64 A8

Northbrook 179 E1
Northend 82 A5
Norton 41 D5
Norton Bavant 194 A6
Notton 86 B8
Nunton 152 D1
Nursteed 214 E1
Nutbane 193 A4
Nythe 51 C7

O

Oaksey 15 F7
Oare 174 B2
Odstock 152 A1
Ogbourne Maizey 213 C7
Ogbourne St Andrew . .168 F3
Ogbourne St George . .169 A5
Okus 50 A4
Old Town 50 D3
Oldbury on the Hill . . .24 B5
Orcheston 196 D8
Outmarsh 102 F7
Outwick 210 D4
Overtown 64 D4
Oxenwood 184 E6

P

Park 51 A5
Park Corner 99 A4
Patney 180 F5
Paxcroft 102 C3
Pear Ash 137 C4
Peckingell 71 B2
Penhill 35 C5
Penknap 112 E8
Penleigh 108 D2
Penselwood 137 B4
Penton Corner 193 A1
Penton Grafton 193 A2
Penton Mewsey 193 B2
Pentridge 208 E4
Perham Down 191 F4
Perry Green 29 B7
Petersfinger 152 E7
Petty France 38 B8
Pewsey 215 D5
Pewsey Wharf 215 B7
Pickwick 76 E2
Pinckney Green 90 E5
Pinehurst 35 D3
Pinkney 25 E2
Pitton 148 C3
Plaitford 212 E6
Plaitford Green 212 F8
Poole Keynes 5 C4
Portash 201 B2
Porton 133 D6
Potterne 179 D5
Potterne Wick 179 E4
Poulshot 179 B6
Preston 60 D1
Preston 170 B4
Purlpit 93 A8
Purton 33 B4
Purton
   Common 33 A5
Purton Stoke 19 C1

Q

Queen Oak 138 A3
Queen Street 31 B3
Quemerford 89 D8
Quidhampton 145 A2

R

Ragged Appleshaw 192 F3
Ram Alley 175 B2
Ramsbury 170 A2
Ratford 80 E5
Ratfyn 217 C5
Redenham 192 D4
Redlands 22 F3
Redlynch 211 D8
Redstocks 95 A2
Restrop 33 A2
Reybridge 86 D7
Ridge 200 F2
Rivar 184 F8
Rockbourne 210 A5
Rockley 168 C2
Rodbourne 35 A1
Rodbourne 43 A3
Rodbourne Bottom 43 A2
Rodbourne Cheney 35 B2
Rode Hill 103 F1
Rodmarton 3 C8
Rollestone 196 F6
Rollestone Camp 197 B7
Rood Ashton 106 D4
Rook Street 139 A4
Roughmoor 34 B1
Roundway 214 D7
Rowde 96 D2
Rudge 107 D5
Rudloe 76 B1
Rushall 181 E2

S

St Edith's 96 D5
St James 202 C1
St Katharines 175 F4
Salisbury 152 C7
Salterton 131 D4
Sambourne 116 F5
Sandleheath 210 B2
Sandy Lane 88 B4
Sanham Green 177 B5
Sawyers Hill 17 A2
Sedgehill 202 C7
Seend 178 E7
Seend Cleeve 178 C7
Sells Green 95 E1
Sem Hill 202 E5
Semington 102 E5
Semley 202 F5
Serrington 129 D7
Sevenhampton 23 B2
Sevington 55 A2
Shaftesbury 202 A1
Shalbourne 176 F2
Sharcott 182 A6
Sharpstone 99 A4
Shaw 49 B7
Shaw 93 D7
Sheepdrove 165 B2
Shefford Woodlands . . .171 F4
Sherrington 194 F1
Sherston 25 C1
Shipton Bellinger 199 D8
Shipton Moyne 26 E8
Shorncote 6 A6
Shrewton 196 E6
Sixpenny Handley 208 A3
Slaughterford 76 A8
Sodom 59 C7
Somerford Keynes 5 F3
Sopworth 24 D1
South Brewham 122 A4
South Cerney 7 A6
South Marston 36 F5
South Marston Park . . .36 D7

South Newton 130 B2
South Tidworth 216 D4
South Wraxall 91 D6
Southbrook 139 B4
Southcott 215 D3
Southend 168 F4
Southwick 104 F3
Spirthill 73 B4
Standerwick 107 B2
Stanley 80 A6
Stanton Fitzwarren 22 B1
Stanton St Bernard . . .173 A1
Stanton St Quintin 56 B4
Stapleford 129 E7
Startley 43 D1
Staverton 101 C6
Steeple Ashton 178 B3
Steeple Langford 128 D8
Stert 180 B6
Stibb Green 175 D1
Stitchcombe 175 D8
Stockley 89 C4
Stockton 195 B1
Stoford 130 A3
Stoke Farthing 205 D4
Stonebridge 110 C7
Stormore 112 A8
Stourton 123 F1
Stourton 123 F1
Straight Soley 171 A3
Strangways 198 A6
Stratford sub Castle . . .145 F5
Stratford Tony 150 C2
Stratton St Margaret . . .36 A3
Studley 80 B3
Studley Green 104 F7
Sturford 115 E6
Sunton 183 E1
Sutton Benger 57 C2
Sutton Mandeville 204 C8
Sutton Row 204 B7
Sutton Veny 117 F1
Swallett Gate 59 A6
Swallowcliffe 204 A6
Swanborough 22 C4
Swindon 50 E4

T

Tangley 193 A7
Tanis 96 F2
Teffont Evias 201 C2
Teffont Magna 201 C3
Tellisford 103 E4
Temple 115 C6
The Causeway 139 C4
The Common 46 B7
The Common 93 B5
The Common 149 C6
The Fox 33 F3
The Gibb 53 F3
The Green 141 A3
The Ham 108 E5
The Linleys 85 B6
The Pitts 205 F5
The Ridge 85 B5
The Shoe 66 F1
The Spa 94 C2
The Stocks 178 C7
The Strand 178 B6
Theobald's Green 172 A8
Thickwood 75 D6
Thingley 77 F1
Thornend 58 C1
Thornhill 61 F1
Tidcombe 184 C5
Tidpit 209 C6
Tidworth 216 E7
Tilshead 188 B3
Tisbury 203 D8
Tockenham 60 E3

Tockenham Wick 60 D7
Tollard Farnham 207 B2
Tollard Royal 207 B4
Toothill 49 C4
Townsend 179 A6
Townsend 180 C3
Trowbridge 101 E3
Trowle Common 100 F2
Tucking Mill 98 D8
Tuckingmill 203 D8
Turleigh 99 F6
Tytherington 194 B4
Tytherton Lucas 71 D1

U

Uffcott 167 E8
Ugford 144 A3
Underhill 140 F2
Upavon 181 F2
Upper Burgate 210 E3
Upper Castle Combe . . .68 B8
Upper Chicksgrove 201 A1
Upper Chute 192 D8
Upper Enham 193 F4
Upper Green 177 E2
Upper Inglesham 12 B5
Upper Lambourn 164 F3
Upper Minety 16 D3
Upper Pickwick 76 C3
Upper Seagry 57 D6
Upper Stratton 35 E4
Upper Street 210 D5
Upper Studley 105 A5
Upper Town 58 D4
Upper Up 6 E6
Upper Upham 169 C8
Upper Woodford 131 C2
Upper Wraxall 66 E2
Upton 141 A5
Upton 185 D2
Upton Lovell 194 E3
Upton Scudamore 112 E5
Urchfont 180 C4

V

Vastern 60 F8
Vernham Bank 185 B3
Vernham Dean 185 C3
Vernham Row 185 B4
Vernham Street 185 D4

W

Wadswick 84 B4
Walcot East 50 F6
Walcot West 50 E5
Wanborough 163 A5
Wardour 203 D6
Warleigh 90 D5
Warminster 116 E7
Warminster Common . .116 E5
Waterhay 18 C7
Wedhampton 180 E4
Well Bottom 206 E3
West Amesbury 198 A4
West Ashton 106 B3
West Chisenbury 189 F7
West Crudwell 14 D7
West Dean 155 F3
West Grafton 183 E7
West Grimstead 154 C2
West Hatch 203 C7
West Kennett 173 D7
West Kington 66 F7

West Kington Wick 67 B6
West Knoyle 140 E6
West Lavington 187 E8
West Overton 173 F6
West Stowell 173 F1
West Winterslow 148 F5
West Yatton 68 D3
Westbrook 95 E8
Westbury 109 B2
Westbury Leigh 108 C5
Westlea 49 D5
Westonbirt 25 D3
Westrop 77 C1
Westwells 84 C6
Westwood 99 C6
Westwood 145 B5
Wexcombe 184 B6
Weyhill 192 F1
Whaddon 102 C7
Whaddon 153 E1
Whitbourne Springs . . .115 E5
White Cross 137 E5
White Hill 139 C2
Whiteparish 161 D4
Whitepits 126 A7
Whitley 85 C1
Whitsbury 210 B5
Whittonditch 170 D1
Wick 210 F8
Widbrook 100 E4
Widham 33 C5
Wilcot 182 A7
Wildhern 193 D5
Willesley 25 C6
Wilsford 181 B4
Wilsford 197 F2
Wilton 144 C3
Wilton 184 A8
Windmills 193 E3
Wingfield 104 C6
Winsley 99 E7
Winterbourne Bassett . .167 B5
Winterbourne Dauntsey 133 B2
Winterbourne Earls . . .133 A3
Winterbourne Gunner . .133 D3
Winterbourne Monkton 167 B3
Winterbourne Stoke . . .196 F4
Wolverton 138 B4
Woodborough 181 D6
Woodcock 117 C6
Woodcutts 207 D4
Woodfalls 211 D7
Woodgreen 211 A4
Woodhouse 193 F3
Woodlands St Mary . . .171 E5
Woodminton 204 E1
Woodsend 169 C8
Woodshaw 48 A2
Woodyates 208 C3
Woolley 100 E7
Woolley Green 100 C5
Wootton Bassett 47 C2
Wootton Rivers 174 F2
Worton 179 B5
Wroughton 64 A5
Wylye 201 F1

Y

Yarnbrook 105 F3
Yatesbury 166 E2
Yatton Keynell 68 E6

Z

Zeals 137 F4

A

Abberd La SN11 ....81 D3
Abberd Way SN11 ......81 C3
Abbess Cl SP4 ....217 B2
Abbey CE Fst Sch The
SP7 ....202 B1
Abbey Cl
Chippenham SN15 ......79 B5
3 Shrewton SP3 ......196 E6
Abbey La BA2 ....99 A3
Abbey Rw SN16 ....28 A3
Abbey View Rd SN25 ...34 E3
Abbey Wlk 6 SP7 ....202 C1
Abbeyfield Sch SN14 ...70 C2
Abbeymeads Com Prim Sch
SN2 ....35 A7
Abbot Rd SP1 ....146 C4
Abbots Wlk GL7 ....2 D4
Abbotsbury Way SN25 ..35 A8
Abbotts Cl SP9 ....216 C7
Abbotts Gdn SN16 .....28 A3
Abbotts Rd SP9 ....216 C7
Abdon Cl BA12 ....195 D6
Abingdon Ct La SN6 ...19 E8
Abington Way SN2 .....35 D5
Abney Moor SN3 ....51 E2
Abotts Cl BA13 ....108 F3
Above Hedges SP5 ....148 C3
Acacia Cl SN14 ....70 A1
Acacia Cres BA14 ....105 A8
Acacia Dr BA11 ....110 C7
Acacia Gr SN2 ....35 C2
Academy Dr SN13 ......76 E2
Acorn Cl SN3 ....51 C5
Acre Cl BA14 ....178 A3
Acres Rd SN10 ....214 C3
Acreshort La BA14 ....178 A3
Activity Zone Leisure Ctr
SN16 ....27 F1
Adam's Grave (Long
Barrow)★ SN8 ....173 D2
Adampur Rd SN9 ......216 A4
Adcroft Dr BA14 ......101 D1
Adcroft St BA14 ......101 C1
Adderwell BA11 ....110 A3
Adderwell Cl BA11 ....110 A3
Addington St SN10 ...214 C2
Addison Cres SN2 .....35 F3
Addison Rd SN12 ......93 F6
Addison Sq 19 SP4 ...198 B7
Adelaide Cl 6 SP4 ...198 F6
Adwalton Cl SN5 ......49 B4
Aelmas Mich Dro
SP11 ....192 E1
Affleck Cl SN5 ....49 C5
Agra Rd SP9 ....216 A4
Agravaine Cl 27 SP10 .193 D2
Ailesbury Cl SN15 .....79 A4
Ailesbury Way SN8 ...183 D8
Ainsworth Rd SN3 .....51 A4
Aintree 7 RG17 ......165 A1
Aintree Ave BA14 ....105 E4
Aintree Dr SN14 ......77 F6
Airman's Cnr SP3 ....197 B5
Aisne Rd SN4 ....65 D1
Akenfield Cl SN25 .....34 F5
Akers Cl SN26 ....21 C2
Akers Way SN2 ....34 E2
Alamein Rd 4 SP11 ..193 E4
Alan Powell La BA13 ..112 B8
Alanbrook Cl SP4 ....217 B4
Alanbrooke Cres SN2 ..35 A2
Alanbrooke Rd SP4 ...197 E6
Alba Cl 11 SN5 ....48 F8
Albany Cl BA14 ....101 F4
Albany Rd SP1 ....146 B1
Albert Cl BA14 ....101 F4
Albert St SN1 ....50 D4
Albion Dr BA14 ....105 B8
Albion Rd 33 SP6 ....210 D1
Albion St SN1 ....50 A5
Aldborough Cl 2 SN5 .49 C6
Aldbourne Cl
Blunsdon St Andrew SN2 .35 C6
27 Hungerford RG17 ..177 B7
Aldbourne Four Barrows★
SN8 ....169 E8
Aldbourne Rd SN8 ...170 D5
Aldeburgh Pl BA14 ...104 F6
Alder Cl Swindon SN2 .34 D4
Trowbridge BA14 .....105 B5
Alder Way SN12 ....94 A4
Alder Wlk 5 BA11 ....110 B7
Alderbury & W Grimstead
Sch SP5 ....153 A3
Alderholt Rd SP6 ....210 B1
Alderney Cl 6 SN4 ...48 A2
Alderton Rd
Grittleton SN14 ....54 D5
Luckington SN14 ......53 D6
Alderton Way BA14 ..105 D5
Aldrin Cl 7 SP10 ....193 D2
Aldworth Dr 3 SP1 ..146 C5
Alexander Fields SN9 .181 F1
Alexander Rd SN16 ...27 F4
Alexander Terr SN13 ..77 A1
Alexandra Cl SP2 ....145 C3
Alexandra Rd
Fordingbridge SP6 ...210 D1
Frome BA11 ....110 A4
1 Swindon SN1 ......50 C7
Alexandra Terr SN8 ..213 D3
Alfred St Swindon SN1 .50 C7
Westbury BA13 ....109 A4
Alfred's Castle★ RG17 .164 B5

Alfred's Twr★ BA10 ..122 F3
All Saints CE Prim Sch
SP5 ....161 D3
All Saints Rd 1 SN10 .187 E7
Allen Rd Corsham SN13 .84 C8
Trowbridge BA14 .....105 B7
Allen Wr Dr SP6 .....210 D2
Allenby Rd SP4 ......133 C2
Allengrove La SN14 ...39 C3
Alley The
Bishopstone SP5 .....205 E4
Woodgreen SP6 ......211 A4
Allington Rd SN2 .....35 B5
Allington Tk SP4 .....198 E4
Allington Way
Amesbury SP4 ....217 D2
2 Chippenham SN14 ..70 A1
Alma Pl SN8 ....213 D3
Alma Rd SN8 ....170 A4
Alma St BA14 ....105 E8
Alma Terr SN11 ......81 B3
Almond Gr BA14 .....105 B5
Alnwick SN5 ....49 B4
Aloeric GM Prim Sch
SN12 ....94 A3
Alpine Cl 6 SN5 .....49 A7
Alton Barnes White Horse★
SN8 ....173 C2
Alton Cl SN2 ....35 C5
Alton Rd SN8 ....181 F8
Altona Gdns 17 SP10 .193 D2
Alvescot Dr SN3 ......50 D5
Alveston Cl SN5 ......49 D6
Amber Ct SN1 ....50 D7
Amberley Cl SN25 ....35 C4
Ambrose House Con &
Management Ctr SN1 .50 B6
Ambrose Rd SN1 .....50 C2
American Mus In Britain★
BA2 ....90 A5
Amersham Rd SN3 ....51 B3
Amesbury Cl 4 SN2 ..35 C6
Amesbury Cty Inf Sch
SP4 ....217 B4
Amesbury Jun Sch
SP4 ....217 B4
Amesbury Rd
Amesbury SP4 ....217 F4
Amport SP11 ....192 A1
Newton Tony SP4 ....199 A3
Shrewton SP3 ....196 E6
Amity Dr SN8 ....175 D2
Amouracre BA14 .....105 F8
Ancaster BA14 ......101 A1
Anchor Rd SN11 ......81 C2
Ancona 12 SN5 ......49 C5
Andeferas Rd 6 SP10 .193 D2
Anderson Cl SN3 ......51 D3
Anderson Rd SP1 ....146 C4
Andover La SP11 .....192 B4
Andover Rd
Amport SP11 ....192 E2
Chirton SN10 ....180 D3
Fyfield SP11 ....192 D3
Upavon SN9 ....181 F1
Andover St 4 SN1 ....50 A5
Andrew Cl 14 SP4 ...198 B7
Andrews Cl SN14 .....78 B7
Andrews Way SP4 ...151 F5
Angel La Hindon SP3 ..200 A3
Mere BA12 ....139 A5
27 Shaftesbury SP7 ..202 C2
Angel Yd SN8 ....213 D3
Angelica Cl 6 SN2 ...34 D4
Angler Rd
Salisbury SP2 ....145 C5
Swindon SN5 ....49 B7
Anglesey Cl 5 SN5 ...49 C6
Anglesey Mead SN15 ..79 A4
Angrove Cotts SN16 ..43 D4
Angus Cl SN5 ....49 B7
Anise Cl 4 SN2 ......34 C4
Ann Edwards Sch GL7 ..6 E6
Anne Cres 24 SP4 ...198 B7
Annett's La RG17 ....176 F7
Annetts Cl SP4 ......217 C4
Anson Ave SN9 ......182 B2
Anson Gr SN12 ....94 C1
Anson Pl SN14 ....56 C7
Ansty Hill BA12 .....195 A6
Ansty Pl SN15 ....79 A4
Anthony Cl SN16 ......25 C1
Anthony Rd SN4 ......64 A7
Anton La SP11 ......193 E4
Antrobus Rd SP4 ....217 B3
Apollo Rd SN15 ......59 E3
Appleford Sch SP4 ..196 E4
Appleshaw CE Jun & Infants
Sch SP11 ....192 E4
Appleshaw Way
Perham Down SP11 ..191 F3
Salisbury SP1 ....146 B5
Appletree Cl SP5 ....211 C8
Appletree Rd SP5 ...211 C8
Applewood Cl SN14 ..78 B8
Applewood Ct SN5 ...49 D6
Aragon Cl SP4 ......217 C4
Archer Cl SN2 ....35 F5
Arches La SN16 ......27 C1
Arcot Rd SP9 ....216 B3
Arden Cl SN12 ....94 C5
Argosy Rd SN15 ......60 B1
Argyle Dr SN14 ......70 C3
Argyle St SN2 ....35 D1
Arkwright Rd SN16 ...25 D6
Arley Cl SN25 ....35 A5
Arlington Cl SN3 .....51 B7

Armitage Sq 4 SP4 ...197 E6
Armoury Yd 15 SP7 ..202 C2
Armstrong Rd BA11 ..110 B5
Armstrong Rise 16
SP10 ....193 D2
Armstrong St 2 SN1 ..50 C7
Arn View 2 BA14 ....117 A8
Arney Cl SN13 ....84 E8
Arnfield Moor SN3 ....51 E2
Arnhem Cross SN15 ..60 B2
Arnold Rd BA14 .....104 E3
Arnolds Mead SN13 ...76 F2
Arran Cl 5 SN4 ......48 A2
Arran Way SN6 ....22 F7
Arras Cl BA14 ....105 C6
Artis Ave SN4 ....64 B7
Arun Rd SN25 ....34 F3
Arun Way 6 SO51 ...212 F6
Arundel Cl
Chippenham SN14 ....78 A7
Swindon SN3 ....50 A7
Arundell Cl BA13 ....109 B4
Ascham Rd SN5 ....49 A5
Ascot Cl SN14 ....78 A5
Ash Cl Lyneham SN15 ..60 B2
4 Shaftesbury SP7 ...202 D2
Swindon SN4 ....34 A2
Tidworth SP9 ....216 E7
Ash Cres SP1 ....146 C5
Ash Dr BA14 ....105 C3
Ash Gdns SN3 ....51 A5
Ash Gr 1 Melksham SN12 .94 A2
Swindon SN2 ....35 C2
Ash Rd SN14 ....75 A5
Ash Tree La SP7 ....206 B7
Ash Wlk
Upton Lovell BA12 ...194 E4
Warminster BA12 ....117 A7
Ashburnham Cl 7 SN5 .49 A4
Ashbury Ave SN3 .....51 B7
Ashbury Hill SN6 ....164 A7
Ashcroft Cotts SN8 ..169 B1
Ashdown Dr SN12 ....94 D6
Ashdown Pk★ RG17 .164 C5
Ashdown Terr SP9 ...216 D5
Ashdown Way SN2 ....34 C4
Ashe Cres SN15 ......70 D1
Ashen Copse Rd SN4 ..63 F7
Ashes La Freshford BA2 ..99 A4
Kington Langley SN15 .70 E7
Ashfield Rd
Chippenham SN15 ....70 D1
Salisbury SP2 ....145 E1
Ashford Cl 11 SP6 ...210 C1
Ashford Rd
Fordingbridge SP6 ..210 C1
Swindon SN1 ....50 B4
Ashford Trad Est SP2 .145 E1
Ashgrove BA12 ......139 B4
Ashie Cl SN3 ....34 B2
Ashkirk Cl SN3 ....50 E6
Ashlade Firs Rd SN8 .175 C6
Ashlands SP4 ....146 D6
Ashleigh Cl SP2 .....130 B2
Ashleigh Gr BA14 ...105 C7
Ashley Cl
Atworth/Whitley SN12 .85 D1
Bradford-on-Avon BA15 .100 B8
Swindon SN3 ....50 F6
Ashley Coombe BA12 .117 A4
Ashley Dro SN8 .....185 A7
Ashley La BA15 ....99 F7
Ashley Piece SN8 ...170 C2
Ashley Pl BA12 ......116 F4
Ashley Rd Bath BA1 ..82 C2
Bradford-on-Avon BA15 ..91 B1
Salisbury SP2 ....145 F2
Ashley Wlk SP4 .....217 D2
Ashleycross SP6 ....211 D1
Ashmead BA14 ......105 D6
Ashmead Ct BA14 ...105 C7
Ashmore Bottom
DT11 ....206 E1
Ashmore Cl
Swindon SN3 ....51 C6
Whiteparish SP5 ....161 D4
Ashmore La
West Dean SP5 .....155 E2
Whiteparish SP5 ....161 D6
Ashton Keynes CE Sch
SN6 ....17 F8
Ashton Rd
Ashton Keynes SN16 ..17 E7
Siddington GL7 ....6 D1
Trowbridge BA14 ....102 A2
Ashton Rise BA14 ...102 A2
Ashton St 2 BA14 ...105 E8
Ashtree Rd BA11 ....110 A7
Ashwell Cl SN3 ....50 F5
Ashwicke Rd SN14 ...74 B3
Ashwood Rd SN13 ....76 A1
Ashworth Rd SN5 ....49 E6
Askerton Cl 5 SN5 ...48 F8
Askew Cl 3 SN5 .....48 F5
Aspen Cl Colerne SN14 .74 F6
Frome BA11 ....110 B7
Wootton Bassett SN4 ..47 E3
Assisi Rd SP1 ....146 A4
Astley Cl SN9 ....215 D5
Aston Cl SN9 ....215 C5
Aston Mead SP1 ....146 C3
Astor Cres SP11 ....192 A5
Atbara Cl SN25 ......35 A3
Atcherly St SN5 .....166 A1
Athelstan Mus★ SN16 .28 A3
Athelstan Rd SN16 ...27 F4
Athena Ave SN2 ......35 E1
Atherton Cl 12 SN8 ..170 B2

Atherton Cres 16 RG17 .177 B7
Atherton Pl 11 RG17 .92 B4
Atherton Rd 11 RG17 .177 B7
Athlone Cl 2 SP11 ..193 E4
Atholl Ct 26 SP10 ...193 E2
Attlee Cres SN4 ......35 E3
Attwood Rd SP1 .....146 A3
Atwell-Wilson Motor Mus★
SN11 ....89 D7
Atworth Cl SN2 ......35 B6
Atworth CP Sch SN12 .92 E8
Atworth La SN13 .....84 E4
Atyec Cl BA13 ....112 B8
Atyeo Cl BA13 ......112 B8
Aubrey Rise 8 SN16 ..28 A5
Auckland Cl 6 SP9 ..216 E6
Auckland Rd 3 SP4 ..198 F7
Auden Cl SN25 ....34 F5
Audley Cl 2 SN5 .....48 F4
Audley Gate BA13 ...108 E2
Audley Rd SN14 ......78 C8
Augustine Way 9 SP10 .193 D2
Austen Cres SN3 .....51 D4
Australian Ave SP2 ..145 D2
Ave Cty Prim Sch The
BA12 ....117 B7
Avebury CE Prim Sch
SN8 ....173 C8
Avebury Cl Calne SN11 .81 A3
Westbury BA13 ......108 F4
Avebury Manor★ SN8 .167 B1
Avebury Mus★ SN8 .167 B1
Avebury Rd
Chippenham SN14 ....78 A6
Swindon SN2 ....35 B5
Avebury Stone Circle &
Henge★ SN8 ....173 C8
Avenell Rd 8 SN4 ...163 A6
Avening St SN2 ......35 D1
Avens Cl SN3 ....34 D4
Avenue La Fleche
SN15 ....78 D7
Avenue Rd Frome BA11 .110 A4
Swindon SN1 ....50 C4
Trowbridge BA14 ....105 B8
Avenue The★
Amesbury SP4 ....197 E5
Cherhill SN11 ....166 E2
Claverton BA2 ....90 A4
Durnford SP4 ....131 D1
18 Durrington/Bulford
SP4 ....198 B7
Porton SP4 ....133 D6
Salisbury SP1 ....146 C1
South Tedworth SP9 .216 C4
Stanton Fitzwarren SN6 .22 B1
Tangley SP11 ....193 D5
Tisbury SP3 ....203 E8
Warminster BA12 ....117 A7
Westbury BA13 ......109 A3
Westbury BA13 ......112 B8
Wilton SP2 ....144 F5
Woodford SP2 ....145 A8
Avil's La SN4 ....56 F6
Avocet Cl SN3 ....51 E6
Avon App SP2 ......146 A1
Avon Cl BA15 ....100 E5
Avon Ct BA1 ....82 A4
Avon Dr SP5 ....153 E2
Avon Mdw SP5 ......211 A8
Avon Mdws SP4 .....131 C5
Avon Mead SN15 .....78 F8
Avon Meade 1 SP6 ..210 D1
Avon Mid Sch SP2 ..145 D4
Avon Mills SN16 ......28 B2
Avon Rd Devizes SN10 .179 C8
2 Durrington/Bulford
SP4 ....198 F6
Malmesbury SN16 ....27 F4
Melksham SN12 ......94 A6
Tidworth SP9 ....216 C5
Warminster BA12 ...117 A5
Avon Reach SN15 ....78 D7
Avon Rise SN14 ......39 E4
Avon Sq SN9 ....181 F1
Avon Terr
Devizes SN10 ....214 A4
Salisbury SP2 ....145 F2
Avon View SP6 .....210 F1
Avon Way BA14 ....101 D3
Avoncliff Sta BA15 ...99 E5
Avondale Sch SP4 ..217 C8
Avondown Rd SP4 ..198 C7
Avonfield BA14 .....101 E4
Avonfield Ave BA15 .100 E5
Avonleaze Rd SN9 ..215 D5
Avonmede SN25 ......34 F4
Avonstoke Cl SP4 ..217 B2
Avonvale Rd BA14 ..101 D2
Avonweir La SN15 ...57 F3
Avro Way SN12 ......94 C1
Awdry Ave SN12 .....94 C6
Awdry Cl
Chippenham SN14 ....77 F7
Heddington SN11 .....89 A2
Axbridge Cl SN3 .....51 A5
Axe & Cleaver La BA14 .105 C7
Aylesbury St SN1 ....50 C7
Ayleswade Rd SP2 ..152 A6
Aymer Pl SN3 ....51 C5
Ayr Cl SN14 ....77 F5
Ayrshire Cl
Salisbury SP2 ....145 B5
Swindon SN5 ....49 B7
Azalea Cl SN11 ......81 C1
Azalea Dr
Trowbridge BA14 ...105 A7
Warminster BA12 ...116 E7

Azelin Ct SN3 ....36 B3

B

Babington Pk 9 SN5 ..48 F5
Back La
9 Aldbourne SN8 ...170 A6
Blunsdon St Andrew SN26 .21 B3
Calne Without SN15 ..88 B4
Cherhill SN11 ....166 E2
Great Hinton BA14 ..178 A5
Maiden Bradley with Yarnfield
BA12 ....118 F2
Marlborough SN8 ...213 D3
Penton Grafton SP11 .193 A3
Ramsbury SN8 ......170 B2
Sixpenny Handley SP5 .208 A4
Tilshead SP3 ....188 B3
Vernhams Dean SP11 .185 C3
Back St Calne SN11 ..81 B2
Chitterne BA12 .....195 D7
Back St
Ashton Keynes SN6 ...6 F1
East Garston RG17 ..171 E7
Great Hinton BA14 ..178 A6
Trowbridge BA14 ....101 C1
Bader Pk 10 SN12 ..178 B8
Badger Cl
2 Wootton Bassett SN4 .47 B2
Badgers Cl 3 SN4 ..163 B6
Badminton House★
GL9 ....38 F2
Badminton Pk★ GL9 ..38 F3
Bagbury Rd BA12 ...194 F4
Baghdad Rd 2 SP4 ..198 F7
Bailey Cl SN9 ....215 B5
Bailey's Mead SN4 ...48 A2
Baileys Barn BA15 ..100 D5
Baileys Way SN4 .....64 B7
Bailiffe Piece SN6 ....8 D1
Bainbridge Cl 2 SN5 .49 A5
Bainton Cl BA15 ....100 D7
Baird Cl SN5 ....49 B8
Bakers Field SN15 ...60 A3
Bakers Rd SN4 ......64 B5
Balden Cl SN4 ....63 F6
Baldwin Cl SN4 ......65 D4
Bale Cl 6 SN5 ....48 F5
Ball Rd SN9 ....215 D4
Ballands Castle★ BA9 .137 A2
Balmoor Cl BA12 ....139 B3
Balmoral Cl SN3 .....51 A3
Balmoral Rd
Salisbury SP1 ....146 B4
Trowbridge BA14 ...105 B5
Bampton Gr SN3 .....50 E6
Banbury Cl SN3 ......50 F3
Bancroft BA15 ......100 D7
Bancroft Cl SN15 ....48 F6
Bank Street SN12 ....75 C3
Bank The SN14 ......75 C3
Bankfoot Cl 3 SN5 ..49 B7
Bankside SN1 ....49 F4
Bannerdown Cl BA1 ..82 B4
Bannerdown Dr BA1 ..82 A4
Bannerdown Rd BA1 ..82 C5
Banwell Ave SN3 .....51 A5
Barbara's Rd SN13 ...84 D8
Barber's La SP5 ....151 C1
Barberry SP3 ....201 B3
Barbury Castle★ SN4 .168 A7
Barbury Castle Ctry Pk★
SN4 ....168 B7
Barcelona Cres SN4 ..64 A7
Bardsey Cl 5 SN4 ....47 F2
Barford La SP5 .....159 C1
Barford St Martin CE Fst Sch
SP3 ....143 B3
Bargates SN13 ......83 D6
Barken Rd
4 Chippenham SN14 ..70 A1
Chippenham SN14 ....78 A8
Barkstead Cl 3 SN5 ..49 B4
Barley Cl
Malmesbury SN16 ....28 A2
Warminster BA12 ...117 C5
Barley Hill La SN10 ..179 A7
Barlow Cl SN25 ......35 A8
Barn Cl
Chippenham SN14 ....78 A8
Corsham SN13 ....76 E1
Barn End SN14 ......74 A8
Barn Glebe BA14 ...101 E1
Barn Hill SP3 ....201 A3
Barn Moor Cl SN3 ...51 E3
Barn Owl Rd SN14 ...70 B2
Barn Piece Box SN13 .83 D6
Bradford-on-Avon BA15 .100 D4
Barn St SN8 ....213 D3
Barnack Cl BA14 ....101 A1
Barnard Cl SN3 ......51 B7
Barnard St 1 SP1 ...152 B8
Barncroft SP11 .....192 E3
Barnes Cl BA14 .....105 A7
Barnes Gn SN15 .....45 F6
Barnes Pl BA12 .....139 A5
Barnes Wallis Cl
9 Amesbury SP4 ....217 E3
Melksham Without BA14 .178 B8
Barnetts Hill SN13 ...83 F7
Barnfield Cl SN2 .....49 F7
Barnfield Rd SN2 ....49 E7

Barnfield Way BA1 .....82 B4
Barnstaple Cl SN3 ....51 B5
Barnum Ct SN2 .....50 A4
Baroda Rd SP9 .....216 A4
Baron Cl Lyneham SN15 ...59 C4
  4 Swindon SN3 .....36 B3
Barons Mead SN14 .....78 A8
Barra Cl SN6 .....22 E6
Barracks SN14 .....74 F4
Barrett La SN15 .....57 D2
Barrett Way SN14 .....64 B6
Barrington Cl SN3 .....51 D3
Barrington Rd SP1 ...146 C3
Barrow Cl SN8 .....213 F3
Barrow Gn SN15 .....70 E2
Barrow La BA9 .....136 B5
Barrow St La
  Mere BA12 .....139 F3
  West Knoyle BA12 .....140 A4
Barrow Water La BA9 ...136 A5
Barrowby Gate SN3 .....36 A4
Barrows La SP5 .....212 B7
Barry Glen Cl SN2 .....35 E1
Barry Pl SN11 .....79 F2
Barters La SP7 .....206 D8
Bartlett Cl 11 BA11 ...110 C6
Bartlett Rd SP1 .....146 B4
Bartletts SN10 .....179 C1
Bartletts Mead BA14 ...178 A4
Bartletts The BA12 .....139 B4
Barton Cl 12 SP10 ...193 C2
Barton Farm Ctry Pk★
  BA15 .....100 A5
Barton Heritage Collection★
  SP2 .....145 F1
Barton Hill 22 SP7 ...202 C2
Barton Hill House Sch
  SP7 .....202 C2
Barton La BA12 .....139 A5
Barton Orch BA15 .....100 C6
Barton Way SN16 .....42 E4
Bartons Rd SN25 .....34 E3
Bartons The 29 SP6 ...210 D1
Basil Cl SN2 .....34 D4
Basil Hill Rd SN13 .....84 C7
Basingstoke Cl 5 SN5 ...49 A4
Baskerville Rd SN3 .....51 E2
Bassett Rd OX12 .....165 F8
Bassetts Pasture
  BA15 .....100 D4
Bassetts The SN13 .....83 D6
Batch The BA2 .....98 E1
Bath Acad of Art SN13 ...77 A2
Bath Rd Atworth SN12 ...84 D2
  Atworth/Whitley SN12 ...93 A8
  Box SN13 .....83 A6
  Bradford-on-Avon BA15 ...91 C1
  Chippenham Without
    SN14 .....77 F5
  Colerne SN14 .....74 F3
  Corsham SN13 .....77 B4
  Cricklade SN6 .....19 D3
  Devizes SN10 .....179 C8
  Frome BA11 .....110 A6
  Hungerford RG17 .....176 F7
  Marlborough SN8 .....213 B2
  Melksham SN12 .....94 A5
  Melksham Without SN12 ...93 A7
  Preshute SN8 .....174 C7
  Seend SN10 .....95 C1
  Swindon SN1 .....50 C4
  Upton Scudamore BA12 ...112 D2
  Warminster BA12 .....112 E1
  Westonbirt with Lasborough
    GL8 .....25 D8
  Wootton Bassett SN4 .....47 C1
Bath Rd Ind Est SN8 ...78 B6
Bathampton St SN1 .....50 A6
Bathford CE Prim Sch
  BA1 .....82 C2
Bathford Hill BA1 .....82 B2
Bathurst Rd SN1 .....50 D6
Batt's La SP5 .....183 F7
Batten Rd SP5 .....211 A8
Battens The 3 SN14 .....70 A1
Battlesbury Barracks
  BA12 .....117 E6
Battlesbury Hill Fort★
  BA12 .....117 F8
Battlesbury Rd BA12 ...117 E7
Battlewell SN5 .....33 A3
Baverstock La SP3 .....142 B5
Bawdsey Rd 6 SP4 .....217 C2
Baxter Cl SN25 .....35 A7
Bay Cl SN11 .....89 C8
Baydon Cl BA14 .....105 C5
Baydon Gr SN11 .....81 B4
Baydon Rd
  Aldbourne SN8 .....164 B1
  Great Shefford RG17 ...171 A4
  Lambourn RG17 .....171 A6
Baydons La SN15 .....78 E6
Bayleaf Ave SN2 .....34 D4
Bayliffes Cl SN15 .....79 A7
Baynton Way BA13 .....186 D8
Bayntun Cl SN15 .....96 A7
Baywater SN8 .....213 E4
Bazaar SP9 .....216 B5
Beacon Cl
  Amesbury SP4 .....217 C4
  8 Swindon SN1 .....49 F4
Beacon Ct SN6 .....210 D2
Beacon Hill Rd 7 SP4 ...198 E4
Beacon View BA12 .....116 D6

Beaconsfield Way
  BA11 .....110 B7
Beale Ct SN14 .....78 A7
Beale's Barton BA14 ...101 F8
Beales Cl SN1 .....50 B7
Beales Farm Rd 15
  RG17 .....165 A1
Beamish Cl 2 SN11 ...166 A1
Beanacre Manor★
  .....94 A8
Beanacre Rd
  Melksham SN12 .....94 A3
  Melksham Without SN12 ...86 A1
Beanlands The SN4 .....163 A6
Bear Cl BA15 .....100 B7
Bearfield Bldgs BA15 ...100 C8
Bearfield La RG17 .....171 A4
Beatrice Rd SP1 .....146 A4
Beatrice St SN2 .....50 C8
Beauchamp Dr 10 SP4 ...217 D3
Beauclerc St SN3 .....179 D8
Beaufort Cl 5 SN12 ...178 B8
Beaufort Gn SN3 .....51 B5
Beaufort Rd SN4 .....64 A7
Beauchamp Cl 9 SP7 ...202 D2
Beaulieu Cl SN5 .....49 C4
Beaulieu Rd 2 SP4 ...217 C2
Beaumaris Rd SN5 .....49 B5
Beaumont Rd SN3 .....50 B6
Beaumont Way SP4 .....217 D2
Beaven Cl SN15 .....78 F4
Becket Way SP1 .....146 D1
Beckett St 14 SP3 .....203 E8
Beckett's La SP3 .....201 A3
Beckford Cl
  Tisbury SP3 .....200 D1
  Warminster BA12 .....117 B6
Beckhampton (Long
  Barrow)★ SN8 .....173 A8
Beckhampton Rd SN8 ...173 B8
Beckhampton St SN1 ...50 C6
Beddington Ct SN2 .....36 A5
Beddoe Cl BA15 .....100 E4
Bedford Cl 2 SP6 .....210 D2
Bedford Rd
  Salisbury SP2 .....145 C2
  6 Swindon SN3 .....50 F6
Bedwin St SP1 .....146 B1
Bedwyn Cl SN2 .....35 C3
Bedwyn Dyke★ SN8 ...176 C3
Bedwyn Sta SN8 .....176 B3
Bedwyn Stone Mus★
  SN8 .....176 B2
Beech Ave
  Melksham SN12 .....94 A3
  Swindon SN2 .....35 A2
  Warminster BA12 .....116 F6
Beech Cl Andover SP11 ...193 B1
  Porton SP4 .....133 C6
Beech Ct BA11 .....110 B7
Beech Dr SN5 .....34 A2
Beech Gr Highworth SN6 ...22 F5
  Trowbridge BA14 .....105 B6
Beech Grange SP5 .....212 C5
Beech Hanger SP4 .....199 C5
Beech Hill Rd SP9 .....216 E7
Beech Lea
  Broad Blunsdon SN26 ...21 C1
  Meysey Hampton GL7 ...1 A4
Beech Rd Colerne SN14 ...75 A5
  Corsham SN13 .....83 E7
Beech Sq 12 RG17 .....177 B6
Beech Wlk SN4 .....131 C1
Beech Wood 13 SN10 ...179 F1
Beechcroft Inf Sch
  SN2 .....35 D4
Beechcroft Rd
  Salisbury SP1 .....146 D1
  Swindon SN2 .....35 E4
Beeches Cl SP5 .....148 C3
Beeches La SN15 .....59 A5
Beeches The
  Bradford-on-Avon BA15 ...101 A7
  Coombe Bissett SP5 ...156 F7
  Lydiard Millicent SN5 ...33 B1
  Melksham Without SN12 ...93 F2
  5 Salisbury SP1 .....152 C8
  15 Shaftesbury SP7 ...202 C2
  Trowbridge BA14 .....101 F2
  Warminster BA12 .....116 F6
  4 West Wellow SO51 ...212 F6
Beechfield SP4 .....199 B3
Beechfield Dr SN10 .....214 E5
Beechfield Rd SN13 .....76 E1
Beechgrove BA12 .....117 B8
Beechwood 18 SP6 .....210 C5
Beechwood Ave BA11 ...110 A5
Beechwood Cl BA11 .....110 A5
Beechwood Rd SN14 .....78 B8
Beehive Cl 1 SN5 .....49 A8
Belcombe Ct★ BA15 ...100 B6
Belcombe Rd BA15 .....100 B6
Belfast Mead SN15 .....60 C2
Belfry Dr SN14 .....41 E1
Belgrave St SN1 .....50 C5
Bell Gdns SN3 .....36 E4
Bell Hill Seend SN12 ...178 E7
  Warminster BA12 .....116 F5
Bell La Inkpen RG17 .....177 E2
  Lechlade GL7 .....2 C3
  Liddington SN4 .....163 A4
  Sutton Benger SN15 .....57 D2
Bell Piece SN15 .....57 D2
Bell Rd SP4 .....197 F7
Bell St
  4 Ludgershall SP11 ...192 B5
  Shaftesbury SP7 .....202 C2

Bellamy La SP1 .....152 B8
Belle Vue Rd
  Salisbury SP1 .....146 A1
  Swindon SN1 .....50 D4
Bellefield Cres BA14 ...101 D1
Bellinger Cl SN15 .....70 C3
Bellingham La SN6 .....23 A2
Bellot Dr
  3 Corsham SN13 .....76 E1
  Corsham SN13 .....84 E8
Bells La BA12 .....137 F7
Bellver SN5 .....49 B5
Belmont Cl
  10 Shaftesbury SP7 ...202 C1
  Swindon SN3 .....36 A4
Belmont Cres SN1 .....50 A3
Belsay SN5 .....49 C4
Belvedere Rd SN3 .....51 A3
Bembridge SN3 .....51 B4
Bemerton Prim Sch
  SP2 .....145 C1
Ben La SP5 .....154 F7
Bences La SN13 .....77 A2
Bendy Bow SN16 .....15 F7
Benin Rd SP11 .....191 F3
Bennett Cl SP5 .....211 C7
Bennett Hill Cl 3 SN4 ...47 F2
Bentham Cl SN5 .....49 C6
Bentham La SN5 .....33 A8
Bentley Cl SN3 .....51 A6
Bentley Gr SN11 .....81 C2
Bentley Way SN5 .....149 D5
Benwell Cl SN5 .....49 C6
Beranburh Field SN4 ...64 E2
Berenger Cl SN1 .....50 D3
Beresford Cl 1 SN3 .....51 C4
Bergamot Cl SN8 .....174 C7
Bergman Cl SN2 .....35 B6
Berhills La SN10 .....95 F2
Bericot La SN4 .....65 E6
Berkeley Cl
  Melksham SN12 .....94 A2
  South Cerney GL7 .....6 A6
Berkeley Lawns SN3 ...50 F3
Berkeley Rd
  Trowbridge BA14 .....105 A8
  Wroughton SN4 .....64 B7
Berkely Cl 2 SN14 .....78 A7
Berkley CE Sch BA11 ...111 A7
Berkley Cl BA11 .....110 D8
Berkley La BA11 .....110 D8
Berkley Rd BA11 .....110 A5
Berkley St BA11 .....107 B1
Berkshire Dr SN5 .....49 A7
Berkshire Rd SP2 .....151 E7
Berrington Rd SN3 .....51 A3
Berry Cl 4 SP4 .....190 A3
Berry Rd BA13 .....186 D8
Berry Wood La SP7 ...203 A3
Berrycroft
  Ashbury SN6 .....164 C5
  Mildenhall SN8 .....175 B8
Berryfield Cl SN12 .....93 F1
Berryfield La SN12 .....93 F1
Berryfield Pk SN12 .....93 F1
Berryfield Rd BA15 .....100 D8
Bertha's Field GL9 .....24 B4
Berton Cl SN26 .....21 C2
Berwick La SP3 .....128 D7
Berwick Rd
  Berwick St James SP3 ...196 F2
  Stapleford SP3 .....129 E7
Berwick St John SP7 ...207 B8
Besomer Dro SP5 .....211 D6
Bess Rd SN5 .....48 F4
Bessemer Cl SN2 .....35 A1
Bessemer Rd E SN2 .....35 A1
Bessemer Rd W SN2 ...34 F1
Best's La BA12 .....194 A5
Bethel Rd SN13 .....76 E1
Betjeman Ave SN4 .....47 E3
Betjeman Rd SN8 .....213 A4
Betony Cl SN25 .....34 E5
Bettertons Cl GL7 .....1 F7
Bevan Cl SN2 .....35 F3
Beverley SN5 .....49 C4
Beverley Cl SN12 .....94 C1
Beverley Cres SN9 .....182 B2
Beverley Way SN14 .....77 F5
Beversbrook Rd SN11 ...81 B5
Beverstone Gr SN3 .....50 F4
Bevil SN5 .....49 A3
Bevisland SN3 .....51 C3
Bewley La SN15 .....86 F5
Bewley Rd 1 BA14 .....105 C5
Beyer Rd 5 SP4 .....217 D2
Bibury Rd SN3 .....50 E5
Bicton Rd SN25 .....34 F6
Biddel Springs SN6 .....23 B6
Bidden La BA12 .....195 D6
Biddesden La SP11 .....192 C5
Biddestone La SN14 .....68 E3
Biddulph Rd SP4 .....198 A7
Bideford Cl SN3 .....51 A5
Big La RG17 .....165 A2
Bilbury Rd SN3 .....50 E5
Bimport SP7 .....202 B1
Bincknoll Castle★ SN4 ...62 F6
Bindon Cl SN5 .....49 A5
Bingham Rd
  Durrington SP4 .....197 E7
  Salisbury SP1 .....146 C4
Birch Gdns BA14 .....102 B2
Birch Glade SN6 .....17 F8

Birch Gr Bower Hill SN12 ...94 C1
  Chippenham SN15 .....70 E1
Birch St SN1 .....49 F5
Birch Wlk 4 BA11 .....110 B7
Birchenleaze BA14 .....105 C3
Birches The SN3 .....51 B2
Birchill La BA11 .....110 A1
Birchwood Cl BA12 .....115 C7
Birchwood Dr 4 SP4 ...198 E1
Birchwood Rd SN3 .....36 B2
Birdbrook Rd SN2 .....35 E5
Birdcombe Rd 1 SN5 ...49 C5
Birds Marsh View SN15 ...70 E2
Bishop Rd SN1 .....81 B4
Bishop Wordsworths Sch
  SP1 .....152 A8
Bishop's Pal★ SP1 .....152 A7
Bishop's Wlk SP1 .....152 A8
Bishopdale Cl 2 SN5 ...34 A1
Bishopdown Rd SP1 ...146 B4
Bishops Cannings Prim Sch
  SN10 .....172 B3
Bishops Cl
  Chippenham SN15 .....78 F4
  Mere BA12 .....139 A6
  Tidworth SP9 .....216 D4
Bishops Dr SP2 .....151 F6
Bishops Mead SP1 .....146 E4
Bishopsfield 6 SN6 .....19 D8
Bishopstone CE Sch
  SN6 .....163 E6
Bishopstone Hollow
  SP5 .....205 E3
Bishopstrow Rd BA12 ...117 E4
Bisley SN16 .....29 A6
Bisley Cl SN3 .....51 A5
Biss Cl BA12 .....112 F4
Biss Mdw BA14 .....105 A8
Bitham Brook CP Sch
  BA13 .....109 B4
Bitham La RG17 .....177 A3
Bitham Pk BA13 .....109 B4
Bittern Rd SN3 .....51 E6
Black Bridge Rd SN15 ...78 F8
Black Dog Hill
  Calne Without SN11 .....80 D2
  Chapmanslade BA13 ...111 C6
Black Horse La
  Westbury BA13 .....108 D1
  Winterbourne SP4 .....146 E6
Black La
  Pitton & Farley SP5 ...148 C4
  Redlynch SP5 .....211 E6
Blackbarn Rd SP4 .....134 B5
Blackberry Cl SN14 .....70 A2
Blackberry La
  Potterne SN10 .....179 D5
  Winsley BA15 .....90 C1
Blackbird Way BA11 ...110 B6
Blackboard La SN10 ...180 B4
Blackcross SN15 .....78 F6
Blackcross Rd SP4 .....217 C2
Blackdown Cl 10 BA12 ...117 A8
Blackford La SN6 .....10 C4
Blackfriars Way SN1 ...152 B8
Blackhill Rd SO51 .....212 F3
Blackland Pk★ SN11 ...89 E7
Blacklands Crossroads
  SN11 .....89 C8
Blackman's La 4 SN8 ...183 D8
Blackmore Cl 1 SN3 .....51 E7
Blackmore La SN8 .....192 A7
Blackmore Rd
  Melksham SN12 .....94 C4
  3 Shaftesbury SP7 ...202 D2
Blackstone Ave SN3 .....51 C4
Blackthorn Cl SN4 .....47 E4
Blackthorn Mews SN15 ...78 F1
Blackworth SN6 .....22 F8
Blagdon Wlk BA11 .....110 C7
Blair Rd BA14 .....105 B7
Blake Cres SN3 .....36 C2
Blakeney Ave SN3 .....51 B7
Blakesley Cl 3 SN3 .....50 F4
Blakey Rd SP1 .....152 C8
Blandford Alley SN6 ...23 A5
Blandford Rd SP5 .....150 F1
Bleak St BA9 .....137 C3
Bleke St SP7 .....202 C2
Blendon Dr SP10 .....193 C1
Blenheim Gdns SN14 ...56 C6
Blenheim Pk 15 SN12 ...178 B8
Blenheim Rd SN4 .....64 A7
Blenheim Cl BA12 .....116 F7
Bletchley Cl 5 SN3 .....51 C4
Blick's Hill SN16 .....28 B4
Blicks Cl SN14 .....41 F1
Blicks Hill SN16 .....28 B3
Blind La Ansty SP3 .....203 F5
  Berwick St John SP7 ...207 B8
  Southwick BA14 .....104 F2
Blissford Rd SP6 .....210 F1
Bloody Shard Gate
  DT11 .....207 A1
Bloomsbury Cl 2 SN5 ...49 B4
Blounts Ct SN10 .....179 D5
Blowhorn St SN8 .....213 D4
Blue Boar Row SP1 .....146 A1
Bluebell Cl SN14 .....70 B3
Bluebell Gr SN11 .....81 B5
Blunsdon Rd SN25 .....34 F4
Blyth Way SP1 .....146 D4
Boar St BA12 .....139 A5
Bobbin La SN14 .....99 F4
Bobbin Pk BA15 .....99 F3
Bockhampton Rd
  RG17 .....165 A1

Bockhampton Village★
  RG17 .....165 B1
Bodiam Dr SN5 .....49 D4
Bodiam Dr N 4 SN5 .....49 D5
Bodiam Dr S 3 SN5 .....49 D4
Bodman Cl SN15 .....78 F4
Bodmin Cl SN3 .....51 A6
Bodyhorse Hill SN4 .....163 C6
Bohemia La SN3 .....51 B6
Bokerley Ditch★ SP6 ...209 A5
Bokerley Junc SP5 .....208 E6
Boldrewood SN3 .....51 D3
Boleyn Cl SN5 .....49 A6
Bolingbroke Cl SN5 .....47 F6
Bolingbroke Rd SN2 .....34 F2
Bolland's Hill SN12 .....178 D8
Bolton Dr SP4 .....133 D6
Bonaker Cl SP4 .....133 D6
Bond St
  Durrington/Bulford SP4 ...198 E6
  Trowbridge BA14 .....105 C3
Boness Rd SN4 .....64 A7
Bonham La BA12 .....137 E7
Bonner Cl 10 SN5 .....48 F5
Bonners Cl SN16 .....28 A5
Boothmead SN14 .....78 B8
Borage Cl SN2 .....34 D5
Border Cl SN25 .....34 C5
Bore Hill BA12 .....116 F4
Boreham Cl BA12 .....117 C6
Boreham Field BA12 ...117 D6
Boreham Rd BA12 .....117 E5
Borkum Cl 8 SP10 .....193 C2
Borough Fields SN4 .....47 D2
Borough The SP5 .....211 A8
Boscombe Down Airfield
  SP4 .....198 E3
Boscombe Rd
  Amesbury SP4 .....217 C2
  Swindon SN25 .....34 E4
Bosham Cl 6 SN5 .....49 B4
Boswell Rd BA15 .....99 F3
Bosworth Rd SN5 .....49 A5
Botany SN6 .....22 E5
Bothwell Rd SN3 .....50 F7
Botisdone Cl SP11 .....185 C3
Botley Copse SN5 .....34 A2
Bottlebush La BH21 .....208 E1
Bottom La
  Ogbourne St George
    SN8 .....169 A5
  1 West Wellow SO51 ...212 F6
Bouchers Way SP2 .....152 A5
Boulton Cl BA13 .....108 E1
Boundary Ave BA11 ...110 B5
Boundary Cl
  Lyneham SN15 .....59 C3
  Swindon SN2 .....35 F6
Boundary Rd
  Chippenham SN15 .....78 F8
  Salisbury SP1 .....146 E2
Bourbon Cl BA12 .....117 B5
Bourne Ave SP1 .....146 C2
Bourne Cl Porton SP4 ...133 D6
  1 Salisbury SP1 .....152 D8
  Warminster BA12 .....117 A5
  3 West Wellow SO51 ...212 F6
Bourne Gdns SP4 .....133 D6
Bourne Hill SP1 .....146 B1
Bourne La 6 SP9 .....199 D8
Bourne Lake Pk 18 E6
Bourne Rd Swindon SN2 ...34 F2
  Tidworth SP9 .....216 D6
Bourne Ret Pk SP1 .....152 D7
Bourne Rise SN8 .....183 E1
Bourne Vale RG17 .....177 B7
Bourne Valley Cl SP4 ...133 E5
Bourne View SP4 .....199 A1
Bourne Way SP1 .....152 D8
Bournmil Cl BA15 .....99 D7
Bourton Ave SN3 .....36 B2
Bourton La SN10 .....172 C3
Bourton Prim Sch
  SP8 .....137 E1
Bouverie Ave
  Salisbury SP2 .....152 A6
  Swindon SN3 .....50 D3
Bouverie Ave S SP2 .....151 F6
Bouverie Cl SP2 .....151 F6
Bouverie Dr 17 SN10 ...179 F1
Bouverie Pk SN4 .....56 B5
Boveridge House Sch
  BH21 .....209 B1
Bow Wow GL7 .....7 A7
Bowd's La SN15 .....60 A6
Bowden Cres SN12 .....94 C6
Bowden Pk★ SN15 .....87 B5
Bowdich Cl SP4 .....198 C7
Bower Gdns SP1 .....152 C8
Bower Hill Rd SP1 .....146 C2
Bower Rd SN8 .....175 D5
Bowerhill CP Sch SN12 ...94 C1
Bowerhill La SN12 .....94 E1
Bowers Hill SP5 .....211 D8
Bowers La SP11 .....185 B4
Bowes Lyon Ct SP2 .....145 D3
Bowldown Rd GL8 .....25 C8
Bowles Rd SN25 .....35 A5
Bowleymead SN3 .....51 D5
Bowling Gn La
  Pentridge SP5 .....208 D2
  Swindon SN1 .....50 C4
Bowls Barrow (Long
  Barrow)★ BA12 .....186 E1
Bowman Cl 5 SN3 .....36 B3
Bowood Cl SN11 .....79 F3

Bowood Golf & Ctry Club
SN11 . . . . .88 A8
Bowood House★ SN11 . .88 C8
Bowood Rd SN1 . . . . .50 B4
Box CE Sch SN13 . . . . . .83 D6
Box Dr SN8 . . . . .213 D8
Box Highlands Sch
SN13 . . . . .84 B8
Box Hill Box SN13 . . . . .76 A1
Corsham SN13 . . . . .83 E7
Box Rd BA1 . . . . .82 C3
Box View SN14 . . . . .75 B2
Boxbush Rd GL7 . . . . .7 A7
Boxfields Rd SN13 . . . . .83 F7
Boydell Cl SN5 . . . . .49 B8
Boyle Ave 4 SN11 . . . .166 A1
Boyne's La DT11 . . . . . .206 B1
Boyton Manor★ BA12 . .194 E2
Bozley Hill SN4 . . . . . . .206 A8
Bracken Cl SP5 . . . . . . .153 D3
Brackenbury 8 SP10 . .193 C1
Brackenbury Rd SP4 . . .197 D4
Brackland SN10 . . . . . . .180 A2
Bradbury Cl SN15 . . . . . .79 A5
Bradene Cl 3 SN4 . . . . .47 E2
Bradenham Rd SN5 . . . . .49 A5
Bradenstoke Abbey★
SN15 . . . . .59 B3
Bradfield Cl BA12 . . . . .117 D5
Bradford Rd
Atworth SN12 . . . . .92 E4
Bathford BA1 . . . . .82 B2
Box SN13 . . . . .83 F3
Broughton Gifford SN12 .93 F4
Corsham SN13 . . . . .76 C1
Holt BA14 . . . . .101 D8
Melksham SN12 . . . . . . .94 A5
Rode BA11 . . . . .103 F1
Swindon SN1 . . . . .50 C4
Trowbridge BA14 . . . . .101 B1
Winsley BA15 . . . . .99 D6
Bradford-on-Avon Com
Hospl BA15 . . . . .100 D8
Bradford-on-Avon Golf Club
BA15 . . . . .100 E5
Bradford-on-Avon
Swimming Pool
BA15 . . . . .100 C6
Bradley Cl Holt BA14 . .101 F8
Warminster BA12 . . . . .116 E4
Bradley La Holt BA14 . . .92 F1
Maiden Bradley with Yarnfield
BA12 . . . . .118 C3
Bradley Mound★
BA12 . . . . .118 F2
Bradley Pk★ BA12 . . . .118 F1
Bradley Rd
Southwick BA14 . . . . . .105 B2
Swindon SN2 . . . . .35 D4
Trowbridge BA14 . . . . .105 C5
Warminster BA12 . . . . .116 E4
Bradon Forest Comp Sch
SN5 . . . . .33 C3
Bradwell Cl 2 SP10 . . .193 C2
Bradwell Moor SN3 . . . .51 D2
Braemar SN3 . . . . .50 E7
Braemar Rise SP1 . . . .146 B4
Braemor Rd SN11 . . . . .81 A4
Braemore CE Prim Sch
SP6 . . . . .210 E4
Braithwaite Way 3
BA11 . . . . .110 C6
Brake Mead SN15 . . . . .78 F7
Brakspear Dr SN13 . . . .76 E1
Bramble Cl SN2 . . . . . . .35 E1
Bramble Dr SN5 . . . . . . .79 A4
Bramble Rd SN2 . . . . . . .35 E1
Brambles The
Hinton Charterhouse BA2 .98 E1
Salisbury SP1 . . . . .146 C2
Bramdean Cl SN25 . . . .34 F5
Bramley Cl
Pewsey SN9 . . . . .215 D6
4 Warminster BA12 . . .116 E7
Bramley Dr BA11 . . . . .110 C6
Bramley Hill BA12 . . . .138 C5
Bramley La BA14 . . . . .105 D7
Bramley Way SN4 . . . .217 C3
Bramleys The SP5 . . . .161 D3
Brampton Ct 8 SN4 . . .178 B8
Bramptons The SN5 . . .49 B7
Bramshaw Golf Club
SO43 . . . . .212 E1
Bramshaw Telegraph★
SP6 . . . . .211 F3
Bramwell Cl SN2 . . . . . .35 E6
Brancaster Ave 1 SP10 193 C2
Branch Rd BA2 . . . . .98 F2
Branders 4 SN6 . . . . . .19 D8
Brandon Cl SN5 . . . . . . .49 A5
Branksome Rd SN25 . . .34 E3
Branscombe Dr SN4 . . .47 F5
Bransdown Hill
Easton Grey SN16 . . . . .26 A3
Sherston SN16 . . . . .25 F2
Brassknocker Hill BA2 . .90 A1
Bratch La SP3 . . . . .201 D8
Bratton Camp★ BA13 . .186 A6
Bratton Cl SN2 . . . . .35 E4
Bratton CP Sch BA13 . .186 B7
Bratton Rd
West Ashton BA14 . . . .106 B4
Westbury BA13 . . . . . . .109 C4
Bray St SN4 . . . . .173 A8
Braybrooke Cl 2 SN5 . .48 F8
Braydon La SN6 . . . . . . .18 F4
Breach La SP8 . . . . .137 E2
Breach La Chute SP11 . .192 E8

Breach La continued
1 Shaftesbury SP7 . . . .202 B1
Southwick BA14 . . . . . .105 A3
Wootton Bassett SN4 . . .61 B5
Breach The SN14 . . . . .214 B2
Bread St BA12 . . . . .116 F5
Bream Cl SN14 . . . . .94 D6
Breamore Countryside Mus★
SP6 . . . . .210 E5
Breamore House★
SP6 . . . . .210 E6
Breamore Rd SP5 . . . . .210 F7
Brecon Cl
Melksham SN12 . . . . . . .94 D4
Swindon SN3 . . . . .50 E2
Bremen Gdns 21 SP10 .193 D2
Bremeridge Cl BA13 . . .109 B3
Bremhill Cl SN2 . . . . . . .35 C4
Bremhill View SN11 . . . .81 A4
Bremilham Rd SN16 . . . .27 E3
Bremilham Rise SN16 . .27 E3
Breton Rd BA14 . . . . . . .108 F2
Brettingham Gate SN3 . .64 F8
Brewer Mead SN15 . . . .78 F4
Brewers La SN11 . . . . . .81 C1
Brewery St SN6 . . . . . . .23 A4
Briar Cl Frome BA11 . . .110 B7
Westbury BA13 . . . . . . .108 F4
Briar Fields SN1 . . . . . .50 E7
Briar Leaze SN11 . . . . .166 B3
Briars Cl SN4 . . . . .47 E3
Briary Rd GL7 . . . . .2 C6
Brick Hill SN15 . . . . .95 D6
Brick La Salisbury SP2 . .145 C3
Trowbridge BA14 . . . . .101 D3
Brickham Rd 1 SN10 . .214 D5
Brickley La SN10 . . . . . .214 D2
Bricksteed Ave SN10 . .214 C3
Brickworth La SP5 . . . .160 E4
Bridewell La SP7 . . . . . .202 A6
Bridge Ave BA14 . . . . . .105 A8
Bridge End Rd SN3 . . . .51 F1
Bridge Rd SP5 . . . . .205 E4
Bridge St Bourton SP8 . .137 E2
Bradford-on-Avon BA15 .100 D6
Fordingbridge SP6 . . . .210 D1
26 Hungerford RG17 . .177 B7
Marlborough SN8 . . . . .213 D3
Salisbury SP2 . . . . .152 A8
Swindon SN1 . . . . .50 B6
3 Trowbridge BA14 . . .105 D7
Bridge The SN15 . . . . . .78 B7
Bridgeman Cl SN3 . . . . .36 B2
Bridgemead Cl SN5 . . . .49 D7
Bridgewater Cl SN2 . . . .50 A7
Bridport Rd SN3 . . . . . .51 B4
Briery Cl SN3 . . . . .36 A4
Bright Cl 8 SN15 . . . . . .78 F5
Bright St SN2 . . . . .50 D8
Brighton Way SN14 . . . .77 F6
Brimble Hill SN4 . . . . . .64 D5
Brimble Hill Specl Sch
SN3 . . . . .51 B5
Brimhill Rise BA13 . . . .111 D4
Brind Cl SN3 . . . . .51 E6
Brind Rd SP4 . . . . .197 F1
Brindley La SN2 . . . . . . .34 E1
Brington Rd SN3 . . . . . .51 B8
Brinkworth Cl SN14 . . . .77 F7
Brinkworth Earl Danbys CE Prim Sch
SN15 . . . . .45 E5
Brinkworth Golf Club
SN15 . . . . .45 C8
Brinkworth Rd SN15 . . .45 C3
Brinscombe La 8 SP7 . .202 D1
Brionne Way 13 SP7 . .202 D2
Brisbane Gdns 7 SP4 . .198 F6
Bristol Rd
Chippenham SN14 . . . . .78 C8
Chippenham Without
SN14 . . . . .69 E2
Luckington SN14 . . . . . .39 D3
Bristol St
3 Malmesbury SN16 . . .28 A3
Swindon SN1 . . . . .50 A6
Britannia Ave SN9 . . . .182 B2
Britannia Cres SN15 . . .60 B2
Britannia Pl SN1 . . . . . .50 D4
Britford La SP2 . . . . . . .152 B6
Britford La W 1 SP2 . .152 A6
Britford Prim Sch
SP5 . . . . .152 D5
British Row BA14 . . . . .101 C1
Britmore La SP7 . . . . . .202 F4
Brittain Cl SN14 . . . . . . .77 F7
Brittox The SN10 . . . . . .214 B3
Brixham Ave SN3 . . . . . .50 E5
Broad Chalke Prim Sch
SP5 . . . . .205 C4
Broad Hinton (Hackpen)
White Horse★ SN4 . . .167 E5
Broad St Swindon SN1 . .50 C7
Trowbridge BA14 . . . . .101 C1
Broad Stones BA15 . . . .90 E7
Broad Town CE Prim Sch
SN4 . . . . .62 B1
Broadacres SN4 . . . . . . .62 B2
Broadbury Banks★
SN9 . . . . .181 B2
Broadcloth E La BA14 . .105 E4
Broadcloth La BA14 . . .105 E7
Broadfield Rd SP4 . . . . .133 D2
Broadfields SN9 . . . . . .215 B4
Broadlands SP1 . . . . . . .146 B4
Broadleas Cl SN10 . . . .214 A2
Broadleas Cres SN10 . .214 A2

Broadleas Gdns★
SN10 . . . . .214 A1
Broadleas Rd SN10 . . . .214 A2
Broadleaze
Down Ampney GL7 . . . . . .8 E4
Seagry SN15 . . . . .57 D6
Broadly Pk BA14 . . . . . .105 D3
Broadmead
Corsham SN13 . . . . .85 B7
Warminster BA12 . . . . .116 A1
Broadmead La BA12 . . .116 A1
Broadmoor Rd SN3 . . . .36 D7
Broadtown La
Broad Town SN4 . . . . . .62 B3
Wootton Bassett SN4 . . .61 F5
Broadway
Market Lavington SN10 .179 D2
Warminster BA12 . . . . .116 E5
Broadway Cl GL7 . . . . . .10 D7
Broadway E BA13 . . . . .108 D6
Broadway La GL7 . . . . . . .7 A5
Broadway The SN25 . . . .35 A3
Broadwood Ave SN13 . . .84 B8
Broadwood Cl 1 BA12 .117 A8
Brockley Rise SN2 . . . . .36 A5
Brocks Orch 8 SP3 . . .196 E6
Broken Cross
Calne SN11 . . . . .81 B3
Laverstock SP4 . . . . . . .146 F6
Brokerswood Rd
BA14 . . . . .105 A1
Bromley Cl 2 SN3 . . . . .50 E6
Bronte Cl 1 SN3 . . . . . .51 D4
Brook Cl 16 SP3 . . . . . .203 E8
Brook Dr SN13 . . . . .85 B7
Brook Dro BA13 . . . . . .108 C4
Brook Hill
Donhead St Andrew SP7 .203 B2
Sherston SN16 . . . . .40 C8
Brook La
Westbury BA13 . . . . . . .108 D4
Woodgreen SP6 . . . . . .211 A4
Brook Rd BA14 . . . . . . .101 B1
Brook St
Chippenham SN14 . . . . .78 B8
Fovant SP3 . . . . .204 D7
Great Bedwyn SN8 . . . .176 C3
Warminster BA12 . . . . .116 E5
Brook Way SN11 . . . . . .81 C3
Brookdene SN25 . . . . . .34 E4
Brookfield SN6 . . . . .22 F7
Brookfield Prim Sch
SN5 . . . . .49 A8
Brookfields SN12 . . . . . .85 D1
Brookfields SO51 . . . . .212 F6
Brooklands SN15 . . . . . .45 E5
Brooklands Ave SN2 . . .34 C1
Brookleaze SN13 . . . . . .84 E5
Brooklime Cl 1 SN2 . . .34 D4
Brookmead BA14 . . . . .105 A3
Brooks Cl SN2 . . . . .35 E6
Brooksby Way SN3 . . . .51 B8
Brookside
Crudwell SN16 . . . . .14 E6
Hullavington SN14 . . . . .41 F2
Brookwell Cl SN14 . . . . .70 C2
Broomcroft Rd SN9 . . . .215 C5
Broome Manor La SN3 . .50 F2
Broomfield SN15 . . . . . .70 D2
Broomground BA15 . . . .99 E2
Broomhill SP5 . . . . .212 C5
Brotherton Cl SN15 . . . .78 F5
Broughton Gifford Sch
SN12 . . . . .93 B3
Broughton Grange 6
SN3 . . . . .51 B8
Broughton Rd 2 BA14 .105 C5
Brouncker's Well★
BA12 . . . . .186 F5
Brow The SN25 . . . . . . .34 E4
Brown St
3 Salisbury SP1 . . . . . .146 B1
Salisbury SP1 . . . . .152 B8
Trowbridge BA14 . . . . .105 D7
Brown's Folly★ BA1 . . .82 C1
Brown's La SN8 . . . . . . .176 B3
Browning Cl 1 SN3 . . . .36 B3
Brownings The SN3 . . . .83 D5
Brownleaze La SN10 . . .179 D6
Browns La Alton SN8 . . .173 C1
Damerham SP6 . . . . . . .209 E3
Broxburn Rd BA12 . . . .116 D6
Bruce St SN2 . . . . .49 F7
Bruddel Gr SN3 . . . . . . .50 E2
Bruges Cl SN15 . . . . . . .78 F7
Brunel Ct SN15 . . . . . . .78 B6
Brunel Rd SP2 . . . . .145 D1
Brunel Way Box SN13 . .83 D6
Frome BA11 . . . . .110 C7
Brunkard's La SN9 . . . .215 D6
Brunswick St SN1 . . . . .50 C4
Brushy Bush La SP5 . . .207 F3
Bruyn Rd SP6 . . . . .210 E1
Bryans Cl Rd SN11 . . . .81 B3
Bryanston Way SN3 . . . .51 C6
Bryant Rd SP2 . . . . .145 C5
Brydes Rd 21 SP11 . . .192 A5
Brympton Cl 5 SP6 . . .210 C1
Brynards Hill SN4 . . . . .47 E1
Bryony Way SN2 . . . . . .34 D4
Bryworth La GL7 . . . . . . .2 A6
Buckhurst Cres SN3 . . . .51 A6
Buckingham Rd
Chippenham SN15 . . . . .79 A5
Swindon SN3 . . . . .50 E6
Buckland Cl SN3 . . . . . .51 A6
Buckleaze Cl BA14 . . . .105 D5
Buckleaze La SN9 . . . . .215 C5

Bucklebury Cl SN3 . . . . .36 A1
Buckthorn Dr SN2 . . . . .34 D4
Budbury Circ BA15 . . . .100 C7
Budbury Cl BA15 . . . . .100 C7
Budbury Pl BA15 . . . . .100 C7
Budbury Ridge BA15 . .100 C7
Budbury Tyning BA15 . .100 C7
Budge La SN16 . . . . . . .114 A8
Buettell Way SN16 . . . . .27 F5
Buie SN5 . . . . .34 B2
Bulbridge Rd SP2 . . . . .144 B1
Bulford Droveway
SP4 . . . . .198 D7
Bulford Hill SP4 . . . . . . .217 C8
Bulford Rd Bulford SP4 .217 E8
Durrington/Bulford SP4 .198 B7
Shipton Bellinger SP9 . .199 C8
South Tedworth SP9 . . .216 A4
Bull La BA12 . . . . .116 F2
Bull Pit BA15 . . . . .100 D6
Bulldog La SN10 . . . . . .180 C3
Buller St SN2 . . . . .35 D1
Bullfinch Cl SN3 . . . . . . .51 D6
Bullock's Horn La
Charlton SN16 . . . . .29 D7
Hankerton SN16 . . . . . . .15 D1
Bulls La Box SN13 . . . . .83 D6
Broad Chalke SP5 . . . . .205 B4
Bulpit La RG17 . . . . . . .177 B6
Bulpits SP11 . . . . .185 C3
Bumper's Batch BA2 . . .98 A8
Bumpers Way SN14 . . . .70 A1
Bunce Rd SN3 . . . . .36 A2
Bunnies La SN10 . . . . . .96 D2
Bunns La BA11 . . . . . . .114 A2
Bunny La SP5 . . . . .162 C4
Buntings The SN5 . . . . .51 D7
Bupton Village★
SN11 . . . . .166 D7
Burbage CP Sch SN8 . .183 D8
Burbage Rd
Easton SN9 . . . . .183 A8
Milton Lilbourne SN9 . . .182 F7
Swindon SN2 . . . . .35 C6
Burbage Wharf★ SN8 . .175 C2
Burcombe La SP2 . . . . .144 B2
Burden Cl SN3 . . . . .36 C1
Burderop Cl
1 Trowbridge BA14 . . .105 D5
Wroughton SN4 . . . . . . .64 B8
Burderop Pk★ SN4 . . . .64 F5
Burdett St 4 SN8 . . . . .170 B2
Burford Ave
Salisbury SP2 . . . . .152 A6
Swindon SN3 . . . . .50 E6
Burford Rd SP2 . . . . . . .152 B6
Burford St GL7 . . . . .2 C4
Burford's 2 RG17 . . . . .171 E7
Burgate Fields SP6 . . . .210 D2
Burgess Cl SN3 . . . . . . .36 A1
Burgess Gn SP1 . . . . . .146 C4
Burghley Cl SN3 . . . . . .51 A6
Burlands Rd SN15 . . . . .78 E6
Burleaze SN15 . . . . .78 D5
Burn Rd SN13 . . . . .76 E1
Burnet Cl
Melksham SN12 . . . . . . .94 B2
Swindon SN2 . . . . .34 D5
Burnet Way SN1 . . . . . .146 D4
Burnett Rd BA14 . . . . . .105 D6
Burnham Rd
5 Fordingbridge SP6 . .210 D2
4 Malmesbury SN16 . . .28 A4
Swindon SN3 . . . . .51 B6
Burnhams Cl 1 SP10 . .193 E2
Burnivale SN16 . . . . . . .28 A3
Burns Way SN2 . . . . . . .35 E4
Burnston Cl SN14 . . . . . .94 D5
Burr La SN8 . . . . .176 F1
Burroughs Dro 2 SN8 . .183 D8
Burton Cl 11 SP7 . . . . .202 D2
Burton Farm Cl SN14 . . .53 B3
Burton Hill Sch SN16 . . .28 A1
Burton Rd GL9 . . . . .52 F6
Burton St SN13 . . . . .83 C5
Burtons SN13 . . . . .83 C5
Burwood Cl 7 SP4 . . . .217 E3
Bury Camp (Hill Fort)★
SN14 . . . . .67 B1
Bury Fields SN5 . . . . . . .33 D1
Bury Hill (Settlement)★
SN6 . . . . .18 B1
Bury La BA13 . . . . .186 B7
Bury Mead BA12 . . . . . .195 A2
Burycroft SN4 . . . . .163 A6
Burytown La SN26 . . . . .21 C2
Buscote Old Parsonage
(National Trust) SN7 . . . .2 E1
Bush Barrow★ SP4 . . . .197 D4
Bush Farm Bison Ctr★
BA12 . . . . .140 B3
Bustlers Hill SN16 . . . . .40 D8
Bute Cl SN6 . . . . .22 F7
Butler Cl SP2 . . . . .152 B6
Butler's Field GL7 . . . . . .2 C5
Butler's Gdns BA11 . . .110 A4
Butlers SN16 . . . . .25 C1
Butt Cl SP11 . . . . .192 A6
Butt La SP5 . . . . .205 E4
Butt St SP11 . . . . .192 A5
Butt's La BA15 . . . . .90 F7
Butter Furlong Rd
SP5 . . . . .154 C3
Buttercup Cl SN14 . . . . .70 B3
Butterfield Dr SP4 . . . . .217 D3
Buttermere SN3 . . . . . . .51 E3
Butterworth St SN1 . . . .50 A5
Buttons Yd BA12 . . . . . .117 B7

Butts (Tumuli) The★
SP6 . . . . .211 E2
Butts Cl SN14 . . . . .76 E7
Butts Hill SP3 . . . . .129 E7
Butts La
Kilmington BA12 . . . . . .123 E6
Steeple Ashton BA14 . .178 A3
Butts Mead 3 SP7 . . . .202 D1
Butts Rd Chiseldown SN4 . .65 D5
Salisbury SP1 . . . . .146 A2
Butts Terr SP2 . . . . .146 A2
Butts The
Aldbourne SN8 . . . . . . .170 A6
Biddestone SN14 . . . . . .76 D7
Bratton BA13 . . . . .186 B7
Chippenham SN15 . . . . .78 E6
Crudwell SN16 . . . . .14 E6
Lydiard Millicent SN5 . . .48 C8
Potterne SN10 . . . . . . .179 D5
Shaftesbury SP7 . . . . . .202 B2
Shrewton SP3 . . . . .196 E7
Steeple Ashton BA14 . .178 A3
Westbury BA13 . . . . . . .109 A2
Bydemill Gdns SN6 . . . .22 E5
Byfield Way SN3 . . . . . . .51 B8
Byrd Cl 18 SN5 . . . . . . .48 F5
Byron Ave SN4 . . . . .47 F2
Byron Cl 11 SP11 . . . . .192 A5
Byron Ct SN3 . . . . .36 E5
Byron Rd SN10 . . . . . . .214 B1
Byron St 3 SN1 . . . . . . .50 C5
Bythebrook SN14 . . . . . .70 B1
Bythesea Rd BA14 . . . .105 C8
Byways Cl 4 SP1 . . . . .152 C8

C

Cabot Dr SN5 . . . . .48 F6
Cabul Rd SP9 . . . . .216 B5
Cadby Cl BA14 . . . . . . .105 F6
Caddy La BA12 . . . . . . .138 F5
Cadley Cl SN2 . . . . .35 D2
Cadley Rd SN8 . . . . . . .183 E1
Cadnam Cres SP4 . . . . .217 E2
Caen Hill SN10 . . . . . . .179 C8
Caen Hill Gdns SN10 . .179 C8
Caen Hill Locks★
SN10 . . . . .179 C8
Caen View SN1 . . . . .49 C8
Caerleon Dr 4 SP10 . . .193 E2
Caesar Rd SP10 . . . . . .193 E2
Caesar's Camp (Fort)★
DT11 . . . . .206 A7
Cagney Dr SN25 . . . . . .35 A5
Caird Lawns SN10 . . . .214 C2
Cairndow Way SN2 . . . .35 E5
Calcutt St SN6 . . . . .19 E8
Calder Cl SN25 . . . . . . .34 F5
Callaghan Cl 2 SN3 . . . .36 B2
Callas Hill SN4 . . . . . . .163 B5
Callas Rise 7 SN4 . . . .163 B6
Callenders SN5 . . . . . . .49 E5
Callow Croft 6 SN8 . . .183 D8
Callows Cross SN15 . . . .46 C6
Calne Coll SN11 . . . . . . .81 B2
Calne Dunstan CE Jun Sch
SN11 . . . . .81 C4
Calne Rd SN15 . . . . .60 A1
Calves La SP7 . . . . .202 A2
Calvert Rd SN3 . . . . .50 E6
Cambrai Rd SN4 . . . . . .65 D1
Cambria Bridge Rd
SN1 . . . . .50 A5
Cambria Pl SN1 . . . . . . .50 A5
Cambridge Cl SN3 . . . . .50 F4
Cambridge Rd SP1 . . . .146 B3
Camden Cl SN5 . . . . . . .49 A5
Camellia Dr BA12 . . . . .116 E7
Camelot Cl 28 SP10 . . .193 E2
Cameron Cl SP4 . . . . . .217 D8
Camilla Cl SP4 . . . . .217 D8
Camomile Dr 25 SP11 . .192 A5
Campbell Rd SP1 . . . . .146 B2
Campden Rd SN3 . . . . . .50 E5
Campion Cl SN11 . . . . . .81 B5
Campion Dr
Melksham SN12 . . . . . . .94 C2
Trowbridge BA14 . . . . .105 D6
Campion Gate SN5 . . . .48 F5
Camton Rd SN5 . . . . . . .48 F7
Canada Rd SO51 . . . . .212 F6
Canada Rise SN10 . . . .179 F1
Canadian Ave SP2 . . . .145 D2
Canal Cl Calne SN11 . . .81 A2
Wilcot SN8 . . . . .182 A8
Canal La SP5 . . . . .153 E2
Canal Mus★ SN10 . . . .214 B4
Canal Rd
Chippenham SN15 . . . . .78 F5
Trowbridge BA14 . . . . .101 E4
Canal Way SN10 . . . . . .214 E6
Canal Wlk
Hungerford RG17 . . . . .177 B7
Swindon SN1 . . . . .50 B6
Canalside SP5 . . . . .153 E2
Canberra Dr SP4 . . . . . .198 F6
Candown Rd SP3 . . . . .188 B2
Canford Cl SN3 . . . . . . .51 C6
Cann Hill SP7 . . . . .206 A7
Canney Cl SN4 . . . . .65 D4
Cannimore Rd BA12 . . .116 D5
Cannon Sq SN12 . . . . . .94 A4
Cannon St SN1 . . . . .50 C5
Cannwood La BA10 . . . .122 D8

Canons Cl
Tidworth SP9 ....216 D4
Warminster BA12 ......117 C5
Cantax Hill SN15 ....86 C6
Canterbury Cl
🔟 Amesbury SP4 .....217 D3
Swindon SN3 ....50 F5
Canterbury St SN14 .....78 C8
Cantors Way SN16 .....17 C2
Capesthorne Dr SN25 ...34 E6
Capitol Cl SN3 ....36 D1
Capps La BA13 ....109 E7
Caprice Cl 🔳 SN5 ....49 A7
Capulet Dr SN5 ....145 F4
Caraway Dr SN2 ....34 C4
Carders Cnr 🔳 BA14 ..105 D7
Cardigan Cl SN3 ....50 E4
Cardigan Rd SN8 ......213 C3
Cardwell Cl 🔳 SN3 ....51 B7
Carey Cl SN5 ....49 A5
Carfax Cl 🔳 SN1 ......50 C6
Carfax St 🔳 SN1 ......50 C6
Carisbrook Rd SN12 ....94 B2
Carisbrook Terr SN4 ....65 C3
Carisbrooke Cres
BA14 ....101 E5
Carleton Pl SP4 ....217 A4
Carlisle Ave SN3 ....50 D3
Carlton Cl 🔳 SP4 .....217 D3
Carlton Gate SN3 ....50 F1
Carlton Row BA14 .....105 C6
Carman Cl SN3 ....36 B3
Carmelite Way SP1 ....152 B2
Carnarvon Cl SN14 .....78 A7
Carnation La SN12 .....178 C8
Carpenter Cl 🔳 SN15 ...78 F5
Carpenter's Cl 🔳 80 F4
Carpenters Cl SN16 ....25 D1
Carpenters La
🔳 Bratton BA13 ......186 B7
Swindon SN2 ....50 D8
Carr St SN1 ....50 B6
Carrick Cl SN3 ....79 A8
Carrion Pond Dro
SP2 ....151 D7
Carroll Cl SN3 ....51 D4
Carronbridge Rd SN5 ...49 B6
Carshalton Rd SN3 .....51 B3
Carstairs Ave SN3 .....51 A3
Carter's Cl SP6 ....211 C6
Cartway SN10 ....180 E4
Cartwright Dr SN5 ......49 B8
Carvers Hill SN8 ......176 E1
Cary Glen SN15 ....79 A4
Casley La BA11 ....107 C7
Casson Rd SN3 ....36 A2
Casterbridge La 🔳
SP11 ....192 F1
Casterley Camp ★
SN9 ....189 D8
Castle Barrow ★ BA12 ..195 A4
Castle Combe Golf Club
SN14 ....68 A8
Castle Combe Motor Racing
Circuit ★ SN14 ......68 C6
Castle Combe Motte &
Baileys ★ SN14 ......67 F8
Castle Ct SP11 ....192 A6
Castle Ditches Hill Fort ★
SP3 ....204 A7
Castle Dore SN5 ....49 A5
Castle Hill (Fort) ★
SN26 ....21 D3
Castle Hill Cl 🔳 SP7 ..202 B2
Castle Hill Cres BA12 ..139 A6
Castle Hill La BA12 ....139 A5
Castle Keep
Salisbury SP1 ....145 E4
🔳 Wilton SP2 ....144 D3
Castle La Alderbury SP5 .153 E1
Devizes SN10 ....214 A3
Wilton SP2 ....144 D3
Castle Mdw SP5 ....211 A8
Castle Prim Sch SP11 ..192 B5
Castle Rd Bratton BA13 ..186 A6
Devizes SN10 ....214 A3
🔳 Great Bedwyn SN8 ..176 B3
Salisbury SP1 ....146 A3
Castle St
Aldbourne SN8 ....170 A6
Calne SN11 ....81 B2
🔳 Ludgershall SP11 ...192 A5
Mere BA12 ....138 F5
Salisbury SP2 ....146 A2
Trowbridge BA14 ....105 D8
Castle View
West Tisbury SP3 .....203 B8
Westbury BA13 ......109 B3
Castle View Cl SN4 .....65 E4
Castle View Rd
Chiseldown SN4 ....65 E4
Swindon SN3 ....36 C1
Castle Woods 🔳 SP5 ...211 C6
Castledown Comp Sch
SP11 ....191 F5
Castlefield Cl 🔳 SN5 ...49 C6
Castlefields SN11 ....81 A3
Castlehaven Cl SN15 ....79 A5
Castleton Rd SN5 ....49 A7
Castley Rd BA14 ....102 A2
Catalina Ct 🔳 SN12 ...178 B8
Cathedral Sch SP1 .....152 A7
Catherine Cres
Dinton SP3 ....201 E2
Downton SP5 ....210 F8

Catherine Ford La
Dinton SP3 ....201 E1
Fovant SP3 ....204 E8
Catherine St
Salisbury SP1 ....152 B8
🔳 Swindon SN1 ....50 B6
Catherine Waite Prim Sch
SN25 ....34 F6
Catherine Way BA1 .....82 A5
Catherine Wayte Cl
SN25 ....34 F6
Catmint Cl SN2 ....34 D4
Cator Rd 🔳 SP4 ......197 E2
Cats Hill La SP7 ......203 A1
Catterick Cl 🔳 SN14 ...77 F6
Caulfield Rd SN2 ....50 D6
Causeway The SN15 .....45 D6
Caversham Cl SN3 ......50 F5
Cavie Cl SN5 ....49 A8
Caxton Cl
🔳 Andover SP10 ......193 C1
🔳 Swindon SN3 ....50 F4
Caxton Rd BA11 ......110 A3
Cayenne Pk SN2 ....34 C4
Cecil Ave SP2 ....152 A5
Cecil Rd SN3 ....51 A6
Cecil Terr SP2 ....145 D1
Cedar Cl Melksham SN12 .94 A3
Salisbury SP2 ....145 B4
Worton SN10 ....179 B4
Cedar Gr
Chippenham SN15 ......70 E1
Trowbridge BA14 .....105 B6
Cedars Cl SN2 ....35 A2
Celandine Way SN14 ....70 B2
Cemetery La BA15 .....100 F7
Central St SN1 ....192 A5
Centre The SP4 ....217 A4
Centurion Cl
Chippenham SN15 ......79 A5
🔳 Salisbury SP2 .....145 D2
Centurion Way SN3 .....51 C8
Cerney Wick La GL7 .....7 D5
Chaddenwick Hill
BA12 ....140 B7
Chaffeymoor Hill SP8 ..137 B1
Chaffinch Ave BA14 ....110 B6
Chaffinch Dr 🔳 BA14 ..105 B8
Chafyn Gr Sch SP1 ....146 C2
Chain Dro
South Newton SP3 ....130 B6
Stapleford SP3 ......129 F7
Chain Hill SP3 ....129 E7
Chain La BA12 ....117 C6
Chalcot La
Chapmanslade BA13 ...111 F5
Upton Scudamore BA13 .112 A6
Chalet Specl Sch The
SN1 ....50 E6
Chalfield Cres SN12 ....94 C5
Chalfont Cl BA14 .....105 A8
Chalford Ave SN3 ......51 B7
Chalk Hill 🔳 SP3 .....196 F6
Chalk Pyt Rd SP5 .....205 B4
Chalk's Cl 🔳 SP5 .....211 C8
Chalkcroft La SP11 ....193 A2
Challis Cl 🔳 SP11 ....192 B5
Chamberlain Rd
Chippenham Without
SN14 ....77 F7
Swindon SN3 ....36 A2
Chambers Ave SP4 .....217 C2
Chambon Cl SN16 ....17 A2
Champney Rd 🔳 BA11 ..110 A7
Chancel Way GL7 ....2 C4
Chancellor Cl SN5 ......48 F6
Chancery Cl 🔳 SP2 ....145 E2
Chancery La BA12 .....117 C6
Chandler Cl SN3 ....50 D5
Chandler Way 🔳 SN15 ..78 F4
Chandler's La 🔳 SN8 ..170 A7
Chandlers Cl SN10 ....180 F8
Chandlers La
All Cannings SN10 ....180 F8
Bishops Cannings SN10 .172 B2
Chandos Cl SN5 ....49 A6
Chanterelle Pk BA15 ...100 D5
Chantry Gdns BA14 ....104 F3
Chantry La Chute SP11 ..184 C2
Marlborough SN8 .....213 D2
Westbury BA13 ......109 A3
Chantry Mead 🔳 RG17 ..177 B7
Chantry Rd Swindon SN2 ..34 F2
Wilton SP2 ....144 C1
Chantry The ★ BA12 ..139 A3
Chants La 🔳 SP3 .....196 E6
Chapel Cl GL7 ....10 D6
Chapel Cnr SN14 ....41 F1
Chapel Ct 🔳 RG17 ....177 B7
Chapel Hill
Broad Blunsdon SN26 ...21 B2
Grimstead SP5 ......154 B2
Lacock SN15 ....86 C6
Chapel La
Acton Turville GL9 .....53 A6
Andover SP10 ....193 E3
Bishopstone SP5 ....205 E4
Box SN13 ....83 D5
Broad Town SN4 .....167 B8
Chippenham SN15 ......78 E7
Collingbourne Kingston
SN8 ....183 D2
Corsham SN13 ....84 F6
Downton SP5 ....159 B5
Hankerton SN16 ....15 C2
🔳 Lambourn RG17 ....165 A2
🔳 Ludgershall SP11 ...192 A5
Melksham Without SN12 ..86 A1

Chapel La continued
Minety SN16 ....17 A2
Nomansland SP5 .....212 C4
Oaksey SN16 ....15 E8
Pen Selwood BA9 ....137 C3
🔳 Ramsbury SN8 .....170 B2
Redlynch SP5 ....211 D7
🔳 Shrewton SP3 .....196 E6
South Marston SN3 ....36 E5
Stapleford SP3 ......129 E7
Upavon SN9 ....181 F2
🔳 Wanborough SN4 ...163 B6
Wingfield BA14 ......104 C6
Woodborough SN9 ....181 D7
Zennor BA12 ....137 E5
Chapel Orch 🔳 SN4 ....163 B6
Chapel Path SN4 ....75 B3
Chapel Pl 🔳 SP2 ......146 A1
Chapel Rd
Ashbury SN6 ....164 A7
Heytesbury BA12 .....194 C5
Kempsford GL7 ....10 D7
Chapel Rise SN12 ....92 E8
Chapel St
Horningsham BA12 ....119 A7
Swindon SN2 ....50 D8
Warminster BA12 ....116 F5
Chapel Wlk GL9 ....24 B3
Chaplins Pl 🔳 SP4 ....217 B7
Chapmanslade CE Sch
BA13 ....111 C4
Charcoal Burners Rd
SN8 ....175 B4
Charcroft Hill BA10 ...122 A5
Charfield Cl SN3 ....51 A4
Charlbury St SN25 ......34 E3
Charles Garrett Cl 🔳
SP7 ....202 C2
Charles Rd SP4 ....198 B7
Charles St
Corsham SN13 ....76 F2
🔳 Salisbury SP2 .....145 F1
Trowbridge BA14 ....101 C1
Charlham La GL7 ....8 D7
Charlieu Ave SN11 ......89 C8
Charlotte Mews SN3 ....50 D4
Charlotte St BA14 .....101 D1
Charlton Cl SN2 ....35 D5
Charlton Hill BA13 ....186 D5
Charlton La SP7 ....202 F1
Charlton Pk ★ SN16 .....28 C8
Charlton Rd SN16 ....28 E5
Charlwood Rd SN13 .....84 F8
Charnham La RG17 .....177 B8
Charnham Pk RG17 .....177 B8
Charnwood Dr 🔳 SP6 ..210 D2
Charnwood Rd
Salisbury SP2 ....145 E1
Trowbridge BA14 ....101 A1
Charter Cl 🔳 SN10 ....214 D5
Charter CP Sch SN15 ...78 E6
Charter Rd SN15 ....78 D7
Charterhouse Dr 🔳
BA11 ....110 C7
Chartley Gn 🔳 SN5 ....49 A5
Chase Cres SN5 ....207 E4
Chase Wood SN5 ....34 A2
Chatham Cl SP1 ....145 F4
Chatsworth Rd SN25 ....34 F5
Chaucer Ave 🔳 SP10 ..193 C1
Chaucer Cl SN4 ....47 E3
Chaveywell Ct SN11 .....81 B7
Cheapside BA12 ....195 A2
Cheddar Cl BA11 ......110 C7
Cheddar Rd SN25 ....34 E3
Chedworth Gate SN3 ....50 F1
Cheese Mkt 🔳 SP1 ....146 A1
Chelmsford Rd SN5 .....49 C7
Cheltenham Dr SN14 ....78 A5
Cheltenham St SN1 ......50 B7
Chelwood Cl SN14 ......78 B6
Chelworth House SN16 ...4 B1
Chelworth Rd SN6 ......19 B6
Chemical Rd BA13 .....108 C6
Cheney Manor Ind Est
SN2 ....34 E1
Cheney Manor Rd SN2 ...34 F2
Chepston Pl BA14 .....100 F1
Chepstow Cl
🔳 Chippenham SN14 ...78 A5
Swindon SN5 ....49 C3
Cheraton Cl SN3 ....51 B7
Cherhill Prim Sch
SN11 ....166 B1
Cherhill White Horse ★
SN11 ....172 C8
Cherrington Field
SN10 ....180 F4
Cherry Cl Pewsey SN9 ..215 D5
Salisbury SP2 ....145 D1
Cherry Gdns BA14 .....102 A3
Cherry Gr 🔳 RG17 ....177 B7
Cherry Orch
Codford St Peter BA12 ..195 A2
Highworth SN6 ....23 A4
Marlborough SN8 ....213 E2
Cherry Orch La
Cann SP7 ....202 A1
Luckington SN14 ......39 C5
Salisbury SP2 ....145 D1
Cherry Rd SN14 ....75 A5
Cherry Tree Ave SP9 ...216 E2
Cherry Tree Cl SN11 ....81 B4
Cherry Tree Gr SN2 .....35 C2
Cherry Tree Rd SN6 .....19 D8
Cherry Tree Way 🔳
SP4 ....217 C3

Chervil Cl 🔳 SN2 ......34 C4
Chesford Cl SN3 ....51 A3
Cheshire Cl
🔳 Bower Hill SN12 ...178 B8
Salisbury SP2 ....145 C4
Chester St SN1 ....50 B6
Chester Way SN14 ......78 A5
Chesterfield Cl
🔳 Amesbury SP4 .....217 E3
🔳 Swindon SN5 ....49 C6
Chesters The SN5 ....49 C6
Chestnut Ave
Netheravon SP4 .....190 A2
Swindon SN2 ....35 C3
Tidworth SP9 ....216 D7
Chestnut Cl
Down Ampney GL7 .....8 B7
Frome BA11 ....110 B7
Rowde SN10 ....96 D2
Salisbury SP1 ....146 D3
Chestnut Dr SN10 .....178 E5
Chestnut Gr
Trowbridge BA14 ....105 B5
Westwood BA15 ......99 F4
Chestnut Grange SN13 ..76 D1
Chestnut La RG17 .....165 C2
Chestnut Mews SN12 ....94 A3
Chestnut Rd
Chippenham SN14 ......78 B8
Sutton Benger SN15 ...57 D2
Chestnut Springs SN5 ...33 C1
Chestnut Wlk 🔳 RG17 ..177 B6
Chetcombe Rd BA12 ...139 B6
Chevalier Cl 🔳 SN5 ....48 F8
Cheverell Ave SP1 .....146 C3
Cheverell Gn Rd SN10 ..179 C2
Cheverell Rd
Cheverell Parva SN10 ..179 C1
West Lavington SN10 ..187 D8
Cheviot Cl Swindon SN5 ..49 A6
Trowbridge BA14 ....105 E2
Chevral Cl SN14 ....70 B2
Cheyney Wlk BA13 .....109 B4
Chichester Cl SP2 .....152 B6
Chichester Pk BA13 ....109 A4
Chick's La SN8 ....183 E1
Chickerell Rd SN3 ......51 A6
Chicksgrove Rd SP3 ....203 F8
Chicory Cl SN2 ....34 C3
Child St 🔳 RG17 ......165 A1
Chilmark CE Fst Sch
SP3 ....201 B3
Chilmark Rd
Tisbury SP3 ....200 F1
Trowbridge BA14 ....101 A1
Chiltern Cl
Melksham SN12 ....94 C4
🔳 Warminster BA12 ..117 A8
Chilton Foliat Prim Sch
RG17 ....171 A1
Chilton Way RG17 .....177 B7
Chilvester Hill SN11 ....80 E2
Chine Rd SP4 ....131 C7
Chippenham Coll SN15 ..78 E8
Chippenham Com Hospl
SN15 ....78 C6
Chippenham Golf Club
SN14 ....70 B4
Chippenham Hardenhuish
Sch SN14 ....70 B2
Chippenham La SN14 ....77 B2
Chippenham Mus ★
SN15 ....78 E7
Chippenham Rd
Lyneham & Bradenstoke
SN15 ....59 E3
Marshfield SN14 ......74 A8
Chippenham Sta SN15 ..78 E8
Chipper La SP1 ....146 A1
Chirton Pl 🔳 BA14 ....105 D6
Chirton Sch SN10 .....180 F4
Chisbury Camp ★ SN8 ..176 C4
Chisbury La SN8 ......176 C5
Chiselbury Gr SP2 .....152 A6
Chiseldon Cl SN4 ....65 D4
Chiseldon Prim Sch
SN4 ....65 E4
Chitham Cl SN10 ......187 C8
Chitterne Rd
Codford BA12 ....195 B3
Shrewton SP3 ....196 B6
Chittoe Heath SN15 .....88 A2
Chivers Rd SN15 ....78 E5
Chives Way SN2 ....34 C4
Chobham Cl SN2 ....36 A5
Cholderton Rare Breeds
Farm ★ SP4 ....199 A5
Cholderton Rd
Amport SP4 ....199 D5
Quarley SP4 ....199 C5
Chopping Knife La
SN8 ....175 A7
Choristers Sq 🔳 SP1 ..152 A8
Choulston Cl SP4 ......190 B3
Christ the King Sch
SP4 ....217 B3
Christchurch Prim Sch
BA15 ....100 D7
Christchurch Rd BA15 ..100 C6
Christchurch Terr
BA12 ....116 F5
Christian Malford CE Prim
Sch SN15 ....58 A2
Christie Cl SN3 ....51 D4
Christie Miller Rd SP2 ..145 E2
Christie Miller Sports Ctr
SN12 ....94 B1
Christin Ct BA14 ......105 A8

Christopher Cl 🔳 SP2 ..151 F5
Christopher Dr SN15 ....79 A4
Christy's La 🔳 SP7 ....202 C2
Chubb Cl SN16 ....28 A5
Chudleigh SN5 ....49 B4
Chur St SP4 ....198 E6
Church Acre
Bradford-on-Avon BA15 ..100 C7
Seagry SN15 ....57 F6
Church Bottom SN4 ....131 A5
Church Cl Bath BA1 .....82 B2
Bourton SP8 ....137 D1
🔳 Lambourn RG17 ....165 A2
Church Farm La
South Marston SN3 ....36 E4
Woodborough SN9 ....181 D7
Church Fields SP3 .....105 A5
Church Furlong SP3 ....129 E7
Church Hatch 🔳 SP5 ..211 B8
Church Hill
Bromham SN15 ....95 F7
Donhead St Mary SP7 ..203 A3
Limpley Stoke BA2 ....99 B5
Nettleton SN14 ....53 B3
Redlynch SP5 ....211 D7
Shaftesbury SP7 .....202 B2
West Overton SN8 ....173 F7
Wroughton SN4 ....63 F5
Church Hill Rise SN15 ...96 A7
Church La
Amesbury SP4 ....217 A3
Bishopstone SP5 ....150 A1
Bishopstone SN6 ....163 E6
Box SN13 ....83 C5
Bratton BA13 ....186 B6
Britford SP5 ....152 E5
Brokenborough SN16 ...27 D7
Buttermere SN8 .....185 C7
Codford St Peter BA12 ..195 B2
🔳 Cricklade SN6 .....19 D8
Damerham SP6 ....209 F2
Dauntsey SN15 ....44 E1
Downton SP5 ....159 A5
Durrington/Bulford SP4 .217 D8
East Kennet SN8 ....173 D6
Fovant SP3 ....204 D8
Hankerton SN16 ......15 C3
Hawkesbury GL9 ......38 E5
Kington Langley SN15 ...70 E6
Limpley Stoke BA2 ....99 A5
🔳 Ludgershall SP11 ...192 A5
Lyneham SN15 ....60 A2
Marshfield SN14 ......74 A8
Melchet Park & Plaitford
SO51 ....212 C4
Melksham SN12 ....94 C6
Mildenhall SN8 .....175 A8
Norton SN16 ....41 D5
Ogbourne St Andrew
SN8 ....168 E3
Pitton & Farley SP5 ..148 C5
Rushall SN9 ....181 E2
Salisbury SP2 ....145 C2
🔳 Shaftesbury SP7 ...202 C1
Sherfield English SO51 ..162 F3
Sherrington BA12 ....194 F2
Sopworth SN14 ....24 D1
South Cerney GL7 .....7 A5
Stanton St Quintin SN14 .56 B5
Tidworth SP9 ....216 D4
Trowbridge BA14 ....105 A5
Vernhams Dean SP11 ..185 B4
West Lavington SN10 ..187 E8
Westbury BA13 ......108 E1
Wingfield BA14 ......104 C6
Church Piece SN15 .....57 D2
Church Pl
Lydiard Millicent SN5 ...33 C1
Swindon SN1 ....50 A6
Church Rails SP3 ......141 B1
Church Rd
Biddestone SN14 ......76 E7
Bratton BA13 ....186 B6
Calne Without SN11 ...80 A2
Cheverell Magna SN10 ..179 B1
Christian Malford SN15 ..58 A2
Derry Hill/Studley SN11 ..79 F7
Froxfield SN8 ....176 D7
Ham SN8 ....177 A1
Hilmarton SN11 ....73 F3
Idmiston SP4 ....133 F8
Kemble GL7 ....4 F7
Kilmington BA12 .....123 E5
Kington Langley SN15 ..70 E6
Liddington SN4 ......163 A4
Luckington SN14 ......39 E4
Milston SP4 ....198 C8
Pitton & Farley SP5 ..154 E7
St Paul Malmesbury Without
SN16 ....43 A3
Salisbury SP1 ....146 E3
Sherston GL8 ....25 B5
Silton SP8 ....138 A1
Stanton St Bernard SN8 .173 B1
Swindon SN1 ....50 D4
Wanborough SN4 ....163 A5
Woodborough SN9 ....181 D7
Church Rise SN13 ....84 E5
Church Row SN13 ......163 D6
Church St
Amesbury SP4 ....217 A3
Atworth SN12 ....92 D8
Bath BA1 ....82 B2
Berwick St John SP7 ..203 E1
Bower Chalke SP5 ....205 A2
Bradford-on-Avon BA15 ..100 C6
Calne SN11 ....81 B2
Chiseldown SN4 ....65 D4

Church St *continued*
Collingbourne Ducis SN8 ..191 E8
Corsham SN13 ....77 A2
Durrington/Bulford SP4 ..198 B7
Great Bedwyn SN8 .....176 B2
Grimstead SP5 ....154 C2
Horningsham BA12 .....119 B7
Hungerford RG17 ......177 B7
Keevil BA14 ....178 A4
Lacock SN15 ....86 D6
Little Bedwyn SN8 ....176 D5
Longbridge Deverill BA12 .120 F7
Maiden Bradley with Yarnfield BA12 ....118 E2
Market Lavington SN10 ..179 F1
Melksham SN12 ....94 A4
Mere BA12 ....139 A5
Pewsey SN9 ....215 D4
Purton SN5 ....33 C4
Semington BA14 ....102 F6
Sherston SN16 ....25 C1
Southwick BA14 ....104 F3
Swindon SN3 ....36 B3
Tisbury SP3 ....203 E8
Trowbridge BA14 ......101 D1
Trowbridge BA14 ......102 A3
Warminster BA12 ......116 F7
West Lavington SN10 ..187 E7
Westbury BA13 ....109 A3
Winterbourne Stoke SP3 .196 F3
Wootton Bassett SN4 ..47 C2
Wylye SP3 ....201 E8
Church St Cl 15 SP3 ..203 E8
Church Tk SP8 ....137 D1
Church View
Castle Eaton SN6 ......10 B4
Chippenham SN14 ......70 C2
Church Way
Hungerford RG17 ......177 B7
7 Swindon SN3 ....36 B3
Church Wlk
Ashton Keynes SN6 ....6 E1
Bishopstone SN6 ......163 E6
Devizes SN10 ....214 C3
Melksham SN12 ....94 A4
Motcombe SP7 ....202 A4
Redlynch SP5 ....211 E7
Swindon SN2 ....35 E3
Church Wlk N SN25 ...34 F3
Church Wlk S SN2 ....34 F3
Churches BA15 ......100 C7
Churchfield SN25 ....34 F4
Churchfield Upper Sch SN3 ....50 F5
Churchfields Ind Est SP2 ....145 E1
Churchfields Lower Sch SN3 ....50 F4
Churchfields Rd SP2 .145 E1
Churchill Ave
Broad Blunsdon SN26 ..21 C2
Durrington/Bulford SP4 .217 D8
Melksham SN12 ....94 D5
Churchill Cl Calne SN11 ..81 C1
North Tidworth SP9 ....216 B8
9 Tisbury SP3 ....203 E8
3 Wootton Bassett SN4 ..47 F3
Churchill Ct SP2 ....144 D3
Churchill Est SP3 ...203 E8
Churchill Way E SP1 .146 B1
Churchill Way N SP1 .146 A2
Churchill Way S SP1 .152 B7
Churchill Way W
Charlton SP10 ....193 C1
Salisbury SP2 ....146 A1
Churchlands BA14 ....105 D2
Churchward Ave SN2 ..35 A1
Churchward Dr BA11 ..110 C7
Churchway SN26 ......21 C2
Churn Cl GL7 ....6 F7
Chute Cswy SP11 ....184 E2
Circle The SN2 ......35 C2
Cirencester Rd
Fairford GL7 ....1 F6
Latton GL7 ....7 E8
Cirencester Way SN2 ..50 D8
City Cnr SN4 ....163 C6
City The SN12 ....94 A5
Clack La SP6 ....210 B3
Clanfield Rd SN3 .....51 B5
Clap La SP5 ....207 B4
Clardon La SN5 ....33 C6
Clare Wlk SN5 ....49 B4
Clarence Cl 18 SP11 ..192 A5
Clarence Rd
Chippenham SN14 ......77 F7
Trowbridge BA14 ......105 E8
Clarence St SN1 .....50 C6
Clarendon Ave BA14 ..105 E8
Clarendon Cl SP3 ....201 F2
Clarendon Cty Jun & Inf Sch SP9 ....216 D6
Clarendon Dr SN4 ....47 E1
Clarendon La 1 SN1 ..50 A5
Clarendon Pal ★ SP5 ..147 C1
Clarendon Rd
Alderbury SP5 ....153 D3
Clarendon Park SP5 ...152 F6
Grimstead SP5 ....154 A4
Salisbury SP1 ....146 C1
Trowbridge BA14 ......105 E8
Clarendon Sch The BA14 ....105 C6
Claridge Cl 3 SN8 ...170 A6
Clark Ave SN11 ......81 C5
Clark's Gdns 25 RG17 .177 B7
Clark's Pl 3 BA14 ...49 C8
Clarke Dr SN5 ....49 B8

Clarke's La SP11 ....193 A7
Clarkes Leaze SN14 ..68 F6
Clary Rd SN2 ....34 D5
Classics The 16 RG17 .165 A1
Claudius Cl 15 SP10 ..193 E2
Claverton Pumping Sta★ BA1 ....90 C5
Clay Cl BA13 ....112 C8
Clay St
Little Somerford SN15 ...4 C6
Longbridge Deverill BA12 ....116 E1
Whiteparish SP5 ......161 C3
Clay The SN10 ......180 A1
Clayfurlong Gr GL7 ...4 F8
Clayhill Copse SN5 ..34 A2
Clays Cl SN2 ....35 E3
Clays The SN10 .....179 F1
Clayton Rd SP4 .....217 E8
Clearbury Ring★ SP5 .158 C5
Clearwood BA13 .....111 F8
Clearwood View BA13 .111 D4
Cleasby Cl SN5 ......49 D6
Cleavers The 1 SN8 ..183 D8
Cleaves Ave SN14 ....75 A3
Cleeve Lawns SN3 ....50 F3
Cleeve The BA12 .....140 A6
Cleevedale Rd SN13 ..85 A8
Cleeves Cl SN5 ....49 A6
Cleeves The SP3 .....143 B3
Clement's La SN14 ...139 B4
Clevedon Cl SN3 .....51 A6
Cleveland Gdns SN14 ..101 E2
Cleveland Way BA11 ..108 C2
Cley Hill (Hill Fort)★ BA12 ....116 A6
Cley View 6 BA12 ....116 E6
Cleyhill Gdns BA13 ..111 D5
Cliff Rd SN16 ....40 C8
Cliffe Dr BA2 ....99 A6
Cliffords SN6 ....19 C8
Clift Ave SN15 ......70 E1
Clift Cl SN13 ....84 A8
Clifton Cl SN14 .....78 B8
Clifton Rd SP2 ......145 F2
Clifton St SN1 ......50 B5
Clink Farm Ct 6 BA11 .110 C6
Clink Rd BA11 ......110 C6
Clinton Cl SN5 ......48 F4
Clipsham Rise BA14 ..101 A1
Clivey BA13 ....107 E1
Cloatley Manor★ SN16 ..15 D2
Cloatley Rd SN16 ....15 C3
Cloche Way SN2 .....35 E3
Cloford Cl BA14 .....101 A1
Close End 8 RG17 ....165 A1
Close La Marston SN10 ..179 A3
Rowde SN10 ....96 A3
Close The
Bulkington SN10 ......178 E5
Corsham SN13 ....85 C6
Kington St Michael SN14 ..70 A8
Laverstock SP4 ....146 D8
Lechlade GL7 ....2 C5
Lydiard Millicent SN5 .48 D8
Melksham SN12 ....94 B3
Tangley SP11 ....193 C5
Warminster BA12 .....117 A7
Cloth Yd 1 BA14 .....105 E7
Clothier Leaze 2 BA14 .105 D7
Cloudberry Rd SN25 ..34 E5
Clough La SP5 ....149 B7
Clover Cl SN12 ......94 C3
Clover Dean SN14 ....78 A6
Clover Mead 22 SP11 ..192 A5
Clover Pk SN2 ....34 D4
Cloverlands SN25 ...34 D4
Club La SP9 ....216 C4
Club Rd 1 SP4 ......198 B7
Clydesdale Cl
5 Swindon SN5 ....49 A7
Trowbridge BA14 .....105 C5
Clydesdale Rd SN13 ..83 D5
Coach Barton BA14 ...178 A3
Coach Hill SP11 .....192 E6
Coach Ho Mews SP4 ..217 B3
Coach Rd
Bradford-on-Avon BA15 ..100 C6
Westbury BA13 ....109 B5
Coalpit Rd BA1 ......82 A4
Coate Agricultural Mus★ SN3 ....51 B2
Coate Rd SN8 ....173 B1
Coate Water Ctry Pk★ SN3 ....51 A1
Cobbett Cl SN2 ......35 A7
Cobbett Pl BA12 .....116 E7
Cobbett Rise BA12 ...117 E4
Cobden Rd SN2 ......50 A8
Cobley Cl SP5 ....208 D6
Cock Hill BA14 ......101 A1
Cock Rd
Horningsham BA12 ....118 F8
Rowde SN10 ....95 F2
Cock-a-troop La SN8 ..175 B8
Cocklebury La SN15 ..70 F1
Cocklebury Rd SN15 ..78 E8
Cocks Cl 5 SP4 ......197 E7
Codford Circ or Wilsbury Ring★ SP4 ....195 C3
Codford Rd BA12 .....195 C6
Codford Rising Sun (Hill Figure)★ BA12 ...195 C2
Codford St Mary CE Sch BA12 ....195 A3
Coker's La BA12 .....123 F7
Colbert Pk SN25 .....34 F6

Colborne Cl SN15 ....79 B5
Colbourne St SN1 ....50 D7
Colchester Cl SN5 ...49 D4
Cold Harbour SP4 ...217 B3
Coldharbour La
Marlborough SN8 .....213 E4
Salisbury SP2 ....145 F2
Coldharbour Rd RG17 .177 B6
Cole Cl 2 Andover SP10 ..193 E2
Swindon SN3 ....51 D6
Cole's La SP7 ....202 A1
Colebrook Rd SN3 ....36 B3
Coleridge Cl
Warminster BA12 .....116 D6
Wootton Bassett SN4 ..47 E3
Coleridge Rd SN25 ...34 F6
Colerne Airfield SN14 ..74 E3
Colerne CE Prim Sch SN14 ....75 B3
Colerne Pk★ SN14 ...75 F6
Coles's La SP4 ......212 A7
Colesway Coll SO51 ..212 F5
College Cl SN15 .....78 F8
College Fields SN8 ..213 C2
College Gdns BA14 ..105 D3
College Gr 1 SN4 ....163 A6
College Rd
1 Durrington/Bulford SP4 ....198 B7
Purton SN5 ....33 C4
Trowbridge BA14 .....105 B6
College St
Salisbury SP1 ....146 B1
Swindon SN1 ....50 C6
College Way 4 RG17 ..171 E7
Collen Cl 1 SN14 ....78 A7
Collett Ave SN2 .....35 A1
Collett Way BA11 ....110 C7
Collingbourne CE Prim Sch SN8 ....191 E8
Collingbourne Cl 2 BA14 ....105 D5
Collingsmead SN3 ...51 C5
Collins Cl 15 SP10 ..193 D2
Collins Ct SP9 ......216 C8
Collins La SN5 ......33 E5
Coln Cres SN25 ......35 A4
Coln Ho Specl Sch GL7 ..1 F6
Colquhoun Rd 2 SP4 ..198 A6
Colston Cl SN3 ......51 A4
Colston Rd SN10 ....214 A4
Coltsfoot Cl SP4 ....217 C3
Column Ride SN8 ....175 E3
Combe La
Bratton BA13 ....186 B7
Hilmarton SN11 ......73 F6
Combe View
10 Hungerford RG17 ..177 B6
Yatton Keynell SN14 ..68 F5
Comet Ave SN9 ......182 B2
Comet Cl SN15 ......60 B2
Comfrey Cl SN2 .....34 D4
Commercial Rd
Devizes SN10 ....214 A4
Swindon SN1 ....50 B5
Common Dro DT11 ...207 B3
Common Hill
Cricklade SN6 ....19 B7
Great Hinton BA14 ...102 F2
Steeple Ashton BA14 ..106 F8
Common Rd
St Paul Malmesbury Without SN16 ....27 D1
Sixpenny Handley SP5 ..207 F4
Whiteparish SP5 .....161 E1
Common Slip SN15 ..78 E7
Common The
Bromham SN15 ....95 E6
Holt BA14 ....92 F1
Kington Langley SN15 ..70 E6
Marlborough SN8 ....213 D4
Minety SN16 ....17 C1
Shrewton SP3 ....196 E6
The Common SP5 .....149 D6
Commonweal Rd SN1 ..50 B3
Commonwealth Rd SN1 ..50 B3
Commonwood La SN16 ..40 D5
Compton Abbas Airfield SP5 ....206 C5
Compton Cl
4 Swindon SN3 ....51 C4
Trowbridge BA14 .....101 E4
Compton Gdns BA11 ..110 C7
Compton Pk★ SP3 ...142 C1
Compton Rd SN11 ....73 F3
Compton's Dr SO51 ..212 A7
Conan Doyle Wlk SN3 ..51 D4
Conference Cl 1 BA12 .116 F7
Congreve Rd 4 SP4 ..197 E7
Conholt Hill SP11 ...185 A2
Conholt La SP11 ....185 B2
Conholt Pk★ SP11 ..184 F1
Conifer Crest 5 SN8 ..183 D8
Coniger The (Tumuli)★ SP3 ....196 F5
Conigre Cl SN12 ....94 A3
Conigre Hill BA15 ...100 C7
Conisborough SN5 ...49 C5
Coniston Cl 5 SP4 ...217 E3
Coniston Rd
Chippenham SN14 ....77 F6
Trowbridge BA14 .....101 E2
Conrad Cl SN3 ......51 D4
Consciences La SN10 .214 A7
Constable Rd SN2 ...35 E2
Constable Way SP2 ..151 D4
Convent The★ BA10 ..123 B2
Conway Cres SN12 ..94 B2

Conway Rd
Chippenham SN14 ....78 A7
Swindon SN3 ....51 C2
Conyers Cl 5 SN5 ...48 F4
Cooks Cl
Hullavington SN14 ...56 D6
Salisbury SP2 ....145 B5
Seend SN12 ....178 E8
Cooks La SO51 ......162 F7
Coombe Barn La BA12 ....124 D5
Coombe Bissett Sch SP5 ....150 F1
Coombe Cl SN4 ......64 C5
Coombe La
Atworth SN12 ....92 C7
Enford SN9 ....190 C6
Coombe Rd
Salisbury SP2 ....151 F5
Swindon SN25 ....34 F3
Coombe St BA9 ......137 D3
Coombe View BA12 ..194 D3
Cooper Fields SN25 ..35 A5
Coopers Cl
Amesbury SP4 ....217 B4
2 Malmesbury SN16 ..28 A5
Cop Croft SN11 .....81 B3
Copheap La BA12 ....117 B7
Copheap Rise BA12 ..117 B8
Copper Beeches SN6 ..22 F5
Coppice Cl SN2 .....34 D3
Coppice Hill BA15 ...100 D7
Coppice St SP7 .....202 C1
Copse Ave SN1 ......50 E8
Copse Dro SN8 ......169 B5
Copse The
Alderbury SP5 ....153 D2
Frome BA11 ....110 B6
Copyhold 2 SN8 .....176 B3
Corbin Rd BA14 .....101 F1
Corby Ave SN3 ......50 E3
Corfe Cl SN25 ......35 A4
Corfe Cres SN11 ....81 A4
Corfe Rd Melksham SN12 ..94 B3
Swindon SN5 ....49 B4
Coriander Way SN2 ..34 D5
Corinthian Cl 14 SP10 .193 E2
Corn Gastons SN16 ..27 E3
Cornbrash Rise BA14 ..102 A4
Corner Gd BA12 .....117 E5
Corner La SP7 ......202 B5
Cornfield Rd SN10 ..214 D3
Cornflower Cl SN11 ..81 C5
Cornflower Rd SN25 ..34 D5
Cornflower Way
31 Ludgershall SP11 ..192 A5
Melksham SN12 ......94 B3
Cornmarsh Way SN3 ..51 E7
Cornpits La SP6 .....209 E2
Cornwall Ave SN2 ...35 A1
Cornwall Cres SN14 ..94 C4
Cornwall Rd SP1 ....146 A3
Cornwell Cres SN10 ..214 A4
Coronation Cl
Christian Malford SN15 ..58 A1
Donhead St Mary SP7 ..203 A1
2 Pewsey SN9 ....215 C5
Sutton Benger SN15 ..57 F1
Coronation Dr SP7 ..203 A1
Coronation Rd
Atworth/Whitley SN12 ..92 E8
Durrington/Bulford SP4 .198 B7
Frome BA11 ....110 B5
3 Ludgershall SP11 ..192 B5
Melksham SN12 .....94 B3
Salisbury SP2 ......145 D1
Tidworth SP9 ....216 C8
Wroughton SN4 ......64 A6
Coronation St
Fairford GL7 ....1 F7
4 Trowbridge BA14 ..105 D7
Corporation St SN2 ..50 C7
Corral Cl SN5 ......34 A1
Corry The 1 SP3 ....203 E8
Corsham CP Sch SN13 ..77 A1
Corsham Ct★ SN13 ..77 A2
Corsham Pk★ SN13 ..77 B2
Corsham Rd
Atworth/Whitley SN12 ..85 D1
Lacock SN13 ....85 B8
Swindon SN2 ....35 C5
Corsham Regis Sch SN13 ....76 F2
Corsham Sch The SN13 .76 F1
Corsham Sports & Cricket Club SN13 ....77 A1
Corsley CE Prim Sch BA12 ....111 D2
Corton (Long Barrow)★ BA12 ....194 D3
Corton Cres SN8 ....49 B6
Coster View 5 SN8 ..176 B3
Coster's La SP5 .....205 A2
Cote La BA12 ....123 E4
Cotley Pl 4 BA12 ...194 D3
Cotswold Cl Calne SN11 ..81 D2
Melksham SN12 .....94 A4
8 Warminster BA12 ..117 A8
Cotswold Wr Pk★ SN6 ..6 F4
Cottage Mews 13 SP6 .210 D1
Cottars Cl 3 SN3 ...36 B3
Cottington Cl SN5 ...49 A4
Cottle Mead SN13 ...84 E8
Cottles La BA15 .....99 F6
Cotton House Gdns BA12 ....117 B7
Couch La SN10 ......214 A4

Coulston Hollow BA13 .186 F8
Coulston Rd SN13 ...77 A3
Council Houses The SN15 ....44 A4
Countess Rd SP4 ...217 A4
County Rd SN1 ......50 D7
County Way BA14 ....101 E1
Court Farm Cl 8 SP4 .190 A4
Court Farm Rd 1 SP4 .190 A3
Court Gdns Bath BA1 ..82 A3
Stanton St Quintin SN14 ..56 B4
Court Hill
Damerham SP6 ....209 F2
Potterne SN10 ......179 C5
Court La Bathford BA1 ..82 B1
Bratton BA13 ....186 B7
Corsley BA12 ....111 B1
Edington BA13 ......186 D8
Court St Sherston SN16 ..25 C1
Tisbury SP3 ....203 E8
Trowbridge BA14 ....105 D8
Court St Cl SP3 ....203 D8
Courtenay Rd 1 SN3 ..51 A6
Courts Gdns (National Trust) The★ BA14 ......101 E8
Courtsknap Ct 7 SN1 ..50 A5
Courtwood Cl 3 SP1 ..152 C8
Coventry Cl SN4 ....64 B7
Covingham Dr SN3 ...51 C8
Covingham Pk Cty Jun & Inf Sch SN3 ....51 D7
Cow Dro SP3 ....201 B4
Cow La Kimpton SP11 ..192 B2
Laverstock SP1 .....146 C1
Cow St SN5 ....19 B1
Cowbridge Cres SN16 ..28 C1
Cowdrey Cl SN5 .....49 B4
Cowleaze Cres SN4 ..63 F6
Cowleaze La BA13 ...186 D8
Cowley Way SN15 ...57 D1
Cowslip Gr SN11 ....81 B5
Cowslip Way SN14 ..70 B3
Cox's Hill
Ashton Keynes SN6 ..6 E2
Calne SN11 ....81 B2
Cox's La SN8 ......176 F1
Coxhill La SN10 ....179 D5
Coxstalls SN4 ......47 C2
Crab La Zennor BA12 ..138 A7
Zennor BA12 ....138 B6
Crab Mill La SN16 ..28 E1
Crabtree Copse SN5 ..34 A2
Crampton Rd SN3 ...51 A7
Cranborne Chase SN4 ..34 C4
Cranborne Dr 1 SP7 ..202 C2
Cranbury Cl SP5 ....211 A7
Crandon Lea BA14 ...92 F1
Crane Furlong SN6 ..23 A7
Cranebridge Rd SP2 ..152 A8
Cranesbill Cl SN10 ..214 D5
Cranfield Univ SN1 ..50 C6
Cranmore Ave SN3 ...51 A3
Cranmore Cl BA14 ...101 A1
Cratchcroft La BA14 ..178 A6
Crate La SP7 ....202 C7
Craven Rd RG17 ....177 D3
Crawford Cl SN5 ....49 A4
Crawlboys La SP11 ..192 B6
Crawley Ave SN3 ....36 B1
Crawley Cres BA14 ..105 A8
Craybourne Rd SN12 .94 C5
Crays The SN12 ....94 C5
Crescent Rd
Durrington/Bulford SP4 .217 D7
Melksham SN12 .....94 C6
Crescent The
Bromham SN15 .....96 C7
Calne SN11 ....89 F8
Chiseldown SN4 ....65 C3
4 Durrington/Bulford SP4 ....198 F7
Pewsey SN9 ....215 B4
Swindon SN5 ....33 F2
Westbury BA13 .....109 A3
Wilton SP2 ....144 B2
Cresswell Dr BA14 ..102 B2
Cresswell La SP15 ..44 B8
Crestmount Dr SP2 ..145 C3
Creswells SN13 .....84 F8
Cricketts La SN15 ..78 F5
Cricklade Leisure Ctr SN6 ....19 C8
Cricklade Mus★ SN6 ..19 E8
Cricklade Rd
Highworth SN6 .....22 F5
Purton SN5 ....19 C2
Swindon SN2 ....35 D1
Cricklade St SN1 ...50 D5
Crieff Cl SN3 ......51 B6
Crispin Cl 6 SN3 ...36 B3
Crockerton Cofe Sch BA12 ....116 D2
Crockford Rd SP5 ..154 B2
Croft Hts SP5 ......161 D3
Croft La SN6 ....8 C4
Croft Rd
6 Hungerford RG17 ..177 B2
Swindon SN1 ....50 C1
Wroughton SN1 .....50 B1
Croft Sports Hall SN1 .50 D1
Croft The
Bishopstone SP5 ....205 E5
Broad Hinton SN4 ...167 D7
Milston SP4 ....198 C8
Newton Tony SP4 ...199 B3

Croft The continued
Trowbridge BA14 ....105 C6
Urchfont SN10 ....180 C3
Crofton Beam Engines★
SN8 ....176 A1
Crofton Rd SN8 ....176 A1
Crombey St SN1 ....50 B5
Cromhall La SN14 ....69 A7
Crompton Rd SN25 ....35 D6
Cromwell SN5 ....49 B3
Cromwell Rd SN10 ......214 D2
Crook Hill SP5 ....204 A1
Crooked Cnr SN8 ....170 A6
Crookhays SP7 ....202 C2
Crooks La SN10 ....180 C4
Crookwood La SN10 ....179 F4
Crosbys 3 SN8 ....183 D8
Croscombe Gdns
BA11 ....110 D6
Cross Hayes La SN16 .....28 A3
Cross Keys Rd SN13 .....77 A3
Cross La SN8 ....213 D3
Cross St Swindon SN1 ....50 C5
Trowbridge BA14 ....101 D1
Cross The
Bishopstone SP5 ....205 E4
Ebbesborne Wake SP5 ..204 D3
Crossing La SN15 ....71 B3
Crossways SN4 ....46 D6
Crossways Ave SN25 .....35 C3
Crosswood Rd SN3 ....51 A3
Croucheston Dro SP5 ...205 C3
Croucheston Hollow
SP5 ....205 C4
Crowdys Hill Sch SN2 ....35 D2
Crowe Hill BA2 ....99 B6
Crowe La BA2 ....99 B5
Crowle Rd 11 RG17 .....165 A1
Crown Cl
Chippenham SN15 ....79 A5
Salisbury SP1 ....145 D3
Crown La 4 SP11 ......192 A5
Crowood La SN8 ....170 B2
Crudwell La
Crudwell SN16 ....14 B6
Long Newnton GL8 ....13 D6
Crusades The 6 SP1 ...146 C5
Cruse Cl SN14 ....77 F8
Cswy The
Broad Chalke SP5 ......205 B4
Chippenham SN15 ....78 E7
The Common SP5 ....149 C7
11 Tisbury SP3 ....203 E8
Cuckoo La BA11 ....110 A8
Cuckoo Pen Cl SN8 ....183 D3
Cues La SN6 ....163 E7
Cuffs La SP3 ....203 E8
Cullerne Rd SN3 ....36 C1
Cullerns The SN6 ....23 A6
Culver Cl SN15 ....100 E5
Culver St 7 SP1 ......152 B8
Culvermead Cl SN8 ....213 E3
Culverwell Rd SN14 .....78 A7
Cumberland Rd SN3 .....50 E6
Cumberwell Pk Golf Club
BA15 ....91 B3
Cunetio Rd SN3 ....51 C8
Cunnage La BA12 ......139 F1
Cunningham Rd SN2 .....35 A2
Curlcroft Rd SN13 ......84 D7
Curlew Dr SN14 ....70 A2
Curnicks The SN4 ....65 C4
Cursus The★
Amesbury SP4 ....197 D6
Lechlade GL7 ....2 C5
Curtis Orch SN12 ....93 B4
Curtis St SN1 ....50 B5
Curzon Cl SN11 ....81 A3
Curzon St SN11 ....81 A3
Cusance Way BA14 .....102 A1
Cuthwine Pl GL7 ....2 C5
Cutting Hill RG17 .....177 A2
Cuttle La SN14 ....76 E8
Cutts Cl SN15 ....46 A7
Cuxhaven Way 10 SP10 .193 D2
Cvnieto Roman Town★
SN8 ....175 B8
Cygnet Dr SP4 ....217 C8
Cyppa Ct SN1 ....78 E6
Cypress Gr SN2 ....35 A3
Cypress Way 7 BA11 ..110 C7
Cypress Wlk SN14 ......74 F6

D

Dacre Cl 13 SP10 .....193 C2
Dacre Rd SN3 ....51 A6
Dairy Cl 8 SP5 ....211 C7
Dairy Mdw La SP1 .....152 D7
Dairy Rd
Barford St Martin SP3 .143 A4
Chiseldon SN4 ....64 F4
Daisy Cl Melksham SN12 .94 C3
Swindon SN2 ....34 C3
Dales Cl SN25 ....35 A7
Dales Rd BA13 ....108 E2
Dalewood Rise SP1 ....146 E2
Dallas Ave SN3 ....51 B7
Dallas Rd SN14 ....78 C8
Dalton Cl SN3 ....50 F7
Dalwood Cl SN3 ....51 B3
Damask Way BA12 .....117 A5
Dammas La SN3 ....50 D4
Damy Gn SN13 ....84 E5

Dando Dr SN8 ....213 B2
Dane Cl BA15 ....99 E7
Dane Rise BA15 ....99 E7
Danegeld Cl 9 SP10 ..193 E2
Danes Cl SN15 ....78 F5
Danestone Cl SN5 ......48 F7
Daniel Cl 9 SN1 ....49 F4
Daniel's Well★ SN16 ...28 A3
Daniell Crest BA12 ....116 A5
Danvers Mead SN15 .....79 A4
Danvers Rd SN13 ....76 E1
Danvers Way BA13 .....109 B4
Darby Cl SN2 ....34 E1
Darcey Cl SN5 ....48 F6
Darcy Cl SN15 ....78 F8
Darius Way SN25 ....35 A6
Dark La Berkley BA11 ..110 E8
Castle Combe SN14 .....68 B7
Grafton SN8 ....175 F1
Kintbury RG17 ....177 D8
Limpley Stoke BA2 ......99 B5
Malmesbury SN16 ....27 C3
Mere BA12 ....139 A5
Dark La N BA14 ....178 A3
Dark La S BA14 ....178 A3
Darnley Cl SN3 ....50 F6
Darrell Rd SP4 ....217 C4
Dart Ave SN25 ....35 A3
Dartmoor Cl 7 SN1 ....49 F4
Darwin Cl
4 Durrington/Bulford
SP4 ....198 C6
Swindon SN3 ....51 B7
Dasna Rd SP9 ....216 B5
Daunch Cl SP9 ....216 B7
Dauntsey Dro SP11 ....192 C1
Dauntsey La SP11 .....192 E1
Dauntsey Pk★ SN15 ....44 E2
Dauntsey Rd SN15 ......44 C2
Dauntseys Prim Sch
SN10 ....187 E8
Dauntseys Sch
Market Lavington SN10 .179 E1
West Lavington SN10 ..187 D8
Davenham Cl SN3 ....51 A3
Davenwood SN2 ....35 F4
David's Gdn SP5 ......148 C3
Davies Cl SN8 ....213 A2
Davis Pl SN1 ....50 B6
Davis Rd 11 SN10 .....179 F1
Dawlish Rd SN3 ....51 B5
Dawneys The SN16 .....14 E6
Day Ho La SN3 ....51 C2
Day's Cl SN3 ....36 A1
Day's La SN15 ....56 D2
Deacon Cl SN3 ....14 E6
De Havilland Pl 4 SN12 178 B8
De Montfort Gr 8 RG17 177 B6
De Vaux Pl SP1 ....152 A7
Deacon St SN11 ....192 B2
Deacon St SN1 ....50 B5
Dean Cl Frome BA11 ...110 C6
Melksham SN12 ....94 C6
Dean La Fovant SP3 ...204 D7
Sixpenny Handley SP5 .207 F6
Whiteparish SP5 ......161 D1
Dean La Dro SP5 ......207 F4
Dean Rd SP5 ....155 B3
Dean St SN1 ....49 F5
Dean Sta SP5 ....155 F3
Deans Cl SN9 ....216 D4
Deansfield SN6 ....19 D7
Deansway SN15 ....70 D2
Deben Cres SN25 ......34 F5
Deburgh St SN2 ....49 F6
Deep La BA12 ....111 D2
Deer Pk★ SN8 ....175 E2
Deerhurst Way 1 SN5 ..49 D4
Delamere Dr SN3 ....36 A4
Delamere Rd BA14 ....101 D2
Dell The SP11 ....185 B3
Denbeck Wood SN5 .....49 B6
Denbigh Cl SN3 ....50 E3
Dene The SP3 ....200 B3
Denes Ave BA12 ......139 A6
Denford La RG17 ......177 D8
Denholme Rd SN3 ......51 A3
Denison Rise SP1 .....146 C3
Dennis La SP7 ....203 B1
Derby Cl
Chippenham SN15 ....78 F5
Lambourn RG17 ....165 A1
Derriads La 3 SN14 ....77 F6
Derry Hill CE Sch SN11 .80 A2
Derry Pk SN3 ....17 C2
Derry The SN6 ....17 F8
Derwent Dr SN2 ....35 F4
Desborough SN5 ....49 A3
Deva Cl SN3 ....51 D8
Deverell Cl BA15 .....100 E4
Devereux Cl 8 SN5 ....48 F5
Devereux Rd SP4 .....217 B3
Deverill Rd
Sutton Veny BA12 .....117 E1
Warminster BA12 ......116 F4
Devils Bed & Bolster The★
BA11 ....107 A8
Devizes Castle★ SN10 .214 A3
Devizes Com Hospl
SN10 ....214 B4
Devizes Gdn Trading Est
SN10 ....214 C4
Devizes Leisure Ctr
SN10 ....214 B3
Devizes Rd Box SN13 ...83 E4
Bromham SN15 ....88 B4
Calne Without SN11 .....87 F7

Devizes Rd continued
Charlton SN9 ....181 D2
Derry Hill/Studley SN11 .79 F1
Hilperton BA14 ....102 C3
Potterne SN10 ....179 D6
Poulshot SN10 ....179 B7
Rowde SN10 ....96 F2
Salisbury SP2 ....145 E2
Swindon SN1 ....50 D4
Trowbridge BA14 ......102 B3
Wroughton SN4 ....64 B6
Devizes Sch SN10 .....214 B3
Devizes Sports Club
SN10 ....214 C4
Devon Cl 5 SN14 ......77 F6
Devon Dr BA13 ....109 A5
Devon Rd Swindon SN2 .35 B1
Upavon Down SN9 .....182 B2
Devonshire Pl SN12 ....94 C5
Devonshire Rd SP1 ...146 A3
Dew Cl SN13 ....85 A8
Dew's Rd SP2 ....145 F1
Dewell Mews SN1 ......50 D3
Dewey Cl SN4 ....65 D4
Deweys La SP11 ......192 A5
Dexter Cl SN5 ....49 B7
Dial Cl SN12 ....178 E8
Dianmer Cl SN4 ....47 F5
Dickens Ave SN13 .....76 F2
Dickens Cl SN3 ....51 D3
Dickenson Rd SN25 ....34 C5
Dicketts Rd SN13 ......85 A7
Dickson Rd SN15 ......60 A1
Dickson Way 2 SN15 ...78 F5
Diddlebury Rd 8 SP4 .217 C2
Dilton Ct BA13 ....112 B6
Dilton Marsh CE Cont Prim
Sch BA13 ....112 B8
Dilton Marsh Sta
BA13 ....108 C1
Dinah's Hollow SP7 ...206 B7
Dingle The 3 SN4 ....163 A6
Dinmore Rd SN25 ......34 F6
Dinton CE Fst Sch
SP3 ....201 F2
Dinton Rd Fovant SP3 .204 E8
Wylye BA12 ....201 E8
Discover Salisbury (Medieval
Hall)★ SP1 ....152 A8
Divinity Cl 2 SN4 ....163 B6
Dixon St SN1 ....50 B5
Dixon Way SN11 ....81 B4
Dobbin Cl SN3 ....51 E7
Dobson Cl SN25 ....35 A8
Dockle Way SN2 ....35 F4
Doctors Hill SN13 .....83 B5
Doctors Pl 3 SP3 ....203 E8
Dodford La SN15 ....58 D6
Dodgson Cl SP6 ......211 A4
Dog Kennel La BA13 ..109 A3
Dog La SP7 ....203 E1
Dog Trap La SN16 .....16 E1
Doggetts La BA13 ....109 A4
Dogridge SN5 ....33 A3
Dolphin Ind Est SP1 ..152 D7
Dolphin St SP1 ....152 B8
Don Cl SN25 ....35 A4
Donaldson Rd SP1 ....146 A2
Doncombe Hill SN14 ...74 F7
Doncombe La SN14 ....75 A6
Donhead Hollow SP7 ..206 E8
Donnington Gr SN3 ....50 F4
Dorcan Tech Coll SN3 .51 D6
Dorcan Way SN3 ......51 A8
Dorchester Rd SN3 ....50 F7
Dores Ct SN2 ....35 E3
Dores Rd SN2 ....35 D3
Dormers The SN6 ......23 A6
Dorney Cl BA13 ......108 F1
Dorset Cl SP4 ....217 E8
Dorset Cres SN12 .....94 C3
Dorset Dr BA13 ......109 A5
Dorset Rd SP1 ....146 B3
Double Hedges SP4 ...217 E2
Doubledays SN6 ....19 D8
Doughty's La BA12 ...195 A2
Douglas Brown's Wlk 6
SP4 ....197 E6
Douglas Haig Rd SP1 .146 A3
Douglas Rd 5 SN3 .....50 F6
Dovecote Cl 3 BA14 ..105 B8
Dovecote Dr SN13 .....76 F2
Dover St
Chippenham SN14 ......78 C7
Swindon SN1 ....50 C5
Dovers La BA1 ....82 C2
Dovers Pk BA1 ....82 C2
Doves La SP5 ....161 C3
Dovetrees SN3 ....51 D7
Doveys Terr SN15 ......70 E7
Dowding Ave SN13 .....84 B8
Dowding Dr 5 SN11 ..166 A1
Dowding Way SN12 ....94 C1
Dowling St SN1 ....50 C5
Down Ampney CE Prim Sch
GL7 ....8 E7
Down Ampney House★
GL7 ....8 B6
Down Ampney Rd GL7 ...8 B6
Down Barn Cl SP4 ....133 B4
Down Barn Rd SP4 ....132 F6
Down Rd Kimpton SP11 .192 D2
Marshfield SN14 ....66 C2
Down The Hindon SP3 .200 B3
Trowbridge BA14 ......101 D2
Down View Rd SP1 ....146 C2
Downavon BA15 ....100 D5
Downham Mead SN15 ...78 F8

Downhayes Rd BA14 ..101 D2
Downing St SN14 ......78 C8
Downland Rd
Calne SN11 ....81 A2
Swindon SN2 ....34 D4
Downland Sch SN10 ...214 B1
Downland Way 12 SP4 .198 B7
Downlands 1 RG17 ....171 E7
Downlands Cl SP5 ....211 A7
Downlands The BA12 ..117 B7
Downleaze 7 SP4 .....198 B7
Downs Cl
Bradford-on-Avon BA15 100 B7
Lambourn RG17 ....171 C8
Downs La SN8 ....185 B8
Downs Rd SN4 ....65 E4
Downs The SN8 ....170 A5
Downs View
Bradford-on-Avon BA15 100 B7
Highworth SN6 ....23 A6
1 Netheravon SN9 ....190 A4
Warminster BA12 .....117 C6
Wootton Bassett SN4 ..47 D1
Downs View Rd SN3 ...50 F2
Downside Cl BA12 ....139 A6
Downside Pk BA14 ...101 E2
Downslands Rd SN10 .214 B1
Downsmead SN8 ......164 B1
Downsview BA13 .....186 C1
Downsview Rd BA13 ..109 A4
Downsview Way SP11 .191 F3
Downsway SP1 ....146 B4
Downton CE Prim Sch
SP5 ....211 A8
Downton Cty Sec Sch
SP5 ....211 A8
Downton Hill SP5 ....211 C8
Downton Meml Gdns★
SP5 ....211 A8
Downton Rd
Salisbury SP2 ....152 B5
Swindon SN2 ....35 B5
Downview Rd BA14 ...209 B6
Downwood Cl 7 SP6 ..210 C1
Doyle Cl SN25 ....34 C5
Dragon La SN9 ....181 F6
Drain Hill RG17 ......165 A2
Drake Cres SN14 ......77 F6
Drake's Way
Swindon SN3 ....50 E6
Swindon SN3 ....50 E6
Drakes Ave SN10 .....214 C2
Draycot Rd SN4 ....65 C3
Draycott Cl SN3 ....51 A5
Drew St SN2 ....49 E7
Drew's Pond La SN10 .214 B1
Drewitts La SN10 .....180 E8
Drifton Hill SN14 ......66 E7
Drive The
Melchet Park & Plaitford
SO51 ....162 C1
Swindon SN3 ....51 B7
Drove Cl SP5 ....150 F2
Drove Infs Sch The
SN1 ....50 D6
Drove Jun Sch The
SN3 ....50 D6
Drove La
Coombe Bissett SP5 ..150 F3
Market Lavington SN10 179 F1
Steeple Ashton BA14 ..178 A2
Drove Rd SN1 ....50 D5
Drove The
Amesbury SP4 ....217 B4
Andover SP10 ....193 C1
Druley Hill BA10 .....123 B7
Drury Cl SN5 ....47 F6
Drury La SN8 ....175 D4
Dry Hill BA12 ....116 E2
Dryden Cl SP2 ....152 B5
Dryden St SN1 ....50 B5
Drynham La BA14 .....105 C5
Drynham Pk BA14 ....105 D6
Drynham Rd BA14 ....105 D6
Duchess Way SN2 .....35 D5
Duchy Manor Mid Sch
BA12 ....139 B6
Duck La
Barford St Martin SP3 143 B3
Laverstock SP1 ....152 E8
Salisbury SP1 ....146 D2
Duck Pool La BA11 ...107 B6
Duck St
Berwick St James SP3 196 F2
Ebbesborne Wake SP5 204 C3
Potterne SN10 ....179 D5
Steeple Langford SP3 128 D2
Sutton Veny BA12 ....194 A4
Tisbury SP3 ....203 E8
West Lavington SN10 .187 E8
Duck's Nest (Long Barrow)★
SP6 ....209 F7
Ducks Mdw SN8 ......213 D2
Dudley Ave SP6 ......210 D2
Dudley Rd SN3 ....50 F6
Dudmore Rd SN3 ......50 D6
Duke St BA14 ....101 D1
Dukes Cl BA12 ....118 A1
Duke's Way SP4 .....217 C8
Dukes Cl SN2 ....35 E5
Dulverton Ave SN3 ...51 A5
Dumbarton Terr 2 SN1 .50 C5
Dummer La SP11 .....184 E1
Dummer Way SN15 ....79 A5
Dunbar Rd SN4 ....64 A7
Dunbeath Ct SN2 .....35 E1
Dunbeath Rd SN2 .....35 E1
Duncan St SN11 ....81 B5

Duncan's Cl SP11 ....192 D1
Dunch La SN12 ....93 F7
Dundas Aqueduct★
BA2 ....90 B2
Dundas Cl SN10 .....179 C8
Dunedin Cl SP9 .....216 C6
Dunford Cl BA14 .....105 D6
Dunhills La SP11 ....193 F4
Dunkirk Hill
Devizes SN10 ....179 A8
Rowde SN10 ....97 A1
Dunley Way SP1 .....146 C5
Dunn's La SP8 ....138 A1
Dunnet Cl SN11 ....81 B4
Dunnington Rd SN4 ...61 D8
Dunns La SN14 ....68 B8
Dunraven Cl SN3 ......50 F4
Dunsford Cl SN1 ......49 F4
Dunspit La DT11 .....207 B1
Dunstable Cnr SP5 ..148 E7
Dunstan's Dro SP11 .185 E1
Dunster Cl SN3 ....50 E3
Dunwich Dr SN5 ....49 D4
Dunworth Rise 6 SP3 203 E8
Durham St SN1 ....50 C5
Durlett Rd SN10 ......95 F2
Durley Pk SN13 ....84 D6
Durnford Rd SN2 ......35 B1
Durrington All Saints Inf Sch
SP4 ....198 C7
Durrington Jun Sch
SP4 ....198 C7
Durrington Swimming Pool
SP4 ....198 C7
Durrington Walls★
SP4 ....217 A8
Dursden La SN9 .....215 E6
Dursley Rd
Heywood BA13 ....108 F8
North Bradley BA13 ..105 E4
Dutts BA13 ....108 B1
Duxford Cl 11 SN12 .178 B8
Dyehouse La SN10 ...214 A4
Dyer La BA12 ....201 E8
Dyer's Cl SN15 ....79 A6
Dyke Mews SN4 ....65 D4
Dymocks La BA12 ....121 F8
Dymott Sq BA14 .....102 A3

E

Eagle Cl SN3 ....51 E7
Eagle Field SP2 .....145 D4
Earl Cl SN5 ....48 F7
Earl's Rise SP4 .....133 A1
Earls Cl SP4 ....217 E2
Earls Cnr SN16 ....15 E8
Earls Ct Rd SP4 .....217 B3
Earthpits La SP5 ....208 E4
East Dunley Cotts SN14 40 E1
East End BA12 ....117 B6
East End Ave BA12 ..117 B6
East End La SN15 .....44 D5
East Gomeldon Rd
SP4 ....133 E4
East Kennett (Long
Barrow)★ SN8 ....173 D5
East La SN15 ....93 B3
East Portway SP10 ..193 C1
East Sands SN8 .....183 D8
East St Bourton SP8 .137 E1
Hindon SP3 ....200 A4
Lacock SN15 ....86 D6
Salisbury SP2 ....145 F1
Swindon SN1 ....50 B6
Warminster BA12 ....117 B6
East Town Rd BA14 ..106 D3
East Woodlands Rd
BA11 ....114 A7
East Yewstock Cres
SN15 ....70 C1
Eastbourne Gdns
BA14 ....101 E1
Eastbourne Rd BA14 101 E1
Eastbury Shute RG17 171 C5
Eastcott Comm SN10 180 A2
Eastcott Hill 5 SN1 ..50 C5
Eastcott Rd SN1 ......50 C5
Eastcourt SN8 ....183 D8
Eastcourt Rd SN8 ...183 D8
Eastern Ave
Chippenham SN15 ....78 F8
Swindon SN3 ....50 E6
Easterton La SN9 ...215 D4
Eastfield
Ashton Keynes SN6 ....6 F1
2 Littleton Panell SN10 187 E8
Easthill BA11 ....110 B4
Eastleaze Rd SN5 ....49 C6
Eastleigh Cl 4 BA11 .110 A7
Eastleigh Rd SN10 ..214 D2
Eastman Cl SP5 .....211 B7
Eastmere SN3 ....51 E3
Easton Comm Hill
SP5 ....149 E6
Easton Hollow SP5 ..207 B3
Easton La SN14 ......77 C7
Easton Royal Sch SN9 183 A7
Easton Sq SN16 ......25 C1
Easton Town SN16 ...25 C1
Eastrip La SN14 ......75 C3
Eastrop SN6 ....23 B5
Eastrop Cty Inf Sch
SN6 ....23 A5
Eastview Rd BA14 ...105 A7
Eastville Rd SN25 ...35 C5
Eastwell Rd SN10 ...179 C5

Eastwood SO51 .....162 E1
Eastwood Ave SN4 .....47 E1
Eaton Cl **1** SN3 .....51 A4
Ebbesborne Hollow
  SP5 .....204 D2
Ebble Cl SP9 .....216 D7
Ebble Cres BA12 .....117 A5
Ebor Cl SN25 .....34 F7
Ebor Gdns SN11 .....89 C8
Ebor Paddock SN11 .....89 C8
Eccleston Cl SN3 .....51 B3
Ecklington SN5 .....51 C5
Eddington Hill RG17 .....177 C8
Edelweiss Cl **29** SP11 .....192 A5
Eden Gr SN2 .....85 D1
Eden Pk Cl BA1 .....82 A4
Eden Pk Dr BA1 .....82 A4
Eden Vale Rd BA13 .....108 F3
Edencroft SN6 .....23 B8
Edgam Pl SP2 .....144 F3
Edgar Cl **6** SP10 .....193 E2
Edgar Row Cl **1** SN4 .....64 A6
Edgehill SN5 .....49 B3
Edgeware Rd SN1 .....50 C6
Edgeworth Cl **4** SN5 .....49 B7
Edinburgh Rd SN11 .....81 F1
Edinburgh St SN2 .....35 D1
Edinburgh Way SN13 .....84 E7
Edington Cl SN5 .....49 B5
Edington Priory★
  BA13 .....186 C8
Edington Rd BA14 .....178 A3
Edison Rd
  Salisbury SP2 .....151 E8
  Swindon SN3 .....51 D5
Edmund St SN1 .....50 C5
Edric's Gn SP4 .....199 C5
Edridge Cl SN15 .....78 F8
Edridge Pl **1** SN13 .....76 E1
Edward Rd SN10 .....214 B2
Edward St BA13 .....109 A3
Edwards Hill **12** RG17 .....165 A1
Edwards Mdw SN8 .....213 B3
Edwards Rd SP4 .....217 B3
Egerton Cl SN3 .....51 B7
Eider Ave SN15 .....60 A1
Elbe Way SN4 .....193 D2
Elborough Rd SN2 .....34 D3
Elcombe Ave **3** SN4 .....64 A6
Elcombe Cl BA14 .....105 C5
Elcombe La SP5 .....204 D2
Elcot Cl SN8 .....213 F3
Elcot La SN8 .....213 F3
Elcot Orch SN8 .....175 A8
Elden Rd SP9 .....191 D5
Eldene Dr SN3 .....51 C4
Eldene Jun & Inf Sch
  SN3 .....51 C5
Elder Cl SN2 .....34 C3
Eleanor Ct **16** SP11 .....192 A5
Elgin Dr SN2 .....35 E1
Eliot Cl SN3 .....51 D3
Elizabeth Cl
  3 Downton SP5 .....210 F8
  Melksham Without SN12 .....93 F1
Elizabeth Dr SN10 .....214 C4
Elizabeth Gdns GL7 .....1 A5
Elizabeth Pl SN15 .....79 A4
Elizabeth Rd
  16 Durrington/Bulford
  SP4 .....198 B7
  Wilton SP2 .....144 B5
Elley Gn SN13 .....84 C7
Ellingdon Rd SN4 .....63 F7
Elliott Ct SN10 .....214 B1
Elliott Gn SP4 .....133 C3
Elliott Pl BA14 .....101 A1
Elm Cl Bower Hill SN12 .....94 C1
  Calne SN11 .....89 C8
  8 Ludgershall SP11 .....192 A5
  Lyneham SN15 .....60 B2
  Motcombe SP7 .....202 A5
  Pitton & Farley SP5 .....148 C4
  Rowde SN10 .....96 D1
  Salisbury SP1 .....146 D3
  Staverton BA14 .....101 D6
  Trowbridge BA14 .....105 C3
  Wootton Bassett SN4 .....47 E4
Elm Gr Corsham SN13 .....76 F1
  Salisbury SP1 .....146 C1
  Swindon SN5 .....49 A8
Elm Gr Rd SP1 .....146 B1
Elm Hayes SN13 .....85 A7
Elm Hill BA12 .....113 C1
Elm Leigh BA11 .....110 C6
Elm Pk SN4 .....47 D1
Elm Rd Colerne SN14 .....75 A5
  Swindon SN2 .....35 A2
Elm Tree Cl SN10 .....214 D2
Elm Tree Gdns SN10 .....214 D2
Elm View GL7 .....5 F4
Elmdale Rd BA14 .....105 A7
Elmer Cl SN16 .....28 A5
Elmfield BA15 .....100 C7
Elmfield Cl **7** SP5 .....211 C7
Elmina Rd SN1 .....50 C7
Elmore SN3 .....51 C5
Elms Cl SP5 .....210 B1
Elms Cross Dr BA15 .....100 C5
Elms The
  Bradford-on-Avon BA15 .....100 B8
  Highworth SN6 .....22 F5
  Holt BA14 .....92 E1
  Swindon SN5 .....48 F8
Elmswood Cl SN2 .....35 E5
Elmwood SN1 .....70 E2

Elmwood Ave **6** SP6 .....210 C1
Elsham Way SN25 .....35 A5
Elston La SP3 .....196 E2
Elstree Way
  Haydon Wick SN8 .....34 F6
  Swindon SN25 .....34 F6
Ely Cl SN5 .....49 C4
Embankment SN1 .....50 D3
Embry Cl **3** SN11 .....166 A1
Emden Rd **18** SP10 .....193 D2
Emerson Cl SN2 .....35 A6
Emery La SN15 .....78 E7
Emlyn Sq SN1 .....50 B6
Emmanuel Cl SN25 .....35 A4
Emms La **10** BA13 .....186 B7
Empire Rd SP2 .....145 C2
Empress Way SP11 .....192 A5
Emwell St BA12 .....117 A7
Endless St SP1 .....146 A1
Enford Ave SN2 .....35 C6
Enford Hill SN9 .....189 F6
Engineer Rd BA13 .....108 C6
Englefield SN8 .....47 E1
Enham Sp10 .....193 C3
Eningen View SN11 .....81 B1
Ensor Cl SN25 .....35 A8
Epping Cl BA12 .....117 A8
Epping Dr SN12 .....94 C6
Epsom Cl SN14 .....77 F6
Epsom Rd BA14 .....105 E4
Erin Ct **2** SN1 .....50 A5
Erleigh Dr SN15 .....78 C7
Erlestoke Sands Golf Club
  SN10 .....186 F8
Ermin Cl SN8 .....170 C8
Ermin St **1** Baydon SN8 .....164 C1
  Baydon SN8 .....170 C8
  Blunsdon St Andrew SN26 .....20 F2
  Swindon SN2 .....35 F4
Erneston Cres SN13 .....76 F1
Ernle Rd SN1 .....81 C4
Erskine Barracks SP2 .....144 F4
Escott Cl **4** SN15 .....78 F4
Esmead SN15 .....78 F8
Essex Pl **7** RG17 .....165 A2
Essex Sq SP2 .....151 D6
Estate Yard The SN10 .....172 B3
Estcourt Cres SN10 .....214 B4
Estcourt Rd SP1 .....146 B1
Estcourt St SN10 .....214 B3
Eston Medieval Village of★
  SN14 .....69 D8
Ethelbert Dr **4** SP10 .....193 C2
Ethelred Pl SN13 .....76 E1
Ethendun **11** BA13 .....186 B7
Euclid St SN1 .....50 C6
Evans Cl SN15 .....70 E1
Eveleigh Rd SN4 .....47 E2
Evelyn St SN1 .....50 D3
Even Swindon Sch SN2 .....49 E7
Eveque Ct SP2 .....144 F3
Evergreen Way SP4 .....217 C2
Evergreens Cl SN3 .....36 C1
Everland Rd **18** RG17 .....177 B7
Everleigh Barrows★
  SN9 .....182 E3
Everleigh Cl BA14 .....105 D5
Everleigh Rd
  Collingbourne Ducis
  SN8 .....191 D8
  Pewsey SN9 .....215 C3
  Swindon SN25 .....35 C5
Eworth Cl SN5 .....48 F5
Exbury Cl **2** SN25 .....35 A6
Exe Cl SN25 .....35 A4
Exeter Cl SN14 .....77 F5
Exeter House Specl Sch
  SP1 .....146 B3
Exeter St Salisbury SP1 .....152 B7
  Swindon SN1 .....50 A6
Exmoor Cl **1** SN2 .....34 C4
Eyres Dr SP5 .....153 E2
Eyres Way SP1 .....152 B8

F

Factory Hill SP8 .....137 F3
Factory La BA12 .....116 F6
Fair Mile
  Collingbourne Kingston
  SN8 .....183 F3
  Grafton SN8 .....184 A3
Fair View Rd SP2 .....144 E4
Fairdown Ave BA13 .....109 B3
Fairfax Cl
  Amesbury SP4 .....217 A4
  Swindon SN3 .....50 F7
Fairfield **1** Cricklade SN6 .....19 D8
  4 Great Bedwyn SN8 .....176 B3
  Rode BA11 .....103 F1
  Wootton Bassett SN4 .....47 E3
Fairfield Cl SN14 .....74 A8
Fairfield Mdws BA14 .....104 F3
Fairfield Rd
  Salisbury SP1 .....146 A4
  Warminster BA12 .....117 B7
Fairfields **22** RG17 .....177 B7
Fairfoot Cl SN14 .....78 A7
Fairford Airfield GL7 .....1 E1
Fairford Cres SN25 .....35 C3
Fairground The **2** SP11 .....192 F1
Fairhaven BA13 .....108 D1
Fairholm Way SN2 .....35 F4
Fairlane SP7 .....202 C1
Fairlawn SN3 .....51 B3
Fairleigh Rise SN15 .....70 F7
Fairview Colerne SN14 .....75 C6

Fairview continued
  Swindon SN1 .....50 B5
Fairview Rd
  1 Andover SP11 .....192 F1
  Hungerford RG17 .....177 B7
  Salisbury SP1 .....146 C1
Fairway Calne SN11 .....89 C8
  Melksham SN12 .....94 C5
Fairway The SN10 .....214 A1
Fairways Amport SP11 .....192 E1
  Dilton Marsh BA13 .....108 D1
Fairwood Cl BA14 .....102 A2
Fairwood Rd
  Dilton Marsh BA13 .....108 C3
  North Bradley BA13 .....107 F5
Falcon Cl SP9 .....216 D7
Falcon Rd SN11 .....81 D3
Falcon Way SN12 .....94 D1
Falconscroft SN3 .....51 C8
Falconsway SP2 .....152 A5
Falconwood Cl **8** SP6 .....210 C1
Falkirk Rd SN4 .....64 A7
Falkner Cl SN8 .....213 B3
Fallow Field Cl SN14 .....70 B2
Falmouth Gr SN3 .....50 E4
Fanshaw Way BA12 .....117 A5
Fanstones Rd SN3 .....51 C4
Fantley La SP8 .....138 B1
Far View Rd SP3 .....196 F7
Faraday Rd
  Salisbury SP2 .....145 E1
  Swindon SN3 .....51 E5
Fareham Cl SN3 .....51 B5
Farfield La SN6 .....19 E4
Fargo Cl SP4 .....198 A6
Fargo Rd SP4 .....217 A7
Faringdon Rd **2** SN1 .....50 B6
Farleigh Ave
  Melksham SN12 .....94 B3
  Trowbridge BA14 .....105 A7
Farleigh Castle★ BA2 .....103 E8
Farleigh Cl
  1 Chippenham SN14 .....77 F6
  Westbury BA13 .....108 F4
Farleigh Coll BA2 .....103 D6
Farleigh Cres SN3 .....50 E3
Farleigh Pk★ BA2 .....103 D5
Farleigh Rd BA2 .....103 A5
Farleigh Rise BA1 .....82 D1
Farley Cl BA14 .....110 C6
Farley Rd SP1 .....152 C7
Farleys All Saints Prim Sch
  SP5 .....154 C8
Farm La Aldbourne SN8 .....170 A6
  Great Bedwyn SN8 .....176 B3
  Salisbury SP2 .....145 E1
Farman Cl SN3 .....51 C4
Farmer Cl SN15 .....70 E1
Farmhouse Cl SN15 .....78 F4
Farnborough Rd SN3 .....51 B3
Farne Way SN4 .....48 A2
Farnsby St SN1 .....50 B6
Farrar Dr SN8 .....213 A2
Farrells Field SN14 .....68 F4
Farrfield SN2 .....35 E4
Farriers Cl SN1 .....50 E8
Farriers Field SN9 .....181 F2
Farthing Row BA11 .....103 C1
Faulkner Sq RG17 .....177 C7
Faverole Way BA14 .....102 A2
Feather Wood SN5 .....49 D5
Featherbed La SN6 .....163 F7
Fell Rd BA13 .....108 E2
Feltham Dr BA11 .....110 A3
Feltham La BA11 .....110 A2
Fenland Cl
  8 Swindon SN5 .....48 F8
  5 Swindon SN5 .....49 A8
Fennel Cl SN2 .....34 D4
Fennel Rd BA12 .....139 B6
Ferguson Rd SN10 .....214 D1
Fermoy BA11 .....110 B6
Ferndale Rd SN2 .....49 F8
Ferne Hollow SP5 .....207 A8
Ferne Wall Cnr SP7 .....203 B1
Fernham Rd SN25 .....34 E3
Ferozeshah Rd SN10 .....214 E6
Ferrers Dr SN5 .....48 F4
Ferris Gr SN12 .....94 C4
Ferris Mead BA12 .....117 A6
Festival Ave SP2 .....145 C3
Feversham Rd SP1 .....146 B3
Fiddington Clay SN10 .....179 F1
Fiddington Hill SN10 .....180 A1
Fiddle The SN6 .....19 C7
Field Barn La SP3 .....201 F3
Field Cl South Cerney GL7 .....7 A3
  Westbury BA13 .....109 A4
Field La BA9 .....137 B3
Field Rise SN1 .....50 A3
Field View
  Chippenham SN15 .....78 D7
  Enford SN9 .....190 A6
Field Way BA14 .....104 F3
Fieldfare SN3 .....51 D7
Fieldings BA15 .....99 E7
Fields The BA12 .....139 B6
Fieldside SN10 .....187 E8
Figgins La SN8 .....213 D2
Figsbury Rd SP4 .....133 B1
Figsbury Ridge SP4 .....133 C2
Figsbury Ring★ SP4 .....147 D8
Finchdale SN3 .....51 D8
Finches La
  2 Baydon SN8 .....164 C1
  Baydon SN8 .....170 C8
Finchley Rd SN2 .....145 E2
Finkley Rd SP11 .....193 F2

Finnis Rd **1** SP4 .....217 C3
Fir Gn La SN8 .....183 D8
Fir Gn SN11 .....89 D8
Fir Rd SN14 .....74 F6
Fire Tree Cl SN2 .....35 A2
Firbank Cres BA12 .....117 D8
Fire Brigade Mus★
  SN10 .....179 C5
Firecrest View **3** SN3 .....51 E6
Firs Cl SP5 .....148 C7
Firs Hill Way SN10 .....179 C5
Firs Rd Alderbury SP5 .....153 C2
  Firsdown SP5 .....148 B7
Firs The Inkpen RG17 .....177 F2
  Limpley Stoke BA2 .....99 A5
First Broad Dr
  Barford St Martin SP3 .....129 A1
  Wilton SP2 .....144 A7
First La SN12 .....85 C1
Firth Cl SN25 .....35 A3
Fisherton Island SP2 .....145 F1
Fisherton Manor Mid Sch
  SP2 .....145 E2
Fisherton St SP2 .....145 F1
Fitzmaurice Cl
  Bradford-on-Avon BA15 .....100 E4
  Calne Without SN11 .....79 F2
  Swindon SN3 .....51 D7
Fitzmaurice Pl BA15 .....100 D5
Fitzmaurice Prim Sch
  BA15 .....100 D5
Fitzroy Rd SN1 .....50 C2
Fitzwarren Cl SN15 .....79 A4
Five Ash La BA12 .....117 C2
Five Stiles Rd SN8 .....213 F2
Five Thorn La SN15 .....57 D6
Flamstone St SP5 .....205 A4
Flashett The SP5 .....149 D6
Flaxfields End **15** SP6 .....210 D1
Fleece Cotts **2** BA14 .....105 E7
Fleet Rd SN15 .....78 D8
Fleet St SN1 .....50 B6
Fleetwood Cl SN13 .....84 E6
Fleetwood Rise SN12 .....93 B8
Fleming Cl SP11 .....192 A5
Fleming Way SN1 .....50 C6
Flensburg Cl **20** SP10 .....193 D2
Fleur De Lys Dr BA14 .....105 A4
Flint Hill SN5 .....49 C4
Flint La SN11 .....193 A4
Flintjack Pl **2** RG17 .....165 A1
Flisteridge Rd SN16 .....16 C3
Flit Croft **4** SP4 .....217 C2
Flood The SP5 .....149 B7
Florence Ct **21** SP10 .....193 D2
Florence St SN2 .....50 C8
Flower La
  Amesbury SP4 .....217 A3
  Melchet Park & Plaitford
  SO51 .....212 F7
Flowers Mead **6** BA13 .....186 B7
Foghamshire SN15 .....78 D7
Folkestone Cl SN14 .....78 A6
Folkestone Rd SN1 .....50 B4
Folkstone Rd SP2 .....151 F6
Folly Barrow★ DT11 .....206 B2
Folly Cl Highworth SN6 .....23 A7
  Salisbury SP2 .....151 F5
Folly Cres SN3 .....23 A7
Folly Dr SN6 .....23 A7
Folly La Alderbury SP5 .....153 C3
  Melksham Without SN12 .....93 B8
  Salisbury SP2 .....145 D3
  Warminster BA12 .....116 B5
Folly La E SN15 .....86 C5
Folly La W SN15 .....86 B5
Folly Rd Inkpen RG17 .....177 F1
  Lambourn SN8 .....164 F1
  Roundway SN10 .....214 C7
Folly The SN15 .....44 A2
Folly View SN15 .....145 C5
Folly Way SN6 .....23 A7
Follyfield
  Bradford-on-Avon BA15 .....100 D4
  Hankerton SN16 .....15 B2
Foot's Hill Cann SP7 .....206 A7
  Salisbury SP2 .....145 A3
Ford St SN1 .....50 A5
Fordingbridge Hospl
  SP6 .....210 D1
Fordingbridge Jun & Inf Sch
  SP6 .....210 D2
Fordson Rd SN10 .....214 D1
Fore St Ashton Keynes SN6 .....6 F1
  Trowbridge BA14 .....101 D1
  Warminster BA12 .....116 F5
  Westbury BA13 .....109 A4
  Wylye BA12 .....201 E8
Forest Dale Rd SN8 .....175 A8
Forest Dr SP9 .....216 E2
Forest Hill SN8 .....176 B3
Forest La
  Chippenham SN15 .....78 E3
  Chute SP11 .....192 D8
  Melksham Without SN12 .....86 F2
Forest Rd
  Bramshaw SP5 .....212 B3
  7 Frome BA11 .....110 B7
  Horningsham BA12 .....118 D8
  Melksham SN12 .....94 B5
  Redlynch SP5 .....211 D8
  Wootton Rivers SN8 .....174 F2
Forest Rd Cnr BA12 .....118 C7
Forest Wlk BA13 .....111 C4
Forester Cl **5** SN3 .....51 D4
Foresters Pk Rd SN12 .....94 C4
Forge Cl
  Milton Lilbourne SN9 .....182 E7

Forge Cl continued
  South Newton SP2 .....130 B1
Forge Fields SN5 .....48 D8
Forge La
  West Overton SN8 .....173 D8
  Zennor BA12 .....137 F3
Forge The RG17 .....177 C7
Forman St SN11 .....81 C3
Forrester Gn SN14 .....75 B3
Forsey Cl **4** SN3 .....51 E7
Fortis Hill SP7 .....203 C3
Fortune Way SN15 .....78 F5
Fortunes Field SN4 .....167 C2
Forty Acres Rd SN10 .....214 C5
Forty The SN6 .....19 D7
Forum Cl SN3 .....51 C8
Fosbury Hill Fort★
  SN8 .....185 A3
Fosse Cl SN2 .....49 F6
Fosse Cotts SN16 .....27 A6
Fosse La BA1 .....82 A4
Fosseway Cl SN14 .....75 B3
Foster Rd BA11 .....110 A3
Fosters Bushes **4** SP4 .....207 B3
Fotherby Cres SP1 .....146 C4
Foundry La SN15 .....70 E1
Foundry Rd
  3 Malmesbury SN16 .....28 A4
  2 Redlynch SP5 .....211 C8
Fountain Mead **3** SP7 .....202 C1
Four Acre Cl SN6 .....18 A8
Fourmile Hill SP4 .....132 B3
Fovant Cl SN5 .....34 A1
Fovant Regimental Badges★
  SP3 .....204 F7
Fowey SN5 .....49 A3
Fowler's Hill SP1 .....152 C8
Fowler's Rd SP1 .....152 B8
Fowlers La SN8 .....173 B1
Fox Brook SN4 .....47 F2
Fox Cl SN14 .....70 B1
Fox Croft Wlk SN15 .....78 F4
Fox Talbot Mus★ SN15 .....86 C2
Fox Wood SN5 .....49 D5
Foxbridge SN3 .....51 D7
Foxbury **4** RG17 .....165 A1
Foxcote Gdns **2** BA11 .....110 C2
Foxcott SN6 .....8 C4
Foxcotte Cl SP10 .....193 C1
Foxcotte La SP11 .....193 C2
Foxcotte Rd SP10 .....193 C2
Foxglove Cl SN12 .....94 C3
Foxglove Dr BA14 .....101 E4
Foxglove Rd SN25 .....34 D5
Foxglove Way SN11 .....81 B5
Foxgrove SN14 .....70 A2
Foxleaze SN6 .....8 D1
Foxley Cl SN2 .....35 E4
Foxley Cnr SN10 .....180 C4
Foxley Fields SN10 .....180 C4
Foxley Rd Norton SN16 .....41 B8
St Paul Malmesbury Without
  SN16 .....27 D2
Foyle Hill SP7 .....202 B1
Foyle Rd SP11 .....192 C2
Foyle's Mead BA12 .....201 E8
Frampton Cl SN5 .....49 B6
Frampton Ct BA14 .....105 A6
Francis Rd **10** SN10 .....179 F1
Francis St SN2 .....101 C1
Francis Way SP2 .....152 A5
Francomes SN25 .....34 E4
Francomes Field **17**
  RG17 .....165 A1
Frank Warman Ct **8** SN3 .....36 B3
Frankenbury★ SP6 .....210 F2
Frankland Rd SN1 .....48 E3
Frankton Gdns **2** SN3 .....36 B2
Fraser Cl SN3 .....51 B7
Frederick Taylor Ct
  BA12 .....116 F4
Free's Ave SN3 .....213 B5
Freegrove Rd SN15 .....73 F8
Freemans Cl **4** RG17 .....177 B7
Freesia Cl **2** BA12 .....116 E7
Fremantle Rd SP11 .....191 F4
French Mill La SP7 .....202 C1
French Mill Rise **16** SP7 .....202 C1
Frensham Way SN9 .....215 D6
Freshbrook Prim Sch
  SN5 .....49 A3
Freshbrook Way SN5 .....49 A4
Freshford BA2 .....99 A4
Freshford Sta BA2 .....99 C5
Freshford VC Prim Sch
  BA2 .....99 B5
Friar's Orch **4** SP1 .....152 B8
Friars Cl BA13 .....112 C8
Friars The SN12 .....94 C6
Friary Cl BA15 .....99 E4
Friary La SP1 .....152 B7
Friary The SP1 .....152 B8
Fricker's La SP3 .....200 F3
Friday La SN9 .....181 D3
Friday St SN15 .....58 C3
Fridays Ham La SN6 .....7 B3
Friesian Cl SN5 .....49 A7
Friesland Cl SN5 .....49 A7
Friggle St BA11 .....110 D1
Frilford Dr SN3 .....36 A1
Frith Copse SN5 .....34 A2
Frobisher Dr SN3 .....50 F6
Frog La Avebury SN8 .....173 B8
  Chilmark SP3 .....201 A3

Frog La continued
Great Bedwyn SN8 . . . .**176** C3
Great Somerford SN15 . . . .**44** B3
Hullavington SN14 . . . .**41** F1
Longbridge Deverill
    BA12 . . . .**121** A6
Motcombe SP7 . . . .**202** A4
West Overton SN8 . . . .**173** A2
Frogmore Rd BA13 . . . .**108** F5
Frogwell
Chippenham SN14 . . . .**77** F8
Chippenham Without
    SN14 . . . .**77** E8
Frogwell Pk SN14 . . . .**78** A8
Frogwell Prim Sch
SN14 . . . .**78** A7
Frome Com Coll BA11 . .**110** A7
Frome Leisure Ctr
BA11 . . . .**110** A7
Frome Mkt BA11 . . . .**107** C1
Frome Rd
Bradford-on-Avon BA15 . .**100** C5
Maiden Bradley with Yarnfield
    BA12 . . . .**118** D5
Southwick BA14 . . . .**104** F3
Swindon SN25 . . . .**34** A4
Trowbridge BA14 . . . .**105** C2
Westwood BA15 . . . .**100** C3
Wingfield BA14 . . . .**104** C6
Frome Sta BA11 . . . .**110** B4
Frome View BA12 . . . .**118** E3
Front Horse Hill La
SP7 . . . .**203** A1
Front La SN26 . . . .**21** A4
Front St RG17 . . . .**171** E7
Fry Cl **2** SN1 . . . .**49** F4
Fryern Ct Rd SP6 . . . .**210** D4
Fugglestone SP2 . . . .**144** F3
Fulford Rd BA14 . . . .**101** E2
Fuller Ave SN13 . . . .**84** E8
Fuller Cl SN2 . . . .**35** F5
Fuller's Cl SN12 . . . .**94** B5
Fullers Ave SN6 . . . .**19** D8
Fullerton Wlk **6** SN1 . . . .**49** F4
Fulmar Cl SN12 . . . .**94** D1
Fulney Cl BA14 . . . .**101** F2
Furlong BA12 . . . .**117** B6
Furlong Cl Rowde SN10 . . .**96** E1
Swindon SN25 . . . .**34** E5
Furlong Cres SP3 . . . .**196** F7
Furlong Gdns BA14 . . . . . .**101** E1
Furlong Way SP3 . . . .**196** F7
Furnax La BA12 . . . .**112** F1
Furse Hill Rd SP9 . . . .**216** D5
Furze Cl SN5 . . . .**34** A2
Furze Dr SP11 . . . .**191** F3
Furze Hill La SN10 . . . .**179** D7
Furzehill SN13 . . . .**84** F8
Furzley La SO51 . . . .**212** F3
Furzley Rd SO51 . . . .**212** F2
Fussells Lodge (Long
    Barrow)★ SP5 . . . .**147** B8
Fyfield Ave SN2 . . . .**35** C5
Fyfield Cl **2** SP1 . . . .**146** D5
Fyfield La SP11 . . . .**192** D1
Fyfield Rd SP11 . . . .**192** E1
Fyfield Way SP11 . . . .**191** F3
Fyne Cl **3** SN5 . . . .**34** B2

G

Gable Cl SN2 . . . .**35** B6
Gables Cl SN10 . . . .**214** D2
Gabriel Cl **4** BA11 . . . . . .**110** C6
Gains La SN10 . . . .**214** B4
Gainsborough Ave SN4 . . .**47** F3
Gainsborough Cl SP2 . . . .**145** C3
Gainsborough Rise
BA14 . . . .**105** A6
Gainsborough Way
SN5 . . . .**49** A3
Gairlock Cl SN5 . . . .**34** B2
Gaisford Chase SN10 . . . .**179** B4
Galahad Cl **2** SP10 . . . . .**193** E2
Gales Cl SN15 . . . .**78** E8
Gales Gd SN8 . . . .**213** F2
Galley La SN8 . . . .**176** C3
Gallipoli Rd **8** SP4 . . . . . .**198** F7
Galloway Cl **13** SN5 . . . . .**49** A4
Galloway Dr SN2 . . . .**34** C5
Gallows Barrow★ SP4 . . .**190** B3
Galsworthy Cl SN3 . . . .**51** D4
Galton Way SN2 . . . .**49** F8
Gambia St SN1 . . . .**50** D6
Gamekeepers Cl SN25 . . .**34** F7
Gantlettdene SN3 . . . .**51** E6
Ganton Way SN2 . . . .**35** E1
Gardeners Gn **2** SP9 . . . .**199** C5
Gardiner Rd **2** SP4 . . . . . .**197** E6
Gardners Dr SN14 . . . .**55** E8
Garendon Ct **2** SP6 . . . . .**210** D1
Garfield Cl SN3 . . . .**51** C3
Garlings The **6** SN8 . . . .**170** A6
Garrard Way SN3 . . . .**51** A8
Garraways **6** SN4 . . . .**47** C2
Garsdon Mill SN16 . . . .**28** F5
Garston La **3** BA11 . . . . .**110** A4
Garston Rd BA11 . . . .**110** A4
Garstons The BA1 . . . .**82** D2
Garth Cl SN14 . . . .**70** B3
Gartons Rd SN5 . . . .**48** F7
Gas La Cricklade SN6 . . . . . .**19** D8
Salisbury SP2 . . . .**145** F1
Gascelyn Cl SN14 . . . .**78** A7

Gascoigne's La SP7 . . . .**202** C1
Gason Hill Rd SP9 . . . . . .**216** C8
Gasper St BA12 . . . .**137** C6
Gassons Rd GL7 . . . .**2** C5
Gassons Way GL7 . . . .**2** C4
Gaston La SN16 . . . .**40** C8
Gaston's Rd SN14 . . . .**78** C8
Gastons Rd SN16 . . . .**27** F3
Gaters La SP4 . . . .**133** A2
Gauntlet Rd SP4 . . . .**217** B4
Gawaine Cl **3** SP10 . . . . .**193** E2
Gawthorne Dr SP2 . . . .**151** F6
Gay's Pl SP4 . . . .**35** F4
Gaynor Cl SN25 . . . .**35** A6
Gaza Rd SP4 . . . .**198** F2
Gdn The SN9 . . . .**181** E3
Geneville Rise **3** SP4 . . .**217** C3
Genoa Ct **16** SP10 . . . . . .**193** E2
Gentle Cl BA12 . . . .**119** C7
George Cl SN11 . . . .**81** C3
George La SN8 . . . .**213** D2
George St (South) **6**
SP2 . . . .**145** F1
George St
Salisbury SP2 . . . .**145** F1
Swindon SN1 . . . .**50** A6
Trowbridge BA14 . . . .**101** D1
Warminster BA12 . . . .**117** A7
George VI Rd SP9 . . . .**216** C8
George Ward Comp Sch
SN12 . . . .**93** F6
Gerard Wlk SN5 . . . .**49** A6
Germain's La SN14 . . . .**76** A8
Geys Hill BA12 . . . .**115** A7
Giant's Cave (Long Barrow)★
SN14 . . . .**39** C2
Giant's Chair The
    (Tumulus)★ SP5 . . . . .**158** E2
Giant's Grave★
Breamore SP6 . . . .**210** C7
Aldbourne SN8 . . . .**169** E7
Downton SP5 . . . .**158** E3
Milton Lilbourne SN9 . . . . .**182** E5
Wilcot SN8 . . . .**174** C2
Gibbs Cl **2** Salisbury SP1 **146** C5
Swindon SN3 . . . .**51** E2
Gibbs La SN14 . . . .**55** F8
Gibbs Leaze BA14 . . . .**102** A1
Gibson Cl SN12 . . . .**94** C1
Gifford Rd SN3 . . . .**36** B3
Gigant St Salisbury SP1 . .**152** B8
Swallowcliffe SP3 . . . .**204** A6
Gilbert Way SP1 . . . .**146** C4
Gilbert's Gn **3** SP9 . . . . .**199** D8
Gilberts Hill Sch SN1 . . . . .**50** C5
Gilberts Piece SN8 . . . . . .**183** E1
Giles Ave **1** SN6 . . . .**19** D7
Giles La SO51 . . . .**212** E7
Gilling Way SN3 . . . .**51** D6
Gilman Cl SN25 . . . .**35** A8
Gipsy La
Chippenham SN15 . . . .**78** D6
Frome BA11 . . . .**110** B7
Holt BA14 . . . .**92** F2
Hungerford RG17 . . . .**177** C8
Swindon SN2 . . . .**50** E8
Warminster BA12 . . . .**117** B5
Gisbourne Cl SP9 . . . .**216** E6
Gladstone Rd
Chippenham SN15 . . . .**78** D7
Trowbridge BA14 . . . .**105** B7
Gladstone St SN1 . . . .**50** C7
Glass's La SP3 . . . .**204** D7
Glebe Cl
7 Aldbourne SN8 . . . . . .**170** A6
Pitton & Farley SP5 . . . . . .**148** C4
Glebe Field BA12 . . . .**117** A6
Glebe Gdns SP7 . . . .**202** A4
Glebe La Kemble GL7 . . . .**4** F7
Landford SP5 . . . .**212** C6
Glebe Pl RG17 . . . .**171** A1
Glebe Rd
2 Durrington/Bulford
    SP4 . . . .**198** B7
Trowbridge BA14 . . . .**105** A7
Wootton Bassett SN4 . . . . .**47** D1
Glebe The
All Cannings SN10 . . . .**180** F8
Calne SN11 . . . .**81** C3
Freshford BA2 . . . .**99** B5
Hinton Charterhouse BA2 . .**98** D2
Glebe Way SN13 . . . .**76** E1
Glebelands **3** BA12 . . . .**194** C5
Glendale Cres SP1 . . . . . .**152** D8
Glendale Rd SP4 . . . .**198** C2
Gleneagles Cl SN15 . . . . . .**78** F7
Glenfield Cl SP5 . . . .**149** D6
Glenmore Rd
Haydon Wick SN25 . . . .**34** C5
Salisbury SP1 . . . .**146** C3
Glenside SN12 . . . .**94** C6
Glenville Cl SN4 . . . .**61** E8
Glenwood Cl SN1 . . . .**50** C2
Glevum Cl SN5 . . . .**33** C5
Glevum Rd SN3 . . . .**36** C1
Globe St SN1 . . . .**50** B6
Gloucester Cl **3** SN14 . . .**78** A6
Gloucester Rd
Calne Without SN11 . . . .**81** F1
Malmesbury SN16 . . . .**28** A4
Trowbridge BA14 . . . .**105** B7
Gloucester Sq SN12 . . . . . .**94** C4
Gloucester St SN1 . . . .**50** B7
Gloucester Wlk BA13 . . . .**109** A4
Glover Rd SP4 . . . .**197** F7
Glyn Pl SP7 . . . .**206** B7

Glyndebourne Cl SP2 . . .**145** C3
Goatacre La SN11 . . . .**73** F7
Goddard Cl **1** SN9 . . . . . .**215** C5
Goddard Pk Prim Sch
SN3 . . . .**51** A4
Goddard Ave SN1 . . . .**215** C5
Goddards La SN8 . . . .**170** A6
Godley Rd SP2 . . . .**152** A6
Godolphin Cl SN5 . . . .**49** A3
Godolphin Prep Sch
SP1 . . . .**146** C1
Godolphin Sch SP1 . . . . . .**152** C8
Godolphin Sch Douglas
    House SP1 . . . .**146** C1
Godwin Rd SN3 . . . .**36** B3
Godwins SN12 . . . .**84** E1
Gogg's La SP5 . . . .**211** D7
Gold Hill **8** SP7 . . . .**202** C1
Gold View SN1 . . . .**49** F4
Golden Cross SP6 . . . .**211** E4
Golding Ave SN8 . . . .**213** A2
Goldney Ave SN14 . . . .**78** C7
Goldsborough Cl SN5 . . . .**49** B6
Gomeldon Medieval Village
    of★ SP4 . . . .**133** C4
Gomeldon Rd SP4 . . . .**133** D5
Gomeldon Sch SP4 . . . . . .**133** C4
Gooch Cl BA11 . . . .**110** D6
Gooch St SN1 . . . .**50** B4
Goodbody Rd **1** SP4 . . . .**198** A6
Goodes Hill
Corsham SN13 . . . .**85** D3
Melksham Without SN12 . . .**85** D2
Goodings La RG17 . . . .**171** D6
Goodwin Cl BA12 . . . .**117** E8
Goodwood Cl BA14 . . . . . .**105** E4
Goodwood Way **3** SN14 . .**77** F5
Goodwyns Cl **5** SP9 . . . .**199** C8
Goor La SN8 . . . .**164** B2
Goose Gn RG17 . . . .**165** A2
Goose St Marston SN10 . . .**179** A3
Southwick BA14 . . . .**105** A2
Gooselands
Crudwell SN16 . . . .**14** D5
Westbury BA13 . . . .**108** F2
Gordon Gdns **4** SN1 . . . . .**50** C6
Gordon Rd **5** SN1 . . . .**50** C6
Gore Cross SN10 . . . .**187** E5
Gore La BA13 . . . .**111** B4
Gore Rd SP4 . . . .**197** E7
Gores La SN9 . . . .**181** C5
Gorringe Rd SP2 . . . .**145** D1
Gorse Hill Jun Sch
SN2 . . . .**35** D1
Gosditch
Ashton Keynes SN6 . . . .**17** E8
Latton SN6 . . . .**8** C4
Goughs Way SN4 . . . .**47** C2
Gould Cl **1** SP11 . . . .**192** A5
Goulding Cl **3** SN3 . . . . . .**36** B2
Gower Cl Swindon SN2 . . . .**35** F2
1 Swindon SN5 . . . .**48** F5
Gower Rd **12** SP7 . . . .**202** D2
Grace Cl SP2 . . . .**145** B5
Grace La SP6 . . . .**211** A4
Graemar La SO51 . . . .**162** E1
Grafton Pl SN8 . . . .**183** F7
Grafton Rd
Burbage SN8 . . . .**183** D7
Swindon SN2 . . . .**35** C5
Graham St SN1 . . . .**50** D7
Grailey Cl SN3 . . . .**51** C4
Gramp's Hill OX12 . . . . . .**165** F7
Gramshaw Rd **2** SP2 . . .**145** D2
Granary Cl **4** SN5 . . . .**48** F8
Granary Rd SN8 . . . .**176** B3
Grand Ave SN8 . . . .**175** E3
Grand Trunk Rd SP4 . . . . .**216** B4
Grandison Cl SN5 . . . .**49** A6
Grange Cl
Atworth/Whitley SN12 . . . . .**85** D1
Fyfield SP11 . . . .**192** D1
Highworth SN6 . . . .**23** A5
Grange Dr SN3 . . . .**36** B1
Grange Gdns SP1 . . . .**146** C2
Grange Inf Sch SN3 . . . . . .**36** B3
Grange Jun Sch SN3 . . . . .**36** B2
Grange La
St Paul Malmesbury Without
    SN16 . . . .**43** B5
Warminster BA12 . . . .**117** C5
Grange Pk Way SN5 . . . . . .**48** F5
Grange Rd BA11 . . . .**110** A7
Grange View BA15 . . . . . .**100** E7
Granger Cl SN15 . . . .**78** F4
Granham Cl SN8 . . . .**213** D1
Granham Hill SN8 . . . .**213** D1
Grans Barrow (Long
    Barrow)★ SP6 . . . .**209** E6
Grantham Cl SN5 . . . .**49** B3
Granthams The **4**
RG17 . . . .**165** A2
Grantley Cl SN3 . . . .**51** A3
Grants Rd SN9 . . . .**190** A6
Granville Gdns **28** SP7 . .**202** C2
Granville Rd SN12 . . . .**94** A6
Granville St SN1 . . . .**50** C6
Grasmere
Bower Hill SN12 . . . .**94** D1
Swindon SN3 . . . .**51** E3
Trowbridge BA14 . . . .**101** E2
Grasmere Cl **1** SP2 . . . .**151** F6
Graspan Rd **12** SP11 . . .**192** B5
Grateley Rd SP4 . . . .**199** C5
Gravel Cl SP5 . . . .**211** A8
Gravel The BA14 . . . .**92** E1
Grays Cl SP7 . . . .**202** A4

Grays Leaze BA14 . . . . . .**105** C2
Graythwaite Cl **3** SN25 . .**34** F6
Great Barn★ SN8 . . . .**167** B1
Great Bedwyn C of E
    Controlled Prim Sch
    SN8 . . . .**176** C4
Great Chalfield Manor
    (National Trust)★
    BA14 . . . .**92** D3
Great Croft SP5 . . . .**148** C7
Great Dro SP4 . . . .**132** F1
Great Hall BA9 . . . .**137** B3
Great La SP7 . . . .**202** C1
Great Lodge Dr SN8 . . . . .**175** B5
Great Parks SP4 . . . .**92** F1
Great Roc Rd BA13 . . . . . .**108** E3
Great Western Ave
    SP3 . . . .**200** B1
Great Western Way
    SN5 . . . .**48** F3
Great Wethers (National
    Trust)★ SN8 . . . .**174** A7
Greater La BA14 . . . .**186** C8
Greatwoods BA13 . . . .**186** C8
Green Acres **13** SN8 . . . .**170** B2
Green Beeches SN12 . . . . .**93** D8
Green Cl
East Grafton SN8 . . . .**183** F7
Holt BA14 . . . .**101** F8
Whiteparish SP5 . . . .**161** D4
Green Dro Fovant SP3 . . . .**204** D4
Grimstead SP5 . . . .**154** B4
Pewsey SN9 . . . .**215** D3
Smannell SP11 . . . .**193** E5
Green Farm Rise SN8 . . .**176** D7
Green Gate Rd SN10 . . . .**180** D4
Green La Ashmore SP5 . . .**206** E4
Cheverell Magna SN10 . . .**179** C1
Codford BA12 . . . .**195** A3
Colerne SN14 . . . .**75** A3
Devizes SN10 . . . .**214** B1
Downton SP5 . . . .**211** A8
Fordingbridge SP6 . . . .**210** D1
Hinton Charterhouse BA2 . .**98** E1
Laverstock SP4 . . . .**146** D8
Rockbourne SP6 . . . .**210** C3
Salisbury SP1 . . . .**146** D6
Sherston SN16 . . . .**25** C1
Southwick BA14 . . . .**104** D2
Steeple Ashton BA14 . . . .**102** C1
Trowbridge BA14 . . . .**105** E8
Westbury BA13 . . . .**108** F2
Winsley BA15 . . . .**99** E6
Green La Hospl SN10 . . . .**214** B1
Green Mdw Ave SN25 . . . .**34** F4
Green Pk La BA11 . . . .**107** A6
Green Rd Codford BA12 . . .**195** A3
Corsham SN13 . . . .**85** B4
Swindon SN2 . . . .**35** E3
Green Ride BA12 . . . .**123** E5
Green St SN8 . . . .**167** C1
Green The
Alderbury SP5 . . . .**153** C3
Biddestone SN14 . . . .**76** E8
Brokenborough SN16 . . . . .**27** D7
Calne SN11 . . . .**81** B2
Cheverell Magna SN10 . . .**179** C2
Dauntsey SN15 . . . .**59** A8
Fairford GL7 . . . .**1** F7
Highworth SN6 . . . .**22** F5
1 Liddington SN4 . . . . . .**163** A4
Lyneham & Bradenstoke
    SN15 . . . .**60** A4
Oaksey SN16 . . . .**15** F7
Pitton & Farley SP5 . . . . . .**148** C3
Salisbury SP1 . . . .**146** D2
Whiteparish SP5 . . . .**161** D4
Green Valley Ave SN25 . . .**34** F4
Green's Ct **3** SP1 . . . . . .**152** B8
Green's La SN4 . . . .**64** B5
Greenacres
Dilton Marsh BA13 . . . .**112** A8
2 Downton SP5 . . . .**210** F8
Greenacres Way SN11 . . . .**80** F4
Greenaway **4** SN3 . . . . .**163** A5
Greenbridge Ind Est
    SN3 . . . .**51** A7
Greenbridge Rd SN3 . . . . .**51** A7
Greenbridge Ret Pk
    SN3 . . . .**51** A8
Greencroft St SP1 . . . .**146** B1
Greenfield Rd SN10 . . . . . .**214** C4
Greenfields
Grimstead SP5 . . . .**154** C2
Smannell SP11 . . . .**193** F4
South Marston SN3 . . . .**36** E5
Greenhill Gdns BA14 . . . .**102** A4
Greenhill Rd SN2 . . . .**34** E2
Greenhills BA13 . . . .**186** C8
Greenhouse Rd SN10 . . . .**180** F8
Greenland Cl SN10 . . . .**92** E8
Greenland View BA15 . . . .**100** D6
Greenlands **1** BA12 . . . .**194** C5
Greenlands Cl **20** SP4 . .**198** B7
Greenlands Rd SN2 . . . . . .**35** E3
Greenlane Cl SP4 . . . .**146** C6
Greenmeadow Prim Sch
    SN25 . . . .**35** A4
Greens Cl SN14 . . . .**41** F1
Greens La SN11 . . . .**172** A8
Greens Meade **6** SP5 . . .**211** C7
Greensand Cl SN25 . . . . . .**34** F7
Greenway SN4 . . . .**60** F2
Greenway Ave SN15 . . . . . .**70** D1
Greenway Cl SN3 . . . .**51** B7
Greenway Dr SN15 . . . .**73** F8
Greenway Gdns
Chippenham SN15 . . . .**70** D1

Greenway Gdns continued
Trowbridge BA14 . . . .**101** E3
Greenway La SN15 . . . .**70** D2
Greenway Pk SN15 . . . .**70** D1
Greenway Rd SN8 . . . .**169** B1
Greenways RG17 . . . .**165** A1
Greenwich Cl SN25 . . . .**35** A5
Greenwood Ave SP1 . . . .**146** D1
Greenwood Rd SN12 . . . . .**94** A3
Gregory Cl SN15 . . . .**57** C1
Grenadier Cl **2** BA12 . . .**116** F7
Gresham Cl SN3 . . . .**50** F6
Grey Wethers or Sarsen
    Stones★ SN8 . . . .**167** C2
Grey's Cnr BA9 . . . .**136** A5
Greyfriars Cl SP1 . . . .**152** B7
Greyhound La **1** SP2 . . .**144** D3
Greystones SN15 . . . .**96** B8
Greywethers Ave SN3 . . . .**50** E3
Grierson Cl SN11 . . . .**81** B3
Griffin Alley **6** SN16 . . . . .**28** A3
Griffins Ct **3** SP2 . . . . . .**146** A1
Griffiths Cl SN3 . . . .**36** B1
Grimstead Beeches (National
    Trust)★ SP5 . . . .**160** C3
Grimstead Rd SP5 . . . .**153** F1
Grindal Dr SN5 . . . .**48** F5
Grittleton House Sch
    SN14 . . . .**54** E4
Grocyn Cl SN14 . . . .**75** B3
Grosmont Dr SN5 . . . .**49** B5
Grosvenor Rd
Shaftesbury SP7 . . . .**202** C2
Swindon SN1 . . . .**50** A4
Ground Cnr BA14 . . . .**101** D8
Groundwell Rd SN1 . . . .**50** D5
Grove Hill SN6 . . . .**23** A7
Grove La
Kington St Michael SN14 . . .**69** F8
Redlynch SP5 . . . .**211** D8
Yatton Keynell SN14 . . . . . .**69** A6
Grove Leaze BA15 . . . .**100** B6
Grove Orch SN6 . . . .**22** F7
Grove Prim Sch The
    BA14 . . . .**105** B5
Grove Rd Corsham SN13 . . .**77** A1
Market Lavington SN10 . . .**179** F1
Sherston SN16 . . . .**40** C8
Grove The
Codford St Peter BA12 . . .**195** A4
Crudwell SN16 . . . .**4** C1
Penton Mewsey SP11 . . . .**193** A2
Warminster BA12 . . . .**117** A7
Grovelands Ave SN1 . . . . . .**50** C3
Grovelands Way BA12 . . .**116** E7
Groveley Rd SP3 . . . .**143** B3
Grovely Castle★ SP3 . . . .**128** F4
Grovely Rd SP3 . . . .**129** E2
Grovely View SP2 . . . .**144** B1
Groves St SN2 . . . .**49** F6
Grundys SN3 . . . .**51** D3
Gryphon Cl BA13 . . . .**108** E3
Guilder La SP1 . . . .**152** B8
Guildford Ave SN3 . . . .**50** F3
Gullet The SN13 . . . .**83** F7
Gulliver's La BA14 . . . .**178** A4
Gundry Cl
Chippenham SN15 . . . .**78** F5
Devizes SN10 . . . .**214** C4
Gunner St SP4 . . . .**198** E6
Gunsite Rd SN8 . . . .**173** C6
Gunville Hill SP5 . . . .**149** E6
Gunville Rd SP5 . . . .**149** D6
Guppy St SN2 . . . .**49** F7
Gurston Mdw SP5 . . . .**205** A4
Gurston Rd SP5 . . . .**205** A4
Guthrie CE Inf Sch
    SN11 . . . .**81** C4
Guthrie Cl SN11 . . . .**81** C4
Guyers La SN13 . . . .**76** D2
Gwyns Piece **14** RG17 . .**165** A2

H

Ha'penny Bridge★ GL7 . . .**2** C3
Habrel's Cl SN15 . . . .**78** F6
Hackett Cl SN2 . . . .**35** E4
Hackleton Rise SN3 . . . . . .**51** B8
Hackpen Cl SN4 . . . .**64** B7
Hackthorne Rd SP4 . . . . . .**198** B7
Haddon Cl **14** SN5 . . . . . .**48** F5
Haddons Cl SN16 . . . .**27** E2
Haden Rd **6** BA14 . . . . . .**105** D7
Hadleigh Cl SN5 . . . .**49** C6
Hadleigh Rise SN2 . . . .**36** A5
Hadrian Rd **20** SP10 . . . .**193** E2
Hadrians Cl
Salisbury SP2 . . . .**145** C3
Swindon SN3 . . . .**51** C8
Haig Cl SN2 . . . .**35** E4
Haig Rd SP4 . . . .**217** C3
Haimes La **20** SP7 . . . . . .**202** C2
Hale House★ SP6 . . . .**211** A5
Hale La SP6 . . . .**211** C6
Hale Prim Sch SP6 . . . . . .**211** C6
Hale Rd SP6 . . . .**211** A5
Hales Castle★ BA11 . . . . .**114** D5
Hales Rd **6** SP4 . . . .**190** A4
Half Hide Down SP5 . . . . .**207** B3
Half Mile Rd RG17 . . . .**171** A5
Halfpenny La SP5 . . . .**206** A4
Halfpenny Row BA11 . . . .**103** E1
Halfway Cl BA14 . . . .**101** F2
Halfway La SN8 . . . .**170** C2
Halifax Cl SN4 . . . .**64** A7
Halifax Rd SN12 . . . .**94** C1
Hall Cl SN4 . . . .**64** A6

Hallam Moor SN3 ......51 E2
Hallsfield SN6 ....8 D1
Hallum Cl SP1 ....146 D4
Halton Rd SP11 ....191 F4
Halve The BA14 ....101 D1
Ham Cl SN8 ....183 D3
Ham La Biddestone SN14 ..76 C8
  Kempsford GL7 ....10 E6
  South Cerney GL7 ......6 F6
Ham Rd Ham RG17 ....177 A2
  Liddington SN4 ......163 A5
Ham The
  Durrington/Bulford SP4 .198 C2
  Kington St Michael SN14 ..70 A8
  [9] Market Lavington SN10 179 F1
  Westbury BA13 ....108 E5
Hambidge La GL7 ....2 C5
Hamble Rd SN25 ....34 F4
Hambleton Ave SN10 ..214 E6
Hamblin Mdw RG17 ...177 C8
Hamilton Cl
  Amesbury SP4 ....217 E3
  Swindon SN3 ....50 F4
Hamilton Dr
  Chippenham SN14 .....77 F5
  [2] Market Lavington SN10 179 F1
Hamilton Pk [3] SP1 ..211 B8
Hamilton Rd SP1 .....146 A2
Hamlet Cl SN15 ....70 D1
Hamlet The SN15 ......70 E1
Hammer St BA10 .....122 C7
Hammond Way BA14 ..101 D4
Hammonds SN6 ....19 E8
Hampshire Cl
  Durrington/Bulford SP4 .217 E8
  [7] Swindon SN3 ......49 A7
Hampshire Gdns
  BA13 ....109 A4
Hampshire Pl SN12 ...94 B5
Hampstead Way SN25 ..34 F7
Hampton Cl SN12 .....94 C1
Hampton Ct SP2 ......144 F2
Hampton Dr SN5 ....48 F5
Hamptworth Rd SP5 ..211 F6
Hamshill Ditches*
  SP3 ....143 B7
Hamworthy Rd SN3 ...51 C6
Hanbury Rd SN3 ......51 A4
Hancock Cl SN15 ......79 A5
Handel St SN2 ....50 C8
Handley St SP5 ......204 D3
Hanging Bushes La
  SP11 ....193 A1
Hanging Langford Camp*
  BA12 ....201 F6
Hanging Stone* SN9 .181 B7
Hangman's Stone*
  RG17 ....164 F4
Hankerton Priory SN16 ..15 B4
Hankerton Rd SN16 ...16 C2
Hanks Cl SN16 ....28 A5
Hannington Cl SN2 ...35 B6
Hanover Cl BA14 ....101 E4
Harbour Cl SN25 .....34 F3
Harcourt Mews [5] BA11 110 A4
Harcourt Rd SN2 .....50 A8
Harcourt Terr SP2 ..115 F7
Hardenhuish Ave SN15 ..70 C1
Hardenhuish La SN14 ..70 B1
Hardenhuish Pk*
  SN14 ....70 C1
Hardens Cl SN15 .....79 A5
Hardens Mead SN15 ..79 A6
Hardhams Rise SN13 ..84 F8
Hardie Cl SN3 ....36 A1
Harding St [6] SN1 ...50 B6
Hardwick Cl SN25 ....35 A5
Hardyfair Cl [5] SP11 .192 F1
Hare Cl SN2 ....35 F5
Hare Knapp BA15 ...100 B6
Hare La Bremhill SN15 ..72 C5
  Pewsey SN9 ....182 A7
Hare Warren Cl SN2 ..144 C1
Harebell Cl SN25 ....34 D5
Harefield Cres SP4 ..190 A2
Harepit Way* SN11 ..172 F7
Hares Patch SN14 ....70 B2
Harford Cl SN3 ......78 F5
Harford St [4] BA14 ..105 E8
Hargreaves Rd SN25 ..35 D6
Harlech Cl SN5 ......49 B4
Harlestone Rd SN3 ...51 B8
Harmony Pl [8] BA14 ..105 D7
Harnham CE Jun & Inf Sch
  SP2 ....151 F6
Harnham Rd SP2 ....151 F7
Harnham Trad Est
  SP2 ....151 D7
Harnish Way SN14 ...70 B2
Harnwood Rd SP2 ...151 E6
Harper Rd SP2 ......145 D2
Harper's La SN16 ....27 F3
Harptree Cl SN5 .....49 A8
Harriers The SN3 ....51 C1
Harrington Dr [4] SP4 .198 E6
Harris Cl [5] RG17 ..165 A2
Harris La SN9 ....183 A7
Harris Rd
  Ashton Keynes SN6 ...7 A1
  Calne SN11 ....81 C5
  Swindon SN2 ....35 A2
Harrow Cl SN3 ......36 A1
Harrow Rd SN5 ......60 B2
Harrow Way SP11 ...193 B1
Harrow Way Com Sch
  SP10 ....193 C1
Harroway La SP11 ..193 B1

Hartfield SN10 ....214 A2
Hartham La SN13 .....76 E5
Harthill Dro SP5 ....211 D7
Hartington Rd SP2 ..145 E2
Hartland Cl SN3 .....51 A5
Hartley Way SP1 ....146 D5
Hartmoor Cl SN10 ..214 A2
Hartmoor Rd SN10 ..214 A2
Harts La SN14 ....76 E8
Harvard Cl
  [16] Bower Hill SN12 ..178 B8
  [1] Salisbury SP2 ....151 F1
Harvest La SP5 .....205 F4
Harvester Cl [7] SN5 ..48 F8
Harvey Gr SN2 ......34 F2
Hastings Ave SN9 ..182 B2
Hastings Cl SN9 ...182 B2
Hastings Dr SN15 ...60 B2
Hastings Rd SN13 ...85 A8
Hatch La SP3 ....203 C8
Hatchbury La SP11 ..185 C3
Hatcher's Cres SN26 ..21 B2
Hatches La SN2 ....152 D7
Hatchet Cl SP6 ....211 C6
Hatchet Hill SN4 ...163 D6
Hatchet La SP11 ...193 E5
Hatfield Cl SN25 ....34 E6
Hathaway Cl SP1 ...145 F4
Hathaway Rd SN2 ...35 C5
Hathaway Ret Pk SN15 ..78 E8
Hatherden CE Prim Sch
  SP11 ....193 C5
Hatherell Rd SN15 ..78 F4
Hatherhall Cl SN3 ...36 C2
Hatherley Rd SN3 ...51 B7
Hathersage Moor SN3 ..51 D5
Hattem Pl [28] SP10 ..193 D2
Hatton Gr SN3 ......50 F4
Hatton Way SN13 ...76 E1
Havard Way [2] SP4 ..217 D2
Havelock St
  Swindon SN1 ....50 B5
  Trowbridge BA14 ...105 C7
Haven Cl SN3 ......51 B8
Havering La SN9 ...182 B2
Hawcroft BA14 .....92 E1
Hawfinch Cl SN3 ...51 E5
Hawk's Worth Cl [6]
  BA11 ....110 C7
Hawker Rd SN3 ....51 C4
Hawkeridge Pk BA13 ..108 E5
Hawkeridge Rd BA14 ..105 E2
Hawkesdene [17] SP7 .202 C1
Hawkesdene La SP7 ..202 C1
Hawkins Cl SN15 ....78 F5
Hawkins Mdw SN8 ..213 B2
Hawkins Rd [16] SN8 ..170 A6
Hawkins St SN2 ....50 A7
Hawksridge [4] SP2 ..152 A5
Hawkswood SN3 ....51 D8
Hawksworth Way SN2 ..50 A7
Hawthorn Ave SN2 ...35 C2
Hawthorn Cl
  Pewsey SN9 ....215 D5
  [1] Salisbury SP2 ....145 F1
  [4] Shaftesbury SP7 ..202 C1
Hawthorn Gr BA14 ..105 C5
Hawthorn Rd
  Chippenham SN15 ...70 C1
  Frome BA11 ....110 A6
  Tidworth SP9 ....216 D7
Hay La Swindon SN5 ..48 F6
  Wroughton SN4 ......48 F1
Hay St SN14 ....74 A8
Haydock Cl [4] SN14 ..77 F5
Haydon Ct SN25 ....34 E5
Haydon Ct Dr SN25 ..34 E5
Haydon End La SN25 ..34 D6
Haydon St SN1 .....50 B7
Haydon View Rd SN25 ..35 C3
Haydonleigh Dr SN25 ..34 E5
Haydonleigh Sch SN25 ..34 E5
Haydown Leas SP11 ..185 C3
Haye's La GL9 ......38 E2
Hayes Cl BA14 .....101 E4
Hayesdown Fst Sch
  BA11 ....110 B5
Hayfield SN14 ......74 A8
Haynes Cl SN3 .....51 C4
Haynes Rd BA13 ...109 A3
Haywain [6] SP4 ...217 B3
Hayward Cl
  Chippenham SN15 ...78 F5
  Swindon SN25 ......35 A6
Hayward Pl BA13 ..108 E3
Haywards Pl SN10 ..179 F1
Hazel Cl
  Marlborough SN8 ...175 A7
  Salisbury SP2 .....145 B3
Hazel Copse [2] SN14 ..77 F6
Hazel End SN4 .....47 E1
Hazel Gr Calne SN11 ..81 B1
  Swindon SN2 ....35 C3
  Trowbridge BA14 ...105 B5
Hazel Way SN14 ....75 A5
Hazelbury Cres SN3 ..51 C7
Hazelbury Hill SN13 ..83 D6
Hazeldon La SP3 ...203 D6
Hazelwood Rd SN12 ..94 A3
Hazlemere Cl SN3 ...51 B4
Hazzard's Hill BA12 ..139 B5
Headlands Comp Sch
  SN2 ....35 D3
Headlands Gr SN2 ...35 E3

Headquarters Rd
  [8] Durrington/Bulford
  SP4 ....198 F6
  Westbury BA13 .....108 C6
Heale Gdn* SP4 ....131 D5
Heath Cl BA12 .....115 B8
Heath La
  Buttermere SN8 ....185 C7
  Great Somerford SN15 ..43 D2
Heath Rd SP4 ......145 D4
Heath Sq [1] SP4 ...197 E6
Heath Way SN3 ....51 B8
Heathcote Rd SN12 ..94 C5
Heather Ave SN4 ...94 C4
Heather Cl BA13 ...108 F4
Heather Shaw BA14 ..105 E8
Heather Way SN11 ...81 C1
Heathfield SN15 ....70 E2
Heathfields Way [2] SP7 202 C2
Heathlands The BA12 ..116 F5
Heathway BA12 ....115 C8
Heaton St [3] SN4 ..35 A6
Heaven's Gate* BA12 .115 C1
Hebden Rd BA15 ....99 F3
Heddington CE Prim Sch
  SN11 ....89 B1
Heddington Cl
  Swindon SN2 ....35 B5
  Trowbridge BA14 ...105 C5
Hedge Row SN15 ...79 A4
Hedgeditch La GL8 ..26 D7
Hedges Cl
  [1] Shipton Bellinger SP9 199 C8
  Swindon SN3 ....36 B3
Hedges The [4] SN4 ..163 A6
Hedgesparrow La SN13 ..83 F8
Hei-lin Way [2] SP11 ..192 A5
Helena Terr SP1 ...146 B1
Helmdon Rd BA14 ..101 A1
Helmsdale SN25 ....34 F4
Helps Well Rd BA14 ..102 B2
Helston Rd SN3 ....51 A5
Henderson Cl BA14 ..105 B7
Henfords Marsh BA12 ..117 B4
Hengest Cl [5] SP10 ..193 C2
Henley La SN13 ....83 C4
Henley Rd [2] SN3 ..51 A4
Henman Cl SN25 ...35 A5
Henn La SN15 ......57 C6
Henry St [1] SN1 ...50 B6
Henry's Garth [7] SN8 183 D8
Hepworth Rd [5] SN25 ..34 F6
Herbert Rd
  [3] Redlynch SP5 ...211 C7
  Salisbury SP2 .....145 C3
Hercules Way [1] SN12 178 B8
Herd St SN8 ....213 D4
Hereford Cl SN14 ...78 A5
Hereford Lawns SN3 ..50 F3
Herepath SN8 .....167 C4
Herman Miller Ind Est
  SN14 ....78 B5
Hermitage La SN2 ..35 E3
Hernsham St SP7 ..203 C4
Herd Prim Sch SN2 ..34 E3
Heron Cl SN11 .....81 D3
Heron Way SN14 ...77 F6
Heron Wlk [12] SP4 ..198 C7
Heronbridge Cl [2] SN5 ..49 C5
Herongate RG17 ...177 B8
Herons Ct [6] SN12 ..178 B8
Heronscroft SN3 ...51 D7
Heronslade BA12 ..117 D5
Heronswood SP2 ..152 A5
Hertford Cl
  [1] Fordingbridge SP6 ..210 D2
  [4] Swindon SN3 ....50 F4
Hesketh Cres SN1 ..50 D3
Hewitt Cl Swindon SN3 ..51 C4
  Trowbridge BA14 ...105 E7
Hewlett Cl SN15 ...79 A5
Hexham Cl
  [4] Chippenham SN14 ..77 F6
  Swindon SN5 ....49 B5
Heyford Cl [8] SP4 ..217 E3
Heytesbury CE Sch
  BA12 ....194 C5
Heytsbury Gdns [4] SN5 ..48 F4
Heywood Cl SN2 ...35 B5
Heywood Prep Sch The
  SN13 ....77 A2
Hicks Cl SN4 ......64 A6
High Bannerdown BA1 ..82 B4
High La SP5 ....205 B4
High Lawn SN10 ...179 D8
High Mead SN4 ....47 F2
High Post Golf Club
  SP4 ....132 C5
High Rd
  Ashton Keynes SN6 ...6 F1
  Bishopstone SP5 ...205 E4
  Britford SP5 ......152 D3
High St Alderbury SP5 153 C3
  Amesbury SP4 .....217 A3
  Ansty SP3 ....203 F6
  Ashbury SN6 ....164 A8
  Ashmore SP5 ......206 E4
  Avebury SN8 ....173 B8
  Badminton GL9 .....38 E2
  Bath BA1 ....82 B2
  Berwick St James SP3 196 F2
  Bishopstone SN6 ...163 E6
  Box SN13 ....83 C5
  Broad Blunsdon SN26 ..21 B1
  Bromham SN15 ......96 A7
  Bulford SP4 ....217 D8

High St continued
  Burbage SN8 ....175 C1
  Calne SN11 ....81 B3
  Chapmanslade BA13 ..111 B4
  Cheverell Magna SN10 ..179 C1
  Chippenham SN15 ...78 D7
  Chiseldown SN4 ....65 D4
  Codford BA12 ......195 A2
  Colerne SN14 ......75 B3
  Collingbourne Ducis SN8 191 E8
  Compton Chamberlayne
  SP3 ....205 A8
  Corsham SN13 ......77 A1
  Cricklade SN6 .....19 E8
  Damerham SP6 .....209 F3
  Devizes SN10 ......214 A3
  Downton SP5 ......211 B8
  Durrington/Bulford SP4 198 B7
  Erlestoke SN10 ....187 A8
  Figheldean SP4 ....190 B1
  [24] Fordingbridge SP6 210 D1
  Fovant SP3 ....204 E7
  Great Bedwyn SN8 ..176 B3
  Heytesbury BA12 ..194 C5
  Highworth SN6 .....23 A5
  Hindon SP3 ....200 A4
  Hinton Charterhouse BA2 ..98 E1
  Hungerford RG17 ..177 B7
  Idmiston SP4 ......133 D5
  Kempsford GL7 .....10 C7
  Lacock SN15 ....86 D5
  Lambourn RG17 ...164 F3
  Lechlade GL7 ....2 C4
  Limpley Stoke BA2 ..99 B5
  Little Bedwyn SN8 ..176 D4
  Littleton Panell SN10 ..187 D8
  [9] Ludgershall SP11 ..192 A5
  Maiden Bradley with Yarnfield
  BA12 ....118 E3
  Malmesbury SN16 ..28 A3
  Market Lavington SN10 179 F1
  Marlborough SN8 ..213 A1
  Melksham SN12 ....94 A4
  Meysey Hampton GL7 ..1 A5
  Netheravon SP4 ...190 A3
  Ogbourne St George
  SN8 ....168 F5
  Pewsey SN9 ....215 D5
  Pitton & Farley SP5 ..148 C3
  Porton SP4 ....133 D6
  Purton SN5 ....33 B4
  Ramsbury SN8 ....170 B2
  Rode BA11 ....103 F1
  Rowde SN10 ....96 D2
  Salisbury SP1 .....152 A8
  Seend SN12 ....178 E8
  Semington BA14 ...102 F6
  [18] Shaftesbury SP7 ..202 C1
  Sherston SN16 .....40 C8
  Sherston SN16 .....40 C8
  Shipton Bellinger SP9 199 D8
  Shrewton SP3 .....196 E7
  Sixpenny Handley SP5 208 A4
  South Cerney GL7 ....6 F6
  Steeple Ashton BA14 ..178 A3
  Stourton with Gasper
  BA12 ....123 F1
  Sutton Benger SN15 ..57 C2
  Sutton Veny BA12 ..117 F1
  Swindon SN25 .....34 E4
  Swindon SN3 ......50 D4
  Tilshead SP3 ......188 B2
  Tisbury SP3 ....203 E8
  Upavon SN9 ....181 F2
  Urchfont SN10 ....180 C4
  Wanborough SN4 ..163 B6
  Warminster BA12 ..117 A7
  West Lavington SN10 ..179 D1
  Westbury BA13 ....109 A3
  Westbury BA13 ....112 C8
  Winterbourne Stoke SP3 197 A4
  Woodgreen SP6 ...211 B4
  Wootton Bassett SN4 ..47 D1
  Worton SN10 ......179 B4
  Wroughton SN4 ....64 A5
  Wylye BA12 ....201 E8
  Zeale SP8 ....137 F2
High St Brow SN8 ..169 A6
High View SP3 .....203 E7
Highbury Ave SP2 ..145 E2
Highbury Cl [2] SP2 ..145 E2
Highbury Fst Sch SP2 145 E2
Highbury Pk BA12 ..117 C6
Highclere Ave SN3 ..50 F4
Highdown Way SN25 ..35 A7
Higher Barn Cl SP7 ..206 B7
Higher Blandford Rd [2]
  SP7 ....202 D1
Higher Mere Pk*
  BA12 ....202 A8
Highfield SN16 .....96 C7
Highfield Cl BA14 ..102 F5
Highfield Cres SP7 ..149 B6
Highfield La [10] SP5 ..211 C7
Highfield Rd
  Amesbury SP4 .....217 B3
  Bradford-on-Avon BA15 100 D7
  Salisbury SP2 .....145 D2
Highfield Rise [1] SP3 196 F6
Highfold SN4 ......47 F1
Highgate Cottage SN4 ..46 F5
Highgrove Cl SN11 ..81 D2
Highland [8] SN5 ...49 A7
Highland View SP2 ..130 A2
Highlands SN10 ....179 D5
Highlands Cl SN13 ..84 A8
Highlands Rd SP2 ..152 A6
Highlands Way SP5 ..161 D4

Highmoor Copse SN5 ..34 A1
Highnam Cl SN3 ....36 A1
Highridge Cl SN5 ...33 A3
Highway Comm SN11 ..166 B6
Highway The SP5 ..158 F5
Highwood Cl [4] SN2 ..34 D4
Highworth Golf Club
  SN6 ....22 F4
Highworth Rd
  Highworth SN6 .....22 D1
  Shrivenham SN6 ....23 E1
  South Marston SN3 ..36 E6
  Swindon SN3 ......36 A4
Highworth Recn Ctr
  SN6 ....22 F5
Highworth Warneford Comp
  Sch SN6 ....23 A5
Hill Beech Rd SP9 ..216 C8
Hill Cl [4] SP3 .....203 E8
Hill Cnr Rd SN15 ...70 E2
Hill Deverill Manor*
  ....120 F5
Hill Deverill Medieval Village
  of* BA12 ....120 F5
Hill Hayes La SN14 ..41 E1
Hill Moody's SP5 ..155 E3
Hill Rd SP1 ....146 E2
Hill Rise SN15 .....70 E2
Hill Side SP3 .....129 E8
Hill St BA14 ......101 C1
Hill The
  Limpley Stoke BA2 ..99 C5
  Little Somerford SN15 ..44 B6
Hill Top Ave SP9 ..216 C8
Hill Top Cl SP4 ...190 B2
Hill View SN8 .....181 B8
Hill View Rd
  [6] Salisbury SP1 ..152 B8
  Swindon SN3 ......36 C1
Hillary Cl SN25 ...35 C4
Hillbourne Cl BA12 ..117 B7
Hillcrest Colerne SN14 ..75 C6
  Malmesbury SN16 ..28 B2
Hilldrop Cl [1] SN8 ..170 B2
Hilldrop La
  Lambourn RG17 ...171 A6
  Ramsbury SN8 ....169 F3
Hilliers Yd SN8 ...213 D3
Hillingdon Rd SN3 ..51 B4
Hillmead Dr SN5 ...34 B1
Hillocks The SN4 ..60 B5
Hillside Leigh SN6 ..18 C5
  Nettleton SN14 ....53 A4
Hillside Ave SN1 ..50 A4
Hillside Cl
  Heddington SN11 ...89 B1
  Mere BA12 ....138 E5
  West Tytherley SP5 ..155 F2
Hillside Cl SN1 ....50 A4
Hillside Dr SP4 ...133 D3
Hillside Pk BA13 ..109 B3
Hillside Rd
  [4] Hungerford RG17 ..177 B6
  South Newton SP2 ..130 B2
Hillside Way SN26 ..21 A1
Hilltop Cl [2] SP3 ..196 F6
Hilltop Way SP1 ...146 A5
Hillview SP5 ......204 C3
Hillview Cl SP4 ...217 B4
Hillwell SN16 .....15 B2
Hillwood Cl BA14 ..116 F5
Hillwood La BA12 ..116 F5
Hillwood Rd [15] SN8 ..170 A6
Hillworth Gdns SN10 ..214 A3
Hillworth Rd SN10 ..214 A2
Hillyard Cl [3] SN5 ..48 F4
Hilmarton CP Sch
  SN11 ....166 A6
Hilperton Dr BA14 ..102 A2
Hilperton Prim Sch
  BA14 ....102 A4
Hilperton Rd BA14 ..101 E1
Hinde's Mdw SP3 ..196 F7
Hindon La SP3 ....200 D1
Hindon Rd
  Chilmark SP3 .....201 B3
  East Knoyle SP3 ..141 C2
  Kingston Deverill BA12 126 D7
Hinton Hill
  Bishopstone SN4 ..163 D6
  Hinton Charterhouse BA2 ..98 A1
Hinton Ho* BA2 ...98 E1
Hinton La SN14 ...178 A5
Hinton Priory* BA2 ..98 F3
Hinton Springs SN6 ..163 D6
Hinton St SN2 ....50 D8
Hitchings Skilling SN14 ..75 B3
Hither Cl SN14 ....78 A8
Hither Spring SN13 ..84 F8
Hither Way SN15 ..86 D5
Hoadley Gn SP1 ...146 D4
Hobbes Cl SN16 ...27 F4
Hobbs Hill BA14 ..178 B5
Hobhouse Cl BA15 ..100 E4
Hobley Drive SN3 ..36 A3
Hocketts Cl SN15 ..60 A3
Hodds Hill SN5 ....34 B2
Hodge La SN16 ....27 F4
Hodges Barn Gdns*
  GL8 ....26 F8
Hodson Rd SN4 ...65 D3
Hoggington La BA14 ..104 D4
Hoggs La SN5 .....33 A4
Holborn Hill OX12 ..165 E8

Holbrook La BA14 . . . . .105 D6
Holbrook Sch BA14 . . . . .105 D5
Holbrook Vale SN12 . . . . .93 F1
Holbrook Way SN1 . . . . .50 B6
Holcombe La BA2 . . . . . .82 A1
Holdcroft Cl SN26 . . . . . .21 C2
Holden Garson Rd SN2 . . .35 B6
Holders Rd SP4 . . . . . . .217 C4
Holford Cres SN5 . . . . . . .10 E6
Holinshed Mews 3 SN5 . . .49 A5
Holland Cl SN15 . . . . . . .79 A4
Holland Dr 11 SP10 . . . . .193 D2
Holliday Cl SN25 . . . . . . .35 A6
Hollies La BA1 . . . . .82 A6
Hollins Moor SN3 . . . . . .51 D2
Hollis Gdns SN14 . . . . . . .39 E4
Hollis Way BA14 . . . . . .104 F3
Hollow La SN8 . . . . .184 A7
Hollow St SN15 . . . . .43 F2
Hollow The
  Bratton BA13 . . . . . . .186 A7
  Chirton SN10 . . . . . . .180 F4
  Corsley BA12 . . . . . . .111 B1
  Dilton Marsh BA13 . . . .112 C8
  Shrewton SP3 . . . . . . .196 E7
  Sixpenny Handley SP5 . .208 A4
  Steeple Langford SP3 . . .128 C5
Hollow Way SN15 . . . . . . .59 D3
Holloway SN16 . . . . .28 A3
Holloway Hill SN14 . . . . . .66 E8
Holloway La SP3 . . . . . .141 B1
Hollows The SP2 . . . . . .144 B4
Hollows Cl SP2 . . . . . . .151 F6
Holly Cl Calne SN11 . . . . .81 C1
  Pewsey SN9 . . . . .215 D6
  Swindon SN2 . . . . .35 C4
Holly Ct BA11 . . . . .110 B7
Holly Dr SN14 . . . . .74 F6
Hollybush Cl
  Acton Turville GL9 . . . . .53 A6
  Chippenham Without
    SN14 . . . . .70 A2
  Winsley BA15 . . . . .99 E7
Hollybush La SN9 . . . . . .215 D6
Hollybush Rd BA12 . . . . .117 A8
Holmbury Cl BA11 . . . . . .110 C6
Holme La 7 BA13 . . . . . .186 B7
Holmeleaze BA14 . . . . . .178 A4
Holmes Cl SN15 . . . . .78 F4
Holmfield 1 SN10 . . . . . .187 E8
Holmleigh SN25 . . . . .34 E4
Holmoak Ct SN3 . . . . . . .50 D4
Holt La Tangley SP11 . . . .193 B8
  Teffont SP3 . . . . .201 C2
Holt Prim Sch BA14 . . . . .92 F1
Holt Rd
  Bradford-on-Avon BA15 . .100 E6
  Witham Friary BA11 . . . .123 C8
Holy Family RC Jun & Inf Sch
  SN3 . . . . .51 B6
Holy Rd Church★ SN3 . . .50 E4
Holy Rood Inf Sch SN1 . . .50 D5
Holy Trinity Sch
  Calne SN11 . . . . .81 C1
  Cheverell Magna SN10 . .187 B8
Holyrood CI BA14 . . . . . .105 B5
Holyrood RC Jun Sch
  SN3 . . . . .50 D5
Home Cl Chiseldown SN4 . .65 C4
  Trowbridge BA14 . . . . .105 D7
Home Farm Cl
  Mildenhall SN8 . . . . . .175 B8
  Steeple Ashton BA14 . . .178 A3
Home Farm Gdns 10
  SP10 . . . . .193 C2
Home Farm Rd SP2 . . . . .144 C1
Home Fields SN14 . . . . . .68 F5
Home Gd Cricklade SN6 . . .19 C8
  Wootton Bassett SN4 . . .48 A2
Homefarm SN6 . . . . .22 F6
Homefield Mere BA12 . . . .138 F5
  Motcombe SP7 . . . . . .202 C2
  Wootton Bassett SN4 . . .47 E2
Homefield Way RG17 . . . .177 B7
Homefields
  Longbridge Deverill
    BA12 . . . . .120 F6
  Marlborough SN8 . . . . .213 F2
Homelands The 1
  BA12 . . . . .116 E5
Homington Rd
  Britford SP5 . . . . .151 D3
  Coombe Bissett SP5 . . . .157 B8
Honey Garston SN11 . . . . .81 C3
Honey Hill 2 RG17 . . . . .165 A2
Honey Knob Hill SN14 . . . .55 F1
Honey La Norton SN16 . . . .41 E6
  Westbury BA13 . . . . . .112 C8
Honeybrook Cl SN14 . . . . .78 B8
Honeybunch Cnr SN8 . . . .164 C6
Honeyfields 10 RG17 . . . .177 B7
Honeylight View 3 SN25 . .35 A6
Honeymans BA14 . . . . . .105 F8
Honeymead SN11 . . . . . . .81 C3
Honeysuckle Cl
  Calne Without SN11 . . . .80 F4
  Chippenham Without
    SN14 . . . . .70 B3
  Swindon SN2 . . . . .34 D5
  4 Trowbridge BA14 . . .105 E7
Honiton Rd SN3 . . . . .51 B5
Hook Cl SN5 . . . . .34 A1
Hook St SN5 . . . . .48 F4
Hooks Hill SN5 . . . . .33 C4
Hooks La SN10 . . . . .179 A7

Hookwood La SP11 . . . . .192 E8
Hoopers Pl SN1 . . . . .50 D4
Hopgood Cl SN10 . . . . . .214 F6
Hopkinson Way SP10 . . . .193 B1
Hops Cl SP3 . . . . .201 A3
Hopton Cl SN5 . . . . .49 B3
Hopton Ind Est SN10 . . . .214 E7
Hopton Rd SN10 . . . . . . .214 D6
Horace St SN2 . . . . .49 F7
Horcott Rd GL7 . . . . .1 F6
Horham Cres SN3 . . . . . . .51 A4
Horn's La SN4 . . . . .167 B8
Hornbeam Cl 1 BA11 . . . .110 C6
Hornbeam Cres SN12 . . . .94 A3
Hornbury Cl SN16 . . . . . . .17 A2
Hornbury Hill SN16 . . . . . .17 A2
Horne Rd SP4 . . . . .198 E6
Horningsham CP Sch
  BA12 . . . . .119 B7
Hornsey Gdns SN2 . . . . . .36 A5
Horse Barrow★ SP4 . . . .133 D3
Horse Fair La SN6 . . . . . .19 E8
Horse Rd BA14 . . . . .101 F4
Horse Shoe La SP3 . . . . .142 C3
Horsebrook Pk SN11 . . . . .81 B2
Horsebrook The SN11 . . . .81 C2
Horsefair La SN15 . . . . . .59 C3
Horsell Cl 2 SN4 . . . . . . .47 C2
Horseponds 8 SP7 . . . . .202 B2
Horsepool SN15 . . . . .96 B8
Horseshoe Cres SN5 . . . . .34 A1
Horseshoe La SP11 . . . . .193 F8
Horton Ave SN10 . . . . . .214 C6
Horton Cl BA15 . . . . . . .100 E4
Horton Rd
  Bishops Cannings SN10 . .172 B2
  Devizes SN10 . . . . . . .214 F7
  Swindon SN2 . . . . .35 E6
Hospital Rd BA13 . . . . . .109 A2
Hossil La SN6 . . . . .22 B1
Houldsworth Ave
  BA12 . . . . .117 D8
Howard Cl SN3 . . . . .50 F6
Howard-Vyse Rd SP4 . . . .197 F7
Howgare Rd SP5 . . . . . . .205 B2
Hubert Hamilton Rd
  SP4 . . . . .198 E6
Huddleston Cl SN2 . . . . . .50 D8
Hudson Rd
  Amesbury SP4 . . . . . . .217 C4
  Malmesbury SN16 . . . . .27 F4
  Salisbury SP1 . . . . . . .145 F3
Hudson Way SN25 . . . . . .35 A5
Hudswell La SN13 . . . . . .84 C8
Hughes La SN8 . . . . .213 A2
Hughes St SN2 . . . . .49 F7
Hugo Dr SN25 . . . . .35 A6
Hulbert Cl SN13 . . . . .76 E1
Hullavington Airfield
  SN14 . . . . .56 A7
Hullavington Sch SN14 . . .41 F1
Hulse Rd SP1 . . . . .146 A2
Humber La SN9 . . . . .216 B4
Humphrey's La 3 RG17 . .171 E7
Hungerdown La SN14 . . . .78 A6
Hungerford Ave BA14 . . . .105 A7
Hungerford CP Sch
  RG17 . . . . .177 B7
Hungerford Hill
  Great Shefford RG17 . . .171 A4
  Lambourn RG17 . . . . . .165 A1
Hungerford La
  Andover SP10 . . . . . . .193 E3
  Chute SP11 . . . . .185 A1
  Kintbury RG17 . . . . . . .177 F5
  Tangley SP11 . . . . . . .193 A8
Hungerford Leisure Ctr
  RG17 . . . . .177 D7
Hungerford Rd
  Buttermere SN8 . . . . . .185 B7
  Calne SN11 . . . . .81 B4
  Chippenham SN15 . . . . .70 D1
  Grafton SN8 . . . . .184 A7
  Hungerford RG17 . . . . .177 D7
Hungerford Sta RG17 . . . .177 C7
Hunsdon Cl SN3 . . . . .51 A6
Hunt Cl The BA14 . . . . . .102 F5
Hunt St SN1 . . . . .50 B7
Huntenhull La BA13 . . . . .111 D4
Hunter's Gr SN2 . . . . .35 B1
Hunters Mdw SN14 . . . . . .68 F5
Hunters Mead SP7 . . . . . .202 A5
Huntingdon Pl BA15 . . . .100 C7
Huntingdon Rise
  BA15 . . . . .100 C7
Huntingdon St BA15 . . . .100 C8
Huntingdon Way SN14 . . . .78 A6
Huntley Cl SN3 . . . . .50 F7
Hunts Hill SN26 . . . . .21 B2
Hunts Mead SN15 . . . . . . .96 A7
Hunts Mill Rd SN4 . . . . . .61 A8
Hunts Rise SN3 . . . . .36 C7
Huntsland SN4 . . . . .47 F2
Hurdcott La SP4 . . . . . . .146 F8
Hurley Cl 5 SP4 . . . . . . .217 C3
Hurricane Rd SN12 . . . . . .94 C1
Hurst Cres SN2 . . . . .35 C3
Hurst's La SN9 . . . . .181 C7
Huxley Ct GL7 . . . . .7 A7
Hyam Cotts SN16 . . . . . . .27 C4
Hyde La
  Marlborough SN8 . . . . .213 C3
  Purton SN5 . . . . .33 C4
Hyde Rd Swindon SN25 . . .35 D6
  Trowbridge BA14 . . . . .101 C2
Hyde The SN5 . . . . .33 D4
Hylder Cl SN2 . . . . .34 D4
Hyson Cres 6 SP11 . . . . .192 B5

Hysopp Cl SN2 . . . . .34 C4
Hythe Rd SN1 . . . . .50 B5

I

Icknield Way
  Andover SP10 . . . . . . .193 E2
  Bishopstone SN6 . . . . .163 E6
Icomb Cl SN5 . . . . .49 C4
Idlebush Barrow★
  SN7 . . . . .164 E7
Idmiston Prim Sch
  SP4 . . . . .133 C6
Idmiston Rd SP4 . . . . . . .133 E6
Idovers Dr SN5 . . . . .49 C4
Idstone Hill SN6 . . . . . . .163 F7
Idstone Rd SN6 . . . . .164 A7
Iffley Rd SN2 . . . . .49 F8
Iford Hill BA15 . . . . .99 E2
Iford La BA15 . . . . .99 D3
Iles Cl SN11 . . . . .73 F7
Ilynton Ave SP5 . . . . . . .148 C7
Imber Ave
  Amesbury SP4 . . . . . . .217 D2
  Warminster BA12 . . . . .117 C7
Imber Pl SP3 . . . . .188 B3
Imber Rd Bratton BA12 . . .186 C6
  10 Shaftesbury SP7 . . .202 D2
  Warminster BA12 . . . . .117 D8
Imberwood Cl BA12 . . . . .117 C7
Imby Cl BA12 . . . . .117 F1
India Ave SP2 . . . . .145 E2
Indigo Gdns BA13 . . . . . .108 F3
Indigo La BA13 . . . . .108 F3
Ingles Edge RG17 . . . . . .177 E2
Inglesham Cl 3 BA14 . . . .105 D5
Inglesham Rd SN2 . . . . . .35 C4
Inglesham Village★ SN6 . . .2 B1
Inglewood Rd RG17 . . . . .177 E5
Ingram Pl BA13 . . . . . . .108 F4
Ingram Rd SN2 . . . . .94 D5
Ingram St SN16 . . . . .28 A3
Inkpen Prim Sch
  RG17 . . . . .177 E3
Inkpen Rd RG17 . . . . . . .177 C5
Inlands Cl SN9 . . . . .215 C5
Inmarsh La SN12 . . . . . .178 E7
Inmead BA13 . . . . .186 C8
Innox Mill Cl BA14 . . . . . .101 B1
Innox Rd BA14 . . . . .101 B1
Inverary Rd SN4 . . . . .64 A7
Ipswich St SN2 . . . . .50 C8
Irston Way 4 SN5 . . . . . . .49 B4
Irving Way SN8 . . . . .213 C2
Isbury Rd SN8 . . . . .213 E2
Isis Cl SN25 . . . . .35 A3
Islandsmead SN3 . . . . . . .51 C6
Islay Cres SN6 . . . . .22 F6
Isles Rd 6 SN8 . . . . .170 B2
Islington BA14 . . . . .101 D1
Islington St SN1 . . . . .50 C6
Itchen Cl 2 SO51 . . . . . .212 F6
Ivies The SN9 . . . . .181 F5
Ivy Field SN13 . . . . .77 A2
Ivy La
  Broad Blunsdon SN26 . . . .21 B2
  South Wraxall BA15 . . . .91 E5
Ivy La Prim Sch SN15 . . . .78 D7
Ivy Lane SN15 . . . . .78 D7
Ivy Mead BA12 . . . . .139 B5
Ivy Rd SN15 . . . . .78 D7
Ivy St SP1 . . . . .152 B8
Ivy Terr BA15 . . . . .100 D7
Ixworth Cl 10 SN5 . . . . . .49 A7

J

Jack Paul Cl BA12 . . . . . .139 A6
Jack Thorne Cl SN5 . . . . . .34 A4
Jack's Hedge Cnr
  BH21 . . . . .208 A2
Jackaments Barn GL7 . . . . .4 B6
Jackson's La SN15 . . . . . . .70 D5
Jackson Cl SN12 . . . . . . .214 C2
Jacob's Barrow★ SP5 . . .211 E4
Jacobs Wlk SN3 . . . . .51 D4
Jagdalik Rd SP9 . . . . . . .216 C4
Jaggard View SP4 . . . . . .217 C3
Jaggards La SN13 . . . . . . .84 D5
James Cl SN15 . . . . .79 A4
James Rd SP4 . . . . .217 C4
James St Salisbury SP2 . .145 F1
  Trowbridge BA14 . . . . .101 D2
James Watt Cl SN2 . . . . . .50 A7
James's Hill BA10 . . . . . .122 A7
Jamrud Rd SP9 . . . . .216 B5
Jarvis St SN9 . . . . .181 F2
Jasmine Cl Calne SN11 . . .81 B1
  Chippenham Without
    SN14 . . . . .70 A1
  Swindon SN2 . . . . .34 D4
Jasmine Way BA14 . . . . .105 E7
Javelin Cl 6 SP4 . . . . . . .217 D3
Jay Cl BA11 . . . . .110 B6
Jeanneau Cl 24 SP7 . . . .202 C2
Jefferies Ave SN2 . . . . . . .35 C2
Jefferies Cl SN8 . . . . . . .213 A2
Jenkins St SN2 . . . . .49 F6
Jennings St SN2 . . . . .49 F6
Jersey Pk SN5 . . . . .49 B8
Jewel Cl SN5 . . . . .48 F5
Jewell Cl SP1 . . . . .146 D4
Joanna Cl 4 SP5 . . . . . . .210 F8
Jobbers La SP3 . . . . .203 E7
Jockey La SN15 . . . . .96 A7
John Aubrey Cl SN14 . . . . .68 F6

John Bentley Sch The
  SN11 . . . . .81 B1
John Betjeman Cl 1
  SN16 . . . . .28 A5
John French Way SP4 . . . .217 E8
John Gay Rd 5 SP4 . . . . .217 B3
John Herring Cres SN3 . . .36 A1
John O'Gaunt Sch
  RG17 . . . . .177 B6
John of Gaunt Rd GL7 . . . .10 D6
John of Gaunt Sch The
  BA14 . . . . .105 B7
John Rennie Cl
  Bradford-on-Avon BA15 . .100 E4
  Devizes SN10 . . . . . . .214 A4
John Rumble Cl SN10 . . . .214 C3
John St SN1 . . . . .50 B6
Jole Cl SN2 . . . . .35 E5
Joles La BA11 . . . . .110 F1
Jolliffe St 8 SN1 . . . . .50 A5
Jones Hill BA15 . . . . .100 C5
Jordan Cl SN15 . . . . .78 F5
Joseph St 5 SN1 . . . . .50 A5
Joule Rd 3 SP10 . . . . . . .193 D2
Joyce Cl SN2 . . . . .35 A6
Jubb's La SN8 . . . . .169 A5
Jubilee Cl
  3 Sandleheath SP6 . . .210 C1
  Westbury BA13 . . . . . .109 A3
Jubilee Ct 3 SP2 . . . . . . .145 F2
Jubilee Gdns GL7 . . . . .6 F7
Jubilee Hill SP4 . . . . . . .197 F1
Jubilee Rd
  Sandleheath SP6 . . . . .210 C1
  Swindon SN2 . . . . .34 D3
Juggler's La SN11 . . . . . .166 C2
Juliana Cl 2 SN5 . . . . . . .49 A4
Jump Farm Rd SN10 . . . .214 C3
Junction Rd
  Alderbury SP5 . . . . . . .153 E2
  Bradford-on-Avon BA15 . .100 D6
Juniper Cl SN3 . . . . .51 B8
Juniper Dr SP1 . . . . .146 A5
Juniper Rd SP5 . . . . .148 C7
Juno Way SN1 . . . . .49 F4
Jutland Cres 3 SP10 . . . .193 D2

K

Kandahar SN8 . . . . .170 A7
Kandy Rd 3 SP4 . . . . . . .198 E6
Karachi Cl SP9 . . . . .216 C4
Karslake Cl 6 SN3 . . . . . .51 C4
Kashmir Rd 1 SP4 . . . . . .198 E6
Katherine's Wlk GL7 . . . . . .2 C4
Katifer La SN16 . . . . .28 A3
Keates Cl BA14 . . . . .101 D1
Keats Cl SN4 . . . . .47 F3
Keble Cl Lechlade GL7 . . . . .2 D5
  Swindon SN3 . . . . .51 C2
Keels SN6 . . . . .8 C1
Keevil Airfield BA14 . . . . .178 C4
Keevil Ave SN11 . . . . .81 A3
Keevil CE Sch BA14 . . . . .178 B5
Kelham Cl 8 SN3 . . . . . . .50 F4
Kelham Gdns SN8 . . . . . .213 E3
Kellsborough Rd SN4 . . . . .63 F7
Kelly Gdns SN5 . . . . .34 F6
Kelmscot Rd SN25 . . . . . .35 C3
Kelsey Rd SP1 . . . . .146 B1
Kelso Ct 3 SN14 . . . . .78 A5
Kelston Rd SN8 . . . . .176 C4
Kelvin Rd SN3 . . . . .51 A7
Kemble Cl BA12 . . . . . . .117 A5
Kemble CP Sch GL7 . . . . . .4 F7
Kemble Dr SN2 . . . . .50 A7
Kemble Sta GL7 . . . . .4 E8
Kembles SN16 . . . . .28 C2
Kembrey Bsns Pk SN2 . . . .35 E2
Kembrey St SN2 . . . . .35 D2
Kemmel Rd SP11 . . . . . . .191 F4
Kemp Cl SN10 . . . . .214 C3
Kemp's La BA11 . . . . . . .110 F7
Kempsfield SN10 . . . . . . .214 C1
Kempton Pk Ct 10 SN14 . . .77 F6
Kendal SN5 . . . . .49 B4
Kendrick Cl BA13 . . . . . .109 A3
Kenilworth Gdns SN12 . . . .94 B3
Kenilworth Lawns SN3 . . . .50 F3
Kennedy Ave SN12 . . . . . .85 D1
Kennedy Dr SN3 . . . . .51 D4
Kennet Ave SN25 . . . . . . .35 B3
Kennet Cl
  Melksham SN12 . . . . . . .94 A6
  Warminster BA12 . . . . .117 A5
Kennet Ct RG17 . . . . . . .177 C5
Kennet Gdns BA15 . . . . . .100 D5
Kennet Mews SN8 . . . . . .213 E3
Kennet Pl SN8 . . . . .213 E3
Kennet Rd
  South Tedworth SP9 . . .216 E6
  Wroughton SN4 . . . . . . .64 A7
Kennet Way
  Hungerford RG17 . . . . .177 B8
  Trowbridge BA14 . . . . .101 C1
Kensington Cl BA14 . . . . .101 D2
Kensington Fields
  BA14 . . . . .104 F7
Kensington Rd 1 SP2 . . . .145 F2
Kensington Way SN14 . . . .77 F7
Kent Cl SN14 . . . . .78 A6
Kent End SN6 . . . . .7 C5
Kent Rd Salisbury SP2 . . .151 E6
  Swindon SN1 . . . . .50 B4
Kenton Cl SN3 . . . . .51 B6
Kenton Dr BA14 . . . . . . .105 B7
Kents Hill SP3 . . . . .201 F1

Kenwin Cl SN3 . . . . .36 E2
Kenwood Cl BA14 . . . . . .105 F8
Kerby Ave SP4 . . . . .190 B3
Kerrs Way SN4 . . . . .64 A5
Kerry Cl
  Derry Hill/Studley SN11 . .79 F2
  Swindon SN5 . . . . .49 A7
Kershaw Rd SN3 . . . . .51 C4
Kestrel Cl SP9 . . . . .216 E7
Kestrel Dr SN3 . . . . .51 E6
Keswick Rd SN3 . . . . .51 B3
Ketton Cl BA14 . . . . .106 A2
Kettle La SP4 . . . . .101 A1
Kew Dr 4 BA14 . . . . .105 A7
Kewlake La SO51 . . . . . .212 F1
Keynes Ctry Pk★ GL7 . . . .6 B3
Keynston Down SN5 . . . . .50 F5
Kibblewhite Cl SN5 . . . . . .33 B3
Kickdom Cl SP4 . . . . . . .217 C2
Kidston Way SN13 . . . . . .84 A8
Kiel Dr SP10 . . . . .193 D2
Kilben Cl SN5 . . . . .48 F1
Kilda Rd SN6 . . . . .22 E7
Kill Barrow (Long Barrow)★
  BA12 . . . . .187 D3
Kilmington CE Fst Sch
  BA12 . . . . .123 E6
Kiln Cl SP5 . . . . .153 F1
Kiln La Redlynch SP5 . . . .211 D8
  Swindon SN1 . . . . .34 F1
Kilns The SN11 . . . . .81 C4
Kilsby Dr SN3 . . . . .51 B8
Kilsyth Cl SN5 . . . . .49 B5
Kilverts Cl SN14 . . . . .78 A6
Kimberley Rd SN3 . . . . . . .51 A4
Kimbolton Cl 6 SN5 . . . . . .49 A4
Kimmeridge Cl SN3 . . . . . .51 C8
Kimpton CE Prim Sch
  SP11 . . . . .192 C1
King Alfred St SN9 . . . . . .215 D5
King Alfred Cl SN15 . . . . . .78 C8
King Alfred Way BA15 . . . .99 D7
King Alfred's Mid Sch
  SP7 . . . . .202 D2
King Alfreds Cl 2 BA12 . . .126 B7
King Arthur's Way
  SP10 . . . . .193 E2
King Barrow★
  Bishopstrow BA12 . . . . .117 F5
  Winterbourne Stoke
    SP4 . . . . .197 C4
King Charles Rd SN5 . . . . .49 B4
King Henry Dr
  Chippenham SN15 . . . . .79 A4
  Swindon SN5 . . . . .48 F4
King John St SN1 . . . . . . .50 D4
King John's Ho★ SP5 . . . .207 B1
King La BA12 . . . . .116 E5
King Oak★ SN8 . . . . .175 C4
King St Melksham SN12 . . .94 A3
  3 Swindon SN1 . . . . . . .50 B6
  Warminster BA12 . . . . .116 C5
  Wilton SP2 . . . . .144 D4
King William St SN1 . . . . . .50 C4
King William St CE Prim Sch
  SN1 . . . . .50 C4
King's House★ SP1 . . . . .152 A7
King's La SP3 . . . . .203 E5
King's Rd SP1 . . . . .146 A2
King's Wall SN16 . . . . .28 A3
Kingdown Comp Sch
  BA12 . . . . .117 D6
Kingfisher Cl SP2 . . . . . .152 A5
Kingfisher Dr
  Bower Hill SN12 . . . . . . .94 D1
  Devizes SN10 . . . . . . .214 E5
  7 Durrington/Bulford
    SP4 . . . . .198 C7
  Swindon SN3 . . . . .51 D7
  Westbury BA13 . . . . . .109 A4
Kingfishers 2 SN9 . . . . . .199 D8
Kingham Cl SN14 . . . . . . .78 C7
Kings Ave
  Chippenham Without
    SN14 . . . . .77 F6
  Corsham SN13 . . . . . . .76 F2
  Highworth SN6 . . . . . . .23 A5
Kings Cl 5 BA12 . . . . . . .116 E5
Kings Dr SN8 . . . . .175 C8
Kings Gate SP2 . . . . .144 E4
Kings Gdns BA14 . . . . . . .101 E5
Kings Hill 18 SP7 . . . . . .202 C2
Kings Lodge Sch SN15 . . . .79 A5
Kings Mdw SN16 . . . . .14 D5
Kings Paddock SP5 . . . . .149 A5
Kings Rd
  Easterton SN10 . . . . . .180 A2
  Enham Alamein SP11 . . .193 E4
  Market Lavington SN10 . .179 F2
Kings Rise BA12 . . . . . . .116 E5
Kingsbere La 5 SP2 . . . . .202 D2
Kingsbourne Cl SP4 . . . . .133 B1
Kingsbury Cl SN12 . . . . . .94 B3
Kingsbury Hill House Sch
  SN8 . . . . .213 D3
Kingsbury Sq 3 SP2 . . . . .144 D3
Kingsbury St
  Calne SN11 . . . . .81 B2
  Marlborough SN8 . . . . .213 D3
Kingscote Cl 1 SN5 . . . . . .48 F8
Kingsdown Golf Club
  SN13 . . . . .83 A3
Kingsdown Gr BA1 . . . . . .82 F2
Kingsdown La SN2 . . . . . .35 D8
Kingsdown Rd
  Stratton St Margaret SN2 . .36 A6
  Swindon SN2 . . . . .35 F5
  3 Trowbridge BA14 . . . .105 C5

Kingsdown Sch SN2 ....35 F5
Kingsettle Hill BA10 ..122 C2
Kingsfield BA15 ......100 D7
Kingsfield Grange Rd
 BA15 ....100 E7
Kingsford Cl 9 SP5 ..211 C2
Kingshill Rd SN1 ....50 A4
Kingsland Rd SP2 ....145 F2
Kingsley Ave SN4 ......47 E3
Kingsley Gdns SN10 ..214 C3
Kingsley Pl BA14 .....100 F1
Kingsley Rd
 Chippenham SN14 ....78 B6
 Devizes SN10 ....214 C3
Kingsley Way SN2 ......35 D5
Kingsman La 13 SP7 ..202 C1
Kingsmanor Wharf
 SN10 ....214 D5
Kingsmead GL7 ....2 C5
Kingsmead House
 SN15 ....44 A5
Kingsmead Mill* SN15 ..43 F6
Kingston SN16 ....43 F8
Kingston Ave BA15 ...100 E5
Kingston La BA12 .....118 F2
Kingston Rd
 Bradford-on-Avon BA15 100 D6
 Shalbourne SN8 ....176 F1
 Swindon SN3 ....51 A4
Kingsway Preshute SN8 168 B1
 Wilton SP2 ....144 E5
Kingsway Cl 1 SN3 .....50 A4
Kingswood BA14 ......104 F6
Kingswood Ave SN3 ....51 A5
Kington La SN14 ....56 B4
Kington St Michael CE Prim
 Sch SN14 ....70 A8
Kingway Wine SN16 .....42 E4
Kintbury Rd RG17 ....177 F3
Kipling Gdns SN2 ......35 E4
Kirby Cl SN3 ....50 F4
Kirby Rd SN13 ....76 E1
Kirkstall Ct SN5 ......49 C4
Kirktonhill Rd SN5 ....49 D6
Kishorn Cl 5 SN5 ......34 B2
Kitchen Barrow*
 SN10 ....172 E3
Kitchener Rd SP4 ....217 B4
Kitchener St SN1 ......50 C8
Kite Hill SN4 ....163 A5
Kite's Nest La SP8 ...137 C6
Kitefield 2 SN6 ....19 D8
Kivel Ct SP2 ....146 A2
Kiwi CP Sch SP4 .....198 E6
Kiwi Rd 6 SP4 ....198 F7
Kiwi The* SP4 ....198 F6
Knap Barrow (Long
 Barrow)* SP6 ....209 D6
Knap Hill (Causewayed
 Enclosure)* SN8 ....173 E2
Knap La SP3 ....200 F2
Knapp Cl SN2 ....35 A2
Knapp Hill SP5 ......205 A4
Knapp The Calne SN11 .81 C3
 Great Bedwyn SN8 ...176 B3
 7 Shaftesbury SP7 ..202 B2
Knapps The BA14 .....102 F5
Knighton Barrow (Long
 Barrow)* SP4 ....197 E8
Knighton Rd SP5 .....205 E4
Knights Cl
 1 Chippenham SN15 ..78 F4
 West Overton SN8 ...173 F6
Knights Enham Inf Sch
 SP10 ....193 E2
Knightsbridge Rd
 SP11 ....193 F4
Knockdown Rd SN16 ...25 C1
Knoll Cl OX12 ....165 F8
Knoll The
 12 Aldbourne SN8 ...170 A6
 Kempsford GL7 ......10 D7
 Westbury BA13 .....109 B4
Knook Barrow (Long
 Barrow)* BA12 ......194 F7
Knook Castle* BA12 ..195 B7
Knook Manor* BA12 ..194 D4
Knowlands SN6 ....23 A7
Knowle The SN13 ......84 F8
Knowledge Hill 2 SN8 170 B2
Knowsley Rd SN3 ......51 A4
Kohat Cl SP9 ....216 B7
Komat Rd SP9 ....216 C5
Kyneton Way SN14 .....70 A8

L

La Retraite Sch SP1 ..146 B2
Labour-in-Vain Hill
 SN11 ....172 A8
Laburnum Dr SN4 ......47 E3
Laburnum Cl 3 BA11 ..110 B7
Laburnum Dr SN12 .....94 A3
Laburnum Gr BA14 ....105 B6
Laburnum Rd SN2 ......35 C3
Lacemakers Rd SN16 ...28 A5
Lackham Cir SN14 .....78 B6
Lackham Coll SN15 ....78 E1
Lacock Abbey* SN15 ...86 D5
Lacock Gdns BA14 ....102 B3
Lacock Prim Sch SN15 .86 D5
Lacock Rd
 Corsham SN13 ....85 D8
 Swindon SN2 ....35 C4
Ladbrook La SN13 .....77 C1

Ladds La SN15 ....78 E7
Lady Coventry Rd SN15 .78 F7
Lady Diana Ct 15 SP11 192 A5
Lady Down View 5 SP3 203 E8
Lady Godley Cl SP9 ..216 C5
Lady Jane Wlk 22 SP11 192 A5
Lady La SN25 ....21 B1
Lady Mead SN6 ....19 D8
Ladyfield Rd SN14 ....78 B7
Ladysmith SP4 ....133 D3
Ladysmith Rd
 Chiseldon SN4 ....65 D1
 Salisbury SP2 ......145 D3
Ladywood 8 SN10 ....179 F1
Laggar The SN13 ......77 A2
Lagos St 3 SN1 ....50 C7
Lahore Cl SP9 ....216 C7
Lahore Rd SP9 ....216 C5
Laines Head SN14 .....70 C2
Lainey's Cl SN8 .....213 D4
Lainsmead Jun & Inf Sch
 SN3 ....50 E5
Lake Group (Tumuli)*
 SP4 ....197 D3
Lake House* SP4 ....197 F1
Lakeside Fairford GL7 ..1 F6
 South Cerney GL7 .....7 B7
 Swindon SN3 ....50 E3
Lakeside Cl SP10 ....193 C1
Lamb Ale Gn SN14 ...105 D6
Lambdown App SP11 ..191 F3
Lambdown Terr
 North Tidworth SN11 216 F6
 Perham Down SP11 ..191 F4
Lambert Cl SN5 ....49 B3
Lamberts SN14 ....78 A8
Lambourn Ave SN5 ....50 E3
Lambourn CE Prim Sch
 RG17 ....165 A1
Lambourn La BA13 ...186 C8
Lambourn Pl 10 RG17 165 A2
Lambourne Cres 94 B4
Lambrok Cl BA14 .....104 F6
Lambrok Rd BA14 ....104 F6
Lammas Cl SN11 .....166 A6
Lamora Cl 12 SN5 .....48 F8
Lanac Rd SN3 ....36 A1
Lancaster Cl RG17 ...177 B6
Lancaster Mews SN3 ..36 C5
Lancaster Pl SN3 .....36 C5
Lancaster Rd
 Bower Hill SN12 .....94 B1
 Kempsford GL7 ......10 E6
 Wroughton SN4 ......64 A6
Lancaster Sq
 Hungerford RG17 ....177 B6
 Lyneham SN15 ....60 A2
Landale Cl 3 SP11 ...193 E4
Landford CE Prim Sch
 SP5 ....212 A4
Landor Rd SN25 ....34 F8
Lane The SN4 ....163 C7
Lane's Cl SP4 ....217 C4
Lane-side 9 SP7 .....202 C2
Lanes End SN13 ....85 D5
Lanes End Hill BA12 .115 A8
Lanfear Cl SP4 ......217 C4
Langdale Dr SN5 ......49 B3
Langet GL7 ....6 E6
Langford Gr SN3 ......50 E6
Langford La SP5 .....160 A3
Langford Rd
 Great Wishford SP2 .129 F4
 Trowbridge BA14 ...101 C2
Langfords La 3 SP7 ..202 B1
Langham Pl BA11 ....103 F1
Langholm Ave BA12 ..116 D6
Langholm Cl BA12 ...116 D6
Langley Fitzure CE Sch
 SN15 ....70 E6
Langley Gdn SP6 ....210 E2
Langley Rd
 Chippenham SN15 ....70 E1
 Swindon SN5 ....34 B1
 Trowbridge BA14 ...105 C5
Langport Cl 1 SN5 ....49 B4
Langstone Way SN5 ...49 C6
Lanham's Cl BA13 ...109 A2
Lanhill (Long Barrow)*
 SN14 ....69 B2
Lanhill View SN14 .....70 A8
Lanhydrock Cl 9 SN5 ..49 A4
Lansbury Dr SN2 ......35 F4
Lansdown Cl
 Melksham SN12 ......94 D6
 Trowbridge BA14 ...105 B7
Lansdown Gr SN15 ....70 D1
Lansdown Rd SN1 .....50 B4
Lansdowne Cl SN11 ...81 A4
Lansdowne Cres SN11 .79 F2
Lapwing Cl 1 SN3 .....51 E6
Lapwing Cres SN14 ...70 B2
Larch Cl SN12 ....94 A3
Larch Gr BA14 ......105 B6
Larch Rd SN14 ....74 F6
Larch Row SP6 ......210 F1
Larchfield Cl BA11 ..110 B7
Larchmore Cl SN25 ...35 A3
Lark Cl SP9 ....216 D7
Lark Down SN14 .....101 E1
Larkham Rise SN15 ...78 F6
Larkhill CP Sch SP4 .197 E7
Larkhill Rd SP4 .....198 B7
Larkrise Sch BA14 ...101 F1
Larksfield SN3 ....51 C8

Larmer Tree Victorian
 Pleasure Garden*
 SP5 ....207 B3
Late Broads BA15 .....99 D7
Latimer Gdns SN14 ....41 E1
Latton Cl SN2 ....35 B6
Laughton Way SN25 ...35 A6
Launcelot Cl 22 SP10 193 E2
Laundry La 5 SP7 ....202 B1
Laurel Cl BA11 ......110 B7
Laurel Dr Colerne SN14 74 F6
 Marlborough SN8 ...213 F2
Laurel Gr BA14 .....105 C6
Laurels The
 Hungerford RG17 ...177 C8
 Melksham Without SN12 86 A1
 Westwood BA15 ......99 F3
Laurence Ct 10 SP11 192 A5
Lavender Cl
 Melksham SN12 ......94 C3
 5 Trowbridge BA14 .105 E7
Lavender Ct BA11 ...110 B7
Lavender Dr SN11 .....81 B1
Laverstock Pk SP1 ...146 E1
Laverstock Pk W SP1 146 D2
Laverstock Rd SP1 ...146 C1
Laverton Gn 3 BA13 .108 F1
Laverton Rd BA13 ...108 F1
Lavington Cl 10 SN10 183 D8
Lavington Hill SN10 .187 F8
Lavington La SN10 ..187 E8
Lavington Sch SN10 .179 E1
Lawn Farm Cl SN9 ...182 E7
Lawn Jun & Inf Sch
 SN3 ....50 F2
Lawns The SN4 ....47 D2
Lawrence Cl
 4 Amesbury SP4 ....217 C3
 Devizes SN10 ......214 C1
 Swindon SN3 ....50 E6
Lawrence Mead 3 SN8 170 B2
Lawrence Rd SP4 ....197 F7
Lawson Rd 3 SP4 ....198 A6
Lawton Cl SN3 ....51 A3
Layton Cl SP7 ....202 C1
Le Marchant Cl 2 SN10 214 D5
Lea Cl SN25 ....35 A7
Lea House SN16 ....28 D1
Leaden Hall Sch SP2 152 A7
Leafield Ind Est SN13 .84 E6
Leafield Pl BA14 ....100 F1
Leafield Rd SN13 .....84 E6
Leafield Way SN13 ....84 E6
Leafy La SN13 ....76 A1
Leamington Gr SN3 ...50 F2
Leap Gate
 Hilperton SN8 ......213 C4
 Trowbridge BA14 ...106 A8
Leatler Cl SP3 ......204 D8
Leaze Rd
 Marlborough SN8 ...213 C4
 Melksham SN12 ......94 C4
Leaze The
 Ashton Keynes SN6 ....6 F1
 Durrington/Bulford SP4 217 E8
 South Cerney GL7 .....6 F6
Lechlade Rd Buscot SN7 .2 E2
 Highworth SN6 ....23 A7
 Inglesham SN6 ....12 A6
Ledge Hill SN10 .....179 E2
Ledger Hill Cl SP4 ..217 D8
Lee Cres SN3 ....57 C1
Legate Cl SN15 ....79 B5
Leicester St SN1 .....50 D6
Leigh CE Sch SN6 ....18 C5
Leigh Cl BA13 ......108 E1
Leigh La SP3 ....202 E8
Leigh Pk Rd BA15 ...100 D8
Leigh Rd
 Bradford-on-Avon BA15 91 E1
 Holt BA14 ....92 C1
 Swindon SN3 ....35 C4
 Westbury BA13 .....108 F2
Leighton Ave SN3 .....50 F4
Leighton Gn SN3 ....109 A4
Leighton La BA13 ...109 A1
Leighton Pk N 4 BA13 108 F1
Leighton Pk Rd 5 BA13 108 F1
Leighton Pk W 2 BA13 108 F1
Leighton Recn Ctr
 BA13 ....109 A2
Leland Cl 5 SN16 .....28 A5
Lena 26 SP11 ....192 A5
Lennards The GL7 ......7 A7
Lennox Dr SN3 ....50 E6
Lenton Cl SN14 ....77 F7
Leonard Cheshire Cl 4
 SP4 ....217 D2
Leslie Cl SN5 ....49 A4
Leslie Rise BA15 .....99 F3
Lethbridge Prim Sch
 SN1 ....50 C3
Lethbridge Rd SN1 ...50 C3
Letterage Rd SN5 ....34 A2
Levell Ct 12 SP11 ...192 A5
Leven Cl SN5 ....49 A3
Leversedge Rd 2 BA11 110 A7
Leverton Gate SN3 ...50 E1
Leverton La RG17 ...171 B1
Lewington Mews 14
 RG17 ....177 B6
Lewisham Castle*
 SN8 ....169 E4
Lewisham Cl SN25 ....34 F3
Ley The SN13 ....83 D5
Leylands Rd SN13 ....76 B1
Leys Hill BA11 ......110 A6
Leys La BA11 ....110 A6

Leystone Cl BA11 ....110 A6
Lichen Cl 3 SN2 ......34 D4
Lickhill Rd SN11 ......81 A4
Lidbury Camp* SN9 ..190 C6
Liddiards Gn SN8 ....168 F5
Liddington Castle (Fort)*
 SN4 ....163 A2
Liddington St SN2 ....35 C3
Liddington Way BA14 105 D5
Liden Dr Swindon SN3 .51 D4
 Swindon SN3 ....51 E4
Liden Infs Sch SN3 ...51 D3
Liden Jun Sch SN3 ...51 D3
Lidenbrook 2 SN4 ...163 A4
Light Cl SN13 ....77 A2
Light's La SP5 ....153 C2
Lightfoot Rd SP4 ....197 F7
Lightning Rd 1 SP4 ..217 D2
Liguiel Cl 9 RG17 ...177 B6
Lilac Cl BA14 ....105 B5
Lilac Gr BA14 ......105 B5
Lilac Way SN11 ....81 B1
Lillywhite Cres 1 SP10 193 E2
Lily Wlk 11 SP4 .....198 C7
Lime Ave Badminton GL9 38 C1
 Melksham SN12 ......94 A3
Lime Cl Colerne SN14 .75 A5
 Frome BA11 ....110 B7
Lime Kiln SN5 ....60 C2
Lime Kiln Sports Ctr
 SN4 ....47 D3
Lime Kiln Way SP2 ..152 A5
Lime Tree SN11 ....81 A3
Lime Trees SN15 ......58 A2
Limekiln Rd SP11 ...192 E6
Limes Ave SN2 ....35 B3
Limes Pl SN6 ....8 C4
Limes Rd GL7 ....4 F7
Limes The
 Badminton GL9 ......38 E2
 Motcombe SP7 ......202 A4
 Porton SP4 ....133 E6
Limpley Stoke Rd BA15 99 D6
Lincoln Gn SN12 ......94 C7
Lincoln Gr SN12 ......94 C1
Lincoln St SN1 ....50 C6
Linden Ave SN2 ....35 C3
Linden Cl Calne SN11 .81 B2
 Colerne SN14 ....74 C6
 Ludgershall SP11 ...192 B5
 Salisbury SP1 .....146 D1
 Wootton Bassett SN4 .47 C3
Linden Cres BA15 ...100 A3
Linden Gr 2 SN12 ....94 A2
Linden Pk BA14 .....101 B1
Linden Pl SP7 ....202 C1
Linden Way SN5 ......34 A2
Lindford Rd SP1 ....146 D5
Lindisfarne 1 SN4 ....48 A2
Lindlar Cl 13 SP7 ...202 C2
Lineacre Cl SN5 ......48 F4
Lingen Cl 12 SP10 ...193 D2
Lingfield Cl 6 SN14 ..77 F5
Link Ave SN5 ....49 B5
Link Leisure Ctr SN5 .49 B5
Link Rd BA13 ....108 E7
Link Way SP1 ....146 C3
Links The Corsham SN13 84 B7
 Pewsey SN9 ....215 B4
Linley Cl SN1 ....50 C2
Linley Rd SN26 ....21 C2
Linnet Way BA11 ....110 B6
Linnetsdene
 6 Salisbury SP2 ....152 A5
 Swindon SN3 ....51 C8
Linslade Cl SN4 ......50 A7
Linslade St SN2 ......49 F6
Linsvale Cl BA11 ....110 C5
Linsvale Dr BA11 ...110 C5
Lipgate SN10 ....180 F8
Liskeard Way SN5 ....49 B4
Lisle Cl SN5 ....49 A5
Lismore Rd SN6 ......22 E6
Lister Gr BA15 ....99 F3
Lister Rd SN4 ....64 B7
Litchfield Cl 11 SP10 193 C2
Little Ave SN2 ....35 A1
Little Badminton La
 SN16 ....28 F2
Little Challows SN14 .76 D7
Little Clarendon (National
 Trust)* SP3 ....201 F2
Little Comm BA14 ...105 D3
Little Content La 17
 SP7 ....202 C2
Little Ct La SP3 ....186 D8
Little Down SN14 .....78 D8
Little Dro SP6 ......211 A4
Little Hill BA12 ....116 E2
Little London
 Heytesbury BA12 ...194 C5
 Swindon SN1 ....50 D4
Little Mead SN8 ....176 F1
Little Pk Cl SN15 ....59 F1
Little Rose La SN26 ..20 F5
Little Sands SN14 ....68 C5
Little Woodbury*
 SP5 ....152 B4
Little Woodfalls Dr
 SP5 ....211 C6
Littlecote Cl 3 SN5 ..49 D5
Littlecote Rd
 Chippenham SN14 ....78 A6
 Froxfield SN8 .....176 D7

Littlecote Roman Villa*
 RG17 ....170 D1
Littledown SP7 ......202 C2
Littlefield La SP5 ...208 A4
Littlejohn Ave SN12 ..94 C6
Littlemead SN13 ......83 B5
Littlemill La SP6 ...209 F3
Littleworth La SN12 ..85 C2
Livery Rd
 West Dean SP5 .....155 B7
 Winterslow SP5 ....149 B4
Livia Cl 18 SP10 ....193 E2
Lock's Hill BA11 ....110 A3
Lock's La SP2 ....145 A3
Locke's Dro SP11 ...193 E8
Lockeridge Cl BA14 .105 D5
Lockeridge La SN8 ..174 B7
Lockeridge Sch SN8 174 A6
Locking Cl SN12 .....178 B8
Locks La SN5 ....33 B5
Locks The SN10 .....179 D8
Locksgreen Cres 1 SN2 34 E3
Lockside 1 SN15 ......78 F5
Lockswell Cl SN15 ....79 A4
Loddon Way BA15 ...100 E5
Lode Hill SP5 ....211 B8
Loder's La SP3 ......204 A5
Lodersfield GL7 ....2 C4
Lodge Cl SN11 ....81 A3
Lodge Dr 6 SP1 .....192 F1
Lodge Dro SP5 ......211 C6
Lodge Hill BA11 ....110 F5
Lodge La SP11 ......192 E6
Lodge Rd
 Chippenham SN15 ....79 A5
 Horningsham BA12 ..119 A8
Lodowicks SN11 ......80 D7
Logan Cl 1 SN3 ......50 E6
Lomond Cl SN5 ....34 B2
London La SN5 ....17 C1
London Rd
 Amesbury SP4 ......217 B4
 Bishops Cannings SN10 214 E6
 Box SN13 ....83 D7
 Calne SN11 ....81 B2
 Chippenham SN15 ....78 F6
 Marlborough SN8 ...213 F6
 Salisbury SP1 .....146 C3
 Shrewton SP3 ......196 F7
London Rd E BA1 .....82 A3
London Ride SN8 ....176 A5
London St SN1 ....50 B6
Londonderry Gdns
 SP4 ....198 E7
Long Acre SN5 ....33 B4
Long Barrow Rd SN11 .81 A3
Long Bottom SP11 ...192 D6
Long Cl
 Chippenham SN15 ....78 F6
 Downton SP5 ......211 A8
Long Cl Ave SN13 ....76 B1
Long Cl W SP5 ......211 A8
Long Cross
 Bramshaw SO43 ....212 C2
 Shaftesbury SP7 ...202 B2
Long Dro Burbage SN8 183 D8
 Grimstead SP5 .....154 B4
Long Harry SN8 .....213 F1
Long Hedge RG17 ...165 B1
Long Hill BA12 .....138 F5
Long Hollow BA13 ..186 D7
Long La Bourton SP8 137 B1
 Cann SP7 ....206 A8
Long Leaze La SN12 ..94 C3
Long Ridings SN14 ...70 C2
Long River Rd BA13 .109 D2
Long Row SN6 ....10 B4
Long St SN10 ....214 B3
Long Steeple La SP5 210 C6
Long Stones* SN8 ...173 A8
Longbarrow Cross Roads
 SP4 ....197 C4
Longcombe Dr BA12 .115 E3
Longcroft Ave SN10 .214 C3
Longcroft Cres SN10 214 C3
Longcroft Rd SN10 ..214 C3
Longfellow Cl SN25 ..35 A8
Longfellow Cres SN4 .47 F3
Longfield Cl 11 SP4 .198 B7
Longfield Rd BA14 ..105 D2
Longfields SN8 .....173 B8
Longfields Wlk SN10 214 C2
Longford Castle*
 SP5 ....153 A2
Longford Pk* SP5 ..152 C2
Longford Rd SN12 ...94 A2
Longhill Dr 1 SP2 ...152 B5
Longland SP2 ....145 E1
Longlands Cl BA13 ..186 C7
Longleat House*
 BA12 ....114 F3
Longleat Safari Pk*
 BA12 ....115 B4
Longleaze SN4 ....47 E3
Longleaze CP Sch SN4 47 E3
Longmead SP7 ......202 C2
Longsplatt SN13 ......83 D3
Longstock Ct SN5 ....49 B6
Longstone Rd 1 SN14 70 A1
Longthorpe Cl SN5 ...49 D4
Lonsdale Cl SN26 ....21 C2
Loop Dr SN8 ....175 A7
Lopcombe Cnr SP4 ..135 D3
Lopes Way BA13 ....108 F4
Lord's La SN15 ....78 E7

Lord's Mead SN14 . . . . . .**78** A8
Lords Croft SP4 . . . .**217** B4
Lordsmead Rd BA12 . . . . .**139** B4
Lorne St SN1 . . . .**50** A5
Lottage Rd SN8 . . . .**170** A7
Lottage Way **2** SN8 . . . . .**170** A7
Lotts The SN6 . . . .**17** F8
Loughborough Cl **1** SN5 48 F4
Louviers Way SN1 . . . .**50** C2
Love La Box SN13 . . . .**83** F7
  Salisbury SP1 . . . .**152** B8
  4 Shaftesbury SP7 . . . .**202** B1
  Woodgreen SP6 . . . .**211** A4
Love's La SN8 . . . .**170** B3
Loveage Cl **5** SN2 . . . . . .**34** D4
Lovel Rd BA12 . . . .**194** E3
Lovell Cl SN3 . . . .**51** D7
Lover's La SN16 . . . .**28** A4
Loveridge Cl
  5 Andover SP10 . . . . . .**193** E2
  Swindon SN2 . . . .**35** E6
Loves La BA14 . . . .**104** C7
Lovett Gn SP1 . . . .**146** C4
Low La SN11 . . . .**81** D2
Low Rd SN10 . . . .**179** C1
Lowa Cl SP9 . . . .**216** C6
Lowa Rd SP9 . . . .**216** B6
Lowbourne SN12 . . . .**94** B4
Lowbourne Sch SN12 . . . . .**94** B5
Lowden SN15 . . . .**78** C7
Lowden Ave SN14 . . . .**78** C8
Lowden Hill SN15 . . . .**78** C7
Lower Alma St SN14 . . . . .**105** E8
Lower Backway **7** SP3 . .**196** E6
Lower Bartons **30** SP6 . . .**210** D1
Lower Blandford Rd
  Cann SP7 . . . .**206** A8
  5 Shaftesbury SP7 . . . .**202** D1
Lower Church Fields
  SN8 . . . .**213** D2
Lower Ct BA14 . . . .**101** D1
Lower Densome Wood
  SP6 . . . .**211** A4
Lower Folly SP2 . . . .**144** B1
Lower Goatacre SN11 . . . .**166** A7
Lower Gr SP6 . . . .**210** B5
Lower Ho SN16 . . . .**15** B8
Lower Kingsdown Rd
  SN13 . . . .**83** A4
Lower Marsh Rd BA12 . . . .**117** A5
Lower N Rd SP5 . . . .**207** C5
Lower Prospect SN8 . . . . .**213** E3
Lower Rd Bratton BA13 . . .**186** B7
  Britford SP5 . . . .**152** B3
  Coombe Bissett SP5 . . . .**151** C1
  Downton SP5 . . . .**159** B4
  Edington BA13 . . . .**186** C8
  Erlestoke BA13 . . . .**178** F2
  Netheravon SP4 . . . .**190** A3
  Odstock SP5 . . . .**152** D4
  Salisbury SP2 . . . .**144** F2
Lower S Rd SP5 . . . .**207** C4
Lower St
  Donhead St Andrew SP7 . .**203** B3
  Netheravon SP4 . . . .**190** A4
  Rode BA11 . . . .**103** E1
  Salisbury SP2 . . . .**151** E7
Lower Stoke
  Limpley Stoke BA2 . . . . . .**99** A4
  Monkton Combe BA2 . . . . .**90** A1
Lower Westbury Rd
  BA13 . . . .**109** E5
Lower Wharf SN15 . . . . . .**214** A4
Lower Woodrow SN12 . . . . .**86** F1
Lowes Cl **2** SN5 . . . .**34** B2
Lowmead BA14 . . . .**101** E1
Loxley Cl SN12 . . . .**94** B6
Loyalty St SN14 . . . .**78** C7
Lubeck Dr **22** SP10 . . . . . .**193** D2
Lucerne Cl
  10 Swindon SN5 . . . .**48** F8
  Wootton Bassett SN4 . . . .**47** D4
Lucewood La SP5 . . . .**154** C7
Luckett Way SN11 . . . .**81** C4
Luckington CP Sch
  SN14 . . . .**39** E5
Luckington Ct★ SN14 . . . .**39** F5
Lucknam Pk★ SN14 . . . . . .**75** B6
Luddesdown Rd SN5 . . . . .**49** C4
Ludgershall Castle★
  SP11 . . . .**192** A6
Ludgershall Rd
  Collingbourne Ducis SN8 . .**191** E8
  4 Swindon SN1 . . . .**49** F1
  Tidworth SP9 . . . .**216** D7
Ludgershall Sports Club
  SP11 . . . .**192** A5
Ludlow Cl
  Chippenham SN15 . . . .**79** A5
  10 Frome BA11 . . . .**110** C4
  Swindon SN3 . . . .**50** F4
  Warminster BA12 . . . .**116** F4
  Westbury BA13 . . . .**108** F4
Ludmead Rd BA14 . . . .**85** A8
Ludwell Fst Sch SP7 . . . . .**203** A1
Ludwell Hill SP7 . . . .**203** A1
Lugbury (Long Barrow)★
  SN14 . . . .**53** E2
Luke St SN1 . . . .**203** E1
Lulworth Rd SN25 . . . .**34** E3
Lumley Cl **2** SN5 . . . .**49** A4
Lumley Wlk **8** SP4 . . . . . .**217** D3
Luxfield Rd BA12 . . . .**116** F2
Lyall Cl SN25 . . . .**34** F8
Lyburn Rd SP5 . . . .**212** A5

Lydford Cl **4** SN5 . . . .**49** A8
Lydiard Ctry Pk★ SN5 . . .**48** E6
Lydiard Rd SN14 . . . .**78** A6
Lydiard Way BA14 . . . .**105** D5
Lye The SN12 . . . .**178** E8
Lyes Gr BA13 . . . .**112** B8
Lyme Ave BA12 . . . .**116** F6
Lyme Way SN25 . . . .**35** A5
Lymers The SN11 . . . .**166** E2
Lynch Cl BA12 . . . .**139** B5
Lynch Field The **5** SN4 . .**163** A5
Lynch La **6** RG17 . . . . . .**165** A2
Lynch The SN1 . . . .**176** F1
Lynchet Cl **7** SN10 . . . . . .**179** F1
Lynchets Rd SP4 . . . .**217** B3
Lynchfield Rd **7** SP4 . . . .**217** B3
Lynden Cl SN3 . . . .**184** A7
Lyndhurst Cres SN3 . . . . . .**51** A6
Lyndhurst Rd
  Amesbury SP4 . . . .**217** C3
  Landford SP5 . . . .**212** C6
Lyneham Cl SN2 . . . .**35** B6
Lyneham Jun & Inf Sch
  SN15 . . . .**60** B2
Lyneham Way BA14 . . . . . .**105** F8
Lynt Rd SN6 . . . .**12** A5
Lynton Rd SN2 . . . .**34** E1
Lynwood Gr SN2 . . . .**34** D3
Lynwood Rd BA14 . . . .**101** A1
Lyons Wlk **1** SP7 . . . .**202** C1
Lypiatt SN13 . . . .**84** F6
Lypiatt Mead SN13 . . . .**85** A8
Lypiatt Rd SN13 . . . .**85** A7
Lysander Rd
  Bower Hill SN12 . . . .**94** B1
  Laverstock SP4 . . . .**146** C8
  Melksham Without SN12 . .**178** B4
Lysley Cl SN15 . . . .**79** A5
Lyster Rd SP6 . . . .**210** E1
Lytchett Way SN3 . . . .**51** C6
Lytham Cl SN15 . . . .**78** F7

M

Macadam Way SP10 . . . .**193** B1
Maccullum Rd SP11 . . . . .**193** E4
Mackenzie Cl **1** SN3 . . . .**51** D4
Macklin Cl **21** RG17 . . . .**177** B7
Macklin Rd SP2 . . . .**145** E2
Macneice Dr SN8 . . . .**213** A2
Maddington **2** SP3 . . . . .**196** E6
Maddington St SP3 . . . . . .**196** E7
Maddle Rd RG17 . . . .**164** E4
Maddock's Hill **4** BA12 116 E5
Magdalen La BA14 . . . . . .**104** B7
Magdalen Rd SN4 . . . . . .**163** A6
Magdalene La **7** SP7 . . . .**202** C1
Magister Rd SN12 . . . .**94** D1
Magnolia Cl **1** BA11 . . . .**110** C7
Magnolia Rise
  Calne SN11 . . . .**81** B1
  Trowbridge BA14 . . . . . .**105** E7
Magnon Rd BA15 . . . .**100** B7
Magpie La SN3 . . . .**51** E6
Maiden La SN11 . . . .**166** B1
Maidstone Rd SN1 . . . .**50** B4
Main Rd Amesbury SP4 . . .**217** D2
  Ogbourne St Andrew
  SN8 . . . .**213** D8
  Cherhill SN11 . . . .**166** B1
  St Paul Malmesbury Without
  SN16 . . . .**42** E4
  Christian Malford SN15 . . .**58** E5
  Sutton Benger SN15 . . . . .**57** F2
Main St
  Great Hinton BA14 . . . . . .**178** A6
  Westbury BA13 . . . .**108** C6
Maitland Cl SN15 . . . .**79** A4
Maitland Rd SN3 . . . .**51** A7
Majestic Cl **4** SN5 . . . . . .**49** A7
Maldwyn Cl **9** SN5 . . . . . .**48** F8
Mall The
  South Tedworth SP9 . . . . .**216** A4
  Swindon SN1 . . . .**50** B3
Mallard Ave SN15 . . . .**60** B1
Mallard Cl
  7 Bower Hill SN12 . . . . .**178** B8
  Calne SN11 . . . .**81** D2
  Salisbury SP2 . . . .**151** F7
  Swindon SN3 . . . .**51** E6
  Westbury BA13 . . . .**109** B4
Mallards The **20** SP3 . . . .**203** E8
Mallow Cl **2** Swindon SN2 34 D4
  5 Trowbridge BA14 . . . .**105** D6
Malmesbury Abbey★
  SN16 . . . .**28** A3
Malmesbury C of E Prim Sch
  SN16 . . . .**27** F6
Malmesbury Com Hospl
  SN16 . . . .**28** B1
Malmesbury Rd
  Chippenham SN15 . . . .**70** C1
  Leigh SN5 . . . .**17** E3
Malmesbury Sch SN16 . . . .**27** E3
Malmesbury Swimming Pool
  SN16 . . . .**27** E4
Malmpit Hill BA12 . . . .**195** B2
Malt House La SP11 . . . . .**193** F4
Malt Shovel La RG17 . . . . .**164** F2
Malthouse Cl
  Ashbury SN6 . . . .**164** A8
  Broad Blunsdon SN26 . . . .**21** C1
Malthouse La
  Chute SP11 . . . .**192** E8
  4 Salisbury SP2 . . . . . .**146** A1
Maltings The
  Malmesbury SN16 . . . .**28** A3

Maltings The continued
  Salisbury SP2 . . . .**146** A1
  8 Wanborough SN4 . . . .**163** B6
  Warminster BA12 . . . .**116** F6
  Wootton Bassett SN4 . . . .**47** D1
  Yatton Keynell SN14 . . . . .**68** F6
Malvern Cl
  Melksham SN12 . . . .**94** D4
  7 Warminster BA12 . . . .**117** A8
Malvern Rd SN2 . . . .**35** C1
Malvern Way SP4 . . . .**133** D6
Mampitts La SP7 . . . .**202** D1
Manchester Rd SN1 . . . . . .**50** C7
Mand Wood BA14 . . . .**101** F8
Manning Cl **8** SP1 . . . . . .**146** C5
Mannington La SN5 . . . . . .**49** D5
Mannington Pk SN2 . . . . . .**49** F7
Mannington Ret Pk
  SN1 . . . .**49** E4
Manor Bridge Ct SP9 . . . .**216** D7
Manor Cl
  Broad Blunsdon SN26 . . . .**21** C2
  28 Fordingbridge SP6 . . .**210** D1
  Semington BA14 . . . .**102** F5
  Sherston SN16 . . . .**25** C1
  4 Shipton Bellinger SP9 . .**199** D8
  Trowbridge BA14 . . . . . .**105** A6
  Wroughton SN4 . . . .**64** B5
Manor Copse SP11 . . . . . .**193** E3
Manor Cotts SN14 . . . .**24** D1
Manor Cres SN2 . . . .**34** F2
Manor Dr BA1 . . . .**82** B2
Manor Farm Cl SP5 . . . . . .**205** C4
Manor Farm Ct SN8 . . . . .**173** D6
Manor Farm Dr SN15 . . . . .**57** C2
Manor Farm La
  Great Wishford SP2 . . . . .**129** F4
  Patney SN10 . . . .**180** D5
Manor Farm Rd
  Salisbury SP1 . . . .**146** C1
  1 Sandleheath SP6 . . . .**210** C1
  Swindon SN3 . . . .**50** D3
Manor Fields **5** BA13 . . .**186** B7
Manor Gdns
  Swindon SN2 . . . .**34** F1
  Warminster BA12 . . . .**117** A7
Manor Ho SN14 . . . .**68** E5
Manor La Baydon SN8 . . . .**170** C8
  Broad Hinton SN4 . . . . . .**167** C7
Manor Orch SN6 . . . .**19** E8
Manor Pk
  Froxfield SN8 . . . .**176** D6
  Great Somerford SN15 . . .**44** A2
  South Marston SN3 . . . . . .**36** E4
Manor Rd
  Chippenham SN14 . . . .**78** A8
  Corsham SN13 . . . .**76** F2
  7 Great Bedwyn SN8 . . .**176** B3
  Mere BA12 . . . .**138** F7
  Salisbury SP1 . . . .**146** C1
  Swindon SN1 . . . .**49** F5
  Trowbridge BA14 . . . . . .**105** A6
  Upton Lovell BA12 . . . . . .**194** E3
Manor The★
  Keevil BA14 . . . .**178** A4
  Longbridge Deverill
  BA12 . . . .**120** F5
Manor View SN16 . . . .**28** F2
Manton Cl
  Marlborough SN8 . . . .**213** A1
  Trowbridge BA14 . . . . . .**105** C6
Manton Dro SN8 . . . .**174** C6
Manton Hollow SN8 . . . . .**213** A2
Manton Rd SN8 . . . .**174** C7
Manton St SN2 . . . .**49** F7
Maple Cl Calne SN11 . . . . .**81** B1
  Melksham SN12 . . . .**94** D5
  Pewsey SN9 . . . .**215** D5
  5 Shaftesbury SP7 . . . .**202** C2
Maple Cres
  7 Ludgershall SP11 . . . .**192** B5
  Wilton SP2 . . . .**144** F3
Maple Ct **8** BA11 . . . . . .**110** A4
Maple Dr Firsdown SP5 . . .**148** C2
  Wootton Bassett SN4 . . . .**47** E4
Maple Gr Swindon SN2 . . . .**35** C2
  Trowbridge BA14 . . . . . .**105** C6
Maple Way
  Chippenham SN15 . . . .**70** D2
  3 Durrington/Bulford
  SP4 . . . .**198** B7
Maplecroft **3** SP2 . . . . . .**152** A5
Mapperton Hill SP8 . . . . . .**138** E1
Marbrean Cl **4** SP6 . . . . .**210** C1
March Cl SN25 . . . .**35** A6
Marden Henge★ SN9 . . . .**181** B5
Marden Way SN11 . . . .**81** A2
Marden Wlk **2** BA14 . . . .**105** D6
Margaret Stancomb Inf Sch
  BA14 . . . .**101** C1
Margha Rd SP9 . . . .**216** C6
Marie Ave **5** SP5 . . . . . .**210** F8
Marigold Cl
  Melksham SN12 . . . .**94** C3
  Swindon SN2 . . . .**34** D4
Marina Dr BA14 . . . .**101** D4
Marina Rd
  28 Durrington/Bulford
  SP4 . . . .**198** B7
  Salisbury SP2 . . . .**152** C7
Marine Cl SN4 . . . .**64** B7
Maristow St BA13 . . . .**109** A3
Marjoram Cl SN2 . . . .**34** D5
Markan Rd SP4 . . . .**133** F4
Markenfield **2** SN5 . . . . .**49** D4
Market Hill SN11 . . . .**81** B3
Market Lavington Mus★
  SN10 . . . .**179** F1
Market Pl Box SN13 . . . . . .**83** D6

Market Pl continued
  Chippenham SN15 . . . .**78** E7
  Colerne SN14 . . . .**75** B3
  Lechlade GL7 . . . .**2** C4
  18 Market Lavington SN10 179 F1
  Marshfield SN14 . . . .**74** A8
  Warminster BA12 . . . .**117** A7
  Westbury BA13 . . . .**109** A4
Market Place The
  SN10 . . . .**214** A4
Market Sq SN3 . . . .**50** D4
Market St
  Bradford-on-Avon BA15 . . .**100** D7
  4 Malmesbury SN16 . . . .**28** A3
  Swindon SN1 . . . .**50** B6
  Trowbridge BA14 . . . . . .**105** D8
Markham Cl SN3 . . . .**50** F7
Markham Rd SN4 . . . .**64** A5
Marl La SP6 . . . .**210** D1
Marlborough Cl SN10 . . . .**214** F7
Marlborough Coll
  SN8 . . . .**213** C2
Marlborough Ct SN14 . . . . .**78** C7
Marlborough Golf Club
  SN8 . . . .**213** D4
Marlborough La SN1 . . . . . .**50** D3
Marlborough Leisure Ctr
  SN8 . . . .**213** C3
Marlborough Rd
  5 Aldbourne SN8 . . . . .**170** A6
  Bulford SP4 . . . .**198** E6
  Burbage SN8 . . . .**175** C1
  Chiseldon SN3 . . . .**51** C2
  Chiseldon SN4 . . . .**65** E7
  Chiseldown SN4 . . . .**65** E7
  Collingbourne Ducis SN8 . .**183** E1
  Everleigh SN8 . . . .**183** A1
  Liddington SN4 . . . .**51** E1
  Pewsey SN9 . . . .**215** B6
  Salisbury SP1 . . . .**146** A2
  Swindon SN3 . . . .**50** D3
  Wootton Bassett SN4 . . . .**61** B3
  Wroughton SN4 . . . .**64** B6
Marlborough St **6** SN1 . . .**50** A5
Marlborough White Horse★
  SN8 . . . .**213** D5
Marlowe Ave SN3 . . . .**50** F7
Marlowe Way SN4 . . . .**47** F3
Marne Rd **3** SP4 . . . .**198** F6
Marney Rd SN5 . . . .**49** A5
Marsh La
  Breamore SP6 . . . .**210** E4
  Cherhill SN11 . . . .**166** A1
  Coombe Bissett SP5 . . . .**150** F2
  Hungerford RG17 . . . . . .**177** A7
  Nettleton SN14 . . . .**53** C4
  Pen Selwood BA9 . . . . . .**137** A4
  Rowde SN10 . . . .**96** D2
Marsh Rd Berkley BA11 . . .**107** C1
  Rode BA11 . . . .**103** F1
  Trowbridge BA14 . . . . . .**101** E5
Marsh St BA12 . . . .**117** A5
Marsh The SN4 . . . .**51** F3
Marshall Rd
  Roundway SN10 . . . .**214** D1
  Swindon SN5 . . . .**49** B8
Marshall St SN14 . . . .**78** C7
Marshfield Prim Sch
  SN14 . . . .**74** A8
Marshfield Rd SN15 . . . . . .**78** C8
Marshfield Way SN3 . . . . . .**36** A2
Marshgate SN1 . . . .**50** F8
Marshmead BA14 . . . .**101** F4
Marshmead Cl SP5 . . . . . .**152** F6
Marshwood SP3 . . . .**201** E3
Marsland Rd SN2 . . . .**35** D2
Marston Ave SN2 . . . .**35** D4
Marston Rd BA14 . . . .**105** B4
Marsum Cl **1** SP10 . . . . .**193** C4
Martha's La SP2 . . . .**144** F4
Marti Cl SN12 . . . .**94** C4
Martigny Rd SN12 . . . .**94** B3
Martin Cl SP9 . . . .**216** E6
Martin Crest BA12 . . . . . .**116** E5
Martin Dro End SP6 . . . . .**209** F2
Martin Way SN11 . . . .**81** D3
Martin's Cl SN9 . . . .**181** C5
Martin's St **4** SP7 . . . . . .**202** C1
Martinbushes Rd SP4 . . . .**198** A7
Martinfield SN3 . . . .**51** D7
Martingale Rd SN8 . . . . . .**183** D7
Martins Cl
  Chippenham SN15 . . . .**79** A8
  2 Salisbury SP2 . . . . . .**152** A5
  Steeple Ashton BA14 . . . .**178** C4
Martins Croft SN14 . . . .**75** B3
Martins La BA14 . . . .**178** C4
Martins Rd BA14 . . . .**178** C5
Martins Rise SP5 . . . .**161** C4
Martinsell Gn SN9 . . . . . .**215** D5
Martinsell Hill (Fort)★
  SN8 . . . .**174** D2
Martlesham Rd SP4 . . . . .**217** C3
Martlet Cl SN12 . . . .**94** D1
Martor Ind Est SN14 . . . . .**66** A2
Marvins Cl SP3 . . . .**188** B2
Mary Barters La SP3 . . . . .**204** E8
Maryland Cl SP2 . . . .**145** B5
Masefield Cl SN4 . . . .**47** F3
Masefield Ave SN2 . . . .**35** E3
Masefield Rd BA12 . . . . . .**116** E6
Maskeleyne Way SN4 . . . . .**63** F7
Masons Cl BA15 . . . .**100** D7
Masons The SN5 . . . .**33** A3
Masons Way SN13 . . . .**76** D1
Matford Hill SN15 . . . .**79** A8
Matilda Way SN10 . . . . . .**214** D4

Matley Moor SN3 . . . .**51** E2
Matravers Cl BA13 . . . . . .**108** F3
Matravers Sch BA13 . . . . .**108** F2
Matrons Cotts SP5 . . . . . .**153** F1
Matthews Cl SN10 . . . .**172** F1
Maud Cl SN10 . . . .**214** D4
Maud Heath Prim Sch
  SN15 . . . .**72** A2
Maud Heath's Cswy
  Chippenham SN15 . . . .**70** D1
  Langley Burrell Without
  SN15 . . . .**71** B3
Maud Heath's Mon★
  SN11 . . . .**80** C8
Maud Heath's Stone★
  SN11 . . . .**80** C8
Maulton Cl BA14 . . . .**101** D4
Maundrell Cl SN10 . . . .**96** D2
Maundrell Rd SN11 . . . .**81** C3
Maunsell Way SN4 . . . .**63** F7
Maur Cl SN15 . . . .**78** C7
Maurys La SO51 . . . .**212** F6
Maxey Cl SN5 . . . .**49** B8
Maxwell St SN1 . . . .**50** A4
May La SP5 . . . .**204** D3
May Tree Rd **9** SP10 . . . .**193** C1
May's La SN4 . . . .**65** D4
Mayenne Pl SN10 . . . .**179** C8
Mayfair Rd SP1 . . . .**146** D1
Mayfield **1** SN4 . . . .**163** B6
Mayfield Ave Ind Pk
  SP11 . . . .**192** E1
Mayfield Cl
  4 Shipton Bellinger SP9 . .**199** C8
  Swindon SN3 . . . .**51** B7
Mayfield Rd **2** SP6 . . . . .**210** C1
Mayfly Cl **4** SP6 . . . .**210** D1
Mayo Cl SN13 . . . .**76** E2
Mays Firs SP6 . . . .**211** D5
Maytree Cl **6** BA11 . . . . .**110** B7
Mc Neill Rd SP4 . . . .**198** A4
Mckie Rd **3** SP4 . . . .**217** D2
Mead Com Prim Sch The
  BA14 . . . .**101** F2
Mead Pk SN12 . . . .**84** F1
Mead The
  Ashton Keynes SN6 . . . . . .**17** F5
  Warminster BA12 . . . .**117** A7
  Westbury BA13 . . . .**109** A5
  Winsley BA15 . . . .**99** E7
Mead Way Swindon SN5 . . .**34** B2
  Swindon SN5 . . . .**49** D6
Meade Rd **2** SP11 . . . . . .**192** B5
Meadens La SP5 . . . .**151** B1
Meadland SN13 . . . .**76** E1
Meadow Ave **10** SP6 . . . .**210** D1
Meadow Cl
  Chippenham SN14 . . . .**78** A7
  8 Fordingbridge SP6 . . .**210** D1
  Yatton Keynell SN14 . . . . .**68** F6
Meadow Ct
  11 Fordingbridge SP6 . . .**210** D1
  Whiteparish SP5 . . . .**161** C4
Meadow Dr SN10 . . . .**214** C3
Meadow La
  Little Somerford SN15 . . . .**44** A5
  Westbury BA13 . . . .**109** A4
Meadow Pk BA1 . . . .**82** B3
Meadow Rd (South) **5**
  SP2 . . . .**145** F1
Meadow Rd
  Durrington/Bulford SP4 . . .**217** E8
  Melksham SN12 . . . .**94** C7
  3 Salisbury SP2 . . . . . .**145** F1
  Swindon SN2 . . . .**49** E2
Meadow Springs SN5 . . . . .**48** E3
Meadow View **5** SP4 . . . .**190** A4
Meadow Way
  Chiseldon SN4 . . . .**65** E7
  South Cerney GL7 . . . .**6** F7
Meadow Well SN8 . . . .**183** D1
Meadowcroft SN2 . . . .**35** F3
Meadowfield BA15 . . . . . .**100** B6
Meadows The
  Lydiard Tregoze SN5 . . . . .**47** F5
  Salisbury SP1 . . . .**152** D8
Meadowsweet Cl **2**
  SN25 . . . .**34** E5
Meadowsweet Dr SN11 . . . .**80** F3
Meads Rd SP4 . . . .**198** B7
Meads The SN14 . . . .**53** B3
Medway
  4 Shrewton SP3 . . . . . .**196** F6
  Wingfield BA14 . . . .**105** A4
Mears Dr SN5 . . . .**49** B8
Mears Rd **4** SP4 . . . .**198** A6
Medbourne SN4 . . . .**163** A3
Medbourne Rd SN4 . . . . . .**163** A4
Medbury Pl SN1 . . . .**50** D6
Medgbury Rd SN1 . . . .**50** C6
Medina Way SN25 . . . .**35** F4
Medway Rd SN25 . . . .**34** F4
Meerut Rd SP9 . . . .**216** C6
Melbourne Cl SN3 . . . .**50** F3
Melbourne Gdns **5** SP6 . .**198** F6
Melbourne St BA13 . . . . . .**186** B7
Melbury Abbas Mill★
  SP7 . . . .**206** A7
Melbury Down (National
  Trust)★ SP5 . . . .**206** C6
Melbury St SP7 . . . .**206** B6
Melbury Way **12** SP2 . . . .**202** D2
Melchet Cl SO51 . . . .**162** D1
Melfort Cl SN5 . . . .**34** B2
Meliot Rise **12** SP10 . . . .**193** E2
Melksham Cl SN2 . . . .**35** C1

Melksham Com Hospl SN12 94 B3
Melksham La SN12 93 C4
Melksham Rd Holt SN12 93 A2
Lacock SN15 86 D5
Melksham Sta SN12 94 A6
Mellow Gd SN25 34 E5
Melrose Ave BA12 116 E6
Melrose Cl
1 Swindon SN5 49 C6
4 Warminster BA12 116 E6
Melsome Rd SN15 59 F1
Melton Rd BA14 101 C2
Melville Cl 3 SN3 50 F6
Melvin Cl SP1 146 D1
Mendip Cl
3 Frome BA11 110 A7
Melksham SN12 94 C4
Swindon SN25 35 C3
6 Warminster BA12 117 A8
Mendip Dr BA11 110 A7
Menham Cl SN2 35 D2
Merchants House The★ SN8 213 D3
Mercia Ave SP10 193 C2
Mere Ave SN14 41 F1
Mere Castle★ BA12 138 F6
Mere Fst Sch BA12 139 B5
Meridian Wlk BA14 105 A8
Merlin Cl 23 SP10 193 E2
Merlin Way
Bower Hill SN12 94 B1
Stratton St Margaret SN3 51 D8
Swindon SN3 36 D1
Merrifield Rd SP4 146 C6
Merrivale Gr SN3 50 E5
Merton Ave SN2 35 D4
Merton Cl 6 SP6 210 D2
Merton St 2 SN1 50 C6
Mervyn Webb Pl SN2 50 D8
Mesh Pond SP5 210 F8
Methuen Ave SN12 94 B6
Methuen Cl BA15 100 E4
Methuen Dr 1 SP1 152 C8
Methuen Pk 5 SN14 77 F5
Mews The
Highworth SN6 23 A6
Lydiard Millicent SN5 48 D8
Warminster BA12 117 A7
Meyrick Ave SP2 152 A5
Meysey Cl GL7 1 A5
Michael Pym's Rd 3 SN16 28 A5
Middle Field Cl SN10 214 C3
Middle Gd Cricklade SN6 19 C8
Fovant SP3 204 E7
Wootton Bassett SN4 48 A2
Middle La
Atworth/Whitley SN12 85 D1
Cherhill SN11 166 B1
Martin SP6 209 A7
Trowbridge BA14 101 F2
Middle St SP2 151 E7
Middle Stoke BA2 99 A6
Middleleaze Dr SN5 48 F8
Middlemass Gn SN9 215 D5
Middleton SP5 149 B7
Middleton Cl
Swindon SN3 50 F6
5 Warminster BA12 116 E6
Middleton Medieval Village of★ BA12 194 A7
Middleton Rd
Salisbury SP2 145 F2
The Common SP5 149 B7
Middletons Cl RG17 177 C8
Middlewick La SN13 76 D3
Midford Hill BA2 98 C4
Midford La BA2 98 E7
Midford Rd BA2 98 B7
Midhurst Ave SN3 51 B5
Midlands Ind Est The BA14 92 E1
Midlands The BA14 92 E1
Midwinter Cl SN5 34 B2
Milbourne La SN16 28 C4
Milbourne Pk SN16 28 C4
Mildmay Cl 12 SN5 48 F5
Mile Dr SN15 44 E1
Miles's La SP5 161 E5
Milestone Way SN15 70 C2
Milford Hill SP1 152 B8
Milford Hollow 6 SP1 152 C8
Milford Ind Est SP1 152 C8
Milford Manor Gdns SP1 152 D8
Milford Mill Rd SP1 152 D8
Milford Pk SP1 152 D8
Milford St
Salisbury SP1 152 B8
Swindon SN1 50 C6
Milford Way SN15 78 F4
Mill Cl Devizes SN10 214 C1
Longbridge Deverill BA12 120 F6
South Cerney GL7 7 A7
Winterbourne SP4 133 B4
Wroughton SN4 64 B6
Mill Ct 18 SP6 210 D1
Mill Dro SN8 183 C1
Mill End SP6 209 F2
Mill Head SN10 179 A4
Mill Hill Ave SP9 216 C8
Mill Hollow La SP7 206 A7
Mill La Bishopstone SP5 150 A1
Bourton SP8 137 E2
Box SN13 83 C7
Bradford-on-Avon BA15 100 D6
Mill La *continued*
Broughton Gifford SN12 93 C3
Bulkington SN10 178 E5
Cherhill SN11 166 B1
Chilmark SP3 200 F2
Fairford GL7 1 F7
Fovant SP3 204 D8
Heytesbury BA12 194 C5
Lambourn RG17 165 B1
Lechlade GL7 2 F4
Little Somerford SN15 43 F5
Malmesbury SN16 28 A3
Melbury Abbas SP7 206 A7
Mere BA12 139 B5
Monkton Combe BA2 98 E8
Poulshot SN10 179 A5
Ramsbury SN8 170 B2
St Paul Malmesbury Without SN16 42 E5
Salisbury SP1 145 E5
Selwood BA11 114 F8
Shalbourne SN8 176 F2
Stanton Fitzwarren SN6 22 A2
Swindon SN1 50 A3
The Common SP5 149 E6
West Lavington SN10 187 E8
Westbury BA13 112 D8
Winterbourne Monkton SN4 167 C3
Winterslow SP5 149 D7
Zeale SP8 137 F2
Mill Rd Devizes SN10 214 C1
Netheravon SP4 190 A4
Potterne SN10 179 D5
Salisbury SP2 145 F1
Worton SN10 179 A4
Mill Rise SP8 137 E2
Mill Sch The SN10 179 C6
Mill St Calne SN11 81 B2
Fontmell Magna SP7 206 A3
Heytesbury BA12 194 C5
Trowbridge BA14 105 D8
Mill Stream App SP2 146 A1
Milland Cl SN25 35 B6
Millard Cl 2 SN15 78 F4
Millbrook 2 SP1 146 B2
Millbrook La SP3 141 C1
Millbuck Cl SN2 35 E1
Millennium Pk Ctr★ GL7 6 B3
Millennium Way SP2 152 B5
Miller Cl Chirton SN10 180 F4
Salisbury SP1 145 E5
Swindon SN5 48 F8
Miller's La DT11 207 D1
Millfield 5 RG17 165 A1
Millgreen Rd 1 SP4 217 C2
Millhand Villas BA14 105 E7
Millington Dr 3 BA14 105 A7
Mills Rd SN12 94 C4
Mills Way SP4 217 D4
Milne Cres 3 SP4 197 E6
Milne Rd SP4 198 E6
Milston Ave SN2 35 C5
Milston Down (Long Barrows)★ SP4 198 E8
Milston Dro SP4 190 E1
Milston Rd Bulford SP4 198 C7
Durrington/Bulford SP4 217 D8
Milston View 2 SP4 198 C7
Milton Ave
6 Andover SP10 193 C1
Melksham SN12 94 B4
Milton Pl GL7 1 F6
Milton Rd
Amesbury SP4 217 E2
Pewsey SN9 215 E5
Salisbury SP2 152 B6
Swindon SN1 50 B6
Milton St GL7 1 F6
Milton's Way SN4 47 C1
Minden Cl 13 SP10 193 D2
Minety CE Sch SN16 17 B2
Minety La SN16 16 A7
Minety Rd SN2 35 B5
Minster Cl SN25 34 F7
Minster St
7 Salisbury SP1 146 A1
Wilton SP2 144 D3
Minster View BA12 116 F7
Minster Way SN14 78 A5
Mint Cl SN2 34 D4
Minty's Top SN15 96 A7
Mitchell Cl 3 SP10 193 C1
Mitchell Dr SN12 178 B8
Mitchell Rd SP2 151 D8
Mitchells Cl 5 SP5 211 C7
Mizmaze★ SP6 210 D7
Moat Rd BA13 108 D6
Moberly Rd SP1 146 B3
Moffat Rise SN16 28 A5
Moggs La SN11 172 A8
Mompesson Ho★ SP2 152 A8
Monastery Rd BA13 186 C8
Monet Cl SN25 34 F6
Moneyer Rd 5 SP10 193 D2
Monk's La SN13 85 B6
Monkley La BA14 104 C1
Monks Cl SP9 216 C7
Monks Pk SN16 28 D4
Monks Pk Gdns SN13 85 B5
Monks Way SN15 79 A4
Monkton Cl SN3 51 B4
Monkton Dro BH21 208 D1
Monkton Farleigh Prim Sch BA15 90 E7
Monkton Hill SN15 78 D7
Monkton House★ SN12 93 C1
Monkton Pk Prim Sch SN15 78 E7
Monmouth Cl 4 SN3 50 F4
Monmouth Dr BA11 110 B5
Monmouth Rd SP3 203 D8
Mons Ave SP4 198 E6
Mons La SN15 86 D8
Montagu St SN2 49 F7
Montague Cl SN15 79 A7
Montague Ct BA14 102 A1
Montague Pl SN12 94 C5
Montague Rd SP2 151 D7
Monteagle Cl SN5 49 A4
Montessori Sch SP2 144 D3
Montgomery Ave SN2 35 B2
Montgomery Gdns SP2 145 E2
Montrose Cl SN2 34 E2
Monument Hill SN10 214 E1
Monxton Cl 3 SP1 146 D5
Moody's Hill SP5 155 E2
Moon Cl SN14 75 B3
Moonrakers SN10 214 D5
Moor Barton SN13 84 D6
Moor Hill SP3 204 D8
Moor La SP5 161 A1
Moor Pk SN13 84 C6
Moore Cl SN4 64 C8
Moore's Pl 12 RG17 177 B7
Moorgate GL7 2 B4
Moorhen Cl SN3 51 E5
Moorlands SN15 70 E2
Moorlands The SN10 214 A2
Moormead Rd SN4 64 B6
Moors Cl SN15 70 C5
Moot (Motte & Bailey) The★ SP5 211 B8
Moot Cl 7 Andover SP10 193 E2
Downton SP5 211 B7
Moot Gdns SP5 211 A7
Moot La SP5 211 A7
Mopes La SN5 33 C7
Moray Rd SN2 35 E1
Moredon Jun Sch SN2 34 E2
Moredon Pk SN2 34 D3
Moredon Rd SN25 34 F3
Moresby Cl SN5 49 C6
Morgan Wlk BA13 108 E2
Morgan's La
Pentridge SP5 208 E5
Winterbourne SP4 133 A2
Morgans Rise Rd 3 SP5 211 C8
Morgans Vale & Woodfalls Prim Sch SP5 211 C8
Morgans Vale Rd SP5 211 C7
Morie Cl SN5 34 B1
Morley Field BA12 117 C7
Morley Pl 23 RG17 177 B7
Morley St SN1 50 C5
Morris La Bath BA1 82 B3
Devizes SN10 214 B3
Morris Rd SN8 213 B2
Morris St SN2 49 E6
Morrison St SN2 49 F7
Morse Cl SN15 78 E4
Morse St SN1 50 B5
Morstone Rd SN4 61 D8
Mortimer Cl 5 SN5 49 B7
Mortimer St BA14 105 C7
Moss Mead SN14 77 F8
Motcombe CE Sch SP7 202 A4
Motcombe Grange Prep Sch SP7 202 A5
Motcombe Rd SP7 202 B3
Moulton Dr BA15 100 D4
Mount Carmel Rd SP11 199 F3
Mount La
Barford St Martin SP3 143 B4
Warminster BA12 117 A5
Mount Pleasant
Atworth SN12 85 A1
Atworth/Whitley SN12 93 A8
Bradford-on-Avon BA15 100 D7
Lechlade GL7 2 C4
South Newton SP2 130 A4
Mount The BA14 101 D2
Mountain Wood BA1 82 B2
Mountford Manor Jun & Inf Sch SN3 50 F6
Mountings The SN4 64 B8
Mountpleasant SP3 203 D8
Mountsfield BA11 110 A2
Moxhams 21 SP6 210 D1
Moyne Cl SN10 179 D8
Moyne Gdns 7 SP4 217 D3
Mud La SN5 32 F2
Muddyford Rd SP5 211 C8
Mulberry Cl SN14 70 B1
Mulberry Ct
Frome BA11 110 B7
Sixpenny Handley SP5 208 B4
Mulberry Gr SN2 35 A2
Mulcaster Ave SN5 48 F5
Mulling Cl SN14 75 A3
Mundy Ave SN3 51 C4
Munks Cl 2 SP2 151 E7
Munro Cl SN3 50 E6
Murdock Rd SN3 51 E6
Murray Rd BA14 101 D2
Murray Wlk SN12 94 B5
Murrayfield SN15 70 E1
Muscott Cl 3 SP9 199 C8
Muscovey Cl SN15 60 A2
Mustons La 26 SP7 202 C2
Myrrfield Rd 7 SP1 146 D5
Myrtle Ave BA12 116 F6
Myrtle Gdns SN2 35 C2
Mythern Mdw BA15 100 E5

N

Nadder CE Mid Sch SP3 203 E8
Nadder Cl 13 SP3 203 E8
Nadder La SP2 144 F2
Nadder Rd SP9 216 D6
Nadder Terr SP2 144 C2
Naini Tal Rd SP9 216 C6
Nantwich SN5 49 A3
Napier Cl Swindon SN2 50 A7
Tidworth SP9 216 E6
Napier Cres SP1 146 D1
Napiers 1 SN8 176 B3
Nash Cl SN25 35 A8
Nash Rd SN8 173 A8
Naughton Ave SN10 214 E6
Naunton Rd SN3 51 A6
Navigator Cl BA14 101 E4
Neal Cl 1 SP1 146 C5
Neale's Barrow★ SP2 150 A6
Neeld Cl SN14 68 F6
Neeld Cres SN14 78 B8
Neigh Bridge Ctry Pk★ GL7 5 F2
Nell Hill SN6 22 A7
Nelson Cl 1 SP4 198 F6
Nelson Rd SP2 146 A2
Nelson St SN1 49 F5
Nepaul Rd SP9 216 C7
Ness Cl 1 SN5 34 B2
Neston Cres SN13 84 E6
Neston Pk★ SN13 84 E3
Neston Prim Sch SN13 84 E5
Nether Leaze SN9 215 B5
Netheravon Rd
Durrington SP4 198 B7
Figheldean SP4 190 B1
Salisbury SP1 146 B2
Nethercote Hill SN15 86 D6
Netherhampton Rd
Netherhampton SP2 150 F8
Quidhampton SP2 144 F1
Netherstreet SN15 96 D6
Netherton CE Prim Sch SP4 190 A3
Netherton Cl SN3 51 B4
Netherton House★ SP11 185 F4
Nett Rd SP3 196 F6
Nettlebed Nursery 14 SP7 202 C2
Nettlecombe 6 SP7 202 D2
Nettlemead La BA12 201 F8
Nettleton & Burton CE Prim Sch SN14 53 B3
Nettleton Rd SN14 53 B3
Netton St SP5 205 E4
Neville Cl SP1 146 C4
Neville Terr SN15 57 D1
Nevis Cl SN5 34 B2
New Bottom Rd SP4 145 E7
New Bridge Cl 4 SN1 50 C7
New Bridge Rd SP1 152 A7
New Broughton Rd SN12 94 A5
New Canal SP1 152 A8
New Cl Bourton SP8 137 E2
West Knoyle BA12 140 E7
New Cl CP Sch BA12 117 B6
New Coll SN3 50 F5
New Cres SP11 192 A5
New Cut BA12 139 A6
New Dro SP11 192 A5
New Haig Rd 7 SP4 198 E6
New Hall Hospl SP5 158 F8
New Harnham Rd SP2 152 A6
New House La SP11 192 E4
New King Barrows★ SP4 197 F5
New La Cann SP7 202 D1
Seend SN12 178 D7
New Lawns SN12 94 B4
New Pk Rd SN10 214 B4
New Pk St SN10 214 A4
New Rd Bath BA1 82 C2
Bradford-on-Avon BA15 100 E7
Bromham SN15 96 A5
Calne SN11 81 B2
Calne Without SN11 79 F3
Chippenham SN15 78 D7
Chiseldon SN4 65 D3
Codford BA12 195 A3
Donhead St Andrew SP7 203 B4
22 Durrington/Bulford SP4 198 B7
East Knoyle SP3 141 B3
Erlestoke BA13 179 A2
Kilmington BA12 123 D6
Landford SP5 212 D5
Limpley Stoke BA2 99 B5
Maiden Bradley with Yarnfield BA11 123 D8
Marlborough SN8 213 D3
Melksham Without SN12 94 E7
Purton SN5 33 C5
Rockbourne SP6 210 A5
2 Shaftesbury SP7 202 B2
1 Trowbridge BA14 105 D7
Wootton Bassett SN4 47 D1
Zeale SP8 138 A3
New Severalls The SN9 182 E7
New St
16 Market Lavington SN10 179 F1
Salisbury SP1 152 A8
Winterbourne Stoke SP3 196 F3
New Terrace BA14 101 C7
New Town La SN6 163 E6
New Ward Rd SP4 198 E7
New Zealand Ave SP2 145 D2
Newall Tuck Rd SN15 78 F7
Newark Cl SN5 49 B3
Newbourne Gdns SN14 56 D6
Newburgh Pl SN6 22 F6
Newburn Cres SN1 49 F5
Newbury Dr
Chippenham SN14 77 F5
Swindon SN5 49 B3
Newbury Rd
Enham Alamein SP11 193 E4
Lambourn RG17 165 B1
Newbury Road SP10 193 E2
Newbury St RG17 165 A1
Newby Acre SN8 213 D4
Newby Cl 4 SN10 187 E8
Newcastle St SN1 50 D6
Newcombe Dr SN2 50 A7
Newcroft Cl SN11 81 B4
Newcroft Rd SN11 81 B4
Newhall St SN1 50 B5
Newhurst Pk BA14 102 A2
Newland Rd SN25 35 A3
Newlands Cl SN15 70 E7
Newlands Rd SN13 77 A1
Newleaze
Steeple Ashton BA14 178 A4
Trowbridge BA14 101 F4
Newleaze Pk SN12 93 B4
Newmans Way SP4 217 E7
Newmarket Ave BA14 105 E4
Newmarket Cl 9 SN14 77 F6
Newmeadow Copse SN5 34 A1
Newopaul Way BA12 116 F8
Newport BA12 117 A7
Newport St SN1 50 D3
Newstead Cl 1 SN25 34 F6
Newth's La SN5 19 D2
Newton Abbot Cl 6 SN14 77 F6
Newton Barrow★ SP2 130 E3
Newton Cl SP5 161 C3
Newton La SP5 161 B3
Newton Rd SP2 145 D1
Newton Toney Sch SP4 199 B3
Newton Way SN2 35 C4
Newtown
Bradford-on-Avon BA15 100 C6
Heytesbury BA12 194 C5
Hullavington SN14 41 F1
Trowbridge BA14 105 C8
Westbury BA13 109 C3
Newtown CP Sch BA14 105 C8
Newtown Rd SN8 170 C2
Nicolson Cl 6 SP4 217 E3
Niebull Cl SN16 28 A5
Nightingale Ave BA11 110 B6
Nightingale Cl 8 SO51 212 F6
Nightingale Dr BA13 109 B4
Nightingale La
South Marston SN3 36 F4
Tisbury SP3 203 C6
Nightingale Rd BA14 105 A8
Nightwood Copse 3 SN5 34 A1
Nindum Rd SN3 36 C1
Nive Rd SN4 168 E8
Noade St SP5 206 E4
Noble St SN16 40 C8
Nolan Cl SN25 34 F8
Nolands Rd SN11 166 D2
Nomansland & Hamptworth CE Prim Sch SP5 212 B4
Norcliffe Rd SN3 51 B4
Nore Marsh Rd SN4 47 E1
Noredown Way SN4 47 E1
Noremarsh Jun Sch SN4 47 E1
Norfolk Cl 1 SN3 50 F6
Norfolk Rd SP2 151 E7
Norley La SN11 80 C3
Norman Cl SN15 79 A4
Norman Rd SN2 35 C1
Normandy Way 14 SP6 210 D1
Norney Rd BA13 179 A4
Norridge View 4 BA12 116 E7
Norrington La SN12 93 C6
Norrington Manor★ SP5 204 A2
Norris Cl SN4 65 C3
North Bank Rise SN4 47 F2
North Bradley CE Sch BA14 105 D2
North Charford Crossing SP6 210 F6
North Charford Dro SP6 210 C8
North Comm La SP5 212 B7
North Cote SN11 81 A4
North End SN11 81 A4
North End Gdns SN16 25 C1
North Farm Cl RG17 165 B2
North La SP5 212 C4
North Leaze Cl SN2 34 F3
North Mdw Rd SN6 8 C1

North Rd
Amesbury SP4 ....**217** E2
Ashmore SP5 ....**206** E5
Mere BA12 ....**139** A6
North Row BA12 .....**117** A7
North St
Broad Chalke SP5 .....**205** B4
Calne SN11 ....**81** B4
Mere BA12 ....**139** A5
Pewsey SN9 ....**215** C5
Salisbury SP2 ....**145** E1
Swindon SN1 ....**50** C5
Wilton SP2 ....**144** D3
North Standen Rd
RG17 ....**177** A6
North Star Ave SN2 .....**50** B8
North View
Berwick St James SP3 ..**196** A2
Highworth SN6 ....**22** F5
North View Hts RG17 ..**177** C7
North View Pl SN8 .....**213** D4
North Wall SN6 ....**19** D8
North Way Calne SN11 ..**81** A4
Trowbridge BA14 .....**105** A7
North Wilts Golf Club
SN11 ....**172** A5
North Wlk SP1 ....**152** A8
Northampton St SN1 .....**50** D6
Northbourne Rd SN25 ...**35** A7
Northbrook SN10 .....**179** F1
Northbrook Cl 1 SN10 ..**179** F1
Northbrook Rd SN12 ....**93** F7
Northcote Cres 7 BA11 **110** A7
Northcroft Rd SN13 .....**76** B1
Northen Cl GL7 ....**10** E6
Northen Terr
Durrington SP4 ....**197** F7
Larkhill SP4 ....**198** A7
Northern Rd SN2 ....**35** A1
Northfield BA15 ....**99** F7
Northfield La SN14 ......**66** A2
Northfield Way SN3 .....**51** B7
Northfields
Bulkington SN10 ....**178** E5
Calne SN11 ....**81** A4
1 Lambourn RG17 .....**165** A2
Northgate Gdns SN10 ..**214** A4
Northgate St SN10 .....**214** A4
Northlands Ind Est
BA12 ....**117** B7
Northleigh BA15 ....**91** E1
Northmoor La GL7 ....**6** F8
Northside SP4 ....**146** D8
Northview 20 RG17 .....**177** B7
Northview Prim Sch
SN6 ....**23** A7
Northway SP4 ....**134** B7
Northwood SN15 ....**70** E2
Norton Dr SP4 ....**146** D6
Norton Gr SN3 ....**50** D5
Norton Rd BA12 ....**117** F1
Norwood Castle (site of) ★
SN16 ....**4** F2
Norwood Cl 3 SN3 .....**51** D4
Noyes Cl
Chippenham SN14 ....**77** F8
Haydon Wick SN2 ....**34** C5
Nuffield Cl SN5 ....**49** B8
Nunns Pk SP5 ....**161** D4
Nunton Dro SP5 ....**152** D1
Nurseries The
Christian Malford SN15 ..**58** A2
Swindon SN1 ....**50** A5
Nursery Cl
4 Amesbury SP4 ......**217** B3
Atworth/Whitley SN12 ...**92** E8
Trowbridge BA14 ....**102** A3
Nursery Gdns
Corsham SN13 ....**85** A8
Mere BA12 ....**139** A5
Nursery Rd
Colerne SN14 ....**75** A3
Salisbury SP2 ....**145** E1
Nursery The SN16 ....**27** F6
Nursteed Cl SN10 .....**214** C2
Nursteed Pk SN10 .....**214** C2
Nursteed Rd SN10 .....**214** C2
Nutbane La SP11 ....**193** A4
Nuthatch Cl 4 SN3 .....**51** E6
Nutley Ct 8 SN8 ....**183** D8
Nutmeg Cl 7 SN2 ....**34** D4
Nyland Rd SN3 ....**51** C7
Nythe Prim Sch SN3 ....**51** C7
Nythe Rd SN3 ....**36** B1

O

O'Donnell Cl SN15 ......**70** E1
Oak Ash Gn SP2 ....**144** C2
Oak Cl
Bishops Cannings SN10 **172** B2
Pitton & Farley SP5 ....**154** E7
South Newton SP2 .....**130** B2
Tidworth SP9 ....**216** E7
Oak Dr Alderbury SP5 ..**153** D2
Highworth SN6 ....**22** F5
Trowbridge BA14 .....**105** C3
Oak Gdns SN3 ....**36** A4
Oak Hill SN8 ....**176** E6
Oak La Easterton SN10 ..**179** F2
Figheldean SP4 ....**190** B2
Oak Lodge Cl SN14 .....**78** C8
Oak Pl SP4 ....**217** C4

Oak Rd
Chippenham Without
SN14 ....**77** F6
Colerne SN14 ....**74** F5
Down Ampney GL7 ......**8** E6
Oak St GL7 ....**2** C4
Oak Tree Ave SN4 ......**35** D3
Oak Tree Cl BA14 .....**101** B1
Oak Way GL7 ....**6** F6
Oakapple Cl 4 SN4 .....**163** B6
Oakbournes The 5 SP1 **146** C5
Oakes Ct 9 SP1 ....**177** B7
Oakes La GL9 ....**52** B5
Oakford La SN14 ....**74** B2
Oakham Cl SN5 ....**49** C5
Oakie Cl SN25 ....**35** A5
Oaklands SN15 ....**70** D2
Oaklands Cl 12 SP6 ...**210** D1
Oaklea La SP5 ....**153** E2
Oakleaze SN16 ....**17** B2
Oakleigh Dr SP5 ....**212** C5
Oakley Flats GL7 ....**10** D6
Oaks La DT11 ....**207** D2
Oaks The
Chippenham SN15 ....**70** D2
Kemble GL7 ....**4** F7
Warminster BA12 ......**117** A8
Oaksey Prim Sch SN16 ..**15** F8
Oaksey Rd Minety SN16 ..**16** C4
Swindon SN3 ....**35** C4
Oakwood Dr SN12 ......**94** B4
Oakwood Gr SP5 ....**153** D3
Oakwood Rd SN5 ....**49** C7
Oamaru Way SN10 .....**214** D3
Oare Hill SN8 ....**174** C2
Oasis Leisure Ctr **50** B7
Oasthouse Cl 3 SN5 ....**49** A8
Oate Hill SN15 ....**78** F6
Oathill La SN10 ....**84** F8
Oathills SN13 ....**84** F8
Obelisk Terr 6 BA12 ...**116** F7
Oberon Way SN25 ......**35** A5
Ocotal Way SN1 ....**50** D8
Odcroft Cl SN15 ....**79** A7
Oddford Vale 17 SP3 ..**203** E8
Odstock Jun Sch SP5 ..**152** B1
Odstock Rd
Britford SP2 ....**152** B4
Swindon SN2 ....**35** C6
Ogbourne SN14 ....**75** B3
Ogbourne St George & St.
Andrew CE Sch SN8 ..**168** F5
Ogbury Camp ★ SP4 ...**198** A1
Ogilvie Sq SN1 ....**81** C3
Okebourne Pk SN3 ......**51** C3
Okeford Cl SN3 ....**51** C7
Okus Gr SN2 ....**35** D4
Okus Rd SN1 ....**49** F3
Olaf Cl 10 SP10 ....**193** E2
Old Alexander Rd SN16 ..**27** F4
Old Bakery Cl SN15 .....**28** F2
Old Barn GL8 ....**3** C5
Old Batch The BA15 ...**100** B8
Old Beasants SN8 .....**174** A6
Old Blandford Rd SP2 ..**151** F6
Old Boundary Rd 5
SN12 ....**94** A5
Old Brickyard Rd SP6 ..**210** D1
Old Broughton Rd
SN12 ....**94** A5
Old Cann Sch SP7 .....**202** C1
Old Castle Rd SP1 .....**146** A5
Old Chapel Cl SP5 .....**153** D3
Old Chase Rd SN8 .....**169** A4
Old Coach Rd
Durrington/Bulford SP4 ..**217** D8
North Wraxall SN14 .....**67** D2
Shipton Bellinger SP11 ..**191** F1
Old Comm Way 18 SP11 **192** A5
Old Ct SN4 ....**47** D1
Old Dames Sch SP6 ...**211** C6
Old Derry Hill
Calne Without SN15 ......**79** D2
Calne Without SN11 ......**79** E2
Old Dilton Rd BA13 ....**112** E7
Old Down Rd GL9 ....**52** C8
Old English Dr 2 SP10 **193** D2
Old Granary La SP4 ....**217** B3
Old Hardenhuish La
SN14 ....**70** B1
Old Hayward La RG17 ..**171** B1
Old Hollow BA12 ....**139** B6
Old Hospl Rd SN9 .....**215** B6
Old King Barrows ★
SP4 ....**197** F5
Old Malmesbury Rd
SN4 ....**47** E4
Old Malthouse La SP4 ..**147** E7
Old Midford Rd BA2 ....**98** A7
Old Mill La SN3 ....**50** D3
Old Orch The SN16 ......**28** A6
Old Post Office La 5
SP4 ....**190** A3
Old Pound Ct SP8 .....**137** D1
Old Rd Alderbury SP5 ..**153** D4
Chippenham SN15 ....**78** D8
Derry Hill/Studley SN11 ...**80** B2
Old Rly Cl 1 SN4 ....**28** A4
Old Sarum ★ SP1 .....**145** F6
Old Sarum Barracks
SP4 ....**146** C8
Old Sarum Pk SP4 .....**146** D8
Old Sawmills The
RG17 ....**177** F3

Old Sch Cl SN15 ....**96** C7
Old Severalls The SN9 ..**182** E7
Old Shaft Rd SN14 ......**84** C7
Old Shaftesbury Dro
SP2 ....**150** A6
Old Shaw La SN5 ....**48** F8
Old Sodom La SN15 .....**59** B8
Old St SP2 ....**152** A6
Old Sta Yd The 14 RG17 **165** A1
Old Tk BA2 ....**98** F7
Old Vicarage La GL7 ....**4** F7
Old Vineries The 10
SP6 ....**210** C1
Old Ward Rd 5 SP4 ....**198** E6
Old Wardour Castle ★
SP3 ....**203** D5
Oldbury Castle (Hill Fort) ★
SN11 ....**172** C8
Oldbury Prior SN11 ......**81** C1
Oldbury Way SN11 ......**81** A3
Oldfield Pk BA13 ....**108** E3
Oldfield Rd
Salisbury SP1 ....**146** C5
Westbury BA13 ....**108** E4
Oldford Hill BA11 ......**110** A8
Oldhat Barrow ★ SN9 ..**183** A3
Olive Gr SN2 ....**35** B3
Olivemead La SN15 ......**45** C1
Oliver Ave SN13 ....**76** F2
Oliver Cl SN5 ....**48** F6
Oliver's Castle (Fort) ★
SN10 ....**97** C6
Oliver's La 5 SN16 ......**28** A3
Olivers Cl SN11 ....**166** B1
Olivers Hill SN11 ....**166** B1
Olivier Cl SP2 ....**145** C5
Olivier Rd Swindon SN2 ..**35** B6
Wilton SP2 ....**144** B5
Olympia The SN8 ....**168** E3
Olympiad L Ctr ★ SN15 ..**78** E8
Omdurman St SN2 ....**35** B1
Orange Cl SN6 ....**23** A6
Orchard Cl Calne SN11 ..**81** C2
Devizes SN10 ....**214** B1
34 Fordingbridge SP6 ..**210** D1
Lechlade GL7 ....**2** B4
5 Ramsbury SN8 ....**170** B2
2 Wanborough SN4 ....**163** A6
Warminster BA12 ......**117** B8
West Ashton BA14 .....**106** B4
Westbury BA13 ....**112** C8
Westwood BA15 ....**99** F3
Orchard Cres SN14 ......**78** B7
Orchard Ct
Bratton BA13 ....**186** A7
St Paul Malmesbury Without
SN16 ....**28** A2
Orchard Dr BA14 ....**104** E2
Orchard End SP4 ....**217** D8
Orchard Gdns
Melksham SN12 ....**94** A3
Purton SN5 ....**33** A3
Orchard Gr
Bromham SN15 ....**96** D7
Swindon SN2 ....**35** D3
Orchard Mead 3 SN4 ....**48** A2
Orchard Pk Cl 2 RG17 **165** B6
Orchard Pl SN10 ....**187** E8
Orchard Rd
Chippenham SN14 ....**78** B7
Corsham SN13 ....**77** A2
Marlborough SN8 ....**213** E2
Redlynch SP5 ....**211** C8
Salisbury SP2 ....**145** D2
Trowbridge BA14 .....**105** D7
Westbury BA13 ....**109** A3
Orchard The
Chirton SN10 ....**180** F4
Kington St Michael SN14 ..**70** A8
Limpley Stoke BA2 ....**99** C5
Semington BA14 ....**102** F6
Sixpenny Handley SP5 ..**208** B4
Upton Scudamore BA12 **112** F4
Orchard Way
Amesbury SP4 ....**217** C3
Longbridge Deverill
BA12 ....**116** E1
Trowbridge BA14 .....**105** C3
Orchid Dr 30 SP11 .....**192** A5
Ordnance Rd SP9 .....**216** D6
Orford Rd SP4 ....**217** D2
Orkney Cl SN3 ....**49** B7
Orlando Cl 4 SN5 ......**48** F5
Orrin Cl SN5 ....**34** B1
Orwell Cl
Malmesbury SN16 ....**28** A5
Swindon SN25 ....**35** A5
Osborne Rd BA14 .....**101** E3
Osborne St SN2 ....**50** B8
Oslings La BA1 ....**82** B2
Osprey Cl
Bower Hill SN12 ....**94** D1
Swindon SN3 ....**51** E6
Osterley Rd SN25 ....**34** E6
Otter Way SN4 ....**47** F2
Overbrook SN3 ....**51** C3
Overhouse Dr 12 SP3 ..**203** E8
Overton Gdns SN3 ......**36** B2
Overway La SP7 ....**203** B2
Overtown Hill SN4 ......**64** C5
Owl Cl SN3 ....**51** E6
Owlswood 9 SP2 ....**152** A5
Ox Dro
Berwick St John SP5 ...**207** B7
Bishopstone SP5 ....**205** F2
Bower Chalke SP5 .....**208** A8
Kimpton SP11 ....**192** A1
Teffont SP3 ....**201** C5

Oxencroft 8 SP7 ....**202** C2
Oxford Rd Calne SN11 ...**81** B3
Swindon SN3 ....**36** A1
Upavon Down SN9 ......**182** B2
Oxford St
Aldbourne SN8 ....**170** A6
Hungerford RG17 ....**177** C8
Lambourn RG17 ....**165** A1
Malmesbury SN16 ....**28** A3
Marlborough SN8 ....**213** D3
Ramsbury SN8 ....**170** B2
Swindon SN1 ....**50** B6
Oxon Pl SN6 ....**163** E6
Oxyard BA12 ....**195** B2

P

Pack Hill SN4 ....**51** F2
Pack Horse La BA2 ......**98** A7
Packhorse Bridge ★
SN15 ....**86** E5
Packhorse La SN15 ......**33** E8
Packington Cl SN5 ......**49** B7
Packway The
Durrington SP4 ....**197** D7
Shrewton SP3 ....**197** A7
Paddington Dr SN5 ......**49** E5
Paddock Cl Enford SN9 **190** A6
Great Somerford SN15 ...**44** A4
4 Shaftesbury SP7 ...**202** C1
Sixpenny Handley SP5 ..**208** A3
Swindon SN25 ....**34** E5
Winterbourne SP4 .....**133** B2
Paddock End SN14 ......**70** A7
Paddock La
Chilmark SP3 ....**200** F2
Corsham SN13 ....**84** D8
Paddock The
Highworth SN6 ....**23** A5
Market Lavington SN10 ..**180** A1
8 Tisbury SP3 ....**203** E8
Paddock Way SP1 .....**146** E2
Paddocks The
10 Aldbourne SN8 .....**170** A6
Chippenham SN15 ....**78** E6
14 Ramsbury SN8 .....**170** B2
5 Swindon SN3 ....**36** A2
Padfield Gdns SN12 .....**93** F1
Page Cl Calne SN11 .....**81** C3
Chippenham SN14 ....**78** A7
Paget Cl SP9 ....**216** B8
Pagnell La SN10 ....**179** D1
Pains Way 3 SP4 ....**217** C2
Painters Mead BA14 ...**102** A2
Pakenham Rd SN3 ......**51** B4
Palairet Cl BA15 ....**100** D4
Palm Rd SN14 ....**75** A5
Palmer Dr BA15 ....**100** D8
Palmer Rd
Salisbury SP2 ....**145** E2
Trowbridge BA14 .....**101** D2
Palmer St SN14 ....**78** C7
Palmers Way 11 SN4 ..**163** A6
Palmerston Mdw SN9 ..**190** A6
Pampas Ct 1 BA12 .....**116** E6
Pans La SN10 ....**214** B2
Panters Rd SP3 ....**204** C8
Pantiles The 12 SP6 ..**210** C1
Parade The
Marlborough SN8 ....**213** D3
Swindon SN1 ....**50** C6
Paradise La BA12 .....**116** E1
Parham La SN10 ....**179** E2
Parham Wlk 7 SN5 ......**48** F5
Parhams Ct SN4 ....**47** E1
Parhams Hill SP7 .....**203** B1
Park Ave
Chippenham SN14 ....**78** B8
Corsham SN13 ....**84** A8
Highworth SN6 ....**23** A5
Park Cl Calne SN11 .....**81** C2
Salisbury SP1 ....**146** A4
Trowbridge BA14 .....**105** D3
Park Dr SP3 ....**201** B3
Park End SN6 ....**17** F8
Park Field SN10 ....**214** C5
Park Fields SN15 ....**78** C8
Park La
Castle Combe SN14 ......**68** A7
Cherhill SN11 ....**166** C1
Chippenham SN15 ....**78** D8
Corsham SN13 ....**76** D1
Great Somerford SN15 ...**44** A2
Heytesbury BA12 ....**194** D5
Heywood BA13 ....**109** C7
Lea & Cleverton SN16 ...**29** D3
Lydiard Millicent SN5 ....**48** D7
Malmesbury SN16 ....**27** E5
North Wraxall SN14 ......**68** A2
Odstock SN14 ....**152** A4
Salisbury SP1 ....**146** A3
Sutton Benger SN15 .....**57** D2
Swindon SN1 ....**50** A6
West Dean SP5 ....**149** F1
Park Mead SN16 ....**27** F4
Park Pl SN6 ....**6** F1
Park Rd
Fordingbridge SP6 .....**210** D1
Malmesbury SN16 ....**27** F4
Market Lavington SN10 ..**179** E1
Rushall SN9 ....**181** F3
Salisbury SP1 ....**146** D2
Tidworth SP9 ....**216** D5
Tisbury SP3 ....**203** E8
Westbury BA13 ....**112** B8
Park Springs SN5 ....**49** C5
Park St Charlton SN16 ..**29** A6

Park St continued
Heytesbury BA12 ....**194** C5
Hungerford RG17 ....**177** B7
Salisbury SP1 ....**146** B2
Swindon SN3 ....**36** C2
Trowbridge BA14 .....**105** C7
Park The
Erlestoke SN10 ....**179** A1
8 Lambourn RG17 ...**165** A2
Park View
Chirton SN10 ....**180** F4
Devizes SN10 ....**179** D8
Park View Dr
Lydiard Millicent SN5 ....**48** D8
1 Westbury BA13 ....**108** F1
Park Way RG17 ....**177** B6
Parkers La SN15 ....**70** D6
Parkhouse Cnr SP4 ....**199** D6
Parkhouse Rd SP9 .....**199** C8
Parkland Way SP4 .....**133** D6
Parklands
Malmesbury SN16 ....**27** E4
Trowbridge BA14 .....**101** D2
Parklands Cl SN16 ......**27** E4
Parklands Rd SN3 ......**50** D5
Parklands The SN14 ....**55** E8
Parkside
Chippenham SN15 ....**78** D8
Swindon SN3 ....**36** A3
Parkwater Rd SP5 .....**161** E1
Parliament St SN14 .....**78** B7
Parr Cl SN5 ....**49** A6
Parsley Cl SN2 ....**34** D5
Parsonage
31 Fordingbridge SP6 ..**210** D1
Salisbury SP1 ....**145** E5
Parsonage Gn SP2 .....**151** E6
Parsonage Hill SP5 ....**154** D7
Parsonage La
Charlton Musgrove BA9 ..**136** C2
Hungerford RG17 ....**177** B7
9 Lambourn RG17 ...**165** A1
20 Market Lavington SN10 **179** F1
Parsonage Pk Dr 3
SP6 ....**210** D1
Parsonage Pl 9 RG17 **165** A1
Parsonage Rd
Amesbury SP4 ....**217** B3
Swindon SN3 ....**36** A3
Trowbridge BA14 .....**102** A1
Parsonage The SP5 ...**208** B4
Parsonage Vale SN8 ..**183** D2
Parsonage Way SN15 ...**70** F1
Parsons Cl SP4 ....**133** D5
Parsons Gn 4 SP3 ....**196** E6
Parsons La BA12 ....**116** E2
Parsons Pool 19 SP7 ..**202** C2
Parsons Way SN4 ....**47** C1
Partridge Cl
Chippenham SN14 ....**70** B2
Corsham SN13 ....**76** E1
Swindon SN3 ....**51** E6
Partridge Hill SP5 .....**212** E6
Partridge Way SP4 ....**146** C8
Passmore Cl SN3 ....**51** E7
Pasture Cl SN2 ....**49** E7
Pastures The BA15 ......**99** E3
Pat-Yat GL7 ....**4** B5
Patchway SN14 ....**78** B8
Patchway The SN10 ...**214** D3
Patney Rd SN10 ....**180** F5
Paul St SN13 ....**76** F1
Paul's Dene Cres SP1 ..**146** A5
Paul's Dene Rd SP1 ....**146** A5
Paulet Cl 3 SN5 ....**49** A4
Pauls Croft SN6 ....**19** D7
Pavely Cl SN15 ....**78** C6
Pavely Gdns BA14 .....**102** A1
Paven Cl SN5 ....**33** A4
Pavenhill SN5 ....**33** A4
Paxcroft Prim Sch
BA14 ....**101** E5
Paxcroft Way BA14 ....**105** F8
Payne Cl SN14 ....**78** E4
Payne's Hill 2 SP1 .....**152** B8
Peacock SN8 ....**173** E6
Peak The SN5 ....**33** B3
Peaks Down SN5 ....**34** B2
Pealsham Gdns 6 SP6 **210** D1
Pear Ash La SP8 ....**137** C4
Pear Tree Dr SP5 .....**212** C5
Pear Tree La SN10 .....**187** B8
Pear Tree Orch 2 BA13 **186** B7
Pearce Cl SN2 ....**35** E6
Pearce Way SP1 ....**146** D5
Pearl Rd SN5 ....**49** A7
Peartree Cl
Atworth/Whitley SN12 ...**85** C1
Purton SN5 ....**33** C5
7 West Wellow SO51 ..**212** F6
Peatmoor Way SN5 ......**34** A1
Peel Cir SN13 ....**84** D8
Pegasus Way SN12 .....**94** C1
Pelch La SN12 ....**178** D8
Pelham Ct SN8 ....**213** E3
Pembridge Rd SP6 ....**210** E1
Pembroke Cl 1 BA14 ..**105** D6
Pembroke Gdns SN25 ..**34** E3
Pembroke Gn SN16 ......**28** F1
Pembroke Pk Cty Fst Sch
SP2 ....**145** C3
Pembroke Rd
Chippenham SN15 ....**79** A4
Melksham SN12 ....**94** B4
Salisbury SP2 ....**145** C2
Upavon Down SN9 ......**182** B2
Pembroke St SN1 ......**50** B4
Pen Cl SN25 ....**35** A4

Pen Hill BA10 ....122 F1
Pen Mill Hill BA9 ....137 E3
Pendennis Rd SN5 ......49 A3
Penfold Gdns SN1 ......50 C4
Penhill Dr SN2 ....35 C4
Penhill Jun Sch SN2 ....35 C5
Penleigh Cl SN13 ....84 F8
Penleigh Rd BA13 ......108 D2
Penn Hill Rd SN11 ......81 C3
Penneys Piece 2 BA11 .110 C6
Pennine Cl SN12 ....94 D4
Pennine Way SN25 .....34 F7
Penning Rd SP2 ....145 B4
Pennings Dro SP5 ......157 A8
Pennings Rd
  North Tidworth SP9 ...191 D5
  Tidworth SP9 ....216 C8
Penny Hill SN8 ....191 E8
Penny La
  Chippenham SN15 .....78 F4
  Swindon SN3 ....50 F7
Penny Royal Cl SN11 ...80 F3
Penny's Cl 3 SP6 ......210 D2
Penny's Cres 4 SP6 ...210 D2
Penny's La
  Pitton & Farley SP5 ...154 E7
  2 Wilton SP2 ....144 D3
Pennycress Cl SN25 ....34 C3
Pennycress Dr SN2 .....94 C3
Pennyfarthing St SP1 ..146 B1
Pennys La SP6 ....210 D2
Penruddock Cl SP2 ....145 C3
Pensford Way BA11 ...110 D6
Penton La SP11 ....193 A3
Penton Lodge School
  SP11 ....193 B2
Pentridge Cl SN3 ......51 C7
Pentylands Cl SN6 .....22 F7
Penzance Dr SN5 ......49 F5
Pepper Pl BA12 ....117 D7
Pepperacre La BA14 ...101 F1
Pepperbox Hill SN5 ....34 B2
Pepperbox Rise SP3 ...153 E2
Pepperbox The★ SP5 .160 C6
Peppercorn Orch
  BA14 ....178 A6
Percheron Cl 11 SN5 ...49 A7
Percy St SN2 ....49 F7
Peregrine Cl SN3 ......51 D8
Perham Cres 1 SP11 ..192 B5
Periwinkle Cl SN2 .....34 C3
Perrinsfield GL7 ....2 D6
Perry's La Seend SN12 .178 D8
  Wroughton SN4 ....64 A6
Peters Finger Rd SP5 ..152 E7
Petersfield Rd SN3 .....51 B4
Peto Gdn The★ BA15 .99 E2
Petter Cl SN4 ....64 B7
Petticoat La
  Redlynch SP5 ....211 D8
  Westbury BA13 ....112 C8
Pettridge La BA12 .....139 A5
Petty La SN11 ....79 F3
Pevensey Way SN5 ....49 C5
Pewsey Rd
  Marlborough SN8 .....213 D2
  Rushall SN9 ....181 E2
  Upavon SN9 ....181 F2
Pewsey Sports Ctr &
  Swimming Pool SN9 ..215 B5
Pewsey Sta SN9 ....215 B5
Pewsey Vale Gram Sch
  SN9 ....215 B5
Pewsham Lock SN15 ...78 E5
Pewsham Rd SN2 ......35 D5
Pewsham Way SN15 ...78 E4
Pheasant Bsns Pk SN14 .78 B5
Pheasant Cl
  8 Chippenham Without
  SN14 ....77 F6
  Swindon SN3 ....51 E5
  Tidworth SP9 ....216 D6
Pheasantry The GL7 ....8 F7
Philip Cl SN12 ....94 C6
Philip Rd
  21 Durrington/Bulford
  SP4 ....198 B7
  Wilton SP2 ....144 B5
Philipps House & Dinton Pk★
  SP3 ....201 A4
Phillip Cl SN10 ....214 C4
Phillips Cl SN14 ....77 F7
Phillips La
  Salisbury SP4 ....145 E6
  Swindon SN1 ....50 D4
Phipps Cl BA13 ....108 F4
Phoenix Rise BA13 ....108 E3
Picket Cl SP6 ....210 D1
Picket Cnr SP6 ....211 F3
Picket Post Gate
  BA12 ....116 A4
Picketleaze SN14 ......78 A7
Pickford Way SN2 .....35 B6
Pickwick Cl SN2 ....35 E5
Pickwick Rd SN13 .....76 F2
Picquet The 12 BA13 ..186 B7
Picton Rd SN5 ....49 A4
Pictor Cl SN13 ....76 D1
Pig La
  Bishops Cannings SN10 172 C1
  Hullavington SN16 ....41 A3
Pigeon House La SN3 ..36 A3
Pigott Cl 4 SP4 ....190 A4
Pigtrough La SP7 .....203 B4
Pike Cnr SN16 ....17 D7
Pike House Cl SN16 ...19 C8
Pikefield Cres SN16 ...29 A6
Pilgrim Cl SN5 ....49 A7

Pilgrims Mead SP1 ....146 C5
Pill Hill SP5 ....161 C4
Pilots View SP4 ....217 D3
Pilton Cl SN5 ....49 A8
Pimperleaze Rd BA12 .139 F1
Pinckneys Way 13 SP4 .198 B7
Pine Cl Corsham SN13 .76 A1
  Landford SP5 ....212 C5
  Melksham SN12 ......94 A3
Pine Ct 2 BA11 ....110 B7
Pine Wlk SN4 ....105 C3
Pinehurst Infs Sch SN2 .35 B2
Pinehurst Jun Sch SN2 .35 B2
Pinehurst Rd SN2 .....35 C2
Pines Rd SN10 ....214 C2
Pines The SP6 ....211 A1
Pinetree Rise SN2 .....35 B3
Pineview Cl SP5 ......211 C6
Pinewood Way
  Colerne SN14 ....74 F7
  Salisbury SP2 ....145 B4
Pinewoods Cl SP2 ....145 B4
Pinfield La SN15 ......78 F4
Pinhills SN11 ....81 A2
Pink La SN16 ....29 E5
Pinkney Pk★ SN16 ...25 F1
Pinnegar Way SN3 ....51 E6
Pinnocks Pl SN2 ......35 F4
Pintail Ct SN15 ....60 B1
Pintail Way BA13 .....109 B4
Pioneer Cl 3 SN5 .....49 A7
Pipehouse La BA2 ....98 F4
Pipers Cl SN4 ....61 D8
Pipers Way SN1 ......50 C1
Pipitdene SN3 ....51 D7
Piplar Gd BA15 ....100 D4
Pippin The SN11 ......81 B3
Pippins The 3 BA12 ..116 F7
Pipsmore Rd
  5 Chippenham SN14 ..70 A1
  Chippenham SN14 ....78 A8
Pit Wlk SP4 ....199 C4
Pitchens End SN4 .....167 C2
Pitchens The SN4 .....64 B5
Pitman Ave BA14 .....105 B7
Pitton Prim Sch SP5 ..148 B3
Pitton Rd SP5 ....154 D8
Pitts Croft SN13 ......84 E5
Pitts La
  Bishopstone SP5 .....205 F4
  Chitterne BA12 ....195 D7
  Sedgehill & Semley SP7 202 B7
Pittsfield SN6 ....19 D7
Pix Mead Gdns 1 SP7 .202 D1
Place La SN14 ....94 A4
Plane Tree Cl SN12 ...85 C1
Planks The SN3 ....50 D4
Plantation Rd
  Chippenham SN14 ....78 C8
  Tidworth SP9 ....216 D5
  Wellow SO51 ....212 F4
Plantation The SP5 ...149 A5
Plants Gn BA12 ....117 B6
Plassey Rd SP9 ....216 C7
Platford St SN11 ......81 B2
Platt Cl RG17 ....177 C6
Platt La RG17 ....170 E2
Plattes Cl SN4 ....49 B8
Play Cl SN5 ....33 C4
Player Ct 8 SP6 ......210 D2
Pleydell Rd SN1 ......50 C2
Pleydells 3 SN6 ......19 D8
Plough La
  Kington Langley SN15 ..70 C5
  Marston SN10 ....179 A3
Plum La SN10 ....180 E4
Plume of Feathers La
  SN8 ....213 E3
Plummer Cl SN4 ......64 A6
Plumpton Cl SN14 ....77 F6
Plymouth St SN1 .....50 D6
Pockeredge Dr SN13 ..84 C7
Pockeridge Rd SN13 ..84 E7
Polden Rd 1 SP1 .....152 C7
Polebarn Rd BA14 ....105 D8
Pollen Cl SP4 ....190 B2
Pollen La SP4 ....190 B2
Poltondale SN3 ....51 D7
Pomeroy La BA14 ....104 B6
Pond La SN5 ....19 B1
Pond St SN25 ....34 F5
Ponting St SN1 ....50 C2
Ponting's Cl SN26 ....21 C2
Pool Gastons Rd SN16 .27 F3
Pool Gn SN13 ....84 E6
Poole Keynes House
  GL7 ....5 B4
Poole Rd SN25 ....34 E3
Poores Rd 17 SP4 ....198 B7
Pope Cl SN15 ....78 E6
Popham Ct SN15 .....78 E6
Poplar Ave SN2 ......35 C2
Poplar Tree La BA14 ..104 B3
Poplar Way
  Colerne SN14 ....75 A5
  Salisbury SP1 ....146 C5
Poplars The
  Chippenham SN14 ....70 A1
  Fovant SP3 ....204 D8
Popplechurch Dr 5 SN3 .51 E7
Poppy Cl SP11 ....80 F4
Porchester Cl 8 SP10 .193 C2
Port Down RG17 .....177 C5
Port Hill SN8 ....213 D5
Port Regis Sch SP7 ...202 B3
Port Way BA13 ......186 A6

Portal Ave SN13 ....84 B8
Portal Pl SN15 ....60 A1
Portal Rd SN2 ....35 A2
Porte Marsh Ind Est
  SN11 ....81 C5
Porte Marsh Rd SN11 .81 C5
Portfield Rd SP5 ......150 A4
Portland Ave
  Britford SP2 ....151 F5
  Swindon SN1 ....50 A4
Portland Way SN11 ...81 C2
Portman Rd SN12 ....94 A6
Portmore SN15 ....34 C2
Portnell's La BA12 ...137 F4
Porton Rd SP4 ....217 D3
Portsmouth St SN1 ...50 D6
Portway
  Chippenham SN14 ...78 B6
  Frome BA11 ....110 A4
  Laverstock SP4 ......146 B7
  Warminster BA12 ....117 A4
  Winterbourne SP4 ...133 A3
Portway Ind Est SP10 .193 B1
Portway La BA12 .....117 A8
Portwell 3 SN6 ......19 D7
Post Office La
  Broad Hinton SN4 ...167 C2
  Corsham SN13 ....77 A1
Post Office Rd RG17 .177 F3
Poston Way BA15 ....99 D7
Pot La SN11 ....110 F8
Potley La SN13 ......84 E7
Potterdown Rd 3 SN2 .35 C5
Potterne CE Prim Sch
  SN10 ....179 D5
Potterne Rd SN10 ....214 A1
Potters Way SP1 .....152 D8
Pottery La RG17 ......177 E3
Pottle St BA12 ....119 A6
Pottows Field SN11 ..166 B1
Poulsen Cl BA12 .....117 A5
Poulshot Rd SN10 ...179 A5
Poulton BA15 ....100 D5
Poulton Hill SN8 .....213 E4
Poulton La BA15 .....100 E5
Poulton St SN2 ......50 C5
Pound Cl Lyneham SN15 .60 A3
  Semington BA14 .....102 F6
Pound Hill
  Melchet Park & Plaitford
  SO51 ....212 F7
  St Paul Malmesbury Without
  SN16 ....43 A3
Pound La
  Bradford-on-Avon BA15 .100 C5
  Damerham SP6 ......209 E3
  Melchet Park & Plaitford
  SO51 ....212 F7
  Semington BA14 .....102 E6
  Shaftesbury SP7 .....202 D2
  Swindon SN2 ....35 B2
  Wilcot SN8 ....174 B2
Pound Mead SN13 ...84 F8
Pound Piece
  Ashbury SN6 ....164 A8
  5 Hungerford RG17 ..177 B7
Pound Pill SN13 ......77 A1
Pound Rd SN6 ....22 F7
Pound Row BA11 ....116 F6
Pound St
  Ebbesborne Wake SP5 204 D3
  Warminster BA12 ....116 F6
Pound The SN15 .....96 B7
Powell Rise SN16 ....28 B5
Powells Way GL8 ....13 B4
Power Rd SP4 ....197 E2
Pownall Rd SP4 .....198 A6
Poynder Pl SN11 ....166 A6
Poynder Rd SN13 ....76 E1
Poynings Way SN5 ..48 F4
Preshute La SN8 .....213 B2
Preshute Prim Sch
  SN8 ....213 A1
Prestbury Dr BA12 ...117 C5
Prestly Wood 3 SN13 .76 B1
Preston La SN15 .....60 B1
Pretoria Rd 13 SP11 .192 B5
Priddy Cl BA11 ......110 C7
Priestley CP Sch SN11 .81 C2
Priestley Gr SN11 ....81 C2
Priestly Wood Rd 6
  SN13 ....76 B1
Primrose Cl Calne SN11 .81 B5
  Swindon SN2 ....34 D5
Primrose Dr SN12 ...94 C4
Primrose Hill
  Tockenham SN4 .....60 D6
  Wilton SP2 ....144 D4
Primrose La
  Manningford SN9 ...181 F6
  Redlynch SP5 ....211 C7
Primrose Rd
  24 Ludgershall SP11 .192 A5
  Salisbury SP2 ....145 C4
Primrose Way SN14 ..70 B2
Primrose Wlk 1 BA12 .116 E7
Prince Charles Cl 14
  SP11 ....192 A5
Prince Charles Dr
  SN11 ....81 C3
Princecroft CP Sch
  BA12 ....116 E6
Princecroft La 3 BA12 .116 E6
Princes Cl SP5 ....211 D8
Princes Hill SP5 .....211 D8
Princes St SN1 ......50 C5
Princess Anne Rd 9
  BA11 ....110 A4

Princess Gdns
  Trowbridge BA14 ....101 E4
  Warminster BA12 ....117 D6
Princess Margaret Hospl
  Liddington SN3 ......51 D1
  Swindon SN1 ....50 A4
Princess Mary Gdns 19
  SP11 ....192 A5
Prior Pk Sch SN6 .....19 E7
Prior's Hill SN4 ......64 B5
Priorsfield SN8 ......213 E2
Priory Ave RG17 .....177 B6
Priory Cl Alderbury SP5 153 E2
  5 Hungerford RG17 ..177 B6
  5 Shrewton SP3 .....196 E6
  Wilton SP2 ....144 C5
Priory Gn SN6 ....23 A6
Priory New Rd SN13 .76 F2
Priory Pk SN13 ......100 D7
Priory Pl 1 RG17 ....177 B6
Priory Rd
  Hungerford RG17 ....177 B6
  Swindon SN3 ....51 A4
Priory Sq 6 SP2 .....146 A1
Priory St SN13 ......76 F2
Pritchard Cl SN2 .....35 F5
Private Rd BA11 .....123 C8
Privet La SP11 ......192 D2
Proby Pl BA14 ....102 A1
Professions Cnr SP5 .206 D6
Prospect Box SN13 ..83 B4
Prospect
  Corsham SN13 ......85 A7
Prospect Hill SN1 ...50 C5
Prospect Pl
  Bathford BA1 ....82 D2
  Mere BA12 ....138 F5
  Swindon SN1 ....50 C4
  Trowbridge BA14 ...101 D4
Prospect Rd RG17 ..177 B7
Proud Cl SN5 ....33 B3
Providence La SN13 .76 F1
Provis Mead SN15 ..79 A4
Provost St 26 SP6 ..210 D1
Pub La SN16 ....180 F8
Puck Well Nature Reserve★
  BA12 ....140 C4
Pucklands SN10 .....180 E5
Puddleslosh La SP6 .210 C2
Pullman Dr SP2 .....145 B3
Pump La Bathford BA1 .82 B1
  Long Newnton GL8 ..13 C4
Purbeck Cl SN3 .....51 C7
Purbeck Pl SN11 ....81 D2
Purleigh Rd SN13 ...76 E1
Purley Ave SN3 .....51 B3
Purley Rd SN4 ......51 F1
Purley Way SO51 ...212 E6
Purlpit SN12 ....85 A1
Purlyn Acre SN8 ...213 D4
Purslane Cl SN2 ....34 C3
Purton Liby & Mus★
  SN5 ....33 C4
Purton Rd
  Haydon Wick SN2 ..34 C3
  Purton SN5 ....34 B2
  Swindon SN2 ....34 D3
Purvis Cl 4 SP4 ....217 E3
Pyatts Cnr BA14 ...178 C4
Pye La SN4 ....167 A4

Quadrangle The SN15 .78 C6
Quakers Wlk SN11 ...73 F7
Quantock Cl
  Melksham Without SN12 .94 D4
  5 Warminster BA12 ..117 A8
Quarr Barton SN11 ..81 B3
Quarries The SN1 ...50 C3
Quarry Cl BA2 ......99 D6
Quarry Cres SN6 ....22 F6
Quarry Fields Ind Est
  BA12 ....138 E5
Quarry Hill SN13 ....83 E6
Quarry La Colerne SN14 .75 B3
  Melbury Abbas SP7 .206 A3
Quarry Mews SN1 ...50 C3
Quarry Rd SN1 .....50 C4
Quarrybrook Cl SN3 .36 E5
Quarrydale Cl SN11 .81 B2
Quartermaster Rd
  BA13 ....108 D6
Quarterway La BA14 .101 E1
Quavey Rd SP5 .....211 D7
Quebec St SN4 .....168 E8
Queen Alexandra Rd
  SP2 ....145 D3
Queen Elizabeth Dr
  SN2 ....34 C4
Queen Manor Rd
  Clarendon Park SP5 .147 B1
  Laverstock SP5 .....152 E8
Queen Mary Rd SP2 .145 D3
Queen Oak★ SN8 ..175 C4
Queen St Hale SP6 ..211 B5
  Salisbury SP1 ......146 A1
  Swindon SN1 ......50 B6
  Wilton SP2 ....144 D4
Queen's Barrow★
  BA12 ....201 A7
Queen's Dr Swindon SN3 .50 E6
  Swindon SN3 ....50 E6
Queen's Rd
  Devizes SN10 ......214 A2
  Westbury BA13 .....108 E3
  Wootton Bassett SN4 .47 E2

Queenborough SN5 ..49 C4
Queens Ave
  Corsham SN13 ......76 F3
  Highworth SN6 .....23 A6
Queens Cl
  27 Ludgershall SP11 .192 A5
  Sutton Benger SN15 .57 D2
Queens Club Gdns
  BA14 ....105 A8
Queens Cres SN14 ...78 A6
Queens Cres Sch SN14 .78 A6
Queens Dr SN3 ......51 B2
Queens Gdns
  32 Fordingbridge SP6 210 D1
  Trowbridge BA14 ...101 E4
Queens Gr BA9 .....137 C3
Queens Rd
  Hannington SN6 ....21 F8
  Mere BA12 ....139 B6
  Salisbury SP1 ......146 B2
  7 Tisbury SP3 .....203 E8
  Trowbridge BA14 ...101 C2
Queens Sq SN15 ....78 F6
Queens Way SN8 ...213 F2
Queensberry Rd
  Amesbury SP4 .....217 C4
  Salisbury SP4 ......146 B3
Queensfield SN2 ....35 D5
Queensway
  Melksham SN12 ....94 C4
  2 Netheravon SP4 .190 A3
  Warminster BA12 ..117 D6
Queintin Rd SN1 ...50 D3
Quemerford Calne SN11 .81 C1
  Calne Without SN11 .89 D8
Quidham St SP5 ....204 F2
Quilling Cl BA14 ...105 E7

R

Rabley Wood View
  SN8 ....213 E4
Radcliffe Rd SP2 ....152 A6
Radcot Cl SN5 ......34 A1
Radley Bottom RG17 .177 F7
Radley Cl SN3 ......51 C7
Radnor Cl SN10 ....214 C2
Radnor Pk SN16 ....42 E4
Radnor Pl 3 SN12 ..94 A2
Radnor Rd SP1 .....146 A3
Radnor St SN1 .....50 A5
Radstock Ave SN3 ..51 B6
Radway Rd SN3 ....35 F3
Raffin La SN9 ......215 C4
Raggett St SN1 ....50 C5
Raglan Cl SN3 .....50 F6
Ragleth Gr BA14 ..101 E2
Railway Village Mus★
  SN1 ....50 B6
Rainer Cl SN3 ......36 B3
Raleigh Ave SN3 ...50 F6
Raleigh Cres SP4 ..217 E3
Rambler Cl BA14 ..105 A8
Ramblers Mead SP11 193 A2
Rambridge Cres SP2 145 B5
Ramleaze Dr
  Salisbury SP2 ......145 C5
  Swindon SN5 ......49 A7
Rampart Rd SP1 ...146 B1
Ramsbury Ave SN2 .35 B6
Ramsbury Dr RG17 .177 C7
Ramsbury Manor★
  SN8 ....169 F1
Ramsbury Sch SN8 .170 B2
Ramsbury Terr RG17 .177 C7
Ramsbury Wlk BA14 .105 D6
Ramscliff SN10 .....187 F7
Ramsden Rd SN1 ..48 F3
Ramsthorn Cl SN2 .34 D4
Randall Cres SN5 ..49 A8
Randall's Croft Rd
  SP2 ....144 B2
Randolph Cl SN3 ...50 F5
Rank The BA14 ....105 C3
Rannoch Cl 4 SN5 .34 B2
Ransome Cl SN5 ...49 B8
Raspberry La 8 SP7 202 B1
Ratcliff's Gdn 15 SP7 202 C1
Ratcoombe Rd SN5 .34 A2
Ratfyn Barrow★ SP4 217 B4
Ratfyn Rd SP4 .....217 B4
Raven Cl SP9 ......216 D6
Ravenglass Rd SN5 .49 C6
Ravenhurst SN16 ...14 E6
Ravens Wlk SN4 ...48 A1
Ravenscroft
  7 Salisbury SP2 ...152 A5
  Swindon SN3 ......51 C8
Ravenscroft Gdns
  BA14 ....101 F1
Rawlence Rd
  Salisbury SP2 ......145 B3
  Wilton SP2 ....144 C2
Rawlings Cl SN3 ...36 E4
Rawlingswell La SN8 213 E3
Rawlins Rd SN9 ...215 C5
Rawlinson Rd SP4 .198 E6
Rawston Cl SN3 ...51 C6
Ray Cl Chippenham SN15 .78 F5
  Swindon SN25 ....35 A4
Raybrook Cres SN2 .49 E6
Rayfield Gr SN2 ...50 B8
Read St SN1 ......50 A5

Reading St 4 SN1 ....50 B6
Recreation Rd
  10 Durrington/Bulford
  SP4 ....198 B7
  Ludgershall SP11 ....192 A6
Rectory Cl Alton SN8 ....181 C8
  Stanton St Quintin SN14 ...56 B4
  11 Warminster BA12 ...117 A8
Rectory Hill SP5 ....155 F3
Rectory La
  Alderbury SP5 ....153 E2
  Breamore SP6 ....210 E5
  Charlton Musgrove BA9 .136 B1
  Cricklade SN6 ....19 E8
  Letcombe Bassett OX12 .165 F8
Rectory Pl 4 SP11 ....192 F1
Rectory Rd
  Alderbury SP5 ....153 E2
  Salisbury SP2 ....151 F8
  Sutton Mandeville SP3 ..204 C7
Rectory Wood 1 SN8 ..170 A6
Reculver Way 6 SP10 .193 C2
Red Cross House ★
  SN10 ....214 B4
Red La Mildenhall SN8 ..169 B2
  Sixpenny Handley SP5 ..208 A3
Red Lion La SN6 ....19 E8
Red Pit BA13 ....112 A8
Red Post La SP11 ......192 F1
Red Way The BA12 .....115 F3
Redbridge Cl 1 SN1 ...49 F6
Redcliffe St SN2 ....49 F6
Redenham Dro SP11 ...192 E4
Redford Cl SP1 ....146 D3
Redhill Cl SN11 ....79 F2
Redhills SN4 ....62 B1
Redland SN14 ....78 B8
Redland CP Sch SN14 ..78 B8
Redland La BA13 ......108 F2
Redlands 3 BA13 ......186 B7
Redlands Cl SN6 ....23 A4
Redlynch CE Prim Sch
  SP5 ....211 E6
Redlynch Cl SN2 ....35 C5
Redman Rd SN11 ....81 C6
Redposts Dr SN1 ....49 E4
Redruth Cl SN3 ....51 B5
Redstocks La SN12 ......95 A2
Redwing Ave SN14 ......70 B2
Redwood Way SN14 .....75 A5
Reed Wlk 10 SP4 ......198 C7
Reeds SN6 ....19 C8
Reeds Farm Rd SN16 ....28 A4
Reeves Cl 2 SN3 ....51 C4
Reeves Rd SN10 ....214 D1
Regent Cir SN1 ....50 C5
Regent Cl
  15 Hungerford RG17 ....177 B7
  Swindon SN1 ....50 C6
Regent St 6 SN1 ....50 C5
Regents Pl BA15 ......100 D5
Regimental Mus ★
  SP1 ....152 A8
Reid's Piece SN5 ....33 B3
Reith Way 2 SP10 .....193 B1
Rendall's Barn GL7 ......4 E5
Rendells Ct SN10 ......214 B3
Renoir Cl SN25 ....35 A3
Restrop Rd SN5 ....33 A3
Restrop View SN5 ....33 A4
Retingham Way SN2 .....36 A5
Reto Gr BA15 ....99 F3
Revell Cl SN2 ....35 E4
Reynolds Way SN25 .....35 A4
Rhine Cl SN1 ....49 F4
Rhuddlan SN5 ....49 B4
Ricardo Rd SN15 ....78 D8
Richard Jefferies Mus ★
  SN3 ....51 B2
Richards Cl SN4 ....47 D1
Richards Way SP2 .....151 E7
Richborough Dr 3
  SP10 ....193 C2
Richmond Cl 2 BA14 ..105 A7
Richmond Ct SN6 ....6 F1
Richmond Rd
  Calne Without SN11 ......81 A4
  2 Salisbury SP2 ......145 E7
Rickbarton 2 SN10 ....187 E2
Rickfield BA15 ....100 B6
Rickworth Pl BA12 .....195 A3
Ridge Gn SN5 ....49 B7
Ridge Nether Moor
  SN3 ....51 D2
Ridge The
  Broad Blunsdon SN26 ....21 B2
  Redlynch SP5 ....211 C7
Ridge Way SP7 ....202 C3
Ridgemead SN11 ....81 B4
Ridgeway SP3 ....201 A3
Ridgeway Cl SN2 ....34 F2
Ridgeway Hospl The
  SN4 ....64 C6
Ridgeway La SN15 ......44 E1
Ridgeway Rd
  Salisbury SP1 ....146 B2
  Swindon SN2 ....35 E5
Ridgeway Sch SN4 ......64 B7
Ridgeway The
  Chiseldon SN4 ....65 D2
  Crudwell SN16 ....14 E6
  Liddington SN4 ....163 A2
  Warminster BA12 ....117 B6

Ridgmount 6 SP4 ......198 B7
Ridings Mead SN14 ......70 C2
Ridings The SN14 ....70 A8
Rigsby's La SN16 ....16 F5
Ringsbury Camp ★ SN5 .32 E2
Ringsbury Cl SN5 ....32 F3
Ringwood Ave 5 SP4 ..217 C3
Ringwood Cl SN3 ....51 B6
Rinsdale Cl SN5 ....34 B1
Ripley Rd SN1 ....50 C4
Ripon Cl SN14 ....78 A5
Ripple Field SN5 ....49 B4
Rise The SN11 ....89 C8
Risingham Mead SN5 ....49 C5
Rivar Rd SN8 ....176 F1
Rivenhall Rd SN5 ....49 C5
River Pk SN8 ....213 D2
River St SN9 ....215 C5
River Way
  5 Durrington/Bulford
  SP4 ....198 C7
  South Cerney GL7 ....6 F7
  Trowbridge GL14 ....101 C1
Riverbourne Rd
  Laverstock SP1 ....146 D1
  Salisbury SP1 ....152 D8
Riverdale Cl
  9 Fordingbridge SP6 ..210 D1
  Swindon SN1 ....50 C2
Rivermead SP4 ....133 F8
Rivermead Dr SN5 ....49 C7
Rivermead Dr Ind Est
  SN5 ....49 C7
Rivers Reach 6 BA11 ..110 A4
Rivers Way SN6 ....22 F6
Riverside Calne SN11 ...89 D8
  Wilton SP2 ....144 D3
Riverside Cl
  Salisbury SP1 ....146 D2
  South Newton SP2 .....130 A4
Riverside Dr
  Chippenham SN15 ....79 A8
  Melksham SN12 ....94 A6
Riverside Pk SN15 ......44 A2
Riverside Rd SP1 ......146 D2
Riverside Terr SP3 .....129 E8
Roach's La GL9 ....38 C1
Road Hill Box SN13 ......82 E8
  Colerne SN14 ....74 D1
Robbers' Stone ★
  SN10 ....187 E6
Robbins Ridge SP4 .....217 C2
Robert Franklin Way
  GL7 ....7 A7
Robert Le Kyng Sch
  SN1 ....50 A5
Roberts Cl SN4 ....64 B5
Roberts of Kandahar Rd
  BA12 ....113 F1
Roberts Rd
  North Tidworth SP11 ...192 A5
  Salisbury SP2 ....145 D3
Robin Cl BA12 ....117 C6
Robin Hill La SP4 ......217 C8
Robin Hood's Ball ★
  SP4 ....189 C1
Robin Hood's Bower ★
  BA12 ....117 B1
Robinia Cl SN9 ....215 D5
Robins Cl
  Chippenham SN14 ....70 B2
  Wootton Bassett SN4 ....48 A2
Robins Hill RG17 ....177 F3
Robinsgreen SN3 ....51 D7
Robinson Cl SN3 ....51 D6
Rochdale Ave SN11 ......81 B4
Roche Cl SN3 ....51 D4
Roche Ct ★ SP5 ....135 E1
Rochelle Ct 19 SN10 ...179 F1
Rocher Cl BA13 ....108 F3
Rochester Cl 5 SN5 .....49 B4
Rochford Cl SN5 ....49 A5
Rock La BA12 ....117 D6
Rock Rd BA14 ....105 B7
Rockbourne La SP6 .....209 F3
Rockbourne Mus ★
  SP6 ....210 A3
Rockbourne Roman Villa ★
  SP6 ....210 A4
Rockdown Ct SN2 ....35 D4
Rocker Bench SN6 .....163 E6
Rockfel Rd RG17 ......165 A1
Rockfield SN14 ....75 B3
Rockley Rd SN8 ....213 C7
Rockmoor La SP11 .....185 C5
Rodbourne Cheney CP Sch
  SN25 ....35 A3
Rodbourne House
  SN16 ....43 B4
Rodbourne Rd
  St Paul Malmesbury Without
  SN16 ....42 F4
  Swindon SN2 ....49 F7
Rodden Manor ★
  BA11 ....110 D4
Rodden Rd BA11 ......110 A5
Roddenbury Cl BA11 ...110 B5
Roddenbury View
  BA12 ....115 A8
Rode Bridge ★ BA11 ...103 E1
Rode Hill BA11 ....103 F1
Rodsleigh BA14 ....104 F6
Rodway 13 SN4 ....163 A6
Rodwell Cl 3 SN3 ....51 A4
Rodwell Pk BA14 ......101 E2
Roebuck Cl SN4 ....47 F2

Roger Penny Way
  SP6 ....211 C3
Rogers Cl SN1 ....51 A7
Rogers Mdw SN8 ......213 D5
Rogers's La RG17 ......171 D7
Rolleston St 1 SN1 .....50 C5
Rollestone Rd SP3 .....196 E6
Rollestone St 1 SP1 ..146 B1
Roman Cres SN1 ....50 B3
Roman Mdw SP5 ......211 A8
Roman Rd SP2 ....145 D2
Roman Way
  Andover SP10 ....193 E2
  Chippenham SN15 ....79 B5
  Highworth SN6 ....22 F5
  Lechlade GL7 ....2 D5
  15 Market Lavington SN10 179 F1
Roman Way Prim Sch
  SP10 ....193 E2
Romer Rd SP2 ....152 A6
Romney Way SN5 ....49 A6
Romsey Rd
  Amesbury SP4 ....217 D2
  Whiteparish SP5 ....162 B3
Romsey St SN2 ....49 F7
Ron Golding Cl SN16 ....28 A5
Rook St BA12 ....139 A4
Rookery La Ansty SP3 .203 F6
  Breamore SP6 ....210 D5
  Swallowcliffe SP3 .....204 A6
Rookery Mdw SN8 .....174 A6
Rookery Pk SN11 ....89 C7
Rookes La SN10 ....179 D5
Rooks La BA11 ....110 E6
Rooks Nest Cl SN15 ....78 F4
Rookwood Gdns 9 SP6 210 C1
Rope Wlk SN12 ....94 B3
Rope Yd SN4 ....47 D1
Rosary The SN4 ....47 E2
Rose St SN2 ....49 F7
Rosebery St SN1 ....50 D7
Rosebrock Gdns SN12 ...94 C3
Rosedale Gdns BA14 ...101 A1
Rosedale Rd SN3 ....51 B4
Rosefield Way BA13 ...108 F4
Roseland Ave SN10 ....214 C3
Rosemary Cl Calne SN11 .80 F4
  Laverstock SP1 ....146 D1
  Swindon SN2 ....34 D5
Rosemary La
  Freshford BA2 ....99 B4
  2 Salisbury SP1 ......152 A8
Rosenheim Rise 1
  BA13 ....186 B7
Ross Gdns SN2 ....36 A4
Ross Rd SP4 ....197 E2
Rossett Gdns BA14 ....105 A8
Rothe Rise BA13 ......108 F1
Rother Cl SN25 ....34 F5
Rotherstone SN10 .....214 A4
Rotten Row SN4 ....163 A6
Rougemont Cl SP1 .....146 B1
Rough St SN13 ....84 F5
Roughmoor Way SN5 ...34 A1
Round Barrow SN14 .....75 B3
Round Hill 25 SP6 .....210 D1
Round House SN11 ......81 D1
Roundaway La SP11 ....193 A5
Roundhills Mead SN6 ...23 B6
Roundpond SN12 ....93 F6
Roundstone St BA14 ...101 D1
Roundway SN11 ....89 B1
Roundway Down SN5 ....49 B3
Roundway Gdns SN10 ..214 B6
Roundway Pk SN10 ....214 C5
Roundwood View SN15 ..58 A3
Roves La SN6 ....23 B1
Row La SN12 ....178 C7
Row The SP5 ....211 C8
Rowan Cl Colerne SN14 ..75 A5
  5 Durrington/Bulford
  SP4 ....198 B7
  Salisbury SP2 ....145 B4
Rowan Ct Frome BA11 ..110 B7
  Melksham SN12 ....94 A3
Rowan Dr SN4 ....47 E1
Rowan Rd SN2 ....35 A3
Rowans The SN16 ......27 F4
Rowbarrow Cl SP2 .....152 B5
Rowde CE Prim Sch
  SN10 ....96 E2
Rowde Ct Rd SN10 ......96 D1
Rowdeford Sch SN10 ....96 D3
Rowden Hill SN15 ....78 C6
Rowden La
  Bradford-on-Avon BA15 .100 D4
  Chippenham SN15 ....78 C5
Rowden Rd SN15 ....78 C6
Rowe Mead SN15 ....78 E5
Rowe's Hill BA12 ......119 C8
Rowland Hill Cl SN3 .....51 E4
Rowlands Cl BA1 ....82 B2
Rowley Medieval Village of ★
  ...99 F1
Rowley Pl SN12 ....94 B4
Rowton Heath Way
  SN5 ....49 A4
Royal Cl SN15 ....78 D6
Royal Field Cl SN14 .....55 E8
Royce Cl 5 SP10 ......193 B1
Royston Rd SN3 ....51 A4
Rubens Cl SN25 ....34 F8
Ruckley Gdns SN3 ....36 B2
Rudge Hill BA11 ....107 D5
Rudge La
  Beckington BA11 ....107 B6
  Wilcot SN8 ....174 B1
Rudge Rd BA11 ....107 B2

Rumble Dene SN15 .....78 E5
Rune Dr 4 SP10 ....193 D2
Rushall CE Sch SN9 ....181 E3
Rushall Cl SN2 ....35 B5
Rushall Dro SN9 ....181 D1
Rushall Rd SN9 ....181 F1
Rushey La BA15 ....91 F3
Rushmead La SN14 ......66 A3
Rushmore Golf Club
  SP5 ....207 C5
Rushmore Pk ★ SP5 ...207 C5
Rushton Rd SN3 ....51 A3
Ruskin Ave
  Melksham SN12 ....94 B4
  Swindon SN2 ....35 F3
Ruskin Cty Jun Sch
  SN2 ....35 F4
Ruskin Dr
  Warminster BA12 ......116 D6
  Wootton Bassett SN4 ....47 F3
Russell Mill La SN10 ...179 D1
Russell Rd SP2 ....145 E2
Russell St SP2 ....144 D3
Russet Ct BA12 ....116 F7
Russley Cl SN5 ....33 F1
Russley Pk ★ SN8 .....164 A3
Rusty La SN12 ....178 E8
Rutland Cl SN12 ....94 C3
Rutland Cres BA14 .....105 C6
Rutts La 3 SN10 ......187 E2
Ruxley Cl SN4 ....47 D1
Ryan Ave SN14 ....78 A7
Ryan Cl SN5 ....34 B2
Rybury Camp (Hill Fort) ★
  SN10 ....173 A2
Rycote Cl SN5 ....49 A6
Rydal Cl SN25 ....34 F5
Rye Cl SN5 ....49 A7
Ryeland Way BA14 ....105 E7
Ryeleaze SN10 ....179 D5
Rylands Way SN4 ....47 E2
Ryles La SN4 ....174 B6
Ryon Cl 11 SP10 ......193 E2

S

**S Ugford Medieval Village
of** ★ SP2 ....144 A2
Sack Hill BA12 ....113 F1
Sackville Cl SN3 ....50 F7
Saddleback Cl SN11 .....81 C2
Saddleback La SN10 ...179 E5
Saddleback Rd SN5 .....49 A7
Saddlers Mead SP2 ....144 C3
Saddlers Way SN8 .....183 D7
Sadlers Mead SN15 .....78 E8
Sadlers Rd RG17 ......177 C3
Saffron Cl 2 Swindon SN2 34 E3
  Wootton Bassett SN4 ....47 F3
Saffron Mdws SN11 .....80 F3
Sage Cl SN2 ....34 D5
St Albans Cl
  Salisbury SP1 ....146 D5
  Swindon SN3 ....49 E7
St Aldhelm Rd BA15 ...100 C5
St Aldhelms Rd SN16 ...27 F4
St Ambrose Cl SN3 ......51 D6
St Andrew's Cl
  Wilton SP2 ....144 B2
  Wootton Rivers SN8 ...174 F1
St Andrew's Rd
  Melksham SN12 ....94 C5
  Salisbury SP2 ....145 C2
  South Newton SP2 .....130 B2
St Andrews Cl 146 D2
St Andrews Cl SN4 ......64 B7
St Andrews Gn SN3 .....51 E7
St Andrews Rd
  Tidworth SP9 ....216 C6
  Warminster BA12 ......116 D6
St Andrews Sch
  Broad Blunsdon SN26 ....21 C1
  Laverstock SP1 ....146 E3
St Ann Pl SP1 ....152 B8
St Ann St SP1 ....152 B8
St Annes Cl SP4 ......217 C4
St Arild's Rd GL9 ....24 B4
St Athan Cl BA14 .....178 B4
St Augustine's Rd 5
  BA14 ....105 B8
St Augustines RC Sch
  BA14 ....105 B8
St Barnabas Sch SN10 .179 F1
St Bartholomew's St
  SP7 ....203 B4
St Bartholomews CE Sch
  ....47 E2
St Bedes Cl 5 SP1 .....146 D5
St Birinus Rd 4 SP5 ...211 C7
St Catherines Cl SN11 ...81 C4
St Christophers Cl 4
  SP1 ....146 D5
St Clair Rd SP2 ....152 B6
St Clements Way SP1 ..146 C5
St David's Way SN8 ...213 D3
St Davids Cl SP1 ......146 D5
St Dennis Rd 7 SN16 ...28 A3
St Dunstan Cl SN11 .....81 B5
St Edith's Cl SP2 .....144 C1
St Edith's Marsh SN15 ..96 C5
St Edmund's Church St 2
  SP1 ....146 B1
St Edmunds Girls Sch
  SP1 ....146 E3
St Edmunds RC Prim Sch
  SN11 ....81 C6
St Edwards 12 SP7 ....202 C2

St Edwards Mdw SP4 ...133 B2
St Edwards Sch SO51 ..162 B1
St Francis Ave SN15 ....78 C6
St Francis Rd SP1 .....146 A4
St George's Cl
  Ogbourne St George
  SN8 ....169 A5
  Warminster BA12 ......117 E5
St George's Rd
  Salisbury SP2 ....151 D7
  Semington BA14 ....102 E5
  11 Shaftesbury SP7 ...202 C1
St Georges Hospl
  BA14 ....102 E5
St Georges Prim Sch
  BA14 ....102 F4
St Georges RC Prim Sch
  BA12 ....117 E5
St Georges Rd
  35 Fordingbridge SP6 ..210 D1
  Tidworth SP9 ....216 C6
St Giles Cl SN16 ....29 A2
St Gregory's Ave SP2 ..145 D2
St Helens View SN1 .....49 F4
St James SN15 ....59 A7
St James Cl
  Salisbury SP1 ....146 D5
  Swindon SN2 ....35 D5
St James St
  7 Ludgershall SP11 ....192 A5
  Shaftesbury SP7 ......202 B1
St John Rd SN4 ....64 A6
St John's Cl
  Donhead St Mary SP7 ..203 A1
  Marlborough SN8 ......213 D3
  2 Salisbury SP1 ......152 D8
St John's Cres SP2 ....104 F6
St John's Ct SP2 ......144 C3
St John's Hill 7 SP7 ...202 B1
St John's Rd
  Frome BA11 ....110 B5
  Warminster BA12 ......117 C5
St John's St
  Devizes SN10 ....214 A3
  Lechlade GL7 ....2 C4
  Malmesbury SN16 ....28 B2
  Salisbury SP1 ....152 B8
St Johns CE Prim Sch
  BA12 ....117 C6
St John Cl
  Pewsey SN9 ....215 D5
  19 Tisbury SP3 ....203 E8
St Johns RC Sch BA14 .105 B8
**St Johns Sch & Comminity
  Coll** SN8 ....213 D1
St Johns Sch
  Marlborough SN8 ......175 A8
  Tisbury SP3 ....203 D8
St Joseph's Dr SN15 ....78 B8
St Josephs GM RC Lower Sch
  SN3 ....50 E7
St Josephs Sec Sch
  SP1 ....146 E3
St Judes Cl SP1 ......146 D5
St Just Cl SP4 ....199 B3
St Katharines Sch
  SN8 ....175 F3
St Katherine Gn 2 SN3 .51 E7
St Katherines SN4 .....167 C4
St Laurence CE Sch GL7 .2 D3
St Laurence Sch BA15 ..100 B7
St Lawrence Cl SP1 ....145 E1
St Lawrence Cres 6
  SP7 ....202 C2
St Lawrence Rd GL7 .....2 C4
St Lawrence Sq 8
  RG17 ....177 B7
St Leonard's Cl SN16 ...16 D3
St Leonard's Church ★
  BA12 ....194 A4
St Leonards Cl SP4 ....217 D8
St Leonards Cl SN16 ....16 D3
St Lukes Cl 8 SP1 .....146 D5
St Lukes Dr SN15 ....78 C6
St Lukes Sch SN2 ....35 D5
St Margaret's Cl 2 SP1 152 C8
St Margaret's Gdns
  SN12 ....94 C5
St Margaret's Gn 1 SN3 .36 B2
St Margaret's Hill
  BA15 ....100 D6
St Margaret's Mead
  SN8 ....213 F2
St Margaret's Pl BA15 .100 D6
St Margaret's Rd SN1 ...50 D3
St Margarets Rd BA15 .100 D6
St Margaret's Villas
  BA15 ....100 D6
St Margarets Ret Pk
  SN4 ....36 D1
St Margarets Cl SN11 ...81 A4
St Margarets Gdns
  SN15 ....78 C6
St Margarets Hospl
  ....36 B4
St Mark's Ave SP1 ....146 B3
St Mark's Rd SP1 .....146 B2
St Marks CE Jun Sch
  SP1 ....146 B3
St Martin's Chapel ★
  ....176 C4
St Martin's Church St 5
  SP1 ....152 B8
St Martin's St SP3 .....143 A4
St Martins SN8 ....213 E3
St Martins CE Inf Sch
  SP1 ....152 B8

St Martins CE Jun Sch
SP1 . . . .**152** C8
St Martins SP3 . . . .**143** A4
St Mary St SN15 . . . .**78** E7
St Mary's Rd SN4 . . . . . .**178** A3
St Mary's Church (remains of)★ SP7 . . . .**206** A5
St Mary's Cl
Chitterne BA12 . . . .**195** D6
Dinton SP3 . . . .**201** E2
Kempsford GL7 . . . .**10** E6
Lyneham SN15 . . . .**59** C3
Potterne SN10 . . . .**179** D5
Redlynch SP5 . . . .**211** D2
Sixpenny Handley SP5 . . . .**208** A4
Trowbridge BA14 . . . .**101** E4
Wilton SP2 . . . .**144** C1
Wylye BA12 . . . .**201** E8
St Mary's Gdns BA14 . . .**101** E4
St Mary's Pl SN15 . . . . . .**78** D8
St Mary's Rd
Dinton SP3 . . . .**201** E2
Frome BA11 . . . .**110** B5
12 Market Lavington SN10 **179** F1
Salisbury SP2 . . . .**151** F7
St Mary's St ❶ SN16 . . .**28** A3
St Marys & St Johns Fst Sch
SP3 . . . .**200** B3
St Marys CE Inf Sch
SN8 . . . .**213** E2
St Marys CE Sch BA14 . .**178** A3
St Marys Field GL7 . . . . .**1** A5
St Marys Gr SN2 . . . .**35** B1
St Marys La
Dilton Marsh BA13 . . . . . .**108** A3
2 Malmesbury SN16 . . . . .**28** A3
Westbury BA13 . . . .**112** C8
St Marys RC Prim Sch
SN2 . . . .**35** A1
St Marys Sch
Calne SN11 . . . .**81** B3
Chippenham SN15 . . . .**78** C6
Donhead St Mary SP7 . . . .**202** E1
Purton SN5 . . . .**33** C3
St Mathews Cl SN10 . . . .**96** D2
St Matthews Cl 6 SP1 . .**146** D5
St Mellion Cl SN15 . . . . .**78** F7
St Michael's Ave SN6 . . .**22** E6
St Michael's C of E Sch
SN8 . . . .**170** A6
St Michael's Cl
8 Aldbourne SN8 . . . . . .**170** A6
Brinkworth SN15 . . . .**45** E6
3 Lambourn RG17 . . . . .**165** A1
Trowbridge BA14 . . . .**102** A3
Wilton SP2 . . . .**144** B1
St Michael's Rd
Melksham SN12 . . . .**94** A3
Salisbury SP2 . . . .**145** C4
St Michaels CE Prim Sch
SN12 . . . .**94** B4
St Michaels CE Sch
SP4 . . . .**190** B2
St Michaels Cl
Lyneham & Bradenstoke
SN15 . . . .**59** F4
Tidworth SP9 . . . .**216** C5
St Nicholas CE Prim Sch
SN8 . . . .**164** B1
St Nicholas Cl
Calne SN11 . . . .**81** C4
11 Ludgershall SP11 . . . .**192** B5
Trowbridge BA14 . . . .**105** D3
Wilton SP2 . . . .**144** B1
Winsley BA15 . . . .**99** D7
St Nicholas Sch SN14 . . .**70** C2
St Nicholas' Rd SP1 . . . .**152** A7
St Osmonds Sch SP1 . . .**152** B7
St Osmund's Cl SP1 . . . .**146** A5
St Patricks Ave SP9 . . . .**216** B5
St Patricks RC Sch
SN13 . . . .**77** A1
St Paul St SN15 . . . .**78** D8
St Paul's Dr SN3 . . . .**51** E6
St Paul's Rd SP2 . . . . . .**145** F1
St Paul's St SN2 . . . .**35** C1
St Pauls Sch SN15 . . . . .**70** D2
St Peter's Church★
SP3 . . . .**127** D4
St Peter's Cl
Chippenham SN15 . . . .**78** C6
Wilton SN3 . . . .**144** B2
St Peter's Pump★
BA12 . . . .**123** C3
St Peters CE Jun Sch
SN8 . . . .**213** E3
St Peters Cl 5 SP9 . . . .**199** D8
St Peters Rd SP1 . . . . . .**146** C5
St Peters Sch SN14 . . . . .**78** A8
St Philip's Rd SN2 . . . . .**35** E3
St Rumbold's Rd 9 SP7 .**202** C1
St Sampsons Cty Infs Sch
SN6 . . . .**19** D8
St Stephen's Pl BA14 . . .**105** D8
St Teresa's Dr SN15 . . . .**78** C7
St Teresas Cl 7 SP1 . . . .**146** C5
St Thomas A'Becket CE Prim
Sch SP3 . . . .**188** B3
St Thomas 14 SP10 . . . .**193** D2
St Thomas Way SP1 . . . .**146** C5
St Thomas' Rd BA14 . . . .**101** D1
St Ursula's Cl 9 SP1 . . . .**146** D5
Saintes Cl ❶ SP1 . . . . . .**146** C5
Salcombe Gr SN3 . . . . . .**50** E5
Salisbury & S Wilts Golf Club
SP2 . . . .**151** A7
Salisbury & S Wiltshire Mus★
. . . .**152** A7

Salisbury Arts Ctr★
SP1 . . . .**146** B1
Salisbury Bsns Pk
SP1 . . . .**152** D7
Salisbury Cath★ SP1 . .**152** A8
Salisbury Cath Sch
SP1 . . . .**152** A7
Salisbury Cl ❶ SN14 . . .**78** A6
Salisbury Coll of Tech
SP1 . . . .**152** B7
Salisbury District Hospl
SP5 . . . .**152** B3
Salisbury Hill SN8 . . . . .**213** E1
Salisbury Hollow
BA13 . . . .**186** D8
Salisbury Leisure Ctr
SP1 . . . .**145** F3
Salisbury Racecourse
SP2 . . . .**150** E5
Salisbury Rd
Amesbury SP4 . . . .**217** A3
Breamore SP6 . . . .**210** F5
Chilmark SP3 . . . .**201** A4
Downton SP5 . . . .**211** A8
Fordingbridge SP6 . . . . . .**210** E1
Hungerford RG17 . . . .**177** B6
Marlborough SN8 . . . .**213** E2
Netheravon SP4 . . . .**190** A3
Pewsey SN9 . . . .**215** C3
Plaitford/Landford SO51 . .**212** E6
14 Shaftesbury SP7 . . . . .**202** C1
Shaftesbury SP7 . . . .**202** D1
Shipton Bellinger SP9 . . . .**199** D7
9 Shrewton SP3 . . . .**196** E6
South Tedworth SP9 . . . . .**216** C3
Steeple Langford SP3 . . . .**128** C8
Wilton SP2 . . . .**144** E3
Salisbury Sch of English
SP1 . . . .**152** B8
Salisbury St
Amesbury SP4 . . . .**217** A3
Devizes SN10 . . . .**179** D8
26 Fordingbridge SP6 . . .**210** D1
Mere BA12 . . . .**139** A5
3 Shaftesbury SP7 . . . . .**202** C1
Swindon SN1 . . . .**50** D7
Salisbury Sta SP1 . . . . .**145** F1
Salisbury Swimming Baths
SP1 . . . .**146** B2
Sally In the Wood BA1 . .**90** C6
Sally Kings La 5 SP7 . . .**202** B2
Salt La Salisbury SP1 . . .**146** B1
Winterbourne SP4 . . . . . .**133** C3
Salt Spring Dr SN4 . . . . .**47** C1
Saltersford La
Chippenham Without
SN14 . . . .**78** A3
Corsham SN14 . . . .**78** A3
Saltram Cl SN3 . . . .**51** C6
Salzgitter Dr SN25 . . . . .**35** A8
Sambourne Gdns
BA12 . . . .**117** A6
Sambourne Rd
Minety SN5 . . . .**17** D2
Warminster BA12 . . . . . .**117** A6
Sambre Rd SN4 . . . .**65** D1
Sams La SN26 . . . .**21** C1
Sanctuary The★ SN8 . . .**173** D6
Sand Hole La BA13 . . . .**112** E8
Sand La BA12 . . . .**121** A6
Sand's La SN10 . . . .**96** D2
Sandacre Rd
❶ Swindon SN5 . . . .**34** A1
3 Swindon SN5 . . . .**48** F8
Sanden Cl RG17 . . . .**177** B2
Sanders Rd BA14 . . . . . .**101** C2
Sandes Cl SN15 . . . .**78** C7
Sandfield
Littleton Panell SN10 . . . .**187** E8
Sutton Veny BA12 . . . . . .**194** A5
Sandford Pk BA14 . . . . .**104** F7
Sandgate SN3 . . . .**36** B1
Sandhills Rd SP3 . . . . . .**142** A4
Sandle Copse SP6 . . . . .**210** B1
Sandle Manor Sch
SP6 . . . .**210** C1
Sandlea Cl SN14 . . . .**68** F5
Sandleaze SN10 . . . .**179** C4
Sandleheath Rd SP6 . . . .**210** A1
Sandown Ave SN3 . . . . . .**50** E3
Sandown Ctr BA14 . . . . .**105** C4
Sandown Dr SN14 . . . . . .**77** F6
Sandown Pl 7 SP2 . . . .**145** F1
Sandpiper Bridge SN3 . . .**51** E7
Sandpit Hill SP3 . . . . . .**141** A2
Sandpit Rd SN11 . . . .**81** D4
Sandpits La
Sherston SN16 . . . .**25** C1
Steeple Ashton BA14 . . . .**106** C4
Sandridge Common
SN12 . . . .**94** D5
Sandridge Hill SN12 . . . .**95** A6
Sandridge La SN15 . . . . .**95** C7
Sandridge Pk★ SN12 . . .**95** B6
Sandridge Rd SN12 . . . . .**94** B5
Sandridge Sch SN12 . . . .**94** E5
Sandringham Rd
Swindon SN3 . . . .**50** F3
Trowbridge BA14 . . . . . .**105** B5
Sandringhams The
SP5 . . . .**153** A1
Sandroyd Sch SP5 . . . . .**207** C5
Sands The SN9 . . . .**181** C2
Sands' La SP7 . . . .**203** C3
Sandstone Rd SN25 . . . . .**34** F7
Sandwood Cl SN4 . . . . . .**34** B2

Sandy La
Edington BA13 . . . .**186** C7
Redlynch SP5 . . . .**211** D8
Swindon SN1 . . . .**50** B4
Sandy Lea Ave 5 SN13 . .**76** B1
Sandy Leaze BA15 . . . .**100** C6
Sandy Ridge SN11 . . . . . .**81** C1
Sanford St 3 SN1 . . . . . .**50** C6
Sangster Ave SN12 . . . . .**94** B4
Sarsen Cl SN1 . . . .**49** F4
Sarson La SP11 . . . .**192** E1
Sarum Ave SN12 . . . .**94** B4
Sarum Cl Salisbury SP2 . .**145** E3
Shipton Bellinger SP9 . . . .**199** C8
Sarum Coll SP1 . . . .**152** A8
Sarum Dr SN10 . . . .**214** C2
Sarum Gdns BA13 . . . . .**109** A4
Sarum Rd SN14 . . . .**78** A6
Sarum St Pauls CE Sch
SP2 . . . .**145** F2
Sarum Way Calne SN11 . .**81** A3
2 Hungerford RG17 . . . .**177** B6
Sassoon Cl BA12 . . . . . .**116** D6
Saunders Gr SN13 . . . . . .**76** D1
Saunders Mdw SN8 . . . .**183** E1
Savernake Ave SN12 . . . .**94** C6
Savernake Cl 4 BA12 . .**117** A8
Savernake Cres SN8 . . . .**213** F2
Savernake Ct SN8 . . . . .**213** E2
Savernake Hospl SN8 . . .**175** A7
Savernake Rd
Burbage SN8 . . . .**175** D1
Corsham SN13 . . . .**84** D8
Savernake St SN1 . . . . . .**50** B5
Savill Cres SN4 . . . .**63** F7
Sawpit Dr SN8 . . . .**175** C5
Sawpit Hill BA12 . . . . . .**140** B4
Sawyers Hill SN16 . . . . . .**17** A2
Saxby Rd SN15 . . . .**70** E1
Saxifrage Bank SN12 . . . .**94** C3
Saxon Cl Cricklade SN6 . .**19** D7
14 Market Lavington SN10 **179** F1
Westbury BA13 . . . .**109** A4
Saxon Dr BA14 . . . .**101** E4
Saxon Leas SP5 . . . .**149** C6
Saxon Mdw SP5 . . . .**211** A8
Saxon Mill SN4 . . . .**65** D5
Saxon Rd SP2 . . . .**151** F6
Saxon Rise SN8 . . . .**183** E1
Saxon Spur 10 SP7 . . . .**202** C2
Saxon St SN14 . . . .**78** B8
Saxon Way
Andover SP10 . . . .**193** D2
Winsley BA15 . . . .**99** F7
Saxonhurst 4 SP5 . . . . .**211** B8
Saxons Acre BA12 . . . . .**116** D6
Scallows La SO51 . . . . . .**212** F7
Scamell's Rd SP2 . . . . . .**146** A1
Scarborough Rd SN2 . . . .**49** F8
Scarlet Cl SN25 . . . .**34** F7
Scholard's La 16 SN8 . . .**170** B2
School Cl
Chiseldown SN4 . . . .**65** E4
Keevil BA14 . . . .**178** B5
St Paul Malmesbury Without
SN16 . . . .**28** A1
Vernhams Dean SP11 . . . .**185** C1
School Dr 25 SP4 . . . . .**198** B7
School Hill
Alderbury SP5 . . . .**153** C2
Brinkworth SN15 . . . .**45** E5
School La
All Cannings SN10 . . . . .**180** F8
❶ Amesbury SP4 . . . . . .**217** A3
Badminton GL9 . . . .**38** E2
Castle Combe SN14 . . . . .**68** A7
Castle Eaton SN6 . . . .**10** B4
East Garston RG17 . . . . .**171** E8
Grittleton SN14 . . . .**54** E5
Hindon SP3 . . . .**200** B3
Lea SN16 . . . .**29** A2
Little Bedwyn SN8 . . . . .**176** C5
Marlborough SN8 . . . . . .**213** A4
Meysey Hampton GL7 . . . . .**1** A4
South Cerney GL7 . . . .**6** F7
Staverton BA14 . . . .**101** D5
Westbury BA13 . . . .**108** E1
Wroughton SN4 . . . .**64** A6
School View SN9 . . . . . .**215** B5
Science Mus Outstation★
SN4 . . . .**63** F3
Scotby Ave SN3 . . . .**50** E2
Scotchel Gn SN9 . . . . . .**215** D5
Scotland Hill SN15 . . . . .**57** A5
Scotland La
Beckington BA11 . . . . . .**107** C4
Landford SP5 . . . .**212** B8
Scotland Rd SN12 . . . . . .**94** A6
Scotney Cres 2 SN25 . . .**34** F6
Scots Cl SP5 . . . .**146** A1
Scott Cl SN8 . . . .**183** C8
Scott's Hill SP7 . . . .**203** C4
Scotts Cl SN11 . . . .**89** B2
Scratchbury Camp★
BA12 . . . .**194** B7
Scrubbity Barrows★
SP5 . . . .**207** E4
Seaford Cl SN5 . . . .**49** A6
Seagrim Rd SN2 . . . .**49** C7
Seagry Hill SN15 . . . .**57** D3

Seagry Rd
Hullavington SN14 . . . . . .**56** D6
Sutton Benger SN15 . . . . .**57** D2
Seaton Cl SN25 . . . .**34** F5
Second Broad Dr SP3 . . .**128** C2
Sedgebrook SN3 . . . .**51** D2
Sedgefield Gdns SN3 . . .**214** B4
Sedgefield Way SN14 . . . .**77** F6
Seend Hill SN12 . . . .**178** F8
Seend Prim Sch SN12 . . .**178** E8
Selby Cres SN5 . . . .**49** B4
Seldon Cl 4 SN3 . . . .**50** E6
Selions Cl SN14 . . . .**70** B2
Selwood Cres ❶ BA11 . .**110** A7
Selwood Mid Sch
BA11 . . . .**110** B6
Semington Rd
Berryfield SN12 . . . .**94** A1
Melksham Without BA14 . .**178** A8
Senior Dr SP2 . . . .**152** A5
Seth Ward Dr SP1 . . . . .**146** D4
Seven Barrows★
Lambourn RG17 . . . .**165** A5
South Tedworth SP9 . . . . .**191** B3
Seven Fields Jun & Inf Sch
SN2 . . . .**35** C4
Sevenfields SN6 . . . .**23** A7
Severn Ave SN25 . . . .**35** A4
Severn Rd SN12 . . . .**94** A6
Seymour Ct BA14 . . . . . .**101** C1
Seymour Rd
Chippenham SN15 . . . .**78** F8
Swindon SN3 . . . .**50** F6
Trowbridge BA14 . . . . . .**101** C2
Seymours Ct★ BA11 . . .**107** A6
Shady Bower SP1 . . . . . .**152** C8
Shaftesbury Ave SN3 . . . .**51** B4
Shaftesbury Fst Sch
SP7 . . . .**202** D1
Shaftesbury Mus★
SP7 . . . .**202** C1
Shaftesbury Rd
Barford St Martin SP3 . . .**143** B3
Mere BA12 . . . .**139** B4
Motcombe SP7 . . . .**202** A3
Wilton SP2 . . . .**144** B3
Shaftesbury St 19 SP6 . .**210** D1
Shaftesbury Upper Sch
SP7 . . . .**202** C1
Shails La
Melksham Without
SN12 . . . .**178** A8
Trowbridge BA14 . . . . . .**101** C1
Shakespeare Ave
SP10 . . . .**193** C1
Shakespeare Dr SN8 . . .**213** C2
Shakespeare Path SN3 . . .**35** F3
Shakespeare Rd
Salisbury SP1 . . . .**145** F4
Wootton Bassett SN4 . . . .**47** F3
Shalbourne CE Sch
SN8 . . . .**176** F2
Shalbourne Cl RG17 . . . . .**177** A7
Shalford La BA9 . . . .**136** A3
Shallow Wagon La
BA13 . . . .**108** F6
Shallowbrooks La SN14 . .**39** F8
Shallows The SP6 . . . . . .**210** F4
Shambles The BA15 . . . .**100** D7
Shanklin Rd SN2 . . . .**34** E4
Shaplands 4 SN3 . . . .**36** A2
Shapwick Cl SN3 . . . .**51** C7
Sharcott Dro SN9 . . . . . .**215** A4
Share La SP3 . . . .**203** C6
Sharp Cl SN5 . . . .**49** B7
Sharpley Cl SP6 . . . .**210** D2
Sharrat Ave 4 SP1 . . . .**146** C5
Shaston Dro SP2 . . . . . .**151** D5
Shave La BA10 . . . .**122** A4
Shaw CE Sch SN12 . . . . .**93** D8
Shaw Hill
Collingbourne Ducis SN8 . .**191** E7
Melksham Without SN12 . . .**93** D7
Shaw Rd SN5 . . . .**49** B7
Shaw Ridge Leisure Pk★
SN5 . . . .**49** B6
Shaw Ridge Sch SN5 . . . .**49** B7
Shaw Village★ SN8 . . . .**173** B6
Shawgrove SN8 . . . .**176** B3
Shear Cross BA12 . . . . . .**116** E1
Shearman St BA14 . . . . .**105** D7
Shearwater SN13 . . . .**84** D7
Shearwood Rd SN5 . . . . .**34** A1
Sheasby Cl SP5 . . . .**208** A3
Sheen Cl Salisbury SP2 . .**145** B5
4 Swindon SN5 . . . .**49** A4
Sheep Fair Way 13
RG17 . . . .**165** A1
Sheep St Devizes SN10 . .**214** B3
Highworth SN6 . . . .**23** A4
Sheepbridge Rd SP4 . . . .**198** E7
Sheepcote Barton 3
BA14 . . . .**105** E7
Sheepdrove Rd RG17 . . .**165** B2
Sheepridge SN8 . . . .**168** E3
Sheepscroft SN14 . . . . . .**70** B2
Sheepwash La BA12 . . . .**201** E8
Sheerwold Cl SN3 . . . . . .**36** B3
Sheffield La SN13 . . . . . .**84** D8
Shelburne Rd SN11 . . . . .**81** C1
Shelburne Way SN11 . . . .**79** F2
Sheldon Rd SN5 . . . .**60** A1
Shelfinch SN5 . . . .**49** D4
Shelley Ave 2 SN4 . . . . .**47** F3
Shelley Dr SP1 . . . .**145** F4

Shelley Gdns SN12 . . . . .**94** B4
Shelley St SN1 . . . .**50** B5
Shelley Way BA12 . . . . .**116** D6
Shenton SN3 . . . .**36** B3
Shepherd Spring Jun Sch
SP10 . . . .**193** E2
Shepherd's La
Donhead St Andrew SP7 . .**203** B2
Selwood BA11 . . . .**114** D6
Shepherds SN13 . . . .**84** D6
Shepherds Breach ❶
SN4 . . . .**47** E2
Shepherds Cl
Coombe Bissett SP5 . . . .**151** A1
Odstock SP5 . . . .**152** A1
Shepherds Mead
BA13 . . . .**112** A8
Shepherds Rise SP11 . . .**185** C3
Shepherds Spring Cty Infs
Sch SP10 . . . .**193** E2
Sheppard Cl SN15 . . . . . .**78** F5
Sheppard St SN1 . . . .**50** B7
Sheppards Rise SN15 . . . .**46** B7
Shepperton Way SN25 . . .**34** F7
Sherborne Rd BA14 . . . .**100** F1
Sherborne St GL7 . . . .**2** C4
Sherfield SP4 . . . .**133** A2
Sherfield English La
SO51 . . . .**212** F7
Sherfield English Rd
SP5 . . . .**212** E6
Sherfields SN4 . . . .**47** E1
Sherford Rd SN25 . . . . . .**34** E4
Sheridan Dr SN4 . . . .**47** F3
Sherrington La BA12 . . . .**195** A2
Sherrington Mead
SN15 . . . .**79** B4
Sherston Ave SN2 . . . . . .**35** C5
Sherston Rd
Brokenborough SN16 . . . . .**27** E4
Luckington SN14 . . . .**39** E5
Sherston Vc Prim Sch
SN16 . . . .**40** C8
Sherwood Ave SN12 . . . .**94** C6
Sherwood Cl 3 BA12 . . .**117** A8
Sherwood Rd SN3 . . . . . .**51** B4
Shetland Gdns SN5 . . . . .**49** A7
Shipley Dr SN25 . . . .**34** F6
Shipton Bellinger Cty Prim
Sch SP9 . . . .**199** C8
Shipton Gr SN3 . . . .**50** E5
Shipton Hill 2 SN16 . . . .**28** A4
Shiptons La SN15 . . . .**43** F2
Shire Cl SN5 . . . .**49** A7
Shire Ct 3 SN1 . . . .**50** A5
Shire Hill SN14 . . . .**66** A7
Shires Sh Ctr The
BA14 . . . .**105** C8
Shirley Cl SN3 . . . .**50** F7
Shockerwick La BA1 . . . . .**82** D4
Shoddesden La SP11 . . . .**192** B4
Shoemaker La SN15 . . . . .**45** F6
Shop La Badminton GL9 . .**38** C7
Wingfield BA14 . . . .**104** C6
Shore Pl BA14 . . . .**100** F1
Shoreland Cl BA13 . . . . .**108** F3
Short Dro SN4 . . . .**163** C6
Short La Andover SP11 . . .**193** B1
Barford St Martin SP3 . . .**143** A4
Short River Rd BA13 . . .**109** D2
Short St
Ludgershall SP11 . . . . . .**192** A5
Melksham SN12 . . . .**94** C6
Shortlands SP2 . . . .**144** B3
Shorts Gn La SP7 . . . . . .**202** A4
Shoscombe Gdns 3
BA11 . . . .**110** C7
Showfield SN4 . . . .**47** D3
Shrapnel Rd ❶ SP4 . . . .**197** E7
Shrewsbury Rd SN3 . . . . .**50** F6
Shrewton Cl BA14 . . . . .**105** D6
Shrewton Jun & Inf Sch
SP3 . . . .**196** F7
Shrewton Rd BA12 . . . . .**195** E6
Shrivenham Rd
Highworth SN6 . . . .**23** B4
Swindon SN1 . . . .**50** E7
Shropshire Cl
Salisbury SP2 . . . .**145** C5
❶ Swindon SN5 . . . .**49** C5
Shurnhold SN12 . . . .**93** F5
Shute End Rd SP5 . . . . .**153** B4
Shutts La SP5 . . . .**151** A1
Sidbury Circular Rd
SP9 . . . .**216** B7
Sidbury Hill Ave SP9 . . .**216** C8
Sidings The 2 SP5 . . . . .**211** B8
Sidney Cl Swindon SN5 . . .**48** F4
3 Swindon SN3 . . . .**50** E6
Sidney St SP2 . . . .**145** F1
Sidney Wood Ct SN14 . . .**78** C2
Signal St SN1 . . . .**50** D7
Signal Way SN1 . . . .**50** D3
Silbury Cl BA13 . . . .**108** F4
Silbury Hill★ SN8 . . . . .**173** C7
Silbury Rd SN11 . . . .**81** A3
Silchester Way SN5 . . . . .**49** C6
Sillen La SP6 . . . .**209** B6
Sillington La SN10 . . . . .**179** B7
Silman Cl SN13 . . . .**76** D1
Silton Rd SP8 . . . .**137** F2
Silver Barrow★ SP3 . . . .**188** D7
Silver Birch Rd BA14 . . .**105** B5
Silver Cl SN16 . . . .**17** B2
Silver La BA11 . . . .**114** C6

Silver Mdws BA14 . . . . .105 A5
Silver St Alderbury SP5 . .153 B2
  Bradford-on-Avon BA15 . .100 D6
  Calne SN11 . . . . .81 B1
  Calne Without SN11 . . . . .89 B8
  Colerne SN14 . . . . .75 B3
  Corsham SN13 . . . . .85 C6
  Kington Langley SN15 . . .70 F7
  Malmesbury SN16 . . . . . .28 A3
  Minety SN16 . . . . .17 B2
  Potterne SN10 . . . . .179 D5
  Salisbury SP1 . . . . .152 A8
  Sherston SN16 . . . . .40 C8
  South Cerney GL7 . . . . . . .6 F7
  Steeple Ashton BA14 . . .178 A3
  Trowbridge BA14 . . . . . .105 D8
  Warminster BA12 . . . . . .117 A7
  Westbury BA13 . . . . . . .112 C8
  Wilton SP2 . . . . .144 D3
Silver St La
  Bromham SN15 . . . . .87 D1
  Trowbridge BA14 . . . . . .105 B5
Silver Wood SP5 . . . . . .153 C3
Silverless St SN8 . . . . . .213 D3
Silverton Rd SN3 . . . . . . .51 B6
Silverwood Dr SN11 . . . .146 E2
Simmance Way SP4 . . . .217 C3
Simnel Cl SN5 . . . . .48 F5
Simonds Rd [17] SP11 . . . .192 A5
Six Acre La
  Shalbourne RG17 . . . . . .176 F3
  West Knoyle BA12 . . . . .140 A4
Sixpenny Handley Cty Fst Sch
  SP5 . . . . .208 A4
Skew Bridge Cl SN4 . . . . .47 C1
Skew Bridge Rd SN4 . . . .145 C2
Skew Rd SP2 . . . . .145 B2
Skinner's Cl SN6 . . . . . . .22 B7
Skye Cl SN6 . . . . .22 F7
Slab La SP5 . . . . .211 C7
Slade Dr SN3 . . . . .36 B1
Slades The SN1 . . . . .81 C3
Sladesbrook BA15 . . . . . .100 E8
Slag La BA13 . . . . .108 F5
Slate Way SP5 . . . . .148 B3
Slater Rd SN9 . . . . .215 C5
Slaughterford Rd SN14 . . .68 C1
Slay Barrow ★ SP4 . . . .189 A6
Sleight La SN10 . . . . . . .179 F6
Sleight Rd SN10 . . . . . . .214 E1
Slessor Rd
  Lyneham SN15 . . . . .60 A1
  Lyneham & Bradenstoke
  SN15 . . . . .166 A8
Sling Orch SP3 . . . . .204 E7
Sling Rd SP4 . . . . .198 E7
Slipper La SN4 . . . . .65 D4
Slipway The BA14 . . . . . .101 D4
Slodbrook La SP8 . . . . . .138 D1
Slowgrove Cl BA14 . . . . .105 F8
Small St SN10 . . . . .180 F4
Smallbrook Gdns
  BA14 . . . . .101 D5
Smallbrook La BA12 . . . .117 D5
Smallbrook Rd BA12 . . . .117 B5
Smannell Rd SP11 . . . . . .193 F2
Smay Down La SN8 . . . .184 E6
Smeaton Rd
  [1] Andover SP10 . . . . . .193 B1
  Salisbury SP2 . . . . .145 E1
Smitan Brook SN3 . . . . . .51 D6
Smith St SN14 . . . . .67 A6
Smith's Hill OX12 . . . . . .165 F7
Smitham Bridge Rd
  RG17 . . . . .177 B7
Smithfield St [2] SP4 . . . .217 B3
Smithy La SN9 . . . . .181 C6
Smithys La SN8 . . . . . . .183 C8
Smithywell Cl BA14 . . . .105 F8
Snail-Creep Hanging ★
  SP3 . . . . .200 E7
Snails' La SN10 . . . . . . .214 A3
Snap Village ★ SN8 . . . .169 C7
Snappersnipes BA13 . . . .109 A3
Snapps SN4 . . . . .64 B5
Snarlton La SN12 . . . . . . .94 C8
Snoddington Rd
  Fyfield SP11 . . . . .192 D1
  Shipton Bellinger SP9 . . .199 E7
  Hilmarton SN11 . . . . .73 F5
Snow Hill Dinton SP3 . . .201 F2
Snowberry La SN12 . . . . .94 C3
Snowdrop Cl SN25 . . . . . .34 D5
Snowshill Cl SN25 . . . . . .34 F5
Snowswick La SN7 . . . . . .12 E7
Snuff St SN10 . . . . .214 A4
Sobers Sq SP11 . . . . . . .193 F2
Sock's La BA10 . . . . .122 A7
Sodom La SN15 . . . . .59 C7
Soldier's Ring ★ SP6 . . . .209 D4
Solstice Rise SP4 . . . . . .217 B3
Somerdale Cl SN5 . . . . . .49 C6
Somerford Cl SN2 . . . . . .35 C4
Somerford Lakes Reserve ★
  GL7 . . . . .5 D2
Somerset Cl [1] RG17 . . .177 B7
Somerset Cres SN12 . . . .94 B3
Somerset Dr BA13 . . . . .109 A5
Somerset Rd
  Salisbury SP1 . . . . .146 B3
  Swindon SN2 . . . . .34 F1
Somerset Way BA14 . . . .102 F6
Somerton Gdns BA11 . . .110 C7
Somerville Rd SN3 . . . . . .50 F6
Somme Rd SP11 . . . . . . .191 F4

Sopwith Pk [7] SP10 . . . .193 C1
Sopworth Rd SN14 . . . . .39 E5
Sorley Cl SN8 . . . . .213 B3
Sorrel Cl
  Chippenham SN14 . . . . . .70 B3
  Melksham SN12 . . . . .94 B3
  Trowbridge BA14 . . . . . .105 D5
  Wootton Bassett SN4 . . . .47 E4
Sound Copse SN5 . . . . . .34 B2
South Alley [6] BA12 . . . .116 E5
South Bank SN8 . . . . . . .174 F4
South Charford Dro
  SP6 . . . . .210 D6
South Cliffe Rd [6] SN10 179 F1
South Cross La SN10 . . .179 C3
South Dr SP9 . . . . .216 C4
South La Downton SP5 . .211 A8
  Nomansland SP5 . . . . . .212 C4
South Marston Pk Ind Est
  SN3 . . . . .36 C7
South Mdw La SN5 . . . . .19 F3
South Mill Cl SP4 . . . . . .217 B2
South Mill Rd SP4 . . . . . .217 B2
South Pk ★ SP11 . . . . . .192 B4
South Pl Calne SN11 . . . . .81 B2
  Corsham SN13 . . . . .77 A1
South St
  Aldbourne SN8 . . . . . . .170 A6
  Avebury SN8 . . . . .173 B8
  Broad Chalke SP5 . . . . .205 B4
  Corsham SN13 . . . . .77 A1
  Great Wishford SP2 . . . .130 A3
  [8] Salisbury SP2 . . . . . .145 F1
  Swindon SN1 . . . . .50 C4
  Warminster BA12 . . . . . .116 E5
  Wilton SP2 . . . . .144 C1
South View RG17 . . . . . .177 B7
South View Ave SN3 . . . .50 E5
South View Pl SN8 . . . . .213 E3
South Way
  Alderbury SP5 . . . . .153 E2
  Trowbridge BA14 . . . . . .105 D7
South Western Rd
  SP2 . . . . .145 F1
South Wilts Gram Sch For
Girls SP1 . . . . .146 A3
Southampton Rd
  Alderbury SP5 . . . . .153 D3
  Fordingbridge SP6 . . . . .210 E1
  Salisbury SP1 . . . . .152 C7
Southampton St SN1 . . . .50 D6
Southay BA13 . . . . .186 B7
Southbank Gdns RG17 . .165 B5
Southbank Glen 47 F2
Southbourne Way
  SP4 . . . . .133 D6
Southbrook BA12 . . . . . .139 C4
Southbrook Gdns
  BA12 . . . . .139 B4
Southbrook La BA13 . . . .178 B1
Southbrook Rd SN12 . . . .93 F6
Southbrook St SN2 . . . . .35 B1
Southbroom Jun Sch
  SN10 . . . . .214 C2
Southbroom Rd SN10 . . .214 B3
Southcott Dr SN9 . . . . . .215 D4
Southcroft Rd BA13 . . . .111 D4
Southcroft Rd [1] SN13 . . .76 B1
Southdown [3] SN4 . . . . .163 A5
Southdown Dr SN2 . . . . . .34 A5
Southerwicks SN13 . . . . .84 F8
Southey Cl SN25 . . . . . . .34 F8
Southfield
  [2] Aldbourne SN8 . . . . .170 A6
  Southwick BA14 . . . . . . .104 F2
  West Overton SN8 . . . . .173 F6
Southfield Prim Sch
  SN6 . . . . .23 A5
Southgate Cl SN10 . . . . .214 B2
Southleigh BA15 . . . . . . .100 C5
Southleigh View BA12 . . .117 C5
Southmead SN14 . . . . . . .78 B6
Southmill Hill SP4 . . . . . .217 B1
Southside
  Laverstock SP4 . . . . . . .146 D8
  Shipton Moyne GL8 . . . . .26 E7
Southview Rd BA14 . . . . .105 D6
Southville Rd BA15 . . . . .100 E5
Southward La SN8 . . . . .170 A6
Southway SP4 . . . . .134 B7
Southway Rd BA15 . . . . .100 D4
Southwell Cl [2] SN14 . . . .78 A5
Southwick Ave SN2 . . . . .35 C3
Southwick CE Prim Sch
  BA14 . . . . .104 F3
Southwick Ctry Pk ★
  BA14 . . . . .104 F5
Southwick Rd BA14 . . . .105 C2
Southwood Rd BA14 . . . .105 F8
Spa Cl SN6 . . . . .23 B6
Spa Rd SN12 . . . . .94 B3
Spackman La SN13 . . . . .84 E8
Spanbourn Ave SN14 . . . .78 C4
Sparcells Dr SN5 . . . . . . .34 B2
Speedwell Cl
  Melksham SN12 . . . . .94 C2
  [1] Swindon SN25 . . . . . .34 E5
  [3] Trowbridge BA14 . . .105 D6
Spencer Cl
  Melksham SN12 . . . . .94 A6
  Swindon SN5 . . . . .48 F7
Spencers Orch
  Bradford-on-Avon BA15 . .100 D5
  Wroughton SN4 . . . . .64 B6
Spenser Cl SN3 . . . . .51 A7
Spereholt SN5 . . . . .49 D4
Spiers Piece BA14 . . . . .178 B3

Spin Hill SN10 . . . . .179 E1
Spine Rd (East) GL7 . . . . .7 C4
Spine Rd W GL7 . . . . .6 A2
Springfield Rd BA12 . . . .139 B5
Spinners Croft [5] BA14 .105 D7
Spinners Way BA14 . . . .139 B6
Spinney Cl
  Chippenham SN14 . . . . . .78 A6
  [3] Liddington SN4 . . . . .163 A4
Spinney The
  Lechlade GL7 . . . . .2 C4
  [3] Littleton Panell SN10 .187 E8
Spital La SN6 . . . . .19 E7
Spitfire Rd SN14 . . . . . . .146 D8
Spout La SN12 . . . . .178 F8
Spouts La SO51 . . . . . . .212 F7
Spracklands SP3 . . . . . . .201 F2
Spratsgate La GL7 . . . . . . .6 B4
Spray Leaze [10] SP11 . . .192 B5
Spray Rd RG17 . . . . .177 C2
Sprays [9] SN8 . . . . .183 D8
Spread Eagle Hill SP7 . .206 B6
Spreckley Rd [1] SN11 . . .166 A1
Spring Cl SN1 . . . . .50 C6
Spring Gdns Lechlade GL7 . .2 C4
  Swindon SN1 . . . . .50 C6
Spring La SN13 . . . . .84 C7
Spring Mdw SN8 . . . . . . .191 D8
Spring Rd BA11 . . . . .110 A6
Spring The SN10 . . . . . . .187 E8
Springfield BA15 . . . . . . .100 E6
Springfield Cl
  Corsham SN13 . . . . .84 A8
  [7] Shaftesbury SP7 . . . .202 C2
  Trowbridge BA14 . . . . . .101 E2
Springfield Cres
  [11] Redlynch SP5 . . . . . .211 C7
  Wootton Bassett SN4 . . . .47 D2
Springfield Dr SN11 . . . . .81 A3
Springfield Gdns SN12 . .85 C1
Springfield Pk
  [18] Tisbury SP3 . . . . . . .203 E8
  Trowbridge BA14 . . . . . .101 E1
Springfield Rd
  Rowde SN10 . . . . .96 D1
  Swindon SN1 . . . . .50 C3
  Westbury BA13 . . . . . . .108 C4
Springfield Sports Ctr
  SN13 . . . . .76 F1
Springfields Sch SN11 . . .81 A3
Springhill Cl [3] SN5 . . . . .49 C5
Spur Way SP4 . . . . .35 E3
Squalls La SP3 . . . . .203 F6
Square The Calne SN11 . . .81 B3
  Mere BA12 . . . . .139 A5
  Pewsey SN9 . . . . .215 C5
Squarey Cl SP5 . . . . .211 A7
Squires Copse SN5 . . . . .34 A1
Squires Hill Cl
  [7] Wootton Bassett SN4 .47 F2
  [7] Wootton Bassett SN4 .48 A2
Squirrel Cres [1] SN4 . . . . .47 F2
Squirrel's Cnr BH21 . . . .208 C1
Stables Rd SP9 . . . . .216 C4
Stacey's La SN4 . . . . . . .163 B3
Stafford St SN1 . . . . .50 B5
Stag Hill RG17 . . . . .171 A1
Stainers Mead SP7 . . . . .202 A5
Stainers Way SN14 . . . . .70 B2
Stallard St BA14 . . . . . . .105 C8
Stalls The BA12 . . . . .114 F5
Stamford Cl SN5 . . . . . . .49 B5
Stanbridge Pk [9] SN5 . . . .49 A7
Stanbury Rd SP11 . . . . . .192 C1
Stancomb Ave BA14 . . . .101 E1
Stancombe Pk [1] SN5 . . . .49 D5
Standen Way SN25 . . . . . .35 A7
Standings Cl [6] SN5 . . . . .49 A8
Stanier Cl BA11 . . . . .110 D6
Stanier Rd SN11 . . . . .81 C6
Stanier St SN1 . . . . .50 B5
Stanley Cl [9] SN4 . . . . . .163 B6
Stanley La SN15 . . . . .79 D6
Stanley Little Rd SP2 . . .145 B3
Stanley St SN1 . . . . .50 A5
Stanmore St SN1 . . . . . . .50 A5
Stansfield Cl [5] SN5 . . . . .49 D4
Stanton Cl BA14 . . . . . . .105 D5
Stanton La SN14 . . . . .56 A1
Stanton St Quintin Prim Sch
  SN14 . . . . .56 B4
Stanway Cl [5] SN3 . . . . . .51 A4
Stapleford Castle Ring &
Bailey ★ SP3 . . . . .129 D8
Stapleford Cl SN15 . . . . . .78 E4
Staples Hill BA2 . . . . .99 C3
Stapleton Cl SN6 . . . . . . .22 F5
Star La SN14 . . . . .74 D8
Star The BA14 . . . . .101 E7
Staring Cl [6] SN5 . . . . . . .48 F8
Station App
  [4] Frome BA11 . . . . . . .110 A4
  Melksham SN12 . . . . .94 A6
  Minety SN16 . . . . .17 C2
  Swindon SN1 . . . . .50 D3
  Westbury BA13 . . . . . . .108 E4
Station Hill SN15 . . . . . . .78 D8
Station Rd
  Ashbury SN6 . . . . .164 A8
  Badminton GL9 . . . . .38 F1
  Calne SN11 . . . . .81 B2
  Chiseldown SN4 . . . . . . .65 D4
  Christian Malford SN15 . . .58 A2
  Codford SN12 . . . . .194 F3
  Corsham SN13 . . . . .77 A1
  Devizes SN10 . . . . .214 A3
  East Garston RG17 . . . . .171 E7

Station Rd continued
  Great Wishford SP2 . . . .129 F3
  Highworth SN6 . . . . .22 F6
  Holt BA14 . . . . .92 E1
  [19] Hungerford RG17 . . .177 B7
  Kemble GL7 . . . . .4 F7
  [10] Lambourn RG17 . . . .165 A1
  Lechlade GL7 . . . . .2 D5
  Limpley Stoke BA2 . . . . . .99 C5
  Minety SN16 . . . . .17 C1
  Purton SN5 . . . . .33 C5
  Sandleheath SP6 . . . . . .210 C1
  Sedgehill & Semley SP7 .202 D5
  South Cerney GL7 . . . . . .7 B7
  Swindon SN1 . . . . .50 B7
  Tidworth SP9 . . . . .216 D5
  Warminster BA12 . . . . . .117 B7
  Westbury BA13 . . . . . . .108 E5
  Wootton Bassett SN4 . . . .47 E1
Station Terr [4] SP2 . . . . .145 F1
Station Way BA14 . . . . . .105 C8
Staverton CE Sch
  BA14 . . . . .101 D5
Staverton Way [2] SN2 . . .35 C6
Stavordale Priory ★
  BA9 . . . . .136 D5
Steadings The
  Salisbury SP4 . . . . .146 D6
  Wootton Bassett SN4 . . . .47 E5
Steam (Mus of Great Western
Rly) ★ SN2 . . . . .50 A6
Steel's La BA9 . . . . .137 A3
Steele Cl SN10 . . . . .214 D4
Steels Dro SP6 . . . . .211 A4
Steels La SP6 . . . . .209 D7
Steep Hollow SP3 . . . . . .201 E3
Steep St BA12 . . . . .139 A6
Steeple Way SN8 . . . . . . .175 C1
Steeple Langford CE Fst Sch
  SP3 . . . . .128 C8
Stenbury Cl SN25 . . . . . . .35 A7
Stenness Cl SN5 . . . . . . .34 C2
Stephen Martin Gdns [7]
  SP6 . . . . .210 D1
Stephens Cl [1] SP2 . . . . .151 E2
Stephens Rd SN3 . . . . . . .36 A1
Stephens Way BA12 . . . .116 F8
Stephenson Dr BA11 . . . .110 C6
Stephenson Rd
  Salisbury SP2 . . . . .145 E1
  Swindon SN25 . . . . .35 C7
Steplake La SO51 . . . . . .212 F8
Steplake Rd SO51 . . . . . .212 F8
Sterling Pk [1] SP10 . . . .193 C1
Stert Valley La SN10 . . . .180 A6
Stevenson Rd SN2 . . . . . .34 C5
Stewart Cl
  Chippenham SN15 . . . . . .78 F4
  Swindon SN25 . . . . .35 B6
Steway La BA1 . . . . .82 B6
Stibb Hill SN10 . . . . .187 F7
Still Man Cl BA14 . . . . . .101 E8
Stirling Cl
  [3] Bower Hill SN12 . . . .178 B8
  Wroughton SN4 . . . . .64 A7
Stirling Rd
  Market Lavington SN10 . .180 A1
  South Marston Park SN3 . . .36 C6
Stirling Way BA11 . . . . . .110 C6
Stobberts Pl [4] SN10 . . .179 F1
Stobberts Rd [3] SN10 . . .179 F1
Stock La
  Aldbourne SN8 . . . . . . .169 D4
  Landford SP5 . . . . .212 C2
Stock's Cross SO43 . . . .212 D2
Stockbridge Copse
  SN5 . . . . .34 A2
Stockley Hollow SN11 . . .89 C4
Stockley La SN11 . . . . . . .89 C6
Stockley Rd SN11 . . . . . . .89 C2
Stockport Rd SP4 . . . . . .217 C1
Stocks Bridge La SP5 . . .151 A1
Stockton Earthworks ★
  .201 A6
Stockton House ★
  .195 B1
Stockton Rd SN2 . . . . . . .35 C4
Stockwell Rd SN10 . . . . .214 C4
Stockwood Cl SP1 . . . . . .146 C3
Stockwood Rd SN14 . . . . .78 B6
Stoke Comm La SN5 . . . .19 A2
Stoke Mead BA2 . . . . .98 F7
Stokes Rd SN13 . . . . .85 A8
Stokes' Croft SN11 . . . . . .81 B4
Stokesay Dr SN5 . . . . . . .49 C4
Stonar Sch SN12 . . . . . . .93 D7
Stone (site of King's Elm) ★
  SP3 . . . . .142 B1
Stone Ave ★ SN8 . . . . . .173 C8
Stone Cl SP5 . . . . .149 C6
Stone La
  Lydiard Millicent SN5 . . . .33 E1
  Ramsbury SN8 . . . . .175 D8
Stonebridge Cl SN8 . . . .213 F3
Stonebridge Dr BA11 . . . .110 B7
Stonecrop Way SN25 . . . .34 E5
Stonefield Dr SN6 . . . . . . .23 A5
Stonehenge ★ SP4 . . . . .197 E5
Stonehenge Cursus ★
  SP4 . . . . .197 C6
Stonehenge Rd SP4 . . . .198 A4
Stonehenge Sch The
  SP4 . . . . .217 B4
Stonehill Barn GL8 . . . . . .3 D8
Stonehill La GL8 . . . . .3 D6
Stonehill La GL8 . . . . .3 D8
Stonelea Cl SN14 . . . . . . .78 B7
Stoneleigh Rise BA11 . . . .110 A6

Stoneover La
  Lydiard Tregoze SN4 . . . .48 A1
  Wootton Bassett SN4 . . . .47 F1
Stones La SN6 . . . . .8 B2
Stoney Bridge BA12 . . . .140 D1
Stoney Cross [20] SP11 . .192 A4
Stony Gutter BA14 . . . . .102 D1
Stony La
  Damerham SP6 . . . . . . .209 E6
  Lambourn RG17 . . . . . . .171 B6
Stonybeck Cl SN5 . . . . . . .49 D5
Stop St SP3 . . . . .200 C1
Stoppers Hill SN15 . . . . . .46 B6
Stops Hill SP3 . . . . .200 B8
Stormore BA13 . . . . .111 F5
Storridge Rd BA13 . . . . .108 C2
Stour Cl [5] SO51 . . . . . . .212 F6
Stour Wlk SN25 . . . . .35 B1
Stourhead House & Gdns ★
  BA12 . . . . .123 F2
Stourton House Flower Gdn ★
  .123 F1
Stourton La BA12 . . . . . .123 E6
Stourton Pk BA14 . . . . . .102 B3
Stowell Pk ★ SN8 . . . . . .182 A4
Stradbrook BA13 . . . . . . .186 B3
Straight La RG17 . . . . . . .171 C6
Strand The Calne SN11 . . .81 B3
  Steeple Ashton BA14 . . .178 A4
Stranks Cl SN6 . . . . .23 A4
Stratford Cl SN5 . . . . .49 D7
Stratford Rd SP1 . . . . . . .146 A4
Stratford sub Castle CE Sch
  SP1 . . . . .145 E5
Stratford Tony Rd
  SP5 . . . . .150 E3
Stratton Orch [1] SN3 . . . .36 A3
Stratton Rd
  Pewsey SN9 . . . . .215 C4
  Swindon SN1 . . . . .50 F7
Strattons Wlk SN12 . . . . .94 B3
Strawberry Hill SN10 . . .187 E2
Strawberry La GL7 . . . . . . .1 A4
Street La
  Brewham BA10 . . . . . . .122 A4
  Sedgehill & Semley SP7 .202 C6
Street The
  All Cannings SN10 . . . . .172 A1
  Alvediston SP5 . . . . . . .204 B2
  Bishops Cannings SN10 .172 B3
  Brinkworth SN15 . . . . . . .45 F6
  Broughton Gifford SN12 . .93 B4
  Castle Combe SN14 . . . . .68 A2
  Castle Eaton SN6 . . . . . .10 B4
  Charlton SN16 . . . . .29 B6
  Cherhill SN11 . . . . .166 B1
  Chilmark SP3 . . . . .201 A3
  Chirton SN10 . . . . .180 F4
  Crudwell SN16 . . . . .14 E5
  Didmarton GL9 . . . . .24 C3
  East Knoyle SP3 . . . . . .141 C2
  Holt BA14 . . . . .101 D8
  Hullavington SN14 . . . . . .41 F1
  Kilmington BA12 . . . . . .123 F4
  Latton SN6 . . . . .8 C4
  Lea SN16 . . . . .28 F1
  Little Somerford SN15 . . .44 C5
  Luckington SN14 . . . . . . .39 E4
  Lydiard Millicent SN5 . . . .48 E5
  Marden SN10 . . . . .181 A4
  Marston Maisey SN6 . . . . .9 C2
  Milton Lilbourne SN9 . . .182 E7
  Motcombe SP7 . . . . . . .202 A5
  Nettleton SN14 . . . . .53 B4
  Oaksey SN16 . . . . .15 F8
  Pitton & Farley SP5 . . . .154 E7
  Shipton Moyne GL8 . . . . .26 E8
  Swindon SN25 . . . . .34 E3
  West Knoyle BA12 . . . . .140 D5
  Winterslow SP5 . . . . . . .149 A5
  Yatton Keynell SN14 . . . .68 F6
Stroma Way SN6 . . . . . . .22 F7
Strongrove Hill RG17 . . .177 A7
Strongs Cl SN14 . . . . . . .178 C4
Stroud La SN10 . . . . .179 F5
Stroud's Hill SN4 . . . . . . .65 D4
Stuart Cl [2] Swindon SN3 .50 F6
  Trowbridge BA14 . . . . . .101 E4
Stuart Gn BA12 . . . . .117 A6
Stubbs La SN14 . . . . .70 A7
Stubhampton Bottom
  DT11 . . . . .206 C3
Stubsmead SN3 . . . . .51 C5
Stuckton Rd SP6 . . . . . . .210 E1
Studland Cl SN3 . . . . .51 B3
Studland Pk BA13 . . . . . .109 B2
Studley Castle ★ SP6 . . .211 F3
Studley Gn Prim Sch
  BA14 . . . . .105 A6
Studley Hill SN11 . . . . . . .80 A4
Studley La SN11 . . . . .80 A3
Studley Rise BA14 . . . . . .105 D6
Sturford La BA12 . . . . . . .115 D6
Styles Ave BA11 . . . . .110 C4
Styles Cl BA11 . . . . .110 B4
Styles Hill BA11 . . . . .110 B4
Styles Pk BA11 . . . . .110 B4
Styles The SP5 . . . . .205 F4
Sudeley Dr GL7 . . . . .6 F6
Sudeley Way SN5 . . . . . . .49 A5
Sudley Way SN5 . . . . .48 F5
Suffolk Cl SN16 . . . . .29 A7
Suffolk Pl GL7 . . . . .8 D7
Suffolk Rd SP2 . . . . .151 E6
Suffolk St SN2 . . . . .50 C8
Summer Down Wlk
  BA14 . . . . .105 C5

ummer La
Castle Combe SN14 ....53 F3
Monkton Combe BA2 .....98 D8
ummer Rd BA13 ....108 F4
ummerhouse Rd SN4 ....63 F7
ummerleaze BA14 ......105 A6
ummerlock App 2
P2 ....146 A1
ummers La SN4 ....167 C1
ummers St SN2 ....49 F7
umsions SN13 ....76 D1
un La BA13 ....108 E1
underland CI 14 SN12 .178 B8
unningdale CI SN15 .....78 F7
unningdale Rd SN25 .....35 C4
unnyhill SN8 ....191 D8
unnyhill La SN8 ....174 C1
unnyhill Rd SP1 ....146 A4
unnyside SN10 ....187 E8
unnyside Ave SN1 ....50 A4
urrendell Cottage
SN14 ....55 B8
urrey Rd SN2 ....35 A1
ussex Rd SP2 ....151 E6
utherland Cresent
SN14 ....70 B3
uthmere Dr SN8 ....183 D8
utton Benger CE Sch
SN15 ....57 D2
utton Bottom SP3 .....141 B5
utton Hill
herrington BA12 ......195 A2
utton Mandeville SP3 ..204 C7
utton La
angley Burrell Without
SN15 ....71 C5
utton Benger SN15 ......57 D1
utton Pk SN26 ....21 C1
utton Rd Fovant SP3 ...204 D7
ington Langley SN15 ....70 F7
windon SN3 ....51 C4
utton Veny CE Sch
A12 ....194 A4
vla La 6 SP4 ....198 E6
waddon SN11 ....81 B4
wallet House SN15 ......58 D5
wallow CI
idworth SP9 ....216 D6
6 Warminster BA12 ....116 E5
wallow Dr
rome BA11 ....110 B6
1 Trowbridge BA14 ....105 B8
wallowdale SN3 ....51 D7
wallowfield Ave SN3 ....50 F5
wallowmead 1 SP2 ....152 A5
wallows Mead 9 SN4 ...48 A2
wan Barton SN16 ....40 C8
wan CI
1 Durrington/Bulford
SP4 ....198 C2
echlade GL7 ....2 C4
alisbury SP2 ....152 A6
wan Dr BA14 ....101 D5
wan La SN4 ....17 F5
wan Mdw SN9 ....215 D4
wan Rd Corsham SN13 ..76 E1
ewsey SN9 ....215 C4
wan's Bottom 7 SN8 ..170 B2
wan's CI 6 SN8 ....170 B2
wanborough CI 6 SN15 78 F4
wanborough Tump★
N9 ....181 F6
wanbrook SN3 ....51 B8
wangate RG17 ....177 B8
wansfield CI 4 ....2 D6
wattons CI SP4 ....217 A5
wayne CI 6 SN15 ....78 F5
wayne Rd SP2 ....144 C2
waynes CI 1 SP1 ......146 B2
weet Briar Rd SN12 .....94 C3
weetmans Rd SP7 .....202 C5
wift Ave SN2 ....35 A7
wift Mead BA12 ....116 C5
wiftdown 5 SP2 ......152 A5
winburne PI SN4 ....47 E3
windon & Cricklade Rly★
N25 ....33 F8
windon Arts Ctr★
N1 ....50 C4
windon Coll
Marlborough SN8 ......213 C1
windon SN2 ....50 B8
windon Coll of Further Ed
N8 ....213 D8
windon Greendown Sch
N5 ....48 F5
windon Mus & Art Gall★
N1 ....50 D4
windon Rd
ricklade SN6 ....19 F7
ighworth SN6 ....22 F7
ilmarton SN11 ....73 F3
ydiard Tregoze SN4 .....48 C2
windon SN1 ....36 A1
Wootton Bassett SN4 ...47 F3
roughton SN4 ....64 D7
windon SN6 ....23 A5
windon Sta SN2 ....50 B7
windon Town Football Club
N1 ....50 C5
winley St SN3 ....34 A1
word Gdns 5 SN1 ......49 F4
wynford CI GL7 ....10 D6
ycamore CI
yneham & Bradenstoke
SN15 ....60 C2
orth Tidworth SP9 ....216 E6
ixpenny Handley SP5 ..208 A4

Sycamore Dr
8 Frome BA11 ....110 B7
Salisbury SP1 ....146 C5
Sycamore Gr
Swindon SN2 ....35 C2
Trowbridge BA14 ......105 C5
Westbury BA13 ....108 F3
Sydnalls La BA12 .....115 D6
Symonds SN5 ....49 B3
Syon CI Corsham SN13 ..84 E8
Sywell Rd SN3 ....51 C8

T

Tadpole La
Blunsdon St Andrew SN25 ..34 C8
Purton SN5 ....33 F8
Talavera Rd SN4 ......168 E8
Talbot CI
Melksham SN12 ....94 D5
Salisbury SP1 ....146 C4
Talbot Rd SN12 ....105 A7
Talboys (Medieval Hall
House) BA14 ....178 B4
Tallow La 5 SN4 ......163 A6
Tamar CI SN25 ....35 A4
Tamar Rd SN12 ....94 A6
Tamesis Dr GL7 ....4 F7
Tamworth Dr SN5 ....49 A7
Tan La SP8 ....138 A2
Tanarisk CI SN11 ....81 C1
Tangmere CI 13 SN12 .178 B8
Tank La SP5 ....205 B4
Tankard La 16 SN8 ....170 B2
Tankey's CI 5 BA11 ...110 A7
Tanner CI SN15 ....78 F5
Tanners CI
Winterbourne SP4 .....133 A1
Wootton Bassett SN4 ...47 D2
Tanners Field SP4 ....217 D3
Tanners Hill SN16 ......40 C8
Tanners La
Sandleheath SP6 .....210 A1
Shrewton SP3 ....196 E2
Winterbourne SP4 ....133 A1
Tansley Moor SN3 ......51 E3
Tanyard La 5 SP7 ....202 B1
Taramah Gdns 10 SP3 .203 E8
Targetts Mead SP3 ...203 E8
Tarka CI SN25 ....34 F7
Tarragon CI SN2 ....34 C4
Tarrant's Hill 24 RG17 .177 B7
Tarters The SN16 ....40 D8
Tascroft BA12 ....116 B5
Tasker CI SN13 ....84 E8
Taskers La SN8 ....183 D8
Tattershall SN5 ....49 C3
Taunton CI 2 SN14 ....77 F5
Taunton St SN1 ....50 A6
Tavinor Dr SN15 ....78 E4
Tavistock Rd SN3 ....51 B5
Tawny Owl CI SN3 ......51 C8
Taylor Cres SN3 ....36 A4
Taylors Gn SN8 ....174 A7
Taylors La SN4 ....168 B1
Taylors View BA14 ....101 D1
Teal Ave SN15 ....60 A1
Teal CI BA13 ....109 B4
Tealgate RG17 ....177 B8
Tealsbrook SN3 ....51 D7
Teapot St SN4 ....201 E8
Teasel CI 28 SP11 .....192 A5
Teasels The BA12 .....116 F6
Technical Coll BA12 ...117 A7
Tedder Ave SN13 ....84 A8
Tees CI SN25 ....35 A4
Teeswater CI SN5 ....49 A6
Teffont Field Bldgs★
SP3 ....201 D4
Teffont Manor★ SP3 ..201 D2
Telford Rd SP2 ....151 E8
Tellcroft CI SN13 ....84 F8
Tellings Orch SN16 .....16 D3
Tempest Rd 9 SP4 ....217 D3
Templar's Firs SN4 .....61 E8
Temple St SN1 ....50 C5
Ten Acres SP7 ....202 C2
Tenby St SN1 ....50 F3
Tennis Cnr SN2 ....107 D2
Tennyson CI BA12 .....116 E6
Tennyson Rd SN4 ....47 F3
Tennyson St SN1 ....50 B5
Tenzing Gdns SN25 .....35 C3
Tern CI SN11 ....81 D2
Terncliff SN3 ....51 D7
Tetbury Hill SN16 ......27 F6
Tetbury La SN16 ....14 D6
Tetbury Rd SN16 ....25 D2
Tethering Dro SP6 ....211 C6
Tewkesbury Way
Lydiard Millicent SN5 ...48 E7
Swindon SN5 ....49 A6
Thackeray CI SN4 ......51 D4
Thackeray Cres SN12 ...94 B4
Thames Ave SN25 ....34 E5
Thames CI BA12 ....117 A5
Thames Cres SN12 .....94 A6
Thames La SN6 ....19 A3
Thames St GL7 ....2 C3
Thames View SN6 ....17 F8
Thamesdown Dr
Haydon Wick SN2 ......34 C4
Swindon SN25 ....35 A7
Theobald St SN1 ....50 B6
Thestfield Dr BA14 ...101 D4
Thetford Way SN25 .....34 C5

Thicketts Rd SN8 .....169 C1
Thickwood La SN14 .....75 C6
Thirsk CI SN14 ....78 A5
Thistlebarrow Rd SP1 .146 A4
Thistledown 6 SN4 ...163 A6
Thomas Byron Rd
SN10 ....214 C1
Thomas Ct SN11 ....81 C1
Thomas Hardy Dr 8
SP7 ....202 A3
Thomas Mead SN15 .....78 E5
Thomas St SN2 ....49 F7
Thomas Wyatt Rd
SN10 ....214 B1
Thompson CI SP2 .....151 F5
Thompsons Hill SN16 ...40 C7
Thomson Way SN8 ....213 B2
Thornbank SN12 ....94 A3
Thornbridge Ave SN3 ...51 A4
Thornbury Rd BA13 ...108 F4
Thorne CI SP5 ....150 F1
Thorne Rd
2 Netheravon SP4 ...190 A4
Swindon SN3 ....51 C4
Thorneydown Rd SP4 .133 E1
Thornford Dr SN5 ......49 C5
Thornhill Dr SN25 ......35 A8
Thornhill Rd BA12 ....116 D5
Thorns The BA13 .....213 D5
Threadgill Way 6 SP9 .199 C8
Three Barrows★ SN8 .164 B3
Three Oak Hill Dr
SN8 ....175 D4
Three Shire Stones★
SN14 ....74 D1
Three Sisters Rd 1
SN4 ....163 B6
Threshel CI SN5 ....34 E4
Thruxton Motor Racing
Circuit★ SP11 ....192 C1
Thurlestone Rd SN3 ....50 E5
Thurlow CI 10 SP4 ....217 E3
Tibb's Mdw SP11 .....192 D8
Tiberius Rd 24 SP10 .193 E2
Tidcombe (Long Barrow)★
SN8 ....184 D4
Tidling Cnr SN16 ....16 C5
Tidworth CI 3 SN1 .....49 F4
Tidworth Coll SP9 ....216 D6
Tidworth Golf Club
SP9 ....216 A4
Tidworth Leisure Ctr
SP9 ....216 D6
Tidworth Oval★ SP9 .216 C5
Tidworth Rd
Bulford SP4 ....199 A7
Collingbourne Ducis
SN8 ....191 D7
Ludgershall SP11 ....191 F5
Milston SP4 ....191 B1
Porton SP4 ....133 C2
Tile Hill BA10 ....122 A5
Tilley's La SN3 ....36 A2
Timandra CI 1 SN25 ...35 A6
Timber St SN15 ....78 E7
Timberley La SN8 .....211 E7
Timbrell St BA14 .....101 D1
Timor Rd BA13 ....108 E2
Tin Pit SN8 ....213 E4
Tinhead Rd BA13 .....186 C8
Tinings The SN15 ....79 A8
Tinkers Field SN4 ......47 D2
Tinkers Mead SN9 ....215 D4
Tinneys CI SP5 ....211 A4
Tintagel CI
3 Andover SP10 .....193 E2
Swindon SN5 ....49 B4
Tintern Rd SN10 .....214 B1
Tisbury & District Sports Ctr
SP3 ....203 D8
Tisbury CI 1 SN2 ......35 C5
Tisbury Rd SP3 ....204 D8
Tisbury Row SP3 .....203 E8
Tisbury St SP3 ....203 E7
Tismeads Cres SN1 .....50 C2
Titan Barrow BA1 ......82 C2
Titchfield CI 5 SN5 ....48 F5
Tithe Barn Cres SN1 ...49 F3
Tittymouse La SP11 ...192 F1
Tiverton Rd SN2 ....35 C1
Tobruk CI 5 SP11 ....193 E4
Tobruk Rd SP11 ......191 F3
Tobys CI 25 SP7 .....202 C2
Tockenham Cnr SN4 ...60 D6
Toghill Cres SN13 ......76 B1
Tokes La SP7 ....202 E6
Toll Down Way SN14 ...53 A4
Tollard CI SN3 ....51 C6
Tollgate CI SP4 ....217 A5
Tollgate Pk SP7 ......202 C3
Tollgate Rd
Andover SP10 ....193 C1
Salisbury SP1 ....152 B8
Tombs Rd SP4 ....198 A6
Toothill Inf Sch SN5 ...49 C4
Top La
Atworth/Whitley SN12 ...85 C1
Stourton with Gasper
BA12 ....137 D7
Top Rd GL7 ....10 D7
Top St SN15 ....44 A2
Toppers CI SN25 ....35 A3
Tormarton Rd
Acton Turville GL9 .....52 E6
Marshfield SN14 ....66 A2
Tornio CI SN10 ......214 D4
Torr CI SN14 ....70 B2
Torridge CI SN25 ......34 F4

Tottenham Ho★ SN8 .175 F2
Tottenham Pk★ SN8 .175 F3
Totterdown CI 3 SN3 ..51 E7
Totts La SN14 ....75 B3
Touchorne La SP3 ....141 A4
Tournament Rd SP2 ..145 C3
Tout Hill SP7 ....202 B2
Tovey Rd SN2 ....35 B2
Tow Barrow (Long Barrow)★
SN8 ....184 B4
Towcester CI SN14 .....77 F5
Towcester PI 1 SN14 ..77 F5
Towcester Rd
North Bradley BA14 ..105 E4
Swindon SN3 ....51 C8
Towell Rd 5 SP4 .....198 A6
Tower CI Andover SP10 .193 C2
Trowbridge BA14 .....105 A7
Tower Hill
Dilton Marsh BA13 ....112 D7
Iwerne Minster DT11 .206 A1
Tower Mews SP1 .....146 B2
Tower Rd
Melksham SN12 ....94 C5
Stourton with Gasper
BA10 ....122 F3
Swindon SN5 ....34 B2
Tower View SN10 ......96 C3
Town Bridge
Bradford-on-Avon
BA15 ....100 C6
Town CI SN14 ....69 F8
Town Farm PI SP5 ....208 B4
Town Mill SN8 ....213 D2
Town Path SP2 ....151 E7
Townfield 10 SN8 ....170 B2
Townsend
Chitterne BA12 ....195 D7
Pitton & Farley SP5 ..148 C4
Townsend CI BA12 ...138 F5
Townsend La SP6 ....209 A6
Townsend PI SN14 .....77 F8
Towpath BA14 ....101 D4
Tracy CI SN25 ....35 A6
Trafalgar Ho★ SP2 ..159 D4
Trajan Rd SN3 ....36 C1
Tregantle Wlk SN3 .....51 C6
Tregoze Prim Sch SN5 ..49 A6
Tregoze Way SN5 ......48 F6
Trenchard Ave
Box SN13 ....84 A8
Calne Without SN11 ...81 F1
4 Corsham SN13 ....76 B1
Winterbourne SP4 ....133 C2
Trenchard Rd
Lyneham SN15 ....60 A1
Stanton Fitzwarren SN6 ..22 B2
Trent Cres SN12 ....94 A6
Trent Rd SN25 ....35 A4
Trentham CI SN3 ....51 A4
Trevithick CI 5 BA11 .110 C6
Triangle The SP5 .....161 D4
Trimm's Dro SP6 .....211 A4
Trimnells SN14 ....75 B3
Trinity CE Sch GL7 ....53 A6
Trinity CI SN3 ....51 A3
Trinity Pk SN11 ....81 C1
Trinity Rd SP3 ....196 F7
Trinity Rise SP11 ....193 A2
Trinity St SP1 ....152 B8
Tropenell CI 2 SN13 ...76 E1
Tropical Bird Gdns★
BA11 ....103 D2
Trout La SN13 ....84 D7
Trow La Brinkworth SN15 ..59 F8
Maiden Bradley with Yarnfield
BA12 ....118 E4
Trowbridge Com Hospl
BA14 ....101 D2
Trowbridge Mus★
BA14 ....105 D8
Trowbridge Parochial Jun
Sch BA14 ....101 D2
Trowbridge Rd
Bradford-on-Avon BA15 .100 E5
Bratton BA13 ....186 A8
Seend SN12 ....178 C2
Trowbridge BA14 ....102 A2
Westbury BA13 ......109 B5
Trowbridge Sta BA14 .105 C8
Trowle BA14 ....101 A2
Truman CI SN3 ....51 C4
Truro Wlk SN14 ....77 F6
Tryhorn Dr SP1 ......146 C5
Tryon CI SN3 ....51 D2
Tubbs Farm CI 6 RG17 .165 A1
Tucker CI 6 SP4 .....217 C2
Tuckers La SN4 ....163 D6
Tuckwell Rd GL7 ......10 E6
Tudor CI SN15 ....79 A4
Tudor Cres SN3 ....36 B1
Tudor Dr BA14 ....101 E4
Tudor Wlk SN3 ....50 F6
Tugela Rd SN15 ....70 E1
Tuggy's La SN4 ....82 E1
Tulip Tree CI SN2 ......35 C2
Tulse Hill Zeale BA12 .138 A4
Zennor BA12 ....137 F3
Tumlins SN10 ....180 E8
Tunball La SN8 ....184 A4
Tuners La SN16 ....14 E6
Tunnel Hill SP5 ......153 C2
Tupman Rd SN13 ....76 B2
Turf Ho La SN11 ....72 D1
Turin Ct 17 SP10 ....193 C2
Turl St SN1 ....50 C6
Turnball SN4 ....65 C4
Turnberry CI SN15 .....78 F5

Turner CI 2 SP2 ......151 E7
Turner St SN1 ....50 A5
Turnham Gn SN5 ....49 A4
Turnpike 4 SN8 ....170 A6
Turnpike Rd
Blunsdon St Andrew SN26 ..35 C8
Highworth SN6 ....23 A6
Turnpike The SP3 ....202 D8
Turpin Way SN14 ......77 F7
Tutton Hill SN14 ....75 B3
Twatley Cotts SN16 ...27 C4
Tweed CI SN25 ....34 F4
Twickenham Way SN11 ..70 E1
Twineham Gdns SP5 ..153 F2
Twyford CI SN3 ....51 A6
Twynham CI SP5 .....211 A7
Twynnoy CI SN16 ......28 A5
Tyburn CI SN5 ....49 B5
Tydeman St SN2 ....35 D1
Tye Gdns SN5 ....48 F5
Tylers CI SP2 ....151 D7
Tyndales Mdw SP3 ...201 E7
Tyneham Rd SN3 ....51 B6
Tyning CI 1 BA14 ....105 A7
Tyning La 9 BA13 ...186 B7
Tyning Pk SN11 ....81 C1
Tyning Rd
Bathampton BA2 ....82 A2
Winsley BA15 ....99 E7
Tyning The BA2 ....99 B4
Tynings The
Biddestone SN14 ......76 D7
Westbury BA13 ....108 F2
Tynings Way BA15 .....99 F3
Tyrone Ave SP4 ......198 E2
Tytherington Rd BA12 .194 C5
Tytherley Rd SP5 ....149 E6

U

Ullswater CI SN3 ....51 E3
Umbers Hill 2 SP7 ...202 B1
Underdown CI 12 SN4 .163 A6
Underhill Mere BA12 .138 F5
Pen Selwood BA9 .....137 B2
Underwood Dr SP4 ...217 D2
Union Rd
Chippenham SN15 .....78 D8
Tisbury SP3 ....203 E7
Union Row SN1 ....50 D4
Union St Melksham SN12 .94 A4
Ramsbury SN8 ....170 B2
Swindon SN1 ....50 C5
Trowbridge BA14 ....101 D1
Unity St SN14 ....78 C7
Univ of Bath in Swindon
SN3 ....51 A7
Up St BA12 ....194 E4
Upavon Airfield SN9 .182 B1
Upavon Prim Sch SN9 .182 A1
Upcott SN6 ....8 C4
Upfield SN3 ....51 D3
Upham Rd SN3 ....50 E5
Upham Village★ SN8 .169 C8
Upland Rise SP3 ......109 B2
Uplands 28 RG17 ....177 B7
Uplands CI BA2 ....98 F7
Uplands The BA12 ...117 C7
Upnor CI SP11 ....191 F4
Upper Avon Sch SP4 .198 C2
Upper Backway SP3 ..196 F5
Upper Broad St BA14 .101 C1
Upper Church Fields
SN8 ....213 E1
Upper Dro SP10 ......193 C1
Upper Eddington
RG17 ....177 C8
Upper Folly SP7 .....144 B1
Upper Garston La 8
BA13 ....186 B7
Upper Isbury SN8 ....213 E2
Upper La SN13 ....84 D7
Upper Lambourn Rd
RG17 ....165 A2
Upper Ley SN13 ....83 D5
Upper Marsh La BA12 .117 A6
Upper Marsh Rd BA12 .117 A6
Upper N Rd SP5 .....207 C5
Upper Noremarsh SN4 ..47 F1
Upper Pavenhill SN5 ...32 F4
Upper Potley SN13 ....84 C7
Upper Regents Pk
BA15 ....100 D6
Upper Seagry Sch
SN15 ....57 D6
Upper St SP2 ....151 D7
Upper St George BA12 .139 B5
Uppington La SP3 ...129 E8
Upton CI 5 BA12 ....116 E7
Upton Great Barrow★
BA12 ....194 F5
Urchfont Manor Coll
SN10 ....180 B3
Urchfont Prim Sch
SN10 ....180 B4
Utah CI SN1 ....49 F4
Utterson View SN15 ...78 C7
Uxbridge Rd SN5 .....49 A3

V

Vale Leaze SN15 ....44 C5
Vale Rd Pewsey SN9 .215 B5

Vale Rd *continued*
Redlynch SP5 ....**211** C7
Vale View SN14 ....**47** D1
Vale View Rd SP2 ....**130** B2
Valencia Ct SN12 ....**178** B8
Valentia Ct SN12 ....**178** B8
Valiant Cl 9 SN12 ....**178** B8
Valletta Gdns SN14 ....**56** B5
Valley Cl SP5 ....**211** C7
Valley Rd SN13 ....**76** C1
Valley The SP2 ....**145** C5
Valley View SN11 ....**81** A2
Valley Way SN14 ....**75** C6
Valleyside SN1 ....**50** A4
Van Diemen's Cl SN8 ....**213** E2
Vanbrugh Gate SN3 ....**50** F1
Vanessa Ave SP1 ....**146** D1
Vastern Wharf SN4 ....**61** A7
Vasterne Cl SN5 ....**33** B5
Velley Hill
Corsham SN13 ....**85** C5
Corsham SN13 ....**85** C5
Venice Ct SP11 ....**193** F2
Venn The 11 SP7 ....**202** C2
Ventnor Cl SN2 ....**34** E4
Ventry Cl 3 SN12 ....**146** B2
Ventry The 4 SP1 ....**146** B2
Verden Way 19 SP10 ....**193** D2
Verney Cl SN3 ....**51** D6
Vernham Dean Sch
SP11 ....**185** C3
Vernon Cl 2 SP4 ....**217** E3
Verona Rd SP1 ....**145** F4
Verulam Cl SN3 ....**51** D8
Verwood Cl SN3 ....**51** B4
Vespasian Cl SN3 ....**51** C8
Vespasian Rd 19 SP10 ....**193** E2
Vicarage Cl Calne SN11 ....**81** B3
Marlborough SN8 ....**213** E3
Vicarage Cotts SN15 ....**57** F6
Vicarage Gdns 3 SP4 ....**190** A3
Vicarage La
Charlton SN16 ....**29** B7
Colerne SN14 ....**75** C3
Easterton SN10 ....**179** F2
Hankerton SN16 ....**15** B1
Highworth SN6 ....**23** A6
Steeple Ashton BA14 ....**178** A3
Upavon SN9 ....**181** F2
Vicarage Pk 1 SP5 ....**211** C7
Vicarage Rd
Redlynch SP5 ....**211** E7
Swindon SN2 ....**34** F1
Tisbury SP3 ....**203** E8
Vicarage St BA12 ....**116** F7
Vice La SO51 ....**212** E2
Victoria Cl
Lyneham SN11 ....**73** E8
Wilton SP2 ....**144** C4
Victoria Cross Rd SN4 ....**63** F7
Victoria Ct SP1 ....**146** A3
Victoria Dr SN15 ....**60** B1
Victoria Gdns
14 Sandleheath SP6 ....**210** C1
Trowbridge BA14 ....**101** B3
Victoria Hospl SN1 ....**50** B4
Victoria Pk SN10 ....**187** B8
Victoria Rd
Devizes SN10 ....**214** B4
Frome BA11 ....**110** A4
Salisbury SP1 ....**146** A2
Sandleheath SP6 ....**210** C1
Swindon SN1 ....**50** C5
Trowbridge BA14 ....**101** E3
Warminster BA12 ....**116** C6
Wilton SP2 ....**144** C3
Victoria St 21 SP7 ....**202** C2
Victoria Terr SN11 ....**81** B3
Victory Rd BA13 ....**108** C6
Viking Cl SN25 ....**34** F7
Viking Way
Andover SP10 ....**193** E2
Salisbury SP2 ....**152** B5
Vilett St SN1 ....**50** B6
Village Mus The Castle
Combe★ SN14 ....**68** A7
Village St SN8 ....**173** D1
Villiers Cl
Chippenham SN15 ....**78** F7
Lydiard Tregoze SN5 ....**48** F7
Vimoutiers Ct 16 SP6 ....**210** D1
Vimy Cres 8 SP4 ....**198** E6
Vincent Cl SN12 ....**94** C4
Vincients Rd SN14 ....**69** F1
Viner's La GL9 ....**53** B5
Virginia Cl 1 SP4 ....**217** E3
Virginia Dr BA12 ....**116** E2
Viscount Way SN3 ....**36** C6
Vockins Cl SP9 ....**216** C8
Volpe Cl SN5 ....**48** F4
Volta Rd SN1 ....**50** C6
Vorda Rd SN6 ....**23** A7
Vowley View SN4 ....**47** F1

W

Wade Hill SN6 ....**22** F5
Wadswick La SN13 ....**84** B3
Wagtail Cl SN3 ....**51** C8
Waiblingen Way SN10 ....**214** A4
Wain-a-Long Rd SP1 ....**146** C1
Wains Way SP4 ....**190** A3
Wainwright Cl 4 SN3 ....**51** D4
Wainwright Dr 5 BA11 ....**110** C7

Waite Meads Cl SN5 ....**33** C4
Wakefield Cl
Kempsford GL7 ....**10** E6
Swindon SN5 ....**49** A4
Walbury Hill (Fort)★
RG17 ....**185** F8
Walcot Rd SN3 ....**50** E5
Walden Lodge Cl
SN10 ....**214** B2
Waldron Cl 3 SN3 ....**51** C4
Waleran Cl SP5 ....**153** E2
Walker Rd BA11 ....**110** A3
Walker's La 3 RG17 ....**165** A2
Wallbridge BA11 ....**110** A4
Wallbridge Ave 2 BA11 ....**110** A4
Wallbridge Gdns 1
BA11 ....**110** A4
Wallingford Cl SN5 ....**49** C3
Wallingtons Rd RG17 ....**177** F4
Wallis Dr SN25 ....**35** A8
Wallsworth Rd 4 SN3 ....**51** A4
Walmesley Chase
BA14 ....**102** A1
Walnut Cl
3 Netheravon SP4 ....**190** A4
Pewsey SN9 ....**215** D5
Rowde SN10 ....**96** D1
Sutton Veny BA12 ....**121** F8
Walnut Dr SN14 ....**74** F6
Walnut Gr BA14 ....**105** B6
Walnut Tree Gdns SN5 ....**48** D8
Walnut Trees Hill SN6 ....**164** A8
Walnut Wlk 1 BA11 ....**110** B7
Walronds Cl SN8 ....**170** C8
Walsingham Rd SN3 ....**50** F6
Walter Cl SN5 ....**49** A6
Walter Powell Sch
SN5 ....**44** B2
Walter Sutton Cl SN11 ....**80** F3
Walton Cl 5 SN3 ....**50** F4
Walwayne Field SN2 ....**36** A5
Wanborough Rd
Swindon SN3 ....**36** C1
Wanborough SN4 ....**51** F6
Wanborough Sch SN4 ....**163** A6
Wansdyke★ SN11 ....**172** C5
Wansdyke Dr SN14 ....**81** A3
Wansdyke Rd SN8 ....**176** B4
Wansdyke Sch SN14 ....**214** B1
Wanshot Cl SN4 ....**64** C5
Wantage Rd RG17 ....**165** B2
War Meml Ave 13 RG17 ....**177** B6
Waram Cl RG17 ....**177** C8
Warbeck Gate 11 SN5 ....**48** F5
Warbler Cl 1 BA14 ....**105** B8
Wardley Cl SN3 ....**51** A4
Wardour Cl SN3 ....**50** E3
Wardour Pl 4 SN12 ....**94** A2
Wardour Prim Sch
SP3 ....**203** C6
Wardour Rd 4 SN14 ....**78** A6
Wareham Cl SN5 ....**49** B5
Warleigh Dr BA1 ....**82** A3
Warleigh La BA1 ....**82** B1
Warmer's Inn La SN16 ....**27** D8
Warminster Ave 2 SN2 ....**35** C5
Warminster Com Hospl
BA12 ....**117** A7
Warminster Prep Sch
BA12 ....**116** F6
Warminster Rd
Claverton BA2 ....**90** B4
Frome BA11 ....**110** B4
Westbury BA13 ....**108** F1
Wilton SP2 ....**144** D5
Warminster Sch BA12 ....**116** F7
Warminster Sports Ctr
BA12 ....**117** D6
Warminster Sta BA12 ....**117** B7
Warneage Gn 2 SN4 ....**163** A5
Warneford Cl 4 SN5 ....**49** D4
Warner Cl 2 SN3 ....**36** B3
Warren Cres SN11 ....**81** C4
Warrens La SP5 ....**159** A4
Warwick Cl
Chippenham SN14 ....**77** F5
Salisbury SP1 ....**145** F3
Warwick Cres SN12 ....**94** B3
Warwick Rd SN1 ....**50** C5
Washbourne Rd SN4 ....**47** E1
Washern Cl SP2 ....**144** C1
Washers Pit★ DT11 ....**206** D3
Washington Rd BA13 ....**108** C6
Washmeres SN14 ....**75** B2
Washpool La GL7 ....**10** E8
Wason Rd 5 SP4 ....**197** E6
Wastfield SN13 ....**84** F8
Water Ditchampton
SP2 ....**144** C4
Water Field SN4 ....**33** A3
Water Furlongs 2 SN6 ....**19** D7
Water La
Castle Combe SN14 ....**68** A7
Enford SN9 ....**190** B6
Horningsham BA12 ....**119** A8
Water St
Berwick St John SP7 ....**203** E1
Durrington/Bulford SP4 ....**217** D8
Mere BA12 ....**139** B5
Upton Lovell BA12 ....**194** E3
Watercrook Mews 2
SN5 ....**49** D5
Waterdown Cl SN2 ....**34** C4
Watergate La SP4 ....**217** C7
Watergates SN14 ....**75** C3
Waterhouse La BA2 ....**98** F8
Waterloo Rd SP1 ....**152** C7
Watermead SN3 ....**36** C1

Watermeadow La
BA12 ....**195** C1
Watermint Way SN11 ....**80** F4
Waters Bank Rd SN13 ....**84** B8
Waters Edge SN15 ....**78** E5
Waters Rd SP1 ....**146** A4
Watersmeet Rd SP2 ....**152** A6
Waterworks Rd BA14 ....**105** B7
Watery La
Donhead St Mary SP7 ....**203** A3
Shaftesbury SP7 ....**202** C1
Sutton Veny BA12 ....**117** F4
Watling Cl SN2 ....**49** E6
Watson Rd SP4 ....**197** E7
Watt Cl 4 SP10 ....**193** C1
Watt Rd SP2 ....**151** D8
Watt's Way 22 SN10 ....**179** F1
Watts La SN14 ....**41** F1
Wavell Rd
Salisbury SP2 ....**152** A6
Swindon SN2 ....**35** B2
Tidworth SP9 ....**216** B8
Waverley Cl
7 Fordingbridge SP6 ....**210** D2
Frome BA11 ....**110** C6
Waverley Gdns SN12 ....**94** A3
Waverley Rd
Fordingbridge SP6 ....**210** D2
Swindon SN3 ....**36** C1
Waylands Cricklade SN6 ....**19** E7
Devizes SN10 ....**214** D3
Wayne Cl SN25 ....**35** A5
Wayside Cl
Frome BA11 ....**110** C6
Kington Langley SN15 ....**70** E7
Swindon SN2 ....**49** E7
Weaveland Rd 2 SP3 ....**203** E8
Weavern Ct SN14 ....**78** A7
Weavern La SN13 ....**76** A5
Weavers Crofts SN12 ....**94** A5
Weavers Dr BA14 ....**105** D7
Weavers La RG17 ....**177** E3
Weavers Mead SN10 ....**179** C1
Weavers The SN3 ....**50** D4
Webb Cl SN15 ....**78** E5
Webbers Ct BA14 ....**105** A6
Webbington Rd SN15 ....**78** E5
Webbs Ct SN15 ....**60** A3
Webbs Way
Burbage SN8 ....**183** D8
Malmesbury SN16 ....**28** A5
Webbs Wood SN5 ....**34** A2
Wedgewood Cl SN2 ....**50** A7
Wedmore Ave SN15 ....**70** C6
Wedmore Cl BA11 ....**110** C7
Weedon Rd SN3 ....**51** B8
Weeke Cl 1 SP5 ....**210** F8
Weir Hayes Ave 7 SN13 ....**76** B1
Weir La SN14 ....**74** A8
Weir The BA13 ....**186** C8
Weirside Ave SN4 ....**64** B6
Welcombe Ave SN1 ....**51** A5
Welford Rd SN3 ....**51** C8
Well Cl SN4 ....**65** D4
Well House Cl SP6 ....**210** B6
Well La Godshill SP6 ....**211** A1
Hawkesbury GL9 ....**38** E5
4 Shaftesbury SP7 ....**202** B2
Welle Sley Cl 18 SN12 ....**178** B8
Weller Rd SP2 ....**144** C4
Wellhead Dro BA13 ....**109** A1
Wellhead La BA13 ....**109** A1
Wellington Dr
Bishops Cannings SN10 ....**214** F7
Bower Hill SN12 ....**94** C1
Wellington Pl SN14 ....**55** F8
Wellington Rd 5 SP4 ....**198** F7
Wellington Sq SN12 ....**94** C1
Wellington St SN1 ....**50** C7
Wellington Way SP2 ....**145** D3
Wellow Dr BA11 ....**110** C7
Wellow La BA2 ....**98** D1
Wellow Wood Rd
SO51 ....**212** F8
Wells Cl
Chippenham SN14 ....**78** A5
Durrington SP4 ....**198** A6
Wells Rd SP4 ....**198** A6
Wells St SN1 ....**50** C6
Welsh Way GL7 ....**1** D2
Welton Rd SN5 ....**49** D6
Wembley St SN2 ....**49** F8
Wenhill Hts SN11 ....**81** B2
Wenhill La SN11 ....**81** A1
Wensleydale Cl SN5 ....**49** B6
Wentworth Cl SN15 ....**78** F7
Wentworth Pk 1 SN5 ....**49** A4
Were Cl 3 BA12 ....**116** E7
Werg SN8 ....**175** B8
Wesley Cl BA14 ....**104** E2
Wesley La BA14 ....**104** E2
Wesley Rd BA14 ....**105** C7
Wesley St SN1 ....**50** C4
Wessex Cl Calne SN11 ....**81** C3
2 Hungerford RG17 ....**177** B7
Melksham SN12 ....**94** B3
Semington BA14 ....**102** E5
Wessex Pl 23 RG17 ....**177** B7
Wessex Rd
Chippenham SN14 ....**78** B5
Salisbury SP1 ....**146** C1
Wilton SP2 ....**144** C1
Wessex Way SN6 ....**23** B7
Wessex Wlk BA13 ....**109** A4
Wessington Ave SN11 ....**81** C1
Wessington Pk SN11 ....**81** C1
West Ashton Prim Sch
BA14 ....**106** B4

West Ashton Rd BA14 ....**105** E8
West Bourton Rd SP8 ....**137** D1
West Cepen Way
Chippenham SN14 ....**70** D3
Chippenham Without
SN14 ....**77** F5
West Ditch La BA14 ....**106** E4
West End
Bishops Cannings SN10 ....**172** B3
Melksham SN12 ....**94** A3
Westbury BA13 ....**109** A3
West End La
Bishopstone SN6 ....**163** E6
Donhead St Andrew SP7 ....**203** B3
West End Rd SN1 ....**36** A1
West Ennox La SN13 ....**84** A6
West Hay Gr GL7 ....**4** F7
West Highland Rd
SN25 ....**34** F7
West Hill
Broad Blunsdon SN26 ....**21** B8
Melksham Without SN12 ....**85** B1
**West Kennett (Long
Barrow)★** SN8 ....**173** C6
West La Kemble GL7 ....**4** F7
Melbury Abbas SP7 ....**206** A2
West Manton SN8 ....**174** C7
West Mill La SN6 ....**8** C1
West Par BA12 ....**116** F6
West Park★ SP6 ....**210** A3
West Pk SP11 ....**192** E3
West Pk Dr SP4 ....**209** F3
West Pk La SP6 ....**209** F3
West Pk Rd SN13 ....**76** E1
West Portway SP10 ....**193** C1
West St Aldbourne SN8 ....**170** A6
Barford St Martin SP3 ....**143** A4
Castle Combe SN14 ....**68** A7
22 Fordingbridge SP6 ....**210** D1
Great Somerford SN15 ....**43** F2
Great Wishford SP2 ....**129** F4
Lacock SN15 ....**86** D5
Malmesbury SN16 ....**27** F3
Salisbury SP2 ....**145** F1
Trowbridge BA14 ....**105** C8
Warminster BA12 ....**116** E6
Wilton SP2 ....**144** C3
West View SN8 ....**191** A8
West View Cres SN10 ....**214** A3
West View Rd BA1 ....**82** A3
West Way A2 ....**2** C5
West Wilts Golf Club
BA12 ....**113** B1
West Wilts Trading Est
BA13 ....**108** D7
West Wlk SP1 ....**152** A7
Westbourne Cl SP1 ....**152** C8
Westbourne Gdns 6
BA14 ....**105** B8
Westbourne Rd
Trowbridge BA14 ....**105** B8
Westbury BA13 ....**109** A3
Westbrook Cl
Chippenham SN14 ....**78** A7
14 Hungerford RG17 ....**177** B7
Westbrook Gn SN15 ....**95** E8
Westbrook Rd
Bromham SN15 ....**88** A1
Swindon SN2 ....**35** A1
Westbury Com Hospl
BA13 ....**109** A2
Westbury Infs Sch
BA13 ....**108** F3
Westbury Jun Sch
BA13 ....**108** E3
Westbury Leigh BA13 ....**108** E1
Westbury Leigh Prim Sch
BA13 ....**108** E1
Westbury Pk SN4 ....**47** D1
Westbury Rd
Bratton BA13 ....**186** A2
Cheverell Magna SN10 ....**179** C1
Heywood BA14 ....**109** A8
North Bradley BA14 ....**105** E3
Swindon SN2 ....**35** B5
Warminster BA12 ....**113** A2
Westbury Sta BA13 ....**108** E5
Westbury View SN12 ....**94** C4
Westbury White Horse★
BA13 ....**109** F3
Westcombe La BA12 ....**195** E1
Westcott Pl SN1 ....**50** A5
Westcott St SN1 ....**50** A5
Westcroft SN14 ....**78** A5
Westcroft St BA14 ....**101** C1
Westerham Wlk SN11 ....**81** C2
Westerleigh Cl SN14 ....**78** B6
Western Downland Prim Sch
SP6 ....**209** F2
Western Downland Sch
SP6 ....**210** A5
Western St SN1 ....**50** C5
Western Way
Melksham SN12 ....**93** F3
Salisbury SP2 ....**145** B3
Westfield BA15 ....**100** B7
Westfield Chase 13 SN8 ....**170** A6
Westfield Cl
15 Durrington/Bulford
SP4 ....**198** B7
Laverstock SP1 ....**146** D4
Trowbridge BA14 ....**105** A6
Westfield Est BA12 ....**137** F4
Westfield Rd BA14 ....**105** A7
Westfield Way SN2 ....**34** D4
Westgrove 17 SP6 ....**210** D1
Westhill Cl SN6 ....**22** F5

Westlake Pl SN15 ....**57** D
Westland Cl 3 SP4 ....**217** E
Westlands 2 BA12 ....**194** C
Westlands La SN12 ....**85** F
Westlea Dr SN5 ....**49** C
Westlea CP Sch SN5 ....**49** C
Westlecot Rd SN1 ....**50** B
Westmead Cres BA14 ....**105** E
Westmead Dr SN5 ....**49** C
Westmead Ind Est SN5 ....**49** C
Westmead La SN5 ....**78** D
Westminster Cl 1 SP7 ....**202** C
Westminster Gdns
SN14 ....**78** D
Westminster Meml Hospl
SP7 ....**202** B
Westminster Rd
Salisbury SP2 ....**145** F
Swindon SN5 ....**49** C
Westmorland Rd SN1 ....**50** D
Weston Ct 1 SP11 ....**193** E
Weston La SP5 ....**149** B
Westonbirt Arboretum★
GL8 ....**25** B
Westonbirt Sch GL8 ....**25** B
Westrop SN6 ....**23** A
Westrop Sch SN6 ....**22** F
Westside SN4 ....**199** A
Westside Cl SP4 ....**146** C
Westview Orch BA2 ....**99** B
Westwells SN13 ....**84** C
Westwells Rd SN13 ....**84** B
Westwood Manor House★
BA15 ....**100** A
Westwood
Corsham SN13 ....**84** B
Salisbury SP2 ....**145** B
Swindon SN2 ....**35** C
Wingfield BA15 ....**100** C
Westwood St Thomas Sch
SP2 ....**145** A
Westwood With Iford Sch
BA15 ....**99** F
Westwoods BA1 ....**82** B
Wet La BA12 ....**139** C
Wet Pits La SN8 ....**168** E
Wetherby Cl 1 SN14 ....**189** F
Wexland Ave SP4 ....**189** F
Wey Cl SN25 ....**35** A
Weyhill Cl SN3 ....**51** B
Weyhill Gdns 7 SP11 ....**192** F
Weyhill Rd SP11 ....**193** A
Weymouth St BA12 ....**117** A
Whaddon La
Hilperton BA14 ....**102** B
Trowbridge BA14 ....**102** A
Whalley Cres SN4 ....**63** F
Wharf Ct SN12 ....**94** B
Wharf Ctr The★ SN10 ....**214** C
Wharf La Kempsford GL7 ....**10** C
Lechlade GL7 ....**2** D
Wharf Rd SN4 ....**47** C
Wharf St SN10 ....**214** A
Wharf The SN13 ....**83** D
Wharfings The GL7 ....**10** D
Whatcombe Brow
SP3 ....**196** D
Whatleys Cl SN10 ....**179** A
Whatleys Orch SN6 ....**163** E
Wheatlands SN25 ....**34** E
Wheatstone Rd SN3 ....**51** E
Wheeler Ave SN2 ....**35** D
Wheelwright's Cl SP5 ....**208** A
Whelford Rd GL7 ....**10** D
Whilestone Way SN3 ....**51** E
Whinyates Rd 2 SP4 ....**197** E
Whistley Rd SN10 ....**179** C
Whitbourne Ave SN3 ....**50** F
Whitbred Cl 2 SN5 ....**49** B
Whitbred Rd SP2 ....**145** C
Whitby Gr SN2 ....**34** F
Whitchers Mdw SP5 ....**153** D
Whitcombe Cl SN15 ....**73** F
**White Barrow (Long
Barrow)★** SP3 ....**188** B
White Castle SN5 ....**49** C
White Cliff★ BA13 ....**186** B
White Edge Moor SN3 ....**51** D
White Ennox La SN13 ....**83** F
White Farm La SN8 ....**185** C
White Hart La 12 SP7 ....**202** C
White Hill
Bishopstone SN4 ....**163** D
Pitton & Farley SP5 ....**148** C
White Horse Cl BA14 ....**105** D
White Horse Dr 8
BA11 ....**110** C
White Horse Rd
Cricklade SN6 ....**19** D
Winsley BA15 ....**99** F
White Horse Sports Ctr
SN11 ....**81** C
White Horse Way
Calne SN11 ....**81** B
Westbury BA13 ....**109** A
White Lion Pk SN16 ....**27** E
White Pit La SP7 ....**206** B
White Rd Mere BA12 ....**139** B
Savernake SN8 ....**175** A
White Row Hill BA14 ....**105** A
White Sheet Castle★
BA12 ....**124** E
**White Sheet Hill Nature
Reserve★** BA12 ....**124** C
White Sheet La BA12 ....**124** C
White Shute RG17 ....**171** A
White St
Easterton SN10 ....**180** A

White St *continued*
Horningsham BA12 . . . . . .**119** B8
21 Market Lavington SN10 **179** F1
White Way
Broad Town SN4 . . . .**167** A8
Pitton & Farley SP5 . . . . . .**148** C3
White's Hill SN8 . . . .**169** F2
Whitebridge Rd SP1 . .**146** D1
Whitecroft BA13 . . . .**112** C8
Whitefield Cl BA1 . . . .**82** B4
Whitefield Cres SN5 . . . .**34** A1
Whitefriars La SN6 . . . .**6** E3
Whitefriars Rd **1** SP1 .**152** B7
Whitegates SN14 . . . .**68** A8
Whitehead St SN1 . . . .**50** B5
Whiteheads La BA15 . .**100** D7
Whitehill SN4 . . . .**100** D7
Whitehill Cl **11** SN8 . . . .**170** B2
Whitehill La SN4 . . . .**47** B2
Whitehill Way SN5 . . . . . .**48** F3
Whitehorn Cl SN4 . . . .**47** E4
Whitehorn Dr SP5 . . . . . .**212** C5
Whitehouse La GL8 . . . . . .**26** B8
Whitehouse Rd SN2 . . . . . .**50** B8
Whiteland Rise BA13 . .**109** B2
Whitelands Rd SN3 . . . . . .**36** A1
Whitelawn La BA14 . . . .**106** F4
Whitelocks Piece
RG17 . . . .**171** A1
Whiteman St SN1 . . . .**50** C8
Whitemarsh BA12 . . . . . .**139** B4
Whiterow Pk BA14 . . . . .**105** A6
Whites Cnr SN12 . . . .**85** D1
Whitesbury Rd SP5 . . . . .**152** B1
Whiteshoot SP5 . . . .**211** D6
Whiteshoot Hill SP5 . . .**211** D6
Whitestone Rd BA11 . . .**110** B6
Whitfield Cl BA12 . . . . . .**117** C7
Whitgift Cl SN5 . . . .**48** F6
Whitley Golf Club SN12 .**93** E8
Whitley Rd **14** SN8 . . . .**170** A6
Whitlock Rise SP5 . . . . .**205** F5
Whitmarsh Cl **7** SP4 . .**190** A4
Whitmore Cl SN5 . . . .**48** F6
Whitney St SN1 . . . .**50** C5
Whitsbury Rd SP6 . . . . . .**210** D2
Whittington Rd SN5 . . . .**49** C6
Whittle Av SN11 . . . .**166** A1
Whittle Cl SN14 . . . .**78** A7
Whittle Rd
4 Andover SP10 . . . . . .**193** C4
Salisbury SP2 . . . .**145** D1
Whittonditch Rd SN8 . .**170** C2
Whitworth Rd SN25 . . . . .**35** A3
Wichelstok Cl SN1 . . . .**50** C3
Wick Ball Camp ★
SP3 . . . .**201** D3
Wick La Devizes SN10 .**214** A1
Downton SP5 . . . .**210** E8
Lacock SN15 . . . .**85** F4
Manningford SN9 . . . . .**181** F5
Wanborough SN4 . . . . . .**51** F6
Wick Rd SN16 . . . .**16** A8
Wickdown Ave SN25 . . . . .**34** F3
Wicker Hill BA14 . . . .**101** C1
Wickfield SN10 . . . .**214** B2
Wicks Cl SN25 . . . .**34** E5
Wicks Dr SN5 . . . .**78** F5
Wickwater La GL7 . . . .**7** C4
Widbrook Mdw BA14 . . .**105** A8
Widbrook View BA15 . .**100** E5
Widhill La SN26 . . . .**21** A1
Wigmore Ave SN3 . . . .**50** F3
Wilcot Ave SN2 . . . .**35** D5
Wilcot Cl
Amesbury SP4 . . . .**217** D2
Trowbridge BA14 . . . . .**105** C6
Wilcot Rd SN9 . . . .**215** B5
Wilcox Cl SN2 . . . .**35** C2
Wild Acre **9** SN4 . . . . . .**163** A6
Wildern Sq SN3 . . . .**36** A4
Wilderness The SN4 . . .**100** C7
Wildmoorway La GL7 . . . . .**7** B7
Wiley Terr SP2 . . . .**144** D4
Wilkins Cl SN2 . . . .**35** F5
William Cl SP1 . . . .**146** D1
William Rd SN10 . . . .**214** D2
William St 4 Calne SN11 .**81** C4
Swindon SN1 . . . .**50** A5
Williams Gr SN13 . . . .**85** A8
Williamson Cl **3** SP11 .**192** A5
Willis Cl
5 Chippenham SN15 . . .**78** F4
Great Bedwyn SN8 . . . .**176** C3
Willis Way SN5 . . . .**33** B3
Willoughby Cl BA13 . . .**108** E2
Willoughby Rd SP4 . . . .**197** E6
Willow Ave **5** SP6 . . . .**210** D1
Willow Cl
Laverstock SP1 . . . .**146** D2
Melksham SN12 . . . .**94** A3
Willow Cres
Broughton Gifford SN12 . . .**93** A5
Warminster BA12 . . . . .**117** C5
Willow Dr
Devizes SN10 . . . .**214** A5
4 Durrington SP4 . . . .**198** B7
Willow Gr
Chippenham SN15 . . . . . .**70** C6
Trowbridge BA14 . . . . .**105** B5
Westbury BA13 . . . .**108** E3
Willow View BA14 . . . . .**105** C3
Willow View Cl SN16 . . . .**27** F4
Willow Way SP7 . . . .**202** A4
Willow Wlk SN4 . . . .**64** B6
Willowbank SN14 . . . .**70** A2
Willowbrook SN5 . . . .**33** C4
Willowbrook End SN15 . .**57** D2

Willowherb Cl SN25 . . . .**34** E5
Willows Ave SN2 . . . .**35** C3
Willows The Calne SN11 . .**89** E8
Highworth SN6 . . . .**23** A5
Swindon SN5 . . . .**34** A2
Wills Ave SN1 . . . .**50** E8
Wilman Way SP2 . . . .**151** E5
Wilmot Cl SN5 . . . .**48** F6
Wilsford Group (Tumuli) ★
SP4 . . . .**197** D2
Wilsford Rd SN9 . . . .**181** C5
Wilson Rd Larkhill SP4 . .**197** E6
Swindon SN25 . . . .**34** F6
Wilson Sq BA12 . . . .**117** C7
Wilton CE Mid Sch
SP2 . . . .**144** B4
Wilton Dr BA14 . . . .**105** D6
Wilton Fst Sch SP2 . . . .**144** B2
Wilton Ho ★ SP2 . . . . . .**144** D2
Wilton Mus ★ SP2 . . . . .**144** D1
Wilton Pk ★ SP2 . . . . . .**144** D1
Wilton Rd
Barford St Martin SP3 . .**143** C3
East Grafton SN8 . . . . .**184** A7
Quidhampton SP2 . . . . .**144** F3
Wylye BA12 . . . .**201** F8
Wiltshire Ave SN2 . . . . . .**50** A8
Wiltshire Bassett Golf Club
SN4 . . . .**60** F7
Wiltshire Cl
Bulford SP4 . . . .**217** D2
3 Hungerford RG17 . .**177** B7
Wiltshire Coll SN8 . . . . .**105** B6
Wiltshire Cres SN12 . . . .**94** C3
Wiltshire Dr **4** BA14 . .**105** D6
Wiltshire Heritage Mus ★
SN10 . . . .**214** A2
Wiltshire Rd SP2 . . . . . .**151** E6
Wiltshire Way BA15 . . . .**109** A4
Wimpole Cl SN3 . . . .**51** E6
Win Gn View **7** SP7 . . .**202** D2
Winchester Cl
Amesbury SP4 . . . .**217** D2
2 Chippenham SN14 . . .**78** A6
North Bradley BA14 . . .**105** C2
Swindon SN3 . . . .**36** B1
Winchester St SP1 . . . .**146** B1
Wincombe Bsns Pk
SP7 . . . .**202** C3
Wincombe La SP7 . . . . . .**202** D2
Wincombe Pk ★ SP7 . . .**202** D2
Windbrook Mdw SN2 . . .**36** A4
Windermere SN3 . . . .**51** D3
Windermere Rd BA14 . .**101** E2
Windflower Rd SN25 . . . .**34** E5
Winding Way SP2 . . . . . .**145** B3
Windlass Way SN5 . . . . . .**78** E5
Windlesham Rd SP1 . . . .**146** B4
Windmill Cl
3 Aldbourne SN8 . . . .**170** A7
Alderbury SP5 . . . .**153** E2
4 Shaftesbury SP7 . . .**202** C2
**Windmill Hill (Causewayed
Enclosure)** ★ SN4 . . . .**167** A2
Windmill Hill Bsns Pk
SN5 . . . .**48** F3
Windmill Hill CP Sch
SN5 . . . .**49** A3
Windmill La
Hurstbourne Tarrant
SP11 . . . .**193** F8
Winterbourne SP4 . . . .**133** B4
Windmill Piece SN4 . . . . .**65** D4
Windmill Rd GL7 . . . .**4** F8
**Windmill Tump (Long
Barrow)** ★ GL7 . . . .**3** A7
Windrush SN6 . . . .**22** E5
Windrush Rd SN25 . . . . . .**35** A3
Windsor Ave SN12 . . . . . .**94** B3
Windsor Cl
Chippenham SN14 . . . . . .**78** A6
Lydiard Tregoze SN4 . . . .**47** F6
Windsor Cres BA11 . . . .**110** A5
Windsor Dr
Devizes SN10 . . . .**214** D3
1 Trowbridge BA14 . . .**105** B5
Westbury BA13 . . . .**109** B4
Windsor Mews **8** SP4 . .**198** B7
Windsor Rd
Calne Without SN11 . . . .**81** F1
9 Durrington/Bulford
SP4 . . . .**198** B7
North Bradley BA14 . . .**105** C4
9 Salisbury SP2 . . . . .**145** F1
Swindon SN3 . . . .**50** F2
Windsor St **10** SP2 . . . .**145** F1
Windwhistle Cnr SP7 . .**202** E2
Windwhistle La
Alderbury SP5 . . . .**160** B7
Grimstead SP5 . . . .**154** B1
Windwhistle Way SP5 . .**153** F2
Wine St
Bradford-on-Avon BA15 . .**100** C6
Devizes SN10 . . . .**214** B3
Wing Rd SP4 . . . .**198** E6
Wingate Par SN2 . . . .**35** A2
Wingfield SN2 . . . .**36** A5
Wingfield Ave SN2 . . . . . .**35** C6
Wingfield Prim Sch
BA14 . . . .**104** C6
Wingfield Rd BA14 . . . . .**105** A7
Winifred St SN1 . . . .**50** D3
Winkelbury Hill (Hill Fort) ★
SP7 . . . .**207** C8
Winkins La SN15 . . . .**44** A2
Winklebury Cottage
SN16 . . . .**29** C2
Winlaw Cl SN5 . . . .**49** C7

Winscombe Ct BA11 . . .**110** B5
Winsley CE Sch BA15 . . .**99** E7
Winsley Cl SN2 . . . .**35** C4
Winsley Hill BA2 . . . .**99** B6
Winsley Rd BA15 . . . . . .**100** B7
Winstanley Cl **8** SN5 . . .**49** A4
Winston Rd SN12 . . . .**93** F1
Winter Gn SN11 . . . .**80** F3
Winterbourne Earls Sch
SP4 . . . .**133** A1
**Winterbourne Stoke Group
(Tumuli)** ★ SP4 . . . . . .**197** C4
Winterslow Prim Sch
SP5 . . . .**149** B6
Wintersow Rd
Idmiston SP4 . . . .**198** C1
Porton SP4 . . . .**133** D6
Swindon SN2 . . . .**35** B5
2 Trowbridge BA14 . .**105** B5
Winton Cl SP9 . . . .**216** D4
Winwick Rd SN5 . . . .**49** B4
Wirr The SP3 . . . .**128** D7
Wirral Way SN25 . . . .**34** F7
Wise La SP3 . . . .**141** A2
Wiseman Cl **2** SN3 . . . . .**51** E6
Wishart Way SN15 . . . . . .**78** F3
Wishford Prim Sch
SP2 . . . .**130** A4
Wishford Rd SP2 . . . . . .**144** B5
Witan Cl **8** SP10 . . . . . .**193** E2
Witchcombe La SN10 . .**179** B1
Witchell La SN10 . . . .**180** B3
Witfield Cl SN5 . . . .**33** B5
Witham Way SN2 . . . .**35** F4
Witherington Rd
Alderbury SP5 . . . .**153** C2
Downton SP5 . . . .**159** C5
**Witherington Ring (Field
System)** ★ SP5 . . . .**159** D7
Witheys The **10** BA14 . .**163** A6
Withies The SN8 . . . .**175** D1
Withy Bed SN4 . . . .**61** C1
Withy Cl
Trowbridge BA14 . . . . .**101** E3
Wootton Bassett SN4 . . .**47** D3
Withybed La RG17 . . . . .**177** F5
Withymead Rd SN14 . . . .**74** A8
Witt Rd SP5 . . . .**149** D5
Wittenham View **7** SP4 .**217** C2
Wittensford La SO51 . . .**212** F1
Witton Windmill ★
SN8 . . . .**184** B8
Witts La SN5 . . . .**33** B5
Wivenhoe Ct **7** BA11 . .**110** C6
Woburn Cl
Swindon SN25 . . . .**34** F6
Trowbridge BA14 . . . . .**105** A8
Wolferstan Dr SP1 . . . . .**146** D5
Wolfhall Rd SN8 . . . .**183** D8
Wolsely Ave SN3 . . . .**51** A4
Wolverton Cl SN14 . . . . . .**77** F6
Wood H Dr SN2 . . . .**34** D3
Wood La
Brinkworth SN15 . . . . . .**46** D7
Chapmanslade BA13 . . .**111** D4
Chippenham SN15 . . . . . .**78** E6
Fonthill Gifford SP3 . . .**200** C2
Lydiard Millicent SN5 . . .**32** A1
Nettleton SN14 . . . .**67** B8
Purton SN5 . . . .**31** E1
Sherston GL8 . . . .**25** B5
Wood Rd SP4 . . . .**198** A6
Wood St SN15 . . . .**81** B3
Clyffe Pypard SN4 . . . . .**61** D1
Swindon SN1 . . . .**50** D4
Wootton Bassett SN4 . . .**47** D2
Woodborough CE Sch
SN9 . . . .**181** C6
Woodborough Cl
BA14 . . . .**105** D5
Woodborough Rd
Beechingstoke SN9 . . . .**181** B6
Corsham SN13 . . . .**85** B7
Pewsey SN9 . . . .**215** A5
Woodbury RG17 . . . .**165** B1
Woodbury Cl **2** SN5 . . . .**49** A8
Woodbury Gdns SP2 . . .**152** A5
Woodchester SN5 . . . .**49** C5
Woodcock Cl SP9 . . . . . .**216** D6
Woodcock Gdns BA12 . .**117** C6
Woodcock Ind Est
BA12 . . . .**117** D7
Woodcock La BA12 . . . .**117** B7
Woodcock Rd BA12 . . . .**117** C6
Woodcombe SN12 . . . .**94** C6
Woodcote Rd SN8 . . . . . .**185** B8
Woodfern SN2 . . . .**210** F1
Woodfolds SN16 . . . .**15** F7
Woodford Cl **3** SN2 . . . . .**35** C6
Woodford Prim Sch
SP4 . . . .**131** C5
Woodhayes Rd BA11 . . .**110** C6
Woodhenge ★ SP4 . . . . .**217** A7
Woodhill Pk ★ SN4 . . . .**166** E7
Woodhill Rise SN11 . . . . .**81** C4
Woodhill Village ★
SN4 . . . .**166** D8
**Woodhouse Castle (rems
of)** ★ BA12 . . . .**114** E1
Woodhouse Gdns
BA14 . . . .**102** B2
Woodland Dr SP5 . . . . . .**149** B6
Woodland Pk SN11 . . . . . .**81** B6
Woodland Rd
Patney SN10 . . . .**180** F5
2 Warminster BA12 . . .**116** E6

Woodland View
Westbury BA13 . . . .**112** B8
Wroughton SN4 . . . .**50** B1
Woodland Way
Devizes SN10 . . . .**214** A1
Salisbury SP1 . . . .**146** A2
Woodlands SN13 . . . .**76** E2
Woodlands Cty Fst Sch
SP2 . . . .**145** B4
Woodlands La SP7 . . . . .**203** E1
Woodlands Manor ★
BA12 . . . .**139** A3
Woodlands Rd
Chippenham SN14 . . . . . .**78** C8
Mere BA12 . . . .**139** B2
Mildenhall SN8 . . . .**169** A1
Pewsey SN9 . . . .**215** D4
Woodlea SN14 . . . .**75** C6
Woodlea Grange SP5 . . .**153** E2
Woodling Cres SP6 . . . .**210** F1
Woodman Mead **5**
BA12 . . . .**116** F7
Woodmarsh BA14 . . . . . .**105** D4
Woodpecker Mews
SN14 . . . .**70** B2
Woodroffe Sq SN11 . . . . .**81** C2
Woodrow SN12 . . . .**94** D7
Woodrow Rd SN12 . . . . . .**94** C6
Woods Cl SN16 . . . .**25** C1
Woods Hill BA2 . . . .**99** A6
Woods's La SP3 . . . .**200** F2
Woodsage Way SN11 . . . .**80** F3
Woodshaw Mead **3** SN4 .**48** A2
Woodside Ave SN3 . . . . . .**50** E5
Woodside Rd
Salisbury SP2 . . . .**145** C3
South Marston Park SN3 . .**36** C7
Woodstock Gdns SN12 . .**94** B3
Woodstock Rd SP1 . . . . .**146** B2
Woodvill Rd SP1 . . . .**146** B2
Woodway Cotts GL9 . . . . .**24** E5
Woolands La **1** SP7 . . .**202** B2
Wooley Dr SN4 . . . .**47** D3
Woolford Grange **2** SN4 .**48** A2
Woollaton Cl SN5 . . . .**49** A5
Woolley Cl BA15 . . . .**100** E7
Woolley Dr BA15 . . . .**100** E7
Woolley St BA15 . . . .**100** E6
Woolley Terr BA15 . . . . .**100** E7
Woolmer Dro SN8 . . . . . .**168** F6
Woolpack Mdws BA14 . .**105** E7
Wootton Bassett Inf Sch
SN4 . . . .**47** C1
Wootton Bassett Mus ★
SN4 . . . .**47** D1
Wootton Bassett Rd
SN5 . . . .**49** E5
Wootton Bassett Sch
SN4 . . . .**47** D2
Wor Barrow (Long Barrow) ★
SP5 . . . .**208** C4
Worcester Lodge ★
GL9 . . . .**24** A3
Wordsworth Cl **1** SN4 . .**47** F3
Wordsworth Rd SP1 . . . .**146** B2
Worlidge Dr SN5 . . . .**49** B8
Wormcliff La SN13 . . . . . .**83** A4
Worsley Rd SN5 . . . .**49** A4
Worsted Cl BA14 . . . .**105** E7
Wortheys Cl SN16 . . . .**28** A5
Worton & Marston Sch
SN10 . . . .**179** B4
Worton Rd SN10 . . . .**179** C4
Wouldham Cl SP11 . . . . .**191** F4
Wren Cl Frome BA11 . . . .**110** B7
3 Warminster BA12 . . .**116** E5
Wren Ct BA14 . . . .**105** B8
Wrenscroft **8** SP2 . . . . .**152** A5
Wrenswood SN3 . . . .**51** D8
Wroughton Airfield
SN4 . . . .**63** F2
Wroughton Cty Inf Sch
SN4 . . . .**64** A6
Wroughton Cty Jun Sch
SN4 . . . .**64** A7
Wych Elm Rd BA11 . . . .**110** C6
Wychurch Rd **4** SN16 . . .**28** A5
Wyck Village ★ SP3 . . . .**203** E7
Wycombe Cl SN11 . . . . . .**79** F2
Wycombe La SN10 . . . . .**172** F1
Wyke Rd BA14 . . . .**101** E4
Wylye Cl Swindon SN25 . .**34** F4
Warminster BA12 . . . . .**116** F5
Wylye Rd
Steeple Langford SP3 . .**128** B7
Tidworth SP9 . . . .**216** D7
Warminster BA12 . . . . .**117** A5
Wylye BA12 . . . .**201** F8
Wyncies The SN6 . . . . . .**163** E6
Wynd The SN11 . . . .**81** B4
Wyndham Cl SN15 . . . . . .**79** A8
Wyndham La SP4 . . . . . .**199** A2
Wyndham Pk Sch SP1 . .**146** B2
Wyndham Rd
Salisbury SP1 . . . .**146** A2
Swindon SN2 . . . .**50** A7
Wyndham Terr SP1 . . . .**146** B2
Wynford Rd BA11 . . . . . .**110** B6
Wynndale Cl SN3 . . . .**36** A4
Wynsome St BA14 . . . . .**104** F3
Wynwards Rd SN25 . . . . .**35** A5
Wythburn Rd BA11 . . . . .**110** C5
Wyvern Ave SN11 . . . .**81** C3
Wyvern Cl SN1 . . . .**50** C2
Wyvern Coll SP1 . . . .**146** E3
Wyvern Rd SP4 . . . .**198** E6
Wyvern Wlk BA13 . . . . . .**108** E3

Wyville Rd BA11 . . . .**110** C6

Y

Yard La SN15 . . . .**96** D7
Yard's La SN9 . . . .**181** C5
Yardley Cl SN2 . . . .**34** F2
Yarmley La SP5 . . . .**149** B6
Yarmouth Cl SN5 . . . .**49** B4
Yarnbrook Rd
Steeple Ashton BA14 . . .**102** E1
West Ashton BA14 . . . . .**105** F2
Yarnbury Castle (Fort) ★
BA12 . . . .**196** B3
Yarnton Cl SN5 . . . .**49** A8
Yatton Rd SN14 . . . .**68** E1
Yeatmans Cl **6** SP7 . . .**202** B2
Yeatmans La **3** SP7 . . .**202** B2
Yeats Cl SN25 . . . .**35** A8
Yellow Way Rd BA11 . . .**118** A5
Yeoman Cl
5 Market Lavington SN10 **179** F1
Swindon SN5 . . . .**49** A7
Yeoman Way BA14 . . . . .**105** C7
Yeovil Cl SN3 . . . .**51** B5
Yerbury St **1** BA14 . . . .**105** E8
Yew Tree Cl Calne SN11 . .**81** A3
Chirton SN10 . . . .**180** F4
The Common SP5 . . . . .**149** B6
Yew Tree Gdns SN3 . . . . .**36** E4
Yew Tree La SN4 . . . .**167** C2
Yews The BA12 . . . .**139** A6
Yewstock Cres W SN15 . .**70** C1
Yewtree Cl **8** SP4 . . . . .**198** C7
Yiewsley Cres SN3 . . . . . .**36** B2
Yockney Cl SN3 . . . .**76** E1
Yonder Way **7** SN4 . . . .**163** A6
York Bldgs BA14 . . . .**101** D1
York Cl
Chippenham SN14 . . . . . .**78** A6
Corsham SN13 . . . .**76** F2
York Dro SP5 . . . .**212** C4
York La SN15 . . . .**46** A7
York Rd
7 Hungerford RG17 . .**177** B6
Lyneham SN15 . . . .**60** B2
Salisbury SP2 . . . .**145** F1
Stapleford SP3 . . . .**197** B1
Swindon SN1 . . . .**50** D6
Upavon Down SN9 . . . .**182** B1
Youngs Paddock SP5 . .**149** C6
Yule Hill SP3 . . . .**203** F6

Z

Zeals Fst Sch BA12 . . . .**138** A4
Zeals Gn Dr BA12 . . . . . .**138** A4
Zeals Rise BA12 . . . .**137** F4
Zig Zag Hill SP7 . . . .**206** C2
Zion Rd SP11 . . . .**199** F3
Zouch Ave SN9 . . . .**216** C7
Zouch Cl SP9 . . . .**216** C7
Zouch Farm Rd SP9 . . . .**216** C7
Zouch Prim Sch SP9 . . .**216** B8

Using the Ordnance Survey National Grid

G NH	NJ	NK
M NN	NO	NP
R NS	NT	NU
NX NY	NZ	
SC SD	SE	TA
SH SJ	SK	TF TG
M SN SO	SP	TL TM
R SS ST	SU	TQ TR
W SX SY	SZ	TV

Any feature in this atlas can be given a unique reference to help you find the same feature on other Ordnance Survey maps of the area, or to help someone else locate you if they do not have a Street Atlas.

The grid squares in this atlas match the Ordnance Survey National Grid and are at 500 metre intervals. The small figures at the bottom and sides of every other grid line are the National Grid kilometre values (**00** to **99** km) and are repeated across the country every 100 km (see left).

To give a unique National Grid reference you need to locate where in the country you are. The country is divided into 100 km squares with each square given a unique two-letter reference. Use the administrative map to determine in which 100 km square a particular page of this atlas falls.

The bold letters and numbers between each grid line (**A** to **F**, **1** to **8**) are for use within a specific Street Atlas only, and when used with the page number, are a convenient way of referencing these grid squares.

Example   *The railway bridge over DARLEY GREEN RD in grid square B1*

Step 1: Identify the two-letter reference, in this example the page is in **SP**

Step 2: Identify the 1 km square in which the railway bridge falls. Use the figures in the southwest corner of this square: Eastings **17**, Northings **74**. This gives a unique reference: **SP 17 74**, accurate to 1 km.

Step 3: To give a more precise reference accurate to 100 m you need to estimate how many tenths along and how many tenths up this 1 km square the feature is (to help with this the 1 km square is divided into four 500 m squares). This makes the bridge about **8** tenths along and about **1** tenth up from the southwest corner.

This gives a unique reference: **SP 178 741**, accurate to 100 m.

Eastings (read from left to right along the bottom) come before Northings (read from bottom to top). If you have trouble remembering say to yourself "Along the hall, THEN up the stairs"!

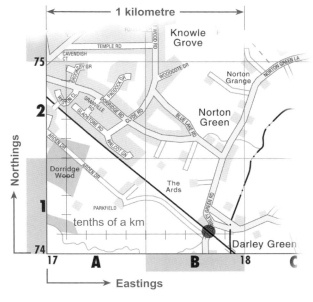

Addresses

Name and Address	Telephone	Page	Grid reference

Name and Address	Telephone	Page	Grid reference

Street Atlases from Philip's

Philip's publish an extensive range of regional and local street atlases which are ideal for motoring, business and leisure use. They are widely used by the emergency services and local authorities throughout Britain.

Key features include:

◆ Superb county-wide mapping at an extra-large scale of 3½ inches to 1 mile, or 2½ inches to 1 mile in pocket editions

◆ Complete urban and rural coverage, detailing every named street in town and country

◆ Each atlas available in three handy formats – hardback, spiral, pocket paperback

'The mapping is very clear... great in scope and value'
★★★★ BEST BUY   AUTO EXPRESS

PHILIP'S
STREET ATLAS
Cambridgeshire
With complete coverage of Peterborough
BEST BUY ★★★★ Auto Express
Unique comprehensive coverage
Ordnance Survey

STREET ATLAS
Glasgow
and West Central Scotland
Ordnance Survey

PHILIP'S
STREET ATLAS
Cardiff, Swansea and The Valleys
Ordnance Survey
Unique comprehensive coverage

Ordnance Survey
STREET ATLAS
London
The definitive London atlas

Ordnance Survey
STREET ATLAS
South Essex
BEST BUY AUTO EXPRESS

PHILIP'S
STREET ATLAS
North Yorkshire
BEST BUY ★★★★ Auto Express
Unique comprehensive coverage

PHILIP'S Ordnance Survey
STREET ATLAS
Bristol and Bath
The definitive Bri
BEST BUY Auto Express

Ordnance Survey
STREET ATLAS
Surrey
Dorking, Epsom, Guildford, Kingston, Leatherhead and Woking at extra-large-scale
Unique comprehensive coverage
BEST BUY AUTO EXPRESS
Includes Heathrow and Gatwick Airports
PHILIP'S

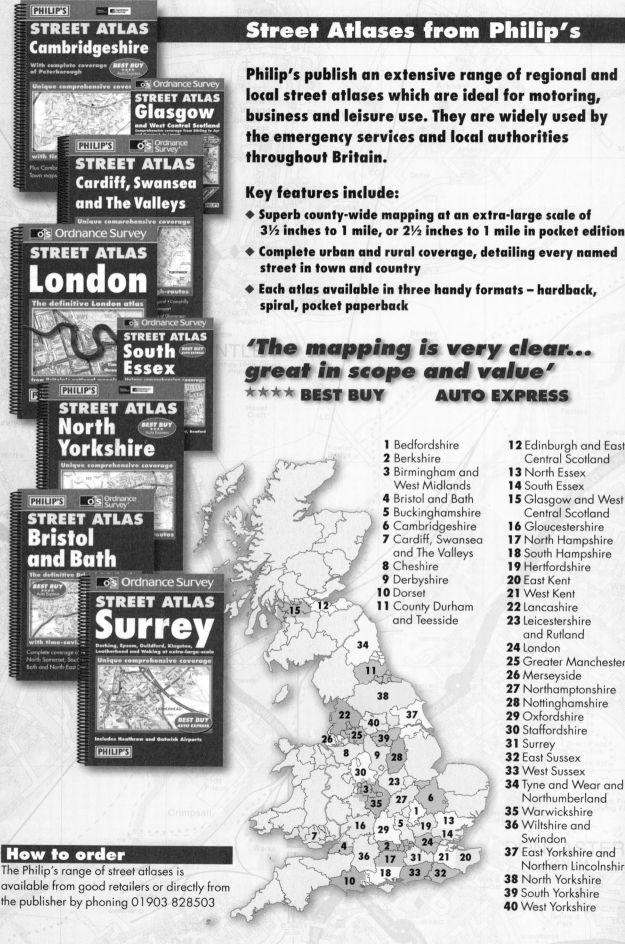

1 Bedfordshire
2 Berkshire
3 Birmingham and West Midlands
4 Bristol and Bath
5 Buckinghamshire
6 Cambridgeshire
7 Cardiff, Swansea and The Valleys
8 Cheshire
9 Derbyshire
10 Dorset
11 County Durham and Teesside
12 Edinburgh and East Central Scotland
13 North Essex
14 South Essex
15 Glasgow and West Central Scotland
16 Gloucestershire
17 North Hampshire
18 South Hampshire
19 Hertfordshire
20 East Kent
21 West Kent
22 Lancashire
23 Leicestershire and Rutland
24 London
25 Greater Manchester
26 Merseyside
27 Northamptonshire
28 Nottinghamshire
29 Oxfordshire
30 Staffordshire
31 Surrey
32 East Sussex
33 West Sussex
34 Tyne and Wear and Northumberland
35 Warwickshire
36 Wiltshire and Swindon
37 East Yorkshire and Northern Lincolnshire
38 North Yorkshire
39 South Yorkshire
40 West Yorkshire

How to order
The Philip's range of street atlases is available from good retailers or directly from the publisher by phoning 01903 828503